Avihu Ronen

CONDEMNED TO LIFE

The Diaries and Life of Chajka Klinger

This book was published under the auspices of the
Center for Research on the Holocaust in Poland,
generously supported by the Aaron Gutwirth Fund and the
Danek Gertner Yad Vashem Scholarship.

Avihu Ronen

CONDEMNED TO LIFE

The Diaries and Life of Chajka Klinger

Translated from the Hebrew by Avital Tsype

יד ושם
YAD VASHEM
THE WORLD HOLOCAUST
REMEMBRANCE CENTER

THE INTERNATIONAL INSTITUTE
FOR HOLOCAUST RESEARCH

The Center for Research on the Holocaust in Poland

Avihu Ronen

Nidona Lechaim

Translation services: Academic Language Experts
Translation from the Polish: Anna Brzostowska, Maria Gajewska, and Jerzy Giebułtowski
Additional translation from the Hebrew: Betsy Rosenberg

Language and Production Editor: Adina Mendelsohn

P.O.B. 3477, Jerusalem 9103401, Israel
publications.marketing@yadvashem.org.il

First published in Hebrew by University of Haifa Press and Miskal–Yedioth Ahranoth Books and Chemed Books, 2011

Unless otherwise indicated, all photos in this publication are courtesy of the Ronen family.

ISBN 978-965-308-706-4

Typesetting: Hava Salzman

Printed in Israel by Offset Natan Shlomo Press

To Mother and her generation

Contents

Chapter One

A Kind of Introduction

In the Citrus Grove: April 19, 1958

We're all in the truck on our way to the old citrus grove. The driver is Boaz (Yankale), the father of a boy in our group. His son is in the cab with him. Maybe he'll let him hold the steering wheel for a while. I'm in the back with the other kids, sitting on those wooden benches that go on the ramp of the cowshed when the dairy products are loaded on the truck heading for Tel Aviv. Every time we take a trip somewhere or drive to the beach, the kibbutz members set the benches up in the back of the truck. Here we are, heading for the citrus grove at this strange hour of the afternoon when we should really be home with our parents. The kibbutz members sent us on an outing because they're burying my mother today. They wanted to keep us away, or maybe they just didn't know what to do with us. A funeral is no place for children.

I'm nine years old and in the "Oren" group of third graders at Kibbutz Haogen in central Israel. Our teacher is Ya'ir, and our housemother is Sarah. During class this morning, Aunt Yaffa walks in and announces that she has to take me home right away. Ya'ir says I can go. It's a little strange, her coming into the room like this all of a sudden, but I'm glad to see her, and I babble cheerfully all the way home. Outside, I see relatives from Tel Aviv sitting on lawn chairs the way they did two months ago at my brother Zvi's bar mitzvah. This is also strange. One of my uncles calls me over and gives me a pocket knife as a present. What's this about—a pocket knife? It's not even my birthday. Then I hear Father calling from inside. As usual, I skip two stairs at a time and call out on the way, "Is

Mother back from the hospital yet?" Father says he has something to tell me. He puts his arms around me and says that Mother is dead.

This is the strangest day. The world seems normal, but it isn't at all. After I cry with Father a while—and even between tears—he starts talking about the school trip to Sha'ar Ha'amakim and things like that. How can one talk about normal things when everything's changing? Then Zvi comes home from the regional school at Kibbutz Ma'abarot, close to Haogen. I go into the other room and hear Father telling him. He cries too.

At noon I go back to the kibbutz's children's house, where all the kibbutz children sleep, and wash up. I'm alone in the bathroom because the other kids have showered already. I start crying again, the water diluting my tears. I think I see them flowing over the tiles. Back in the room, my bed has been turned down for the afternoon nap, and I find a surprise there. The children have collected a bunch of trading cards (the kind city kids call "prizes"), including some really valuable ones that I wanted but couldn't get, and they've given them to me as a present.

And in the afternoon, instead of going home to our parents, we drive to the citrus grove with Boaz (Yankale), one of the fathers. There isn't much to do in the grove. We wander among the trees and practice throwing stones. Avri from the "Rimon" group teaches me how to throw further. You have to fling the stone at a 45-degree angle, he says. The "Rimon" group is two years older than the "Oren" group, and I'm proud that Avri is treating me like a friend. Meanwhile, in a different grove, the newly planted one near the kibbutz, they were burying Mother.

The Book: 1960

Mother died on April 18, 1958, on the eve of the fifteenth anniversary of the Warsaw Ghetto Uprising—it says so on her tombstone, which I visited for the first time with the "Oren" group two years after she died. The young grove where she's buried is now the kibbutz cemetery, although at the time, there was only one other grave there. As I entered the grove, I was met by the overpowering smell of orange blossoms, which would accompany me along the path to her grave each spring for many years to come. My entire group was there with me, and so were Father and Zvi. Grandmother rode in the truck via the dirt byway. My teacher Ya'ir took out a little book with two black lines inked on the cover and began to read aloud from it. This, I realized, was my mother's diary, which had been published the year before. Ya'ir choked up all of a sudden, and I wondered why. Grandmother, a small woman whom I would shortly overtake in height, wiped her eyes. That was baffling too because Grandmother barely understood Hebrew.

On the thirtieth day after Mother's death, the kibbutz published a pamphlet. In it was a photograph of Mother sitting in an armchair, reading the newspaper with a peaceful expression on her face. This was the photo Father had chosen to frame and display on the shelf at home. When the first anniversary of her death came around, her book had been published with the title *Chajka Klinger: Miyoman Bageto* (A Diary from the Ghetto) written on the cover. I devoured the book in one sitting, as was my habit at age ten. I was such a bookworm, Father often had to chase me out of the house and send me off to play with the other children. Not that I didn't like playing games. My favorites were capture the flag and soccer. I kept a meticulous record of our scores in a special diary, with notes about what or who had made us win or lose. Whenever our number of wins went up, I was filled with happiness, although I always preferred to play on the side of the underdogs when we chose teams. To win with the good players seemed too easy. Mother had also chosen to stay with the underdogs. She wasn't afraid. She was a hero.

From Mother's book, I learned that she had been one of the ghetto fighters they used to talk about so reverently in the kibbutz. She had joined the underground resistance in the city of Będzin, Poland, where she lived during the Nazi occupation. The great hero Mordechai Anielewicz came to visit her and her youth movement friends and asked them to join the uprising against the Nazis. The few against the many, the weak against the strong. I read about how Mother was captured with a pistol in her handbag and tortured by the Gestapo. They never broke her, she wrote, although the torture almost killed her. I was proud of my mother. She was the heroine of a book, and her death was somehow connected to the horrors she had endured.

There were times when getting on without her was very hard. Father said it was alright to cry, and he cried too sometimes, but I was ashamed to cry in front of the other children. I discovered a bunker in the kibbutz from the days of the Sinai Campaign in 1956, and I would sometimes sneak in there to cry. Not always on Mother's account, though. Sometimes it was because I was angry at someone or because we had lost a game. Once, I started sobbing as we were being woken up from nap time. The father of another kid who was on "wake-up duty" that day told me I should control myself; that his parents had been killed in the

Holocaust, and he'd learned how to stop himself from crying. That didn't help much.

And there were long nights in the children's house too. Now and then, Father would sit beside my bed after all the other parents had left and play the harmonica. But when he finally had to go, I struggled to fall asleep, lying awake in the dark, trying to understand what death was like. I was afraid to wake the other children, afraid I might discover that they were not really people at all but little demons with chicken legs like in Hayim Nahman Bialik's *The Legend of the Three and Four*. So, I'd get up and go to the bathroom where you could turn on the light or wait for the night guard in the doorway of the children's house. When the guard arrived, he'd look surprised and take me back to bed. One time, I couldn't stand it anymore, so I ran home in the dark. This hardly ever happened with the kids in our group, except maybe Esther did this sometimes. I didn't dare barge in on Father, but our housemother Sarah lived one house away from him, so I woke her instead. She took me back to the children's house and as she explained later on, she was afraid that if she let me stay over, she would have had to let everyone stay over.

Sarah was a strict housemother. It was not unusual for her to raise her voice when we did a sloppy job on cleanup or kitchen duty. But she had a soft spot for me. When I was in fourth grade, she decided to wean me from the habit of sucking my thumb while twisting a curl with my other hand. She promised to get me a gift if I stopped for a week. I was skeptical of this promise, but when a week passed without any thumb-sucking (except maybe once), she came in toting a table-soccer game, the object of our wildest fantasies in those days. When I was in sixth grade, she did something totally out of the ordinary. She waited for me at nap time with a bunch of flowers and took me out to the cemetery. "Chajka was my friend too," she explained.

Father had a difficult time of it too. He'd been left with three children. Zvi was thirteen when Mother died, Arnon was three, and I was nine. For a while, Father continued to work for the building division of Hakibbutz Ha'artzi (the National Kibbutz Movement), which required him to go to Tel Aviv every day. Sometimes I would walk out to the gate and wait for him to arrive with the sports paper he would bring home from the city. He drove a pickup truck provided by the division, and sometimes he would let Arnon sit on his lap and hold the steering wheel on the road leading into the kibbutz. Halfway along, we would swap places, and I'd take Father's lap and the wheel. On one such occasion, Arnon refused to switch and "drove" all the way up to the kibbutz gate. My pleas fell on deaf ears, and Father refused to get involved. Later, after he'd put Arnon to bed in the children's house, he took me out for another spin, and this time he let me drive all the way.

Father never went to the cemetery with me. He found other ways to help me cope with Mother's death. Once when I was in fifth grade, he took me to the cinema in Netanya. It was a special outing for kibbutz members—no children allowed—and everyone was stunned to see me there with him. The film was a Yugoslavian one, called *Valley of Peace*. It told the story of two children who had been orphaned during the war and who wandered over the mountains in search of a mysterious valley where peace reigns eternal. When they came across an African-American soldier on their way, they rejoiced, thinking they'd found the valley, but the next shot showed the notch of a German rifle, and then you saw the Black soldier lying dead. The children went on searching, but they never found the "valley of peace." The next morning in class, our teacher Ya'ir commented that although some parents might consider it appropriate to bring a child to a grown-up film, he did not. It was an opinion undoubtedly shared by the Education Committee, without whose special permission no child was allowed out of the kibbutz.

But the kibbutz also tried to be helpful. Father's room filled up with toys none of the other children had, and he received a large increase in his childcare allowance as well as help from a woman who looked after the three of us in the afternoon. The days went by, and Mother's image grew fainter and hazier. Every time I came back to the room, I would glance briefly at the little photograph on the shelf, afraid I would forget what she looked like.

The Trial: 1963

In seventh grade, I entered the regional school at Kibbutz Ma'abarot. My life overflowed with exciting new activities: being with the big kids, joining the youth movement, meeting classmates from other kibbutzim. Our group was now called "Ma'ayan." I made friends with a boy named Ofer from Ma'abarot. We were both chess enthusiasts. Our beds were next to each other, and we put a chess set on a little chair between them, so we could play whenever we wanted. We held simultaneous matches like the famous chess players Tal and Botvinnik. We read the humorist Ephraim Kishon together and laughed our heads off. In the classroom, I used to cast secret glances at a certain girl, hoping she wouldn't notice. There was already one couple in our group, but I was still shy. When Giora from Ma'abarot asked me who I considered the most lustful boy in our group, I was mortified. What did he mean by "lustful" anyway?

In seventh grade, we usually went home twice a week to our parents' homes at Kibbutz Haogen. Kids in the older classes only went home for Shabbat because of their workload as well as their youth movement activities. My brother Zvi was a junior and only came home for Shabbat. Malka, who later married Father, was living with us by then. She baked cakes and knitted sweaters for all of us. Our four o'clock family tea times were a treat. We always had coffee and freshly baked cakes on the table and talked about important things like politics, the Hashomer Hatzair youth movement to which we belonged, or sometimes about schoolwork. Zvi and Father talked about trigonometric functions. I didn't understand what the strange words meant, but they sounded lovely to my ears. After tea time, we would work in the garden, weeding Father's "jungle," and Father would tell us stories about World War II while we worked. His stories were always funny—he did a lot of running from the police during the war. Mother's name was no longer mentioned, and her picture had vanished from the shelf.

A sudden reminder of Mother came my way when I was in eighth grade. The truck that drove the schoolchildren to work at Haogen stopped unexpectedly outside the dining hall at Ma'abarot. I was told to get off. Malka was waiting for me there. I asked her what the matter was, but she didn't say. She only explained that Lina wanted to see me. Lina was our class teacher, and I had a good relationship with her. I was happy to go to her office despite the strangeness of the invitation. Once we were seated, she asked me whether I'd heard about the Barenblatt trial. I said yes, I'd read about it. I knew that Hirsch Barenblatt was the head of the Judenrat (Jewish Council) in Będzin, where Mother had lived. He was being tried for collaborating with the Nazis during the war. But what was so important about the trial that Lina had to summon me in the middle of the day and make me take time off work? Slowly and gently, she explained that an article about the trial had appeared in the *Al Hamishmar* newspaper that day. The article mentioned Chajka Klinger, member of Kibbutz Haogen, who had committed suicide. My father knew that I usually went to the housemother's room to read the paper and was afraid I would learn how Mother had died. He wanted to soften the blow.

No, I hadn't read the article in the paper. It was there in Lina's room that I first learned that Mother had taken her own life. Lina asked how I felt. It was difficult to come up with an answer. I was confused. After we had talked a while, she suggested that I skip work that day and go back to Kibbutz Haogen.

I walked the two kilometers to Haogen alone with feverish thoughts running through my brain. How could I have missed the article in the paper? I usually read it regularly and rather thoroughly. When I first entered the regional school the year before, I had gone straight to the library to check the shelves, afraid I would read all the books before the year was out and have to reread them in the second and third years. The adults who marveled at my speed reading insisted that anyone who reads that fast probably skims the words and doesn't retain anything. They would test me, but I always remembered what I'd read. And of all the articles, this was the one I had overlooked. How could I have missed Mother's name printed there? A few years later, a girl in our group called Nitza told me that the paper had disappeared from the housemother's room.

Certain things suddenly became clear. Especially Mother's death on the anniversary of the Warsaw Ghetto Uprising. The events of her life in the ghetto and the timing of her death had always seemed linked. The date lent a special significance to the fact that she was a ghetto fighter. It had never occurred to me that this was no coincidence.

At home, Father was waiting for me again, but this time there were no relatives outside. We sat and discussed the matter like adults. I didn't cry this time. I had decided the year before that only little kids cry and that I would never cry at the regional school. I cried five times in seventh grade but not even once in eighth grade. It made me proud that I had managed to stick to my resolve. I was neither angry nor resentful that Father had never told me how Mother had died, but I was shaken up all over again. I didn't say so to Father at the time because I sensed that he wasn't in a good mood either. We went to the dining hall together. There were notices up about the Purim party. While we were eating, I asked Father what costume he was planning to wear this Purim. The year before, he had been a hit as an English bobby. Father said he wasn't going to dress up this year. I stopped asking questions.

The Diaries: October 2, 1985

In February 1985, as I made my way to "Ginger" Ehud's memorial service at Kibbutz Sarid in northern Israel, I suddenly realized that I had begun counting my past in decades. For fifteen years, our "Ginger" had been lying under the trees in that wood. He had been killed during the War of Attrition (1967–1970), and it was Yiftach who came back to tell us about the circumstances of his death. Ehud was standing guard during a bombing raid, and the shockwaves did him in. All through the War of Attrition, we felt as though our entire generation was being wiped out. Every day, a new picture appeared in the paper, and we dreaded setting eyes on yet another familiar name. Kerem Shalom had contributed its own share of casualties—first Ze'evik, then Ehud.

In 1970, Kerem Shalom in southern Israel had been a promise for a better future. The best core group of founders, the most beautiful location, the most radical of kibbutzim. There was a feeling of change in the air, of a veritable leap forward. But then "Ginger" Ehud, whose ready laughter was the epitome of joy, optimism, and all that was possible, was slain. He died before the bitter struggles began, before the disappointments and the desertions from the kibbutz. Only four of us from Kerem Shalom showed up at his graveside. I had come up for the occasion from Tel Aviv.

Ofer said some beautiful things over the tombstone, evoking our earlier faith and our present disappointments. He was the friend I had played chess with in seventh grade. We had entered the army together, formed a core group, and founded Kerem Shalom. Our paths had diverged six years prior to the funeral when Ofer returned to Ma'abarot, and I settled in Tel Aviv to study history and philosophy. Ofer's eulogy did not contain the words "we failed," perhaps because he himself had continued the kibbutz way of life, or because he was more at peace with himself and his past.

It was late in the evening when I returned home to Tel Aviv. My daughter Ayelet was already asleep. She was four years old by then and enrolled in daycare. She loved her preschool teacher Saraleh. While I ate, my wife Raya told me the news. She'd met Uncle Yosef for lunch that day. Yosef was an old cousin of Mother's with whom we had gotten back in touch the previous year. He phoned to ask why we never saw each other, especially now that we lived nearby. So, we went to visit him. He bought a doll for Ayelet and won her affection, much to our surprise. Our little one adopted him as an extra grandfather, even though she had enough grandparents already. None of them lived in Tel Aviv though, and none of them had a magical apartment with electric windows and a music box.

And today, Raya had gone to see him. They dined together at a table set with elegant china and sterling silverware. For a moment, Yosef was back in the role of a charming host with Eastern European manners. And for the first time, he showed Raya the pamphlet Kibbutz Haogen had published in Mother's memory a month after her death. A single word stood out on the cover against a background of small, cramped handwriting in Polish: Chajka.

As evident from Yosef's stories, Mother had been very attached to him. She loved to visit him in Tel Aviv for a break from the rigors of kibbutz life. To sleep in a big soft bed, to go to the cinema, to see a play. Perhaps he offered her consolation for all the family members she had lost somewhere in Poland. There was not much Yosef could tell Raya or was able to recall. But I was in a peculiar mood after "Ginger's" memorial service, and I looked through the familiar pamphlet, reflecting on how little I actually knew about Mother, about her family, and about her life and death.

Mother's private memory had not been preserved in the family. The word "Mother" had long since vanished from the family lexicon. I used to visit her grave every year, sometimes with Father, but we never went together as a family. A few of our relatives—Uncle Yosef among them—continued to visit Kibbutz Haogen, but they were no different from other guests. The details of Mother's life and death were not discussed. They had become an open family secret, something we all knew about but never mentioned.

Mother's memory belonged to the public sphere. On the tenth anniversary of her death, a conference was held in her honor at the kibbutz on the subject "Resistance and Rescue during the Holocaust Era." It was attended by the legendary ghetto fighters Yitzhak (Antek) Zuckerman and Chajka Grossman. The list of participants on the flyer hanging from the kibbutz bulletin board included a certain "Avihu R." with no indication of his connection to the subject of the conference. And there was no connection of which to speak. The various orators spoke solemnly about their personal experience of the Holocaust and in the underground resistance forces, while I, who had spent my first leave from the army boning up on historical literature, remained dumbstruck. I had little to add to their turbulent reminiscences. My eyes were fixed on the auditorium door in the hope that the pretty redhead from my army unit would show up as promised. She did not.

And there was Mother's book, *Miyoman Bageto*. But this book didn't include everything. A few years ago, Father told me that it comprised only excerpts of her diaries, and he wondered whether we might publish them in their entirety one day. This was compounded by a strange passage I had read in another book some years earlier with the long and peculiar title *Post-Ugandan Zionism on Trial*. It kept echoing in my ears:

> One victim of censorship within the framework of the Hashomer Hatzair [Young Guardian] movement was Chajka Klinger (Rosenberg), a Holocaust survivor who had arrived in Israel filled with despair and the need to speak. For a few years, she tried publishing her work through different channels.... On April 18, 1958, just before the anniversary of the Warsaw Ghetto Uprising, she took her own life. After her death, Sifriat Poalim and Kibbutz Haogen brought out her book *Miyoman Bageto* based mainly on the material she had written on the "Aryan" side. The book is shocking in its candor and authenticity, but it had been ruthlessly censored. A reviewer who witnessed the writing of the diary maintains that, due to the various cuts, deletions, and changes made by the editors, "researchers" would do well to inquire beyond the edited and published form of the diary and seek out the original manuscript.[1]

Who was this Shabtai B. Beit Zvi who had written such things? Who was the anonymous reader that had discovered the book was censored? Were his claims factual? I had put the book down under the impression that it blamed Zionism for betraying the Jewish people during the Holocaust era after the Zionist movement's Uganda crisis. The Zionists had been less concerned with rescuing Jews than settling Mandatory Palestine. But when Raya told me about her visit with Uncle Yosef, I began to reflect more deeply on Beit Zvi's troubling claims of censorship.

"Ginger" from Kerem Shalom, an elderly Polish uncle, a book seeking to stir up controversy—loose ends peeking through a tangle of threads. Raya began to unravel a mystery I had never dared touch. What exactly had happened to Mother? Why were her diaries censored? Why did she commit suicide? What had her life been about? Perhaps it was time for me to find out.

Ayelet and Ofer: May 1, 2007

My son Ofer finds a copy of *Miyoman Bageto* on one of his excursions through the second-hand bookstores in Jerusalem. He buys two copies—one for himself and one for Ayelet. They are both students now, he in

1 Shabtai B. Beit Zvi, *Post-Ugandan Zionism on Trial: A Study of the Factors that Caused the Mistakes Made by the Zionist Movement during the Holocaust* (Tel Aviv: Shabtai B. Beit Zvi, 1991), p. 388.

Jerusalem, she in Tel Aviv. It's Ayelet's second time reading the diary of the grandmother she never knew. The first was during a family heritage trip we took to Będzin twelve years ago. Now, over the phone, she talks about her experience reading it this time around. One thing in particular bothers her: Chajka almost never talks about herself. She always speaks in the plural "we."

I am surprised at her surprise. "Of course that's how she speaks, that was the spirit of the time. I've written about this quite extensively, especially in the first big book I wrote about her."

"What book?"

That is how the realization gradually seeps in: I have never shown my daughter the big ring binder collecting dust on the tall bookshelf in my study. Hundreds of typewritten pages that had led me off the beaten academic path all those years ago. Even Raya has no memory of the manuscript anymore, and she is furious: "Why didn't you show us?"

The book. How long has it been since that tempestuous period when I became addicted to research and writing? Interviewing dozens of witnesses, avidly collecting more and more documents, losing myself in tomes upon tomes, pilfering from my small family the few hours I could have spent with them. The book became a foundation for a doctoral dissertation, articles, lectures. Mother was always there as an authentic source, a point of departure from which to seek insight, the underpinning of historiographical approaches but also of disputes and more than a few struggles. Still I have managed to forget her. Again. The book of which she is the protagonist lies unfinished.

Raya is the force that drives me back to the diaries and the book. The moment the book is rediscovered, she takes it upon herself to retype it with Ayelet and Ofer's help. The plan is to surprise me on my birthday. Seven chapters are hastily typed out, although the constant hustle and bustle in the house spoils the surprise. After that, the family enterprise picks up speed. The rest of the typing is done by a professional, and during the summer vacation, I sit down to rewrite and edit. The editing is hard going. At the time, I was attempting to understand my mother, the Jews of Zagłębie, the destruction of Polish Jewry, the Holocaust as a whole. Now, I have to bring the story back to her. Back to her diaries. Back to her death. To write those last, most difficult chapters about her life on the kibbutz. The hospitalization. The suicide. That is where I had stopped back then. In the course of my research, I had interviewed dozens of witnesses who'd known my mother, but I never dared approach even one member of Haogen who had been with her during those last days.

Most of them have passed away in the meantime. Who will I interview now? Not only that, but I also have to catch up with the literature that has been published since, some of it bearing the influence of my work but some containing testimonies that have only recently come to light, new research on the subject. And then there's the unavoidable matter of footnotes, the scientific apparatus that needs substantiating and updating.

In conversations with Raya, Ayelet, and Ofer, I bring up my usual qualms about the book's final form. Is it historical research, a biography, or a personal memoir? Finally, I decide to remain true to the 1986 format: Mother's biography, centered around her diary, with bits of my journey to her woven into it. I already know what the future holds for this book. Should it see the light of day, historians will thumb their noses at all the personal stuff, while literary readers will be perturbed by the proliferation of footnotes. The remaining survivors will be offended by those passages of the diary that ruthlessly reveal every shortcoming and human flaw of heroes and victims alike. Even Father and Malka, both then still alive, might not condone this renewed ransacking of the past.

But that's Mother, and that's me. And this is her past, hers and her comrades', refusing to die.

Chapter Two

The Hasid's Daughter

The Polish Uncle: 1985

Uncle Yosef lives on Hashoftim Street, not far from Ibn Gabirol Street. At one time, this was the upscale north end of Tel Aviv. Now, the north end has drifted across the Yarkon River, though his side of Hashoftim Street remains as it was: small, quiet, and respectable, a worthy abode for the Polish bourgeoisie who built the city.

For me, Yosef is and has always been the archetypal Polish uncle, an elderly, pot-bellied man with a deep-furrowed face. His Hebrew never quite pried itself free of his native Yiddish, and he has the habit of kissing you on both cheeks. When I was a boy, he was my city uncle. On Saturday mornings, he would drive his big car into the kibbutz, and I would stick my nose up with pride—not many kids had uncles with cars. We would drive out to the beach, and in the afternoon, he would sprawl out on the couch and fall asleep, snoring loudly.

Now, Yosef is old, so old he has lost count of his years. According to him, he's eighty-one; eighty-two, according to his daughter. He lives alone in a stodgy apartment crammed full of porcelain and crystal. Yosef's life used to consist of business and family. Sometimes, business and family overlapped, melded together, or inevitably clashed. He would come home for lunch, where his favorite dishes—prepared by his wife Zippora—would be waiting for him, and he would continue to work on the accounts while he ate.

"Yosef, what did you have for lunch today?" Zippora would ask teasingly, but he couldn't answer. At night too, his head kept working. Unable to sleep, he would get out of bed and sit in the living room, doing calculations on a slip of paper until Zippora would join him and press her warm body against his. "Yosef, Yosef," she would remind him, "at night, you belong to me." But Zippora is no longer among the living, and the factories are run by their children and grandchildren.

Yosef has vivid memories of Mother that I will make use of later on. I want to learn something about my close relatives, but he isn't much help on that score: He left Poland in 1924 and never lived in Będzin. Even so, he has two anecdotes for me about Chajka's father and brother.

Chajka's father, Leibel Klinger, was known to be a great Talmudic scholar. When asked to become a rabbi, Leibel declined, saying: "What if a poor woman came to me on the Sabbath eve holding a non-kosher chicken? How could I forbid her to cook it, knowing it was the family's Sabbath meal? No, I am not cut out to be a rabbi." And that is why Leibel Klinger was not appointed rabbi of the congregation. Did this really happen? And was my grandfather Leibel Klinger the person to whom it happened? I don't know. I would later learn that there is much cause for skepticism here. All the same, it's a good story in my opinion, mainly because it transports me to a faraway world with its faraway concerns.

The second anecdote has to do with Chajka's older brother. Aharon-Shmil, yet another Talmudic scholar and Torah prodigy, became a heretic at an early age after falling in with bad company. In other words, he became a socialist. And not just your run-of-the-mill socialist, but one of some renown. Sadly, Aharon-Shmil died young; all the great socialists of Zagłębie and Poland attended his funeral. Uncle Yosef remembers how multitudes filled the streets, and ardent eulogies were pronounced over the grave of the young socialist who had died before his time.

And that is the sum of Uncle Yosef's memories of the Klingers, although at times he says my face reminds him of Chajka's young socialist brother. He suggests that I speak to the other branch of the family living in Israel, particularly Shlomo Swinkelstein,[1] the eldest of Chajka's cousins. I contact Shlomo, another cousin Shaya, and others. Bit by bit, their memories help me to piece together a picture, albeit one that is somewhat blurred as there are no surviving members of the Klinger family.

1 Yosef's original name was Swinkelstein, but he changed it to Sfinkelstein when he arrived in Mandatory Palestine for the convenience of British army personnel with whom he had extensive business dealings.

The Klingers

Leibel Klinger, Chajka's father, was one of eight children born to a Hasidic family from Warsaw. His parents were Esther and Asher-Zelig Klinger, who were scrap metal merchants.[2] Little is known of the family history other than the fact that Leibel (Leibush-Itzik), according to a rare list in the 1939 census of Będzin, was born in 1880.[3] Being one of the older sons, Leibel studied Talmud at the *beit midrash* all his life, but not all the siblings followed "the ways of the fathers." Some became secular, and two brothers—Yosef and Shmuel—immigrated to Mandatory Palestine. One sister ventured as far as America.[4]

Chajka's mother, Perl (Rivka-Perla) Swinkelstein, was also born in 1880 to a Hasidic family from Przedbórz.[5] Her parents ran an inn that accommodated the disciples of the rabbi of Rozprza. The match with Leibel was made through the rabbi's court, which the young couple then joined. This may have had to do with the fact that Perl was a descendent of Rabbi Yeshayele Przedbórzer, the founder of a Hasidic dynasty.[6] Leibel Klinger's rabbi, Avraham Moshe Weltfried, was said to be "so renowned in worldly matters, even Polish noblemen would visit him. A fluent leader of prayers before the ark, he was also a fine musician and a composer of *niggunim* [Hasidic melodies] of great complexity and art that were sung in the courts of other *tzaddikim*."[7]

It was in this court, which was perhaps a little less open and cheerful than most Hasidic courts, that Leibel and Perl lived for a number of years. They also relied on it for support. The rabbi ran a *lotteria*—a lottery coordinated with the national lottery—and Leibel was its manager.[8] It was a suitable livelihood for a young Talmudic scholar, allowing him ample time for studies. This arrangement seems to have served them well.

2 Yitzhak Klinger, interview by the author, Rehovot, 2008.

3 See "Będzin Census of 1939," Jewish Historical Institute Archives (Żydowski Instytut Historyczny, AŻIH), 212/11, https://www.jewishgen.org/databases/holocaust/0128_Bedzin_census.html (accessed June 2024); https://www.ushmm.org/online/hsv/source_view.php?SourceId=20586 (accessed June 2024). The census was taken immediately after the occupation, ostensibly for the use of the German occupation authorities.

4 Yitzhak Klinger interview.

5 "Będzin Census of 1939," AŻIH, 212/11.

6 Yosef Sfinkelstein, interview by the author, Tel Aviv, 1985.

7 Meir Shimon Geshuri (Brukner), "Kloyzim BeBendin" (Hebrew), in Avraham S. Stein, ed., *Pinkas Bendin*, vol. 2 (Hebrew) (Tel Aviv: Irgun Yotzey Bendin BeYisrael, 1959), p. 244.

8 Shlomo Swinkelstein, interview by the author, Tel Aviv, 1985.

During World War I, the rabbi of Rozprza drifted to Piotrków Trybunalski and from there back to Przedbórz where he died at a venerable old age in 1918.[9] It may have been the rabbi's absence or perhaps his death that led Leibel and Perl Klinger to settle in Będzin. A list of Leibel's associates and business records shows how much his fate as a maturing Hasid depended on his proximity to the rabbi. Besides, Perl's brother, the father of Shlomo Swinkelstein, was also living in Będzin at the time.

Was the Będzin Yeshiva a step down for the couple? That is difficult to determine with any certainty,[10] although everyone who was acquainted with them in Będzin describes their life as one of hardship and misery.[11] Things were tough. Leibel Klinger was now far from the rabbi's court, and the community (*kloyz*) of Przedbórz Hasidim in Będzin was small and inconsequential, although it continued the tradition of the rabbi's *niggunim*.[12] After some years, Leibel Klinger left this *kloyz* and joined that of the Amshinov Hasidim, which had a higher standing and was also apparently better off. It was there that the town notables prayed, among them Rabbi Bunim Bonhardt and Nuta Londner.[13]

The Klingers lived at 61 Modrzejowska Street, and their income derived from a small grocery store managed by Perl.[14] Although Modrzejowska was one of the main streets in Będzin, ramshackle one-story houses crowded behind the handsome façade.[15] A small stoop led up to the door of the grocery store,[16] but few customers bothered to ascend it.[17] As Shaya Sfinkelstein observes, "grocery store" is too grandiose a term for the miserable place it was. The Klingers, he says, were abject in heart and soul.[18]

9 Geshuri, "Kloyzim BeBendin," p. 244.

10 According to the account of Chajka's friend Esther Shoshan (Zborowska), the family had apparently gone down in the world. Esther Shoshan, interview by the author, Kibbutz Galon, 1985.

11 Shaya Sfinkelstein, interview by the author, Kiron, 1985; Esther Shoshan interview; Ada Halperin (Neufeld), interview by the author, Tel Aviv, 1985.

12 Geshuri, "Kloyzim BeBendin," p. 244.

13 Ibid., p. 242. See also Shlomo Swinkelstein interview. The importance of this *kloyz* is attested to by its order of appearance in the *pinkas* and the length of the passage that deals with it.

14 "Będzin Census of 1939," AŻIH, 212/11.

15 This assessment is based on the appearance of the street as noted by the author during a visit in 1996.

16 Shalom Herzberg, interview by the author, Ramat Gan, 1986.

17 Chana Lieberman, interview by the author, Kibbutz Galon, 1985.

18 Shaya Sfinkelstein interview.

Yet, poverty did not hamper Leibel in his studies; on the contrary, it spurred him on to greater diligence. He would respond irritably when called to lend a hand in the grocery store and leave his books even for a moment. Anecdotal though Yosef's story about Leibel's refusal of the rabbinical appointment may have been, all evidence points to his seriousness as a Torah scholar.[19] Shaya Sfinkelstein calls Leibel a genius and a prodigy who knew the Talmud inside out: "The greatest Hasidim would come to impose on him so he could teach them some Torah."[20]

And perhaps Leibel's scholarly assiduousness was also a manner of fending off his grief. He and Perl had six children, three of whom—all boys—died before World War II. According to Shlomo Swinkelstein, the oldest son's name was Avraham.[21] Like other Jews of the time, when Avraham was due to be conscripted into the Polish army, he had a finger chopped off to avoid the draft, only the plan went awry, and he died of blood poisoning. Yosef Sfinkelstein relates that his own grandfather had intended to maim him in a similar fashion for the same reason, but he refused and immigrated to Mandatory Palestine instead.[22]

The second son Aharon-Shmil is the protagonist of one of Uncle Yosef's previously mentioned stories. Shlomo Swinkelstein confirms that he was a dedicated socialist, a member of the leftist Poalei Zion party, who died at an early age, and that representatives from all over Zagłębie came to his funeral. They delivered eulogies in Yiddish and named libraries after him. Aharon-Shmil's premature death hit Leibel Klinger hard. Although the youth had turned his back on his father's customs and way of life, he never forgot his learning. Even after becoming a socialist, he would go to his father's house and study a page of the Gemara with him. At the end of these learning sessions, when the son would return to his secular life, Leibel would lament: "A diamond I lost."[23] The third son Menahem-Mendel, born in 1911, died as a child in 1915.

The three daughters gave their parents more peace of mind. All three survived despite the family's poverty and grief. And even though

19 Pessia Neuhouse, telephone interview by the author, Hatzor Haglilit, 2008.

20 Ibid.

21 Shlomo Swinkelstein interview. Avraham Klinger (1900–1924), gravestone in the Jewish cemetery in Czeladź, http://jewishcemetery.czeladz.pl (accessed September 8, 2024).

22 Yosef Sfinkelstein interview.

23 Shlomo Swinkelstein interview. Aharon-Shmuel Klinger (1905–1925), gravestone in the Jewish cemetery in Czeladź, http://jewishcemetery.czeladz.pl (accessed September 8, 2024).

they didn't hold to the faith of their father's Hasidic home, they had found their own way in life. The eldest daughter—the fourth of the six children—Sarah (Sarah-Mindele, born in 1908)[24] was married in the early 1930s to Ya'akov Mgła the *shtaper* (boot-closer), a craftsman skilled in fitting the upper shoe to the sole, so Uncle Yosef told me. This was a highly desirable profession in Poland at the time.[25] The young couple apparently did well, and an earlier photograph of Sarah in profile from the 1920s shows a delicate young woman with a modish, curly hairstyle.[26] She and Ya'akov had two daughters: Malka-Chana, born in 1933,[27] and little Tova-Taube,[28] apparently nicknamed Tamusia,[29] who was born in 1940 just after the start of World War II.

The Klingers' second daughter Chaja-Nacha—nicknamed Chajka—was born in 1916 or 1917, followed in 1919 by Malka, or Mania as she was called by her friends during the war.[30] The two younger girls survived the vicissitudes of post-World War I and grew into well-educated young women. Perl and Leibel's grief was thus somewhat quelled by the pride they could take in their daughters who were succeeding so well in life.

And yet, although their daughters brought them some measure of comfort, the atmosphere at home seems to have been one of bitterness and resentment. In her diaries from the war period—personal and revealing as they are—Chajka rarely mentions her family. Nor do the testimonies relating to her school days at the Fürstenberg Gymnasium and her friends in Hashomer Hatzair afford many glimpses of her parents or visits to her home.[31] Thus, there is a scarcity of information about her childhood and family life, there being no one in her immediate family who survived to testify.

24 "Będzin Census of 1939," AŻIH, 212/11.

25 Yosef Sfinkelstein interview. Ya'akov Mgła was born in 1906.

26 Courtesy of the Ronen family photograph collection.

27 "Będzin Census of 1939," AŻIH, 212/11.

28 Zippora Eisenberg (Szporn), interview by the author, Kibbutz Galon, 1986.

29 Chajka Klinger, *Miyoman Bageto* (Hebrew) (Merhavia: Sifriat Poalim and Kibbutz Haogen, 1959), p. 114.

30 In the Będzin census, the youngest sister appears under the name of Malka-Chana. See "Będzin Census of 1939," AŻIH, 212/11. All other testimonies refer to her as Mania. See, for instance, Tosia Herzberg, interview by the author, Tel Aviv, 1985; Chana Lieberman interview.

31 Karola Bojm, interview by the author, Tel Aviv, 1985; Shraga Fruchtzweig, interview by the author, Tel Aviv, 1985.

All we know so far is this: Chajka was born in Będzin, Poland, the fifth daughter of an impoverished Hasidic family.[32] The few friends who entered the Klinger home during the 1930s would describe Leibel as an ultra-Orthodox Jew with a hoary beard and Perl as a gloomy, nervous housewife. The grocery store was a bleak place with scarcely any customers, and the atmosphere at home was no better, according to the girls' friends.[33] Their home was reminiscent of the atmosphere in Yiddish writer Kadya Molodowsky's poems:

> In a Warsaw neighborhood dingy and black
> find a swamp, a fence, and a shack.
> There lives Elke—a little girl
> With a light blue parasol.[34]

Kadya's Elke seeks to escape from the endless chores imposed by her impoverished parents into the world of her dreams, where the buttons she must sew turn into the wheels of a train, and "off she goes / traveling far and wide / to a land no one knows."[35] But Kadya, whose poems were an attempt to inspire the poor children of Israel, reveals nothing of the girl's feelings toward her parents. It would appear that a similarly dreary reality filled Chajka with rancor toward the parents who had brought her into such a world.

The Fürstenberg Gymnasium

A major transformation came about with Chajka's entry into secondary school. It was a surprising, almost revolutionary step for the daughter of a poor Hasidic family to attend a modern school that defied the society she had grown up in, a society that still questioned the need to send girls to school and viewed education as the greatest threat to the tradition of "ancestral Israel."

32 September 25, 1917, is the date that appears on Chajka's passport, her death certificate, and also her grave. A different birth date—September 28, 1916—appears in the "Będzin Census of 1939" and on her birth certificate in the Będzin registrar's office. The second date is most likely the correct one.

33 Esther Shoshan interview; Shraga Fruchtzweig interview; Ada Halperin (Neufeld) interview; Chana Lieberman interview.

34 The original Yiddish: "vint dart Elke / mit dar bleuer parasalke." Kadya Molodowsky, *Pithu Et Hasha'ar* (Hebrew) (Tel Aviv: Hakibbutz Hameuchad, 1979), p. 7.

35 Ibid.

The school Chajka attended—the Fürstenberg Gymnasium—reflected the flourishing Jewish society in Będzin at that time. In 1931, over half of the 21,000 inhabitants of the city were Jewish. With roots in the Middle Ages, Będzin had enjoyed a real surge of commercial development starting at the end of the nineteenth century, thanks to the rapid development of the nearby mining region called Zagłębie. There were a number of towns and cities with large Jewish populations in the vicinity of Będzin. The biggest of them was Sosnowiec, which was only a few kilometers away from Będzin and had an even larger Jewish community. Some saw the two as twin cities, but according to Będziners, Będzin was the "Zagłębien Jerusalem."[36] Here was the very heart of Jewish life in the region. Hasidim like Leibel Klinger could find the court of their choice in one of the eighteen *kloyzn* then active in Będzin. Leibel's sons could join one of twenty or more Jewish, Zionist, or socialist organizations. And one of the most conspicuous and highly developed centers of Jewish culture was the Fürstenberg Hebrew Gymnasium.

The Gymnasium, originally called Yavne, was established at the end of World War I. Wealthy Będziner Jews who wished to provide their children with a good education sought an alternative to the Catholic Gymnasium. The solution was a bilingual (Hebrew-Polish) school under government supervision. For the Jews of Poland, a Gymnasium of this type paved the way to modernity. Here their children could study the same curriculum as their Polish peers while retaining and developing their own national tradition. Student enrollment grew steadily until eventually, to accommodate for the demand, a new school was erected in the 1930s thanks to contributions from a wealthy Jew named Fürstenberg. The three-story building, now named after the philanthropist, became a source of pride for Będziners. The Gymnasium upheld the highest standards. It was considered an A-category school, meaning that it bestowed a first-rate matriculation diploma. Among its staff were teachers with master's and doctorate degrees.[37] Some of its alumni would become famous historians (Professor Joshua Prawer and Professor Joshua Efron), writers (Stanisław Wygodzki), scientists (Professor Natan Goldblum and Dr. Judith Sinai), and successful businessmen (Sigmund Strochlitz and Arno Lustiger).

Chajka entered the Gymnasium in the fourth or fifth grade. Her classmate Tosia Gutman (the future Tosia Herzberg) remembered her as

36 Avraham Stein, "Yerushalayim DeZaglembia" (Yiddish), in Avraham S. Stein, *Pinkas Bendin*, vol. 1 (Yiddish) (Tel Aviv: Irgun Yotzey Bendin BeYisrael, 1959), p. 6.

37 Joshua Efron, interview by the author, Tel Aviv, 1985.

a lovely, curly-haired girl with a mild voice. "There was a gentleness about her," she recalled later, "and she had her own unique approach to things. And sensitivity. She had great sensitivity."[38] Chajka and Tosia shared a room at the summer camp organized by the Gymnasium. At night, they would have long talks and share impressions. During one such conversation, Chajka confided in Tosia that her family had no idea she was attending the Fürstenberg Gymnasium. Ultra-Orthodox parents usually preferred their daughters to be educated at the Polish Catholic Gymnasium because at the Jewish Gymnasium, the classes were mixed. Leibel Klinger believed that his daughter was enrolled in the Polish Catholic Gymnasium. Some of Tosia's other friends practiced similar deception.[39]

Tosia's story provides the first indication of Chajka's estrangement from her family. It is easy to surmise that the Gymnasium represented the antithesis of her upbringing. The tall Gymnasium building—its doors flung open to the wide world, offering a top-rate education and a springboard to a promising career—stood in stark contrast to the meager grocery store and the Hasidic father absorbed in outdated ideas.

There is no evidence of Leibel Klinger's response upon learning that his daughter had lied. Presumably, he was hurt at first but later made peace with her. Chajka's studies were not terminated: After all, he had agreed to her studying in the Polish Catholic Gymnasium. Perhaps he was even proud of her—she was the first of his daughters to receive an education. Yet, he could not afford her tuition. Chajka received a scholarship from the Gymnasium, but when this proved inadequate, she started earning money as a private tutor.[40] In general, though a Gymnasium education was normally a privilege of the middle class, the Fürstenberg Gymnasium offered scholarships and ran a mutual-aid fund based on donations by the parents of wealthier students.[41] It is uncertain whether or not Chajka ever had to avail herself of this fund, but she certainly had to struggle. Chana Lieberman, her friend in the *hachshara* (kibbutz training group) later, was one of the few who visited Chajka's home and was deeply distressed

38 Tosia Herzberg (Gutman), interview with the author. The first interview with Tosia took place in 1985. Over the years—until 2004—many more conversations took place. Apart from the footnotes in this chapter, which refer to her testimony in 1985, the conversations as a whole will be referred to henceforth as Tosia Herzberg interview.

39 Ibid.

40 Tosia Herzberg interview.

41 Joshua Efron interview.

by the poverty and misery she saw there. She often wondered how Chajka had managed to study and succeed under those circumstances.[42]

According to Chajka's classmate Joshua Efron (or Kamiński, as he was known then), the Gymnasium's curriculum followed the Austro-Hungarian model introduced by teachers from Galicia. Most of the teachers at the Gymnasium were graduates of the universities of Lwów (Lviv) or Kraków, which had been part of the Habsburg Empire prior to World War I. Although Fürstenberg was bilingual, it developed into a humanistic Gymnasium where special emphasis was placed on Polish, German, and Latin studies. The study of Hebrew was minimal, and anyone wishing to study it further had to enroll in a special course in which both Chajka and Joshua Efron were participants.[43]

The Hebrew teacher was Dr. Hochwald from Bukovina, and according to some of Chajka's friends, he was one of the reasons for the decline of Hebrew studies at the Gymnasium. Tosia recalled with amusement that "Dr. Hochwald was a dear man. He didn't know Polish, but he insisted on speaking it."[44] Karola Bojm, another alumna of the school, put it more bluntly: "He was just plain ugly." Both women recalled that "Dr. Hochwald didn't like girls," either because the girls lagged behind the boys in Hebrew or because he was afraid of their sharp tongues. Nevertheless, according to Karola, even among the girls he had his favorites, Chajka in particular. He would seek her out between classes, and they would talk as they walked along the long Gymnasium corridors with everyone watching. "They seemed to have so much to say to each other. What did they talk about?" Karola wondered many years later.[45]

Was it Dr. Hochwald's timid love, the Jewish burden she had brought from home, or perhaps the Zionism so openly discussed within the walls of the Gymnasium that influenced Chajka? One thing is clear: Hebrew took on a special importance in Chajka's life. Tosia and Efron remembered her excelling in Hebrew.[46] According to Efron: "She put in a lot of effort and made spectacular progress in spite of not having an adequate basis, unlike the boys who were mostly graduates of the Mizrachi elementary school. She became the best student in the girls' group, particularly in Hebrew."[47]

42 Chana Lieberman interview.
43 Joshua Efron interview.
44 Tosia Herzberg interview.
45 Karola Bojm interview.
46 Tosia Herzberg interview; Joshua Efron interview.
47 Joshua Efron interview.

It seems that his linguistic difficulties and general risibility notwithstanding, Hochwald was very good at his profession. His Hebrew courses included biblical and literary studies. Under his tutelage, the students read modern Hebrew authors like Devorah Baron, Abraham Mapu, and Yosef Haim Brenner. Efron recalls that Dr. Hochwald was also active in the Hebrew Drama Club of which Chajka seems to have been a member and which performed plays on Jewish holidays such as on Purim and Hanukkah.[48]

Generally speaking, Fürstenberg was rather sympathetic to the Zionist movement. Their syllabus included the *Lashon Vesefer* (Language and Literature) textbook,[49] which was also used in Mandatory Palestine and contained prose and poetry by Ahad Ha'am, Bialik, and Shaul Tchernichovsky, among others. In 1930, Bialik himself visited Będzin and made sure to pay a visit to the Gymnasium.[50] It is, therefore, not surprising that many of the Gymnasium's students joined youth movements, particularly Hanoar Hatzioni (The Zionist Youth). Students gathered openly at school to plan activities and shape their future dreams.[51]

The Gymnasium had another feature that would influence Chajka's future—an emphasis on Polish and modern European culture. Tosia marveled at Chajka's proficiency in the Polish language, which was normally frowned upon in Hasidic homes, and she remembered Chajka's exquisite Polish compositions, which surpassed even the high standards of the Fürstenberg Gymnasium.[52] Indeed, Chajka's diaries and their daringly personal entries reveal how deeply influenced she was by Polish culture and the revolutionary romanticism epitomized by several generations of Polish writers. Joshua Efron remembered Chajka reading a great deal of Stefan Żeromski, the most prominent writer of the critical yet romantic Young Poland movement. The character of Tomasz Judym, the idealistic doctor who lives among the people, must have exerted a formative influence on the students at the Fürstenberg Gymnasium. Likewise, *Płomienie* (Flames) by Stanisław Brzozowski also had a powerful effect on the developing personalities of young readers—the story of the soulful

48 Ibid.

49 Yaakov Fichman, *Lashon Vesefer: Sefer Limud Umikra Im Mahlaka Le'avodot Bihtav* (Hebrew) (Warsaw: Central, 1923–1924). It was a four-volume Hebrew-language textbook with a workbook section.

50 Mordehai Hampel, "Bikurey Ishim BeBendin" (Hebrew), in Stein, *Pinkas Bendin*, vol. 2, pp. 318–319.

51 Joshua Efron interview.

52 Tosia Herzberg interview.

struggles and travels of Michael Kaniowski, the Polish aristocrat who joins the Narodniks (late nineteenth-century Russian revolutionaries), which became a cult favorite among Chajka and members of her generation.[53] They also read Zofia Nałkowska, who, at the turn of the century, was among the first Polish intellectuals to fight for women's rights and wrote about gender issues, as well as Wanda Wasilewska, a young communist writer who adopted the socialist-realism style that was entirely innovative at the time.

And there were also European works, particularly from Germany. Students read Goethe and Schiller as part of their studies as well as Thomas Mann, Stefan Zweig, and Erich Maria Remarque, either in the original language or a translation.[54] Chajka also read books translated from French and other European languages: Louis-Ferdinand Céline, Roger Martin du Gard, Romain Rolland, and Jaroslav Hašek, to name a few.[55] Books formed an intimate part of Chajka's world. There are no less than eighteen writers mentioned in her diaries alongside paraphrases of literary passages that particularly impressed her. The silence of the wretched in I.L. Peretz's *Bontshe Shvayg* (Bontshe the Silent), the revolutionary death described in André Malraux's *La Condition Humaine*, and the rebellion of the Armenians in Franz Werfel's *The Forty Days of Musa Dagh* all left their mark on Chajka and her friends.[56]

53 Stanisław Brzozowski, *Płomienie* (Lwów: Połonieckiego, 1908). *Płomienie* (Flames) exerted a formative influence on a generation and a half of leading Poles like Leszek Kołakowski, Czesław Miłosz, and Adam Michnik. More will be discussed later concerning his profound effect on members of Hashomer Hatzair. The book was one of the first to be published by Sifriat Poalim Press, founded by Hashomer Hatzair in Mandatory Palestine. Stanisław Brzozowski, *Lehavot* (Hebrew) (Merhavia: Sifriat Poalim, 1939–1940).

54 The list of works, according to the account of Joshua Efron, included the two most influential books by Thomas Mann among contemporary youth: *Tonio Kröger* and *The Magic Mountain*. Both deal with the power of art and the longing for unattainable beauty. Stefan Zweig's psychological novels (*Amok*, *Fear*, *Twenty-Four Hours in the Life of a Woman*, and others published after World War I) had a particular influence on the educated elites who adopted his fascination with the human psyche. Erich Maria Remarque's novel, *All Quiet on the Western Front* (1929), was considered the greatest anti-war novel of its day.

55 Most of these books were translated from the French and will be discussed further.

56 Most noteworthy here is Franz Werfel's *The Forty Days of Musa Dagh*, tr. by Geoffrey Dunlop (New York: Modern Library, 1934), which deals with the Armenian genocide during World War I, published in German in 1933, in Hebrew in 1934, and in Yiddish in 1939. No Polish translation from the 1930s can be found. Malraux's *La condition humaine* (The Human Condition) was published in France in 1933 and

She absorbed the values of the postwar-generation writers with their hatred of war, their apprehension of a strange, alienating, and predatory world, and their faith in the possibility of transforming it into a better, more just world. In a rare essay, probably composed during her Gymnasium days,[57] Chajka's clear, round hand describes a reluctant stroll through town. Her feet carry her while her eyes follow obediently, submitting to their will:

> But I don't want to go, to look back, something is screaming inside me, something keeps rebelling. I don't want to go, I don't want to look at anything, but my legs keep on walking without any conscious effort. All that noise and bustle around me, the city is alive, people walking hurriedly in all directions. I see so many people. They have fat, sated faces. Their eyes are thoughtless, greedy, stupid, and evil. They are dressed elegantly: coats, suits, furs, silk stockings and lace.... Among the crowd, I occasionally glimpse a different face: thin, sallow, swollen, filled with worry, sadness, and grief. Their clothes are dirty, full of patches and spots; you walk on, but they are everywhere around you, right behind you or right in front, there is no getting rid of them. They chase you down and eventually catch up, and I cannot help but wonder: Will it always be like this? Will the world always be like this?
>
> A sudden silence, then a noise, footsteps, people running, shouting as they run. The flow of humanity carries me along, I can feel the crowd around me, hear an ambulance wailing in the distance. There is an elegant luxury car in the street; next to it there is a small boy lying in a pool of blood. My heart tightens, I turn away. I cannot look, but there are people gathering next to the car. The same sallow, thin, sunken cheeks, but so entirely changed, full of hatred, the desire for revenge. I can imagine myself sitting in that car. I imagine knowing that, in one moment, the crowd will attack us, destroying everything in their path. The car, however, turns back and drives off, while everyone else looks sheepish, standing in the street, blaming each other, swearing. When will they finally confront

translated into Polish in the mid-thirties. It, too, had a special influence on Chajka, which will be discussed later on.

57 Chajka Klinger, "Unititled essay," Moreshet Archive, Avihu Ronen collection, 235. The essay's date of composition is unknown. It would be published in a *hachshara* pamphlet later, but its contents and style point to a Gymnasium-period composition. The handwritten manuscript was preserved by Esther Shoshan in Kibbutz Galon.

> the "others" and destroy them? When will it happen?—the question keeps surfacing in my mind. But then a new surge of strength, I can feel it in my legs, my legs walk on. Or perhaps they are no longer walking, they are running, running away. I am running faster and faster. I am sprinting home, racing to get away from the street. My thoughts are racing too, one after the other. Can I just close myself off, cushion myself with peace and security, hear only distant echoes of the street? No, I cannot run away, cannot close myself off, I will not forget them, I will, undoubtedly, be back.[58]

In her sensitive soul, the fear of poverty clashed with a revolt against the world that gave rise to it; the desire to shut herself away from injustice clashed with the impulse to fight it. For the rest of her life, she would waver between the two poles of this duality.

58 Ibid.

Chapter Three

"Hearken Not, My Son, to the Father's Lesson"

Hashomer Hatzair

Most pupils at the Fürstenberg Gymnasium tended to join Hanoar Hatzioni, the strongest Jewish youth movement in Będzin and Zagłębie. They normally came from well-to-do families, and Hanoar Hatzioni with its strong affinity to the Tzionim Klaliyim (General Zionists) movement was ideologically attuned to the moderate views they brought from home.[1] But Chajka had ideas of her own. She joined the socialist Hashomer Hatzair movement.

Hashomer Hatzair was the classic youth movement of its day. It began as one of various Jewish scout movements that sprouted up all over Galicia and Poland on the eve of World War I and took its name from the Jewish defense organization Hashomer (The Guardian) in Mandatory Palestine. The youth movement adopted a paramilitary program and the ideals of life in nature as the condition for mental and physical health according to the Scout Movement founder Robert Baden-Powell. An element of Jewish nationalism was added—a prevailing trend among the youth of the era that saw ideas of nationalism spread throughout Europe. In 1916, these Jewish scouts joined the movement that was closest to them in spirit—Hashomer—to form the Hashomer Hatzair youth movement.[2]

1 Karola Bojm interview; Tosia Herzberg interview; Naftali Tzachar, interview by the author, Tel Yitzhak, 1986; Joshua Efron interview.

2 Levi Dror and Israel Rosenzweig, eds., *Sefer Hashomer Hatzair*, vol. 1 (Hebrew) (Merhavia: Sifriat Poalim, 1956), p. 32.

One of the earliest branches of this group emerged in Będzin. Known for its staunch autonomy, this *ken* (branch) never joined the nationwide movement, notwithstanding the name Hashomer Hatzair that it adopted in 1918. This state of affairs displeased the heads of the movement, and when certain branch leaders were arrested during the 1920s, they shut down the Będzin branch. Three years later, a new *ken* was formed, which maintained closer ties with the nationwide movement. That is, until 1927.[3]

The stubbornness of Hashomer Hatzair in Będzin was a manifestation of the growing pains the movement was undergoing during those years. Although new youth movements were springing up everywhere in the 1920s, Hashomer Hatzair was unique among them. Its young members were reading Sigmund Freud and Friedrich Nietzsche, whose intellectual merits were still disputed in Vienna and Berlin. They drew their concept of youth culture (*Jugendkultur*)—as the antithesis of the tired and tainted world of adults—from the German educator Gustav Wyneken and the back-to-nature, German Wandervogel youth movement. From Hans Blüher, the Wandervogel ideologue, they learned about Eros, the emotional affinity that binds groups of young men in the idolization of a charismatic leader.[4] From Karl Marx, they drew their faith in the revolutionary might of the proletariat; from Theodor Herzl—faith in a Zionist utopia; from Gustav Landauer, the German-Jewish anarchist who rejected Marxism and called for a humanistic socialism—the ideas of the anarchist commune; and from the philosopher Martin Buber—the culture of dialogue and the aspiration of "personal fulfillment."[5] This strange commixture was far from synthesized at the time. It epitomized the soul-searching and questing of youth who refused to grow up.

Immigration to Mandatory Palestine did not put an end to this search. In Bitania Illit, on a hilltop overlooking the Sea of Galilee, a group of *shomrim* (members of Hashomer Hatzair) sought to combine socialist labor and the reclamation of the land with the most deeply intimate and open communal life possible. As the sweat of the workday evaporated and their aching backs uncurled, the youthful members gathered at night for the rite of the Hashomer discussion in a hut on the otherwise barren

3 Haim Wolgryn, "Hashomer Hatzair" (Hebrew), in Stein, *Pinkas Bendin*, vol. 2, pp. 280–281.

4 Hans Blüher, *Die Deutsche Wandervogelbewegung als Erotisches Phänomen: Ein Beitrag zur Erkenntnis der Sexuellen Inversion* (Berlin-Tempelhof: Weise, 1912).

5 Martin Buber met Hashomer Hatzair members during World War I in Vienna and urged them to consolidate their ideas by immigrating to Mandatory Palestine.

hilltop. There was an elitist desire for individualism among these young intellectuals, the will to emphasize their uniqueness and difference from all the other indigent laborers working on building roads. *Kehilatenu* (Our Community) was the name of the anthology they published in 1922, in which they expressed their youthful longings, their spiritual yearnings, and the erotic anguish of which they were reluctant to let go.[6]

The man who stood at the head of this group would soon put an end to this youthful romanticism. Meir Ya'ari—scion of a Hasidic family, a former officer in the Austro-Hungarian army, and the charismatic leader of those wild confessional nights—left Bitania suddenly following a long vigil when the group turned sharply against him.[7] Ya'ari was unforgiving. In an article published in 1923, he called for a rejection of "the detached symbols" of the Bitania youth movement in favor of the values of work and personal fulfillment espoused by A.D. Gordon.[8] Thus, he reshaped his role as leader and ideologue of the youth movement and outlined its future course in *Eretz Israel*—moving away from "youth culture" with its quasi-mystical symbolism toward "the long gray road" of integrating into the masses toiling to build the Land of Israel.[9]

By 1927, the movement's direction was clear. With the establishment of Hakibbutz Ha'artzi, which united all the kibbutzim of Hashomer Hatzair in Mandatory Palestine, Hashomer Hatzair accepted the yoke of Marxist Socialism combined with pioneering Zionism and an irrevocable commitment to the establishment of kibbutzim in Mandatory Palestine as the sole means of personal fulfillment.[10] These principles were to become obligatory for those who came out of the movement in Europe. Members who rejected these principles or wished to find their own paths toward personal fulfillment—students for example—were expelled from the movement.

This turn of events was not met with approval by the *bogrim* (veteran members) of the Hashomer Hatzair branch in Będzin: "When

6 *Kehilateinu* (Hebrew) (Jerusalem: Yad Ben Zvi, 1922).

7 For a detailed description of Ya'ari's place in Bitania, see Aviva Halamish, *Meir Ya'ari: Biografia Kibbutzit Hamishim Hashanim Harishonot, 1897–1947* (Hebrew) (Tel Aviv: Am Oved, 2009), pp. 56–72.

8 For the full article, see David Zayit and Yosef [Josef] Shamir, eds., *Me'ir Ya'ari: Diyukano shel Manhig Ke'adam Tza'ir—Pirkey Hayim, 1897–1929* (Hebrew) (Givat Haviva: Yad Ya'ari, 1992), pp. 124–132.

9 Ibid., pp. 131–132.

10 Margalit Elkana, *Hashomer Hatzair: Medat Ne'urim Lemarksism Mahap'hani, 1913–1936* (Hebrew) (Tel Aviv: Hakibbutz Hameuchad, 1971), pp. 135–150.

our council emissaries returned from the conference [of 1927] and reported its rulings, stormy arguments broke out in the *ken*, leading to a serious crisis and ultimately to a schism."[11] The Będzin *ken* effectively fell apart. Many left to join movements like Hashomer Haleumi (The National Guard), which in time became Hanoar Hatzioni. This movement flourished in Będzin and was more tolerant of the choices made by its *bogrim*. *Aliya* (immigration) to the Land of Israel was considered important but remaining in Poland and participating in local Zionist activities was acceptable too and viewed with understanding. Socialism was likewise interpreted along more moderate lines. Hanoar Hatzioni intended to establish its own kibbutzim in Mandatory Palestine but did not peremptorily reject nonsocialist paths toward personal fulfillment.[12]

The Founding of the Będzin *Ken*

In 1932, Esther Zborowska's family moved to Będzin. Esther (later Esther Shoshan) was a member of Hashomer Hatzair in nearby Zawiercie, but when she arrived in Będzin, she found no active branch of the movement there. Esther's family were staunch adepts of the movement, and the three children—all members of Hashomer Hatzair—set about organizing a *ken* in Będzin. Their first step was to contact a group of Hashomer Haleumi veterans, among whom Esther remembered Ada Neufeld (later Ada Halperin). Very soon, they established a *ken* and began regular activities.[13]

The founding of the *ken* in Będzin became a point of prestige for Hashomer Hatzair members in Zagłębie. From the solid, well-organized *ken* in the nearby town of Dąbrowa Górnicza, Shraga Fruchtzweig—already a member of the *hachshara*—came to offer help and guidance. Every Shabbat, he and his friends would show up to breathe life into the budding *ken*.[14] A student from Będzin at the Vilna Polytechnic Institute took it upon himself to lead the group during school breaks, and within a short time, the *ken*'s membership grew to a total of roughly 150. Their most important activity was recruiting new *chanichim* (junior members), and to this end, they turned to the Gymnasium. Their efforts paid off:

11 Mordehai Hampel, "Hanoar Hatzioni" (Hebrew), in Stein, *Pinkas Bendin*, vol. 2, p. 292.

12 Ibid.

13 Esther Shoshan interview.

14 Shraga Fruchtzweig interview.

Between 1934 and 1935, a group of Gymnasium students joined the *ken*, among them the sisters Irka and Lea Pejsachson, and Chajka Klinger.[15]

We have no direct testimony about what might have motivated Chajka to join Hashomer Hatzair and can only infer it from her character and activities during this period. In 1934, Chajka was seventeen years old. Photographs of the period show her boldly facing the camera with the trace of a smile. Friends from her days in the *hachshara* remember her as happy and markedly extroverted.[16] She was easily animated and easily enamored. This may have been an expression of the rebellious side of her nature, which surfaced during those Gymnasium days in the company of the lively Esther and her friends. Or perhaps it was the shy young love that had developed between her and Shraga Fruchtzweig. Shraga was Chajka's first boyfriend. He was slightly older, a *boger* of the movement and the *hachshara*. When they first met, she had never heard of Hashomer Hatzair, or as he put it, "She was intelligent but knew nothing about the movement."[17] The young couple would stroll through the town hand in hand or see a film at the cinema. According to Shraga they were "very close."[18]

And there was another equally important factor for Chajka. Hashomer Hatzair had absorbed the Marxist ideology that had been adopted by the kibbutzim in *Eretz Israel* without forsaking the spirit of youthful rebelliousness, which had characterized the movement from its inception. Ya'ari's proclamation notwithstanding, the Polish branches of the movement were loath to give up the "detached symbols" of youth culture. Thus, while more and more kibbutzim in *Eretz Israel* took the "long gray road" toward the realization of the socialist ideal, Hashomer Hatzair in Poland preserved their romantic ideals and the myth of Bitania.[19] There was plenty of Eros in the intimate friendships that developed between members, in their adulation of male and female leaders, even in their personal commitment to the movement's values. The norms they adopted expressed a fervent idealism and an unceasing

15 Ibid.

16 Shmaryahu Milinsky, interview by the author, Kibbutz Galon, 1985; Abrashka Eisenberg, interview by the author, Kibbutz Galon, 1985.

17 Shraga Fruchtzweig interview.

18 Ibid.

19 The book *Sefer Hashomrim*, which was published in Warsaw in 1934, can serve as clear evidence for this. See Yehuda Gotthelf and Avraham Cohen, eds., *Sefer Hashomrim: Antologia Leyovel Hashomer Hatzair, 1913–1933* (Warsaw: Hahanhaga He'elyona Lehistadrut Hashomer Hatzair, 1934).

protest against the decadent world of the adults: "A *shomer* is a person of truth," they are an "*Ahiezer*" (helping brother) and an "*Ahisamah*" (trustful brother), "faithful to nation and fatherland", a *shomer* does not drink or smoke and preserves sexual purity.[20] For many junior members, the *ken* provided a surrogate family.

Hashomer Hatzair retained its youthful autonomy at the institutional level as well. Unlike other youth movements, it chose not to affiliate itself with a political party.[21] On an ideological level, it associated the Marxist hope of creating a new world with the youth revolution. On the walls of Hashomer Hatzair branches hung a poem by David Shimonowitz (Shimoni):

> Hearken not, my son, to the father's lesson
> Nor incline thine ear to the mother's law
> For the lesson of the father is line upon line
> And the law of the mother moves ever so slow.[22]

Other youth movements were also inspired by this intergenerational conflict, but only Hashomer Hatzair turned it into a manifesto. Presumably, it was the rebellious, if not revolutionary elements, that contributed to Chajka's immediate affiliation with this particular youth movement. It was a direct extension of her rebellious impulses vis-à-vis tradition, which she had first expressed by enrolling at the Fürstenberg Gymnasium.

According to the available testimonies, Chajka took on her educational work in the movement with enthusiasm. Before long, she was appointed counselor for a group of Gymnasium girls and later as editor of the *ken* newspaper and a member of its leadership.[23] Though the *ken* was originally founded on the idea of youth labor, it also needed the skills and education of the Gymnasium students. From Chajka's perspective, she needed the warmth and youthful merriment that abounded in the *ken*. As mentioned, Chajka never spoke about her family and was not in the habit of inviting friends to her home. Esther, for one, found this puzzling: She expected Gymnasium students to hail from broadminded, well-to-do families. On the one or two occasions when Esther happened by the

20 "Aseret Hadibrot," in Dror and Rosenzweig, *Sefer Hashomer Hatzair*, vol. 1, p. 44.
21 This decision was reached at the Danzig Conference of 1927. Ibid., pp. 166–168.
22 As cited in ibid., p. 53.
23 Esther Shoshan, letter to the author, Kibbutz Galon, August 22, 1985.

Klinger house, she came away dejected. Even though she had never made it past the doorway, she could sense the gloom inside. She remembered the sight of Chajka's father absorbed in prayer and her impoverished-looking mother.[24] Esther's home was altogether different. Although she herself was motherless and her father worked as a tailor, their home was "open" and "filled with light." There was always singing as well as conversations about the movement. In her family, the father deferred to the children, voting Hashomer Hatzair in the Zionist Congress elections on their behalf. When Hashomer Hatzair leadership members visited Będzin, they stayed with the Zborowski family rather than with Chajka's family, despite the prestige of her Gymnasium education or idealistic fervor.[25] Home and *ken* were two different worlds, and the distance between them grew ever greater.

Enter David

It was Esther who brought David Kozłowski into the *ken*. She had gone to buy something at a stationary store and happened to catch sight of a Hashomer Hatzair badge on the lapel of the tall, young salesman. When she asked about the badge, it turned out that he was a member of Hashomer Hatzair from Pińczów. Esther invited him to the *ken* and became his girlfriend sometime later.[26]

Chajka described David's arrival at the *ken* and her subsequent relationship with him in one of the loveliest passages she wrote:

> Nobody paid any attention to him when he first visited our Hashomer Hatzair office. A tall, slim boy. I can only remember that all his pockets were stuffed with newspapers.
>
> I glanced at him once in the library, where I was with a group of my schoolmates. I asked the librarian for a book, but she refused me for the first time, saying, "No, I've promised this one to Mr. Kozłowski. You must excuse me, but I have to give it to him. He's in a privileged position because he's our first reader."
>
> Discontented, I turn back and he's standing behind me, smiling mockingly. I turn around quickly to avoid the risk of my friends

24 Esther Shoshan interview.
25 Ibid.
26 Ibid.

> jeering me, "Oh, it's your *shomer* friend." I pretend that I don't know him. He never forgave me for that.
>
> He had a stutter. I never had the patience to hear him out.
>
> I was carefree, joyful, and loved to smile and frolic, while he was serious. He didn't exist for me.
>
> I didn't know him. They were saying that he had come for Esterka [Esther], that as a matter of fact he was a communist and that he would not stay.
>
> Esterka left for the *hachshara*, whereas he stayed. We were publishing a newspaper, of which I was the editor. He gave me a poem—a beautiful one with a wonderful rhythm and composed with artistic taste. It was a song filled with sadness and longing, about a lonely, lost soul. So much emotion and lyricism emanated from it and so much sadness and pain.
>
> Everybody was wondering who had written it and I was the only one who knew that it was Dawid [David]. And that was the first time I noticed him. The first time I saw his eyes, brown and deep-set. They were so beautiful, so velvety, brown, and oblong. So much unfathomable sadness was apparent in them.
>
> "Those are the eyes of a dreamer," I said to myself.[27]

As one door closed, another seemed to open. In 1936, Esther went off to the *hachshara*, and Shraga was recruited to the Polish army shortly after. Chajka was nineteen years old by then, and she had a *ken*, a youth movement, and a new great love. What she wrote about David paints a picture of her own world. In David's image, her youthful romanticism found its perfect expression. In him she saw Goethe's famous character of Werther combined with a young Marx and a socially conscious Narodnik. A young man bearing the troubles of the world on his shoulders, wishing to redeem the world of its miseries one minute and the next, redeemed from it by taking his own life. His spiritual world became hers:

> He intrigued me. He used to read a lot. He simply devoured books, each leaving its imprint on him, each depositing something in his

27 Chajka Klinger, *I Am Writing These Words to You: The Original 1943 Diaries, Będzin 1943*, ed. by Avihu Ronen (Jerusalem and Givat Haviva: Yad Vashem and Moreshet, 2017), pp. 166–167. All names of people and localities quoted from the original diaries were retained in their original forms. A clarification for each name appears in square brackets in the text.

soul. Once it was *Jean-Christophe* speaking through him. Another time it was *Antoinette* or phantoms that caused unrest in his soul. Another time it was Shakespeare who made a tremendous impression on him.

He was consuming books chaotically: ancient classics, poetry, and Celine's *Voyage au bout de la nuit* [Journey to the End of the Night].[28] Consequently, he often shifted from a fine mood into sheer depression. One minute he wanted to embrace the whole world and everybody and love them in his heart, and then he thought that the entire world was one big mess, men—degenerates, women—whores, muck, corruption, and decadence. He didn't want to live.

He wanted to fall asleep, die, commit suicide and not exist.[29] [...]

What was both touching and beautiful about him? It was the fire constantly burning in him, the fire of emotions, the reverence for heroism and that constant readiness, that readiness to fight for liberation. At first [he yearned for] vague, *Weltschmerz* [world weariness], liberation of all mankind and then [for] liberation of the proletariat based on a thorough knowledge of Marxism.

I remember him talking beautifully about Malraux's *Man's Fate*, the revolution in China, Chen, and Mary. One could feel that he was standing by them, that he was ready to go with them, and that he was one of them.[30]

28 The books Chajka mentions, most of them translated from the French, are a mixture of classical literature, romanticism, and nihilistic pessimism. While Romain Rolland's *Jean-Christophe* and *The Enchanted Soul* were cult classics among young Europeans of the 1920s and 1930s who were intrigued by the psychological development of a rebellious genius and a young woman struggling for spiritual freedom, the influence of Celine's dark novel in which the world perceived as absurd is irredeemable even by love, seems particularly curious. The fact that Celine would go on to become a racist, an antisemite, and a Nazi sympathizer is likewise not without interest with regard to this book. *The Nightmares* is apparently the name of a novel by the Polish journalist Tadeusz Jaroszyński (1862–1917). Chajka and David could have read Romain Rolland either in the Polish, Yiddish, or Hebrew translations that appeared during this time.

29 Klinger, *I Am Writing These Words to You* (1943 diaries), p. 167.

30 The Polish translation of Malraux's novel (*La condition humaine*, published in French in 1933) appeared during the 1930s. The book describes the struggles of the Chinese communists during the civil war against the forces of Chiang Kai-shek and invests the idea of the heroes' revolutionary death with a romantic aura. Chan, the book's hero, believes that dying for the sake of the revolution is the only way he can fulfill his life's purpose.

> When Dawid was speaking long and inspiringly, one forgot his stutter.
>
> And then during the revolution in Spain he wrote an excellent article, and once again you felt your soul reaching out to them, to those fighting for freedom. There was no posturing or insincerity in him. One felt that he was ready to join them on the barricades that day or the next. His words were not idle chatter, platitudes, nor were they dry, Marxist populism. He was a revolutionary.
>
> Dawid kept abreast of the times and was always on the side of those who were fighting for liberation.[31]

Chajka fell in love. Her words reveal just how deeply she herself was immersed in that romantic, revolutionary state of mind. In the figure of David, conflicting elements of youth culture and Hashomer Hatzair came together as one unified manifestation of the Zeitgeist of that place and time. The tempestuous spirit of French literature after World War I replaced the turn-of-the-century Viennese literary and artistic movement Sturm und Drang, and staunch Marxism turned into more general yet fervent aspirations for world change. Yet despite its volatile nature, this new cultural brew retained its former groundbreaking defiance.

The moment David entered her life, Chajka lost interest in her family. Had Leibel and Perl Klinger known about David, they would have had to reconcile themselves to their daughter's otherness. At any rate, there is no evidence of friction between Chajka and her parents. In the *ken*, David was a questioning young intellectual who reminded her of the heroes in the books she read. She felt that his soul cried out for help. As the stronger and more practical one, Chajka felt that she had to protect him, to shield him from the pricklier elements of their circle and help him bring out his hidden potential:

> He was in need of a kindred spirit and support. I offered him my hand. He was like a young tree, blown by winds yet tall, slender, and growing up toward the sky, the sun. To bloom and grow he needed strong, down-to-earth support—also a sun, a kindred feeling, and spirit and love and caresses. I saw his soul in his speech, which was emerging with such difficulty.
>
> He suffered greatly on account of his speech [impediment]. Few people realized it as he didn't have a fixed *Minderwertigkeitsgefühle*

31 Klinger, *I Am Writing These Words to You* (1943 diaries), pp. 170–171.

> [inferiority complex]. Nonetheless, he did suffer for he had to remain silent when so many beautiful words during ceremonies, or so many factual arguments during discussions—for he was very knowledgeable—were springing to his lips too late.
>
> And that was why in his heart he dreamed about writing. Talented, he wanted to continue learning and to excel, to learn more and more. He wanted to fathom, absorb, know, and comprehend everything. His heart was insatiable too. He wanted to embrace and absorb every feeling, all pain, longing, joy, sadness, and love in all their shades.
>
> His heart was so insatiable.
>
> Dawid could love madly for he knew no half measures and gave his entire self. He loved with all his senses and his passionate soul. One minute he was passionate, the next moment delicate like a most affectionate friend.
>
> Dawid could not live without a girl, could not live without love.[32]

When the two became a couple, David was twenty.[33] It would appear that even within the movement he was considered eccentric, whether because of his absentmindedness or his leftist leanings. He stretched the inherent radicalism of Hashomer Hatzair to the dangerous point of "deviation." A case in point would be his eagerness to fight in the Spanish Civil War. While Hashomer Hatzair sympathized strongly with the Republicans, it expelled those who joined the International Brigade. The members were expected to wage the class war in one place only, and that place was *Eretz Israel*.[34] Chajka noted:

> He had a difficult life—away from his family home and having experienced neither warmth nor protection. His father came once a year, collected his annual salary, and left—he [the father] was selling a servant.
>
> Dawid didn't complain and was happy to support his family. But rebellion was welling up within him, rebellion against his father.

32 Ibid., pp. 167–168.

33 In the 1939 Będzin census, Didia (David) Kozłowski appears with the birth year of 1916. See "Będzin Census of 1939," AŻIH, 212/11.

34 In the Hashomer Hatzair *ken* in Warsaw, two veteran members, Moshe Kopito and Jakob Fliderbaum ("Dutens") were ousted from the movement for joining the International Brigade. See Israel Gutman, *Mered Hanetzurim: Mordechai Anilevitz Vemilhemet Geto Varsha* (Hebrew) (Jerusalem and Givat Haviva: Yad Vashem and Moreshet, 2013), pp. 51–53.

> He did not want to follow in the footsteps of his father, for whom money was the greatest power. He had all the predispositions to work his way up and earn a fortune, but was unwilling to become a servant of money.
>
> He was talented and lucky as hell, but he despised money and was careless with it. When the kibbutz purse was empty, he filled it. When somebody fell deeply into debt, Dawid would provide some secret help.
>
> All of his friends owed him money, but he kept forgetting about those debts. He would only wave his hand. He was criticized for that, but that was how he was. "You can even strip him of his trousers," people used to say.
>
> He was so kind that it bordered on gullibility.[35]

Is it a coincidence that this description is the earliest reference in her diaries to the prewar period? Leibel and Perl, the Hasidic family, the house on Modrzejowska Street, childhood games—there is no mention of any of these in her diaries. David, Hashomer Hatzair, and her budding young love seem to have overshadowed all previous memories.

35 Klinger, *I Am Writing These Words to You* (1943 diaries), pp. 168–169. No further biographical details of David's origins have been found. For more on Pińczów, see Mordehai Shenar, ed., *In Pintshev Togt Shoyn Nisht / Sefer Zikaron Lekehilat Pintshev* (Yiddish and Hebrew) (Tel Aviv: Irgun Yotzey Pintshev BeYisrael U'vatefutzot, 1970).

Chapter Four

A Melody of Sorrow

The *Hachsharot*

In the 1930s, the *hachshara* was "the central link in the lengthy process of transitioning from the community of the town *ken* to settlement in [Mandatory] Palestine."[1] Graduates of the movement would organize into *aliya* kibbutzim in nearby cities or towns in order to train for communal labor and life in the Land of Israel. By 1933, the Hashomer Hatzair movement had thirty-four *aliya* kibbutzim consisting of 4,000 members in total, 1,500 of whom were participating in *hachshara* programs.[2]

This seemingly dry statistic reveals part of the problems encountered by the *hachsharot*. Clearly, they could not accept all the members knocking on their doors. Poland was not spared the financial crisis that gripped the world in the 1930s, and the *hachshara* programs were unable to provide an income for unemployed *shomrim*. Many members had no choice but to hang around while they waited for their turn to go through the *hachshara* and immigrate to Mandatory Palestine.

Yet despite the economic hardships and suffering, the *hachshara* remained an exciting and rewarding experience. Years later, Shmaryahu Milinsky, a member of the Hapo'el Lakfar *hachshara* program in Kalisz and later a member of Kibbutz Galon, would remember not only the hunger and destitution but also the fervor of faith in the movement and

1 Levi Aryeh Sarid, *Hehalutz Vetnu'ot Hano'ar BePolin, 1917–1939* (Hebrew) (Tel Aviv: Am Oved, 1979), pp. 589–590.

2 Ibid., p. 589.

the desire to move forward toward a new future.[3] His eyes sparkled as he testified to his experience, while from behind the armchair in which he was seated, the eyes of a young man looking out of a framed black-and-white photograph implied that his woes would not end in Kalisz.

Hapo'el Lakfar

Hapo'el Lakfar (the worker to the countryside). This strange name tells us quite a bit about the vision of Jewish productivization espoused by members of the *haschshara* programs as inspired by the Marxist Zionist Ber Borochov's philosophy. Jewish youth was seeking to flip the "upside-down pyramid" of the Jewish "anomaly": to fundamentally change the existing socioeconomic structure of European Jewry wherein most Jews worked in "unproductive" professions (mainly in the mercantile or administrative sectors) and among whom the peasants and laborers who formed the foundation of any "normal" society were a minority.[4] The youth movements that had wholeheartedly embraced Borochov's vision wished to realize it through agricultural settlement in the form of kibbutzim. However, due to the shortage of agricultural training farms, most of the *hachshara* kibbutzim were established in urban centers. If they could prepare themselves for field labor in the kibbutz, they would be "workers" going out to the "countryside."

The *hachshara* program began in the town of Mława where approximately twenty-five graduates from Zagłębie and Volhynia gathered in May 1935. At this first meeting, "the operations of the kibbutz in the near future and our role at this time" were discussed, the first committees were elected, and the name of the first "worker" kibbutz was picked.[5] The youngsters were in for a tough time in Mława as they lacked both guidance and work. In mid-July, they got into a spot of trouble when a Christian child and an elderly woman were injured in a work accident caused by one of the members. The town turned against them. Fearing for their safety, the group put guards on the doors at night, and they dreaded the walk to work in the mornings.[6] A few members began reconsidering their options, and the first walkouts began. Yet, "even in

3 Shmaryahu Milinsky interview.

4 Ber Borochov, *Selected Works of Ber Borochov* (n.p.: CreateSpace Independent Publishing Platform, 2011).

5 "Hapo'el," *Hayovel*, May 1937, Kibbutz Galon Archive, p. 26.

6 *Hayovel*, May 1937, Kibbutz Galon Archive, pp. 3, 27–28.

this state of affairs, we saw the necessity of distancing the few people who could not go forward with us."[7]

The long-awaited turning point came with the move to Kalisz in April 1936. Here, they were welcomed by members of Lamifal (to the factory), another *hachshara* kibbutz. However before long, the warm welcome gave way to tensions between the two kibbutzim on the subject of labor and economic arrangements. Finally, they merged into one kibbutz: Hapo'el Lakfar. In May 1937, the Kalisz *hachshara* celebrated its one-year anniversary, while the kibbutz celebrated its second year.

A few months later, David Kozłowski arrived at the *hachshara*.[8] As was also the case with many others, his participation in the program involved a difficult decision. David's father was opposed to the pioneer way of life and offered to pay for his son's *aliya* expenses as long as he did not immigrate under a pioneer immigration certificate. Alternatively, he offered to pay his son's university tuition.[9] David refused and joined the *hachshara*. There, he met a few familiar faces, such as Esterka (Zborowska) from Będzin and Abrashka (Eisenberg) from the nearby town of Żarki. Others were less familiar. According to Chajka's diaries, the *hachshara* members recognized him immediately as an intellectual, which apparently did not play in his favor:

> The first days were difficult and full of disappointments.
>
> Dawid had imagined and dreamed of everything differently in his mind. He had expected that the people would be ideal, that there would not be any petty, stupid, and trivial issues. That life would be bustling with new content and that it would sweep him away with its fullness. But there were days that were monotonous, dead, and horribly empty. [...]
>
> He had to be taught life like a little child. And he needed to be brought down to earth from the clouds again and again.[10]

The above description may have been exaggerated as it was written years later and informed by a great dose of compassion. David, the ever-daydreaming man of the mind, became friends with the practical and

7 Article by Shayke Goldrin in *Hayovel*, May 1937, Kibbutz Galon Archive, p. 5. This is a euphemism for removing people from the group.

8 The exact date of David's arrival is unknown. At any rate, he did not participate in the publication of the *Hayovel* newspaper.

9 Klinger, *I Am Writing These Words to You* (1943 diaries), p. 169.

10 Ibid.

decisive Shayke Goldrin—of all people—who had already made his way into the inner circle. He was an *amud tavech* (a pillar), as they used to say in those days. The two young men shared a bed, as was the custom among the humble pioneers.[11] Shmaryahu Milinsky, the son of a devout family from Volhynia, also felt a spiritual connection to David, as did Abrashka. We can therefore surmise that David's first days at the *hachshara* were marked by new friendships as well as initial disappointments and probably difficulties getting accustomed to the hard, physical labor.[12]

He was ashamed of his stutter. Chana Lieberman remembered him walking to and fro in preparation for a mock public trial of Jewish youth at the *hachshara*. "What are you buzzing around for like a *meshuga*?" she asked, and he replied, "If only I was better at expressing myself."[13] But despite his speech impediment, David was impressive in conversation: "When he talked, everybody would listen with their mouths agape," Shmaryahu would recall many years later.[14] He became a *tarbutnik*, a "culturehead." He was made responsible for the Shabbat festivities. Abrashka remembered that once David asked him to give a lecture on some topic or other, and Abrashka had acquiesced. Later, after the lecture, David told him: "That was good, but superficial."[15] In his eyes, David had become somewhat of a spiritual leader. That is, until the arrival of Zvi Brandes on the scene.[16]

Enter Chajka

Chajka entered the *hachshara* in the winter of 1937. Shayke remembered her approaching him at the Hashomer convention in Warsaw and telling him she would like to get to know the kibbutz and to see how David was settling in. It was a harsh winter, and Chajka and Shayke drove down to Kalisz in a freight truck. On the way, Chajka continued interrogating him about the ways of the kibbutz. Shayke came to the conclusion that Chajka sincerely wished to dedicate herself to kibbutz life, but in light of the housing and job shortage, her position as David's girlfriend was not

11 Shayke Goren (Goldrin), interview by the author, Kibbutz Galon, 1985.
12 Abrashka Eisenberg interview.
13 Chana Lieberman interview.
14 Shmaryahu Milinsky interview.
15 Abrashka Eisenberg interview.
16 Ibid.

enough to make her a natural candidate for the *hachshara* program.[17] She stayed in Kalisz for a few days before returning to Będzin.[18] It would seem that she joined the *hachshara* shortly after.

The dilemma she faced in making this decision had more to do with giving up her studies and career than overcoming any resistance at home.[19] A few of her peers from the Gymnasium had already immigrated to Mandatory Palestine and were occupying the benches of the Hebrew University's lecture halls. Some of them would become scholars of considerable renown. Others went on to higher education in Poland or integrated the business and community life of the bourgeoisie class in Będzin. Immigrating as a pioneer meant long periods of ascetic life during the *hachsharot* followed by the austerity of socialism in Mandatory Palestine. But the *hachshara* was the choice David had made, and Chajka's faith, which she had internalized through her complete identification with him, made her follow suit.

She was accepted straightaway. Her friends from this period remember her as a chipper and playful young woman, and she clearly enjoyed being seen that way.[20] Various accounts of her paint a picture even describing her as an extrovert. She was not shy about making her happiness and her love for David visible to all, conduct that went starkly against the mores of the time, which dictated timid restraint in relations between the sexes.[21]

The Freudian revolution and the son's rebellion aside, the tenth commandment of the movement stated: "The *shomer* is pure in thought, speech, and action," with an explicit emphasis on the prohibition of alcohol, nicotine, and sexual promiscuity.[22] Although most of the codes of the Jewish household were dropped by the wayside, the same did not apply to the spirit of modesty. It was far easier to rebel against the Talmud and the laws of *kashrut* (Jewish dietary laws) than to embrace freedom when it came to interactions between the sexes.[23] Chajka, perhaps as a

17 Shayke Goren interview.

18 Ibid.

19 Klinger, *I Am Writing These Words to You* (1943 diaries), p. 27.

20 Shayke Goren interview; Abrashka Eisenberg interview; Esther Shoshan, in *Chajka: Hoveret Zikaron* (Hebrew) (Kibbutz Haogen: Haogen, 1958), p. 7.

21 Abrashka Eisenberg interview; Esther Shoshan interview.

22 "Aseret Hadibrot," in Dror and Rosenzweig, *Sefer Hashomer Hatzair*, vol. 1, p. 44.

23 For more on the question of family and the relations between the sexes in the *hachshara* kibbutz, see Israel Oppenheim, *Tnu'at Hehalutz BePolin, 1929–1939* (Hebrew) (Be'er Sheva: Hamerkaz Lemoreshet Ben Gurion, Ben-Gurion University, 1993), pp. 141–143; Sarid, *Hehalutz Vetnu'ot Hano'ar BePolin*, pp. 498–500.

way of thumbing her nose at her family, perhaps as a desperate attempt to hide the pain inside—she never mentioned her father's home in this context either—broke ground in this area. Abrashka never dared hug his girlfriend in public,[24] and when Zvi Brandes arrived in the *hachshara*, he never went on a walk alone with Dorka Herzberg but would always invite other friends along to avoid any suspicion that his intentions were anything less than completely honorable.[25] Chajka and David, however, made no such concessions.

It is not hard to picture the sexual frustration that fermented within the *hachshara* in Kalisz. Participants were housed in large rooms containing several beds, each of which would sleep two young men or two young women, sometimes more. Chajka shared her bed with Chana Lieberman from Sosnowiec, who would become her good friend.[26] As mentioned, David shared his bed with Shayke. Based on the statistics of membership in the kibbutz in 1937, each member was entitled to 40 percent of a bed, however two years later, things improved, and each member enjoyed 80 percent of a bed.[27] Like most of their friends, Chajka and David were already past the age of twenty. Hiding would have been awkward and unwise—the individual, even when in love, always remained part of the group and part of the kibbutz. They would therefore read together. A young man and a young woman hunched together over a book, sometimes on his bed, sometimes on hers, depending on the circumstances. Shayke recalled that upon returning from his travels in the late hours of the night, he would often find Chajka and David reading together in his and David's bed. Upon Shayke's arrival, the two would close the book and retire each to their own bed.[28] Yet despite all this, Chajka did not draw David out of the circle of activity, according to Shayke. Their relationship seems to have been of no detriment to kibbutz life.[29]

24 Abrashka Eisenberg interview.

25 Aharon Brandes and Haim Reshef, *Zvi Brandes: Mirashey Hamahteret Hehalutzit BeZaglembia* (Hebrew) (Tel Aviv: Moreshet and Sifriat Poalim, 1978), p. 32.

26 Chana Lieberman interview.

27 *Der Kibbutz, Ein Hachshara Ein Aliya, 1932–1939: 7 Yar Hachshara—4 Dorot Kibbutzim in Kalish*, issued by the kibbutz in Kalisz, May 1939, Kibbutz Galon Archive, p. 13.

28 Shayke Goren interview; Abrashka Eisenberg interview.

29 Shayke Goren interview.

Proletarianization

And yet, they had to work. According to Shayke, Chajka worked in a toy factory along with a few other female friends.[30] Chana Lieberman attested that she also worked as a nanny and probably also a tutor for a family in town. The kibbutz's records from 1937 show that seven of its members worked as tutors.[31] Abrashka remembered Chajka's constant smile, the jokes she would make first thing in the morning.[32] There are no reports of her suffering any particular difficulties at work, beyond the usual strife of the working woman.

The experience of working was both hard and exciting. As a rule, Jewish boys and girls were not the spoiled sort. Few among them came from well-off households. Nevertheless, it was one thing to help Mother out at the store or do some light tailoring with Father and another thing to bend one's back at the factory or over housework for ten hours or more every day. About half of the members of Hashomer Hatzair's *hachsharot* had been trained in a profession, and we can assume that the same was true for Hapo'el Lakfar.[33] However, these were traditional Jewish professions—most of the members were the sons and daughters of grocers, small merchants, and craftsmen, mainly in the textile industry.[34] Now they were forced to undergo the difficult and painful process of proletarianization.[35] In an article that appeared in the 1939 *hachshara* pamphlet signed by "K.," which can be attributed with some certainty to David Kozłowski, this process was described as follows:

> The first time I put on secondhand work clothes, got up with the sunrise and walked to work down the paved street with proud and confident strides, I beamed a smile up at the sun: I was a proletarian. Without knowing anything about the metabolic process or the meaning of "new soul," I sent out blessings of gratitude onto the world. Everything within me cried out: "World, I have important news for you: I am a proletarian!"

30 Ibid.

31 *Der Kibbutz, Ein Hachshara Ein Aliya, 1932–1939*, Kibbutz Galon Archive, p. 13.

32 Abrashka Eisenberg, in *Chajka: Hoveret Zikaron*, p. 8.

33 Sarid, *Hehalutz Vetnu'ot Hano'ar BePolin*, p. 240.

34 Ibid., p. 243.

35 Ibid., p. 592.

> Today, sometimes, when I stand at my machine and feel a terrible hatred toward it, I think that my joy on the occasion of my first venturing out to work was premature.... It is a brutal and difficult thing for a Jewish lad raised in the lap of the Torah to become a proletarian. And it is even more difficult for a lad whose head has been made accustomed to thinking to align his thoughts with the rhythm of the machine.[36]

Two years earlier, the *Hayovel* newspaper of May 1937 contained a "Reportage from Life in the *Hachshara*" in which the author Ya'akov described the soap factory, at the center of which stood the saponification vat—a massive wooden tub in which the soap was cooked. Above the vat, a thick rope hung down from the ceiling, at the end of which was a pile with a bucket tied to it. The workers would service the soap vat—two of them would let down the rope, and another two would draw up the hot soap and pour it into pipes. From the pipes, the soap would be poured into molds where it would solidify into giant slabs weighing 120 kilograms each. From there, "Onto the shelves! No easy task! You have to hold the slab carefully and bravely, otherwise it could topple onto the ground and into the mud. Then, beside the enormous workload, there's the shouting, squabbling, and the constant threat of being fired." In the evening, sitting at his desk alone, propping his head on his hands and looking out at the rain outside, the worker would feel a wave of self-pity: "And you feel yourself alone, a miserable nothing, and the raindrops fall ceaselessly, mercilessly.... And you ask yourself once more—will the rain ever stop? Will the weather be clement? Will I go to the factory tomorrow?"[37]

The loneliness experienced by the youths who had just torn themselves away from their family homes was assuaged by a feeling of camaraderie. Life in the kibbutz did not end at hard physical labor. For many members, Shmaryahu among them, it only began once the latter was done for the day. One member, referred to only as Rivkale, recounted in the *Hayovel* newspaper the events of a typical night in the *hachshara*. She returned from work early since her job—a relatively easy one—required she only put in eight hours a day. On her way home, she had already started planning her evening. First, she popped into the common room (the dining hall) and chatted with the members on duty. Then,

36 "K.," "Bay Der Arbet," in *Der Kibbutz, Ein Hachshara Ein Aliya, 1932–1939*, Kibbutz Galon Archive, p. 3.

37 *Hayovel*, Kibbutz Galon Archive, May 1937, pp. 18–19.

she took a shower and joined a few friends reading together seated in a semicircle in their room:

> Eight o'clock. Outside, night has already begun falling and we cannot continue reading. And so, as we sit there holding hands, the conversation begins to unfold. "How was your day?" Before you know it, they've moved on to speak about the current economic situation of the kibbutz, then someone asks: "What time is dinner tonight?" Everyone falls silent. Only one person answers quietly: "I do not know, fellow, if there will even be a dinner as there is no money." Again, total silence.[38]

Then, Rivkale writes, "from our heart bursts a melody of sorrow," followed by melancholy Ukrainian songs and then by other, more enthusiastic songs, sung with full-throated fervor, from the heart. Only at ten o'clock in the evening did there arise "shouting from the kitchen. The workers on duty began calling the comrades in for dinner."[39]

Cultural and educational activity occupied a central place in the *hachshara*. The *Hayovel* newspaper proudly remarked that over the past two years, the kibbutz had held no less than 546 classes, among which Hebrew accounted for 164, Zionism for 111, and sociology for 96. There had also been no less than 293 assemblies, which came out to at least two or three *hachshara* get-togethers and parties per week.[40] According to testimonies, cultural activity was central to David and Chajka's lives. Chajka gave David more than a helping hand in organizing social events and publishing the kibbutz's newspaper.[41] Even though the members came from mostly similar socioeconomic backgrounds, it appears that those hailing from Zagłębie were more educated than others. They came from a more urban and industrial setting thoroughly steeped in German culture. Chajka was fluent in German as were David and Esther. The youths from Volhynia, on the other hand, coming as they did from the small towns and villages of eastern Poland, checked the Westerners' pride with their superior knowledge of Hebrew, which they had acquired thanks to their Gemara studies.[42]

38 Ibid., p. 15.

39 Ibid.

40 Ibid., p. 30.

41 Shmaryahu Milinsky interview; Esther Shoshan interview.

42 Esther Shoshan interview. According to the *Hayovel* newspaper, of the forty-five kibbutz members, twenty-five "know and use the language," twenty "understand it," and ten "don't understand it." *Hayovel*, May 1937, Kibbutz Galon Archive, p. 30.

This along with the struggle for productivization served as the background to an incident that shook the kibbutz. Shayke, who had served as the kibbutz's secretary at the time, recounted it as follows. David approached him to report having taken offense at something he heard another member say. There was talk of him being spoiled and unfit for a life of labor. Unable to forgive himself for giving such an impression, David decided to leave.[43] Chajka's version of events was far more prosaic:

> A stupid incident made Dawid want to leave the kibbutz. He was denounced once. He did not want to, could not continue to live with these people, because they did not understand him. They said that he got angry whenever food was brought to him too late when he was working. They accused him, for whom food was completely unimportant and who was always ready to give it to somebody else. Dawid wanted to leave the kibbutz. Being sensitive, he did not wish to live among people who did not understand him.
>
> It was a major shock in the life of our kibbutz. In the end, his departure was averted. He was already well-respected and very popular.[44]

Yet, her account reveals little—if any—of the personal crisis she herself was undergoing at the time. Many years later, Shayke would remember how much she had been hurt by the whole affair. She was deeply in love with David and could not imagine staying in the kibbutz without him.[45] David's departure would have meant having to face a difficult choice, and her future in the movement hung in the balance. Shmaryahu's testimony is somewhat less clear, but he, too, related—in hushed tones, even all those years later—that Chajka was having a difficult time with David, and she would often come to pour her heart out to him.[46]

It was a very tough moment for the group as a whole. Friends tried to talk sense into David and prevent him from leaving. Shayke did his share too. David, this shoddily clad "Werther," would have to make peace with day-to-day life and realize that taking offense at personal affronts was a luxury of the petty bourgeoisie, which the collective could not afford. Whatever the case, it was clear to all that they mustn't

43 Shayke Goren interview.

44 Klinger, *I Am Writing These Words to You* (1943 diaries), pp. 169–170.

45 Shayke Goren interview.

46 Shmaryahu Milinsky interview.

give up on David, his dogged individualism and pro-Soviet leanings notwithstanding.[47]

In the end, David retracted his decision, and Shayke announced at one of the group conversations that David had been offended by a personal remark but did not intend to leave the kibbutz, which was met with general cheer and relief. In Shayke's mind, David's final choice had much to do with Chajka,[48] and in hindsight, the ordeal would prove to Chajka how much David depended on her. Members of Kibbutz Galon clearly remembered the extent to which her life in Kalisz was occupied with constant worries about David's status and well-being. The same emerges from her own writings:

> He was already nicknamed "*Chamele*."
>
> This is what he had once called one of the young kibbutz members. They gave the nickname to him instead and it stuck.
>
> He was just a *Chamele*, an ordinary stutterer, *Dawydka* in unkempt clothes. Trousers without creases and baggy like two sacks, particularly at the knees. Holes near the elbows. And he used to pick his nose. On familiar terms with everybody, including the stupidest and the worst. Guileless and candid. A simple, ordinary *Chamele*.[49]

Zvi Brandes

Zvi Brandes showed up at the *hachshara* in the winter of 1937–1938. His arrival was preceded by much talk and expectation but kept being put off due to his intense activity in the *ken* in Żarki, another Zagłębien town.[50] Zvi was not a tall man. He was a stocky fellow who weighed his words thoroughly before speaking. He, too, had come from a traditional Jewish home, but one—like Esther's—which was open to the movement and its people. He had studied in a *heder*, then later at a Polish school. He never made it to a Gymnasium. Situated midway between Będzin and Częstochowa, Żarki was a small town of 5,000 inhabitants, yet despite its size, it was home to a highly energetic little *ken*. Abrashka recalled that the Brandes family were closely identified with this *ken*.[51] Later, Chajka

47 Ibid.; Shayke Goren interview.

48 Shayke Goren interview.

49 Klinger, *I Am Writing These Words to You* (1943 diaries), p. 170.

50 Brandes and Reshef, *Zvi Brandes*, p. 32.

51 Ibid., p. 15; Abrashka Eisenberg interview.

would compare him to a picture published in one of the movement's newspapers of a man brandishing his fist in the air:

> I don't know why but when I think about him I see the image we often used on the cover of our newspapers: a man with a raised fist.
>
> Can you recall that cover?
>
> I don't know why my mind makes that association!
>
> It might be because he had thick, sinewy, muscular arms. It might be because his features were coarse, as if chiseled from stone or granite—stern, sharp, and simple. Thick, bristly eyebrows standing out on his face, appearing to be grown together into one. They testified to his energy and strong will.
>
> Cwi [Zvi] used to step heavily and clumsily, yet confidently. His feet were firmly on the ground as if wanting to press into it. And that was also how he was in life. He took life as it was and was never beguiled or disappointed. No depression or hesitation.
>
> Cwi looked at the world and people in a wise and reasonable way and he knew what he wanted and where he was going. He was rarely angry, irritated, or upset.[52]

The arrival of Zvi took some of the luster out of the halo surrounding David. Zvi, too, was highly knowledgeable and intelligent, but he also had a quality that David apparently lacked: leadership. When Zvi talked, silence would settle over the room; when he had finished speaking, it would be clear to all that the subject had been exhausted, and there was nothing to add to the matter.[53] Work was a considerable effort for him. His friends described him as having two left hands, a real *schlimazel*. He got injured in a work accident, spent some time in the hospital, and then later returned to work with heroic tenacity, his head still wrapped up in bandages.[54] As often happens in such instances, the rivalry between David and Zvi never became overt. On the contrary, it turned into a friendship. From the vantage of time, perhaps slightly anachronistically, Abrashka described David, Zvi, and Chajka as a solid trio.[55] However, it is more likely that the great friendship between them blossomed only later, during the war.

52 Klinger, *I Am Writing These Words to You* (1943 diaries), p. 177.

53 Abrashka Eisenberg interview.

54 Brandes and Reshef, *Zvi Brandes*, p. 30.

55 Abrashka Eisenberg, in *Chajka: Hoveret Zikaron*, p. 8.

Zvi's arrival coincided with a pivotal moment in the *hachshara*. Having united with Hapo'el and recruited members from the peripheral areas, its membership stood at seventy. A year later, in 1939, it had close to twenty large rooms, including sanitary necessities (the *hachshara* members finally had their own showers and toilets), workshops, a reading room with a large library, and a small farm plot where they grew vegetables for their own consumption.[56] This turnaround came as a result of illegal immigration to Mandatory Palestine, which had regained momentum in the late 1930s. These new prospects of making *aliya* had a positive impact on the *hachsharot*. A circular memo from Hashomer Hatzair's *Brit Hakibbutzim* of July 1939 stated that "our kibbutz has once again reached its former size, as in the years of prosperity."[57]

This boost in immigration was influenced by the steadily deteriorating situation in Europe. If the Europeans could still turn a blind eye after the Munich Conference in September 1938, the Germans' march through Prague shattered all remaining illusions. In Great Britain, Chamberlain's reaction was not unlike that of a spurned lover. Having bailed on Czechoslovakia, he now hastened to provide Poland with one-sided guarantees. By doing so, he made it known to one and all that the British were willing to fight for every last drop of Polish blood. The Zbąszyń incident in October 1938 implied that the Jews would not make it out of the war unharmed. Some 17,000 Jews with Polish citizenship who were living in Germany—5,000 of whom had neither residence nor relatives in Poland—were deported from Germany to Poland and concentrated in an internment camp in the town of Zbąszyń. The Jews of Poland hasted to the refugees' aid. The Jewish relief organization the Joint took charge of providing for their basic needs, while the youth movements took care of their education.[58]

Were the youth movements' charges able to read the signs of what was to come? According to Rivka Perlis, it would appear so. The flurry of activity around the Zbąszyń Jews in the summer of 1939 as well as the increased educational and emigration efforts point to a deeply felt sense of urgency—an awareness that time was running out.[59] The Hashomer

56 Shmaryahu Milinsky interview; Zvi Brandes, in *Der Kibbutz, Ein Hachshara Ein Aliya, 1932–1939*, Kibbutz Galon Archive, p. 1.

57 As quoted in Sarid, *Hehalutz Vetnu'ot Hano'ar BePolin*, p. 603.

58 Based mainly on Rivka Perlis, *Tnu'ot Hano'ar Hehalutziyot Bepolin Hakvusha* (Hebrew) (Tel Aviv: Ghetto Fighters' House and Hakibbutz Hameuchad, 1987), pp. 19–22.

59 Ibid., p. 22.

Hatzair memo quoted above explains the increase in the number of *hachshara* members by the fact that "day by day the snake slithers around the ankles of the Jewish youth, wanting to bite and to poison."[60] Even Hashomer Hatzair, which had traditionally been wary of uncontrolled emigration, decided to amplify its *aliya* efforts.[61]

Meanwhile, the *hachshara* in Kalisz celebrated three years since its establishment in the town. As a sign of the movement's strength at the time, its newspaper came out for the first time in print rather than a hand-copied pamphlet. The main articles in the issue were written by Zvi, Shayke, and David. The back pages featured advertisements for various commercial establishments in the town.[62] Zvi Brandes got the honor of writing the ideological position article, as befitting his leadership role in the kibbutz. His opening remarks proudly summed up the history of the *hachshara* in Kalisz:

> We left Jewish homes where fathers and mothers worried about their children's future. We left behind us the hum of the small town, the atrophy and decadence of Jewish intelligentsia; we rebelled against the conventional models and the diaspora tradition, and true to our youthful dreams, to the vision of a better and finer life, we created our *hachshara* enterprise. Jewish society looked upon us…as dreamers taking youthful romanticism seriously, as lambs straying onto twisting paths.… But we knew that the Jewish distress is great and tragic, and that there are vast desolate marshlands waiting to be recovered, that danger still lurks everywhere—and only the calloused hands of the pioneer can drain the swamps, pave the roads, lay the rails, and turn the malaria-stricken land [of Israel] into flourishing and fruitful Jewish settlements ready to receive hundreds of thousands of Jews from all over the world.[63]

Soon after, a literary fair was organized by the kibbutz in the nearby town of Błaszki. Among other works, the event included readings of texts by the famous Yiddish writers Sholem Aleichem and

60 Sarid, *Hehalutz Vetnu'ot Hano'ar BePolin*, p. 603.

61 Eli Tzur, *Lifney Bo Ha'afela: Hashomer Hatzair Bepolin U'veGalitzia, 1930–1940* (Hebrew) (Sde Boker: Ben Gurion Institute, Yad Ya'ari, and Ben Gurion University, 2006), pp. 316–317.

62 See the back pages of *Der Kibbutz, Ein Hachshara Ein Aliya, 1932–1939*, Kibbutz Galon Archive.

63 Zvi Brandes, in *Der Kibbutz, Ein Hachshara Ein Aliya, 1932–1939*, p. 1.

I. L. Peretz. Zvi Brandes again took the stage as the representative of the kibbutz and pronounced:

> These are bleak days. Who knows what lies in store for us in the coming months. We must hurry to leave Poland and immigrate [to Mandatory Palestine]. This is the path of the pioneer youth. We must leave here whatever the cost. Whatever the means, even if it means taking illegal ways. The time is short. The hour is pressing, and everyone must take advantage of the moments we have left.[64]

The first members had already started making *aliya*. Shmaryahu immigrated to Mandatory Palestine in February 1939. The order of *aliya* was determined by seniority, and newer members worried that their turn would never come. Chajka would often tell Shayke: "You'll make your *aliya* yet." When his turn finally came, she approached him and said: "Take David's hat and coat with you." David had one of the finer coats in the kibbutz, lined with thick lamb's wool, and the kibbutz treasurer would regularly take it with him on his travels. Shayke went back to his hometown to bid his parents farewell but made it back in time to say goodbye to his friends in Kalisz as well. He looked around him with his leader's eyes and saw that the young laborers were working well. He wished to say his goodbyes to Chajka and David right there and then, but they insisted on accompanying him to the train station. It was somewhat unorthodox, but they refused to give up on the idea. Shayke had no girlfriend to wave him off from the platform. Before the train left the station, Chajka and David said to him: "You're going to make it. It's too late for us."[65] Shayke left in late April 1939.

64 Brandes and Reshef, *Zvi Brandes*, p. 34.
65 Shayke Goren interview.

Chapter Five

So This Is War

Sacred History: 1985

The road to Givat Haviva passes by orchards, kibbutzim, and villages all squashed up side by side. A comfortably crowded piece of countryside bathed in the sweet odor of citrus. What more does one need, as the German dramatist Heinrich von Kleist would say: plant a tree, build a house, have a child. He himself, of course, in the grand tradition of people who say grand things, never did any of it. He shot himself and his terminally ill female companion to death in 1811.

Givat Haviva— the national education, archival, and research center of Hakibbutz Ha'artzi and my destination—is where Mother's original diaries are preserved, in the archive building erected by Father. "The last building," he promised himself and us, a promise he had made and broken time and time again. The archive building is probably not the most handsome among them, but it was certainly a fine seal on a forty-year building career. Clean, precise lines, meticulous finish, double doors to maintain a steady temperature, comfortable reading rooms, even a little coffee nook. No detail left unattended.

A year ago, a pamphlet published by the Hakibbutz Ha'artzi movement featured photos of the archive building on its chrome-paper front page. Inside was an interview with Arnon, my younger brother, a member of Kibbutz Kramim in the Negev. On another page in the same pamphlet were two texts of my own about Kerem Shalom, without mention of the author's present whereabouts in Tel Aviv. A real family pamphlet, I chuckled to myself. Still, I was proud. Father's edifices continue to breathe, always constructed with an awareness of their surroundings, and their form never gives in to the routine conformity of the matchbox-style buildings. When he switched to exposed concrete in the early sixties, it caused uproar in the kibbutz. The members wished to have the concrete painted in bright "country" colors, but he objected and stood his ground.

We used to go to Givat Haviva to attend Hakibbutz Ha'artzi seminars and education councils, dressed in blue and white, faces donning masks of seriousness and maturity, as is proper when one is dealing with important matters. Take the twelfth-grade seminar, for instance. Yuval Luria lectured on Marx, Gabriel Moked on the French philosopher Jean-Paul Sartre. In the evenings, the core group gathered to make plans, to weave dreams. Aharoni from Kibbutz Sarid was there, and we lowered him on a rope from the pool house roof to write the group's name up high in big letters. We sang a song in Russian to encourage him, but he suddenly panicked, lost his celebrated sense of humor entirely, and screamed to put him down immediately or he would stop what he was doing and come settle the score with whoever was responsible.

And the girl with the long braid and the upturned nose from Emek Hayarden, she was there too. Four of us walked to the Karkur Junction so as not to reveal our intentions, not to expose ourselves to ridicule. Then we split up, two by two, hands beginning to slowly stutter toward each other, toward the possibility of youthful flesh. *Nu tov*, oh well, as Abrashka or Shmaryahu would say.

On my visit to Givat Haviva, I run into trouble with Mother's diaries. As a history student at Tel Aviv University, I had the occasion to rifle through various narratives about Saint Francis of Assisi, amazed at the importance the younger order had given to their spiritual father's life story. All those versions, the contradictions between them, the systematic editing, the severe censorship to which several of them had been subjected, and best of all—the burning of the unauthorized versions by Cardinal Bonaventure in 1260. You see, the history of the Franciscans was to be based on a single, canonical version.

The fact that Saint Francis himself had left behind very few manuscripts—all of them highly cryptic and susceptible to a multitude of interpretations—played a big part in the controversy surrounding his personage and teachings. More importantly, it revealed the significance of the manner in which one's story is told. What if mother's diary had been similarly manhandled, as suggested by the line in Beit Zvi's strange book? It was one thing to deal with the hagiography of a distant Christian saint, but it was another thing to delve into the historiography of my mother in a place that was also part of my own past.

Mother's diaries are hard to crack. Even the term "diaries" is a less-than-ideal fit. Most of them were written in hindsight in 1943—after the events in question had taken place but still in relative temporal proximity—with few segments describing events at the time of writing. They were written while Mother was hiding in a little village near Będzin, shortly after the decimation of the local ghettos. The composition of the diaries—as she referred to them already back then—was fueled by an emotional storm, and their contents reveal an author rushing to put her impressions down on paper before the vividness of what she had lived through could fade from her memory or before her capture. As such, chronological order was not a priority. The diaries served as a medium for deep and incisive personal reckoning rather than a measured and objective witness account. However, in the spring of 1944, shortly after arriving in Mandatory Palestine, Mother began working on an amended version, still in Polish but one that filled in the gaps left open in the first draft. Yet the text remained unfinished. She did not return to it again.

The two versions were translated into Hebrew by Zvi Arad in the 1950s and served, in various permutations, as the basis for articles that appeared in her name, some with and some without her consent. After her death, the book *Miyoman Bageto* was published. According to the editor David Hanegbi, it relied on the entirety of the materials available but differed from the previous publications.[1] He did not mention the exact sources on which it was based, and in an attempt to shape the contents into a coherent chronological sequence, he made numerous mistakes when it came to situating events in the correct place. This was compounded by literary, ideological, and political considerations. The various editors who worked on Mother's diaries took it upon themselves to make their contents fall in line with the spirit of the time. Like the hagiography of Saint Francis, Mother's diaries were a part of *historia sacra*.

Here I am now, looking at Mother's 1943 notebooks. They are school notebooks wrapped in coarse kraft paper, frayed wooden fibers sticking out beyond their edges. One of the notebooks is yellow, the other is green. The handwriting within them is round and neat; only the amount of ink in the pen varies from paragraph to paragraph. The emotional turmoil behind the words did not affect the pleasing shape of the foreign letters. There is almost nothing crossed out, almost nothing added. The words seem to flow in an uninterrupted stream. The outward appearance of the

1 David Hanegbi, "Editor's comment," in Klinger, *Miyoman Bageto*.

straight lines clashes with the bitter questions that opens their sequence: "So, I am alive? Am I?"[2]

The cardboard box before me also contains the notebooks written at Haogen, the various translations—handwritten and typed—as well as different edited versions and loose pages. Not all of them are intact.[3] With the help of several Polish speakers, I am trying to piece together Mother's story. The mythological figure is beginning to emerge from beneath its calcified layers.

War

At the end of August 1939, with the Ribbentrop-Molotov Pact in place, it seemed inevitable to all that the German-Soviet agreement would make Poland—that wide and fertile expanse between the two cagey giants—the stage for the next round of hostilities. In the meantime, Hapo'el Lakfar members tried to get out while they still could, some more successfully than others. Esther Zborowska set out for Mandatory Palestine in June, leaving behind her boyfriend Zelig Shoshan, whose turn had not yet come. In Romania, she boarded the ship *Tiger Hill* that sailed in defiance of the agreement with the British. The boat was caught, and its passengers were transferred to an internment camp, only to be released on September 2, 1939, as the British now had bigger fish to fry.[4] Abrashka had also left a girlfriend in Poland—Zippora Szporn from

2 Klinger, *I Am Writing These Words to You*, p. 25.

3 The different versions of the diaries, as preserved in the Moreshet Archive according to the approximate order of writing, translation, and publication, are as follows: notebooks in Polish written in hiding in Poland between August 26, 1943, and September 17, 1943, D.2.211; notebooks in Polish written in Kibbutz Haogen, starting May 22, 1944, D.2.211; Hebrew translation of the 1943 notebooks by Zvi Arad (probably in 1955), pp. 1-11, C.36.3.1; pp. 11–110; C.36.3.2; pp. 111–143, C.36.3.3; printout of the Hebrew translation of the 1943 notebooks in preparation for publication as part of the book *Hashomer Hatzair* in 1955 or 1956 (the printout has many editing and erasure marks, probably made by the editors Israel Rosenzweig and Levi Dror), C.36.2; an article by Chajka Klinger (Rosenberg), "Hashomrim Bebendin Al Mishmar Kavod Atzmam"(Hebrew), in *Sefer Hashomer Hatzair*, vol. 1, pp. 691–706; Hebrew translation of the 1944 diaries, pp. 1–100, 201–225, manuscript by Zvi Arad (early 1959), C.36.2; an article by Chajka Klinger (Rosenberg), "Hashomrim BeBendin Al Mishmar Kavod Atzmam," in Stein, *Pinkas Bendin*, vol. 2, pp. 360–362.

4 Esther Shoshan interview.

his hometown of Żarki, also a member of the kibbutz. In fact, Zippora had joined the kibbutz before Abrashka, but she missed her turn because she had gone on vacation. Abrashka wished to stay so the two could emigrate together, but Zippora put her foot down: "You will go." He left, carrying Zelig's suitcase, and he managed to send her a postcard from Warsaw. Zelig was more optimistic and promised Esther that he would join her shortly. Zippora was also supposed to leave on September 4–5, 1939, the same date as David and Chajka.[5]

This is where Chajka's diaries begin. In the chronological version of 1944, the one that appears in *Miyoman Bageto*, she describes the first days of the war in a fluid stream of details:

> War has broken out. Nobody wants to believe it's true. The enemy's airplanes are in the air, right above our heads, the alarms keep blasting one after another, yet many still have doubts. Is it true that these are false alarms, they ask the Polish police passing by. More and more people gather in front of the mobilization posters, entire crowds. People are racking their brains, they can't figure out where they should go, to what category they belong, to which regiment they should report.
>
> Later we were told this was the first betrayal of the Polish command. A poorly edited mobilization poster caused much confusion across the country. All the train carriages were taken up by men going to their regiments. One could see half-armed men everywhere, as they were being sent running around from one mobilization center to another. And not just freshly mobilized soldiers—entire armed squads, following orders and heading to their prescribed positions. Civilians are following the army and the mobilized men, especially those in proximity to the German border. The roads and paths to Warsaw, Sandomierz, Lwów are filled with people. […]
>
> But the Jewish people have suffered the most. Happy were those who managed to squeeze into cars, already so stuffed with people they may well have suffocated. But these were the lucky few. The Jews are taking any means of transport they can manage to get as far from the border as possible. That's where the Germans will come first. The horror of Hitler's Germany is pushing the Jews out, further and further away, as far as their feet can carry them. […]

5 Abrashka Eisenberg interview.

Very few have managed to squeeze onto buses. The owners do not want to rent the spaces. They take all their belongings out to the countryside, then they come back and take their families. A spot in a car costs thousands. [...]

I too have walked one of the roads from Będzin to Pińczów. David walks by my side with a heavy suitcase in his hand. No matter how much I ask, beg, threaten, he does not want to give me half to carry. Sweat is pouring down his face, he is panting heavily. "Leave it," I shout, "I don't need these rags," but he will not listen. This is our journey, the journey we are making to *Eretz Israel*. On September 5, 1939, we were meant to make our *aliya*. [...]

My legs are swollen; my shoes are falling apart. Suddenly the bombing begins again. There is a forest nearby, hastily we jump in. But the army must have passed through here, as more and more planes are circling the forest. We hear the sound of anti-aircraft weapons firing. This is the Polish army's response. Only now have they begun to shower the small forest with a hail of bombs. There were many civilians in the forest. I have never heard such screaming, such laments. A bomb fell right next to us, maybe half a meter behind us; it left a huge crater, uprooted a tree. David lies on top of me, trying to protect me from the bomb. "Get off," I shout and kick him. Later we laugh about it. It must have been some kind of instinctual reaction on his part.

So this is war. I recall all the books I've read: Remarque, Hašek, du Gard.[6] The reality is far worse. The forest is strewn with corpses, injured people. Moans, the rattling breath of the dying. The Red Cross ambulance arrives and gets to work. [...]

It was already dark when suddenly rockets began flying over our heads, shining a light on us and exploding. We jump off the wagon and run into some nearby cottages. Finally, as we almost run out of breath, we reach a cottage. It's empty, there's no one inside. We sit on the floor. I lean against a wall and feel an unusual, sudden warmth. "What is this?" I shout. The cottage is burning, quickly, we must run away. David cannot find his case in the dark. Finally, we ditch it and run away into the field. We spend the whole night there. In the morning, we move on. In the nearby village, they tell us to not go any further; they say the Germans have arrived, but we don't want to

6 These were pacifist books about World War I. Chajka read Remarque and Hašek in Yiddish, and Martin Du Gard in Polish.

> hear any of it. Yet we barely manage to walk a few steps before we see two huge tanks marked with a large Hakenkreuz [swastika]. Calmly we walk through mud, water, hills. The peasants watch us from afar. We have seen German tanks, seen them with our own eyes, but we don't want to believe it.
>
> Soon we arrive. We are standing in front of Pińczów. All at once, it's not the town we see but one massive flame. Pińczów is burning. The Germans have begun their work. Tears well up in my eyes. One cannot get into Pińczów. So, this is what we've suffered so much for over the last two weeks. We've crossed the entire length of the Kieleckie [Kielce] Voivodeship on foot, which is as large as the whole of [Mandatory] Palestine, only to witness one of our family's homes burning. I want to console David, tell him not to worry, that maybe his parents had left Pińczów before the fire, maybe everything's fine, but I cannot find the right words.[7]

"So this is war"—the description of those few days (most likely just over a week in total), as startling and dense as they might have been, shows Chajka and David undergoing a process of coming to terms with their new situation. They had known that the world was at war, but this fact had failed to penetrate their consciousness until an actual bomb went off right next to them. They had sensed that their people were in danger, but only standing at the gates of the flaming town of Pińczów did they perceive the magnitude of the threat. Before then, it was but a rumor spread by enemy agents. The sorrow evident in the description of Jews running for their lives is always accompanied by a slight note of contempt; only when she is faced with this burning wreckage does the tragedy turn personal.

Modern research confirms Chajka's assessment of the Polish army and administration as inefficient at best. The military forces that were ostensibly meant to protect Będzin, among other places, retreated on day two of the war. German battalions quickly swept through the Kielce region, easily defeating the ill-prepared Polish defenders. As early as September 6, the Polish army had already received orders to retreat in the direction of Warsaw.[8]

7 Chajka Klinger, 1944 diaries, Haogen I notebook, Moreshet Archive, D.2.211, pp. 9–14.

8 Katri'el Ben-Aryeh, *September 1939* (Hebrew) (Tel Aviv: Lavi, 1987), pp. 158–167.

The Return Home

Chajka looked at the Germans in shock and disbelief. Polish Jewry had fond memories of the German occupation during World War I, and one can safely assume that as a native of Zagłębie, a region steeped in German culture, Chajka's natural inclination would be to view the German soldiers as representatives of an advanced and refined civilization. There is a certain note of admiration that creeps into her description of the manly German soldiers. Moreover, the pacifist literature she consumed—Remarque's novel in particular[9]—depicts German soldiers as being forced to fight on the enemy's side despite themselves. Yet the sight of Jewish towns on fire snapped Chajka out of her romantic idealism and into a bitter reality. She feared for her home. The parental abode from which she had deliberately distanced herself now seemed like a refuge in a world gone mad:

> David is worried. He doesn't know what to do—try to reach Pińczów at any cost, stay in the village, wait until an opportunity comes along and sneak into the city, see what's happened to his family, or go back to Będzin. We meet a peasant. David asks if we could stay at his place for two weeks, he says he will pay, that he could work for him as a farmhand. No, he's not interested. It's a shame, we have to go back. I'm happy, I want to be close to home even if that home has turned to ash.
>
> We are going back. We enter the first village occupied by the Germans. A soldier guards the place, many children crowding around him. He gives them chocolate. They bring him German money from that other war, from the time of inflation, they ask if it's any good. He laughs. No, it's no good. He eyes us with pity. Go back home, he says. We will not harm you, we want to live alongside you as friends, and he directs our attention to a huge poster in German and in Polish. It's an appeal to the Polish people. A declaration of friendship and sympathy, a plea for loyalty. See, he says, that's the kind of sentiment we bring to you. We don't wish to harm you. He

9 Pacifist and antiwar literature was popular among Hashomer Hatzair members and its influence remained potent at the start of the war. *Płomienie* (Flames), Hashomer's underground newspaper in Warsaw, published an elegy by the pacifist poet and writer Józef Wittlin (1896–1976) in October 1940. See "Płomienie, issue 2, October 10, 1940," in Tikva Fatal-Knaani, ed., *The Jewish Underground Press in Warsaw: Vol. One, May 1940–January 1941* (Jerusalem: Yad Vashem, 2018), pp. 260, 270.

believes it, he must be a good man, there is truth in his eyes. They told him so, and he believes it.[10] [...]

We've rented a cart; we are on our way. But pretty soon we have to get off the main road. There are entire army divisions marching ahead of us. I stand there with my mouth agape and watch them, curiously. Never have I seen such an army. Big men, every single one of them as strong as an ox. Tall, strong, healthy, beautiful, like young oak trees, and what uniforms! All of them new, made of the best broadcloth, corduroy, leather. And what technology! Everything is motorized—tanks, motorcycles, trucks, heavy artillery.

Now it is clear how much the anti-Hitler propaganda has been lying to us. This army does not seem hungry or poor. Rather the opposite. They have put all their energy, all their strength and ambition into this army—and they can be proud of it. The danger that Hitler's Germany poses to all of Europe has been underestimated, it has been minimized on purpose. And now, I will pay for it. The German army has been marching for three days and three nights. Occasionally, I heard shouts of "Juden nach Palästina. Verfluchte Juden" [Jews, go to Palestine. Cursed Jews], but mostly they responded to the cart driver's greetings in kind. We were very scared, there were so many of them. One shot and we would have been dead. But they did not touch us.

We are going back... After a few days, we arrive in a small town. As I walk down the street, suddenly someone shouts "Chajka, Chajka." It's Shoshana Neuman. So, we are in Żarki. When she saw me in my worn-down shoes, my legs swollen, she cried. Chaotic questioning ensued—where are Zvi, Frumka, Shimshon, Abrashka, Zippora, Hedva?[11]

10 This seems to be paraphrased from Leonhard Frank's *Der Mensch ist gut* (Man is Good), first published in 1918. This collection of pacifist short stories, which denounced the senseless slaughter of the Great War, on the one hand, and affirmed faith in humanistic values, on the other hand, was widely read in Hashomer circles. See "El Al: Iton Hatzofim, issue 1, April 1941," in Tikva Fatal-Knaani, ed., *The Jewish Underground Press in Warsaw: Vol. Two, February–June 1941* (Jerusalem: Yad Vashem, 2019), pp. 346–347.

11 Klinger, 1944 diaries, Haogen I, pp. 9–12. These people were trainees from the Żarki *ken* who were also part of the *hachshara* farm in Kalisz. See "Hamesh Shanim Lekibbutz Hashomer Hatzair Gal-on," Nes Ziona, January 1944, Kibbutz Galon Archive, 51.

Forty-six years later, that meeting was still fresh in the mind of Isaac Neuman, then a lad of sixteen, today a carpenter living in Israel. Isaac recalled that after the German invasion, his family had moved to a temporary home without any furnishings or kitchen equipment. His older sister Shoshana had been a member of the Hapo'el Lakfar *hachshara* in Kalisz. He remembered that his sister had been walking down the street when she suddenly spotted Chajka. She invited her and David to stay with them, even though the house was already crowded with eight people under its roof. They slept on the floor for a few days, gathering strength for the rest of their journey ahead.[12] Shoshana took advantage of their time together to tell Chajka about the fate of their mutual friends. This account, which Chajka reproduced in her 1944 diary, tells us a few things about her attitude toward the war:

> Still no news from Shimshon. Mendek is dead, he fell for another's cause.[13] Do you remember when he wrote from the army how he only had to last another month, how he could see the day of freedom on the horizon. Asking to write and tell him what his emigration budget was. How he wanted to make his *aliya* the moment he was discharged from the army. He is gone. We will never hear him discuss Marxism again. He was so straightforward, untarnished by falsehoods and lies. He could have run away; he could have deserted. He didn't want to. My place is here, he said, while the struggle against fascism goes on. He did not wish to desert. He sacrificed his life in the struggle for a new world, a better world. Will anyone ever remember his sacrifice? Will this world of ours ever pay us back for the thousands, millions of victims, of youths who fell at various parts of the front? Surely, they will forget, just as the Polish soldiers did, those Polish soldiers with whom Mendek fought side by side against fascism, but also for their fatherland. Abrashka is heavily wounded, Shoshana has to go on. The Germans rounded up Zvi, Shmuel, and all the other men of the town at the synagogue. We don't know what will happen to them.[14]

From Chajka's notes, it is unclear which parts of the account conveys what she heard from Shoshana and which reflect her own thoughts. Nevertheless, we can visualize the two young women sitting and talking

12 Isaac Neuman, interview by the author, Ramat Hasharon, 1985.

13 There are no other mentions of Mendek.

14 Klinger, 1944 diaries, Haogen I, pp. 15–16.

about their friends. From what they have to say about Mendek, we can discern a hint of criticism regarding his chosen path—"he fell for another's cause." Before the war, the Polish army draft had disrupted the *hachsharot*, raising complex questions of belonging and seniority.

The passage quoted above reveals that Mendek was apprehensive about the budget required for his *aliya*. Beyond that, it also implies that even in this dire hour of struggle against the German invaders, the movement had no consensual position regarding service in the Polish army. Mendek could have dodged the draft but chose not to do so. A touch of bitterness creeps into Chajka's writing when she talks about his unnecessary sacrifice. Though she may not state it explicitly, in her eyes the war was a Polish struggle between two reactionary blocks.[15] And yet, as we learn from Shoshana's account, the war was already hitting Polish Jewry particularly hard:

> The very next day after the Germans entered the town, they gathered all the Jews together and told them that from now on, they all had to wash themselves every day and clean their apartments. And that they could no longer live like parasites, they had to work. This is what they had been told about Polish Jews back in Germany, that they were savage creatures, completely set apart from European culture. How can one be surprised then that this is how they approach these people, these half-beasts?[16]

The soldier giving out candy and the Nazi troops greeting passersby now seemed threatening rather than friendly. Reading Chajka's description of the treatment suffered by her people at the hands of these representatives of German culture, one can feel the seeping sense of insult. It was the smallest things that hurt the most: the obligation to bathe and clean the house.[17] Chajka and David decided to get back out on the road homeward:

> Shoshana has given me a pair of stockings and on we go. Even before reaching Będzin, we are told that the town has been burnt down and that they are not letting anyone in. [...]

15 This is according to Sarid, *Hehalutz Vetnu'ot Hano'ar BePolin*. Nevertheless, Hashomer trainees enlisted to participate in civil defense actions across Warsaw. Gutman, *Mered Hanetzurim*, pp. 53–54.

16 Klinger, 1944 diaries, Haogen I, pp. 16–17.

17 Ibid., p. 17.

> But we are not deterred. I might at least see the ashes. We enter the suburbs [of Będzin]—nothing, no trace of war happening anywhere in the world. Everything looks just as before. Only there are huge queues of people standing in front of the bakeries. Never-ending rows of people. I approach. I recognize one of those queuing as my mother. "Mama," I say, and suddenly find myself in her embrace. "I have cried a thousand tears for you," she says. "So many people died on the way. Where is your bag?" she asks. I look down. She understands. "What is happening back home? Is everyone safe?" "Yes, everything is fine." I breathe a sigh of relief.[18]

Unlike Żarki 30 kilometers away, Będzin and its neighboring towns remained unharmed during these battles. The Germans circled this industrial and mining area, intending to keep it intact in order to use its enormous resources to their benefit later. General Wilhelm List's 14th Army completed its mission of enclosing the region in six days, and its reserves entered the towns of Zagłębie and took over without encountering resistance.[19] As part of the Zagłębie region, Będzin was to be annexed by the Reich and become part of Germany over the next five years.

Chajka's parents Leibel and Perl Klinger were alive and living at 61 Modrzejowska Street with their youngest daughter Mania, now aged twenty. She had just finished her studies at the Gymnasium, and even though she had joined Hanoar Hatzioni,[20] she maintained a close emotional relationship with her older sister. Some thought she was even brighter than Chajka.[21] Their eldest daughter, Sarah, now aged thirty-one, lived at 24 Joselewicza Street with her husband Ya'akov Mgłą and their six-year-old daughter. She was expecting another daughter at the time.

The warmth of the reunion erased the memory of all past resentments. Even the lost suitcase. The prodigal daughter had come home.

18 Ibid.

19 Mieczysław Norwid Neugebauer, *The Defence of Poland* (London: M.I. Kolin Ltd, 1942), pp. 70, 108–118.

20 Tosia Herzberg interview.

21 Chana Lieberman interview.

Chapter Six

And Then Everything Went Quiet

Occupation and Annexation

At the outset of the war, the Jewish population of Zagłębie and its neighboring regions amounted to roughly 95,000. Będzin and Sosnowiec, the two major cities in the district, were home to approximately 27,000 Jews each.[1] In Będzin, Jews accounted for about half the general population,[2] and in Sosnowiec, just over a quarter. Many of them—like Chajka and David—attempted to flee the region, primarily to the east, according to most testimonies available to us from this time.[3] The Jews of Zagłębie, situated

1 These numbers are according to Perlis, *Tnu'ot Hano'ar Hehalutziyot*, p. 278.

2 "Będzin Census of 1939," AŻIH, 212/11.

3 Ka-Tzetnik 135633 (Yehiel De-Nur), *Sunrise over Hell* (London: W.H. Allen, 1977), pp. 3–8; Eliezer Schönker testimony, in Haim Volnerman, Aviezer Burstein, and Meir Shimon Geshuri, eds., *Sefer Oshpitsin: Oshviyentshim-Oshvits* (Hebrew and Yiddish) (Jerusalem: Irgun Yotzey Oshpitsin BeYisrael, 1977), p. 162; Cypora (Plawner) Kohav testimony, Yad Vashem Archives (YVA), O.3/3020; Fredka Mazia, *Re'im Basa'ar: No'ar Tzioni Bema'avak im HaNatzim* (Hebrew) (Jerusalem: Yad Vashem, 1964), pp. 12–14; Frumka Perchi (Skuchilak) testimony, Moreshet Archive, A.473; Shoshana Sternfeld-Egozi testimony in Meir Shimon Geshuri, ed., *Sefer Sosnowitz Vehasviva BeZaglembia*, vol. 1 (Hebrew) (Tel Aviv: Igud Yotzey Zaglembia Vehasviva BeYisrael, 1973), p. 139; Josef Jacobowitz, "Miyoman," in Shlomo Even-Shoshan, Haim Dan, and Yishayahu Stavi, eds., *Gushey Hachshara Mesaprim: Kibbutz Al Shem B. Borochov, Gushey Kiltz VeBendin* (Hebrew) (Tel Aviv: Ghetto Fighters' House and Hakibbutz Hameuchad, 1983), pp. 251–252; Eliyahu Miron, ed., *Bielitz-Biala (Bielsko-Biala): Bruchschnitte aus vergangenen Zeiten* (German and Hebrew) (Jerusalem: E. Miron, 1973), p. 109.

in close proximity to the German border, hoped to outrun the German war machine. However, like Chajka and David, they underestimated both its strength and efficiency. Poland surrendered to the Reich in late September 1939, and on October 3, German boots were already marching through Warsaw. When the Nazi battalions had caught up with them, most of the fleeing Jews returned to their hometowns. Most, but not all. When the Germans surveyed the population of Będzin at the end of 1939, they found only 22,167 Jews living in the city.[4]

Hitler's troops entered Będzin on September 5, 1939. The Jews hunkered down in their homes. Through a locked window, Jochanan Ranz, a member of the local Kibbutz Dror, watched them pass by.[5] For three days, he and his friends had been deliberating whether to pack their things and join the refugee convoys headed east. They decided to wait for the fog to clear. Now, Ranz was watching a motorized column pass through the heart of the city:

> Motors roaring, the column circled the town a few times in a show of strength designed to inspire fear in the hearts of the townspeople. The dust on their long leather coats suggested they had been on the warpath for several days now and their silent faces boded no good. After completing their circuit of the city, they drove on, leaving a *Kommandant* and his staff in charge of the town.[6]

The *Kommandant* in question was none other than *SS-Obergruppenführer* Udo von Woyrsch, head of the Einsatzgruppe zur besonderen Verwendung (z.b.V)—one of the special death squads assigned to exterminate Polish Jewry.[7] It took him only a few days to gain complete control of the city. On September 6, two bakers were executed for unlawful baking of bread and price gouging, the Jews were told.[8] The symbolic act of burning down

4 "Będzin Census of 1939," AŻIH, 212/11.

5 Jochanan Ranz, *In Nazi Claws: Bendzin 1939–1944* (New York: unknown publisher, 1976), pp. 4–5.

6 Ibid., p. 5.

7 *SS-Obergruppenführer* Udo von Woyrsch was a particularly tough SS officer who earned his reputation during the Night of the Long Knives in 1934. See Helmut Krausnick and Hans-Heinrich Wilhelm, *Die Truppe des Weltanschauungskrieges: Die Einsatzgruppen der Sicherheitspolizei und des SD, 1938–1942* (Stuttgart: Deutsche Verlags-Anstalt, 1981), pp. 51–52.

8 David Liwer, *Ir Hametim* (Tel Aviv: Twersky, 1946), p. 18. The names of the bakers were Stavsky and Katz. Von Woyrsch reported on numerous actions taken against Jewish-owned businesses that were supposedly price gouging as well as disturbers

the synagogue sent an even more unequivocal message. Będzin's Jews were proud of their beautiful house of worship, the walls of which were adorned with murals painted by Jewish artists:

> [The Germans] burned down the synagogue and some of the nearby houses, almost the entire street. They did this at 2 AM, having cordoned off the street. They stationed guards in front of every house. They didn't let any men out of the burning houses, just women. Some men escaped disguised as women, some managed to sneak through, but most were burned alive. There was a Catholic church right next to these houses. One could only get to the church through a back exit, which some of the houses had. A priest had stayed in the church, a young man; he let in everyone who came and hid them in the church's cellars. Next morning, after everything had calmed down, he let them all out.[9]

Chajka's testimony, based on the accounts of her family, is true to history. A similar version of events is recounted by David Liwer with the addition of one important detail: The Polish locals took part in burning the synagogue and set fire to Jewish houses intentionally.[10] Chajka herself was unwell due to the tribulations she had experienced on her journey home during the first days of the war: "I felt ill for a long time afterwards. I began to suffer from rheumatism. For a long time, I had a fever."[11] It would take a while for her to get better and grow accustomed to this new reality.

Meanwhile, the Nazi onslaught continued. That same month, during the Days of Repentance, seventeen Jewish men were shot to death after being dragged out of a house on Piłsudski Street. The reason for their execution was unknown, as was the exact day of their demise. Only later did it come to light—thanks to the testimony of the undertaker at the Christian cemetery—that seventeen bodies had been brought to the cemetery in a truck one night. The bodies were stripped of all valuables and buried with their clothes on. "The undertaker was threatened not to say a word to anyone lest he encounter a similar fate," David Liwer

of the peace, and the execution of three people. Krausnik and Wilhelm, *Die Truppe des Weltanschauungskrieges*, pp. 51–52.

9 Klinger, 1944 diaries, Haogen I, pp. 18–19.

10 D. Liwer, *Ir Hametim*, p. 18. There is no testimony regarding the number of victims.

11 Klinger, 1944 diaries, Haogen I, p. 18.

recounts.[12] The incident was likewise mentioned in Chajka's diaries.[13] Later, it would come to light that von Woyrsch was worried about a possible uprising of the Jewish population and ordered the executions as part of what he termed "emergency directives."[14]

The fate of Będzin during the first month of the German invasion was no different than that of other towns in the occupied areas. A synagogue was similarly blown up in the nearby Sosnowiec, and the Germans spent two whole days tormenting the town's Jewish men who had been rounded up in the town square. Several Jews were shot and killed.[15] "Everywhere the Germans organized pogroms, rounding up the non-Jewish population to witness and learn how to mock, abuse, injure, and murder Jews. Unbridled killing and senseless violence became daily commonplaces for the Jews."[16] This was rampant and deliberate—though not yet systematic—terror aimed at exterminating Polish Jewry.[17] The Jewish refugees flocked to the big cities or returned to their hometowns to try and keep their heads down and adjust to this new, frightening reality. Many painful lessons lay ahead. Wasn't this yet another twentieth-century blight that they would weather just as they had its predecessors? Weren't they better off keeping their nose to the grindstone and carrying on with their daily lives? Their collective memory and lust for life drove

12 David Liwer even remembered the names of some of the men put to death: Hamburger and his son, Spiegler, Malah, Grossman, Itzkovitz, Safirsztajn. D. Liwer, *Ir Hametim*, p. 19.

13 Klinger, 1944 diaries, Haogen I, p. 18.

14 Krausnik and Wilhelm, *Die Truppe des Weltanschauungskrieges*, p. 51.

15 See the anonymous testimony of a woman from Sosnowiec, YVA, O.12/26; Ka-Tzetnik, *Sunrise over Hell*, pp. 26–27; Mazia, *Re'im Basa'ar*, p. 24; Emanuel Ringelblum, *Notes from the Warsaw Ghetto: The Journal of Emanuel Ringelblum* (New York: Ibooks, 2006), pp. 32–33; Pawel Wiederman, *Płowa Bestia* (Munich: Eucom, 1948), p. 40.

16 Lucy Dawidowicz, *The War Against the Jews: 1933–1945* (Toronto: Bantam Books, 1986), p. 200.

17 Von Woyrsch's rampage through Zagłębie was excessive even in the opinion of his fellow military commanders in the region. On September 8, *Generalfeldmarschall* Wilhelm List himself was forced to intervene and issued an order prohibiting the looting of property, the burning of synagogues, the rape of women, and the killing of Jews. Fourteen days later, on September 22, after the intervention of General Wagner, von Woyrsch was finally removed from the rear battalions of the 14th Army. The army commanders were mainly concerned that this terror would possibly lead to unrest in the region and would loosen military discipline. Krausnik and Wilhelm, *Die Truppe des Weltanschauungskrieges*, p. 54; Raul Hilberg, *The Destruction of the European Jews* (New York: Holmes & Meier, 1985), pp. 54, 190.

the Jews to keep going, to content themselves with whatever bread crust they could find, and to do their best to outsmart the Germans. Chajka, who made a full return to form, would later write:

> And then everything went quiet. Life went along its usual tracks. The prices of basic necessities keep going up, reaching preposterous heights. Profiteering is spreading at an unthinkable pace. The bread they bake at the bakeries is inedible, and it's impossible to find potatoes at all.
>
> All day long, nothing but long queues in front of the shops. Technically, we're only allowed to go out into the streets at 5 AM, but people do not obey. As early as three in the morning, they leave their homes to queue. Day after day, I am woken up by the sound of gunshots and fearfully, I try to listen and hear whether these are Germans shooting the ephemeral shadows of the people who go out into the streets. But no, they all just shoot into the air, though there are those who do aim at people, and some shots attain their targets. This week, ten Jewish bakers have been shot. They were accused of profiteering. Germans hate profiteering, they care for social justice. The hunger grows day by day. The bakers don't want to bake more than usual or necessary, they don't want to risk their lives. Only a few small bakeries bake bread from dark flour with all kinds of stuff mixed in. They sell this on the black market.[18]

Chajka's eye, with its decidedly Marxist vision sharpened by her literary talent, could not but observe the unfolding social injustice. Do we discern a hint of covert criticism aimed at her parents' store? It is hard to tell. The store was too small to be involved in daring acts of profiteering. And after all, the Jews could not be blamed for the terrible circumstances befalling them. It was all they could do to stay alive faced with rations, shortages, and hunger. Any scruples about "unkosher" means now had to be left by the wayside as one had to resort to previously unthinkable acts in order to survive. This included using the new borders established with the annexation of Zagłębie—including Będzin—to the German Reich and its separation from the central Polish territory, which was now under the control of the Generalgouvernement. Chajka looked around her and saw:

18 Klinger, 1944 diaries, Haogen I, pp. 19–20.

> Little children, with Aryan kerchiefs pulled over their heads, used to go to Żarki and Częstochowa, which are in the Governorate, by the border. They would buy eggs, butter, exchange their Rentenmarks[19] for the złoty then used for payment in the Governorate. They pay for the goods and bring them back, putting it into small bags made especially so that the eggs wouldn't crack. These they tie to their bodies, put their clothes over them and cross the border. These children know a great deal about trade. As you walk down the street, you can hear how much a dollar costs in paper money, how much in gold; how much for a pound. In their Jewish tongue, this is called "hard" and "soft." Children walk down the street saying among themselves: "The price of the dollar has risen, as has the price of gold. How much did you earn this week? I cheated a peasant, gave him a fake złoty." These children are progressively more and more demoralized. They have no schooling, no upbringing, no care. They grow up in the street. Children of the streets, under German control.[20]

But children were not the only ones affected. When they first took control of Będzin, the Nazis directed their efforts toward stripping the Jews of their financial security, even though few of the town's Jewish residents would have been considered wealthy. Nevertheless, several of the richer members of the community were arrested on November 11, 1939, and forced to sign a document forfeiting the rights to their property.[21] Similarly, numerous businesses were confiscated and transferred to German custody. The economic disenfranchisement process was executed swiftly and efficiently.[22] It is therefore not surprising that a hint of glee can be detected in Chajka's descriptions of all the ways in which Jewish grocers exploited the ignorance of the Germans and their loyalists in order to cheat them. Some Jews even managed to profit off the new situation, with the black market becoming an unavoidable necessity.

19 The Rentenmark was the official currency in the German Reich.

20 Klinger, 1944 diaries, Haogen I, pp. 27–28.

21 Alfred (Alf) Schwarzbaum testimony, Alfred Schwarzbaum Personal Archive, Massuah Archive, AR-A-00054-020.

22 Over 4,000 Jewish businesses were registered at the conservatorship office in the Katowice area. See Jerzy Jaros, "Grabież mienia Żydów przez wladze hitlerowskie w swietle akt Urzędu Powierniczego w Katowicach," *Biuletyn Żydowskiego, Instytutu Historycznego*, 38 (1961), pp. 105–117.

Nevertheless, the terror employed on the weaker classes and Jewish street merchants was relentless. The numbers of beggars and charity cases rose sharply, and some trades were increasingly turned over to children. Being small and agile, the little ones could do what their parents could not:

> Whenever a German appeared on the street, they'd give one another quick signals. One whistle, then another—and everyone hid inside the houses. Sometimes, some bitter, drunken sadist would chase them into their homes. And then he would drag people out of the apartment and start beating them, hitting their faces, arms and bodies with a rubber club. He would turn red, redder and redder, you'd think blood would come springing from his face, foam would show on his lips. And the child would grow progressively more black and blue, and the scream would turn into a moan, and only when he would grow completely silent the beating would cease.[23]

At this time, it appears that Chajka also underwent a humiliating experience. Walking down the street with David, they were accosted by a thug—probably a member of the Hitlerjugend (Hitler Youth)—who struck Chajka in the chest. She was enraged, and David bunched up his fists, intending to hit the man back. But then, a blade gleamed in the attacker's hand. Chajka grabbed David's hands and placed her body in between the two men, thus preventing further fighting and the possibility of serious injury. The lovers continued on their way, mortified. It was the first time they felt the desire for vengeance.[24]

The harsh winter of 1939–1940 found Będzin Jewry mostly alive but much afflicted economically and afraid for their lives. At this point, however, their fortune took a turn, because in late October 1939, the area was annexed to the German Reich. Thenceforth, the Jews of Zagłębie became subjects of an area called *Ostoberschlesien* (Eastern Upper Silesia). This administrative shift would have far-reaching implications for the fate of the Jews living in the region. Yet, at the time, it seemed to have some advantages. As mentioned earlier, the new border created new smuggling opportunities. On the other hand, it also accelerated the process of financial disenfranchisement, since German subjects in Zagłębie could now remain there as full-fledged citizens. There were also

23 Klinger, 1944 diaries, Haogen I, pp. 33–34.
24 Ibid., p. 34.

local Germans who now became *Volksdeutsche*, a high-ranking category within the Polish population according to the Nazi racial hierarchy, which came with many rights and privileges.[25]

The annexation of Zagłębie placed its local Jews under the direct supervision of the Gestapo, headed at the time by Kommissar Hans Dreier, often cited as "Dr." Dreier. Dreier was director of the Jewish Affairs Department at the Gestapo headquarters in Katowice. As a sign of things to come, immediately following the annexation in late October 1939, he issued an order stating that Jews must hand over all radio devices in their possession to the authorities. Those who refused to obey could expect execution. The aforementioned arrests of Będzin's eminent Jews were also the work of the Gestapo. In late December 1939, the town's Jewish community was placed under the obligation to "donate" 5 kilograms of gold and 10 kilograms of silver.[26] This operation involved the participation of a newly established institution, which would become a central part of the Nazi machine in Zagłębie and the rest of occupied Poland: the Judenrat.

Merin's Ascension

Chajka disliked the idea of the Judenrat from the start; however, she also saw it as a direct continuation of the legacy of Jewish institutions from before the occupation. In her diary, she refers to it as a "community" (*gmina*) or a "community council." Her negative sentiment centered on its leader: "The Germans created a Jewish municipality. Its leader is Moniek Merin, a gambler, a clown, and a brawler who always bets all or nothing—well, now he's betting on collaborating with the Germans."[27]

Who was Moniek (Moshe) Merin? There is not one testimony from this era painting him in any kind of positive light. According to David Liwer, Merin was a member of the World Zionist Organization, a commercial agent, albeit one in whom the mercantile circle had little trust. "He was a fickle man with no conscience and spent his time sitting in cafés, always in close proximity to a game of card or billiards."[28]

25 According to Jaros, the number of Germans living in Sosnowiec increased from a few hundred in 1939 to around 10,800 in 1942. Jaros, "Grabież mienia Żydów," pp. 105–117.

26 D. Liwer, *Ir Hametim*, pp. 25–26.

27 Klinger, 1944 diaries, Haogen I, pp. 21–22.

28 D. Liwer, *Ir Hametim*, p. 42.

According to Emanuel Ringelblum, the chronicler of the Warsaw ghetto who appears to have known him before the war, Merin was a small-time politician who switched camps on a regular basis: from Poalei Zion Right to the General Zionists, also with some time as a supporter of Rabbi Hager. He had always been a wheeler-dealer and an avid card player who was constantly in debt. His wife had divorced him, although on the eve of the war, he did make an effort at reconciliation.[29] He has also been described as a smallish, energetic young man with a mousy face and skittish eyes.[30]

Merin's appointment as head of the Judenrat in Sosnowiec came as a surprise. Later, Yehiel De-Nur (Ka-Tzetnik)[31] would include this event in his description of the public humiliations of the Jews of Sosnowiec in the town square:

> A black-uniformed officer, trailed by his retinue, strode around the compound, viewing the dead and beaten lying along the margins and in the corners. Suddenly, he turned on the terrified mass:
>
> "Which one of you is on the Community Council?"
>
> No answer. Then a skinny little man of about thirty elbowed his way through the cowed silence, and in an effeminate voice, nervously piped up: "Me…"
>
> The officer looked him over, ordered him to follow and they left.
>
> The witnessing crowd was aghast: Monyek Matroz! Shafran's employee! What made him jump up? What did he have to do with the Community Council? But this was no place for puzzlement, reaction or response. Only silence.[32]

Ka-Tzetnik's depiction matches David Liwer's portrait of Merin on most points, except that the latter states the man's real name: Moniek Merin. In Liwer's version of events, however, Merin had received a beating from the Germans before being appointed for the job.[33]

At any rate, it appears that the appointment was arbitrary in nature. The Germans needed a representative who would force the Jews to submit to their orders or, according to Liwer, to transport the Germans' belongings to their temporary military camp in Będzin and to shave

29 Ringelblum, *Notes from the Warsaw Ghetto*, p. 32.

30 Ya'akov Ronen, interview by the author, Kibbutz Haogen, 1986.

31 Yehiel De-Nur was born Yehiel Feiner in Sosnowiec in 1909.

32 Ka-Tzetnik, *Sunrise over Hell*, pp. 27–28. Monyek Matroz is the fictional name used by Ka-Tzetnik to depict Moniek Merin.

33 D. Liwer, *Ir Hametim*, p. 33.

off Jewish beards.[34] However, Ka-Tzetnik writes that the beards had already been shorn and that Merin's main task was to clear the corpses littering the town square.[35] Liwer also mentions the presence of the pre-occupation community council chairman, Szlomo Lejzerowicz, and the latter's apprehension at the thought of crossing the Germans. Another account describes Merin's ascension as the result of his procurement of forged documents in which Lejzerowicz seemingly entrusted Merin to represent the Jews before the German authorities.[36] The forged documents episode, albeit unsupported by further evidence, is enough to paint a picture of the public perception of Merin at the beginning of his career—as a crook who had obtained his position within the community leadership by fraudulent means.

Merin's political ambitions played a central role in his rise.[37] As far as the Germans were concerned, he was the right man for the job—power-hungry and willing to wield the authority placed in his hands to execute their harshest decrees. The Jews distrusted him but obeyed him nonetheless, fearing for their lives. Nevertheless, it is unclear whether they saw him as a collaborator from the start. Initially, Merin sought to gain the Jewish public's approval, even though he acted on German orders. In Chajka's description of events:

> Moniek Merin wanted to create a Jewish municipality that included all the political parties active among the Jews. He wanted to be able to say that this institution was rooted in all the classes of Jewish society and their struggle. Yet he failed to do so, even though, at the time, no one knew exactly what the role of this municipality would be or how far it would extend. He was given all sorts of competencies, space, money.
>
> But there were also those who did not want to be involved in this, those who knew all too well that they would have to pay the Germans dearly for this kind of leeway. They did not ask for much at first—get some Jews together for public works. 10 kilograms of gold, 10 kilograms of silver. Initially, the Germans would grab people off the street, anyone they could get their hands on: young, old, children.

34 Ibid.

35 Ka-Tzetnik, *Sunrise over Hell*, pp. 28–29.

36 M. Parasal, "Der Judenrat in Zaglembia," in Izaac Rappaport, ed., *Pinkas Zaglembia* (Yiddish) (Tel Aviv: Hamenora, 1972), p. 329.

37 Philip Friedman, "Two 'Saviors' Who Failed: Moses Merin of Sosnowiec and Jacob Gens of Vilna," *Commentary*, 26 (1958), pp. 479–491.

> They had to remove half-exploded bombs, clean rubble and debris, get rid of any sign of the burned down houses, which often still had burnt corpses inside. Those who had the right kind of document signed by the German commissar, attesting that this-here-Jew worked for them, were then let off to do other kinds of work.[38]

There were, however, a few people who refused to cooperate with Merin, such as Alfred Schwarzbaum, a wealthy merchant and Zionist activist.[39] Other Zionist militants, especially those who were members of socialist parties, also stood their ground.[40] Notably alongside them, we find Yitzhak Pejsachson, the father of Chajka's friends Irka and Lea. Pejsachson, a Bund[41] man and veteran revolutionary who had done more than one stint in prison, was a well-known and respected personality in Będzin thanks to his position as community secretary before the war. Like the representatives of the General Jewish Labor Bund in Warsaw and his friends in Będzin, Pejsachson categorically dismissed the idea of any participation in or collaboration with the Judenrat.

Yet, despite his dubious character, Merin was well-connected in the local political circles. Within a short time, a good portion of the Sosnowiec community elite had joined the Judenrat, including Lejzerowicz, the former community leader.[42] Some of the more notable people among them included Fania (Fanny) Czarna, secretary of the Sosnowiec Gymnasium, who became his personal secretary, as well as several relatively young politicos from the General Zionists party, most of them graduates of the local branch of Hanoar Hatzioni.[43] Liwer mentions

38 Chajka Klinger, 1944 diaries, Haogen I, pp. 22–23.

39 Alfred Schwarzbaum testimony, Massuah Archive, AR-A-00054-020.

40 Such militants included: Gedalia Sowkowski of Poalei Zion—see Arie Liwer, "Asher Lo Yishkach" (Hebrew), in Stein, *Pinkas Bendin*, vol. 2, pp. 349–350; Moshe Rosenkier from the leadership of the World Zionist Organization in Będzin—see Rachel Rosenkier (Schwarz), interview by the author, Haifa, 1987.

41 The Bund was a revolutionary Jewish socialist party that believed in national and social liberation for the Jews within Poland. They were against the use of the Hebrew language.

42 A rare testimony by Jerzy Olszewski, a Polish teacher appointed to represent the Sosnowiec city hall in the local Judenrat, claims that Lejzerowicz had collaborated with Merin at the beginning of his career. See Jerzy Olszewski testimony, Holocaust Remembrance and Beyond, https://isurvived.org/TOC-III.html#III-2 (accessed 2011).

43 Shalom Herzberg interview. Herzberg remembered taking part in a special assembly convened by Merin prior to the establishment of the Central Judenrat.

that Merin "managed to convene a suitable council of people to work with him as president of the Sosnowiec community."[44] Other sources reveal that the people who formed the Judenrat leadership had distinctly Zionist leanings: Most of the central positions in Sosnowiec and later in Będzin were held by members of the Zionist parties.[45] Merin also had authority over other local Judenrat leaders, and he made it a habit to periodically fire them and replace them with people he deemed loyal. After many such upheavals, the leadership of the Judenrat in Będzin coalesced under the direction of Chaim Mołczadski—former head of the local branch of the Jewish National Fund—and included four more Zionist politicos out of a total of six members.[46]

The recruitment of the political elite to the Judenrat was largely due to Merin's second guiding imperative—the establishment of an organizational structure that could rapidly respond to the essential needs of the various communities. Most of the politicians active in the Judenrat saw their involvement as a way of serving Jewish communities in their hour of distress.[47] In turn, Merin—the shady hustler—revealed himself to have extraordinary organizational capacities.[48]

The establishment of Merin and the institution of which he was in charge in Sosnowiec was indeed remarkably quick. In December 1939, the Germans created a regional Judenrat called the Ältestenräte der Jüdische Kultusgemeinde in Ostoberschlesien

It was attended by about fifty people, most of them graduates of Hanoar Hatzioni and members of the General Zionists party from Będzin and Sosnowiec. Merin informed those present about the appointment he had received and asked for their help in establishing his departments. According to Herzberg's testimony, most of those present at the meeting accepted Merin's proposal, and only four of those present—Herzberg himself, Yehezkel Krener, Moshe Rubin, and Yisrael Gelbart—signaled their reticence to participating in the Judenrat, saying that "the Germans should do their own dirty work."

44 D. Liwer, *Ir Hametim*, p. 33.

45 Shalom Herzberg interview; Anonymous Judenrat clerk testimony, YVA, O.12/3; Mazia, *Re'im Basa'ar*, p. 55; D. Liwer, *Ir Hametim*, p. 40.

46 Arie Liwer describes a meeting of the leaders of the Zionist parties, which was held in the spring of 1940 and in which some of the participants supported participation in the Judenrat, except for Gedalia Sowkowski. Chaim Mołczadski refused to participate in this meeting on the grounds that "there is no Zionism during wartime." A. Liwer, "Asher Lo Yishkach," p. 349. See also anonymous Judenrat clerk testimony, YVA, O.12/3.

47 A. Liwer, "Asher Lo Yishkach," p. 349; Abraham Manela, interview by the author, Netanya, 1987; Mazia, *Re'im Basa'ar*, pp. 36–40.

48 Chajka Klinger, 1944 diaries, Haogen I, pp. 22–23.

(The Jewish Council of Elders of East Silesia) and placed Merin as its chairman.[49] As head—or *Leiter*—of the council, Merin was in charge of roughly 100,000 Jews scattered across approximately thirty-five communities, including Będzin.[50] By 1941, this Central Judenrat—or the Zentrale as it was referred to by Jews in the district—was already operating nine departments, including those dedicated to welfare, health, and labor. The Welfare Department ran twenty-eight public kitchens, large clothes warehouses, about a dozen feeding stations for children, five shelters for the elderly, and several orphanages.[51] The Health Department operated two hospitals with the help of only thirteen Jewish doctors, nineteen general clinics as well as a dozen dental clinics, and performed close to 15,000 house calls by sanitation agents for the purpose of maintaining hygiene standards in residential areas.[52] The Labor Department arranged jobs for thousands of Jews in factories run by "German loyalists," but it was also in charge of providing the Germans with forced labor.[53] The Zentrale also established a Jewish Order Service (Jüdischer Ordnungsdienst) or as it would later become known, the Jewish police or Jewish militia. The Jewish Order Service was staffed by about 200 men, and the Będzin branch was outfitted with blue-and-white hats.[54]

Merin also appears to have been rather successful in his third area of responsibilities—negotiations with the Germans. He had a close relationship with the Gestapo commander Dreier, and on one occasion showed a community leader documents signed by the SS, according to

49 Central Judenrat report, September 3, 1940, Ringelblum Archive, AŻIH, I/II.

50 Central Historical Commission (CHC) document, YVA, M.1.Q 2388/603.

51 Jüdische Fürsorge in Ostoberschlesien (Jewish Welfare in Eastern Upper Silesia), March 25, 1941, YVA, O.6/853.

52 Head of the Council of Elders of the Jewish religious community in Eastern Upper Silesia, Central Health department, activity report for 1940, Ringelblum Archive, AŻIH, AGDC 254. See also Mazia, *Re'im Basa'ar*, pp. 36–40; Amos Kenigstein Avni testimony, YVA, O.3/3794. Mazia was a nurse in one of the hospitals, and Avni was a hygienist.

53 Central Judenrat report, Ringelblum Archive, AŻIH, I/II; Mazia, *Re'im Basa'ar*, p. 49; Szymon (Shimon) Balicki, YVA, O.3/1246; Mordechai Bochner, ed., *Sefer Kheshanov [Chrzanów]: Lezihram shel Kedoshei Ha'ir Shenisfu Bashoah* (Hebrew) (Tel Aviv: Hotza'ot Avivim and Irgun Yotzei Kheshanov BeYisrael, 1992); Natan Eliasz Szternfinkiel, *Zagłada Żydów Sosnowca* (Katowice: Centralnej Żydowskiej Komisji Historycznej w Polsce, 1946), p. 27.

54 Aharon Weiss, "Dfusey Hatguva Hayehudit BeZaglembia Betkufat Hashoah" (Hebrew), *Dapim Leheker Tkufat Hashoah*, 1 (1979), p. 57.

an oral testimony recorded by Ringelblum. For the purpose of fulfilling his role as head of the Judenrat, he was given a private bank account, a personal car, and freedom of movement—in the years 1940 and 1941, he visited Warsaw and even Slovakia.[55] According to Merin, it was thanks to his connections that he was able to prevent both the expulsion of Zagłębie's Jews in the first few months of the war and then later the establishment of ghettos in the region.[56]

And indeed, as the months went by, things in Zagłębie certainly seemed relatively calm and quiet compared to other regions. As is known today, the district's Jews were slated for expulsion to Generalgouvernement-controlled areas, where during the first months of the war, Adolf Eichmann had instituted the forced emigration policy he had previously employed in both Austria and the Protectorate of Bohemia and Moravia.[57] Merin established an Emigration Department in Sosnowiec with the probable aim of facilitating the execution of this policy. In early 1940, the expulsion of the Jews of Zagłębie was on the agenda of the higher echelons in the Nazi hierarchy, but the plan fell through, mainly due to opposition from Hans Frank, the head of the Generalgouvernement. it would seem that he already had enough Jews of his own.[58] It was therefore decided to harness the Jewish labor force in Zagłębie for the benefit of the German war economy. Thus, although the Jewish population in the area was subjected to forced labor,

55 Eliezer Schönker testimony, in Volnerman, Burstein, and Geshuri, *Sefer Oshpitsin*, p. 78; Friedman, "Two 'Saviors' Who Failed," p. 138; Cyril Rakocz, in *Sefer Sosnowitz*, vol. 2, p. 129; David Jakubowicz, "Beyamey Avera Veshoah," in David Jakubowicz, ed., *Sefer Zikaron Lekehilot Vadovitze, Andrihov, Kalvarya, Mishlenitze, Suka* [*Wadowice, Andrychów, Kalvarija, Myslenice, Sucha*] (Hebrew) (Givata'im and Ramat Gan: Massada Press, 1967), p. 189; Isaiah Trunk, *Judenrat: The Jewish Councils in Eastern Europe under Nazi Occupation* (New York: Stein and Day, 1977), pp. 141–142; Jaros, "Grabież mienia Żydów," p. 117; Wiederman, *Płowa bestia*, p. 157; Jakub Sandzer (Sander) testimony, http://polishjews.org/shoahtts/007one.htm (accessed April 30, 2024).

56 Ringelblum, *Notes from the Warsaw Ghetto*, p. 33. It later came to light that the Jews of Zagłębie were indeed due for expulsion in the first months of the war and that Merin had spoken with Eichmann on the subject.

57 Ze'ev Goshen, "Mivtza Nisko" (Hebrew), *Dapim Leheker Tkufat Hashoah*, 2 (1982), pp. 179–183.

58 Janusz Gumkowski and Kazimierz Leszczynski, *Poland Under Nazi Occupation* (Warsaw: Polonia Publishing House, 1961), pp 133–135; Władysław Bartoszewski, *War Crimes in Poland: Erich Von dem Bach* (Sudbury: Chilton Books, 1961), pp. 15–18; Hilberg, *The Destruction of the European Jews*, p. 207.

Zagłębie remained a ghetto-free zone and was spared the epidemics and rising death tolls that plagued other regions.[59] As mentioned previously, this was mostly due to Zagłębie's annexation to the Reich, but the local Jewish population could not help but attribute at least some of their good fortune to Merin.

59 Head of the Council of Elders of the Jewish religious community in Eastern Upper Silesia, Central Health department, activity report for 1940, Ringelblum Archive, AŻIH, AGDC 254.

Chapter Seven

The Movement's Order

Censorship: 1986

"Censorship?" a puzzled Zvi Arad says on the phone. "I don't know. I was just the translator. David Hanegbi edited. He used to correct everybody," he chuckles, "he corrected [Friedrich] Engels once." Zvi Arad was the movement's main Polish and German translator. His elegant style floats over Mother's diaries. But as for editing decisions, he is none the wiser.

"Stuff and nonsense," Ya'akov Hazan[1] decrees conclusively when I finally muster the courage to call him up and ask about one of the murkier points I stumbled across in my research: the ties between the Yishuv (the Jewish community in Mandatory Palestine) and members of Hashomer Hatzair in the Polish ghettos, in particular concerning the Tabenkin telegram.[2] Even in his twilight years, Hazan is always in the right.[3] The leader of Hakibbutz Ha'artzi does not admit mistakes, except one: defining the Soviet Union as a "second homeland."

1 Ya'akov Hazan, telephone interview with the author, 1985.
2 For more on the Tabenkin telegram, see chapter 16.
3 In a collection of articles and speeches published by the leader of Hakibbutz Ha'artzi Ya'akov Hazan in the late 1980s, he admitted to closely following the debate that broke out from time to time regarding the attitude of the Yishuv in *Eretz Israel* to that of the European Jews during the Holocaust. Yet, he stated, "I do not belong to the partisans in this field either," and described the many actions of the Yishuv for the Jews of Europe—the paratroopers, those who joined the British army, Aliya Bet, and more. Ya'akov Hazan, *Reshit Hadasha* (Hebrew) (Tel Aviv: Sifriat Poalim, 1988), pp. 15–16.

"This part hasn't been translated," wrote the Jewish partisan leader Różka Korczak in the margins of one of Chajka's notebooks, "and that's for the best."[4] The section dealt with a problematic subject—a Marxist analysis of life in the Jewish ghetto. Różka was all for reissuing the diaries, but she, too, was uncomfortable with some of Chajka's statements. "It will, however, be necessary to approach with intelligence and integrity a number—albeit a small one—of particularly sensitive issues in the public eye," wrote Abba Kovner in 1959, as he gave the final go-ahead for Sifriat Poalim to publish Mother's diaries. The movement's publisher had not been thrilled at the opportunity to publish Chajka's diaries—even after her death—and passed on the decision to him.[5] Kovner also had reservations about the diaries, but the more he read it, the more it became clear to him that "this legacy, as it is given, deserves to be published, in spite of all the perplexities certain ideas expressed in the diary may raise in the heart of the contemporary reader."[6]

An entry in Hanegbi's work diary from January 21, 1959, reads: "Chajka's diaries in the *affirmative* [emphasis in the original], special attention to phrasing (so as not to offend), David Kna'ani to read."[7] He worked swiftly as the book had to be published before Chajka's first *yahrzeit* (anniversary of her death).[8] Hanegbi was an experienced editor working for a kibbutz publisher who had earned a reputation for quality. However, he was also one of the movement's literary commissars. A few years later, he published an article in support of the Zhdanov Doctrine, the rigid communist cultural policy named after Stalin's head of agitprop Andrei Zhdanov.

Upon the book's release in 1959, Hashomer Hatzair member Shmuel Ron (Rozencwajg) wrote the following:

> Chajka was incapable of just laying out the facts in chronological order. Her testimony is informed by emotion alone, without

4 Różka Korczak, handwritten notes to the original diaries of Chajka Klinger, Moreshet Archive, C.36.

5 Letter from Chajka Grossman to Benito, September 9, 1958, Moreshet Archive, C.36.18.

6 Letter from Abba Kovner to the management of Sifriat Poalim, January 30, 1959, Hashomer Hatzair Archive, Yad Ya'ari, 7.24 (3).

7 Work diaries of David Hanegbi: 1959–1960, Hashomer Hatzair Archive, Yad Ya'ari, 24.59. The letter preceding Kovner's appears to have been written on the basis of this approval.

8 Letter from David Hanegbi to Yoshko Baumer, February 6, 1959, Moreshet Archive, C.36.21.

> succumbing to the discipline of the historiographer. Accordingly, there are some who claim that the time is not yet right to publish the "Diary".... The editing, as usual, has moved parts around and rejoined them, erased and deleted. Thus, the researcher will not settle for the "Diary" as it is published, but will turn to the original."[9]

Ron's review would later serve as the basis for Shabtai B. Beit Zvi's claim that Chajka's diaries were censored.[10]

Mother's diaries, it must be said, were very challenging to edit. As mentioned, she left two unfinished versions and never really put a seal on the writing process. Their contents were also difficult to digest: The diaries included humiliatingly detailed documentation of Hashomer Hatzair's oversights; the failures and later betrayals of the Jewish underground; harsh accusations against Zionists members of the Judenrat, against Jews who had gone as lambs to the slaughter, against the communications bureau of Hechalutz (the pioneering movement) in Geneva, and finally against the Yishuv. Some of these materials had significant political ramifications in the 1950s. Certain passages of Mother's diaries were as good as dynamite at a time when the Kasztner trial[11] had set off an exchange of bitter disputes and accusations. And, as was already known at the time, the diaries also had legal implications. Years later, they would serve as important evidence in the Barenblatt trial.

Mother's diaries had to be edited into a homogenous whole and in a way that would both preserve the memory of the dead and spare the pride of the survivors. Above all, they had to be adapted to conform to the legacy of Hashomer Hatzair and to the memory of the heroes of the resistance. Accordingly, problematic lines were redacted, events were presented in mitigated form, and names that were too well known were sometimes abbreviated to initials only.[12] Sometimes, whole passages were omitted, such as the detailed and revealing description of the Jews' conduct on the brink of extinction. On the other hand, *Miyoman Bageto* included Chajka's literary depictions of her comrades' demise, even though she was not there to witness them. Yet the editor, who was of course aware of this

9 Shmuel Ron, "Im Hofa'at Yoman Hageto shel Chajka Klinger" (Hebrew), *Yediot Yad Vashem*, 21–22 (1959), p. 21.

10 See Beit Zvi, *Post-Ugandan Zionism on Trial.*

11 For more on the Kasztner trial, see chapter 26.

12 Such initials included, for example: M.Y. instead of Meir Ya'ari; N.S. instead of Nathan Schwalb; Z. and Y. instead of Zivia Lubetkin and Yitzhak (Antek) Zuckerman.

fact, chose not to alert the reader to their fictional nature because they were in line with the heroic legacy of the movement. And so, one after the other, jarring failures became daring feats of audacity, critical analyses were replaced by myth, and imagined last moments were transformed into historical facts. That was the Zeitgeist of the time.

Mother's diaries were not the only ones to have been altered and censored. Paragraphs considered embarrassing were also edited out of the testimony of Mordechai Tenenbaum-Tamaroff, leader of the uprising in the Białystok ghetto, and it would be years before an unredacted edition of his writings would see the light of day.[13] Accusatory lines were omitted from Tosia Altman's famous letter "Israel is dying before my eyes."[14] Sometimes it was self-censorship, as in the case of Yitzhak Zuckerman, Mordechai Anielewicz's legendary second-in-command, who recorded his full memoirs during his lifetime but only agreed that they be published after his death.[15] The sacred writings of the ghetto fighters had to be published, but only in a form that made the past serve the present.

And yet, they wanted Chajka's diaries to be made into a book. Without the encouragement of her resistance friends when she had been alive, and especially after her death, none of the published materials would have seen the light of day. Chajka Grossman was the one to urge Mother to publish her memoirs, and it was she who cried injustice over her grave when they remained unpublished.[16] Abba Kovner gave Mother's diaries the final push when he wrote:

> This is, after all, a shocking testament to the purity of heart of the Holocaust generation, all those noble souls whose terrible concern for others made them know no fear. And for all of it—perhaps most importantly—it is yet another authentic and encouraging document attesting to the primal virtues of the movement's educational enterprise.[17]

13 See Mordechai Tenenbaum-Tamaroff, *Dapim Min Hadlika* (Hebrew) (Jerusalem: Yad Vashem, 1985).

14 Tosia Altman, "Yisrael Geviya Le'eynai," in Dror and Rosenzweig, *Sefer Hashomer Hatzair*, vol. 1, pp. 523–524.

15 Yitzhak (Antek) Zuckerman, *A Surplus of Memory: Chronicle of the Warsaw Ghetto Uprising* (Berkeley: University of California Press, 1993), p. ix.

16 Chajka Grossman, in *Chajka: Hoveret Zikaron*, pp. 39–40.

17 Letter from Abba Kovner to the management of Sifriat Poalim, January 30, 1959, Hashomer Hatzair Archive, Yad Ya'ari, 7.24 (3).

Later, in the 1980s, Różka Korczak, who saw it as a settlement of debts to the dead, sought to publish the unabridged version of the diaries,[18] as did the researcher Eliyahu Stern at the Ghetto Fighters' House in northern Israel in the 1970s.[19] Stern stumbled upon the text by accident when he was trying to prove that a certain paragraph in Chajka's diaries—one that was extremely politically and ideologically problematic in terms of how it reflected on his movement's leader, Yitzhak Tabenkin—strayed from the historical truth. Even in the late 1970s, Stern still felt the need to protect the great leader's honor.[20] Any way you look at it, the diaries were supposed to be part of a "sacred history," one that delivered a lesson and conveyed explicit ideological values.

But Then an Order Came

While the later 1944 version of the diaries opens with the war, the 1943 version begins by tracing the history of the Hashomer Hatzair movement. Overwhelmed by her experiences, Chajka tried her best to detach herself from the recent shock and go back to the early days of the war in order to properly fulfill her role as eyewitness:

> I'm still so stuck in what I went through not so long ago. What we lost causes me so much pain that I'm still unable to draw a line and separate myself from all of it and say that it's all over. I am still unable to treat it as history. It is so difficult for me to look dispassionately at everything that happened during those four years of war and make an objective judgment. My eyes simply can't see that far. I cannot forget the present and assume the spirit of that period, which seems so distant, already so unreal and unimportant.[21]

Directly following this paragraph, she begins to describe—as objectively as possible—the origins of Hashomer Hatzair in Będzin:

18 Różka Korczak, handwritten notes to the original diaries of Chajka Klinger, Moreshet Archive, C.36.

19 Eliyahu Stern testimony, 1985, Ghetto Fighters' House Archive (GFH); Chajka Klinger file, C.36.01, Moreshet Archive. See also Moreshet Archive, Avihu Ronen collection, 235.

20 Eliyahu Stern, "Hamivrak shel Tabenkin el Hamahteret Hehalutzit BeBendin" (Hebrew), *Mibifnim*, 41 (1979), pp. 323–325.

21 Klinger, *I Am Writing These Words to You* (1943 diaries), p. 80.

> The war broke out. Disappointed hopes. Everything interrupted in the middle. Some during *hachshara*, others just before *aliya*.
>
> The thread of life cut off right in the middle. What will the conditions and life be like? Nobody knows. At first all of us wanted to flee from here and follow the movement's route, go toward Równe and then toward Vilna. All *bogrim* [senior members, adults] of the movement followed that route.
>
> But then an order came—"Stop. Stay put. Everybody stay where you are."
>
> The Yishuv of Polish Jews remained, was in Poland, the former Congress Poland, so our [Yishuv] must stay here as well.[22] It had to stay with the Yishuv—live, grow, and die with it.[23]

One line in this version—the command "Stop. Stay put," which was omitted from the later diaries as well as the book—hints at a long and intricate tale that remains partially obscure to this very day. What did this order actually mean? Who gave it? What was the effect of this order on Chajka's fate? In her 1944 diaries, Chajka describes the decision to stay in Będzin after her recovery from illness in a different way:

> At the time, almost all the *bogrim* went to Równe, then to Vilna. We also wanted to go to Vilna. Every week, we, the people of Dror or Gordonia, would receive a letter telling us how more and more people were gathering in Vilna to make their *aliya* from there. People around us also started to leave. One day, Zvi [Brandes] came by and told David, "I am going, if you want, come with me." They had everything arranged, how they would dress, where they would put their money. I didn't want to go, my health was still frail, I could still see that perilous journey at the beginning of the war before my eyes. At home, whenever we began talking about going, there would be an uproar. So, I kept postponing the decision to tomorrow and the next day. Let's wait, I told David, and he said he didn't want to go without me, so we waited. Dorka [Herzberg] felt the same, so Zvi also decided to wait. Meanwhile, a ferocious winter rolled around, so he really didn't want to go anywhere anymore.[24]

22 This is the part of Poland that according to the decisions of the Congress of Vienna (1815), was under Russian rule during the nineteenth century.

23 Klinger, *I Am Writing These Words to You* (1943 diaries), pp. 80–81.

24 Klinger, 1944 diaries, Haogen I, pp. 28–29.

Yet, even this excerpt falls short of explaining why Chajka chose to remain in Będzin following the winter of 1939–1940. As shown in the two above-quoted passages, young people with any sense of affiliation with a youth movement had the option of escaping the German occupation area at the beginning of the war, and this option had been available to Chajka and David not only in September 1939 but also in the following months. Why did they not set out again?

In the earlier version of the diaries—the one written in hiding—Chajka and her friends appear to have followed an order to stay put, despite the renewed possibilities of escape. In the second version, written in Mandatory Palestine, the decision to stay was attributed to personal motives and thought processes. Did Chajka herself choose to emphasize her private considerations and omit the order received from the movement, or was this an editorial consideration that covered up a complicated affair, which for years would remain an open wound in the movement's historiography? To elucidate this subject further, we must turn the spotlight on the Hashomer Hatzair gathering in Vilna at the end of 1939.

The Vilna Gathering

In October 1939, shortly after Poland was occupied by Germany and the Soviet Union, Lithuania concluded an agreement with the USSR in which Lithuania, a small Baltic state that still maintained its independence, agreed (under considerable duress) to accept Russian military presence on its soil. As compensation, Lithuania would annex the city of Vilna to its territory, thus joining the club of states eating into Poland. For a considerable portion of Polish Jewry, in particular for the Zionists among them, this opened a door to hope. Lithuania had a small passage to the Baltic Sea, and it seemed that this might make it possible for Jews to slip through the fingers of the two totalitarian giants obstructing their path to *aliya*. There was also the possibility of continued Jewish and Zionist activity under the relatively liberal Lithuanian regime while waiting for the war to end. These hopes explain the mass influx of Polish Jews to Vilna from mid-October onward. About 15,000 Jews arrived there during the fall and winter months, including about 2,000 youth movement members.[25]

25 Perlis, *Tnu'ot Hano'ar Hehalutziyot*, p. 83.

The gathering of the *bogrim* in Vilna was an organized operation. Vilna offered a chance to maintain and even bolster the strength of the movement. The leadership's emissaries would travel to different cities and towns, making arrangements with the *bogrim* for their arrival in Vilna.[26] In the border towns of Vilna, local Hashomer branches set up smuggling stations, and in February 1940, there were already 657 *shomrim* from thirteen *hachshara* kibbutzim gathered in Vilna, among them some members of Hapo'el Lakfar.[27] One of them was Zelig Shoshan, the boyfriend of Esther Zborowska (she had already immigrated to Mandatory Palestine).[28] And yet, on the eve of the war, most of the movement's members remained in both German- and Soviet-occupied territories: Hashomer Hatzair in Poland counted 18,000 trainees, of which 3,500 were *bogrim*. In Galicia there were another 7,000 trainees.

The main leadership of Hashomer Hatzair in Poland also attended the Vilna gathering. In a first letter to the secretariat of Hakibbutz Ha'artzi—the kibbutz movement to which they belonged in *Eretz Israel*—they wrote that the rescue operations from occupied Poland were limited: "We didn't want to save individual people, or even dozens, and endanger the entire movement. If the whole movement is condemned to death, it is not important to save individuals. On the other hand, it is imperative to maintain the integrity of the movement."[29]

This principle, according to which the collective stands above the individual, was one of the distinct hallmarks of Hashomer Hatzair. Nevertheless, maintaining the "integrity of the movement" would prove difficult now that the war had cut up the organization's operating area into three parts: the German-occupied territory, the Russian-occupied territory, and Lithuania. The same attitude was true for both continued immigration to *Eretz Israel* and the movement's activities in general. With the coming of winter, in December 1939–January 1940, the misgivings multiplied. Along with convening the kibbutzim in Vilna and looking for ways to immigrate to *Eretz Israel*, emissaries of Hashomer Hatzair

26 Ibid., pp. 60–63.

27 Ibid.

28 Esther Shoshan interview.

29 Letter from the leadership in Vilna to the secretariat of Hakibbutz Ha'artzi, November 9, 1939, Hashomer Hatzair Archive, Yad Ya'ari, March 28 (2); Hanhagat Hareishit [the main leadership], "Hayad Ro'edet," in Dror and Rozenzweig, *Sefer Hashomer Hatzair*, vol. 1, p. 455.

ventured into the two occupied territories. Tosia Altman[30] was followed by Mordechai Anielewicz to the German-occupied territory.[31] Other emissaries operated in Russian-occupied territory.[32] Their goal was to renew contact with the bulk of the movement's members who remained in the two occupied parts of Poland.

At that time, the Hashomer leadership in Vilna began to consider the possibility of their own emigration from Lithuania. Echoes of these deliberations reached *Eretz Israel* and Meir Ya'ari. The forty-two-year-old Ya'ari was the undisputed leader of Hakibbutz Ha'artzi in *Eretz Israel*, and his charismatic authority extended to branches of Hashomer Hatzair in Poland as well. In the years that had passed since the Bitania experiment in the early 1920s,[33] he had expanded his influence to thirty-nine kibbutzim in the Land of Israel[34] and to tens of thousands of Hashomer instructors and trainees in Europe.[35] A polemicist by nature, he was not above whipping them into shape using the harshest of words. Being a scion of Rabbi Elimelech of Lizhensk, his Marxist rhetoric was saturated with Hasidic terminology. His abundant gifts of idealism, toughness, and sharpness of mind allowed him to dominate his followers with reproving yet loving command.

On January 10, 1940, Ya'ari wrote words of tough encouragement to Vilna:

> We have come to the conclusion that the movement must not allow itself to be annihilated by any means. We understand that it will be diminished. There will certainly be many victims, there will certainly be incidents of betrayal and provocation. But underground resistance is not a game, and it demands risk and dedication. We cannot afford to behave like some countries that have surrendered without firing a shot for excess tactical and strategic cleverness.

30 Letter from Zalman Gayer to the Action Committee of Hakibbutz Ha'artzi, December 7, 1939, Hashomer Hatzair Archive, Yad Ya'ari, March 28 (2).

31 Gutman, *Mered Hanetzurim*, p. 91.

32 Letter from Haim Holtz and Ya'akov Griksgorn to the Action Committee of Hakibbutz Ha'artzi, January 13, 1940, Hashomer Hatzair Archive, Yad Ya'ari, March 28 (2).

33 For more on Bitania, see chapter 3.

34 Only twenty-four kibbutzim actually got off the ground. The rest of the kibbutzim stayed at temporary locations, waiting to move to permanent settlements.

35 The movement's numbers at the time were estimated at 35,000, including approximately 25,000 *shomrim* in Poland and Galicia and another 8,000–10,000 instructors and apprentices across the rest of Europe.

> He who is ready to be wiped out without any resistance loses not only this world but also the right to rise up and flourish again when the time comes. We will not follow in the footsteps of the workers' movement in Germany.[36]

Like its author, readers of this letter were readying themselves for the sorry decline of socialism with Hitler's rise to power.

Later in his letter, Ya'ari made several practical decrees that did not please the movement's leadership. The most controversial among them was the ruling that none of the leadership members could leave their positions without express permission from Hakibbutz Ha'artzi in *Eretz Israel*. This was clearly Ya'ari's reaction to rumors about the desire of several leadership members to resign from their positions and immigrate to *Eretz Israel*. "In emergency conditions," he wrote, "each member of the leadership is an emissary."[37] It is possible that, with his choice of words, Ya'ari was also hinting at a painful fact known to both him and the representatives in Vilna: Immediately following the outbreak of the war, fourteen emissaries of the pioneering movements from *Eretz Israel* had left Warsaw and returned to Mandatory Palestine, including three members of Hashomer Hatzair—Israel Rosenzweig, Avraham Lipsker, and Jacob Friedman.[38]

Some of the movement members in Vilna did not take kindly to the letter, and echoes of their reactions later reached Ya'ari.[39] However, they did feel somewhat reassured: contact with *Eretz Israel* had been renewed after all. The harsh but loving hand of the distant leader managed to reach them. On March 22, 1940, the Vilna Gathering Council was held. The keynote speech of the evening was given by Josef Shamir and included an optimistic note in the spirit of the directives given by the sage of Merhavia:

> We are young. Our generation must now make good on the deal we signed in our early days, during evenings of long conversations and heated arguments, nights spent by the fire, weeks of youthful fervor, dreams of the future, of a new tomorrow. We knew: a time of trials

36 Letter from Meir Ya'ari to the Leadership in Vilna, January 10, 1940, Hashomer Hatzair Archive, Yad Ya'ari, March 28 (2a). This letter was not included in Sefer Hashomer Hatzair, and its discovery was somewhat of a surprise.

37 Ibid.

38 Perlis, *Tnu'ot Hano'ar Hehalutziyot*, pp. 34–35.

39 Letter from Meir Ya'ari to the Leadership in Vilna, May 28, 1940, Hashomer Hatzair Archive, Yad Ya'ari, March 28 (2).

> would come. We believed: we will prevail. Now the great hour has come. Will we bear the weight of the load?[40]

Regarding the future of the gathering in Vilna, Shamir said:

> Many from this area write to us to say: "When spring comes, we will go." What is our council and our opinion?—Not to leave, for now, because: 1) The passage is already very difficult; 2) The juridical arrangement here [in Vilna] teeters in the balance; 3) The chances of *aliya* from there [occupied Poland] do not seem any less than they are from here [Vilna].[41]

As usual, the council's decisions supported Shamir's remarks. This was the movement's order. Chajka, David, Zvi, and many others were made to stay put and resume the movement's activity. The leadership in Vilna knew about them, and the decision it made took them into account: "In Będzin, a group of our comrades have organized themselves for kibbutz life," said Shamir during his speech. "These are the members of 'Galon.' A group that will surely grow."[42]

In Vilna, however, the emigration efforts continued. From November 1939 to June 1940, about 600 immigrants from the German occupied area of Poland arrived in *Eretz Israel*, most of them businessmen and Zionist leaders.[43] There were few pioneers among the immigrants, but these included most of the members of the old leadership of Hashomer Hatzair, including Josef Shamir himself.[44] And this, despite Ya'ari's order, despite the instructions given to members of the movement in occupied Poland. In fact, among Hashomer veterans, only Josef Kaplan returned to Poland. Only many years later would Abba Kovner point out that despite his understanding of the old guard's emigration, "it is an objective fact that the old leadership of Hashomer Hatzair and of the majority of the

40 *Al Masu'ot Polin* (Hebrew) (Merhavia: Hakibbutz Ha'artzi and Hashomer Hatzair, 1940), pp. 176–177.

41 Ibid.

42 Ibid., p. 145.

43 Perlis, *Tnu'ot Hano'ar Hehalutziyot*, p. 102.

44 The members of the leadership who made *aliya* were: Zelig Geyer, Adam Rand, Yitzhak Zalmanson, Chaim Holtz (Alon), and Josef Shamir. As mentioned, from the ranks of the old leadership, only Josef Kaplan returned to Warsaw. Tosia Altman, Mordechai Anielewicz, Mira Fuchrer, and Shmuel Breslaw, who would make their way back to Warsaw, belonged to the young leadership.

older echelon departed and immigrated to *Eretz Israel*, leaving not even one emissary of Hakibbutz Ha'artzi in the circle of fire when the critical hour came."[45]

Chajka was among those who stayed. Whether she wanted to or not, she complied with the movement's order.

The First Meeting

In the 1943 diaries, a note of acrimony creeps into Chajka's description about the beginning of work in the Będzin ghetto:

> Then they came from Vilna to work in the movement in Poland. Josef Kaplan [came]. And after a while he visited us in Zagłębie.
>
> "I'm [illegible]," he said. "We've become stuck, we—the old-timers. There's no path to *aliya*. We have to make sure that this... is worthy of our movement. We have to start work, rebuild the movement, the branches, and the groups."
>
> And I forgot what I once promised myself during *hachshara*, that is, that I would never return to being an educator.
>
> *Hatnua doreshet* [the movement demands]—it's so simple and obvious by itself.[46]

This passage was not included in the published book. In the movement's tradition of heroic tales, Kaplan's return to the occupied territories and the renewal of the movement's work was a symbol of the movement's resilience. The fact that he was the only member of the old leadership to return to Poland was simply "forgotten," and his bitterness regarding this fact was not made public. In an article Chajka published in 1945, she emphasized Kaplan's courage: "'How does he travel by train with a face as Jewish as his?' we inquired awkwardly, and he explained with a smile that facial features are not important, it is the person's posture, behavior, confidence that count."[47]

Kaplan's visit was the harbinger of a fresh start. In Chajka's later version of events—the one included in *Miyoman Bageto*—this idea takes on a nostalgic tone:

45 Abba Kovner, *Al Hagesher Hatzar: Masot Be'al Pe* (Hebrew) (Tel Aviv: Sifriat Poalim, 1981), p. 74.

46 Klinger, *I Am Writing These Words to You* (1943 diaries), pp. 81–82.

47 Chajka Klinger, "Hara'ayon Shehasir et Ruhenu" (Hebrew), *Mishmar*, April 20, 1945.

> I remember that first evening when all of us, all the remaining *bogrim* from our *ken*, gathered together like it was yesterday. It was at Lea's place, there were nine of us: Lea, Nacia Klugman, Irka Pejsachson, Ada Neufeld, Rachel (Rachelka) Rosenkier, Bronka Lipszyc, Hela Kacengold, David Kozłowski—the only man present—and me.
>
> Well, we said, bad luck, we are weak, and the war has messed up our plans. Some had intended to join a *hachshara*—Nacia, Irka, Hela—while we wanted to go to *Eretz Israel*. The *ken* had fallen apart, there were no platoons, no groups, really there was no one but us. Just us, and we could count on no one but ourselves, we had to build everything anew. Those promises of not returning to pedagogical work would also soon ring hollow, we had to return. The Będzin *ken* had been one of the worst before the war—only an address really, nothing more. Sometimes there was no venue, other times we had a venue but no people. Usually, there were many *bogrim*, but none of them wanted to join the *hachshara*. We were always arguing, there were always problems, everything was disorganized.[48]

Only three of the nine participants in that meeting survived to testify: Chajka, Ada Neufeld (Halperin), and Rachel Rosenkier. The Pejsachson sisters were the daughters of the aforementioned Yitzhak Pejsachson, a veteran Bund man and a known personage in Będzin who, despite his radical stances, was very popular and well-respected among the townsfolk. He was an open-minded man, and his house served as a meeting place for the Hanoar Hatzioni youth movement. Lea, the eldest of the Pejsachson girls, was Chajka's best friend. She followed her to join Hashomer Hatzair and became a loving mother figure to her friends and trainees. Idzia, the second eldest daughter, belonged to the Bund's youth movement Zukunft (Future) and appears to have joined Hashomer Hatzair only after the onset of the war. She was a serious, bespectacled intellectual with radical leftist views.[49] Irka, the youngest Pejsachson daughter was best friends with Nacia Klugman. The two were golden-haired Gymnasium students with a mischievous streak.[50] Like Idzia Pejsachson, Nacia was considered

48 Klinger, 1944 diaries, Haogen I, pp. 30–31.

49 Ranz, *In Nazi Claws*, p. 95.

50 Ibid.; Klinger, 1944 diaries, Haogen I, pp. 27–28; "Będzin Census of 1939," AŻIH, 212/11.

highly intelligent and an eloquent speaker.[51] Ada Neufeld left Hanoar Hatzioni to join Hashomer Hatzair. Her boyfriend from the movement Joshua Kamiński had already immigrated to Mandatory Palestine. Later, he would become known as Professor Joshua Efron, the famous historian.[52] Rachel Rosenkier (later Schwarz) was the daughter of Moshe Rosenkier, head of the Hitachdut (Union) party in the town, and she, too, had transferred from Hanoar Hatzioni.[53] There is no additional testimony regarding the two other girls present.[54]

It seems that Chajka and David held leadership positions in this group, if only because of their age: They were about twenty-two or twenty-three at the time, while most of the girls had not yet turned twenty. The youthful—and mostly female—brigade set to work. Chajka describes it thus:

> So, we decided to either create a strong *ken* built on a solid foundation, or to do nothing at all and not waste our energy and effort. We were the first organization to begin our work out in the Jewish street. We brought together two groups of students, boys and girls, who could then become our instructors. Almost all of them were very worthy young people, intelligent boys and girls. We put a lot of effort into bringing them together. We recruited them. We had to work fast, even though we knew it was not advisable, as they had no legacy of the Hashomer tradition and, sadly, this would prove a lasting influence on the Będzin *ken*.
>
> We organized oral and written seminars. Nacia took the lead on this, and over the course of the year she gave them a momentous, beautiful, and thorough pedagogical and ideological education. It was hard work, as they were all at an age that comes with its own, significant problems. Then we began to organize *tzofim* [scouts] and *bnei midbar* [sons of the desert] groups. David, Lea, and Hela took charge of the pedagogy there. The other organizations followed suit and also began to work with the youths.[55]

In the Hashomer Hatzair hierarchy in Poland, the rank of *menahalim* (youth leaders) was filled with the oldest members (sixteen to eighteen

51 Klinger, 1944 diaries, Haogen I, p. 36. Like her friend Irka, Nacia Klugman was seventeen years old at the time.

52 Ada Halperin (Neufeld) interview.

53 Rachel Rosenkier (Schwarz) interview.

54 For further mentions of Hela Kacengold, see chapter 18.

55 Klinger, 1944 diaries, Haogen I, pp. 31–32.

years old), and they provided the recruitment pool for instructors. The *tzofim* were the intermediate rank (fourteen to sixteen years old), while the youngest, the *bnei midbar,* were ten to fourteen years old. The work done with the younger ranks of the organization is well-documented in the 1943 diaries:

> The young, particularly the children, are suffering from neglect. Extreme poverty. All trade in is children's hands. They sell pretzels, rolls, sweets, corsets and stays, mercers' goods, and shoelaces. They travel, trade, smuggle. Dirty, neglected, they do not go to school. No guardians or teachers.
>
> A new generation is growing up—children of the street.
>
> Children must not be left on the street at the mercy of fate. We won't let them become a generation of *amei ha'artzim* [ignoramuses, illiterates]. The children must not forget the Hebrew language, but more importantly they cannot become illiterates. We shall not let that happen. [...]
>
> I still remember the first joys and concerns: How can we teach children and play with them when they are hungry, dirty, and barefoot?
>
> We began trying to obtain shoes and clothes, and to ensure that the children would be clean and well-fed—common funds, lunch eaten together. But all that was palliative medicine.
>
> Będzin had broad prospects. Young *menahalim* [youth leaders] came to us. We have to work on a larger scale and with more momentum. Let us open a kind of day care center. But where can we obtain the resources, premises, and money? The only thing we have is teachers.
>
> Let's turn to the *gmina* with a plan to open a day care center. A detailed plan was prepared, specifying the premises we needed, the meals, the curriculum, and the games. We went to the distinguished gentlemen and they liked the idea.... They did open common rooms and day care centers, but without our participation. But we had no regrets. We were happy that we had initiated the idea of care for Jewish children.[56]

The importance that Chajka and her friends attached to the establishment of the kindergarten and the school was not driven by philanthropy

56 Klinger, *I Am Writing These Words to You* (1943 diaries), pp. 82–83.

alone. As she herself later explained in the 1944 diaries: "The Germans forbade the existence of Jewish schools, and there was a foreseeable danger that the People of the Book would raise a generation of complete ignoramuses."[57] Scholar Isaiah Trunk, who expands on this subject in the context of Poland as a whole, notes that part of the Nazis' policy was to turn Poland—particularly its Jews—into a weak and ignorant nation. Already by the end of November 1939, the civilian German authorities in Poland had ordered the closure of Jewish schools, the last of which shut its gates on December 4, 1939.[58]

Hashomer Hatzair was not the only organization trying to deal with this problem, but Chajka and her friends' application to the Judenrat regarding the establishment of a school was of particular importance. For the first time, youth movement members sought to take on a role that under normal conditions would have been entrusted to the state and the community. The *shomrim* wanted to bring their revolutionary spirit to this new role and offered a replacement for the schools that were closed. The Judenrat, however, was worried about rattling their German supervisors. The first seed of conflict had thus been planted. Despite this, Chajka viewed the operation of the Judenrat's children's clubs in a positive light:

> The Judenrat had a lot of money at their disposal, and they did a lot for some aspects of Jewish life. In no time, common rooms and clubs for older children, crèches for little ones, and kindergartens for children five or six years old were set up all over Zagłębie. The Judenrat implemented many of our projects, with slight adjustments, but they did not employ our educators. They were afraid of our influence. They also did not accept our children as an organized group, but individually. Still, we were happy that we had managed to do something. Tens of children who until then were out in the street, horribly demoralized by their condition, were now spending three or four hours under adult care.
>
> The children were given a meal, and we tried to find clothes for those who looked particularly shabby. Once the children gained a bit more discipline, various games were also organized, and they were taught to eat with a spoon and fork. Initially, the children pounced on their food like small, hungry, feral animals. They would

57 Klinger, 1944 diaries, Haogen I, p. 43.

58 Trunk, *Judenrat*, p. 197.

> shout if their neighbor was given more; they fought over every slice of bread. There was so much noise in the dining hall that the educators had to shout to hear each other. It was like dealing with a river, which, having overflown its natural channel, had to be tamed and redirected back to its old conduit.[59]

Despite opposition from the Judenrat, the young instructors were able to incorporate their spiritual baggage from the youth movements into their work. Chajka wrote:

> The children were hardly recognizable after just a few weeks. They were cleaner, able to participate in games and go out for walks. They sang a lot of Hebrew songs. There were some members of youth organizations among their instructors and educators. Following Batya's example [probably Batya Schiff, A.R.], the instructors decided, almost as an afterthought, with no direction from any authorities, to raise the children in the spirit of Zionism, as far as possible under the circumstances. More and more frequently, one would hear Hebrew songs, single Hebrew words spoken by the children in the playgrounds, on the streets. This made us very happy—it was as if the living Hebrew word had descended from its pedestal and settled among us, among the people.[60]

The bitterness of the movement's struggles against the Judenrat had been somewhat dimmed by the joy of educational action, the latter fueling and filling Chajka's entire existence in the near future.

59 Klinger, 1944 diaries, Haogen I, pp. 45–47.

60 Ibid., pp. 47–48.

Chapter Eight

Breathe with Ease

Kibbutz Dror and the Slovakia Affair

This period also saw the formation of Kibbutz Dror in Będzin, which differed from the Hashomer Hatzair group in several ways. The Dror movement, or Dror-Freiheit as it was sometimes called,[1] was established in 1938 through the merger of two preexisting youth movements: Freiheit and Hechalutz Hatzair.[2] These movements mainly appealed to young workers. They had a higher percentage of laborers than other movements, although not by much (as a rule, there were few laborers among Polish Jewry).[3] The proletarian nature of these movements mainly manifested itself in the low number of Gymnasium students among their members.[4]

Kibbutz Dror in Będzin was one of the movement's training kibbutzim. It counted roughly sixty members who had returned and reassembled in Będzin, having failed to make their escape with the outbreak of the war.[5] In October 1939, they were visited by Frumka Płotnicka, the emissary of the Dror movement from Warsaw.[6] The

1 Both the words "Dror" and "Freiheit" mean freedom—the first in Hebrew, the second in German.

2 Sarid, *Hehalutz Vetnu'ot Hano'ar BePolin*, pp. 264–267.

3 Perlis, *Tnu'ot Hano'ar Hehalutziyot*, p. 4; Sarid, *Hehalutz Vetnu'ot Hano'ar BePolin*, p. 243.

4 Sarid, *Hehalutz Vetnu'ot Hano'ar BePolin*, p. 245.

5 Hanna Ben Nun, *Behazara Lesham* (Hebrew) (Dalia: Ma'arehet, 1997), p. 13.

6 Pnina Jacobowitz, in Even-Shoshan, Dan, and Stavi, *Gushey Hachshara Mesaprim*, p. 257; Perlis, *Tnu'ot Hano'ar Hehalutziyot*, p. 80.

central figure in the kibbutz was Herszel Szpringer, whose big curls and innocent, boyish face belied an outstanding aptitude for leadership and community organization. Herszel became the main spokesman for Kibbutz Dror.

Another prominent character in the kibbutz was Baruch Gaftek. With his athletic physique and Aryan looks, Gaftek was one of the rare youth movement activists to have undergone military training. On the other hand, he retained a sensitive, intellectual side, as expressed in both his participation in the teachers' seminar in Warsaw and his poetry.[7] Along with Frumka, who became more and more attached to the kibbutz, they would play an important role in its future: Herszel with his captivating folksiness and inexhaustible energy; Gaftek with his courage and coolness; and the thin, dark-skinned, chain-smoking Frumka with her authority and experience.[8]

In the winter of 1939–1940, the Dror community in Będzin discovered an escape route to Slovakia, thanks to a local initiative of the head of the Judenrat in the nearby town of Oświęcim by the name of Leon Schönker. On the outskirts of which the Auschwitz death camp would later be established, Oświęcim was a respectable town with a small Jewish community of several thousand people. As part of the deportation plan designed for the local Jews, Schönker was tasked with establishing an Eretz Israel Office (a regional emigration bureau) in Oświęcim to deal with emigration matters.[9] This initiative was a remnant of the forced migration plans that Eichmann had tried to implement in the region.[10] While dealing with legal options of emigration, Schönker also considered the possibility of crossing the border illegally into Slovakia.

News of Schönker's activities reached Kibbutz Dror, and Frumka and Herszel began organizing groups of pioneers—in Warsaw and

7 Ranz, *In Nazi Claws*, pp. 88–89.

8 See Naomi Shimshi, "Frumka Płotnicka," in Avihu Ronen and Joachim Kohavi, eds., *Guf Shlishi Yahid: Biographiyot shel Havrey Tnu'ot No'ar Betkufat Hashoah*, vol. 1 (Hebrew) (Haifa: Ghetto Fighters' House, Moreshet, Yad Ya'ari, 1994), pp. 165–220.

9 Eliezer Schönker testimony, in Volnerman, Burstein, and Geshuri, *Sefer Oshpitsin*, pp. 179–180.

10 See ibid.; Goshen, "Mivtza Nisko," pp. 179–183. It is interesting to note that until now, researchers have failed to notice the connection between the Nisko plan for the deportation of the Jews of Upper Silesia and the Eretz Israel Office that was established concurrently in Oświęcim. Eichmann's presence in the implementation of the Nisko plan indicates that the Germans did not abandon the forced emigration programs that Eichmann had begun operating before the war (mainly in Austria) until early 1940.

Będzin respectively—to cross the border into Slovakia. Their efforts expanded rapidly, and when Herszel turned to Merin for help, Merin offered to transfer around 200 pioneers to Slovakia legally. With the consent of the Germans, Merin even established an emigration office in Sosnowiec for this purpose.[11] It seems that this office was also part of the Germans' forced emigration plans, which were still in effect at that time. The degree of seriousness with which youth movement activists regarded Merin's influence is evidenced by the fact that one of the officials in the emigration office was Kalman Tencer, the head of the Hashomer Hatzair *ken* in Sosnowiec. Merin even corresponded in writing with representatives of Hechalutz in Switzerland, and representatives of the movements regularly sent him copies of their letters. Later, this emigration attempt, for which the heads of Hechalutz and Hashomer Hatzair in Warsaw had such high hopes, would become known as the "Two Hundred Affair."[12]

In light of Merin's promises and his energetic involvement in the issue of emigration, several Dror groups left Warsaw for Zagłębie. From there, they hoped to get to Slovakia and then to Hungary, which was still free of German presence on the ground, despite being a de facto German colony. These groups arrived in Będzin and Oświęcim, where they were to await Merin's signal.[13] However, no signal ever came. Merin's plan turned out to be a wild goose chase, his promises empty. At the same time, the escape route discovered by Schönker was blocked. Schönker confronted Merin and was fired from his position, to be replaced by Merin's brother Chaim, the family's go-to problem-solver.[14] The word among Kibbutz Dror members was that conflict arose over border smuggling, and Merin—who did not tolerate private initiative—got fed up with Schönker and fired him. Some claimed that the smuggling operation failed because Merin had tipped off the Germans,[15] despite the lack of evidence to support this assertion. At any rate, two years later, leaders of the youth movements in Warsaw

11 Josef Korniański, *Shlihut Halutzim* (Hebrew) (Tel Aviv: Hakibbutz Hameuchad and Ghetto Fighters' House, 1979), p. 46; Perlis, *Tnu'ot Hano'ar Hehalutziyot*, p. 283.

12 Letter from the leadership in Vilna to the Action Committee, March 30, 1940, Hashomer Hatzair Archive, Yad Ya'ari, March 28 (2); "Correspondenzia Pnimit" (Hebrew), *Dapim Leheker Hashoah Vehamered*, 1 (April 1951), p. 153.

13 Ibid.

14 Weiss, "Dfusey Hatguva Hayehudit BeZaglembia," p. 62.

15 Ranz, *In Nazi Claws*, p. 38. See also "Correspondenzia Pnimit," p. 153.

still regarded Merin as someone who could help with smuggling people out of Poland.[16] Furthermore, despite the operation's evident failure, it was not a total loss for Kibbutz Dror, as its ranks were supplemented by those members stuck in Będzin.

The Youth Movements

By the spring of 1940, any attempts to escape or emigrate were deemed futile. Instead, the Hashomer Hatzair girls worked full steam ahead on the establishment of a new, strong *ken*. The first groups began to form, and this initial success made them optimistic.

The nearby town of Sosnowiec also saw a flurry of Hashomer activity, however unlike in the past, the Będzin *ken* took the lead. Most of the Sosnowiec *bogrim* had managed to reach Vilna, and only Kalman Tencer remained to hold the fort in Sosnowiec. Tencer, a bespectacled young man who, according to Chajka, was so "meticulous that it bordered on pedantry," worked in a quiet and orderly manner with "no excesses, no hesitation."[17] With the help of members from Będzin, he was able to report about seventy-five trainees in his *ken* to the Hashomer Hatzair liaison office in Geneva by the end of April 1940. He also reported on the convention of the first regional council, a clear sign of extensive movement activity.[18]

Kibbutz Dror apparently did not engage in any special educational activities during this period, being preoccupied with its internal structuring instead. Gaftek, who had recently joined the movement, organized Hebrew classes, renovated the library, and coordinated poetry evenings. The kibbutz had its own means of production, and its laundry, which must have shut down with the outbreak of war, resumed its operations. As a general rule, the kibbutz served as a kind of social center for youth movement activists, in particular members of Hashomer Hatzair.[19]

At the same time, activity also began in the Gordonia movement. This youth movement was associated with the Hitachdut party in Poland,

16 For more on this, see chapter 11.

17 Klinger, *I Am Writing These Words to You* (1943 diaries), p. 130.

18 Perlis, *Tnu'ot Hano'ar Hehalutziyot*, p. 281, according to a letter from Tencer, dated April 29, 1940.

19 Klinger, 1944 diaries, Haogen I, p. 25.

which was linked to the Mapai party in *Eretz Israel*. This was another pioneering youth movement, which relied mainly on the teachings of A.D. Gordon with an emphasis on constructive Zionism rather than class warfare.[20] According to Arie Liwer, the activity of the local Gordonia branch recommenced after a conversation between him and Shlomo Zimmerman, the head of the *ken* at the time. Liwer advised Zimmerman to start organizing operations without the help of the Judenrat, even if it meant going underground. The head of the *ken* accepted his recommendation, and within a few days, a meeting was arranged and activity resumed.[21]

Chapters of Hanoar Hatzioni, the largest youth movement in the region, also renewed operations. Even though Hanoar Hatzioni—associated with the General Zionists party—was not considered a pioneer youth movement, it was one in essence, if "pioneer" is defined as a person preparing oneself for a life of labor in *Eretz Israel*. With the beginning of the war, members of Hanoar Hatzioni began to gather in private apartments and gradually decided on two main lines of action: establishing a school for children and starting a self-help fund. The fund was a great success. Similar to Chajka and her friends, they submitted a memorandum to the Judenrat concerning the establishment of a special soup kitchen for children. When their request was accepted, they began operating such an establishment, which also provided educational services, teaching the children to read and write, as well as mathematics and the stories and songs of *Eretz Israel*.[22] Members of Hanoar Hatzioni were less radical than their counterparts in Hashomer Hatzair and more willing to compromise. Azriel (Józek) Kożuch, head of the *ken* in Sosnowiec, was a prominent figure among them.[23]

The fifth largest youth movement in Będzin was Hashomer Hadati (The Religious Guard), a religious Zionist youth movement that had split from Hashomer Hatzair in 1927. According to diverse testimonies, Hashomer Hadati was also very active during this period under the leadership of Yeshayahu Erlich.[24]

20 Sarid, *Hehalutz Vetnu'ot Hano'ar BePolin*, pp. 272–275.

21 A. Liwer, "Asher Lo Yishkach," p. 348.

22 Fredka Mazia, in *Sefer Sosnovitz*, vol. 2, p. 197.

23 Ibid., p. 204.

24 Michael Drexler and Moshe Orbach, interview by the author, Ramat Gan, 1989.

The Farm

Spring 1940 found Chajka, Hashomer, and the other Polish youth movements busy organizing and operating educational activities, without waiting for the Judenrat to initiate the same. However, when they were offered the opportunity to establish an agricultural farm on behalf of the Judenrat, they quickly realized the possibilities contained therein. The farm would be established on land assigned to the Będzin Judenrat. The lot in question was located in Środula, close to the city suburbs. According to Arie Liwer, the farm was the brainchild of the youth movements, and it was Herszel Szpringer who had brought it up initially.[25] However, Chajka's testimony indicates that it was a Judenrat initiative. Here is how she describes the establishment of the farm and its first days:

> At this time, the municipality reached out to a youth movement representative claiming that they had received about 100 acres of land from the Germans to be worked by the Jews. We decided that this land would go to Zionist youth movements of all persuasions, so that they could set up a farm and start toiling the land. We accepted this unconditionally and with great enthusiasm. It was, after all, a type of *hachshara*. The land was about 3 kilometers outside the city and had not been worked for thirty years. [...]
>
> We began work with almost no experience, no proper tools, no means, and no help. Every day, a group of young boys and girls left the town for the field, spades propped up over their shoulders. The field, dead until then, came to life. We had no ploughs and no horses; the digging was done with spades alone. Picture this, a group of twenty young men and women in scouts' shorts. They are standing in a neat row and evenly, rhythmically, plunge their spades into the ground, turning the dead, bleak stretch of fallow land into rich, black soil. The spade keeps dipping into the soil, faster, more frequently. The youths are drenched in sweat, but there are more of them every day. The village peasants stand at a distance and cannot help laughing. This one here doesn't know how to hold a spade, that row is crooked, and how dare the girls work in shorts! The village women, especially, are scandalized, worried that the girls will spread bad morals. Some girls prefer

25 A. Liwer, "Asher Lo Yishkach," p. 352.

to wear less comfortable clothes, but most stick to it, undefeated. "We have to get them used to this," we say. "What is there to be afraid of? We will not give up!"

We did not give up. Now we have an apartment, two rooms, and an attic rented from a peasant woman. One room is the kitchen, the other has been turned into the bedroom. Some sleep in the attic, and we set up the dining room outside. It only gets tricky when it rains and everyone tries to squeeze into the corridor and into this one room of ours, which is both a bedroom and a library. People arrive from the fields soaking wet, but they forget about any trouble or discomfort once they've had their food. Laughter and singing soon fill the room, and they sing Hebrew songs. The villagers have never heard such songs before. Soon afterwards we push the beds aside and begin the wild hora dance. [...]

But, most importantly, we are learning to work. Every day the work improves. We need to show these villagers what scrappy Jewish kids can do. We have already ploughed and sown a significant stretch of land. Neat, even rows stretch far into the distance, already beginning to turn green. The farm has become the center of pioneer life in Zagłębie. All the organizations, their groups and squadrons, gather here. There must be some force in this farm that draws the youths in. In the city, they find only hunger, sadness, disease, epidemics; one cannot see the faintest scrap of sky. And so many Germans in uniforms, military and civilian, more and more of them. As a result, the youths run to the farm right after work, with barely enough time to change out of their work clothes. There is joy, laughter, fun. It's so nice to see these boys and girls in their shorts working away with such enthusiasm. There is fresh air and there is happiness, and one can hardly see any Germans around. Occasionally one might walk past, but even then, the laughter and song do not stop. These young Jews have much *chutzpa*, they do not even wear the "Jude" armband, even though the municipal representatives remind them about it all the time, while the passing Germans think that us, working Jews, do not need to wear it. Do you know what it means to be able to take off the "Jude" sign, if only for a moment? It is as if a great burden falls off one's shoulders. Your heart feels lighter, and you can breathe with ease.[26]

26 Klinger, 1944 diaries, Haogen I, pp. 32–37.

Chajka's enthusiasm is easily understandable. In the ocean of hardship and suffering, the youth movements had stumbled upon an island of freedom. Nevertheless, it is important to remember that the farm—from the day of its foundation until its final demise as part of the liquidation of the ghetto—was a Judenrat institution through and through under the auspices of the Economic Department headed by Herman Sztrochlic.[27] Arie Liwer, who had been chosen as the farm manager, received his salary from the Judenrat, and Merin's officials would sometimes visit the farm, accompanied by Germans.[28] Farmworkers were likewise considered Judenrat workers. As far as the Judenrat was concerned, the farm was just another community enterprise that provided a source of livelihood for young people and fresh garden produce for its kitchens. From the point of view of the Germans, the farm was legitimized as an attempt at *Umschichtung*— the process across Europe by the German authorities to increase the so-called productivity of Jews.

In practice, however, the farm was a distinct youth movement institution, as Chajka described it. Arie Liwer, who formally functioned as a Judenrat man but was, in fact, one of its prominent opponents, recounted that he conditioned his agreement to take over the management of the farm on its operation as an autonomous body. This meant that all of its procedures, including any decisions regarding employees, work arrangements, and protocols, would be determined by members of the youth movements.[29] The movements insisted on being solely responsible for determining who would work on the farm. The farm workers carried work certificates that protected them from deportation to forced labor camps. However, there were not enough places for everyone. Essentially, the farm could house about sixty live-in workers, supplemented by a few dozen temporary workers, most of them coming from the youth movements.[30]

Apart from providing employment, however, the farm's most important contribution was the creation of an ideal setting for educational

27 A. Liwer, "Asher Lo Yishkach," p. 352; Letter from Motek Krzesiwo to Nathan Schwalb, Będzin, June 20, 1940, Gordonia Archive, S/150.

28 Arie Liwer testimony at the Barenblatt trial, Moreshet Archive, D.1.5366.

29 A. Liwer, "Asher Lo Yishkach," p. 352.

30 Letter from Motek Krzesiwo to Nathan Schwalb, Będzin, November 29, 1941, Gordonia Archive, S/150; "Operations of Hechalutz in European countries at the end of 1941" (based on the report of the liaison office of Hechalutz in Geneva), GFH, Hechalutz Archive, 1056. This report is likely to have been written by Nathan Schwalb based on information from Będzin.

and ideological activity. Had Merin foreseen this in advance, or did it come as a slap in the face? The answer is difficult to determine. On the one hand, it was convenient for him to remove an organized element, which might have agitated against him, from Będzin and Sosnowiec. On the other hand, he was still threatened by its activity, which he could now only monitor from afar. As the farm's operations expanded, he tried to limit the number of its employees and even minimize and prevent educational and cultural activities. Despite this, neither Merin in Sosnowiec nor Mołczadski in Będzin ever tried to close the farm.[31]

As far as the youth movements were concerned, this was the desired situation. A new strategy was taking shape: take from the Judenrat as much as possible and give back as little as possible. The autonomy they had carved out for themselves made the farm a perfect environment for opposition to the Judenrat to ferment. Rather than following the path paved by Merin, the youth movements had other things in mind.

The Youth Council

The first evidence of attempted opposition to Merin dates to the winter of 1940–1941. By that time, the farm had already been operating for around six months, and Merin attempted to monitor the activities of the youth movements by establishing a Youth Council. The youth movement members opposed this. However, at the same time, Aron Menczer, a delegate of the Aliyat Hanoar (Youth Aliya) movement in Vienna arrived in Sosnowiec, and after talking with Merin, he became convinced of the importance of establishing this advisory body.[32] Arie

31 It is interesting to compare the Będzin farm with the Marysin farm established by Mordechai Chaim Rumkowski in the Łódź ghetto, and where approximately 1,000 youths—most of them youth movement members—were concentrated. The role of the farm in Marysin was similar to the one in Będzin—growing and supplying fresh vegetables to the starving ghetto. There, too, the youth movements engaged in extensive autonomous activity, organizing themselves according to customary Zionist frameworks and even establishing a kind of kibbutz. Nevertheless, Rumkowski closed the Marysin farm about a year after its establishment due to his desire to integrate the young people into work at "resorts"—the term used for the workshops in the Łódź ghetto (May 1940–March 1941). Sarah Stern-Katan testimony, YVA, O.3/10236. See also Michal Unger, *The Last Ghetto: Life in the Lodz Ghetto, 1940–1944* (Jerusalem: Yad Vashem, 1999).

32 Aron Menczer's visit was unusual in that he had managed to break through the almost complete isolation of Polish Jews. It seems that this was made possible due

Liwer, Herszel Szpringer, and Chajka, who had traveled to Sosnowiec to meet with the envoy, were surprised by his sympathetic attitude toward Merin and tried to convince him to reconsider. Menczer appeared to have heeded their warnings, but eventually sided with Merin's approach.[33]

Menczer's final decision seems to have tipped the scales. He was seen as a connecting factor between the youth and the pioneer movements in Zagłębie and the Hechalutz institutions in Europe, in particular the liaison office in Geneva, whose support was important to the Polish activists. The council was established in spite of widespread apprehension, with Arie Liwer (Gordonia) and Herszel Szpringer (Dror) representing their respective movements, Kalman Tencer representing Hashomer Hatzair, and Israel Diamant representing Hanoar Hatzioni.[34] The question of oversight remained open: Merin wanted his own man to head the council, while the youth movements naturally wanted their own representative for the position. Finally, the name of Józek Kożuch, the Hanoar Hatzioni leader who worked in the Judenrat, was put forward. Kożuch was deemed acceptable to both sides, and he soon began his activity.[35] Writing in retrospect, Chajka summarizes this chapter with some bitterness:

> A council was set up, under the name *Jugendberatungsstelle* [Youth Advice Bureau]. A representative of every youth organization joined the council. It was headed by a dedicated civil servant from the municipality. Then, a department called *Umschichtung* [productivization] was set up, tasked with organizing courses and lessons for fourteen and fifteen year olds. We wanted to take matters into our own hands and create a space for Hechalutz. We wanted to bring groups of our scouts and teachers, so that independent of the courses and professional training, we could sneak in some lessons in Hebrew and the history of the Jewish

to the annexation of Zagłębie to the Reich, and therefore Menczer, coming from equally annexed Austria, was probably able to obtain the necessary permits. For more on Menczer, see Herbert Rosenkranz, *Verfolgung und Selbstbehauptung: Die Juden in Österreich 1938–1945* (Vienna: Herold, 1978), p. 59.

33 A. Liwer, "Asher Lo Yishkach," p. 350.

34 Perlis, *Tnu'ot Hano'ar Hehalutziyot*, p. 257.

35 A. Liwer, "Asher Lo Yishkach," p. 350; D. Liwer, *Ir Hametim*, p. 50; Fredka Mazia, in *Sefer Sosnovitz*, pp. 56–58.

> nation. Woodworking and welding courses were organized, but they did not accept our children, and they were led by people we didn't know.[36]

Chajka's verdict is slightly too harsh in this case. According to Kożuch's letters to Geneva, the youth movements' plans did partially come to fruition. By the end of 1941, about 900 Jewish teenagers had participated in vocational training, and about 200 pioneers were concentrated in the various farms, although these would turn out to be short-lived enterprises.[37]

The establishment of this Youth Council sealed one chapter in Merin's complicated relationship with the youth movements. Why did Merin devote so much time and effort to these young people, who at that time represented—at most—1.5 percent of the Jews of Zagłębie? There were nearly 100,000 Jews subject to his whims and oversight, yet he chose to devote so much effort to a group of boys and girls, the oldest of whom were in their early twenties. One possible answer concerns Merin's domineering personality. All the measures he implemented aimed to bring all the social factors in the Zagłębie region under his supervision. His policy was part of the general centralization process that the communities in the region underwent. At the end of the first year of the war, the Judenrat was the sole organized social body left in Jewish Zagłębie.

By the spring of 1940, the Judenrat included: Icchak Wygodzki, head of the Zionist Hitachdut in the city; Chaim Mołczadski of Poalei Zion; Moshe Manela of Mizrachi; and Michał Laskier of the General Zionists. The Jewish police in Będzin was initially headed by Moshe Glidman, while its counterpart in Sosnowiec was headed by Klajner, both of them members of the Betar movement. The latter would later be replaced by Romek Goldminc (who was born in Mandatory Palestine).[38] Thus, Merin had managed to gather around him the relatively young Zionist leadership of Będzin and Sosnowiec,[39] and Merin often presented himself as a Zionist too.[40] The Zionist character

36 Chajka Klinger, 1944 diaries, Haogen II notebook, Moreshet Archive, D.2.211, pp. 6–7.

37 See letter from Kożuch to Schwalb, March 8, 1941; Letter from Kożuch to Schwalb, May 9, 1941, Pinchas Lavon Institute for Labour Movement Research, III/52/37 A.

38 Moshe Yarkoni, in *Sefer Sosnovitz*, vol. 2, pp. 167–168; Fredka Mazia, in *Sefer Sosnovitz*, vol. 2, p. 158; Chana Schlesinger-Wiernik, *Hadapim Sheli* (Hebrew) (Ra'anana: self-published, 2004).

39 Shalom Herzberg, interview by the author, Ramat Gan, 1987.

40 Regarding Merin's Zionism, see for example: Merin's connections with the Hechalutz

of the Judenrat leadership in Zagłębie comes up many times in Chajka's writings and in other documents and testimonies.

Whatever his political leanings might have been, in the absence of community elections and elections for the Zionist Congress, and in view of Merin's firm rule and the dependence of the people of Zagłębie on him, it seems that there was no other candidate for leadership. Furthermore, there were those who relied on their role in the Judenrat as a personal source of income—whether by virtue of their previous positions or because they were public servants by profession. Those who remained on the outside were virtually inactive. There was little to no party activity at this time, and Merin's Judenrat reflected a new and different phase in Jewish leadership.

Yet, within this political space over which Merin seemed to have absolute domination, a new factor gradually began to emerge, which took shape alongside the Judenrat, at times cooperating with it, at other times coming up against it, but never for one moment forgetting its own distinct identity: the youth movements. Gradually, they filled the void created by the paralysis of the political parties and the leadership crisis. Someone with such a finely attuned political sense as Merin could not ignore the presence of this social factor and its young leadership: Herszel Szpringer, Arie Liwer, and Chajka Klinger, among others. They were to be dealt with, for better or for worse.

Chajka: A Budding Leader

Chajka herself was a member of that young leadership class that had grown out of the soil of the youth movements. In the fall of 1940, she turned twenty-three. She was a little younger than Josef Kaplan, the leader in Warsaw, and a little older than her comrades in the Będzin *ken*. Only a few years separated her from the young leadership that coalesced around Merin, but unlike them, she chose to follow her own path. She was growing up fast. From a mischievous high school girl and a romantically inclined trainee, she blossomed into a staunch and loyal activist. Despite

in Warsaw (this chapter); his appeal to the heads of youth movements to establish kibbutzim in the labor camps (chapter 10); his direct appeal to the heads of the Yishuv in *Eretz Israel* in February 1943 (chapter 15); his identification as a Zionist before Zvi Dunski (chapter 15). When she came to *Eretz Israel*, Chajka would emphasize this point in her words to the Executive Committee of the Histadrut (chapter 24).

regarding certain orders with a critical eye, she was nevertheless ready to accept them and get to work without hesitation.

Unfortunately, it is difficult to reconstruct her actions during this period from her diaries. At this point, her narrative style changes from the first-person singular (I) to the first-person plural (we). This is not because her own doings were—in her eyes—irrelevant to the history of the movement. It is more likely evidence of her complete identification with Hashomer's activity in Będzin. In this sense, she used the first-person plural just as Ya'ari used it when speaking on behalf of the movement in *Eretz Israel*. Chajka's "we" refers to the leadership of the Hashomer Hatzair branch in Będzin during this period. Within this leadership, a dominant group of similar stature and influence formed, comprising Chajka, David, Nacia Klugman, and the two older Pejsachson sisters—Lea and Idzia. These names come up repeatedly in numerous testimonies. Even though she makes no mention of it in her diaries, it would appear that Chajka was a member of both the leadership of the Będzin *ken* and the district leadership of the movement in Zagłębie.[41] According to the detailed descriptions of the meeting concerning the farm, it seems that she also represented Hashomer at gatherings of the Hechalutz organization.

Nevertheless, this collective "we" certainly obscures her identity as a young woman. The predominance of girls in the Będzin *ken* was indeed a striking phenomenon, but not atypical of Jewish youth movements, within which girls assumed roles far superior in stature and responsibility to the roles generally available to other female activists at the time. As organizations who educated their trainees in the emergent tradition of revolutionary women, such as Vera Figner, Manya Shochat, and Rosa Luxemburg, and who adopted the concept of the intimate group in which the members of a youth movement were akin to brothers and sisters, the youth movements fostered the relatively equal status of women. Female members were encouraged to stand out in the fields of education, self-expression, social liaison, and even leadership and organization, which were at the center of the youth movements' activities.[42] These were areas where Chajka could apply her innate talents and surpass her male friends. Yet, she did not attach any special importance to this.

41 Hakibbutz Ha'artzi membership card, Moreshet Archive, C.36.20.54.

42 See Avihu Ronen, "Women as Leaders in the Jewish Undergrounds in Poland during the Holocaust," in Paula E. Hyman, Dalia Ofer, and Alice Shalvi, eds., *Jewish Women: A Comprehensive Historical Encyclopedia* (Jerusalem: Shalvi Publishing, 2006).

Nor did she write about her relationship with David—her colleague and co-leader—preferring instead to attribute her romantic notions and expressions of emotion to the movement itself. However, it would seem that their work partnership did nothing to harm their intimate bond; on the contrary, it may have deepened it. Testimony relating to the winter of 1940–1941 reveals that in the eyes of the movement and its trainees, Chajka and David were a model couple, embodying the idea of true love.[43] Perl Klinger, Chajka's mother, also grew very fond of David.[44] Yet, whereas the description of the *ken* shows the influence of serious, thoughtful David, the description of the farm is 100 percent Chajka. The enthusiasm for working in the fields, the cheerful spirit of rebellion in the girls' insistence on wearing shorts to work before the judging eyes of the prudish peasants, the hint of self-irony in the depictions of nights of dancing and abandon—all these are distinct signs of Chajka's individual personality peeking through the collective "we." According to the farm manager Arie Liwer, Chajka excelled at her job as labor coordinator.[45] As with her participation in the delegation to Menczer, here we have some evidence of the role she actually played.[46] In photographs that have survived from the farm period, she is always positioned front and center.[47]

Chajka's enthusiasm, however, is mitigated by the serious tone of one on whose shoulders rests the burden of responsibility. Later she would write about the lack of working hands, about the futile debates that took place in the farm secretariat, about the agronomists who lacked expertise in agricultural matters, about the kitchen being run without any account, and about objects stolen from apartments left without supervision.[48] And yet, she ends this passage in the diary in the resigned but optimistic style of a veteran organizer: "The regulars on the farm have already learned a little discipline, while with the new ones, you have to start from scratch."[49]

She was no stranger to criticism, including frequent self-criticism, but she saw the course of affairs through the lens of her movement's ideals and sometimes tended to ignore other sides, other opinions. Her writing traces the outline of the type of young leader who is anxious to protect

43 Chana (Wiernik) and Benjamin Schlesinger, interview by the author, Ra'anana, 1985.

44 Chana Lieberman interview.

45 A. Liwer, "Asher Lo Yishkach," p. 352.

46 Ibid., p. 350.

47 Photograph of Hechalutz in Będzin, Moreshet Archive, Avihu Ronen collection, 235.

48 Klinger, 1944 diaries, Haogen I, pp. 39–40.

49 Ibid., p. 29.

her movement's interests, but one who knows how to infect those who walk beside and behind her with her enthusiasm.

In terms of ideology, the ideas she retained from the Gymnasium and her time as a trainee had matured by then. At this point, she was an ardent Marxist with a favorable orientation toward the Soviet Union. However, the Zionist sentiment ran just as deep within her, and she repeatedly emphasized the connection between the movement's activities on the farm and *Eretz Israel* during this period. Added to this was the influence of Polish romanticism as well as the influence of European culture from the interwar period. On the other hand, the Diasporic Jewish tradition is hardly mentioned. The rejection of the Diaspora was one of the hallmarks of both Chajka's thoughts and of Hashomer Hatzair in general. For Chajka in particular, this rejection had a personal aspect: it was also a rejection of her family. The movement became her only home, a sharp shift from the ultra-Orthodoxy and poverty of the home in which she had been raised. Her intellectual skills found a place here, and she became the spokesperson for the movement in Będzin. According to the Schlesingers' testimony, Chajka and Nacia Klugman were the main speakers on behalf of the movement at assemblies and holiday gatherings.[50]

As such, she exhibited a clear negative attitude toward cooperation with the Judenrat as far back as the winter of 1940–1941, a fact which bears explaining. Having a rebellious character by nature and a dedication to the ideas of youth autonomy and the revolutionary Marxism of Hashomer Hatzair, Chajka was naturally opposed to the policies of Merin and his people who sought to centralize power in their own hands. It is possible that she did not initially see Merin and his men as Nazi collaborators, and it is likely that—like most Jews—she had gotten used to their presence. However, now they represented an establishment that threatened the youth movements' freedom, and this she could not accept. Nonetheless, it would be a mistake to conclude that this meant severing all ties with the Judenrat. As a representative of her movement, Chajka continued to be in contact with Merin and Mołczadski throughout the existence of the Będzin *gmina*, even as the relationship between the two sides grew more and more conflictual.

50 Chana (Wiernik) and Benjamin Schlesinger interview. A photograph from a gathering at the farm shows Nacia Klugman speaking and Chajka standing behind the festive table as she waits her turn. See Schlesinger-Wiernik, *Hadapim Sheli*, p. 154.

Chapter Nine

Bitania in Będzin

On the Farm

Chajka's friend Ada Neufeld would later compare life on the farm in Zagłębie to Bitania Illit, the Hashomer Hatzair farm near the Kinneret in *Eretz Israel* in 1920. The era was different, of course, as was the context, but like in Bitania, the youth movement members on the farm fell under the spell of romantic idealism. Like their predecessors, they also sought to escape an oppressive reality—that of Będzin in the midst of a global war. The farm was a haven of freedom on the outskirts of the occupied city. Removed from the hardships of life in Będzin, the young activists could develop their own, independent culture with a vigor possibly never witnessed before the war. Chajka wrote:

> We have organized a celebration in honor of Herzl and Bialik. Everyone sits together out in the field in the evening. A song carries far, far into the distance through the nighttime silence, it is "Tehezakna" [Heb. Be Strong]. The lyrics are filled with a sense of protest, of revolt against fascism and against the horrible injustice being done to the Jewish nation. We remember those who fell at various parts of the front. Unwittingly, one turns one's head to look around—mightn't someone be eavesdropping? My heartbeat quickens. It is quite a remarkable thing to be here, right in the middle of the field, unafraid. We are a little mad, surely we will have to pay for this one day. I can hear words of longing, longing for a land far away, for a kibbutz, for a brother. Among us are two girls

> who came down from *Eretz Israel* to visit their parents but were met with war. They are singing to us about *Eretz Israel*, about the Galilee, Lake Kinneret—Eastern-sounding, Arabian songs. And the longing, waxing by the moment, washes over you, sorrow and grief for all the years, the youth wasted here, the dreams that will never come true. Yet soon, nostalgia and sadness give way to joy. The young ones start dancing, someone plays the harmonica. They are dancing wildly, with abandon, on and on, and constantly the words are heard: "Mi chai? Am Israel chai" [Heb. Who is alive? The nation of Israel is alive]. And you forget about the whole world, you too are drawn into it. We go on well into the night. The youths are not afraid of anything—no wonder so many come down to the farm. On Saturdays, even the older people come. Hundreds of people. It makes it impossible to normalize life on the farm, but we mustn't forget that this is the only place where Jews can breathe with some semblance of freedom, the only place where they can see a patch of green grass. Some people come for the whole day on Saturdays, they bring food with them and spend the day relaxing. The boys organize various games, matches, sporting exercises. They dare not do this in the city, with no parks or public squares for Jews.[1]

Chajka's writing takes a poetic turn as she describes the experience of life on the farm. Her words express that pioneer desire for settling in *Eretz Israel*, as realized twenty years earlier in Degania and Bitania Illit.[2] In Będzin, however, this desire was realized against the background of an all-out war in Poland, which made the experience that much more vital and liberating.

The solidarity of belonging to a youth movement was an integral part of the pioneering experience. Very quickly, the farm moved from routine work and cultural activity to educational and ideological activity according to the diverse traditions of the different movements:

> We put so much energy into it. We, members of Hashomer, want to be exemplary at everything: work, eating, cleanliness, keeping our rooms tidy. And never letting up during debates. Oh, yes, Jewish youths certainly know how to debate. They never stop debating.

1 Klinger, 1944 diaries, Haogen I, pp. 37–38.

2 See Boaz Neumann, *Land and Desire in Early Zionism* (Chicago: University of Chicago Press, 2011).

> The Jewish society and the youths of Będzin were not really familiar with our movement before. We decided to become clearly visible, audible on the Jewish street, to work our way into people's brains, their consciousness, to sow the seeds of our worldview, our affirmations—but the real ones, not the things certain factions like to falsely attribute to us. We initiated cultural activities at the farm, we helped the young people, hitherto shallow, begin to think and ponder the world. We organized discussions on religion and on socialism. People from Hanoar Hatzioni and from Hashomer Hadati began to join our movement.
>
> A public storm was brewing against us—us who had previously been almost insignificant and now becoming a force to be reckoned with. Many were especially incensed at us having meetings separate from the others.... however, this was the most beautiful time for Zionist work in our entire district. We recruited young people, set up groups, organized scouts' fetes and celebrations; we worked tirelessly on shaping our ideology, issued newspapers, organized many interesting meetings.[3]

As Chajka points out, not everyone was thrilled by Hashomer's upward momentum. Even though Jochanan Ranz from Dror might have been impressed by the indelible energy of the Hashomer girls,[4] others such as Bracha Chmielnicka (later Plotnik), a member of Gordonia, saw the farm as a common enterprise where there was no room for distinct factional activity. Bracha's view was backed by directives coming from Hechalutz headquarters, calling for the pioneer youth to act as a united front. According to her, the Hashomer group went against these instructions time and time again, led by none other than Chajka,[5] who herself mentions the spirit of competitiveness among the movements with a pinch of malice in her earlier diaries:

> It was during the period of rivalry between the organizations, the period of constant discussions and "attraction" of people. That was when we asked ourselves a question: Should we be guided by stupid sentimentalism just to avoid breaking up the organizations? Should we live in harmony and peace? We decided that we had to disband

3 Klinger, 1944 diaries, Haogen I, pp. 40–42.

4 Ranz, *In Nazi Claws*, pp. 95–97.

5 Bracha Plotnik (Chmielnicka), interview by the author, Mishmar Hasharon, 1985.

> Hanoar [Hatzioni] because we pitied those young people, who were wasting their potential there. But it would not be bad either to reduce Gordonia's membership.... Everybody hated us then, but we cared little about that. We were growing stronger, acquiring valuable members every day.[6]

It was not by chance that this paragraph was omitted from the initial published version of the diaries. It contradicts the harmonious spirit of joint action that Chajka's testimony was supposed to project after the war; however, although the antagonism in which Hashomer Hatzair people engaged may have soured the atmosphere at the farm, it did not paralyze the movements' activities. On the contrary, all the evidence indicates that from the summer of 1940 to the spring of 1942, educational work flourished in Zagłębie across all Jewish youth movements. In Będzin alone, the number of youth movement members and trainees reached 1,400 in the spring of 1942. For a moment, the war was completely forgotten, and Jewish Będzin returned to the good old days before the occupation. This time, however, the youth movements were center stage. Their relentless efforts were bearing fruit. Chajka wrote:

> I remember the first meeting organized for the *bnei midbar* during Hanukkah. It was in the orphanage, a big, brightly lit hall, so nice and warm, especially if you were entering from the cold, your nose and ears freezing. Outside, the little *bnei midbar* kept watch over us, ensuring no German would enter. And they demanded a password from every member of Hashomer coming in. They felt so important, looked so stern and dignified. They were learning the art of conspiracy. The watch changed every hour. The room was full of little *shomrim*, smiling in their gray jumpers. This was our first attempt to gather the children, under the guise of serving supper. It was difficult enough to get permission and a suitable space from the Judenrat. Here they are, marching across the room, singing, occasionally the sound of a Hashomer whistle breaks through. Later, they staged a play. I couldn't believe the instructors when they told me the children had written it themselves. It was a story written for the children of *Eretz Israel*, recounting the hardships of exile, how difficult it was, how hungry they were, how they had no school, how unhappy they were. They presented vignettes from their lives:

6 Klinger, *I Am Writing These Words to You* (1943 diaries), pp. 132–133.

> trading in the streets, dealing with a sick mother, getting beaten by the Germans; then they described the lives they longed for in *Eretz Israel*, with the other children, how they wanted to work the land, to be like the Maccabees, fighting the enemy. Did you hear them, children of [Mandatory] Palestine? Then the first full headquarters assembly was held. There was much defiance expressed, words of revolt, and threats of revenge. Many spoke directly to the youths of *Eretz Israel* about how we still remembered Zionism, how we would continue on our path no matter the setbacks, no matter the conditions, we would never let ourselves be uprooted and destroyed.[7]

Among those present that night was Benjamin (Jumek) Szlezinger (Schlesinger), then a youth of about seventeen, who had attended the Yavne Gymnasium until the outbreak of the war. Benjamin remembered that Hanukkah party very well. He remembered how the groups had gone onstage and sang "We Will All Be Pioneers" at the top of their lungs. In their enthusiasm, they forgot the war. The feeling of transcendence was upon them. The party was conducted entirely in Hebrew, he remembered.[8]

The youngsters' admiration for the *ken*'s leaders bordered on worship. Nacia Klugman was the revered instructor, while Chajka and David were perceived by Benjamin as the mother and father of the movement. The trainees saw the love between them—the glances they exchanged, her curling up in his lap—as exemplary. Like other members of the *ken*, Benjamin remembered David's sharp mind and wit, which shone through the stutter. In particular, he remembered a lecture he delivered on Moses Hess, the harbinger of utopian Zionism.[9] When David spoke, Chajka listened; she never interrupted him.[10]

The youngsters seemed to place an unreserved trust in Chajka. According to Benjamin, they could go to her with any problem, including personal matters of the heart. She was a great listener, and the trainees could rely on her for straight answers to their questions. On the other hand, she was one to show flashes of anger in arguments. As Benjamin remembered, Chajka's personality combined an eagerness to listen with a

7 Klinger, 1944 diaries, Haogen I, pp. 43–44.

8 Chana (Wiernik) and Benjamin Schlesinger interview.

9 Moses Hess was said to have preceded Herzl by around thirty years with his vision of humanist nationalism blended with utopian socialism as seen in his original 1862 publication. See Moses Hess, *Rome and Jerusalem: A Study in Jewish Nationalism* (New York: Bloch, 1945).

10 Chana (Wiernik) and Benjamin Schlesinger interview.

loathing of compromise, especially where the movement's principles were concerned.[11] It was from Chajka and David that the youngsters learned what a youth movement was, what it meant to be a member of Hashomer Hatzair, which was not only believing in the movement's principles but also leading a "*shomer* way of life."

To illustrate, Ada Neufeld remembered coming down with a long illness and being attended to by Chajka and Irka Pejsachson. The sickness left her mentally exhausted, and when she recovered she wrote in the farm's communal journal, a practice borrowed from Bitania: "I do not see myself able to carry on doing movement work any longer. I can sing, and recite texts—yes. But not more educational work." The reaction was swift to arrive: The next time she opened the journal, she read a scathing commentary from Chajka and Irka, the gist of which was, "Ada, how could you?"[12]

Indeed, Chajka tended to view things in rather harsh terms:

> Before the war, our education seemed quite normal, but the war changed everything. It became clearer and clearer that we could no longer live according to our ideals, our truths, which, though sacred to us, were completely contrary to the sad reality of life. Those raised by our movement were not ready to fight for their lives, they were at risk of complete obliteration, of dying from hunger. [...]
>
> If we are to raise them, we cannot go against the old truths; they are still truths, and doing so might unsettle our entire socialist worldview. But how can we teach the young people to be more robust, to be able to fight for their livelihoods, to stay above water without going against our values? Without having them lie, steal, humiliate themselves, damage their dignity? We no longer tried to camouflage the dark sides of life; we dragged them out into the light and analyzed them; we explained—"This is life," and we will not lie about it. One needs to be prepared for this, to be tough, strong, capable of fighting, of resisting. One needs to be ready to fight for one's rights, not to give up too soon, to be a revolutionary not just in theory and worldview, but in daily life.
>
> We were against queuing before public institutions. We decided to organize separate kitchens within every headquarters and a communal fund for every *gdud* [brigade]. Everyone who could contributed,

11 Ibid.
12 Ada Halperin (Neufeld) interview.

> and we got on through mutual help, without begging. Such matters became the core topics of discussion at our second *moatza* [council].[13]

Had Chajka been aware of Meir Ya'ari's letter to the leadership in Vilna? We might reasonably assume that she had not;[14] yet her words echo his proclamation that "we will not follow in the footsteps of the workers' movement in Germany." Still, the slogan had to be translated into operative action, and this could not be done from the relative safety of Merhavia. In Będzin, Hashomer Hatzair faced an acute problem: Their commitment to what they called the "*shomer* way of life" was incompatible with the conditions imposed by reality. The movement's commandments dictated that "a *shomer* must be true";[15] however, now, they were forced to lie, steal, and smuggle in order to stay alive. The *shomer* had to always be "helpful and reliable to his fellow";[16] yet the war-imposed conditions in which it was every man and woman for themselves.

Faced with this dilemma, it seems that the Hashomer members opted for a stubborn adherence to the old and familiar values and norms. All evidence points to the fact that in many respects, the movement members acted as if nothing had changed.[17] Paradoxically, therein lay the answer to the demands of this new, ruthless reality. It gave the young people a sense of belonging in a world that was crumbling around them and the opportunity to identify with firm ideals in the midst of a society leaning more and more toward utter nihilism.

Hashomer had always nurtured feelings of identification and belonging among the youth by bolstering their autonomy. Now, the small community turned the youngster's adoration of their instructors and adherence to ideals into a powerful tool for fostering endurance and survival skills in the harsh conditions of the war. The establishment of the common kitchens and cash funds while making concessions bordering on self-sacrifice was another operative act designed to strengthen social cohesion and reduce the movement's dependence on the outside world as much as possible.

13 Chajka Klinger, 1944 diaries, Haogen I, pp. 53–55.

14 There is no evidence of the letter's circulation, probably due to its problematic content. If Chajka had laid eyes on even an edited version of the letter, she probably would have mentioned it.

15 "Aseret Hadibrot," Dror and Rosenzweig, *Sefer Hashomer Hatzair*, vol. 1, p. 44.

16 Ibid., p. 45.

17 Chana (Wiernik) and Benjamin Schlesinger interview.

The same was true on the level of ideology. Chajka and her friends opted for a strategy of strict adherence to the traditional position of Hashomer just as the movement was finding itself on the defensive:

> We wanted a socialist [Mandatory] Palestine. Russia was not a popular model; it had disappointed us. The eyes of the entire global proletarian movement were on it, people thought it would be the first to join the war and free the world of Fascism. There were accusations, complaints. The Jews, who could not see beyond their own interests, were particularly biased. We, however, chose to look beyond them. We perceived the genius of Stalin's policy; we were sure the Soviets would eventually intervene. Until then, we saw our own socialist work as promoting the interests of the only socialist country in Europe. We knew that the fate of socialism would depend on this country for many years to come.[18]

These views were very much in line with the decisions made by the Hashomer Hatzair council that convened in the Warsaw ghetto in May 1941.[19] The ideological outline prepared for the convention declared that "The present war is not a war for securing the freedom of nations from the hands of German imperialism. It is also not a war for democracy and the liberty of the individual. This is a war of certain groups from big industry and wealth over the right to rob the world's riches without interference."[20] The workers' movement, which espoused the tactic of "revolutionary defeatism," had no share in it. When the former would have exhausted the power of the latter, the Soviet Union, having gathered strength in the meantime, would step in and bring socialist salvation to the world entire. *Eretz Israel* too—the promised utopia that the Hashomer people in Warsaw and Będzin dreamed about—would be a "Soviet Israel" in this conception.[21]

The youth movements' stubborn adherence to their ideals and their unshakable belief in the power of the Soviet Union was also an escape

18 Klinger, 1944 diaries, Haogen I, pp. 49–50.

19 Because of the great similarity between the descriptions, it is unclear whether this refers to the convention of Warsaw or Zagłębie.

20 "Neged Hazerem, issue 4 (15), May 1941," in Fatal-Knaani, *The Jewish Underground Press, Vol. 2*, pp. 469–470; "Neged Hazerem, issue 5 (16), July 1941," in Tikva Fatal-Knaani, ed., *The Jewish Underground Press: Vol. 3, July–October 1941* (Jerusalem: Yad Vashem, 2021), p. 60.

21 Ibid.

from reality. The farm in Będzin—like Bitania Illit before it—served as a kind of social bubble for the youth, one through which they bolstered their capacity to deal with reality, but at the same time isolated themselves from it. There was a practical dimension to this isolation: The youth movements, including Hashomer Hatzair, took care of their own people first. Their leaders secured the interests of their members and protected them from the harsh conditions of life in the city. Their activity provided the Jewish youth with a solid shelter, stepping in to replace the social institutions that had disintegrated following the outbreak of the war. The Hashomer Hatzair groups especially flourished in Zagłębie. At the first Hashomer council held at the end of April 1940, only two representatives from each *ken* in Zagłębie were in attendance. By the summer or fall of 1941, a written census conducted for the purposes of a conference of the entire Zagłębie region—with the participation of Tosia Altman—showed that there were about 1,200 *shomrim* in the region, as Chajka proudly reported.[22] And even though this number seems somewhat excessive and does not correspond to another report,[23] it is clear that there was a significant increase in the number of members across all Hashomer groups in the area. In the report of the main leadership in the Warsaw ghetto written at the end of 1940, Zagłębie was commended for its "large and beautiful branches, with their gatherings, councils, newspapers, and multifaceted work."[24]

Tosia's Visit

One event that made an impression—especially on the youth—from that period was Eliezer Geller's visit to Będzin. Geller, a member of the leadership of Gordonia and a prominent figure in the movement during the war, had an Aryan appearance and traveled around Poland, carrying fake certificates in the name of "Eugeniusz." His arrival at the beginning of 1941 was cause for celebration:

> We were so happy about his arrival. We were yearning for news about the movement in Warsaw, the world and Jewry.

22 Klinger, 1944 diaries, Haogen I, p. 61.

23 According to Jochanan Ranz, there were approximately 200 members in the Hashomer Hatzair *ken* in Będzin. See Ranz, *In Nazi Claws*, p. 22.

24 Chajka Rosenberg, "Shana shel Avoda," in Dror and Rosenzweig, *Sefer Hashomer Hatzair*, vol. 1, p. 491.

> He came to our *asefat menahalim* [youth leaders' meeting]. There were already 40–50 *menahalim.*
>
> The room was so full, the faces were so young, the eyes so smart.
>
> He talked about Warsaw and our hearts are swelling. The largest and best movement, just like before the war—Hashomer Hatzair.[25]

Other sources confirm that youth movement activity surged throughout the Generalgouvernement territory. The Dror *ken* in Warsaw had close to 1,000 members at this time, the Hashomer Hatzair *ken*, about 800,[26] and Gordonia, about 300. Dror had about 100 operational branches and a similar number was registered for Hashomer Hatzair.[27] The difference in numbers seems to reflect the competition between the movements, which was always a sign of growth and vitality. Geller's visit was also significant in itself: The envoys of the leadership from Warsaw filled the void created by the return of the emissaries to *Eretz Israel* at the beginning of the war. The main envoy of Hashomer Hatzair was Tosia Altman, the first to return from Vilna to Warsaw. Chajka wrote:

> Soon after Eliezer Geller's visit, Tosia arrived, with no address to go to. She walked down the street looking at people, their faces, their clothes. She was looking for a member of Hashomer, hoping to run into someone. Finally, she took a guess, approached Shoshana and asked: "Excuse me, do you perhaps know where I can find Lea Pejsachson?" Shoshana regarded her with suspicion: What does this non-Jewish woman want with Lea? But then suddenly she decided to trust her. "Yes, I know her, come along." On the way, inside the Jewish quarter, a little *bnei midbar* came up to Shoshana and whispered "hazak" [strong], but Tosia overheard him. "Are you from Hashomer?" "I am. And are you not Tosia from Warsaw?" "Yes, that's me." Shoshana started jumping for joy. "We have been waiting for you for so long," she said. She took Tosia straight to the farm.
>
> Everyone gaped at her, unable to believe their eyes. Yes, that's her, just as she was before the war. The hunger and poverty of Warsaw had not left a single trace. She was still full of life and energy. Only she had become very solemn, one could feel the weight of responsibility on her shoulders. [...]

25 Klinger, *I Am Writing These Words to You* (1943 diaries), p. 88.

26 Perlis, *Tnu'ot Hano'ar Hehalutziyot*, p. 111.

27 Ibid.

> A scouts' meeting was held. Again, we had been given the large hall at the orphanage. Tosia recounted a fable about a snake crawling on the ground and an eagle soaring in the sky. And she told the assembly about the scouts in Warsaw, who did not want to leave their group, which numbered 100–150 strong. Do you know how they would tell each other apart from the crowd? They would organize a walk where they would mix with the crowd, but each wore a predetermined sign: a flower on their shirt, a leather belt, something like that. Every group had a dedicated spot where they would gather, a square, a garden, under a particular lantern in the cemetery. The children listened with rapt attention, their eyes glued to her. Suddenly, there was a commotion. I got a call from the Judenrat, saying we must disperse, the police are coming. Everyone was scared and upset about being disrupted in this manner. We were very sorry to leave, we have enjoyed this bright hall so much, but Tosia tried to make us feel better and said it's no big deal, and that everyone will remember the meeting all the better and hate the Germans all the more for it. She explained all that and everyone dispersed in peace.[28]

That same day, Tosia went to Sosnowiec, and based on her description of things, it would seem that Chajka went with her. Tosia's visit of the Zagłębie *kens* brings to light the vigorous work that was going on in other towns as well. Unlike the Będzin *ken*, which had rebuilt itself at the beginning of the war mainly from the recruitment of high school students, the Hashomer branch in the more industrial and modern Sosnowiec sourced its membership mainly from among working youths.[29] Within its ranks were such members as Zvi Dunski, a simple man of action who was passionate about the ideas of the movement, and Lipek Minc, a recent member and a mechanic by profession. Kalman Tencer's benevolent spirit hovered above them all. He was not much older than most of them and was even somewhat sickly, but his devotion and dedication made him a father to his people. When the tuberculosis he had contracted intensified, the *bogrim* would gather at his house. Even from his sickbed, he continued to give instructions, arrange matters, and advise his friends.[30]

28 Klinger, 1944 diaries, Haogen I, pp. 57–61.

29 Shmuel Ron, in *Sefer Sosnovitz*, vol. 2, p. 176.

30 Ibid., pp. 52–54.

Things were less lively, however, in Dąbrowa Górnicza. As Chajka put it, "in all honesty, what they've got there is not a *ken*, but a few disparate groups."[31] There is no further information about this branch. In Zawiercie, there was another, better organized *ken*, led by Greitzer and Dorka Herzberg—Zvi Brandes's girlfriend.[32] Tosia's visit coincided with a two-month-long Hashomer instructor seminar.[33] It is not clear whether Tosia took part in the entire seminar, but it is reasonable to assume that she did. The envoys' visits tended to be prolonged, especially in Zagłębie, where the youth movements enjoyed a period of particular prosperity and flourishing.

Underground Resistance as a Symbol

The description of Tosia's visit in Chajka's diary is given in close proximity to an account of a local council convention, which in all probability took place in the winter of 1940–1941, prior to Tosia's arrival:[34]

> Everybody knows that there will be a Hashomer meeting at the farm. The members are cleaning up, tidying, scrubbing everything, decorating. There are no tablecloths, so they spread sheets of white paper over the tables. The barracks begin to look festive. It has been snowing again, quite a lot actually, and we worry that people won't be able to get here from the city. If you start wandering about in the fields, you can easily drown in the snow, and the road is completely invisible. Those living on the farm hunker down in their rooms, so we go out to look at the road. We see rows of sleighs, carrying people from everywhere: Dąbrowa Górnicza, Sosnowiec, Będzin. The shouting and laughter can be heard from afar. Members of Hashomer coming from all over. The fields are perfectly white,

31 Klinger, 1944 diaries, Haogen I, p. 60.

32 Inka Wajsbort, *Yahad U'badad Mul Ha'eyma* (Hebrew) (Tel Aviv: Moreshet, 1992), p. 39.

33 Rachel Rosenkier (Schwarz) interview.

34 There is some uncertainty regarding the date of this convention. It appears to have taken place with the first snowfall of the year, meaning at the beginning of winter, but the visit itself is said to have taken place in August according to both Schwalb's letter and Inka Wajsbort's testimony. On the other hand, the details given by Tosia match the circumstances preceding the German attack on the Soviet Union on June 22, 1941. Therefore, there may have been a mix-up between the two conventions.

> nothing but snow, and against this snow you can see black dots: people and their sleighs. As they get closer, the black dots grow larger. The members take up their shovels and go out to clear the road for the incoming guests.[35]

At the meeting, Tosia gave an account of the work being done in occupied Poland, the Soviet occupation area, the Vilna gathering, and the subsequent emigration from there. In fact, at that time, with the occupation of Vilna by the Soviets, the Vilna chapter of Hashomer no longer functioned as a "gathering," but the *aliya* efforts from there continued. When the subject of educational activity came up, so did the question of working underground. A proposal was made to publicly announce the cessation of the movement's educational efforts due to persecution at the hands of the Judenrat and the Germans. In practice, however, the work would continue in small groups of up to five members, with each group unaware of the others' activities. The general enthusiasm that followed was soon quelled by the statement: "This is of course not a feasible proposal, since it has just now been heard by eighty people. Is that what we call going underground?" The assembly erupted in laughter. "Are we to leave at the end of an action and wait for each other on the street?"[36] According to Chajka, it was decided not to institute "strict and precise underground protocols, for the conditions are not such as to call for that."[37] Instead, it was decided to "use it as a symbolic element that carries some degree of attraction."[38]

This attitude toward underground resistance is highly informative. Chajka's diaries reveal that even at this early stage, some underground protocols were already in effect—the covert meetings in basements, the secretive behavior of the *shomrim* accompanying Tosia, the persecution at the hands of the Judenrat and the Germans all indicate as much. Chajka's account is corroborated by testimonies of members of the Sosnowiec *ken*.[39] The youth movements' activity was illegal in the eyes of the Germans, semi-legal in the eyes of the Judenrat. The Judenrat in Będzin was aware of the movements' comings and goings, their members often needing its

35 Klinger, 1944 diaries, Haogen I, pp. 62–63.

36 Ibid., p. 64.

37 Ibid.

38 Ibid.

39 Shmuel Ron (Rozencwajg), interview by the author, Jerusalem, 1985, 1986; Fela Katz (Weintraub), interview by the author, Tel Aviv, 1985; Chana Schlesinger (Wiernik), interview by the author, Ra'anana, 1985.

help, especially in securing large halls for their assemblies. Mołczadski, head of the Będzin Judenrat, was a leftist Zionist and closely involved in the affairs of the movements, especially Dror. But that is where the relatively easygoing Mołczadski differed from Moniek Merin. The latter, who was eager to proclaim his Zionist leanings in public, was also eager to suppress any sign of possible resistance to his domination.

Nevertheless, it appears that there was no strict supervision over the youth movements. Together with Mołczadski's sympathetic attitude, this explains the fact that Hashomer Hatzair did not effectively need to go underground. The idea of underground resistance was mainly useful as a symbol, as an idea with pedagogical merit. Among the Będzin *shomrim*, it was common practice back then to read and reread Stanisław Brzozowski's novel *Płomienie* (Flames). This book was a prime example of the Polish romantic tradition, now revived by the advent of a new kind of romance—that of revolution and resistance. Brzozowski's fiery protest against a world alienated by injustice, robbery, and plunder became their protest.[40] *Płomienie* also carried a strong erotic charge, both directly in the story of the Jewish prostitute or its depictions of youthful love, and indirectly in the revolutionary fervor of its characters, including a fictionalized version of the real-life nihilist Sergey Nechayev. This may also explain the influence of the book on generations of *shomrim*. The youthful Eros that had characterized Hashomer Hatzair from the beginning found a revolutionary outlet in *Płomienie*. The first underground newspaper of Hashomer Hatzair in Warsaw took its name *Płomienie* from the novel, as well as its motto: "As long as even one human has perished in the world, as long as one human life is trampled in the dust, there is no point in living, it is impossible to live, except if you fight."[41] The novel thus became a source of inspiration for mustering an idealistic response to the terrors of war.

Another novel that made an intense impression on the youth movement cadets was *The Forty Days of Musa Dagh* by Franz Werfel, which describes the struggle of a group of Armenians who held out for forty days on a high mountaintop in defense against the Ottoman Turks.[42] This, too, was a symbol of noble resistance to the young Jews of Zagłębie. Inka Puterman (later Wajsbort) had read it in the summer of

40 Brzozowski, *Płomienie*.

41 "Biuletyn, September 1940," in Fatal-Knaani, *The Jewish Underground Press, Vol. 1*, pp. 198–212, especially p. 198.

42 Werfel, *The Forty Days of Musa Dagh*.

1941 over three consecutive days, without leaving her room: "If I lifted my eyes from the book, it was only to shout out: 'Mother, how could this be?'"[43] Chajka would also need to draw on these texts for strength and inspiration: In Werfel's novel, as in Brzozowski's, the romance of resistance was combined with the romance of heroic death.

Longing and Despair

Returning to Będzin, Chajka bid farewell to Tosia, most likely after the convention that took place in early 1941:

> The young people have long since left, Tosia and I are sitting together and chatting. She too belongs to Kibbutz Galon. We are tired and worn-out. It's good that we can lose ourselves so readily in our work. We and Tosia are the only ones left from the older generation. We have no friends; we have no lives of our own. We reminisce about people, about the kibbutz. Our lives have been scarred; we're not sure we'll ever be able to devote ourselves fully to building a kibbutz. Of course, we may well lack the physical strength. Hunger and starvation have left their traces on our minds, but also on our bodies. We cannot forget what's happened, and we talk about food very frequently. Did we ever talk about food before the war? Tosia is filled with optimism—we will meet again at the kibbutz, she has so much to do there. Our faith keeps us strong. Tosia is good at not making things any more difficult than they are; she knows how to accept certain things and how to respond to them.[44]

This description of Tosia, which was also written as a memorial portrait,[45] communicates a sense of momentary loneliness and despair, a kind of sobering chill descending on the fiery enthusiasm of the convention. Tosia helped Chajka, David, and probably also Nacia and the Pejsachson sisters shake off the gloom. Her inherent pragmatism was in stark contrast to the frequently wild passions displayed by David and the Będzin girls. Yet in describing Tosia's activities, Chajka was also writing

43 Wajsbort, *Yahad U'badad*, p. 34.

44 Klinger, 1944 diaries, Haogen I, pp. 66–67.

45 Chajka Klinger, "Shney Bikurim: Kitey Yoman" (Hebrew), *Al Hamishmar*, April 18, 1947.

about herself—her admiration, perhaps even her jealousy, of Tosia's mettle as she wandered the roads and snuck over borders. In the earlier 1943 version of the diaries, however, she did not hesitate to add a note of criticism: "Although she did fulfill her tasks in a timely manner, she did not solve the ideological problems as she postponed [dealing with] those until the planned convention, which had serious consequences for us."[46] One cannot help but notice a hint of intellectual superiority underlying this comment, which Chajka omitted in the later version of the diaries. Her tone here is understandable considering Tosia Altman's characteristic practicality. The same tone would also creep into her descriptions of Mordechai Anielewicz. Chajka, Nacia, and David were intellectuals, but as will become clear later, what they were lacking in these crucial moments was the kind of charisma that has the power to tip the scales in dead-end debates and steer members toward action.

Chajka's expression of longing for *Eretz Israel* is here, but for the first time, accompanied by an echo of despair. In less than a year, Tosia would write in helpless desolation: "[*Eretz*] Israel is dying before my eyes and I open up my hands and can do nothing to help it."[47] The Land of Israel was a dream, a hope, and a source of encouragement for Tosia and Chajka. But it was a land so far away, and it seemed to them that they might never reach it.

In a Faraway Land: *Eretz Israel*

Meanwhile, at that time in Nes Ziona, Chajka's kibbutz Hapo'el Lakfar and Tosia's kibbutz Elgavish had already merged to form Kibbutz Galon. Living in tents among the sand dunes and hiring themselves out for day labor in the nearby moshav (cooperative agricultural settlement), Esther Shoshan, Shayke Goldrin, and Shmaryahu Milinsky built a new home. Over time, they were joined by some of their comrades who came through the Vilna gathering, among them Zelig Shoshan, Esther's boyfriend. In 1943, Esther would bear their first child.

Other friends continued to wander the roads. Among them was Moshe Gal together with other kibbutz members who traveled from Vilna by way of Eastern Russia to the Far East. Those in Galon had not

46 Klinger, *I Am Writing These Words to You* (1943 diaries), p. 129.

47 Ziva Shalev, *Tosia Altman—Mihahanhaga Harashit shel Hashomer Hatzair Lemefakedet Ha'irgun Hayehudi Halohem* (Hebrew) (Tel Aviv: Moreshet and Tel Aviv University Press, 1992), p. 142.

forgotten their comrades; how could they have? Abrashka was still waiting for his girlfriend Zippora who was stuck in Żarki; Shmaryahu was waiting for David and Chajka to resume their joint reading sessions. The entire Kibbutz Galon longed for the war to end so they could be joined by the reserve forces stuck behind closed borders. As things stood, they could not do much. At first, they wrote to Vilna, but this thread of communication was severed from mid-1941. Contact between *Eretz Israel* and occupied Europe was conducted through Geneva alone, but it is unclear whether this was known to Kibbutz Galon as it was a secret shared by a select few.

In Merhavia, the center of Hakibbutz Ha'artzi and Hashomer Hatzair in the Land of Israel, the subject of "comrades in the Diaspora" was not at the top of the list of priorities. The world was at war, and people were stuck. Reports of attacks against Jews would appear in the press from time to time, as well as news of the desperate economic situation of European Jewry. However, it appears that after the initial shock of the war, life resumed its course. The people of *Eretz Israel* had to face other wartime challenges: conscription into the British army, the establishment of the Palmach,[48] and the renewal of settlement efforts. In Merhavia—as in Zagłębie—it seemed that this rupture was temporary, and that one just had to wait for the winds to settle.

Nevertheless, it was a painful separation. Hava Geva demonstrates that during 1939 and 1940, Hashomer Hatzair emissaries from *Eretz Israel* left their posts not only in Poland but also in Europe as a whole: the three envoys to Poland returned immediately after the occupation in the fall of 1939. Aharon Cohen was sent to Romania in October 1939 to make contact with Hashomer Hatzair members who were trying to secure a way to the Soviet Union. However, his efforts failed. In 1940, amid growing fears that Romania would soon join the Axis powers, Cohen and his two fellow mission members decided to return to Mandatory Palestine. The last Hashomer emissary in Europe at the time was Levi Dror in Lithuania, and he began urging Meir Ya'ari to confirm his return to Mandatory Palestine due to the Russian occupation. In a personal letter, Ya'ari begged him to stay but to no avail. Dror returned to Mandatory Palestine in October 1940 along with emissaries from other movements. Other envoys simply returned to *Eretz Israel* without asking permission from their leaders.[49]

48 The Palmach was the elite fighting brigade of the Hagana, the underground army of the Jewish Yishuv in Mandatory Palestine.

49 Hava Geva, *Pe'alo shel Hakibbutz Ha'artzi Le'ezrat Hatnu'a Beshtahey Hakivush ad 1942* (Hebrew) (unpublished).

Back in Mandatory Palestine, the returning envoys were received with mixed emotions. As far as we know, with the exception of Aharon Cohen's case, no inquiries were made into their decision to leave Europe. They were greeted with neither the festive reception that the Hechalutz people usually held for their returning emissaries nor any harsh criticism in the style of the Labor Zionist leader Berl Katznelson.[50] Ya'ari initially commended the envoys on their efforts but retracted his praise a little later, admitting that their mission had been a failure.[51]

While the motives of the emissaries who returned for fear of arrest as subjects of an enemy country in territories of Nazi occupation or influence are understandable, it is difficult to see, even in retrospect, why Mordechai Oren (Orenstein) chose to return to Mandatory Palestine from Geneva. In January 1940, it was decided that a liaison office between the global Hashomer leadership and Hakibbutz Ha'artzi and occupied Europe would be set up in Geneva. At the time, Oren was one of the leading activists in Hakibbutz Ha'artzi. Upon his arrival in Geneva, he formed a clear idea of his role and responsibilities for the coordination and guidance of the movement in the world and for maintaining contact with the German-occupied countries and with Jewish and Zionist institutions around the globe.[52]

However, with the return of the emissaries, which he partly tried to prevent, Oren began to feel that "the meager possibilities afforded to my activity as a coordinator, guide, and helper no longer justify my remaining in the Diaspora."[53] Due to continued pressure on his part, the movement's leadership approved his return to Mandatory Palestine.[54] It was a fateful decision. Two and a half years would pass until another authority figure would come to represent Hashomer Hatzair in Europe. On August 21, 1940, Mordechai Oren left Geneva.[55] Three other emissaries returned

50 Hava Eshkoli, *Ilem: Mapai Lenohah Hashoah, 1939–1942* (Hebrew) (Jerusalem: Yad Yitzhak Ben Zvi, 1994), pp. 130–132.

51 Halamish, *Meir Ya'ari*, p. 209.

52 For more on this, see chapter 8.

53 Letter from Mordechai Oren to the Central Global Leadership of Hashomer Hatzair, August 18, 1940, Yad Ya'ari Archive, as quoted in Geva, *Pe'alo shel Hakibbutz Ha'artzi*, p. 44.

54 Geva, *Pe'alo shel Hakibbutz Ha'artzi*, p. 44; Ariel Horowitz, "Shlihuto shel Menahem Bader BeKushta U'maga'ey Hashomer Hatzair im Yehudey Eropa Hakvusha," *Yalkut Moreshet*, 35 (1983), p. 155; Heini Bornstein, interview by the author, Lehavot Habashan, 1985.

55 Horowitz, "Shlihuto shel Menahem Bader," p. 155; Heini Bornstein, *Ha'i Shvaitz: Pe'ulot Ezra Vehatzala Bashanim 1939–1946* (Hebrew) (Tel Aviv: Moreshet, 1996), p. 26.

with him, including Yosef Burg, who would go on to become a minister in Israel.[56]

From that point on, starting in early 1941, the charge of communication with occupied Europe fell to a young Hashomer trainee in Switzerland named Heini Bornstein. He was joined by two fellow trainees, Bruno Levin and Arthur Rath.[57] Heini did what he could, and the Będzin *ken* would maintain a lengthy correspondence with him in the future. Yet, he had little authority compared to the officials of Hechalutz and the Eretz Israel Office also situated in Geneva at the time. It was only in the summer of 1943 that Heini was made a privileged member of the liaison office of Hechalutz in Geneva, thanks to considerable efforts and political pressure.[58]

Had Meir Ya'ari forgotten about his disciples in Europe? From time to time, he would find himself overwhelmed by feelings of exhaustion and guilt, as he wrote to the people of Vilna in May 1940 and in his book *Bepetach Tkufa* (The Dawn of an Era) in mid-1941.[59] But these episodes were minor and marginal. Like many others, Ya'ari believed at the time that the disconnect was temporary and that with the end of the war, the "youthful forces of the Jewish masses" would emerge again in Eastern Europe. Ya'ari foresaw waves of millions of Jewish immigrants after the war and had already started preparing for the dominant role Hashomer Hatzair would play in this Jewish resurgence.[60] This was his "prognosis," as he termed it, adopting the medical lingo favored by Marxism. In the meantime, in his position as distant commander—to use military terms—Ya'ari could not continue to send his officers to make contact with the troops trapped and encircled behind enemy lines. Despite his demands, his envoys capitulated one by one, resigning themselves to the impossibility of saving their stranded forces. And these forces were significant—the main reserves that would ensure postwar renewal. Even as late as the summer of 1941, Hashomer Hatzair activists continued to

56 Bornstein, *Ha'i Shvaitz*, pp. 36, 103–104.

57 Ibid., p. 42.

58 Ibid., p. 187.

59 Letter from Meir Ya'ari to the central leadership in Vilna, May 28, 1940, Hashomer Hatzair Archive, Yad Ya'ari, March 28 (2); Meir Ya'ari, *Bepetah Tkufa: Prakim Lediyun Likrat Hamo'atza Hashishit shel Hakibbutz Ha'artzi Hashomer Hatzair* (Hebrew) (Merhavia: Hakibbutz Ha'artzi, 1942), p. 128, as quoted in Halamish, *Meir Ya'ari*, p. 211.

60 Meir Ya'ari, *Bederech Aruka* (Hebrew) (Merhavia: Sifriat Poalim, 1947), pp. 117–130.

operate in Poland and occupied Europe in numbers that can comfortably be estimated at over 10,000, the biggest pool of human resources Hashomer possessed at the time,[61] as compared to the roughly 7,000 members of Hakibbutz Ha'artzi.

In Będzin, two such activists, Tosia and Chajka, continued to dream about *Eretz Israel*. Despite the hunger, the restrictions, and the loneliness, they believed they would survive the war. Following the German incursion into the Soviet Union, it is reasonable to assume that they were more worried about their comrades in the Soviet-occupied territories. Nevertheless, their apprehensions were probably mitigated by a note of optimism: At last, the Soviet Union would be roused from its apathy, and despite its initial defeats, the Red Army would certainly prevail.

61 It is, of course, impossible to find precise statistics for this period; however, based on the data from Warsaw, Zagłębie, and Łódź, Hashomer Hatzair membership in these three areas alone amounted to 3,000 people.

Chapter Ten

In the Shadow of War

The Invasion of Russia

In 1944, a year after the tide of war had started to turn in favor of the Soviets, Chajka wrote the following in her diary:

On June 22, 1941, Germany declared war on Russia. This brought much commotion into our little world. The Jews knew this meant the beginning of a period of repression, but they were not afraid—they hoped that perhaps it would also bring about the end [of the war]. They had no more illusions about the Allies—they wouldn't do a thing, just as they hadn't done a thing until then. Soviet Russia was their only hope. One cannot begin to describe the excitement, everyone reading the news, listening to the radio with bated breath. Children were taught how to pronounce "Stalin"; they listened to stories of how they [the Russians] would be received with bread and salt. How all the houses would be decorated with red banners.

I don't think I'll ever forget the Saturday when the town found out that the Germans were leaving, the army had left their barracks, the police were packing, as were the employees of the *Stadtverwaltung* [municipality]. All the Jews went out onto the streets, which they had never done before. Usually, they clung to the shadows, stayed at home so as not to offend the eyes of passersby, not to let them realize just how many Jews there really were in the town. But today, they are not afraid. They are looking at the army marching out, calling out to each other. Orthodox Jews, formerly with beards and payot, walked down the street, with joy in their eyes. "Di Rusn kumen" [Yid. The

> Russians are coming], they said. They were in for a disappointment. One German army brigade left only to have another take its place. The Russians did not come; instead the Jews were persecuted with ever-growing severity.[1]

Contemporary testimonies from Będzin do not relate any comparable experiences, but similar descriptions of expectations regarding the Russians' arrival in the Warsaw ghetto also appear in the writings of Emanuel Ringelblum.[2] The Soviet Union, which until now had remained on the sidelines due to the Molotov-Ribbentrop nonaggression pact, was a source of grave disappointment to those who idolized it, including the Hashomer Hatzair movement. However, when the Soviet Union finally became an active party in the war following the German invasion, there was hope once again. Chajka's fellow movement members in Warsaw published the following placard: "The Hour of Reckoning is near and the Day of Liberation approaches...We believe they will bring freedom to the nation and a global Soviet Union. We believe they will come here to level the walls of the ghetto and free us from the shameful burden of scorn."[3] In the eyes of Hashomer Hatzair, which only a month earlier had talked about "the second imperialistic war,"[4] the image of the war was flipped on its head, and it became a just war—a war of liberation led by the Soviet Union. *El Al*, the underground newspaper of the Hashomer scouts, published a passionate piece titled "A Word to the Soviet Soldier." Its author wrote: "I think of you often these days, Soviet soldier...It was not orders alone that made you go into battle. You know what you are fighting for. You are a man of peace...and for that, the better you shall fight. I understand you. I love you. My heart is with you."[5]

But the movement's optimism soon gave way to concern. The German press and radio—though known to be unreliable—were reporting swift victories on the new Eastern front. The names of the newly conquered places also indicated to the Polish public that the German army was advancing further and further into Soviet territory.[6]

1 Klinger, 1944 diaries, Haogen I, pp. 68–69.
2 Ringelblum, *Notes from the Warsaw Ghetto*, pp. 198–199.
3 Hashomer Hatzair newspaper, 3 (agricultural overview), Moreshet Archive, D.1.173.
4 "Neged Hazerem, issue 5 (16), July 1941," in *Fatal-Knaani, The Jewish Underground Press, Vol. 3*, pp. 60–64.
5 "El Al, issue 3, August 1941," in Fatal-Knaani, *The Jewish Underground Press, Vol. 3*, pp. 258–260.
6 See Gutman, *Mered Hanetzurim*, p. 174.

The Jews of Warsaw and Będzin had no way of knowing that the incursion into the Soviet Union was not just a new phase in World War II—it signaled the beginning of a new phase in Hitler's assault on the Jews. From a process of economic dispossession, concentration, isolation, and occasional murders under the auspices of actual or mob law, the Germans would move on to systematic extermination. The Einsatzgruppen—the special task forces attached to the three army groups charging into the Soviet Union that would later come to be known as death squads—began the systematic elimination of Jews in recently occupied territories.

At the same time, preparations had already begun for the systematic extermination of the Jews in occupied Poland. Near the town of Oświęcim, only 40 kilometers from Będzin, a large complex of camps was being established, later given the German name of Auschwitz. The people of Zagłębie stood witness to this strange activity, the meaning of which they could not yet fathom. As early as April 7, 1941, the Jews of Oświęcim were exiled from their town to other settlements in the region.[7] At that point, of the 8,000 Jews who had lived in Oświęcim before the war, 6,500 remained. Roughly 3,000 of them were displaced to Sosnowiec, and the majority of the rest settled in Będzin.[8] Oświęcim Jewry had long suffered at the hand of the Germans, largely due to the concentration camp that had been established in their town at the beginning of the war. It was public knowledge that Polish prisoners of war were being tortured inside the camp, their cries of agony reaching the nearby houses.[9] Sometimes, Jewish prisoners were brought into the camp. They never came back out.[10] The tall barbed-wire fences around the camp and the giant barracks inside added to the atmosphere of terror. The area around the camp was a no-go zone, while in the rest of the town, there were more and more SS men with skulls emblazoned on their uniforms walking the streets, casually hitting Jews with their rubber clubs.

Thus, the Jews of Oświęcim experienced a sense of relief upon their arrival in Sosnowiec and Będzin. Their fellow Zagłębien Jews came out to greet them, ready to help, moved by their plight.[11] The youth rallied to

7 The official reason for the deportation was to make room for workers of the IG Farben company that was supposed to erect factories in the area. See "Case VI: IG Farben Case," *Trials of War Criminals before the Nuremberg Military Tribunal*, vol. VIII (Washington: IMT, 1952), pp. 334–335.

8 Mina Fortgang nee Kempler testimony, Protocol 5, December 1942, GFH, 13893.

9 Ibid.; Rachel Banit testimony, YVA, O.12/11.

10 Mina Fortgang testimony, GFH, 13893; Rachel Banit testimony, YVA, O.12/11.

11 D. Liwer, *Ir Hametim*, pp. 53–54.

their aid.[12] The poor tormented people of Oświęcim, who felt as if they had left a cemetery, were met by a well-dressed bunch of youngsters. "I couldn't understand how one could primp in those days," wrote one of the deportees, "don't they know what's happening in Oświęcim? Haven't they heard of the giant corpse incinerators in Oświęcim?"[13] The testimonies were true: by then, it had already become customary to burn the bodies of dead prisoners or forced laborers in Oświęcim. The Judenrat, the youth movements, and of course regular, non-affiliated Jews with a sense of compassion took part in the efforts to aid the deportees, efforts for which the deportees were grateful, even though it would appear that their integration was not altogether smooth.[14]

The deportation of the Jews of Oświęcim and the news about the mysterious terror camp did not make much of a stir among the Jews of Będzin and Sosnowiec. The camp was remote and apparently closed-off. The testimonies of the refugees mainly referred to Polish prisoners, and the construction of the new incinerators could not be linked to what would later turn out to be their true purpose. Moreover, the Oświęcim community was neither the first nor the last Jewish community to suffer expulsion. Such things were somewhat par for the course in the Generalgouvernement.

All things considered, in mid-1941, the Zagłębien Jews were relatively well-off compared to the rest of Polish Jewry. On May 1, 1940, the 66,000 Jews of Łódź were cramped into a crowded ghetto, and in November 1940, over 300,000 Warsaw Jews were incarcerated behind the walls of their ghetto.[15] However, in Zagłębie at this time, which was annexed to the German Reich, no ghettos were established. This industrial region provided fertile ground for the erection of factories by entrepreneurs from the Reich or local *Volksdeutsche*. Large workshops were opened, which mainly dealt in tailoring and shoemaking. The largest of them—that of the German entrepreneur Alfred Rossner, which opened on May 5, 1940—produced clothes and coats. Initially, Rossner produced clothes for the German market, but at the beginning of 1941, he began to supply large orders for the German army. Over the course of the year, thousands of employees joined Rossner's workshop. Despite

12 Mazia, *Re'im Basa'ar*, pp. 58–59.

13 Mina Fortgang testimony, GFH, 13893.

14 Mazia, *Re'im Basa'ar*; Mina Fortgang testimony, GFH, 13893; Rachel Banit testimony, YVA, O.12/11; D. Liwer, *Ir Hametim*, pp. 53–54.

15 Dawidowicz, *The War Against the Jews*, pp. 220–221.

the meager wages and the fact that the workers had to bring their own sewing machines, Rossner provided a certain security in those days. As a social democrat, he protected his workers, and they were exempt from forced labor for the most part. Three more workshops were engaged in the production of footwear and another in the production of games for German soldiers.[16]

Aside from the workshops, the Judenrat acted as one of the biggest employers in the regions. Its many branches relied on hundreds of personnel for their operation.[17] Testimonies from this period contain almost no mention of unemployment or deaths due to starvation or lack of means. Food was doled out using a system of ration cards. In addition, the Judenrat operated almshouses and soup kitchens for the needy. Thus, when the Germans began their invasion of the Soviet Union, the Jews of Zagłębie were enjoying a period of relative calm: They could work, eat, take care of the Oświęcim refugees, send parcels to their friends in the work camps, and pay visits to the thriving youth movements' farm.

Resisting the Labor Camps

Chajka's view of life in Będzin, however, was different. Fully immersed in movement work and the collective experience of Hashomer Hatzair, Chajka found herself caught up in two difficult struggles for the movement's survival. The first was the struggle to save Hashomer members from being sent to labor camps, directed outward against the Judenrat. The second struggle was directed inward against the new ideological trends that threatened the integrity of the movement. The first struggle was for the members' physical bodies, the second—for their souls. Around the time of the invasion of the Soviet Union, Chajka wrote:

> The *Arbeitseinsatz* [Ger. (forced) labor deployment] now began in earnest. All of our leaders were on the lists, and we had to fight tooth and nail for each one. We spent hours standing in the corridors of the Judenrat. We will not give them our people. They hid, didn't show up for work on certain days, the Judenrat could have fired everyone but

16 Rapaport, *Pinkas Zaglembia*, pp. 62–64.

17 At its peak—April 1943—the number of Judenrat employees stood at 972. Documents regarding the Jewish community in Bedzin, 1943, YVA, M.54.ZIH/JM/2702.

> didn't want to. We were turning into naughty children who didn't want to listen or continue cooperating with their organization. In vain, Mołczadski called us, pleading, threatening, saying that we were bringing bad fortune on the entire Jewish society, that the Gestapo knew about our [educational] work. Finally, he cracked the ultimate whip and threatened us with *Arbeitslager* [labor camps].[18]

And indeed, during this period, deportations to the labor camps in Germany increased. Forced labor was instituted in Zagłębie in general—and particularly in Będzin—from the beginning of the war. In October 1940, a special office of the SS called the Dienststelle das Sonderbeauftragten des RFSS und Chef der Deutschen Polizei für fremdvolkischen Arbeitseinsatz in Oberschlesien (the Special Commissioner of the *SS-Reichsführer* and Police Commander for Foreign Labor Forces in Upper Silesia) was established. Local Jews referred to this office as the "Special Commissioner" or simply the "Special" (Sonder), whereas German documents referred to it as Organization Schmelt, after its chief officer *SS-Brigadeführer* Albrecht Schmelt. The organization was designed to make intensive and comprehensive use of the Jewish workforce in the region. It turned forced labor into a well-oiled system, based on the operation of a large number of labor camps in Eastern Upper Silesia, Upper and Lower Silesia, and finally even in the Sudetenland. At the same time, the organization was also responsible for the exploitation of the Jewish workforce in urban centers, whether by integrating it into old Polish and German firms or within the framework of the newly established workshops.[19]

Under pressure to supply a large number of workers for the Organization Schmelt labor camps, Merin thought to procure this workforce by enlisting volunteers. In special meetings held with representatives of the youth movements in the fall of 1940, he suggested that they emerge as leaders of the Jewish youth by contributing their social experience to the enterprise and even forming "training kibbutzim" within the labor camps. Chajka wrote:

18 Klinger, 1944 diaries, Haogen I, pp. 69–70.

19 Letter from Schmauser to the RFSS, April 20, 1942, Wiener Library, Tel Aviv University, 1386. For more on Organization Schmelt, see Alfred Konieczny, "Die Zwangsarbeit der Juden in Schlesien im Rahmen der 'Organisation Schmelt,'" in Götz Aly et al., *Sozialpolitik und Judenvernichtung: Gibt es eine Ökonomie der Endlösung?* (Berlin: Rotbuch, 1987), pp. 91–110.

> In the early days of the *Arbeitseinsatz*, we held a very heated discussion at the Hechalutz council. Moniek Merin told us with great enthusiasm that the Germans wanted to allow us to set up kibbutzim. Not for 30–40 people but huge ones, for 300–400 people, to help us reach the goal of productivizing Jewish youth. There were some among us who latched onto this idea. Indeed, wherever the Jewish youth goes, we should go too. [...]
>
> However, most were against it. How could anyone fall for Merin's tall tales? Does anyone for a moment believe that the Germans would allow even the caricature of a kibbutz to exist? It's funny to speak of cultural work or productivization. Who would be brave enough to do that sort of thing right next to the German barracks? Haven't we always, right from the beginning, called for resistance, for sabotage under any circumstances and by any means?
>
> A labor camp is a condemnation and must be treated as such. Not only must we not go ourselves but we must help others escape them as much as we can. The nation stays here, most of our youth stays here, where greater duty awaits.[20]

That was Merin's warped vision of a "Zionist" project—the return to a life of labor, taking the form of life in German forced labor camps. Nevertheless, the idea, to which both Chawka (Havka) Lenczner[21] and David Liwer[22] also attested, turned out to be a success. Roughly 2,500 Jewish youths volunteered to go to the labor camps before the end of 1940, including five members from Dror and a few from Hashomer Hatzair. Among them, notably, was Baruch Gaftek, one of the leading figures of Kibbutz Dror, who mistakenly placed his trust in Merin's promises.[23]

Disillusionment was not long in coming. The work in the camps turned out to be hard labor, and those who had gone soon sent desperate letters asking to be rescued. It took considerable efforts on the part of Herszel Szpringer to free Gaftek from the camp and return him to Będzin.[24] Meanwhile, Chajka wrote:

20 Klinger, 1944 diaries, Haogen I, pp. 75–76.

21 Chawka Lenczner, "Parashat Bendin" (Hebrew), *Mibifnim*, June 1944, pp. 124–125.

22 D. Liwer, *Ir Hametim*, pp. 43–45.

23 According to Max Fischer's testimony, the youth movement members were taken by the German police. See Max Fischer testimony, Budapest, June 16, 1944, GFH, Max Fischer: His Wartime Memoirs file, 11578.

24 Lenczner, "Parashat Bendin," pp. 124–125.

When we finally heard from those first volunteers, people stopped responding even to leaflets threatening repercussions for the entire family if they failed to go. The Judenrat was being squeezed, it had to send a quota of people by a set date.

The Jewish militia gained importance, its tasks and competencies broadened. Initially they were quite insignificant: ensuring order in queues to public institutions, acting as a social help group, helping at the kitchen and the first-aid clinic, and at the cooperatives as well. Now they were given new responsibilities: to recruit the people according to the lists compiled by the Judenrat. Militiamen were given new uniforms: blue caps with white stripes, colors resembling the national Jewish flag. It hurt, this humiliation, this depravation, the growing hatred within the society.

Initially, most people had no idea about the planned blockade. The police would enter their houses, show their papers, and take everything without shame, never mind the screaming and crying. People began to hide in attics, in cellars. It was the Jewish policemen who went looking for them. The German police rarely found anyone, so it became normal to send the Jewish militia instead, as the Germans knew they would do their job well. The Judenrat found a way to make them cooperate: either you bring the people on the list, or you go yourselves. Corruption proliferated. Initially one could bribe a militiaman for 50 Marks, then it became 100, 200. The militiamen protected their families first and foremost. A militiaman who failed to do his job lost it, lost his salary, his ability to survive, and became a potential candidate for *Arbeitseinsatz*. Still, there were some who resisted, who were unable to tear a father away from his children crying at the sight of the militia, or to take a son who was the only source of livelihood for his family. But most found more and more refined ways of doing their job. They came at night, they dragged people out of bed. [...]

Those they took during the night would be taken to shut-off buildings surrounded by militiamen. Crowds gathered in front of these buildings, women tearing out their hair, children crying. Crowds in front of the Judenrat. There were various kinds of selection processes. The doctor would let sick people go, but only when they were really mortally ill. That being said, the Judenrat could influence the doctor and, given the right sign, he would let off healthy people too, because, for example, this one had too many children, or that one already had a few sons in the camp. Furthermore, they only

> took people between the ages of eighteen and fifty. Those employed by the workshops were also set free. On the whole, probably ten to fifty people were let off every day. They always walked back onto the street in a line, shouting "Long live Moniek Merin!" forgetting the thousands of their brothers being sent to the labor camps.[25]

It was in reaction to these events that opposition to Merin first arose. Maks Brzeski, a graduate of Hanoar Hatzioni and head of Merin's Labor Department, resigned from his position.[26] It is possible that the resignation of Moshe Glidman, the head of the Jewish police, was also a consequence.[27] Yet, substitutes were found for both positions, and the forced conscription into the labor camps that began in the spring of 1941 bore real results. According to German records, by spring 1942, there were approximately 6,000 Jewish youths working in forty Organization Schmelt camps.[28] However, because the very same organization also supervised the workshops operating in Zagłębie, it made it possible to evade conscription for forced labor. Most of the workshops were German-owned, and a German factory owner was better able to protect his workers from forced labor than the Judenrat or a Jewish business owner, most of whom were powerless. Chajka wrote:

> Those who worked [in the workshops] for the Wehrmacht were not taken away, nor those employed in military factories. There were some Germans who allowed their workmen to sleep at the factories to avoid being taken away. The Germans [the employers] went to various committee meetings and protested that they needed these people to work for them, that they could not run their factories without them. And their employees were let off, though less frequently if they worked for private companies. No one was taken from Rossner's shop, not a single person; on the contrary, he brought in more staff from the labor camps. He set up a huge tailor shop making clothes for the Wehrmacht. Initially, the shop employed 50–100 Jews, but eventually that number reached 3,000. The town benefitted from this immensely.[29]

25 Klinger, 1944 diaries, Haogen I, p. 77; Haogen II, pp. 1–2.

26 Mazia, *Re'im Basa'ar*, p. 49.

27 Moshe Yarkoni, in *Sefer Sosnovitz*, vol. 2, pp. 167–168.

28 Letter from Schmauser to the RFSS, April 20, 1942, Wiener Library, Tel Aviv University, 1386.

29 Klinger, 1944 diaries, Haogen II, p. 4.

Chajka was grateful to Rossner, as were most of the Jews in Będzin. A German socialist by ideology, Rossner was an extraordinary entrepreneur. While he certainly took advantage of the cheap Jewish workforce available to him, he also protected his workers from being deported to the labor camps and would hire members of the Communist Party as well as many others whom he sought to protect. As Chajka put it, "he did much good for the Jewish people, and he did so not unwittingly."[30] But it was not enough. The massive deportation of the able-bodied workforce threatened the youth movements. Most, if not all, of them were suitable candidates for the camps, and there was growing concern that the movements would sooner or later be forced to stop operating. In her diary, Chajka mentioned that "David was on the list almost perpetually. We had a couch, and whenever they knocked on the door, David would dive under the cushions. No one ever considered looking under there if someone was sleeping on top."[31] Lea Pejsachson, Chajka's best friend and one of the leading figures in the Będzin *ken*, was not so lucky and was captured:

> Lea Pejsachson became the first victim. They could have gotten her out, they knew she was a member of Hashomer, but they didn't even try. Lea wrote to us about the soup she was given there. Hot water and 300 grams of bread. But the worst thing was being treated like a dog. Even girls were beaten up. They often forgot about *Rassenschande* [Ger. racial shame] and tried to get it on with the girls. And the girls were very easy to buy, which hurt the most. There was also a lot of bribery going on in the kitchen. The girls who worked there ate all the best food, to the detriment of everyone else. And they were not beyond telling on others. Other girls rebelled against them, but they were afraid—the kitchen girls had power and support. Lea could not stand this, it kept bothering her and she couldn't find peace of mind. She constantly tried to stir up the other girls to rebel. Finally, it worked. They decided to hold a meeting in every bedroom at 2 AM, when the whole camp was asleep. They went to bed as normal every day, but at two in the morning, they were all sitting upright on top of their beds, even though no one had woken them up. One girl stood guard at the door. Finally, someone said: We cannot keep

30 Ibid., p. 5.

31 Klinger, 1944 diaries, Haogen I, p. 80.

> living like this. Not only are we in prison, after all, we cannot jump over the barbed wire, but even among ourselves we are at each other's throats. We will tell the *Lagerführer*, she says, we will tell him that you steal from the kitchen, that you sell the food, that you are growing fat from overeating, we will tell him. One girl begins to laugh—she is not afraid, she's friendly with the *Lagerführer*. The room grows quiet. So, you're not afraid, are you? Another girl steps forward. She hits her, once, twice, she pummels her face and her body, again and again. The room is still. No one says anything, no one moves, even the girl being beaten up doesn't moan or cry. Suddenly, the girl doing the beating begins to cry. She settles down quickly though and goes back to bed. In this silence, they all go to bed. Next day they are all nervous, unsettled, uncertain whether the beat-up girl will tell on them. She is bruised all over. They ask her what happened. I fell off the bed, she replies, calmly. The relations in the camp slowly change. No one knows how much of that is due to Lea. Whenever I looked at her, I was reminded of the mother from [Maxim] Gorky's novel. [...]
>
> For a long time, she worked as a nurse. It was a difficult job, with the doctor coming in only for the most severe cases. She worked without fixed hours, without rest, and then she had to go help out in the kitchen too. But all the sick people blessed her, she was never short on kindness, and whenever she put her maternal hand on someone's forehead, they instantly felt better. Everyone in the camp liked her singing. She would sing about *Eretz Israel*, about the movement, and then the whole camp would sing her songs as well.
>
> We dragged her out of the camp almost against her will. She was not sure, she wrote, whether she should return. Whether she had the right to leave the camp, when so many people needed her there.[32]

This was Chajka's epitaph for her friend. By the time these lines were put down on paper, Lea was no longer among the living. The passage also highlights the complexity of the youth movements' relationship with the Judenrat and the Jewish public. The forced conscription into the labor camps introduced a new dimension of conflict between the Judenrat and the Jewish community, especially in view of the methods employed by the Jewish police. Chajka saw this as the beginning of the end for both institutions:

32 Ibid., pp. 70–74.

> The Jewish militiamen had to resort to harsher and harsher methods. They locked up apartments, took away furniture, even the beds, they took hostages and threw them in jail for weeks, without any food. The people's hatred toward the Jewish militia grew, without a thought for the Germans behind their actions. A mother only sees the man who takes her son away.[33]

The youth movements' resistance, which was part of the general evasion of forced conscription, created a nucleus of opposition to the Judenrat for the first time. However, the youth movement members found themselves in a trap: In order to free their people from being drafted into the camps, they had to make effort in the corridors of the Judenrat and maintain steady relations with Mołczadski and Merin. The latter, in turn, used this dependence in order to limit the autonomous activity of the youth movements, whose political elements were a constant threat to their power. Nevertheless, the youth movements' struggle against the deportations to the labor camps and for the release of prisoners intensified and continued, and as the days passed, it became clear that the Judenrat and the young activists were positioned in two opposing camps.

The Ideological Struggle

During this very period, Chajka was also engaged in another equally difficult and possibly even more painful struggle. The fight for the physical freedom of her comrades was accompanied by a fight for their souls. On this battleground, she was not facing some reviled enemy but rather the people she loved the most—her Hashomer Hatzair peers. Severe differences of opinion emerged in the Hashomer *ken* in Będzin at this time, threatening to split the group.

The entry of the Soviet Union into the war spurred the hope that salvation was approaching; however, it also raised new questions:

> When Russia joined the war, many heated debates ensued among us. How should we react when Russia approaches and the war front migrates here, right to our doorstep? If we are to follow through on our previous statements, we must join the revolution, but it will not happen as we imagined. There will be no barricades, just the Red

33 Klinger, 1944 diary, Haogen II, pp. 3–4.

> Army gaining ground. Such will be the second wave of the political and economic revolution. Will we stand aside? Will we become insulated, sever our ties with these historic events happening right in front of our eyes? No nation can stand idle at this historic hour, with the whole world caught in the whirlwind. Our organization will only be historically relevant if it opens itself up to these momentous events. If all we do is carry on with our pedagogical efforts in secret and not join the revolution, it will be our death sentence. Will the youths stay loyal to us then? They almost certainly will not.[34]

The questions posed by Chajka were both ideological and practical. The members of Hashomer Hatzair dreamed of revolution, but that revolution was supposed to take place in the Land of Israel. In this new state of affairs, however, that revolutionary energy was to be redirected toward the Soviet Union, and the revolutionaries were to join its military ranks. Whoever did not take part in this struggle could not hope to lead a social struggle in the aftermath of the war, or so Chajka believed:

> And if the Soviets had come and at the same time there would have been a possibility of immigrating to *Eretz Israel*, they [the youth] would have stayed in the Soviet Union. And that was why one could no longer answer "yes" as easily as before the war to the question of whether Zionism would still be relevant after the revolution.[35]

Chajka's way of formulating the dilemma shows how close she came to negating the relevance of Zionism. She and David, the de facto intellectual leaders of the *ken*, found themselves in a bind. At this point in time, a young Trotskyist lawyer by the name of Erlich came to prominence in Będzin and gained significant influence among the Hashomer youths.[36] Chajka wrote:

> And the Trotskyites began to meddle. Negative consequences—the young, whom we valued the most, left us….
>
> And then doubts in the *hanhaga* [leadership] itself.
>
> Long, tiring discussions.

34 Klinger, 1944 diaries, Haogen II, pp. 10–11.

35 Klinger, *I Am Writing These Words to You* (1943 diaries), p. 92.

36 Shmuel Ron interview.

> It was known that Idzia would leave. I planned to forbid her. But a real blow came with [the departure of] Irka.
>
> The branch, which had been built with such effort, disintegrated in our hands and that caused us so much pain. I simply had a feeling that they were ripping a fetus out of my womb—my own child who had grown there.[37]

In the 1944 version of her diaries, Chajka expanded the description of the debates over six pages. With palpable love and pain, she described the personalities and the diverging and changing positions of her two friends Idzia Pejsachson and Nacia Klugman. These two young women in their early twenties were now facing each other and fighting for the soul of the movement among themselves:

> Idzia was the soul of the opposition. She came to us from the Bund, a foreign element among us, and what she brought with her quickly spread. She became the ringleader of the young generation that grew up in the *ken*. They were impressed by her revolutionary nature, her enthusiasm and energy. I see her standing against the wall during a farm council meeting. Tall, shapely, athletic. She is pale, with a pink blush on her cheeks, her eyes sparkle. She talks about Soviet Russia, about the Red Army, getting more and more excited, dealing with her opponents without mercy. She knows no compromise, an extremist. How knowledgeable she is, how far she's come in her time among us. If there's one thing she can do, it's learn. She can stay up reading a book until 2 AM. Even though she is Lea's sister, the two are worlds apart. Idzia can't abide anyone standing up to her, she's a dictator type.[38]

At the leadership meeting, the movement's position was presented by Nacia Klugman. Nacia was deeply attached to the Pejsachsons, especially Irka with whom she had studied at the Gymnasium. The ideological rift between herself and Idzia was therefore painful for her too:

> It was no longer possible to ignore the issue. A tempestuous leadership gathering was called in order to discuss everything. Nacia presented the position of Hashomer Hatzair. Educated at a Hebrew Gymnasium, she had been schoolmates with the daughter of a Hebrew teacher and

37 Klinger, *I Am Writing These Words to You* (1943 diaries), pp. 92–93.

38 Klinger, 1944 diaries, Haogen II, pp. 33–34.

> grew up respecting Hebrew culture. She loved it with all her heart. Just like Idzia, she had seen no Jewish traditions at home. She did fall in love with Bialik though, she knew his poems by heart; she also translated so many poems by Tchernichovsky beautifully. The bible, which she loved to read, lay on her desk alongside Marx. She fell in love with our movement, which became her home, her mother (she lost her real mother when she was young). She yearned for *Eretz Israel*, for the kibbutz. Nacia was Idzia's worthy rival.[39]

The essence of what Nacia had to say was that every nation must fight for socialism in its own way, and that the Jewish nation, as impaired as it may be, must not elect a fate of national suicide. It must preserve its uniqueness. She quoted Josef Kaplan who said: "We must go toward the Soviet Union as one united group whose motto is 'Long live the Soviet Land of Israel.'"[40]

In the evenings, after everyone on the farm had gone to bed, the leaders would stay up to argue in the toolshed:

> Now we organize gatherings by candlelight, debating well into the night. The youths are angry with us. They do not want to hear about what they call "sentimental yearnings for *Eretz Israel*." They simply don't want to understand that one cannot create a new life without some sense of grandeur, a kind of flair, what we call *halutziyut* [Heb. pioneering spirit]. They want to know whether Zionism is a historical necessity or whether it is justified only under certain conditions, and whether such conditions exist under the Soviet regime.[41]

Such reasoning amounted to heresy. According to Hashomer dogma, the role of the youth movements was to serve as role models for the Jewish people and to lead them on their new path of becoming pioneers. However, now that conditions had changed and war had broken out, some were of the opinion that the historical path was leading in a different direction—to the Soviet Union. Was the movement's job to continue pushing for *aliya* to *Eretz Israel* or to prepare for the arrival of the Red Army instead?

39 Ibid., pp. 14–15.
40 As quoted in ibid., p. 16.
41 Ibid., p. 19.

Chajka's partner David had his own answer to this question. He had been swept up in the revolutionary fervor when the Soviets had joined the war. Later, Chajka would describe his ideological evolution during this period as follows:

> The war had a negative effect on him.
>
> Dawid pined away and lost weight; his skin became sallow and a cough began to rattle his lungs more and more often.
>
> His *Weltschmerz* [Ger. world-weariness] disappeared, [giving way to] an outlook well-grounded in Marx's philosophical and economic theories. Dawid was becoming a supporter of Stalin. [...]
>
> Oh, he loved the Red Army more than life.
>
> Totally fixated on it, he would be literally taken ill whenever it suffered defeat—he couldn't eat, sleep, or live.
>
> And when it was victorious, he revived, shone with joy and embraced everybody out of happiness.
>
> "My brother," he would write to the Red Army soldier, "I'm with you. I offer you my hand. Take it."[42]

His position was not far removed from that of the younger members of the *ken* who were now rising up against their leaders and their attachment to *Eretz Israel*, a place that seemed completely irrelevant to the events taking hold of the world. David was looking for a solution that would reconcile the opposing opinions.[43]

The arguments between the two sides became very heated and very personal: "It was so painful. Once Nacia cried during an *asefa* [gathering]. None of us wanted to leave. The fiercest oppositionists, for example, Idzia, wanted to stay with us. They were attached to the movement and they wanted to be convinced that they were wrong."[44] Chajka and David felt like they were not in a position to make any final decisions. "We, the veteran *shomers*, Dawid and I, didn't feel able to do that.... Somebody had to come to us [from the outside] and explain," she wrote.[45] And in May 1942, as if in response to Chajka's wish, someone from the outside did arrive and put an end to the debate. That someone was Mordechai Anielewicz: "Mordechai was appalled. 'Are you all

42 Klinger, *I Am Writing These Words to You* (1943 diaries), pp, 171–172.

43 Klinger, 1944 diaries, Haogen II, p. 19.

44 Klinger, *I Am Writing These Words to You* (1943 diaries), p. 93.

45 Ibid.

living on the moon,' he asked, 'that you are with theoretical matters now, while the ground burns under our feet?' But he soon understood our reasons."[46]

The *ken* was saved. Anielewicz annihilated all seeds of doubt over the course of a few lectures and discussions. A few members either left the movement as a result or were perhaps expelled. Among them were Sawek Merin and probably also Dov (Bobo) Graubart. A Trotskyist cell was emerging in Będzin. Idzia Pejsachson stayed, as did her sister Irka.[47] However, the events that immediately followed soon rendered all this insignificant.

News of Extermination

Indeed, in a certain sense, the people of Będzin were "living on the moon," as Anielewicz had put it. By this point, he had already received verified reports from Vilna and Chełmno via Warsaw about the beginning of the extermination process. Moreover, by the time Anielewicz visited Będzin, the first groups of Zagłębien Jews had already been dispatched to the gas chambers at the strange camp established in Oświęcim.

In fact, Hashomer Hatzair members in Będzin had already received firsthand information regarding the unfolding events but had not yet grasped the significance of the news brought to them by Będzin Judenrat member Michał Laskier. Laskier—a General Zionists man—was a well-to-do and respected figure in town who saw his role in the Judenrat as serving the public good as opposed to a means of procuring personal benefit. He was one of the only members of the Judenrat to be viewed positively by the youth movements throughout the period. In 1944, Chajka wrote:

> That winter [most likely January or February 1942] we received sad news. Michał Laskier was coming back from his visit to the Generalgouvernement. One night he was taking a carriage toward Częstochowa, when suddenly a man jumped on and refused to get off. He said he was a Jew and to leave him alone. After an hour's ride he started talking. He said he used to live in Płock with his family.

46 Klinger, 1944 diaries, Haogen II, p. 20.
47 Ibid.

One day, the Germans came to town with a big truck and took fifty young men and fifty young women. The next week they came back for more and continued to do so every week. They allowed the Jews to take suitcases. They said they were taking them to work. No news ever came from those who had already left. This man was in one such group. They came to Chełmno, a small town, where they were greeted by an older man, an intellectual by appearance. The place looked like a nobleman's residence, a few poplars, a grand house. The elderly man was exceedingly polite. He helped them get into the car, asked if anyone needed to see the doctor, told them they were going to take a shower. They were led into a large room full of clothes and underwear and told to undress. In the corner, one of them saw inscriptions scribbled in Yiddish: "There is no leaving this place," and "Shema Yisrael." They had a sudden premonition that death awaited them here. Suddenly, they heard quick steps and voices. Again, "Shema Yisrael." The voices came from somewhere in the distance, but the steps seemed to come from above. Somehow, the man managed to hide amongst the piles of clothes. He lay there, completely still, for a long time, until suddenly he felt something hard. He was very scared, heard a sigh, raised his head. It was the middle of the night, he only recognized a shadow; he was afraid to move. Suddenly, the shadow spoke, saying "Kum hir" [Yid. Come here]. It was a Jew from another town who had been hiding there for three days. He said that people were taken from there to a field nearby, packed into a car, tightly locked. The car is filled with gas that kills people instantly. He and six others were made to dig graves for the corpses, which are flung from the car directly into pits. He managed to escape and hide here, but they both must run away tonight, as he thinks the Germans will come and sort through the clothes.

We sat there in deadly silence as he recounted this. We felt our skin crawl, the hair on our heads rise, a deadly fear. So, this is what awaits us, this is their plan, to exterminate all the Jews entirely. However, we quickly calculated, each one of us instinctively, that if they can kill a hundred Jews per day, they probably couldn't destroy the entire nation.[48]

48 Ibid., pp. 7–10.

Laskier's account referenced the Jewish underground's report about Chełmno, which was circulating in Warsaw at the time.[49] It is the earliest evidence of the systematic genocide of the Jews to reach Będzin. The way Chajka relates this testimony, with no interpretative comments or reactions, in all likelihood demonstrates the way it was perceived by those who heard it. Chełmno was far away, and even if what was happening there was the fate designated for all Jews, it was still not perceived as a real threat. What Laskier told the Hashomer members seemed unrelated to other events unfolding around them. They were too preoccupied with forced labor camps and preparations for the arrival of the Red Army to worry about the smoke already rising from the chimneys of the camp situated only 40 kilometers away: Auschwitz.

49 Elisheva Shaul, "Gviyat Edut Mikavran Kfiya, Ya'akov Gruyanovsky, Ivica" (Hebrew), *Yalkut Moreshet*, 35 (1983), pp. 101–122.

Chapter Eleven

Mordechai Anielewicz

Gilad: 1985

It is the eve of Yom Kippur, and we are driving to Kibbutz Yad Mordechai to spend the sabbatical—forced upon us secular Jews—somewhere livelier. It is where Gilad lives now with his wife Idit and his daughter Racheli. Gilad is not one for nostalgia. On our way to the dining hall, he declares: "This kibbutz is sandwiched between two gravestones." He is referring to the Anielewicz monument and the collective burial site for the fallen War of Independence soldiers on the hillside opposite it. It is where Idit's father Moshe is buried, along with many others. Yet, Gilad remains firmly rooted in the struggles of the present, rejecting the shadows of the past. He came here after our Kerem Shalom adventure, and although he has retained a firm grasp on his principles, he is done with revolutions.

Was it youthful enthusiasm that had driven us to establish our own kibbutz, a new kind of kibbutz that would avoid the pitfalls to which our parents had succumbed? Or were we perhaps carried out into the expanses of the Negev desert on the winds of the New Left, blowing strong in 1968? Three years earlier, we had met at a young Hashomer Hatzair instructors' course. Gilad, with his mane of curls and upturned nose, was a man of few words but these he spoke with a great deal of self-assurance. The girls would listen enraptured—he had that stamp of natural leadership. When we were in eleventh grade, I went to visit him in Mishmar Ha'emek to discuss some matters, and when that was done, we adjourned to an insulated room to play a Handel duet—we had both played cello in the back row of the Bnei Kibbutzim Orchestra. A girl suddenly appeared in the doorway and stood there listening quietly. Gilad already had a girlfriend; I did not. Both of us were looking for a way to implement the "revolt of the son" we preached to our trainees by establishing a "new kind of kibbutz"—we were seeking to start our own little revolution. Our own homes had been built by the Jewish Agency, but we were far more radical than that organization. We made sure that the Arab construction workers ate with us in the dining hall like everyone else. We protested against the illegal settlements in Pithat Rafiah and the deportations of the Bedouins that had commenced under the command of Ariel Sharon. Remembrance Day was not observed in Kerem Shalom, and Independence Day was celebrated with a humble bonfire.

Gilad, however, was reticent about Kerem Shalom's wild streak. He had probably been right too, as usual. When the dust settled, most of the high school graduates returned to Tel Aviv, while the kibbutzniks returned to their more peaceful, settled kibbutzim, or found another one nearby. We had wanted to shake off the burden of the past, yet we unwittingly continued to carry it on our shoulders: Many of us had parents that had either helped found the Israeli left or died defending it. For me, even the blinding sun of the desert could only blur the memory of my mother but never erase it completely.

"Speak, memory," commanded Vladimir Nabokov in his autobiography.[1] In my ongoing journey to the past, I cannot help but think on this supplication, as the place where our feet tread now is named after a man whose fate was closely bound with that of my mother. She had known Mordechai Anielewicz well, having accompanied him as a representative of the Hashomer leadership in Będzin on a two-month tour of Zagłębie. Her diary contains multiple passages describing his actions, his strengths, and his shortcomings in vivid detail. A meticulous reader looking carefully between the lines might suggest that she was slightly in love with him. Mother was the first to convey the news of Mordechai Anielewicz's death to *Eretz Israel* immediately after the Warsaw Ghetto Uprising. "Did you know Mordechai?" she wrote to her contact in Switzerland. "He was the father of the *Hagana* [resistance] and loved her more than any father has ever loved his daughter." Various—and probably inaccurate—sources quote a different version of this letter: "Had grandfather Meir known his grandson Mordechai? He was the father of the *Hagana* and

1 Vladimir Nabokov, *Speak, Memory* (London: Penguin, 1999).

loved her like no man had ever loved his children."[2] No, Hashomer Hatzair's venerated leader Meir Ya'ari had not known his proverbial grandson Mordechai. Anielewicz was virtually unknown in *Eretz Israel* at the time, and there was a slight dispute regarding the identity of the "Mordechai" referenced in the letter. Two years later, in 1943, there was already a kibbutz named after him—the very same kibbutz in which we are walking now.

Mordechai Anielewicz had made an indelible impression on Mother. Though she sought to describe him as a flesh-and-blood man, she also saw him as the real-life embodiment of the heroes in the books she had read and admired. She fashioned the myth while revolting against it at the same time. Here in Yad Mordechai, however, only the myth has survived: The monument to Anielewicz is a giant figure with a grenade in its hand, silhouetted against a leaning water tower. The damaged tower itself is yet another monument. For five days in May 1948, the Egyptians attacked the small kibbutz, and when the death toll rose to twenty-three and the munitions ran out, the defenders left the kibbutz for the nearby Kibbutz Nir Am. Three more members were killed on the way. For years, those who had withdrawn from the kibbutz named after the Warsaw ghetto commander bore the torment of guilt.[3] Baby Idit, her sister, and her mother then lived in kibbutzim in the central region. A photograph of Moshe Baron, Idit's dead father who was killed in the battles in Yad Mordechai, stands in a modest but prominent place in Idit and Gilad's bedroom. Like the small picture of my mother above my desk in our modest dining room in Tel Aviv.

Chajka: Spring 1942

In the spring of 1942, Chajka was twenty-four and a half years old, a prominent figure among the frontline leadership of the youth movements in Będzin. The first two and a half years of the war had been ones of nonstop activity. According to her diaries, the movement—the farm, the *ken*, David—was her home. She seemed to have no private life at all, unless we consider the life of the movement as, in fact, her most intimate and private life. When the Trotskyist split threatened to tear the *ken* apart,

2 See chapter 16.
3 Margaret Larkin, *The Six Days of Yad Mordechai* (Yad Mordechai: Yad Mordechai Museum, 1975).

she wrote that she "simply had a feeling that they were ripping a fetus out of my womb—my own child who had grown there."[4]

It is not entirely clear where Chajka was living in 1942. It appears that for a long while, she stayed on the farm, where she held organizational roles. It is also likely, however, that she periodically returned to her parents' house. At some point, she may have found a place to live with David, since she wrote about "our house" in the previous section of the diaries. Her parents and their home are not mentioned in the writings concerning this period. According to Ada Neufeld, even at this time members of the movement were never invited there.[5] Nevertheless, it is known that in the spring or summer of 1942, Leibel Klinger fell ill and was hospitalized in Sosnowiec. It appears to have been another instance of blood disease—the family curse—and Leibel's leg was amputated.[6] He was about sixty years old at the time.

This family misfortune is not mentioned in Chajka's diary. Then again, she hardly mentions her own ailment either. Several testimonies as well as her later correspondence point to the fact that she had fallen gravely ill that winter.[7] David and her family took great care of her. It was a time of war, and antibiotics were unavailable. Any minor blood poisoning or even a cold in the harsh Polish winter risked being fatal. Chajka was transferred to the hospital in Sosnowiec, where for many days her loved ones sat by her bed, worried that she would never wake up again. Later David's devoted care was remembered by her tenderly: "He was carrying her in his arms during the fatal illness, and he did not wish to live without her."[8]

Leibel Klinger treated his sick daughter as dictated by Hasidic tradition: He taped a *kvitl*, a note of petitionary prayer blessed by a rabbi as part of Hasidic tradition, to the wall to ensure her recovery. Members of the movement came to donate blood. At the time, donations were made via direct transfusion—vein to vein—rather than using sterile bags. One Hashomer trainee who came to donate blood was reportedly asked if he was afraid of losing too much blood, and he answered with considerable pathos: "I am donating my blood for Chajka and for the Red Army."[9]

4 Klinger, *I Am Writing These Words to You* (1943 diaries), p. 93.
5 Ada Halperin (Neufeld) interview.
6 Shraga Fruchtzweig interview.
7 Letter from Chajka Klinger to Shraga Fruchtzweig, Kfar Saba, February 25, 1947, Moreshet Archive, Avihu Ronen collection, 235; Shmuel Ron interview.
8 Klinger, *I Am Writing These Words to You* (1943 diaries), p. 27. In this quote, she is referring to herself in the third person.
9 Bracha Plotnik (Chmielnicka) interview.

Chajka got better. But as soon as she regained consciousness, she saw the *kvitl* her father had hung on the wall, and she tore it off, crumpled it up, and threw it to the ground. Talk of this act traveled around town.[10]

Despite the lack of detailed evidence, we know that Chajka maintained a close relationship with her two sisters. Sarah's daughters Malka-Chana and Tova-Taube were now two and nine years old, respectively. Chajka used to visit her sister's family, sometimes in the company of friends, to play with the children and take a break from her daily worries. Her younger sister Mania was closer in spirit to Chajka. She was a highly educated girl, whom Chajka's friends saw as the real genius in the family.[11] Mania joined Hanoar Hatzioni, but there is no evidence that Chajka begrudged her for it.[12] On the contrary, later evidence points to a close and spirited relationship between the two sisters.[13] At that time, Mania had a communist boyfriend and her own ideology seems to have shifted under his influence.[14] Their mother Perl Klinger's dream was to get through the war and to celebrate the marriages of Chajka and Mania to their boyfriends.[15] A rare photograph of Perl from the ghetto period shows the image of a woman with black hair and piercing eyes, her mouth bunched up in a frown before the camera capturing her portrait for a German identity card.[16]

Chajka's relationship with David was now stronger than ever. David seems to have gone wherever she went. On the farm, in the *ken*, and apparently at home too. The evidence relating to the period, setting aside Chajka's own testimony, mentions her name more than his. We may conclude from this that her role in both the organization of the farm and the *ken* was more central. When it came to ideological issues, however, she probably ceded the upper hand.

It was at this point that a young man—in many ways cut from the same cloth, yet in many ways very different from them—entered their lives. That man was Mordechai Anielewicz, a delegate of the Hashomer Hatzair leadership in Warsaw, who arrived in Będzin in June 1942.

10 Ibid.
11 Chana Lieberman interview.
12 Karola Bojm interview.
13 Zippora Szporn (Eisenberg) interview.
14 Tosia Herzberg interview.
15 Zippora Szporn (Eisenberg) interview.
16 Collection of passport photos of the Jews of Będzin found by Aryeh Ben-Tov, YVA, K149/1179.

Enter Anielewicz

It is unclear whether Chajka knew Mordechai Anielewicz before his arrival in Zagłębie. He was about two years younger than her. Later, she would repeatedly describe the strong impression he made on her:

> Mordechai came. Such a tall, thin, expeditious boy emanating so much energy. [...]
>
> Mordechai was the pride of the movement. He had unusual, rare abilities—a man of theory and a practical leader. He couldn't stand people's lack of resources and *shlamazel* [incompetence]. [...]
>
> Whenever the tall young man with the open-collar shirt was spotted, people looked at him, saying, "It's him."[17] [...]
>
> Mordechai was brave. Not because he wanted to be brave, but because he truly was brave.[18]

Chajka's romantic enthusiasm had found a new focal point. Although Mordechai could not take David's place in her heart, it would seem that the delegate from Warsaw had something that David was lacking—the makings of a leader. Intellectually, however, Chajka thought him inferior to herself and her beloved. In her 1943 diaries, she wrote that Mordechai had tried to argue a point "awkwardly,"[19] even though elsewhere she referred to him as "the theoretician of our movement in Poland during the war," an epithet that was not quite applicable to Anielewicz at the time.[20] Chajka admired Mordechai because he embodied a new type of *shomer* previously unseen in the movement. He had the militant outlook of a man brought up in the Betar movement, and this shone through the Hashomer Hatzair ideology. David had flinched that time when a German thug hit Chajka in the chest, and she had stopped him from hitting back. But Anielewicz was used to hitting back. Oftentimes he was only too eager for a brawl: Even before the war he had belonged to a group that protected Jews who wished to walk through the Saxon Garden in Warsaw.[21]

17 Klinger, *I Am Writing These Words to You* (1943 diaries), pp. 93, 98.
18 Klinger, 1944 diaries, Haogen II, p. 30.
19 Klinger, *I Am Writing These Words to You* (1943 diaries), p. 134.
20 Ibid., p. 93.
21 For a biography of Mordechai Anielewicz, see Gutman, *Mered Hanetzurim*, pp. 11–97.

Ostensibly, Anielewicz's visit to Będzin was one of those regular visits made by members of the main leadership of Hashomer Hatzair to Zagłębie. The role of the delegate—the leadership representative—during these visits was to get updated on the organizational activity, issue directives, lead seminars, and conduct educational and ideological inquiries. Mordechai's intervention in the Trotskyist dispute was typical of this mode of leadership: He simply tipped the scales and prevented a split in the *ken*.

However, his departure from Warsaw was also spurred by a turn that had taken place in the movement's activity over the preceding months. News brought by the movement's emissaries from the east reported the systematic killing of Jews in German-conquered Soviet territories. In October 1941, *Neged Hazerem* (Against the Current), Hashomer Hatzair's underground newspaper in Warsaw, published a detailed report about the Ponary massacre, which had effectively halved the number of Jews in Vilna from 70,000 to 35,000.[22] These reports were confirmed in the following months by messengers arriving from Vilna and later by messengers departing from Warsaw. In February 1942, news also reached Warsaw about the latest methods of slaughter being employed in Western Poland. A Jew by the name of Jakub Grojanowski managed to escape from Chełmno and brought to Warsaw the shocking news of extermination by gas chamber. His testimony was recorded by Ringelblum and others in the Oneg Shabbat Archive, and excerpts from it were published in the underground press.[23]

The dissemination of Grojanowski's report instigated the preliminary organization of the armed underground. In March 1942, the Anti-Fascist Bloc was established in Warsaw, bringing together the Communists, Hechalutz, Hashomer Hatzair, and Poalei Zion. The armed underground had a distinct communist orientation. The goal was to participate in the fight against the Nazis by attacking the enemy on the home front, thereby helping the Soviet struggle. However, opinions were divided about the best way to do this. The Communists' proposal was to send groups of volunteers to join the partisans, while

22 "Neged Hazerem, issue 7–8 (18–19), September–October 1941," in Fatal-Knaani, *The Jewish Underground Press, Vol. 3*, p. 537.

23 Israel Gutman, *The Jews of Warsaw 1939–1943: Ghetto, Underground, Revolt* (Bloomington: Indiana University Press, 1982), p. 166. The Oneg Shabbat underground archive was established and run by the historian and community figure Dr. Emanuel Ringelblum with the express purpose of documenting the reality of life under Nazi occupation.

the Zionist youth movements argued that the struggle should take place within the ghetto itself.[24]

Hashomer Hatzair thus redirected its efforts from the field of education to preparations for underground warfare. The underground press in Warsaw reflected this development. In March 1942, in the margins of the Chełmno report published in *Neged Hazerem*, the editors noted: "If there are such shocking incidents in Vilna and Chełmno, we cannot remain passive. If there is nothing left to lose, we should at least lose with dignity."[25] In April 1942, the movement's newspaper published an article that read: "As for our role in these days of upheaval: Lest the poet of rage proclaim once again 'The sun rose, the field flowered, the slayer slew'...Prepare to defend in case the enemy tries to destroy your city."[26]

Yet, the days of the Anti-Fascist Bloc in Warsaw were short-lived. On April 18, 1942, fifty-two Jews were dragged from their homes and shot in the streets, an action seemingly directed against underground activity. On May 30, 1942, the three main activists of the Communist Party were arrested, including Andrzej Szmidt (Pinkus Kartin), who was parachuted in by the Russians in December 1941. All three were executed, and the bloc was effectively shut down. Historian Israel Gutman claimed that the bloc continued to exist in the aftermath of these executions, but no evidence has been found of its continued activity after this date.[27]

A few days later, three members of the Hashomer Hatzair leadership—Josef Kaplan, Arie Wilner, and Mordechai Anielewicz—set out for Jewish communities in the provinces. Nothing is known about the deliberations that preceded their departure, but the course of events makes it possible to surmise their contents. It would appear that the leadership of Hashomer Hatzair decided to take a break from internal organizational activity in Warsaw and take advantage of the hiatus to pursue actions outside the capital. The delegates' main objectives were to spread the news about the extermination and create a base for armed underground resistance in the

24 Ibid., pp. 240–242.

25 "*Neged Hazerem*, April 1942," in Dror and Rosenzweig, *Sefer Hashomer Hatzair*, vol. 1, p. 525.

26 "Iton Hatnu'a, issue 3, April 1942," in Joseph Kermish, ed., *Itonut Hamahteret Hayehudit Bageto Varsha, Vol. 6: March 1942–July 1944* (Hebrew) (Jerusalem: Yad Vashem, 1997), p. 61. The quotation refers to the poem "In the City of Slaughter" by Hayim Nahman Bialik.

27 Gutman, *The Jews of Warsaw*, pp. 243–246.

provincial towns. According to the testimony of Abraham Zilberstein, a Hashomer member who assisted Anielewicz in stealing across the border into Reich territory, Mordechai Anielewicz carried with him copies of the movement's bulletins and many reports that included testimonies as well as instructions for defensive action.[28]

Anielewicz's visit to Zagłębie was thus planned as a continuation of the shift in strategy that had been initiated in Warsaw. In Będzin, he found a group of high-level *shomrim* in a state of disarray. The internal problems of the *ken* were now dwarfed by a new and much more worrisome threat: The Jews of Będzin and Sosnowiec were gradually being deported to unknown destinations.

The Beginning of the Deportations

The first deportation of Zagłębien Jews took place roughly two months before Anielewicz's arrival, on March 19, 1942.[29] It likely involved the displacement of several dozen or even hundreds of Jews from Sosnowiec and the surrounding area, although it seems to have been overshadowed by the large deportations that followed. Most of the evidence holds that the first deportation to Auschwitz took place only in May 1942.[30] At any rate, it appears that the Jews of Będzin and Sosnowiec did not attach much importance to the March deportation. They may have believed that this was part of the Germans' punitive policy. Several public hangings that were held in April 1942 only reinforced this impression. The hangings took place in Będzin and Sosnowiec concurrently, and according to the order of the Gestapo commander Dreier, all Jewish residents of the two cities had to be present at the hangings.[31]

28 Abraham Zilberstein (Adam), *Bageta'ot Varsha, Tzenstohov [Warsaw and Częstochowa]* (Hebrew) (Merhavia: Sifriat Poalim, 1945), pp. 43–44.

29 Szewa (Sheva) Ingster testimony, 1944, Moreshet Archive, C.53.1.24.

30 The commandant of Auschwitz Rudolf Höss testified that deportees from Eastern Upper Silesia were brought to Auschwitz in January 1942. See Rudolf Hoess, *Commandant of Auschwitz: The Autobiography of Rudolf Hoess* (London: Phoenix Press, 2000). See also Mazia, *Re'im Basa'ar*, pp. 73–74. Records from Auschwitz show an unknown number of Jews who were deported from Bytom on February 19, 1942. Aleksandra Namysło, ed., *Zagłada Żydów Zagłębiowskich* (Będzin: Instytut Pamięci Narodowej—Komisja Ścigania Zbrodni przeciwko Narodowi Polskiemu, Oddział w Katowicach, 2004), p. 30.

31 D. Liwer, *Ir Hametim*, pp. 64–65.

The mass deportations began in May 1942. A few days earlier, in late April 1942, the Judenräte of Będzin and Sosnowiec sent out thousands of summonses to Jews designated for "resettlement" (*Umsiedlung*). These notices were sent to Jewish families with two or more children, as well as adults who did not work in German-approved factories. Among these were a large number of refugees, elderly people, and women whose husbands were out of town. News spread in Sosnowiec that they would be sent to Theresienstadt, the special ghetto established in the Protectorate of Bohemia and Moravia for elderly Jews and those who had special rights under the Reich. The deportees were ordered to hand over the keys to their lodgings to the Judenrat officials, and they were allowed to take 25 kilograms of luggage and provisions for three days. They were also told that they must equip themselves with a hammer and nails as well as any gear and clothing suitable for a prolonged sojourn—winter clothes, cooking utensils, and so on.[32]

The first deportation from Będzin was conducted quietly, in no small part due to the promise made by the local Judenrat that Fania Czarna, Merin's deputy, would accompany the groups on their journey. On May 12, around 1,000 people arrived at the designated meeting point at the orphanage. Old people were escorted by their sons, disabled people were pushed in wheelchairs by members of the Jewish police. From there, they were led in an organized manner to the train station.[33]

In Sosnowiec, on the other hand, there was some unrest. On May 10, 1942, only a small portion of those selected for deportation—according to the Judenrat's lists—showed up. The Gestapo put pressure on Merin, and Jewish policemen led by Czarna set out to forcibly bring in the defectors, albeit with limited success.[34] The Gestapo lost patience. Its men surrounded a number of large houses in the city and, with the help of the Jewish police, dragged out the Jews living there and took them to the departure point. The hunt continued the next day as well, and on

32 Szternfinkiel, *Zagłada Żydów Sosnowca*, p. 33; Wiederman, *Płowa Bestia*, p. 133; Anonymous Judenrat clerk testimony, YVA, O.12/3; "Kos Hayegonim shel Yehudey Bendin" (Hebrew), Melech Noy collection, Pinchas Lavon Institute, IV/104; Fredka Mazia, *Re'im Basa'ar*, p. 75; D. Liwer, *Ir Hametim*, pp. 56–66.

33 D. Liwer, *Ir Hametim*, pp. 56–66; Anonymous Judenrat clerk testimony, YVA, O.12/3; "Kos Hayegonim shel Yehudey Bendin," Pinchas Lavon Institute, IV/104.

34 Unlike the obliging Fania Czarna, Józek Kożuch, leader of Hanoar Hatzioni and head of the youth council of the Judenrat, refused to take part in locating and handing over candidates for deportation. See Mazia, *Re'im Basa'ar*, p. 75.

May 12, 1942, a train loaded with 1,500 deportees left Sosnowiec.[35] Several hundred young Jews were also deported to labor camps.

During May and June 1942, the Germans extended the deportations to other Zagłębien towns while continuing their operations in Będzin and Sosnowiec. Hundreds of deportees from Będzin were added to the transport of Jews from the Zagłębie communities. Some of them were victims of a manhunt conducted by the Gestapo in several buildings on Modrzejowska Street. Included in this deportation were the mentally ill, the elderly, and even children from the orphanage, according to the lists of the local Judenrat. The second deportation also numbered around 1,000 Jews.[36] In addition to these, hundreds of other young Jews were deported from Będzin to the labor camps in June. Chajka was aware of this:

> It began with posters saying they wanted to resettle 300 Jews in the Generalgouvernement area for labor and that would be that. The Judenrat sent summons to the elderly, to large families without work relying on public institutions. Everyone complied, those who did not come were threatened with sanctions, told that their whole families would be taken. Sons and daughters brought in their elderly fathers and mothers, thinking why should the whole family suffer. On the streets, one could see elderly men in particular making their way with little bundles on their backs, carrying broomsticks or umbrellas. It would be funny if it weren't so tragic. But the Germans were not satisfied with 300. The number increased. For some time, everything was quiet, then the Judenrat began to move against the so-called undesirable elements of society. They were ordered to cooperate with the resettlement efforts. They knew people would not come of their own accord anymore. We never had any news from those who had been resettled. People began to surmise that

35 According to the testimony of a woman from Sosnowiec, the total rose as high as 2,000, and according to the records, 1,500 Jews from Sosnowiec and 586 Jews from Gleiwitz arrived in Auschwitz in May 1942. See the anonymous testimony of a woman from Sosnowiec, YVA, O.12/26. See also Namysło, *Zagłada Żydów Zagłębiowskich*, p. 30.

36 David Liwer estimated the number of deportees at about 1,200. See D. Liwer, *Ir Hametim*, p. 69. Auschwitz records indicate that 2,000 Jews were deported from Będzin in May 1942. See Namysło, *Zagłada Żydów Zagłębiowskich*, p. 30. For more on this deportation, see also Alexander Gutman and Esther Gutman-Herzberg, "Bageto Bendin: Protocol" (Hebrew), Massuah Archive, AR-PS-00089-012 (1973), pp. 172–179. Esther Herzberg's testimony was collected in the fall of 1943.

> they had been taken away to be killed. Everyone remembered Laskier's story of Chełmno.[37]

It is unclear whether the first deportation from Będzin comprised only 300 victims, but as for the manner in which it took place, Chajka's testimony is consistent with others.[38] Nevertheless, the violent nature of the deportations, their definition as "resettlement," and the lack of clear information about the destination of the trains and the fate of the deportees created a sense of terror among the Jewish population in the area. The deportations also highlighted the helplessness of the youth movements, however active they may have been. They found the ground slipping under their feet, and a sense of frustration and depression threatened to paralyze all activity. The educational work in which Chajka and her comrades had invested all their energy for two years appeared to have been for naught. Whom would they educate? And to what end?

> It was a period of stagnation in the life of our young people. After that great blossom[ing] came a period of moral dissatisfaction. Less activity. The educational work had come to a halt. Here and there you hear that everything is falling apart inside a given organization. Everything is resting on feet of clay—the slightest wind will cause it all to collapse. Narrow-mindedness has begun to creep into our ranks. What are its causes?
>
> Every educator has to have their own [personal] aim he's trying to achieve as well as his own educational aim. Toward what goal are we educating the children?
>
> Toward [Mandatory] Palestine? It's ridiculous. Toward the Soviets? Or to be *stam* [simply] men? What for?
>
> It was already clear to us that a systematic, gradual annihilation of Jewry was in progress. So, what was the education toward? Toward death?[39]

The deep despair in these words reflects a process of painful disillusionment. Until now, the youth movement members had been sheltered by their distinctive culture, which acted like a protective shell

37 Klinger, 1944 diaries, Haogen II, pp. 44–45.

38 D. Liwer, *Ir Hametim*, p. 66. Photographs attributed to this deportation document Jewish policemen taking people in wheelchairs to the departure point.

39 Klinger, *I Am Writing These Words to You* (1943 diaries), p. 94.

separating them from reality. However, the values that had guided their actions thus far appeared irrelevant in the face of the nightmare of extermination—the dream of immigrating to the Land of Israel was more distant than ever. A Soviet-oriented education likewise meant futile anticipation of the arrival of the Red Army. Education for the sake of "just being a person" with a universal value system seemed equally pointless. There was nothing left but death.

Anielewicz and the Idea of Jewish Resistance

Amid this atmosphere of despondency, Mordechai Anielewicz arrived like a gust of fresh air, capable of blowing a new flame into dying embers. Faced with despair, he proposed a bold new alternative: the establishment of a Jewish underground. In her 1943 diaries, Chajka wrote:

> There was a need for a new spark, a current that would stimulate, invigorate the young people and incite them to act, to fight.
>
> And Mordechai came and told us about what was happening in the world, about the underground struggle for liberation in the mountains of Serbia, about the grand deed in Czechoslovakia, about the partisans in the Polish forests. And he asked where the young Jews were, for they had to participate in that struggle for liberation as they had always done in every epoch.[40]

In the later 1944 version, she wrote: "Under these circumstances, Mordechai played an exceptional role not only in the life of our movement but also of all the youths in Zagłębie. He was the spark, the electric current that moved us all, gave us new meaning and a new direction in our life and work."[41]

The information Anielewicz brought with him was tough to swallow: He told the youths about the murder of Jews in Ponary, about the slaughter in the streets of Lwów. He confirmed the rumors about Chełmno and said that there was an exact report on its layout and the process of extermination. According to Chajka, he even said that a new slaughterhouse near Warsaw called Treblinka had been established.[42] Her

40 Ibid., p. 95.

41 Klinger, 1944 diaries, Haogen II, p. 23.

42 Wajsbort, *Yahad U'badad*, pp. 59–60.

testimony is consistent with the information that the youth movements in Warsaw had at the time: They knew about Treblinka, although it was not yet clear what exactly was happening there.

Some of Anielewicz's young listeners had a hard time digesting the news. Fela Katz, then a young Hashomer trainee in Sosnowiec, later testified:

> I will never forget the first debate when Mordechai told us about the actions of the Germans...Ina stood up and protested: "It is impossible that they should take young and healthy people and kill them in this way." We were all young. We couldn't imagine it. So, Mordechai read out the names of people we knew and proved his claims with numbers and facts.[43]

A similar experience was reported by Inka Puterman (later Wajsbort), a Hashomer Hatzair member from Zawiercie. The seventeen-year-old Inka, eager to impress the big shot delegate from Warsaw, was excitedly telling him about the educational activities her group had been engaged with, when Anielewicz cut her off saying: "What you're telling me now is no longer important…We are under threat of annihilation. That is the problem we need to deal with. People are being carted out of ghettos in cattle wagons. They're taking away the elderly, the children, and the sick. And they're not being taken to labor camps—but to extermination camps." Upon hearing this, Inka felt dizzy and came close to fainting.[44]

Yet, alongside the terrifying details that justified his current position, Anielewicz also told them the story of the first Jewish revolt. Chajka reported: "And he also mentioned Nowogródek, and how our young people locked themselves in and defended themselves with axes—all of them died, but they didn't walk like sheep to the slaughter. They managed to die a human death."[45] Tales of what happened in Nowogródek made the rounds among youth movement members in Warsaw and was even published in the underground press. But as far as we know, no attempt at self-defense took place there at that time. Nowogródek became a myth, a pedagogically useful illusion, another symbol in the chain of symbols held up by the Zionist youth: the heroes of Brzozowski's *Płomienie*, the fighters of the International Brigade in Spain, the Red Army soldiers.

43 Fela Katz testimony, Moreshet Archive, A.470.

44 Wajsbort, *Yahad U'badad*, pp. 59–60.

45 Klinger, *I Am Writing These Words to You* (1943 diaries), p. 97.

All the girls had tears in their eyes. As one Hanoar Hatzioni member would later write:

> Nowogródek, the small town that until then was only known as the hometown of one of Poland's greatest poets, Adam Mickiewicz, has become a symbol and a sign. Remember? "We longed for peace, but we also prepared for battle," this anthem of our last bastion—Adina whispered to me. Indeed. There was a clear statement being made here, which nestled in our hearts even though we did not know it, did not dare give voice to it.[46]

Anielewicz was thus able to tap into the thought patterns and the value system of Zagłębie's youth culture.

His ideological orientation at that time was aligned with the Anti-Fascist Bloc, which even though already inoperative by then, had shaped the concept of the new underground. Chajka's testimony, as well as others, indicates that Anielewicz's words and actions in Zagłębie were influenced by a Marxist analysis of the events and by an uncompromising belief in the power of the Soviet Union and the Red Army. Anielewicz was also part of the radical wing of the Hashomer leadership in Warsaw and had drafted the council's resolutions in May 1941 calling for a so-called Soviet Land of Israel.[47] Chajka wrote:

> That was when we found out about the Polska Partia Robotnicza (PPR) [Polish Workers' Party] and about our participation in it. And about the importance of partisan warfare during that period of the fighting. And that with the opening of the second front in Europe the struggle behind the frontlines—sabotage of various kinds—would be of the greatest importance. The individual third-front lines of workers would now determine the course of the war. [...]
>
> The only subject of socialism—of actual strength—is the USSR. You can't count on the proletariat. You can only count on existing strength. The titanic struggle that is going on now will settle the fate of socialism for many, many years to come.

46 Mazia, *Re'im Basa'ar*, p. 84.

47 "Neged Hazerem, issue 5 (16), July 1941," in Fatal-Knaani, *The Jewish Underground Press, Vol. 3*, pp. 64–70.

> Every proletarian willing to fight for socialism has to take the side of the USSR and aid it in its heroic fight. Those claiming that the right moment hasn't come yet are opportunists.[48]

Chajka's account in the 1943 diaries documents the operations of the Anti-Fascist Bloc as Mordechai Anielewicz presented them to his listeners in Zagłębie:

> In Poland, the communists set up the Polska Partia Robotnicza (PPR), which was organizing partisan forces under the banner of an independent Poland. Why under the banner of a chauvinistic [slogan]? Because you couldn't come to the Polish masses with other [kinds of] slogans. They hated Soviet Russia as much as the Germans and thought that the Soviet occupier was as hateful as the German one. Masses should be approached with popular slogans. [...]
>
> A delegate from the USSR, who arrived in Warsaw literally from the sky (we were so happy about that) turned to us—the Jewish faction. Attempts were made to form a certain political/theoretical base, but they failed.... A bloc was formed on the basis of practical work in the political sphere.
>
> The committee consisted of Dror, us, communists. The PPR was carrying out intense propaganda activity. The life of the young acquired new meaning.[49]

The myth of the resistance in Nowogródek and the descriptions of the first actions of the Anti-Fascist Bloc had an electrifying effect on Anielewicz's listeners in Zagłębie. Their faith in his narrative was complete: "Mordechai rekindled the flame of hope in their hearts. He ignited a new light in their extinguished eyes."[50] In Chajka's eyes, it was a revelation:

> Our path had already become clear to us. *Hagana* [Heb. resistance or, literally, defense] is an inappropriate term. We didn't want to defend ourselves because we didn't stand a chance of succeeding. But to die an honorable, human death.
>
> We took a social task on our shoulders of not letting it—[the nation]—sleep peacefully, of not letting it delude itself that

48 Klinger, *I Am Writing These Words to You* (1943 diaries), p. 95.

49 Ibid., pp. 95–96.

50 Printout of *Sefer Hashomer Hatzair*, C.K. [Chajka Klinger], p. 28; Chajka Klinger file, Moreshet Archive, C.36.2.

> not everybody would go, that they wouldn't exterminate the entire nation.
>
> We had to bring the naked truth to it and terrify it with our stories about Vilna, Chełmno, Treblinka, Trawniki, Bełżec, Auschwitz—the sites of mass extermination of the Jewish nation.
>
> We organized young Jews brought up on faith in man and his goodness. We, who [had believed] in a caring world and people, the optimists, had become black ravens, pessimists who predicted that the demise of our entire nation was nigh. Yes, we had to open its eyes, prevent it from sedating itself on opium, and show it the naked reality, however horrible it was. Because we wanted to trigger a reaction. No revolutionary movement, let alone [a movement of] the young, had ever faced problems similar to ours—the single, naked fact of annihilation, of death. We stood face-to-face with it and found an answer. We found a path. We were still groping our way but we found a path and this is what was the most important—partisan warfare and *hagana*.[51]

Even though Chajka's mentions of Auschwitz and Bełżec are clearly the product of hindsight as information about these death camps was not yet available, her description of Anielewicz's influence is very much realistic and accurate. Fascinated by the young man's persona—but no less by the novel idea of the *hagana*—she expressed what would become the central motif of her life from that moment on—Jewish resistance. The woes of the "Trotskyist deviation," the frustration she had felt from the futility of educational work, and the fear of deportations all vanished as if they had never existed. And as was her way, once she became attached to an idea, she gave herself over to it wholly and unconditionally.

Anielewicz and Merin

Anielewicz stayed in Zagłębie for about three months, from early June to early September 1942. During this long stay, he dealt with a number of issues, and alongside his participation in the ideological debates and spreading the idea of resistance, he formed a relationship with the Judenrat and met with Merin and Mołczadski several times. The purpose of these meetings was to promote the idea of a mission abroad

51 Klinger, *I Am Writing These Words to You* (1943 diaries), pp. 97–98.

to communicate information about the exterminations taking place in Poland to the free world.

As far we know, this idea circulated in the pioneer movement circles as early as spring 1942 and also the following year. However, it seems that the events that followed immediately had a greater impact on Anielewicz. On July 22, 1942, the great deportation from Warsaw began. Thousands of Jews were gathered every day at the *Umschlagplatz* (transfer point), whereupon they were put on trains going to Treblinka. While the common folk continued to delude themselves, the youth movement activists knew that "Treblinka means death."[52] In August 1942, the first refugees from Warsaw arrived in Będzin, among them well-known public figures.[53] One of them brought a letter addressed to Anielewicz from fellow leadership member Josef Kaplan, which contained a detailed description of the deportations. Chajka, who must have read the letter, would later quote it from memory:

> All our people in the Hashomer Hatzair cell in Warsaw are assembled and ready. No, they will not go anywhere without resistance. They are ready to defend themselves. However, starvation weakens people tremendously. They falter. They realize these might be their last words, that tomorrow they might be dead. I shall say goodbye now. If any of them make it to [Mandatory] Palestine, they may pass along my greetings.[54]

These last lines of the letter caused fresh shock. "We felt an attitude of sanctity toward this letter," wrote Chajka, "it was passed from hand to hand and shook each person who read it to the core."[55] Other testimonies mention that Kaplan's letter was read at the youth movements' assembly and led to a deeper awareness of the exterminations.[56] With the arrival of the first testimonies from Warsaw, Anielewicz wished to return there as soon as possible. Later, Chajka would write:

52 Gutman, *The Jews of Warsaw*, pp. 222–224.

53 Among the refugees from Warsaw were Heini Bornstein, the Joint official, and Nathan Eck. See Nathan Eck, *Hato'im Bedarkey Hamavet: Hav'vai Vehagut Beyemey Hakilayon* (Hebrew) (Jerusalem: Yad Vashem, 1966), pp. 178–182; David Ron, *Hem Yorim: Eliezer Geler Mefaked Ezor Bemered Geto Varsha* (Hebrew) (Tel Aviv: Tarbut Vehinuch, 1960), pp. 62–65.

54 Klinger, 1944 diaries, Haogen II, p. 40.

55 Ibid.

56 Abraham Manela interview.

> Mordechai was running around Będzin like a man possessed. His whole heart was with Warsaw—but he had work to finish in the Reich [Zagłębie]. I asked him once: "Do you have family in Warsaw?"—He said to me: "I have a large family in Warsaw—the movement." He wanted to go back post haste. For days on end he would sit near the telephone linking us with the leadership in Warsaw. This way, the leadership was in constant contact with the provincial towns. There was terrible news: the slaughter of activists,[57] the death of Czerniaków.[58] Then came the message from Josef.[59]

We can assume that Anielewicz used the link with Warsaw to consult with his comrades and even to receive instructions regarding the continuation of his activities in Zagłębie, and that his decision to promote the subject of a mission abroad through Merin was made under the influence of the news from Warsaw, Kaplan's letter in particular.

Mordechai Anielewicz believed in Merin's power, probably because he still remembered cooperating with him on the escape attempt to Slovakia the previous year. The fact that he saw Merin as a Nazi collaborator does not contradict the fact that he continued to believe in the sincerity of his intentions and the strength of his influence. Chajka wrote:

> Anielewicz had one dream. They promised to help him get across the border. They had very good connections, they could have helped. He really wanted to go abroad, to England, America, [Mandatory] Palestine, Switzerland. To tell everyone what was happening here, to shake the world. He could have done that, and he believed it was possible. He was almost set to go as a Polish laborer to France, and then onward, but he couldn't manage it in the end, something went awry. He believed Moniek Merin would help him, but that was naïve. If Merin were to send anyone, it would be one of his own men. But, as Mordechai noted, who among his men would want to go? Didn't they collaborate with the Nazis? No one would understand them outside in the free world.[60]

57 This refers to the imprisonment and murder of the leaders of the Anti-Fascist Bloc on May 30, 1942.

58 Adam Czerniaków was the head of the Judenrat in Warsaw and committed suicide on July 23, 1942, the day after the beginning of the Great Deportation from Warsaw.

59 Chaja Klinger, "Hara'ayon Shehasir et Ruhenu" (Hebrew), *Mishmar*, April 20, 1945.

60 Klinger, 1944 diaries, Haogen II, p. 30.

Managing his relationship with Merin required a deft and delicate touch. After all, the establishment of the underground involved the agitation of the youth against the Judenrat, which Anielewicz himself constantly reiterated and emphasized. Chajka viewed the situation with a critical eye:

> He [Mordechai] would always tell us, first of all, [to liquidate] the Jewish traitors [collaborating with] the Gestapo.
>
> So how could his personal behavior be reconciled with the political struggle that he led? We frowned, but he [Mordechai] had an answer for that: he wanted to get abroad and they had promised him that. He very much wanted to leave but not in order to stay there. He wanted to shock the world. Oh, he would have done that so well! He was the right person for the job. But it wasn't about to happen.[61]

According to the testimony of Shmuel Ron, Anielewicz intended to get retribution against the Germans in a neutral country and thus "wake up the enlightened world and warn of the danger of mass extermination," but Shmuel also believed that Mordechai was wrong in his assessment of Merin's power.[62]

Evidence from Anielewicz's meetings with Merin indicates that Mordechai not only brought up the idea of the mission abroad with Merin but also passed on information about the exterminations. He probably also brought up the idea of defensive action.[63] During his time in Będzin, Anielewicz—in all likelihood—also met with Mołczadski. Chajka's account attests that Anielewicz's attitude toward the Judenrat was somewhat similar to a young child behaving insolently toward his parents:

> And he [Mordechai] didn't lack for moral courage either. He was able to criticize the Będzin *gmina* [Judenrat] chairman Chaim Mołczadski to his face and pass judgment on him before the *Leiter* [director—Merin]. Even though representatives of Jewish communities were afraid of him, they still received and entertained him.

61 Klinger, *I Am Writing These Words to You* (1943 diaries), p. 100.

62 Shmuel Ron interview.

63 Ibid.

> And he was content like a scamp playing a trick—that he was eating in their homes, that they were throwing parties for him, and that they made the effort to visit him on the farm while he was printing anti-German flyers almost right under their noses.[64]

Mołczadski and Merin rejected the idea of defensive action, while the idea of the mission abroad was simply not in their power to implement. And as for the news about the exterminations, we do not know how they reacted to Anielewicz's reports. In public, Merin and Mołczadski were generally careful—even in later periods—not to speak of "exterminations," but of "deportations" only.

Nevertheless, Merin also gained respect for Anielewicz. Dr. Nathan Eck, who arrived in Zagłębie shortly after Anielewicz's departure from there in fall 1942, testified that Merin told him: "Here, in Zagłębie, there are no young people with judgment and status equal to Mordechai Anielewicz."[65] Eck was surprised to hear the infamous head of the Judenrat speaking about Mordechai Anielewicz with sincere and unreserved admiration. He reminded Merin that Mordechai was the architect of the Jewish uprising and a zealous believer in the idea of armed resistance. To this Merin replied that he was not opposed to resistance in principle either and only feared that the young people were reckless and irresponsible and could cause a premature crisis. He then declared that he knew where to get weapons, and when the time came, he would make sure that they would be found in Jewish hands. Yet, only he would determine when such a time arrived, if there was no other way out.[66]

Dr. Eck could not, of course, vouch for the sincerity of Merin's statements, but youth movement members from Będzin also attested to the respect Merin showed Anielewicz. Albeit representative of two radically opposed viewpoints and cultures suspended in open conflict at that point, the two men were, after all, partners in destiny.

64 Klinger, *I Am Writing These Words to You* (1943 diaries), pp. 99–100.
65 Nathan Eck testimony, Moreshet Archive, A.552.
66 Ibid.

Chapter Twelve

The Great *Punkt*

Fiszel Does Not Forgive: 1987

I am interviewing Abraham Fiszel in a modest apartment situated in the heart of a large housing project in Lod. Fiszel is still the portrait of a typical Dror-Freiheit man, a working boy encouraged by the movement to cherish hard labor and straight talk, imbued with a faith in the power of the class struggle to right society's wrongs. His hands are solid, his manner common, his clothes simple. Hebrew tumbles awkwardly from his lips, and he supplements it with frequent words in Yiddish.

Fiszel is the son of a Będzin coachman, and he and his seven brothers and sisters grew up on Modrzejowska Street—like Mother. His father barely earned a living. "What games did you play when you were little?" Fiszel pauses for a long time before replying: "Games? When my first son was born here and I bought him his first toy, I stayed up all night playing with it." It was Zivia Lubetkin who had introduced him to the youth movement. She had given him a revolutionary book in Yiddish and said: "Study it." His father was furious: "No son of mine will read a banned book under my roof." But Abraham held fast: "I will not bring pork into the house, but I will not set foot in the synagogue either." To which Fiszel the elder responded: "I will light black candles in your name." Nevertheless, they eventually managed to reach a compromise, and Abraham became a valuable member of the movement. By the time the war started, he was already a member of the Będzin *ken* leadership.[1]

1 Abraham Fiszel, interview by the author, Lod, 1988.

Fiszel still holds a grudge against the Judenrat as "an instrument in the hands of the Gestapo." The way in which the first deportation was carried out left deep scars on his soul. He was shocked by the actions of the Jewish establishment: "What the Gestapo failed to do, we did ourselves through the Judenrat and the Jewish police. There was no difference between them and their masters, except for the Star of David on their sleeves," he testified shortly after the war.[2]

In 1963, Fiszel was called to testify in the trial of Hirsch Barenblatt, head of the Jewish ghetto police in Będzin. It was an electrifying trial. For the first time ever, a senior Judenrat official was being tried in Israel by the same law previously used to judge the Nazis and their collaborators. Fiszel was a key witness in the trial. He testified to having seen with his own eyes the accused together with other Jewish policemen transferring children from the orphanage where Fiszel had worked to the roundup point for deportation. When the defense attempted to undermine Fiszel's testimony by questioning his reliability and mocking his speech, Fiszel was deeply offended. "He was presenting me as an ignoramus, a primitive savage," he tells me now.

Still, the Tel Aviv District Court believed Fiszel, even though he was the only witness to testify to this particular event. This latter fact served as the grounds for the Supreme Court's later decision to overturn the verdict.[3] Fiszel returned to his home bitter and sore. He now quotes the words of Zivia Lubetkin, who once told him: "Abramaleh, they have never understood us, and they never will." Fiszel remained a Dror-Freiheit man until the end of his days. He also refused to accept compensation money from Germany, despite all he had endured, despite his modest lifestyle. About a year after the interview, Abraham Fiszel died of cancer. A short time before his death, he called me sounding confused, wishing me to find out some more information, perhaps asking that justice finally be done.[4]

At the time of the Barenblatt trial, Mother was no longer among the living; yet, her diaries testified in her place. Barenblatt's name was not

2 Abraham Fiszel, YVA, M.1.E/1150. See also Moreshet Archive, Avihu Ronen collection, 235.

3 Hirsch Barenblatt was sentenced to five years in prison by the District Court and then acquitted by the Supreme Court. "Barenblatt vs. The Legal Adviser, criminal appeal 77/64, verdict 18 (2) 70, 101," *Piskey Beit Din shel Beit Hamishpat Ha'elyon* (Hebrew) (Jerusalem: Nevo, 1989).

4 Abraham Fiszel interview.

mentioned in the diaries, but her position regarding the Judenrat was firm, and the diaries were a serious indictment against the organization and the men who ran it. Mother's name came up in the trial in other contexts as well. In the winter of 1943, after the liquidation of the ghetto, Barenblatt fled across the border to Slovakia with his girlfriend Kasia, who was a Hashomer Hatzair trainee. Barenblatt claimed to have had a hand in Mother's escape at an earlier date. Of course, mother was not there to either confirm or deny this allegation, but Father, who testified on behalf of the prosecution, told the court that when he had first met Mother, after they had both crossed the border into Slovakia, Mother had identified Barenblatt as a Nazi collaborator. Father's testimony continued that later, when Barenblatt had asked Mother to testify in his favor at his trial in Poland, Mother responded with an outburst of rage. Even with the benefit of hindsight, she could not forgive. It was during Father's testimony when he admitted for the first time in public that mother took her own life.

It was intended that Mother's diaries would play an important role in describing the main events that were brought up in the trial. In particular, there was a very detailed discussion of Barenblatt's part in the mass selection of the Jews of Zagłębie on August 12, 1942. On that day, over 10,000 Jews were deported to Auschwitz.[5] It was a terrible day of hope and terror, of expectations and disillusionment, the day when the German intention to exterminate the Jews—though unimaginable—could no longer be denied. Everyone was there: Fiszel as a member of Dror, Barenblatt in his position as the deputy chief of the Jewish police in Będzin, Mother as a youth movement leader helplessly looking on, Ka-Tzetnik in his literary guise as "Harry Preleshnik," David Liwer who was always close to the center of events, as well as Merin, Mołczadski, and over 40,000 other Jews from Będzin, Sosnowiec, and Dąbrowa Górnicza. None of those who survived forgot that day. It is etched in their memory as the day when reality changed beyond recognition. What follows is a detailed description of the days leading up to the mass deportation to Auschwitz, based on the available evidence. Mother's testimony is one of them.

5 This figure ranges from 10,000 to 11,500. See the end of this chapter for more on this number.

The Jews of Zagłębie: August 1942

In August 1942, the wave of deportations in Zagłębie had reached its peak. The deportations were carried out on a selective basis: only those Jews who were considered nonessential to the German system were deported to Auschwitz. While the Judenrat had selected the candidates for the initial deportations, a new deportation method was implemented for the first time in Chrzanów on May 30, 1942. The approximately 8,000 Jews of the town were ordered to report to three central points, and after an extensive selection, they were divided into three groups: The first, which consisted of workers in essential factories, remained in the city; the second, which consisted of young people, was sent to labor camps; and the third group, which consisted mainly of the elderly, women, children, and disabled people—about 3,000 in number—were sent to Auschwitz.[6]

Between March and July 1942, the Germans almost completed the selective deportation process in the region. Out of approximately 95,000 Jews living in Eastern Upper Silesia in 1941, about 17,000 Jews were deported to Auschwitz. By August, there were around 7,000 young Jews working in labor camps, while roughly 67,000 Jews were concentrated in ten large cities in the region.[7] Then came the turn of the largest Jewish communities in this region—Będzin, Sosnowiec, and Dąbrowa Górnicza. According to the estimate, there were approximately 24,000 Jews in Będzin, an equal amount in Sosnowiec, and just over 3,000

6 Bochner, *Sefer Kheshanov [Chrzanów]*, p. 289; Aharon Weiss and Abraham Wein, eds., *Pinkas Hakehilot Polin: Entziklopediya shel Hayishuvim Hayehudiyim Lemin Hivasdam Ve'ad Le'ahar Sho'at Milhemet Ha'olam Hashniya, Vol. 3, Galitziya Hama'aravit VeSileziya* (Hebrew) (Jerusalem: Yad Vashem, 1984), p. 275.

7 Until this time, there had been close to thirty Jewish communities in the area under the administration of the Central Judenrat in Sosnowiec. In the first wave of deportations, most of these communities were wiped out through the selection process. See Shlomo Spivak, ed., *Sefer Zikaron Lekdoshey Zavirtshe [Zawiercie] Vehasviva* (Hebrew and Yiddish) (Tel Aviv: Irgun Yotzey Zavirtshe Vehasviva, 1958), pp. 312–313; Zvi Yashiv, ed., *Olkush [Elkish]: Sefer Zikaron Lekehila Shehuheda Bashoah* (Hebrew) (Tel Aviv: Irgun Yotzey Olkush BeYisrael, 1972), p. 49; Jakubowicz, *Sefer Zikaron Lekehilot Vadovitze, Andrihov, Kalvarya, Mishlenitze, Suka* [*Wadowice, Andrychów, Kalvarija, Myslenice, Sucha*], p. 179; Abraham Wolf Jasny, ed., *Yizker Buch fun der Farpeynikter Klobutsker Kehile* (Yiddish) (Tel Aviv: Irgun Yotzey Klobuck, 1960), p. 245; Pinhas Goldwasser and Elimelech Gross, eds., *Kehilat Tshebin [Trzebinia]* (Hebrew) (Haifa: Irgun Yotzey Tshebin BeYisrael, 1969), pp. 1–9.

in Dąbrowa Górnicza. About a third of these Jews were considered essential workers.[8]

The Central Judenrat in Sosnowiec as well as the Judenrat in Będzin were involved in the deportations from the start. On the eve of the first deportation in Sosnowiec in May 1942, Merin gathered the senior Judenrat officials and presented them with the question of whether or not the Judenrat should take part in the upcoming deportations. Some of the Judenrat members objected, citing Maimonides: "And if the gentiles said to you: Give us one of your own and we shall kill him, lest all of you be killed—let all be killed, and not a single Israelite soul shall be delivered."[9] Yet, Merin disregarded their opinion. To his mind, as a statesman, he was faced with the choice of either ridding the community of the chaff or letting the Germans do the job and risk losing the wheat as well. It was a Realpolitik move through which Merin sought to save part of the community by sacrificing its weakest members. In the end, Merin won the necessary support from the Judenrat and the local rabbis. The rabbis initially responded to Merin's query in the negative, but after much deliberation, Rabbi Grossman of Mizrachi in Sosnowiec informed him that "there is no other way out but to take the path of lesser evil. They hope he proves the savior and redeemer of the remainder."[10] At the beginning of August 1942, when the Germans informed Merin that a document check would be conducted among all the Jews of Będzin, Sosnowiec, and Dąbrowa Górnicza on the twelfth of the month, Merin was already determined to continue on the path he had followed until then.

He thus began preparing for the great inspection. Not satisfied with simply summoning the Jews to the designated assembly points, which were mostly situated in large football fields, he tried to get broad public support for his measures by addressing the community directly in public meetings and making special proclamations calling for obedience to orders.[11] Similar tactics were deployed in Będzin. According to Chajka's

8 These statistical calculations are based on: Letter from Schmauser to *Reichsfuhrer-SS*, April, 20, 1942, Weiner Library, Tel Aviv University, 1386; Geshuri, in *Sefer Sosnovitz*; Stein, *Pinkas Bendin*; Mordehai Gelbart et al., eds., in *Sefer Dombrova Gurnitze* [*Dąbrowa Górnicza*] *Vehurbana* (Hebrew) (Tel Aviv: Irgun Yotzey Dombrova Gurnitze BeYisrael, 1974).

9 Wiederman, *Płowa bestia*, pp. 96–98.

10 D. Liwer, *Ir Hametim*, p. 68.

11 See "Dokumenty o Likwidacji Gett na Śląsku," *Biuletyn Żydowskiego Instytutu Historycznego*, Nr. 38 (1961), p. 114.

testimony, the propaganda had a manifest effect on the members of the youth movements:

> One day, the Judenrat announced that there would be a general registration of all the Jews. They all had to present themselves to the municipal officials, down to the last one. They must not be afraid as nothing bad would happen to them. They had to show up looking clean, well dressed, as if for a wedding. This registration was happening in all the towns and cities across the district simultaneously. This raised our suspicion: If it was a normal registration, why was it happening everywhere at the same time? Unless something else was about to happen and they didn't want word to spread from one town to another.
>
> We felt more and more uneasy. But everyone told us it would be fine. Even the greatest pessimists said the worst that could happen would be another *Arbeitseinsatz* [deportation to labor camps]. But no one even considered that we could be resettled. I was certain it was going be a trap, and indeed it was.[12]

Chajka's description is supported by a wealth of testimonies. At first, the youth movement activists believed that the call for inspection must not be obeyed. Shortly before the appointed time—and possibly due to Anielewicz's influence—leaflets were distributed by Hashomer Hatzair and Hanoar Hatzioni in Sosnowiec, calling on Jews not to report voluntarily. At the next public gathering, Merin addressed their position stating: "The hot-headed youths will bring a holocaust upon us. They will bring on the end I am trying to stave off...If their placards get into the hands of the Germans, we will pay a high price. Will you believe the cowardly and the irresponsible? It is thanks to my efforts and labors that you are here today."[13]

It would appear that the Germans were also aware of unrest in the area, so they performed a misdirection maneuver on the eve of the deportation. On August 11, 1942, one day before the date set for the great roundup, the Germans conducted a certificate-stamping operation in the nearby town of Czeladź, north of Sosnowiec, which was home to roughly 700 Jews at the time. The town's Jews were gathered at the appointed location, where the Gestapo stamped their documents, after which the

12 Klinger, 1944 diaries, Haogen II, pp. 46–47.

13 Mazia, *Re'im Basa'ar*, p. 87.

Jews were allowed to return to their homes. Several testimonies claim that the operation took place in the town of Modrzejów.[14]

On the eve of the great roundup—most likely August 11, 1942—representatives of the youth movements gathered to decide how they would act on the day of the roundup. Anielewicz was also present at the gathering and spoke out against showing up, but the local representatives knew that the Jewish population would present themselves at the designated time and place. If they chose not to come forward, they would be endangering not only themselves but also members of their families, who would be imprisoned as hostages. And so, despite their apprehensions and the presence of Anielewicz, the members of the youth movements decided to obey the orders along with their loved ones.[15]

The *Punkt*: August 12, 1942

5:00 AM in Będzin, Sosnowiec, Dąbrowa Górnicza: Assembly

In the early hours of the morning, the Jews of Będzin, Sosnowiec, and Dąbrowa Górnicza left their apartments and began walking toward the assembly points. The inspection was set to commence at 7:00 AM, but many wished to get there early. Later, Ka-Tzetnik would describe the spectacle he witnessed in Sosnowiec—his fictionalized "Metropolis"—as follows:

> [Jewish] mothers rose early to wash their children's hair, and made sure their families put on their Sabbath best. Houses were locked and shuttered; family by family, all the Jews streamed through the city streets; parents with babies in their arms, pushing infants in prams; a father with a baby's bottle in one hand, while with the other he supported an old grandfather who couldn't for the life of him fathom the purpose of this procession.[16]

14 Ibid., p. 85; D. Liwer, *Ir Hametim*, p. 73; Aharon Gelbart, in *Sefer Sosnovitz*, vol. 2, p. 121; Anonymous Judenrat clerk testimony, YVA, O.12/3.

15 D. Liwer, *Ir Hametim*, p. 73; Abraham Manela interview.

16 Ka-Tzetnik, *Sunrise over Hell*, p. 77.

In Będzin, a similar tableau presented itself before the eyes of a Judenrat clerk:

> As early as five in the morning, the Jews were already rushing to the spot, lest, God forbid, they be late. I was also rushing to be on time, and my sixty-five-year-old mother walked alongside me. The traffic was immense. Mothers carried their toddlers in prams, the elderly and sick were transported in carriages and carts. Everyone was dressed in their best clothes, as if they were going to a festive assembly. Grief nestled in the hearts of each and every one of them. Many openly said that this was them pulling all the Jews into a trap, and still, they all went.[17]

According to this same testimony, the Judenrat received instructions from the Gestapo to allow the nonappearance of sick people upon presentation of an appropriate medical certificate. But the sick were afraid to stay, lest the Gestapo men find them and kill them on the spot as an unproductive element. "Thus, you could say the entire Jewish quarter in Będzin was emptied that day and appeared dead."[18]

Chajka was also among the moving crowd. The youth movements had decided that attendance was necessary, and she acted accordingly. Yet, she bid her invalid sixty-two-year-old father to stay home. Leibel Klinger had no chance of passing the document inspection.[19]

7:00 AM in Sosnowiec, 8:00 AM in Będzin and Dąbrowa Górnicza: Registration

The time set for the start of registration had arrived. At seven o'clock, about 22,000 Sosnowiec Jews were waiting at the municipal sports field and at the city's seven large workshops. In Będzin, by eight o'clock, 20,000 Jews had gathered in the town's two sports fields: Hakoach and Sarmacja. In Dąbrowa Górnicza, 3,000 Jews gathered in front of the community building. They, too, were dressed in Shabbat clothing "as for a meeting among friends and loved ones."[20] The Będzin Judenrat workers began the

17 Anonymous Judenrat clerk testimony, YVA, O.12/3.

18 Ibid.

19 Klinger, 1944 diaries, Haogen II, p. 47; Shmuel Ron interview.

20 The estimates above are based on: D. Liwer, *Ir Hametim*, p. 73; Anonymous Judenrat clerk testimony, YVA, O.12/3; Anonymous testimony of a woman from Sosnowiec,

registration process as soon as people entered the sports fields. At the entrance to the field, everyone was given a serial number, after which they proceeded to one of the small tables set up in the middle of the field to be registered by Judenrat officials. Only a few Germans were to be seen. The Jewish police kept order. It was a beautiful morning, and children were playing on the grass. Everything seemed fine.[21]

Ten-year-old Reuven Wekselman lived near the Hakoach sports field. Throughout the morning, he and his family had watched the stream of people flowing into the field. They were not sure whether to join the walkers. When they saw Jewish policemen passing among the houses to round up latecomers, Wekselman senior grabbed Reuven and his brothers and marched them to the field.[22] Hirsch Barenblatt, the deputy chief of the Jewish police in Będzin, together with about fifty policemen kept order inside the field. Barenblatt also brought his family along as required of Judenrat officials. Things were similar in Sosnowiec and Dąbrowa Górnicza. Thousands stood and waited patiently for the Germans to proceed with the registration.[23]

9:00 AM in Będzin: The Long Wait

The August sun climbed higher in the sky. It was getting rather hot. Those who had remembered to bring water took out their bottles and drank. People were sitting on the grass waiting for whatever was to come.

By ten o'clock in Będzin, the Judenrat officials had completed their registration: over 90 percent of the Jews had shown up for inspection.[24] A few refugees—mainly those from the Generalgouvernement and towns in the Będzin area—chose to hide, frightened by memories of deportation still fresh in their minds. Among them was Mordechai Anielewicz, who opted to hide in Ada Neufeld's house.[25] She herself attended the inspection with her recently widowed mother. A number of elderly and sick Jews

YVA, O.12/26; Gelbart, *Sefer Dombrova Gurnitze* [*Dąbrowa Górnicza*] *Vehurbana*, pp. 395, 397.

21 D. Liwer, *Ir Hametim*, p. 73; Anonymous Judenrat clerk testimony, YVA, O.12/3.

22 Reuven Wekselman testimony at the Barenblatt trial, Moreshet Archive, D.1.5366, pp. 45–50.

23 Hirsch Barenblatt testimony at the Barenblatt trial, Moreshet Archive, D.1.5366, pp. 70–78; Ka-Tzetnik, *Sunrise over Hell*, pp. 76–78.

24 D. Liwer, *Ir Hametim*, p. 73; Anonymous Judenrat clerk testimony, YVA, O.12/3; Anonymous testimony of a woman from Sosnowiec, YVA, O.12/26.

25 Ada Halperin (Neufeld) interview.

also failed to turn up, among them Abraham Manela, the twenty-year-old son of the deputy head of the Judenrat Moshe Manela, who was ill that day. The Germans appeared to be few and far between, and it was assumed that they would not conduct searches for no-shows.[26] The same was true of Sosnowiec and Dąbrowa Górnicza—there were few known cases of refugees and elderly persons who chose not to attend.[27]

10:00 AM in Dąbrowa Górnicza: Selection

While the Jews of Będzin were waiting, the selection began in Dąbrowa Górnicza.[28] Fifteen-year-old Esther Kaminsky, a Hashomer Hatzair trainee, recalled:

> Suddenly, armed SS men appeared. There was pushing, shouting, and threats of murder. We were divided into four groups: The first was designated to go home, the second was young people destined for labor camps, the third was people both young and old taken as the SS man pleased, some despite even having the *sonderkarte* [the Special Commissioner's employee card]. In the fourth group were elderly people who would be sent to Auschwitz.[29]

At the same time, things were starting to look tense in Sosnowiec. They were as of yet unaware of the goings-on in Dąbrowa Górnicza, but an order had come in to transfer to the sports field those who had turned up for inspection at the workshops. The Jewish police were sent to carry out the order. The members of the Klajner family, who had waited for many long hours on their feet, turned to go with the 500 people who were concentrated in their designated workshop. The road was long, and their legs hurt.[30] At the sports field, they noticed the long lines of workshop employees approaching the area. The crowding and nervousness

26 Ibid.

27 Bracha Habas, *Yeladim Mutzalim* (Hebrew) (Tel Aviv: Am Oved, 1945), p. 127; *Sefer Dombrova Gurnitze* [*Dąbrowa Górnicza*] *Vehurbana*, p. 412.

28 Gelbart, *Sefer Dombrova Gurnitze* [*Dąbrowa Górnicza*] *Vehurbana*, p. 395. According to David Liwer, the selection process in Dąbrowa began earlier than in Będzin.

29 Ibid., p. 389.

30 Habas, *Yeladim Mutzalim*, pp. 127–128; Anonymous testimony of a woman from Sosnowiec, YVA, O.12/26.

intensified, as did the heat: "The sun beat down mercilessly on people's heads. Children were running around thirsty and pestering their parents with demands. The noise and commotion grew worse and worse."[31]

Tensions also rose in Będzin. A rumor reached David Liwer in the Hakoach field that armed SS guards and policemen had surrounded the field. No one was allowed to leave, not even the Judenrat officials. They had no knowledge at this point of what was happening in Dąbrowa Górnicza. Jochanan Ranz, a member of Dror, also kept an eye on the armed guards. If he had misgivings about presenting himself at the inspection before, he now realized that it was too late to turn back.[32] Rutka Laskier also realized that the decisive hour was at hand: "We were in a pretty good mood until nine o'clock. Then I looked beyond the fence and I saw soldiers with machine guns aimed at the square in case someone tried to escape (how could you possibly escape from here?)."[33]

12:00 PM in Będzin: Fears

It was now midday, and according to the plan for the day, everyone should have returned to their homes by now; yet nothing was happening. Strewn around the grassy field, the assembled were languishing in the heat. "People fainted, children cried. In short—Judgment Day. People were thirsty, and there was not a single drop of water around."[34] Rumors from Dąbrowa Górnicza reached the Judenrat: The Jews had been sorted into three groups, and only the young men with worker's certificates were being released. Moshe Manela, the deputy chairman of the Judenrat in Będzin, now confided in Liwer that "the Gestapo tricked us."[35] He feared for the fate of the women and children gathered in the field. It was thus clear to the Judenrat in Będzin that a mass selection would be conducted there as well. The only question was who would be in charge: Dreier, the Gestapo man, or Friedrich Kuczyński, the representative of the Special Commissioner. There was still hope that if it was Kuczyński, then the selection would be for the labor camps rather than deportation.[36]

31 Mazia, *Re'im Basa'ar*, p. 89.
32 D. Liwer, *Ir Hametim*, p. 73; Ranz, *In Nazi Claws*, p. 51.
33 Rutka Laskier, *Rutka's Notebook: January–April 1943* (Jerusalem: Yad Vashem, 2007), p. 37.
34 Ibid.
35 D. Liwer, *Ir Hametim*, p. 73.
36 Ibid.

1:00 PM in Będzin: Selection

And indeed, their hopes were answered. At 1:00 PM, Kuczyński and the Special Commissioner officials arrived at the field, accompanied by several aides. A few of the Germans wore uniforms, whereas the rest wore civilian clothing. The mood brightened somewhat as after all, it was the Special Commissioner's office who would be running the operation. With the help of a few SS men and Jewish policemen, the entire Jewish population (around 12,000 people) was concentrated in one-half of the field. Several tables were placed in its center before Kuczyński, Kronau, and a number of Jewish Judenrat officials—Mołczadski apparently one of them—took their seats behind them. The Jews began to file past the tables. The Judenrat official identified them by name, and in accordance with Kuczyński's instructions, they were assigned to one of three different groups assembling in the other half of the field. The Jews waiting in line quickly realized that the first group consisted of workers with work certificates; those with small families, some of whom had work permits, were sent to the second group; and the third group consisted of elderly Jews and large families.[37] The Judenrat clerk awaiting her turn knew immediately that this selection was meant to separate "1) the productive class, whose certificates would be signed immediately; 2) those who were provided for, and whose fate would be determined later; 3) the 'redundant' class who would be deported immediately." Others listed four groups: those who would be allowed to go home, those provided for, those destined for labor camps, and those destined for deportation.[38]

Lipa Klajman barely made it to the selection table. There was great hustle and bustle. At the table, he found himself separated from his ten-year-old sister. He was sent to the group of young people with workers' certificates. His sister disappeared from sight.[39] Ada Neufeld was separated from her mother, who was made to join the group of elderly people and those with large families.[40] Thirteen-year-old Rutka Laskier was separated from her family and assigned to "labor." To her, this was a fate worse than deportation. She approached the group designated for forced labor feeling stunned and defeated. Several of her friends were

37 Hirsch Barenblatt testimony at the Barenblatt trial, Moreshet Archive, D.1.5366, pp. 70–78; Ranz, *In Nazi Claws*, p. 52.

38 Anonymous Judenrat clerk testimony, YVA, O.12/3.

39 Lipa Klajman testimony at the Barenblatt trial, Moreshet Archive, D.1.5366, pp. 66–70.

40 Klinger,1944 diaries, Haogen II, p. 54; Ada Halperin (Neufeld) interview.

already sitting there. "The strange thing was that we didn't cry at all, not even a little bit. We didn't shed a single tear."[41] Hirsch Barenblatt also approached the table in the company of his family members. They showed their papers, were directed to the first group, and were released to their homes immediately afterward. Barenblatt himself accompanied them to the exit, then returned alone.[42] He and his men were busy keeping order on the field, and according to many witnesses, they took special precautions to prevent the different groups from mixing.[43]

Little by little, the Jews had begun to comprehend the meaning of this selection, and there were attempts to sneak out and switch groups. Turmoil erupted. According to Chajka's testimony:

> Soon everyone realized that one set was meant for resettlement, the second was for *Arbeitseinsatz*, the third meant being let go. The Jews became afraid of approaching the Germans. Jewish police began to beat people with clubs to force them to stand in rows and approach the commission, and the Germans were not looking at any papers or documents, but rather at faces. The young were let go, the elderly and children were to be resettled. If they didn't like someone, they screamed right in their face: "Die, you piece of trash!"[44]

3:00 PM in Sosnowiec: Rumors

In Sosnowiec, seven hours had passed since the time set for the beginning of registration, and nothing had happened. The tension was at its zenith. Heat exhaustion and thirst were now exacerbated by hunger. Most people had obeyed the orders of the Judenrat and had not stocked up on food. The Judenrat finally decided to bring loaves of bread to the waiting Jews. Jewish policemen were sent to carry out the mission. When the bread arrived, a riot broke out. The SS officers took the bread, arranged the Jews in rows, and beat with rubber batons anyone who approached in the hope of receiving some. It would appear that news about what was happening in Będzin and Dąbrowa Górnicza had reached Sosnowiec by

41 Laskier, *Rutka's Notebook*, p. 37.

42 Hirsch Barenblatt testimony at the Barenblatt trial, Moreshet Archive, D.1.5366, pp. 70–78.

43 Reuven Wekselman testimony at the Barenblatt trial, Moreshet Archive, D.1.5366, pp. 45–50.

44 Klinger, 1944 diaries, Haogen II, pp. 47–48.

now. The crowd was abuzz with rumors. They were saying that the Jews of Sosnowiec were slated for deportation, yet at that very moment, the owners of the German workshops were calling Berlin, trying to convey their dissatisfaction with the decree. Then they said that Berlin had replied: "The Jews most indispensable to the Germans will be released."[45]

4:00 PM in Będzin and Dąbrowa Górnicza: Rioting and Shots Fired

Meanwhile, the selection process continued in Będzin and Dąbrowa Górnicza. Ranz paints a picture of Kuczyński standing like a statue in the middle of the Hakoach field and screaming at the victim before him: one, two, or three. Mostly three. Whenever anyone tried to show him documents in an attempt to save their lives, he would simply kick them with mad fury. About an hour before, the Gestapo head Dreier had visited to check that everything was going well. The refined figure of the highly educated Dreier stood in stark contrast to the crude and violent Kuczyński. The Judenrat clerk noticed that a group of elegant German ladies had arrived on the field with him. The ladies "enjoyed the sight of the frightened Jewish crowd and strolled there for pleasure for a long time while laughing out loud."[46]

As the hours rolled by, the third group grew larger, and it became evident to all that it consisted of people destined for deportation. Riots broke out in various corners of the field. Chajka wrote:

> Those who still harbored any illusions about resettlement stopped kidding themselves; but the worst was yet to come. The Germans made it into a game: children to be resettled, parents to be let free, or the other way around. This became horrendous. Children would chase their parents, mothers would run after the children, they were separated by force, with clubs and gun barrels. They were dragged apart, the mothers hauled away by their hair. The first shots were fired. The Jewish militia showed what they could do. Those who did manage to join the groups being let go were pulled back by force. A mother with a baby in a pram somehow managed to sneak over to the other side. A Jewish militiaman

45 Mazia, *Re'im Basa'ar*, p. 85.

46 Anonymous Judenrat clerk testimony, YVA, O.12/3.

> found her, grabbed the pram, and threw it. The baby fell out of the pram and onto the stones; it died on the spot. We remembered this militiaman's surname very well.[47]

Rutka Laskier likewise witnessed the murder of an infant, as written in her diary six months later: "I saw, how a soldier tore a baby, who was only a few months old, out of mother's hands and bashed his head against an electric pylon. The baby's brains splashed on the wood. The mother went crazy."[48] A group of Hashomer Hatzair activists congregated around Chajka and David. They were frustrated by the feeling of helplessness. Chajka and David had to respond to their demands:

> It's true that the fields were surrounded by fences guarded by German soldiers; but there were 10,000 people gathered in both fields, and we could have squashed the guards with our bare hands.
>
> Our youths stood in the field and bit their lips in anger. "We have to do something," they said to us. But the instructors didn't know how to respond, because we hadn't prepared anything. They were prevented from deciding anything without the consent of all the other movements. After all, you can't organize anything on your own. You can't trust the crowd. You never know how they will react. Each of them thinks to themselves: maybe I'll get lucky, maybe I'll get out.[49]

4:00 PM in Sosnowiec: Panic

At about 4:00 PM, a riot suddenly broke out in Sosnowiec. SS men were seen encircling the sports field in a long chain. The Jewish police received an order to gather all the people in one-half of the field. They lined up and compelled the frightened crowd in the required direction. Ka-Tzetnik would later describe the scene as follows:

> Gripped by the fear of death, a cry rose from the multitude and it began to move. People pushed and shoved and were tossed about

47 Klinger, 1944 diaries, Haogen II, p. 48.

48 Laskier, *Rutka's Notebook*, p. 39.

49 Excerpt from an unidentified description of the August selection written by Chajka Klinger (translated from the Hebrew, the original Polish document has been lost), Moreshet Archive, C.36.2; Chajka Klinger, *Miyoman Bageto*, p. 81.

> as in the eye of a typhoon. Mothers lost hold of their children, husbands and wives were torn apart, vanished from one another's sight, and were swallowed up in the stormy sea. Women tore at their hair, rending the air with screams for their little ones, as lost children were trampled beneath the pounding feet of the frenzied crowd.[50]

Eight-year-old Rivka Klajner remembered being separated from her mother by the stream of people. She began pinching the adults' legs and biting their arms lest they trample her. No one noticed her. They were too busy staring in the face of death. Finally, she fell and was stepped on repeatedly. She thought she would never get up, until a man lifted her up in his arms and cried: "Save the girl!" Soon after, she recognized her aunt among the crowd, who then brought her over to her mother. Other girls her age were not so lucky—they were trampled to death.[51]

Then, the selection began. It was initially managed by Dreier, with the assistance of Heinrich Lindner, the senior representative of the Special Commissioner of Organization Schmelt. Lindner was well known among the Jews of Zagłębie as the man who had managed the abductions and selections for the labor camps for a long time. Merin was also present on the scene. Dreier stood in the center of the field brandishing a small stick in his white-gloved hands. He smiled with satisfaction. Despite the initial uproar, the selection process was proceeding as expected. He pointed his small stick as a means of instructing the people which way to go, hardly glancing at their certificates.[52]

All the testimonies from Sosnowiec indicate that the Jews were divided into four groups. The first group was mainly made up of necessary workers but also included many Judenrat officials as well as members of the Jewish militia. The second group consisted largely of young people aged sixteen to twenty-eight. The third group was more varied, but it would seem that it included people with a work permit. The fourth group was mostly made up of old people and children. The hypothesis was that group one would be released to go home, group two would be sent to

50 Ka-Tzetnik, *Sunrise over Hell*, p. 78.

51 Rivka Klajner's testimony in Habas, *Yeladim Mutzalim*, p. 127; Anonymous testimony of a woman from Sosnowiec, YVA, O.12/26.

52 Mazia, *Re'im Basa'ar*, p. 89.

the labor camps, group three were provided for because of their work permits, and group four would be deported.[53]

The nightmarish scenes that had played out in Będzin and Dąbrowa Górnicza were witnessed here too. The young Moshe Zielonka passed the selection, but his father, mother, and sister were transferred to group four. Meir Peredalski's heart sank at finding himself with his mother in this same group. The Klajner family, reunited, was sent to group three. Rivka remembered it being a bad number, but better than number four—the group headed for slaughter.[54]

Members of Hanoar Hatzioni had gathered in one corner of the field. Their friend Janek Zimmerman had been assigned to group number four despite his young age. They saw this as Merin's revenge on the youths who had raised their voice against him at the assembly. They decided to organize a rescue mission. Fredka Oksenhendler (later Mazia) and Sara Bergman put on their nurse's aprons and began to move among the groups. Ben Zion (Bolek) Kożuch donned a Jewish policeman's cap and turned to walk among the crowd. Fredka made it to group four and located Janek. She managed to pass to him the nurses' special Star of David ribbon, and under its protection, he escaped to group number one.[55]

9:00 PM in Dąbrowa Górnicza, Będzin, and Sosnowiec: Sweeping Rain

Night descended on Zagłębie, and with it, sweeping rain.[56] The majority of the Jews were still gathered in the four roundup points, where they had to bear the agony of the cold, the wet, and the mud. The vicissitudes of their hopes now seemed to be reflected in the violent swings of weather.[57] Chajka recorded:

> Night came and rain began to fall. Some shots were fired. At night, many people from the "resettlement" [deportation] group sneaked

53 Anonymous testimony of a woman from Sosnowiec, YVA, O.12/26; Mazia, *Re'im Basa'ar*, p. 90.

54 Moshe Yarkoni, in *Sefer Sosnovitz*, vol. 2, p. 303; Rivka Klajner's testimony in Habas, *Yeladim Mutzalim*, p. 127.

55 Mazia, *Re'im Basa'ar*, p. 90.

56 Rutka Laskier describes rainfall beginning in the afternoon. Laskier, *Rutka's Notebook*, p. 37.

57 Anonymous Judenrat clerk testimony, YVA, O.12/3.

> into the "free" group. The selection process was not yet finished. People had not brought any food, they sat there, soaking wet, on the muddy ground. They began to let the freed ones out, pasting a stamp onto each one. They were shouting, crying in the street. How were they to return home without their mother? At least we left our father at home: if we hadn't, he would not have made it back.[58]

On the Hakoach field in Będzin, the sorting operation had stopped. Kuczyński and his friends hurried to take shelter from the rain. Only the armed guards remained on site. The popular estimate was that only around 4,000 Jews had been released to their homes so far. The SS guards turned on spotlights and ordered the Jews to get off the benches and sit on the ground:

> Weak old men lay prostrated in the mud, mothers laid their babies in the mud, people who were close to fainting with thirst began to lap up dirty water from the puddles. Every moment someone else passed out. Shouts of "Nurse!" "Help!" "Save us!"—were constantly heard. The elders seemed to have frozen and no one cried. They were no longer even afraid, because the worst had already happened.[59]

Rutka Laskier also witnessed these sights: "Little children were lying on the wet grass, the storm raging above our heads. The policemen beat them ferociously and also shot them."[60]

The SS men with the help of the Jewish police were supposed to guard the three groups that remained in the field. Under the cover of darkness, attempts to move from group to group multiplied. Benjamin Klajnman, who had been released earlier, now returned to the field. His sister-in-law remained there, and he was determined to get her out. He turned to Barenblatt, who directed him to the Jewish policemen guarding the place. Among them, he knew a certain Kaufman from Vienna. Klajnman pulled a wad of bills out of his pocket and began ransoming people. The price was 50 złotys per person. Among those he had freed were also a number of children. Reuven Wekselman's brother, who had been assigned to the labor camp group, tried to get away but ran into Barenblatt accompanied by several Jewish policemen. Barenblatt stopped him and put him back in his designated group. Later that

58 Klinger, 1944 diaries, Haogen II, pp. 48–49.

59 Anonymous Judenrat clerk testimony, YVA, O.12/3.

60 Laskier, *Rutka's Notebook*, p. 38.

night, his father—a pharmacist—managed to obtain a white coat and thus entered the field as a medic and rescued his son.[61]

The selection process had also ended in Sosnowiec. In the evening, the members of the first group including the Judenrat officials and their families were released to their homes. At nine o'clock, they began to release the men from the third group—the ones carrying a worker's card from the local workshops. In the fourth group—the one destined for deportation—a riot broke out. Many of them tried to move to the third group. They made particular efforts to transfer children from the fourth group to the third. Shots rang out, and blows fell on people's heads. Mina Fortgang who had been assigned to this group remembered that one of the SS men jumped into a baby's carriage during the riot and trampled the baby inside to death.[62]

Rain began to fall in Będzin as well. Dreier and his men hurriedly wrapped themselves in raincoats but soon tired of hanging around. They gathered the men from groups three and four along with those who were still waiting their turn, put them under guard, and left.[63] It continued to rain all night. The Germans aimed searchlights every which way so that no one could escape. Shots were heard.[64] The young Rivka Klajner saw the following:

> [M]any children [who] were covered in mud and did not dare to cry or shout aloud. They whispered their crying. Then someone said: "May God hear the children's cries!" I couldn't fall asleep, and then *mamusia* sat in the mud and took me in her arms. Every time she would wake me up and ask: "Rivka, are you sleeping?" I was afraid I would faint from hunger and thirst, because many children and adults had fainted.[65]

Only at dawn did they notice that among them were lifeless bodies of children who had been trampled under the feet of the terrified crowd.

61 Reuven Wekselman testimony at the Barenblatt trial, Moreshet Archive, D.1.5366, pp. 45–50.

62 Mina Fortgang testimony, GFH, 13893.

63 Mazia, *Re'im Basa'ar*, pp. 91–92; Anonymous testimony of a woman from Sosnowiec, YVA, O.12/26; Mina Fortgang testimony, GFH, 13893. According to Mazia, the selection continued until midnight. Others claim it went on all night.

64 Mazia, *Re'im Basa'ar*, pp. 91–92.

65 Rivka Klajner's testimony in Habas, *Yeladim Mutzalim*, p. 128.

Day Two: August 13, 1942

8:00 AM in Będzin and Sosnowiec: The Selection Resumes

The selection process resumed in Będzin the following morning. Kuczyński was back in action. Some of the people in group three (the group with work permits) were let go. The screening was now much faster; the Germans did not bother checking certificates and based their judgment on looks alone.[66] The group destined for deportation steadily grew.

Many of those released did not go to work that day. Some locked themselves in their homes, some tried to save their relatives. During the night, youth movement activists organized into groups and went into action. Members of Dror gathered a group of children who had been abandoned by their parents to save them from selection for deportation. Among them were also children from the orphanage. At the signal of one of the Dror activists, the children started running, and most of them managed to avoid the Jewish police and the armed SS men. Shots were heard, but most of the children managed to escape the field. Members of other youth movements obtained Jewish police hats and, under their protection, managed to reach the deportation group. Acting tough, they pushed several people from this group to another with kicks and punches.[67]

In Sosnowiec, the selection resumed at 5:00 AM. A little later, Merin arrived on site and announced that at his request, the Jews would not be deported. Those in the field were arranged in groups of eight and taken to four houses on Targowa and Kołłątaja Streets, which had been emptied of their inhabitants. On the way, some took advantage of the opportunity to escape. The SS men opened fire, and several people were killed.[68] In a report to the chief of police in Sosnowiec, the officers of the Schutzpolizei (German State Police, Schupo) headquarters announced the killing of one Jewish woman at around 8:45 AM and another around 11:00 AM. Both were shot while trying to escape.[69]

66 D. Liwer, *Ir Hametim*, p. 75; Anonymous Judenrat clerk testimony, YVA, O.12/3.

67 Ranz, *In Nazi Claws*, pp. 55–56.

68 Anonymous testimony of a woman from Sosnowiec, YVA, O.12/26.

69 "Dokumenty o Likwidacji Gett na Śląsku," *Biuletyn Żydowskiego Instytutu Historycznego*, 38, pp. 114–115.

Hanoar Hatzioni also continued rescue operations. Five of the movement's members—dressed as Judenrat sanitary workers—received a permit to enter the four houses where the Jews had been brought from the sports field. Fredka Oksenhendler and Hypek (Olek) Glitzenstein entered 4 Targowa Street. The house was crowded. The stench was terrible. There were dozens of people crammed into every room, unable to move. Some had defecated on the floor. When Fredka wished to open a window, she was prevented from doing so. The Germans shot anyone who tried to open a window.[70]

12:00 PM in Będzin and Sosnowiec: The End of the Selection

By noon, the selection process had ended in Będzin. Rumors spread about the number of those destined for deportation. David Liwer estimated their number at about 10,000, Chajka at about 8,000.[71] They were taken to three buildings: the Judenrat orphanage; the popular kitchen building at 28 Katowice Street (formerly the offices of Agudat Israel); and the Judenrat headquarters. It was estimated that due to the simultaneous deportations being conducted in Sosnowiec and Dąbrowa Górnicza, there were disruptions in transportation arrangements. Therefore, the Germans decided to keep the deportees in closed buildings for the time being. An SS unit was meant to escort the deportees to the wagons.[72] When the field had been emptied, a number of tarpaulin-covered carts emerged from its gates. A crowd of Jews gathered around them. Their hearts were filled with evil premonitions. Chajka went over and lifted up one of the tarps. The carts were loaded with corpses. The Jewish police made the crowd disperse. The Judenrat clerk learned that some seven or eight dead bodies remained lying on the ground, while David Liwer counted about thirty dead bodies the next day, which he buried with the help of his thirteen-year-old son.[73]

The popular kitchen on Katowice Street, where most of the deportees were concentrated, was terribly overcrowded. Armed guards were placed around the building, and food and medical assistance were

70 Mazia, *Re'im Basa'ar*, p. 93.

71 D. Liwer, *Ir Hametim*, p. 75; Klinger, 1944 diaries, Haogen II, p. 49.

72 Anonymous Judenrat clerk testimony, YVA, O.12/3.

73 D. Liwer, *Ir Hametim*, p. 76; Klinger, 1944 diaries, Haogen II, p. 49; Anonymous Judenrat clerk testimony, YVA, O.12/3.

initially denied entry. Fortunately, some food was found in the kitchen, and the kitchen manager Hadassah Prager tried to cook soup in the huge 2,000-portion-capacity pot. One of the deportees threw herself into the boiler, suffered severe burns, and died. She was a refugee, and her name remains unknown. There were other suicides: a woman jumped from the third floor, and a young man cut his veins.[74]

Outside the kitchen, most of the city's residents were looking for ways to rescue the prisoners or, failing that, to ease their plight. The Judenrat finally obtained permission to bring food and medical aid into the three buildings. The youth movements, however, had their sights set on rescue. Chajka wrote:

> They gathered 8,000 people in three houses. We must get into these houses, no matter what the cost. We stole a [Jewish] policeman's hat and quickly made a few more. Then we sent our boys into the buildings. People were getting in inside closed ambulance trucks, which went into the buildings alongside bread deliveries.[75]

The Hashomer Hatzair activists appealed to the Judenrat and received permission to enter the orphanage to provide the people there with medical assistance:

> Girls in white aprons enter the building, disperse in all directions, and reach every corner. They console the people, calm them down, and bandage the wounded, but that is not their main task—they must remove as many as possible. One of them takes off her apron and says to one woman, "Put it on quickly, take the ID, and leave, straight away, without fear, past the guards, and then send [the apron] back." And every couple of hours somebody disappears in a white apron. They have to watch everything: Which guard is by the gate? Is it the one who was promised a golden watch? Has the *Leutnant* come? And first and foremost, one has to smile beautifully and play innocent. Irka directs the work there. She's Lea's sister. Even though she's younger, she has a lot of experience.
>
> She is tall, shapely, and fit. The Germans find her attractive. She smiles beautifully at them, but hates them bitterly. She would have

74 Klinger, 1944 diaries, Haogen II, p. 49; Anonymous Judenrat clerk testimony, YVA, O.12/3.

75 Klinger, 1944 diaries, Haogen II, p. 49.

> strangled them with her own hands. "The time for that will come. I will pay you back for this smile I am forced to give."[76]

David Kozłowski found another way to extract people:

> Completely by accident, David managed to get into the attic of one of the houses where all these people were kept. The attic of the house next door adjoined this one. David knew the construction of these houses very well, so he began to ram into the wall, and after a few hours, he made a small hole. And indeed, there was the other attic. After that everything happened very quickly. He asked one of the men to stand guard, to look out for anyone coming their way. They had to watch out for the Jewish militia as much as for the Germans. When the hole was large enough for a man to pass through, they began to help some people, especially the parents of Hashomer members (there were no young people there) to get out of the hall downstairs. One pretended to faint, another said he needed the lavatory; they were not under such strict guard inside these houses. Those people then slowly moved up to the attic and began to sneak into the adjacent house. After that, they broke down the door and snuck into other houses. Their documents were checked in the streets, the Germans were making sure they had the correct red stamp, but they got them soon enough: forged stamps that one could have sworn were identical to the authentic stamps the Germans had given us.[77]

At this point, Mordechai Anielewicz had also made it out and rejoined his Hashomer Hatzair comrades. It seems that he was more interested in learning about the deportation proceedings than directing rescue operations. Looking back on those terrible days, Chajka wrote:

> I can remember Mordechai during the deportation days in Będzin. He was extremely curious about everything. A crowd assembled on the street near the deportation center. The Germans were shouting, rushing people with whips, firing [guns], and carrying a corpse. Everybody was fleeing, but Mordechai was pushing in

76 Klinger, *I Am Writing These Words to You* (1943 diaries), p. 139.

77 Klinger, 1944 diaries, Haogen II, pp. 50–51.

> the opposite direction, toward the Germans. He was curious about everything.[78]

Meanwhile, other movements also joined the action: an operation similar to the one devised by David was also conducted by Abraham Mandrowski and Israel Grosfeld of Dror.[79] Elsewhere, Shlomo Zimmerman, head of the Gordonia *ken* who worked as a storekeeper in the Judenrat building, tried to use his job to save a number of Jews. Together with Shraga Fruchtzweig, they were carrying some boards behind which they planned a to hide a few Jews when they ran into officials from the Central Judenrat in Sosnowiec, including Merin's secretary Fania Czarna. Black-haired and energetic, Czarna was known for her toughness. Some said that she was the driving force behind Merin's intransigence. Czarna stopped Shraga and his friends and scolded them: "We will get in a lot of trouble because of you!"[80] In another building, David Kozłowski continued his efforts. Chajka wrote:

> There was one room where they kept only small children. They were left completely uncared for. It's difficult to describe what was happening there and what these children looked like. Many of them died. "We have to save these children," David kept screaming like a madman. Forty children were brought in from the town square, babies really, left by parents who knew they were going to be resettled, so they left their children there.
>
> Once, some girls in white aprons entered the building, carrying food for the children. They were allowed inside; they washed those who were alive and took away the bodies of the dead babies. This room was at the front of the building, the windows overlooking the street grilled with iron bars. The space between the bars was quite large, and the girls began to squeeze the children out through the window. Many children were saved that way. Suddenly, a Jewish militiaman noticed that a German policeman was watching. Frightened, he came up to the window and pushed a baby, which at that point was almost out, back inside. The German saw everything. He bounded up to the Jewish militiaman, slapped him, took off the man's hat and threw it on the ground.[81]

78 Klinger, *I Am Writing These Words to You* (1943 diaries), p. 99.

79 Ranz, *In Nazi Claws*, p. 57.

80 Shraga Fruchtzweig interview.

81 Klinger, 1944 diaries, Haogen II, pp. 51–52.

In Sosnowiec, a similar rescue operation was being conducted by Hanoar Hatzioni. Five members of the sanitary staff infiltrated the holding centers. The girls exchanged aprons with women prisoners, allowing the latter to escape. In the evening, large pots of soup were brought into the buildings. Children were hidden inside these pots and smuggled out. Hypek Glitzenstein discovered that the wall of one of the houses was attached to a house that was not guarded. He recruited a number of people, and a hole was made in the wall. During the night, many people managed to get through. But the rumor spread and crowds gathered, and finally the hole had to be plugged. Others tried to escape through the chimneys and the upper story windows.[82]

4:15 PM in Będzin

The Schupo headquarters reported to the police command in Sosnowiec that the "*Wachtmeister* of the Schupo guarding the Jews has wounded a Jewish woman in her stomach during an escape attempt. The Gestapo man then shot the woman with a bullet to the temple."[83] The name of the Jewish woman is unknown.

Day Three: August 14, 1942

8:00 AM in Sosnowiec: More Rescue Activity

Dawn broke upon the third day of the Great *Punkt*. It seemed that something was gumming up the works of the German deportation system: the trains were slow to come. The detainees were still waiting, locked up in the holding locations. In Sosnowiec, the distress increased. The food provided by the Judenrat was largely insufficient. Hunger grew. The children cried constantly, without a moment's pause. There were three suicides at 4 Targowa Street: two women and one man jumped from the fourth floor.[84]

82 Mazia, *Re'im Basa'ar*, p. 97; Anonymous testimony of a woman from Sosnowiec, YVA, O.12/26.

83 "Dokumenty o Likwidacji Gett na Śląsku," *Biuletyn Żydowskiego Instytutu Historycznego*, 38.

84 Shraga Fruchtzweig interview.

Outside, rescue efforts continued. It came to light that the owners of the German workshops as well as a number of German loyalists and supervisors were making efforts to free their workers. Their success, however, was limited: Braun, the owner of the shoemakers' workshop in Będzin, managed to free several people; yet, Rossner, the owner of the largest workshop, failed. The assumption that Rossner's workers were immune from deportation was thus proven false. On the other hand, a number of Jews who were employed as street cleaners in Katowice were released. In Sosnowiec, Dreier would appear, take a census, and announce the names of the few who would be released thanks to the influence of their employers.[85]

Certain rescue efforts were also conducted by the Judenräte in both Będzin and Sosnowiec. The Judenrat clerk reported seeing members of the Jewish Council running around frantically, trying to save at least some of the unfortunates.[86] However, they cannot be said to have gone above and beyond. When Shraga Fruchtzweig approached Mołczadski with a request to help his parents who were among the deportees, he found him in a gloomy mood. It seemed to Shraga that even Mołczadski had been deceived. He had mistakenly placed his trust in the Germans' promises or perhaps in Merin's power. Mołczadski assented to give Shraga a note to the Jewish police, but they refused to release his parents. In retrospect, they would write it off as a "misunderstanding."[87]

Merin, too, released only a handful of detainees. One of them happened to be Hypek Glitzenstein who, together with a number of Hanoar Hatzioni activists, was caught while smuggling people out of their place of detention. Dreier was there and lined them up against the wall and pointed his gun at them. Merin appeared at that moment and distracted Dreier, thus sparing the group.[88] The Judenrat's main concern was to help the detainees waiting for the deportation trains to arrive. This aid mainly consisted of food provisions and medical help. Under the cover of these, the members of the youth movements continued their own rescue operations. According to David Liwer, around 5,000 people managed to escape in Będzin alone thanks to their efforts. Chajka's estimate was more modest—about 2,000—but

85 Klinger, 1944 diaries, Haogen II, pp. 53; Mazia, *Re'im Basa'ar*, p. 94; Shraga Fruchtzweig interview.

86 Anonymous Judenrat clerk testimony, YVA, O.12/3.

87 Shraga Fruchtzweig interview.

88 Mazia, *Re'im Basa'ar*, p. 94.

even this estimate is excessive. In all likelihood, only a few hundred detainees were rescued.[89]

12:00 PM in Będzin and Sosnowiec: Deportation

At midday, the special brigade in charge of evacuation had arrived in Będzin and began transporting the Jews from the holding points to the train station. The *Landrat* (county commissioner on behalf of the German Ministry of the Interior) of Będzin, Udo Klausa, was having lunch with his wife at that time. From the window of his apartment he had a view of the main street leading to the train station:

> The sound of shouting and orders came to our ears. I almost thought a riot had broken out. I hurried to the street...There, I saw a shocking sight: the terrible parade of Jews, arranged ten in a row, had reached the street; about 1,000 people, in my estimate. They were led by their own Jewish policemen, who, at the slightest provocation, attacked the deviants with wooden sticks. At the head of the parade were two police officers. The parade itself consisted of women, men, children, and babies carried in the adults' arms. They hauled packages on their bodies. A shocking sight! I returned to my house and called the police chief in Sosnowiec. I asked: "Herr Woedtke, what's going on here?" "Don't stick your nose in, Herr K, this is an order from the *SS-Reichsführer*. All the Jews will go to the Jewish Republic in Russia." At a time when our armies were advancing on Stalingrad, the idea of a Jewish Republic sounded credible to me.[90]

However, for the Jews of Będzin, the scenes they witnessed that day hit far closer to home. Through the slats of their closed blinds, those who

89 D. Liwer, *Ir Hametim*, p. 75; Klinger, 1944 diaries, Haogen II, p. 49; Tosia Herzberg interview. In Tosia's opinion, the numbers given by Liwer and Klinger are greatly exaggerated. At most, hundreds of people were rescued, probably around 150. However, it should be noted that Klinger and Liwer's reports were written independently in 1944 and 1945 respectively, and that the numerical estimates provided by Liwer in other cases were found to be reliable after comparing them to other sources. David Liwer, who was close to both the youth movements and the Judenrat circles, had extremely wide sources of information and did not tend to exaggerate. Chajka Klinger, who was actively involved in this rescue operation, also had many sources of information.

90 Udo Klausa, *Erlebt—Überlebt, Erster Teil, 1916–1945* (unpublished).

had made it through the selection looked out at the convoys of the unfortunates making their way to the train station:

> Many people lost their minds and went into strange fits of convulsions and danced as if for joy. Others who were filthy and dirty, threw off their clothes and walked half-naked. The sick and grimy children were placed on freight cars together with the bodies of the dead. To add a special note of solemnity to this procession, the SS men continued shooting at the enemy. One girl was hit by a bullet—bang!—and her bloodstained body was also loaded onto the general deportation train.[91]

Liwer noticed that at the end of the convoy was a long line of children who had been left behind by their parents in the hope that they would be saved from deportation. Two Gestapo men—Freytag and Peikert—ordered sacks to be brought over, stuffed the babies from among the abandoned children into them, and threw the sacks into the train carriages.[92]

The rescue efforts of the youth movements continued until the very last moment. The day before, Jochanan Ranz and Markus Pohorila were caught trying to rescue their friends' parents. That morning, they were also taken to the train station and were added to the crowd of deportees. When they were late to arrive, the SS man who was guarding them turned his back. The young men took the opportunity and escaped.[93]

Witnesses estimate the number of those deported that day to be about 5,000. According to Auschwitz records, this estimate is accurate, although it also includes the deportees from Dąbrowa Górnicza.[94] According to statistical calculations conducted by the Judenrat after the Great *Punkt*, 5,215 Jews were subtracted from the population census from May 1, 1942.[95]

It was now the turn of the Sosnowiec deportees. Here, too, the same scenes repeated themselves:

91 D. Liwer, *Ir Hametim*, p. 76.

92 Ibid.

93 Ranz, *In Nazi Claws*, p. 60.

94 D. Liwer, *Ir Hametim*, p. 76; Anonymous Judenrat clerk testimony, YVA, O.12/3; Namysło, *Zagłada Żydów Zagłębiowskich*, p. 30.

95 Statistische Angaben des Stands über die Jüdische, Bevölkerung 119 Regierungsbezirk Kattowitz, vom August 24, 1942 (Statistical information about the status of the Jews, Population 119 Katowice Region, August 24, 1942), Moreshet Archive, Avihu Ronen collection, 235.

> A long procession of dirty and ravaged shadows dragged on failing legs to the station, with the Germans hurrying them along with blows and shouts. When they reached the train, which was ready and waiting, the people began to run to it, to take seats. They pushed each other. With their last strength, they fought for a place on the death train so that they could rest a little, so that they could sit down and not have to stand on their swollen legs.[96]

The deportations from Sosnowiec took about four days. Opinions differ on the exact number of deportees: Some put the number at 4,000, while others claim that twice as many Jews were deported to Auschwitz. Records from Auschwitz support the higher estimate: 8,000 Jews from Sosnowiec arrived at the extermination camp between August 15 and 18, 1942.[97] The statistical report of the Central Judenrat reported the loss of 7,377 persons since May 1, 1942.[98]

It is unclear on which date exactly the deportees from Dąbrowa Górnicza were sent to Auschwitz. However, it is known that before their transfer to Auschwitz, the Dąbrowa Górnicza deportees were concentrated in the orphanage in Będzin. This could have only been done after the deportation of the Jews from Będzin on August 15, 1942. It is also known that two days later, another train of deportees left Będzin for Auschwitz. It is believed that Dąbrowa Górnicza deportees were among the people on this train. Dr. Samuel Mitelman, a Dąbrowa Górnicza resident, estimated their number at about 1,500. A similar number is recorded by David Liwer.[99] According to the statistical report, the Jewish population of Dąbrowa Górnicza decreased by 2,117 from the census of May 1, 1942. In total, according to the same report, 14,709 people were deported from the three cities. Most of them ended up in Auschwitz.[100]

96 Mazia, *Re'im Basa'ar*, pp. 94–95.

97 Anonymous Judenrat clerk testimony, YVA, O.12/3; Chaya-Ita Goldblum testimony, Central Zionist Archives, S/26 1159; Namysło, Zagłada Żydów Zagłębiowskich, p. 30.

98 Statistische Angaben des Stands über die Jüdische, August 24, 1942, Moreshet Archive, Avihu Ronen collection, 235.

99 Gelbart, *Sefer Dombrova Gurnitze* [*Dąbrowa Górnicza*] *Vehurbana*, p. 386; D. Liwer, *Ir Hametim*, p. 76.

100 Statistische Angaben des Stands über die Jüdische, August 24, 1942, Moreshet Archive, Avihu Ronen collection, 235.

CHAPTER THIRTEEN

Thoughts of Revolt

After the Deportation

The Great *Punkt* marked the day when the Jews of Zagłębie were brutally and forcefully made aware of the prospect of extermination. There was not a Jew in Będzin, Sosnowiec, or Dąbrowa Górnicza who did not lose a family member, friend, or acquaintance in the process. The raw memory of the apprehension, the assembly, the wait, and especially the selection and deportation, made the proximity of the end palpable to everyone. It had been a collective awakening: the Jews of Zagłębie had gone through the most difficult hours of their lives together and at a distance of just hundreds of meters from their homes. Their world, which had up until now retained a certain measure of stability and security, suddenly buckled under their feet. David Liwer's description of the last victim of the Great *Punkt* perhaps illustrates this best:

> The last victim of the deportation was Rabbi Mendel Levin of Będzin. The physical and mental torture of spending a day and a half at the roundup field had undermined his health. He was tormented by feelings of remorse and suffered severe pangs of conscience at having been tempted into trusting the Judenrat and even convinced Jews to show up at the designated assembly point. He was broken and devastated in body and spirit—and he never returned to his previous state. He used to sit motionless in the doorway to his house, absorbed in his own thoughts, uttering not a word and answering no one, consumed by grief and affliction.[1]

1 D. Liwer, *Ir Hametim*, p. 77.

Had Rabbi Levin gone mad, or was sanity no longer possible in a world where people could be exterminated in gas chambers? The quiet nearby town of Oświęcim now emanated terror under the name of Auschwitz. Both the Judenrat clerk and Mina Fortgang, who would arrive in Mandatory Palestine in November 1942, would describe Auschwitz as an extermination camp.[2] The information at their disposal came from a reliable source. The Judenrat clerk in Będzin said that unlike previous deportations in which the names of those sent to forced labor camps were kept on record, they were instructed to delete the names of all deportees from the card catalog. Still, some continued to ask what became of the deportees. The Judenrat, perhaps for the sake of the historical record, addressed this question to the Gestapo. They were answered rudely: "You would be better off asking what your fate, the fate of the remaining Jews, will be." No official reply was received. On the other hand, there were testimonies from eyewitnesses who had seen the trains going into Auschwitz, the concentration camp. There, they reported seeing a narrow side railway leading to the crematorium.[3]

Another macabre piece of evidence indicating the Jewish public's awareness of what was happening in Auschwitz was the appearance of "soap jokes" in Będzin. A girl passing by a cosmetics store would remark: "There's my grandmother. But they will make cream soap out of me, because I am younger and plumper." A Jew who gained weight would have his neighbors tell him: "The Germans will make a decent bath soap out of you." And when two Jews bid each other farewell, they would remark: "See you on the shelves."[4] The rumor that soap was made from human fat has been fundamentally unfounded, and it is doubtful that the people of Będzin attached any importance to it beyond its being a popular joke. And yet, if the story of the gas chambers, which initially sounded like a morbid rumor turned out to be true, couldn't it also be possible that the initials stamped on German soap bars from the war period indicate that it was fabricated out of Jewish fat?[5]

2 The testimonies in section O.12 of the Yad Vashem Archives are Hebrew testimonies collected by Jewish Agency researchers from the two delegations of exchanged subjects who arrived in *Eretz Israel* in November 1942. In these testimonies, Auschwitz is described as a concentration camp where the Jews were being gassed. See also Mina Fortgang testimony, GFH, 13893.

3 Anonymous Judenrat clerk testimony, YVA, O.12/3.

4 D. Liwer, *Ir Hametim*, p. 133.

5 The acronym RIF stands for Reichsstelle für industrielle Fettversorgung (National Center for Industrial Fat Provisioning), the German government agency that made

One man in Będzin, however, was apparently unperturbed by all this, and that man was Moniek Merin. Some said that Merin had known about the Germans' intentions. It is believed that the events in Chrzanów, where his representatives had been present, as well as the selective deportations in other cities, had been a "dress rehearsal" for the *Punkt* and were supposed to teach him about the German deportation methods in the region.[6] From his meetings with Anielewicz, Merin would have also presumably known about the exterminations going on outside Zagłębie.[7] Be that as it may, Merin's attitude toward the Great *Punkt* fell in line with his general philosophy: the survival of the Jews of Zagłębie—partial though it may be—could only be ensured through integration into the German war economy. He told his close associates: "I feel like a captain whose ship is about to sink, and only by throwing a large part of the valuable cargo into the sea can the rest be saved and reach a safe harbor."[8] The fact that most of the workshop employees and their families passed the selection safely proved, in his eyes, that only working for the Germans could save one from death.

Merin's accomplishments until the deportation earned him the nickname "King of the Jews," a title that connoted equal doses of admiration and mockery. After the Great *Punkt*, however, confidence in his leadership wavered. The Jews of Zagłębie still harbored fresh memories of both his and his people's involvement in the call for general mobilization, their instructions to wear Shabbat clothes, their promises that everything would be alright. A lot of anger was also directed toward the Jewish policemen due to their behavior throughout the selection. Chajka wrote:

> Hatred towards the Jewish militia was growing. They will be held accountable for this.... And now, at last, everyone saw the true face of the Judenrat. Everyone understood that they would go on blindly obeying the Germans, that they were only a tool designed to keep the

soap during the war. This was stamped on German soap bars. The Jews used to read this as RJF, which supposedly stood for *Rein Jüdische Fett*—Pure Jewish Fat. The soap, of course, was of entirely unrelated origin.

6 Merin had been present at some of the selective deportations. On May 30, 1942, Merin and Czarna arrived in Jaworzno by car, accompanied by Jewish policemen. They took an active part in the selection, which resulted in the deportation to Auschwitz of roughly 3,000 people from Jaworzno and Chrzanów.

7 See chapter 11.

8 Friedman, "Two 'Saviors' Who Failed," pp. 479–491.

> Jews in the dark, a venom created to poison the Jewish community, day after day. They were there to distract the Jews from the tragic end that awaited them, to weaken any resistance or rebellion. We had to open the eyes of our community, to show them the role that the Judenrat played in all this.[9]

She directed particular criticism at Fania Czarna, Merin's secretary:

> The Germans usually said that they had much respect for a woman they called Black Fania, Moniek Merin's secretary and deputy. They said she was a vampire, a pitiless woman, who spent human life as if she were spending small change. "In historic times such as these one cannot be sentimental," she used to say. But she raised her own child in comfort and luxury.[10]

Other testimonies, in particular that of Paweł Wiederman who worked in the Judenrat, also point to strong feelings of anger and bitterness toward Merin and the Jewish police. Once, when he was passing through a town, stones were thrown at his carriage, but Merin, as an experienced manipulator, was quick to redirect the crowd's anger toward the Jewish police officers (who had initially tried to protect him) and initiated a reorganization of the police force.[11] The move was successful, and the anger subsided somewhat. Moreover, as the days passed and deportations did not resume, most Jews tended to adopted Merin's views on survival. Within a few months, about seven out of every ten Jews in Będzin registered as essential workers.

On the other hand, the youth movement activists came to entirely different conclusions. For them, August 12, 1942, was a day of frustration and discouragement. The rescue operations undertaken during the Great *Punkt* proved that effective organization in well-known field conditions can bring results. Yet they were reeling from the nascent awareness of the destruction awaiting them in Auschwitz and felt powerless to put up any meaningful resistance. It was therefore time to either mount an actual defense or perish.[12]

9 Klinger, 1944 diaries, Haogen II, p. 57.

10 Ibid., p. 58.

11 Wiederman, *Płowa bestia*, pp. 250–254.

12 Mazia, *Re'im Basa'ar*, p. 95; Ranz, *In Nazi Claws*, pp. 61–62.

The Birth of the Resistance

The establishment of the underground resistance in Zagłębie was a seminal event in Chajka's life. Although she took an active part in it, her diaries do not specify the exact date on which the resistance movement was founded, nor does she describe it in any detail. Her process of writing was circular and brought her back to the idea of Jewish struggle time and time again, as she tried to describe how such an idea affected her being. It would appear that the notion of resistance and the discovery it entailed had a more powerful impact on Chajka than the events themselves. She describes the establishment of the underground in a brief sentence within a passage dedicated to describing a turning point for the movement:

> The Jewish Fighting Organization (ŻOB) was established. It was founded on totally different principles than the Hashomer Hatzair educational organization.
>
> Iron discipline, strict military discipline, punctuality, and soldierly fitness.[13]

Another factor behind the lack of accurate documentation may be that the establishment of the resistance did not happen all at once but was a continuous process. The idea and perhaps even some preliminary activity toward building an underground defense force in Zagłębie had occurred before the official decision to establish the resistance was made. Anielewicz's stay in Zagłębie lasted about three months, and his conversations with Hashomer Hatzair and other youth movement members as well as the appearance of placards on the eve of the Great *Punkt* indicate that the notion of struggle had already taken hold during the months of July and August 1942. At any rate, various testimonies indicate that the Jewish underground resistance in Zagłębie—as a body uniting the pioneer youth movements—was organized in the second half of August 1942, shortly after the Great *Punkt*. Aside from the immediate impact of the *Punkt*, contributing factors included the establishment of the ŻOB in Warsaw during the Great Deportation of July–September 1942 and the views held by Mordechai Anielewicz, who initiated the preliminary organization in Zagłębie.

13 Klinger, *I Am Writing These Words to You* (1943 diaries), pp. 96–97.

In Warsaw, on July 28, 1942, at the end of the first week of the *Grossaktion* in Warsaw, representatives of Dror-Hechalutz, Hashomer Hatzair, and Akiva gathered and decided to establish a Jewish Fighting Organization (Żydowska Organizacja Bojowa or ŻOB). The ŻOB differed from the Anti-Fascist Bloc both in its composition and its goals. While the bloc had a clear pro-communist ideology and intended to take part in the anti-Nazi war effort to aid the Soviet Union, the ŻOB was an enterprise undertaken by Jews for Jews within the ghetto.[14]

Diverse testimonies, in particular Josef Kaplan's letter, give the impression that there was continuous contact between the ŻOB in Warsaw and Anielewicz in Zagłębie, and that Anielewicz was well informed about the happenings in Warsaw. One of his companions reported having witnessed Anielewicz telephoning Warsaw.[15] Yitzhak Zuckerman's later testimony shows that in Warsaw, the perception was that Anielewicz was on a mission to organize a local defense force in Zagłębie, since, according to Zuckerman, the list of the organization's goals was headed by the item: "Emissaries must be sent to all major cities to organize the defense of the remaining ghettos."[16] Thus it can be stated with some confidence that the establishment of the resistance in Zagłębie was directly inspired by the ŻOB in Warsaw. In August 1942, as before, the central youth movement headquarters had great influence over local branches.

The most detailed account of the establishment of the resistance comes to us from David Liwer. He remembered that hot August day when he came home from work to find two Gordonia activists in his apartment. They told him that a meeting would be held that night at the farm regarding defense actions, with the participation of an emissary from Warsaw. It was already seven o'clock in the evening, and Liwer wondered how they would have time to discuss everything before the nine o'clock curfew. "The discussions will last all night," they replied. The meeting started at nine. The participants gathered in the farm's large kitchen from which they could escape out into the fields if necessary. Guards were posted around the building. According to Liwer, members of Dror, Hashomer Hatzair, and Gordonia were present, about twenty-five in

14 Gutman, *The Jews of Warsaw*, pp. 236–243.

15 Abraham Manela, interview by the author, Netanya, 1986. See also Klinger, "Hara'ayon Shehasir et Ruhenu."

16 Letter from the ŻOB leadership to London, May 24, 1944, in Melech Neustadt, *Horban U'mered shel Yehudey Varsha* (Hebrew) (Tel Aviv: Hava'ad Hapo'el shel HaHistadrut Hakelalit shel Ha'ovdim Ha'Ivrim BeEretz Yisrael, Va'adat Hagola, 1946), pp. 101–102.

total. These included: Chajka Klinger, David Kozłowski, the Pejsachson sisters, Shmuel Rozencwajg, and Moshe Orbeital from Hashomer Hatzair; Baruch Gaftek from Dror; and Shlomo Zimmerman, Hanka Borenstein, and the Liwer brothers from Gordonia. It can be assumed that Herszel Szpringer, Alter Goldblum, and Hanche Płotnicką (who was in Będzin at the time) of Dror were likewise in attendance, as well as members of Hanoar Hatzioni (for example, Israel Diamant) and Hashomer Hadati (for example, Yeshayahu Erlich).[17]

The meeting was chaired by Baruch Gaftek and conducted in Hebrew. Arie Liwer introduced Mordechai Anielewicz, at which point the special guest gave a two-hour lecture:

> Over two hours, Mordechai Anielewicz gave a detailed account of the defensive preparations of the Hebrew youth in Warsaw, Białystok, and Vilna. The comrades in Vilna decided to be the first to rise up against the Germans and take their weapons, but a decision was made, said Mr. Anielewicz, that the uprising should break out in all locations simultaneously. The Jewish youth in Będzin, whose representatives are gathered here, must also make a decision regarding defensive action at this time. There are serious difficulties in purchasing weapons in Warsaw; the Polish underground is standing idly by and to this day has not offered us any help. We are alone and isolated in our desperate struggle. The Polish underground has plenty of weapons but will not sell them for any amount of money. We are now waiting for an answer on this matter from a communist group we have been talking to lately. One thing is clear: We will defend the honor of Israel with all our might, even if we have to fight with knives and stones against an enemy equipped with modern weapons.[18]

Liwer's account is consistent with the information Anielewicz would have had in August 1942 as well as about the man's passionate, rebellious spirit. The details about Vilna and the communist underground also proved to be true in retrospect. At that time, Tosia Altman and Arie Wilner of

17 D. Liwer, *Ir Hametim*, pp. 81–82; Shmuel Ron, in *Sefer Sosnovitz*, vol. 2, p. 179. Israel Diamant is mentioned as a key activist in Hanoar Hatzioni in Będzin, who was closely associated with the pioneering movements. Yeshayahu Erlich is also mentioned as a key activist of Hashomer Hadati. However, there is no clear evidence of their presence at this meeting.

18 D. Liwer, *Ir Hametim*, p. 82.

Hashomer Hatzair brought the first weapons received from the PPR into the ghetto, consisting of five pistols and eight grenades.[19]

The testimony of Shmuel Ron confirms Chajka's reading of Anielewicz's stance, namely that practically speaking, his vision for Hashomer was that they should join the partisans: "Our idea was to establish Jewish groups within the general partisan movement. It was our opinion that there was no objective possibility of waging a separate Jewish war for Jewish honor, and that we could only accomplish this by integrating the general anti-Nazi forces struggling against the invaders."[20] The differences in Liwer and Ron's testimonies do not necessarily indicate conflicting information. It would appear that one of these witnesses interpreted Anielewicz's remarks in light of his movement's ideological leanings.

This evidence also points to the multitude of notions that must have been running through Anielewicz's mind. The partisan orientation of the Anti-Fascist Bloc, whose influence had not yet faded, was supplemented by the ŻOB's insistence on defending the ghetto. His friends in Warsaw also seem to have been rather unfocused since, despite their intention to fight within the ghetto itself, the ŻOB continued to at least partially follow the direction set by the bloc. Several groups from the labor organizations and the pioneer youth movements—consisting of twenty to thirty people each—had been sent to the forests to join the partisans during the Great Deportation.[21]

That said, both programs owed more to revolutionary romanticism than realism regarding the youths' capacity for operative action. The events that followed in Warsaw itself would soon prove that little practical foundation had been laid both for defending the ghetto and joining the partisans. With loving irony, Chajka recorded some of Anielewicz's remarks from this period:

> But back when he [Mordechai] was with us, we felt that what he was telling us about the guerrillas and forests was more a product of his imagination, of how he wanted to see it, than actual reality. [...]
>
> It made us laugh.
>
> We knew that it was a tiring, tough life of a soldier. Partisans of 1863—ragged, dirty, and starving—stood before our eyes.

19 Gutman, *The Jews of Warsaw*, p. 243.

20 Shmuel Ron, in *Sefer Sosnovitz*, vol. 2, p. 180.

21 Gutman, *The Jews of Warsaw*, pp. 240–241.

> Exhausting, long marches. Gray, tiny graves of unknown soldiers with simple, black crosses.
>
> But you felt a human being there, without the yellow patch on your chest—not a beaten dog with its head hung low, but a free man taking revenge, not with words but through action. And that was attractive.[22]

As these lines indicate, Chajka was also carried away by the revolutionary fervor radiating from Anielewicz. The historical reference she chose here for comparison was one pregnant with meaning. The Polish uprising against the tsarist regime in 1863 was considered in Poland the great national uprising in which people from all walks of life took part under the slogan, "For our freedom, for your freedom." By the time Chajka was writing these words, this slogan had already been adopted by the Bund party in Warsaw.

A similarly romantic view, albeit stemming from other sources, can also be found in the testimony of Abraham Manela, a member of the Gordonia movement:

> We had a very exciting evening at the farm. We stayed overnight as a large group, and spent almost the whole night [together]. We called it [the evening]: "Farewell to life." The idea was that each of us had a death sentence in our pocket, and we wanted to leave a testament. The slogan was: "Better a group...that will kill the enemy and save the honor of the people—than fifty more hoes and pickaxes."[23]

Even among the moderate Hanoar Hatzioni there was marked enthusiasm about the idea of self-defense. Then eighteen-year-old Helena (Halina, Halinka) Goldblum (later Yehudit Sinai) would later recall:

> When I heard about the revolt for the first time, it was as if some most wonderful thing was revealed to me. I knew that it would not have occurred to me.... I remember feeling as if I were in attendance at Mount Sinai. Janek Zimmerman spoke, and he said that maybe we would also participate. It was like an epiphany.[24]

22 Klinger, *I Am Writing These Words to You* (1943 diaries), p. 106.

23 Abraham Manela interview.

24 Yehudit Sinai (Halinka Goldblum), interview by the author, Tzahala, 1986.

For the first time, this zeal took the form of operative plans. According to Shmuel Ron's testimony, it was decided at this meeting to: "a) Establish a joint organization for the pioneering youth movements; b) Recruit about 200 fighters from among the movements' graduates; c) Prepare for work in underground conditions and establish operative groups of five members each."[25] Arie and David Liwer also remembered the first organization established under Anielewicz's influence: "It was called *Lekrav* (Heb. To Battle) and was placed under the leadership of Arie Liwer. His deputies were Baruch Gaftek of Dror, Idzia Pejsachson from Hashomer Hatzair, and Israel Diamant from Hanoar Hatzioni."[26] In Chajka Klinger's diaries, the abbreviation OKW appears twice as the name of the resistance organization in Będzin. Although there is no further confirmation of the composition of the command, most of the evidence indicates that the underground organization was formed under the influence of Mordechai Anielewicz.[27]

The Death of Josef Kaplan

Anielewicz's long stay in Zagłębie implies that he had taken over command of the Hashomer Hatzair chapters in the region and had perhaps even set his sights on becoming the head of the underground resistance there. It seems that Anielewicz found Zagłębie to be a territory ripe for action, replete with youth activists eager to answer his call. Even the news about the Great Deportation from Warsaw failed to motivate Anielewicz to return; yet it did influence both the idea of the mission abroad and the establishment of the resistance in Zagłębie.

Meanwhile in Warsaw, the deportations continued and intensified. Every day thousands of Jews were rounded up at the *Umschlagplatz* and put on trains heading to the Treblinka death camp. A total of 250,000 Jews were exterminated from the end of July to the end of September 1942. About 55,000 Jews remained in the Warsaw ghetto.[28] The ŻOB's activity during the Great Deportation was minimal. The organization was still in its infancy and lacked weapons, trained personnel, and experience. Upon its establishment, the ŻOB concentrated on several types of actions: distributing leaflets

25 Shmuel Ron, in *Sefer Sosnovitz*, vol. 2, p. 180.

26 Arie Liwer testimony at the Barenblatt trial, Moreshet Archive, D.1.5366; D. Liwer, *Ir Hametim*, p. 82.

27 Klinger, *I Am Writing These Words to You* (1943 diaries), pp. 94–95.

28 Gutman, *The Jews of Warsaw*, pp. 211–213.

to warn the population against reporting for deportation; forgery of work certificates that protected holders from deportation; attempts to smuggle partisan members out of Warsaw; executing death sentences pronounced against members of the Jewish police. All of the above failed except for one: On August 20, 1942, Israel Kanal, an Akiva man, shot Józef Andrzej Szeryński, one of the commanders of the Jewish police, and wounded him in the cheek.[29]

In reference to the deportation period, Chajka wrote the following:

> There was no *hagana* [resistance] in Warsaw at that time. It was not long after the formation of a bloc with the PPR, with the intention of waging partisan warfare. The first groups had not yet left.
>
> Consequently, all the energy was put into preparing the people for the woods. That consumed not only much energy and effort but also and predominantly a large sum of money. The people were ragged, short of clothes and lacking boots. [...]
>
> Another group in Międzyrzecze was betrayed by their messenger and handed over to the police. As that group of young people was walking on the streets of Międzyrzecze, evidence was found on them, and they knew they were being taken for interrogation. They didn't want that and preferred to die on the spot, so they decided to provoke the Germans into executing them.
>
> Shouts burst out from the young chests, "Away with Nazism! Murderers! Long live socialism and the USSR!"
>
> It didn't work, so they attacked the soldiers, who finally shot them. The young people died on the spot. They didn't denounce their comrades. [...]
>
> Other groups did not reach their destination either. As there were no messengers who would escort them to the PPR groups, they had to seek contact on their own. Almost all of the groups perished and the girls were raped. That was the bloody price paid for our first attempts to participate in partisan combat.[30]

And that is when the blow came. News reached Będzin that Josef Kaplan, the movement's leader in Warsaw, had been killed. Chana (Hanka) Wiernik, in whose home in Sosnowiec the *ken*'s activities were now conducted

29 Yitzhak Zuckerman, *Bageto U'bamered* (Hebrew) (Tel Aviv: Ghetto Fighters' House and Hakibbutz Hameuchad, 1985), pp. 71–72.

30 Klinger, *I Am Writing These Words to You* (1943 diaries), pp. 147–148.

since her mother had been deported on August 12, 1942, remembered the moment when Mordechai Anielewicz received the tragic news:

> We called Mordechai "Marian" then. I received a note for him. I did not understand its contents. I handed the letter to Mordechai when he first appeared at the door. He remained standing as if frozen, suddenly grown pale. There were only a few of us in the room. When he recovered he said: "Josef has fallen." Then he turned to us and said: "Josef was my friend, my teacher, my comrade, everything. I don't know how I'll go on without him."[31]

Chajka, on the other hand, upon receiving the message, recalled the last letter that had arrived from Josef some time before: "How could he know, sense that those were indeed his last words to us? Soon afterward a terrible blow—Josef is dead, executed at Pawiak."[32]

It is hard to tell whether the letter given by Hanka Wiernik to Anielewicz also included the description of the circumstances of Kaplan's death. Whatever the case, the details soon became public knowledge. In her 1943 diaries, Chajka lamented the loss suffered by her movement: "Why was he executed? I don't want to recall it because it's too painful and it makes me feel ashamed and furious. He died as a result of a denunciation, given away by [Israel] Zelcer—a member of the *merkaz* [central leadership] and Gordonia and one of our 'allies.'"[33] This was the first time she was forced to deal with the failures of the resistance, yet it would become a recurrent theme in her diary. Chajka could not forgive the weak, the cowardly, and especially those she saw as traitors. Elsewhere in her diary, she describes the affair in detail, a description that was, of course, omitted from the published book version:

> And there was also the case of Zelcer. Heading for Lublin (I don't remember exactly), Zelcer and a group of boys were captured at a [train] station and they were to be executed, but Zelcer managed to convince the Germans not to execute him, of course at a certain price. He survived.
>
> He [Zelcer] escorted them to Dror's post on the edge of the woods from where there was to be contact with the partisans. Those

31 Chana Schlesinger (Wiernik) testimony, Moreshet Archive, A.273.

32 Klinger, *I Am Writing These Words to You* (1943 diaries), p. 103.

33 Ibid., pp. 103–104.

> who were with him quickly rushed in to give a warning, but not everybody managed to escape, and 14 people were executed. Zelcer was released. He arrived in Warsaw, where he was captured for the second time. A (false) pass was found on him and when he was asked who had made it, he offered Josef's name.
>
> They drove to Lande's factory to collect Josef [Kaplan], but he wasn't there. The owner of the factory —I will mention him later— did not realize what it was about and Josef was sent for. And he went, despite all his caution.
>
> He was put in a car, where Zelcer was already waiting. Purportedly they did everything to save him. Every single day prisoners from the Pawiak Prison, where Josef was imprisoned, were escorted to the *Umschlagplatz* from where he would have surely been removed. But that day no prisoners were escorted out and Josef was executed in the Pawiak courtyard, where he was supposedly buried.[34]

The main outline of Chajka's account matches the conclusions of the investigation conducted by Yitzhak Zuckerman shortly after the event: Kaplan had been denounced by a man in an overcoat who was sitting in the Gestapo car. Later, the body of Israel Zelcer was discovered next to Kaplan's. Zuckerman was surprised as Zelcer was not supposed to have been in Warsaw. He was a Gordonia man who went out with members of the Dror group to join the partisans. The group was lost, and the news of Zelcer's return to Warsaw had not reached the resistance. Based on this, Zuckerman put two and two together and determined that Zelcer was the man who had betrayed Kaplan. It also turned out that this man hiding in the car was the key to the tragic events that had taken place in Warsaw as well as at one of the stations before Lublin and at the Werbkowice sawmill.[35]

As for Chajka, her anger at Zelcer's betrayal was exacerbated by the feeling that Hashomer Hatzair was now doomed. Not only had Josef Kaplan been killed, but on that same day, Shmuel (Szmuel) Breslaw, the second leader of Hashomer Hatzair in Warsaw, also lost his life. Breslaw was the man who had brought the information about Kaplan's imprisonment to the resistance headquarters in Warsaw on September 3, 1942. He then left to get help, taking a jackknife with him. He was stopped by Germans on the street, and when Breslaw tried to pull out

34 Ibid., pp. 148–149.

35 Zuckerman, *Bageto U'bamered*, pp. 75–79.

the knife, he was shot on the spot.[36] This act was typical of the hotheaded Breslaw, and according to Chajka, he had always dreamed of killing "at least one German."[37] In one day, the Hashomer Hatzair movement lost two of its most prominent leaders—the fatherly and considerate Josef, and the impassioned theoretician Breslaw:

> Even before Josef's death I had a feeling that we—the *shomers*—were being dogged by ill fate.
>
> During the deportation they—[the *shomers* in Warsaw]—tried to get mostly those they wanted to save for after the war out of Warsaw.
>
> Among that group was Rachel, a future genius of the shomer movement, who wrote beautifully, and other very valuable individuals.
>
> They were captured while leaving the ghetto. The first victims. Then Josef, Szmuel [Breslaw], the leadership member who was captured with a switchblade knife and was executed.[38]

Chajka knew the two well. She had met Josef Kaplan at the beginning of the war, possibly even before. As a member of the same graduate class, Chajka had felt an extreme closeness to him. He had been "the last of the Mohicans, the last *shomer* of the old school, from before the war, our last link with the movement in *Eretz Israel*, with the prewar movement."[39] She was likewise acquainted with Shmuel Breslaw, the leading intellectual of Hashomer Hatzair in Warsaw whose somewhat long-winded articles were a staple of the movement's underground press. Though younger than Kaplan and Chajka, Breslaw spearheaded Hashomer's extreme left agenda during the war, and his tendency to overidentify with the struggle of the Soviet Union more than once provoked the anger of Kaplan, who was a moderate in his views. But the sharp-quilled lad was too hasty in his actions as a resistance man, and ended up extinguishing his promise before it could come to any real fruition.[40] Chajka recalled Shmuel Breslaw's last letter to Mordechai Anielewicz: "He wrote about deep hatred, about terrible, horrible revenge,

36 Gutman, *The Jews of Warsaw*, p. 244.

37 Klinger, *I Am Writing These Words to You* (1943 diaries), p. 105. In her diary, this is mistakenly attributed to Josef Kaplan.

38 Ibid. Rachel's identity is unknown.

39 Ibid., p. 103.

40 For more on Shmuel Breslaw, see Eli Tzur, "Shmuel Breslaw," in Ronen and Kohavi, *Guf Shlishi Yahid*, vol. 1, pp. 35–116.

by which we would make up for all the harm done to us. And he asked him to give his regards to Josef Szamir [Shamir]." To this she added: "No, Szmuel, Mordechai won't be able to give him your regards."[41] When she wrote this in hiding in 1943, Anielewicz was no longer among the living. It was Chajka who first reported, in a letter to *Eretz Israel*, that Josef Kaplan was no longer alive. "He has been residing with Ruppin for several months now,"[42] she wrote in coded language permeated with macabre humor, referring to the death of the notable Zionist leader Arthur Ruppin who died earlier that year on January 1, 1943. This letter bore the first of much tragic news Chajka would have to deliver over the next year regarding the deaths of her comrades.

Anielewicz's Departure

The deaths of Josef Kaplan and Shmuel Breslaw had a direct impact on Anielewicz's stay in Zagłębie. The three of them had been at the helm of Hashomer Hatzair in Warsaw, and the murder of the two created a leadership void that needed to be filled quickly. It seems that only later did Anielewicz learn of the full severity of the blow suffered by the ŻOB on September 3, 1942, the day Josef was arrested and Shmuel was killed.

When the news of Shmuel's death arrived, Zuckerman and his friends believed that there was a connection between this incident and Kaplan's arrest, and therefore hurried to transfer the weapons that had just arrived from the PPR to a different hiding place.[43] This was a hasty decision. Regina Justman, a member of Hashomer Hatzair who had been dispatched to transfer the weapons that were bundled in a sack, was caught on the street by a German guard. The weapons were confiscated, and she was taken to the *Umschlagplatz*. Fortunately, her friends managed to help her escape.[44] Yet, the ŻOB's spirits were crushed: in just one day they had lost two of their leaders and the few weapons in their possession. In a conversation held in proximity to these events, the members of the young organization brought up the idea of attacking the Germans with stones and knives as a desperate act of suicide. However, with a bit of effort, the slightly

41 Klinger, *I Am Writing These Words to You* (1943 diaries), p. 105.

42 As seen in Bracha Habas, ed., *Mihtavim Min Hageta'ot* (Hebrew) (Tel Aviv: Am Oved, 1943), p. 38.

43 Gutman, *The Jews of Warsaw*, pp. 244–245.

44 Ibid., p. 245.

Chajka Klinger, 1939.
Ghetto Fighters' House Museum
(GFH), Photo Archive, 27878.

Chajka (center) with friends in Będzin,
c. 1937.

Leibel Klinger, Chajka's father.
Photo Collection, Yad Vashem Archives (YVA), K148/1179.

Perl Klinger, Chajka's mother.
Photo Collection, YVA, K148/1179.

Sarah Mgła née Klinger, Chajka's sister.

The grave of Aharon-Shmil Klinger, Chajka's brother, Czeladź, Poland.

A mother and son, Będzin (item ID 6037).

Two young boys in a bunk, Będzin (item ID 6040).

German soldiers in Będzin escorting Jewish men to forced labor in 1941 (item ID 5969).

Jewish policeman in Będzin: Saporstein (right) and Danziger (left) (item ID 7781).

GFH, Photo Archive

The Central Judenrat, Sosnowiec (item ID 7002/35).

Moshe Merin (second from the left) with other members of the Central Judenrat (item ID 1862/1).

Photo Collection, YVA

Alfred Rossner, German manager of a textile factory in the Będzin ghetto and a Righteous Among the Nations (item ID 14474264).

A group of tailors from one of Rossner's factories, Będzin ghetto, March 4, 1941 (item ID 503/4174).

Photo Collection, YVA

Josef Kaplan, Hashomer Hatzair leader and a ŻOB leader in Warsaw (item ID 503/7357).

Tosia Altman, Hashomer Hatzair leader and a ŻOB leader in Warsaw (item ID 503/7360).

Mordechai Anielewicz, Hashomer Hatzair leader and commander of the ŻOB in Warsaw (item ID 4225/23).

Photo Collection, YVA

A group of female members of Hashomer Hatzair on the agricultural farm, Będzin, July 3, 1941 (item ID 33396).

A group of Zionist youth on the agricultural training farm, Będzin (item ID 6712).

GFH, Photo Archive

Dancing the hora on the farm. Chajka is fourth from the left (item ID 70379).

Harvest Festival on the farm, Będzin.
Baruch Gaftek (left), David Kozłowski (right)
(item ID 6085).

GFH, Photo Archive

Nacia Klugman addressing her comrades.
Chajka is standing in the center.
Courtesy of Chana Shlesinger-Wiernik z"l.

Lea Pejsachson, Hashomer Hatzair member, 1940.
GFH, Photo Archive, 6102.

Members of Kibbutz Dror, Będzin, 1943. Herszel Springer, back row second from the left (item ID 6072).

Meeting of Hechalutz members. Baruch Gaftek and Chajka Klinger are in the center (item ID 6079).

GFH, Photo Archive

The Struggles between the Underground and the Judenrat

Zvi Dunski, Hashomer Hatzair member (item ID 1412/1567).

Lipek Minc, Hashomer Hatzair member (item ID 5020/110).

Judenrat leaders (right to left): Moshe Merin, Fania Czarna, and Chaim Merin (item ID 7002/35).

Photo Collection, YVA

Modrzejowska Street, Będzin, during the relocation to the ghetto (item ID 7743).

Moving to the Będzin ghetto (item ID 5940).

GFH, Photo Archive

The Fighters' Bunker

Baruch Gaftek, member of Hashomer Hatzair and later Dror, ŻOB commander in Będzin.
GFH, Photo Archive, 6092.

Frumka Płotnicka, ŻOB leader in Warsaw and Będzin.
Photo Collection, YVA, 15128436.

The Będzin Ghetto Fighters' memorial, 2024.
From right: Piotr and Karolina Jakoweńko with historian Andrzej Ciepał.
Courtesy of Jonathan Juniper.

The Last Bunker

Aharon Brandes.

Dorka Herzberg.

Chajka Klinger.
GFH, Photo Archive, 40168.

Zvi Brandes.
GFH, Photo Archive, 40168.

Herszel Szpringer.
GFH, Photo Archive, 6093.

Chawka Lenczner.
GFH, Photo Archive, 18389.

Max Fischer.
GFH, Photo Archive, 18389.

Meir Schulman.
Courtesy of Edna Ben-Asher.

Nechama Schulman.
Courtesy of Edna Ben-Asher.

The Kobylec Family

The Kobylec Family.
Courtesy of Jolanta Kobylec-Cyganek.

Klara Banasik.
Courtesy of Jolanta Kobylec-Cyganek.

Jolanta Kobylec-Cyganek sitting outside the house where the Kobylecs hid Jews.
Courtesy of Karolina and Piotr Jakoweńko.

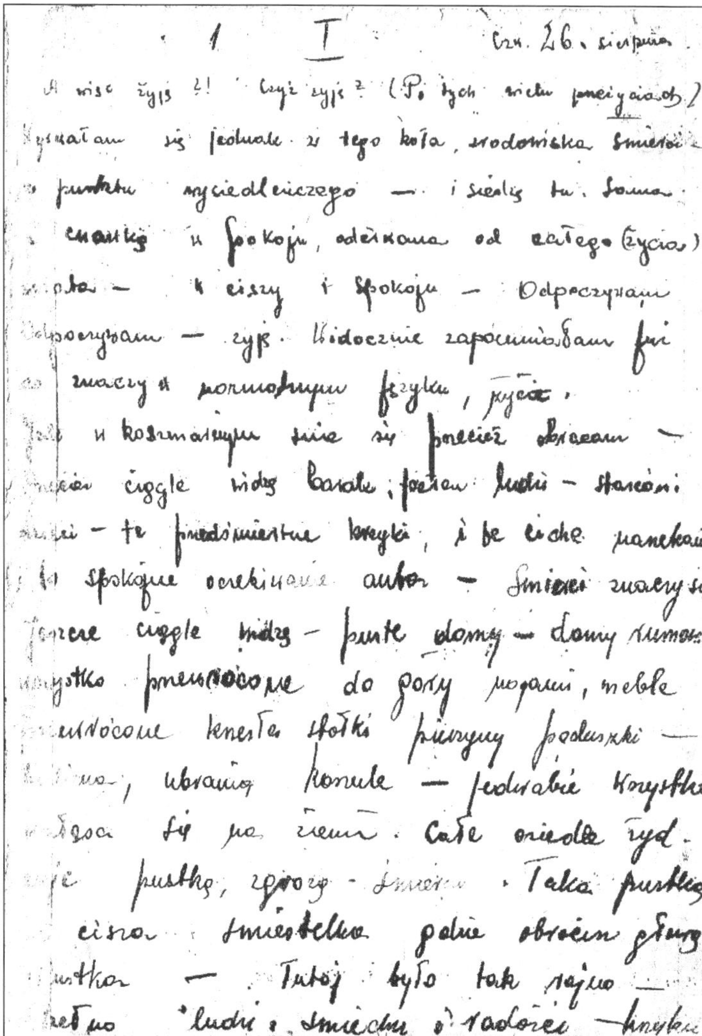

The first page of Chajka's diary, August 26, 1943.
Moreshet Archive, 143640.

older Yitzhak Zuckerman succeeded in dissuading them from doing so and convinced them to try to regroup instead.[45]

Anielewicz in Będzin knew little about all this, but the scarce details that came to his attention were enough to make up his mind: he had to go back to Warsaw. Chajka noted briefly:

> Mordechai had to leave. He couldn't stay here. Josef was dead and somebody had to take his place. He had also left his large family without protection. So, he had to return. They were growing restless in Warsaw because they needed him and needed his guidance, as he was their leader. He left.[46]

In Warsaw, Anielewicz found only one-fifth of the ghetto's Jews remaining—the rest had been destroyed, a crumbling and depressed movement mourning the loss of its leaders, and a militant organization, the operations of which had almost all ended in failure. The youth expected a leader. He would be the man for the job during this difficult period. In Będzin, however, Mordechai's departure left a feeling of emptiness. The resistance, which had just been established and had taken its first steps, was left without a guiding hand. The movement's educational work had most likely stopped with the beginning of the deportations. The *ken* had been dispersed, and the *bogrim* organized themselves into small operative groups of three to five members.

The Dror members were divided into groups of five, although it seemed that they were not the best at conspiring—after all, they had all lived on one kibbutz.[47] It is important to note, however, that Dror had not ceased its educational activities. On the contrary, following the Great *Punkt*, the movement members adopted a group of eighteen children and adolescents who had been separated from their parents and established a children's kibbutz called Atid (Heb. Future).[48]

In Hashomer Hatzair, a movement in which every practical action had to be anchored in well-founded ideological postulations, the transition from educational work to resistance operations raised difficult questions, as documented by Chajka:

45 Zuckerman, *Bageto U'bamered*, pp. 79–81.

46 Klinger, *I Am Writing These Words to You* (1943 diaries), p. 106.

47 Ranz, *In Nazi Claws*, p. 75.

48 Lenczner, "Parashat Bendin," p. 125; Max Fischer testimony, GFH, 11578.

> When Mordechai came to us and told us about the PPR and our participation in it, when he established a fighting organization, he talked about two bodies of Hashomer Hatzair and about that new organization. Back then we sensed and told him, as he was, awkwardly, trying to prove to us the necessity of further educational work, that in fact the educational role of Hashomer Hatzair was already over. [...]
>
> I still have the impression that it was then that Hashomer Hatzair became a political-military organization.
>
> Formally speaking, there were two organizations, but when the one became more active, the other withered.[49]

These lines contain Chajka's first reference to the concept of vanguardism, which was prevalent in Hashomer Hatzair in the years before the war. This revolutionary vanguard assigned to Hashomer Hatzair a leading role in the social and national revolution, similar to the role assigned to the Communist Party.

As Chajka described it, with the establishment of the resistance, the concept of the political vanguard supplanted the movement's educational vision. The argument with Anielewicz, which Chajka mentions, represented the difficulty of this transition.

However, the main activity of the resistance in Zagłębie—similar to that of the ŻOB in Warsaw—consisted of making preparations for heading into the forest to join the partisans. Chajka wrote:

> So much money spent on sending them away, on the equipment, and just on shoes. There was a collection, the first on such a large scale. 100 to 200 Reichsmark per person. The people were simply stealing things from their homes, selling their watches and clothes. Just a new Hashomer Hatzair morality. We collected 2000–3000 RM—an enormous sum at that time.[50]

The funding drive was crowned with success, and vigorous debates took place regarding who would go first:

> We argued as to who would leave in the first group. The boys began to think about the next step. But the girls were worried. "What about

49 Klinger, *I Am Writing These Words to You* (1943 diaries), p. 134.
50 Ibid., p. 105.

> us? Why aren't they taking girls in? Why, we have such brave girls. They're good at everything: working in the field, propaganda, being messengers or paramedics."[51]

Yet, in the absence of any real contact with the partisans, these plans were doomed to remain a youthful pipedream:

> And then those long days of waiting for a letter from Mordechai, for an establishment of contact with the PPR in Zagłębie.
>
> Everything came to a halt again. And the people are whispering and asking what was the purpose of all that empty talk when we can't bring ourselves to do anything.[52]

The main problem was the lack of communication with the local partisans and the PPR. This was a puzzling fact as the industrialized region of Zagłębie was known for its socialist organizations. People spoke of "Red Zagłębie,"[53] which raises the question: How did an underground resistance fail to arise in the region? Due to the ideological disconnect from the Trotskyist group, Hashomer's loose ties with the PPR were not utilized.[54] In Będzin, they were waiting for news from Mordechai in Warsaw, who had promised to obtain a local contact with the help of the PPR Central Committee. However, no such news arrived.

This failure to make contact caused disappointment and frustration. Chajka felt that the quiet preparation work taking place within the operative cells was not enough. She could hear the young men getting angry. They did not want to sit idly by. Disenchanted, she wrote in her diary:

> The young people were becoming restless: How much longer must we wait in vain? Autumn was coming, then winter, they said. We won't be able to leave in time this year. Will anyone ever comprehend the tragedy of our generation, which is not the tragedy of people dying of hunger and exhaustion in labor camps,

51 Ibid., pp. 106–107.

52 Ibid., p. 107.

53 D. Liwer, *Ir Hametim*, p. 124.

54 According to Balicki's testimony, an underground group with a communist orientation called Dimitrov operated from 1940, led by Lieber Brenner and David Bratt. The group consisted of both Jewish and Polish members. Szymon (Shimon) Balicki testimony, YVA, O.3/1246, p. 15.

> nor of the people being resettled, or not as such, but rather of those who died in the gas chambers instead of on the battlefield, like they wanted to. They flailed like caged animals, longing for freedom. We wanted to join the Polish youth in their underground resistance. We wanted to lend them our vital forces, but they didn't want us. [Władysław] Sikorski's men [Armia Krajowa, AK—the Home Army] didn't want us. The PPR didn't want us either—they couldn't even send a guide to help us escape through the forest, they were always late with everything. When their guide finally arrived, the Jews were already gone.[55]

The Arrival of Zvi Brandes

The void left by Anielewicz in Będzin would be filled several weeks later. He sent them a man to fill his place and to take management of affairs into his own hands. That man was Zvi Brandes.

On his way back to Warsaw, Anielewicz passed through Żarki, where a community of 3,000 Jews still existed and where the Hashomer Hatzair farm and the local *ken* operated under the leadership of Zvi Brandes—David and Chajka's old friend. The deportations had not yet reached Żarki, but according to the news coming in from the nearby areas, it was evident that the days of the Żarki community were numbered. Plans to set fire to the city and attempt an uprising during the upcoming deportation were developed but soon abandoned. Brandes preferred to take the advice of the local Judenrat and send his men to work on peasant farms in the vicinity in the hope that this would save them. In retrospect, the decision amounted to the dispersal of the local *ken*.[56] On September 21, 1942, this resolution was granted official approval. Tosia Altman and Arie Wilner, members of the Hashomer Hatzair leadership in Warsaw, had also arrived in Żarki. At the meeting that took place at Brandes's house, it was ruled too risky to stay in the town. It was decided that Tosia, Arie, and Mordechai would return to Warsaw, and Brandes was assigned to Zagłębie.[57]

Zvi set off a few days before the liquidation of the Żarki ghetto on October 6, 1942. He was a man who radiated leadership, albeit a different

55 Klinger, 1944 diaries, Haogen II, pp. 60–61.

56 Brandes and Reshef, *Zvi Brandes*, pp. 51–58.

57 Ibid., p. 59.

brand of it than Anielewicz. As a balanced and moderate personality, he was closer in spirit to the folksy Josef Kaplan. His brother Aharon remembered that at the first news about the extermination, he reacted in a typically Jewish way: "They won't shoot us all..."[58] Yet, by the time he arrived in Zagłębie, he was committed to the idea of underground resistance. Chajka and David were ecstatic: the Hapo'el Lakfar reading club had evolved into a new form of comradeship. For them, Zvi was first and foremost a man of the movement.

Zvi's arrival was like a breath of fresh air to the youths who were frustrated by the failure to go into the forest. It seems that due to the ongoing failure to establish contact with the partisans, perceptions had changed, and the emphasis was now being placed on self-defense and propaganda operations. This change in priorities was motivated mainly by pragmatic considerations. Preparations for defending the ghetto meant that the youngsters were at least engaged in some kind of activity and were not just waiting for news from afar in passive idleness. In her 1943 diaries, Chajka credited the arrival of Brandes in Będzin with the resumption of activities after Mordechai Anielewicz's departure:

> Cwi arrived. We prepared a plan of action. Large-scale propaganda on the Jewish, Polish, and German street. A series of fliers on doors, on the street, in the *gmina* [Judenrat offices]. Letters to German companies—ours [our comrades] left the ghetto and went to the "Aryan" districts. The first walk with hidden fliers. The pounding of the heart, the contained joy—I'm doing something.
>
> Workshops began [to produce] brass knuckles, daggers, knives—cold weapons.
>
> The newspaper, fresh news every day from the radio, a political article, news about the guerrillas, from Jewish ghettos, and about mass deportations of Jews. The newspaper already had a number of subscribers.[59]

A significant part of the movement's efforts during this period focused on propaganda. In the evenings, members of Hashomer would gather in Sosnowiec at Hanka Wiernik's house. In the aftermath of the deportations and the cessation of educational activities, only ten of them remained. Kalman Tencer, head of the *ken*, had died in May 1942 and was replaced by

58 Ibid., p. 56.

59 Klinger, *I Am Writing These Words to You* (1943 diaries), p. 107.

Zvi Dunski. They would sit at Hanka's and compose letters in which they warned of the impending threat Hitler posed to Poland and humanity as a whole. They called for resistance and signed as "The Black Hand." The letters would be sent to lawyers, doctors, and laborers whose addresses they found in the phone books. As Zagłębie was part of the Reich, letters could be sent from there to Germany and to other Polish regions. The letters were taken by the Aryan-looking girls to the surrounding towns in order to dispatch them from there.[60]

Members of Hanoar Hatzioni also engaged in similar activities. They established a makeshift laboratory that set to work producing fake certificates and Molotov cocktails. In terms of announcements and propaganda, they went a step further. Janek Zimmerman printed leaflets in German calling on the German soldiers at the front to throw down their weapons and return to their homes. Workshop employees inserted the photocopied flyers into the shoes and boots headed to the front.[61]

The existence of a daily newspaper is confirmed by Shmuel Ron's testimony. According to him, the publication of the underground newspaper began during Anielewicz's time. It was reproduced using primitive means (a hectograph) by Zvi Dunski, Lipek Minc, and Shmuel Ron himself.[62] Among other things, the newspaper was based on news heard over a secret radio station, an operation of which Lipek Minc was in charge in Sosnowiec and which Zvi Brandes and David Kozłowski carried out in Będzin.[63]

Yet they were still lacking the most important thing of all—weapons. By the end of 1942, most of the movements did not own a single firearm. The only ones who had managed to obtain weapons were the members of Hanoar Hatzioni in Sosnowiec. In November, Leon Blatt managed to get to Częstochowa, where he bought three old pistols and two hand grenades at an exorbitant price. On his way back, he was almost caught at the border, but made it through the search by hiding the weapons among the dirty laundry in his suitcase.[64] Until the beginning of 1943, this haul constituted the only firearms obtained by the young underground resistance. The idea of Jewish rebellion and struggle was still a distant dream.

60 Fela Katz testimony, Moreshet Archive, A.470.

61 Mazia, *Re'im Basa'ar*, pp. 110–112.

62 Shmuel Ron, in *Sefer Sosnovitz*, vol. 2, p. 178.

63 Klinger, 1944 diaries, Haogen II, p. 27.

64 Leon Blatt, interview by the author, Tel Aviv, 1986.

Chapter Fourteen

The Resistance Game

Israel Gutman: 1986

Israel Gutman doesn't like my title for this chapter. He remarks: "One could see the early organization of the resistance as the brash actions of youth, but it all became very serious soon after," by which he means, of course, the Warsaw Ghetto Uprising. I feel somewhat ill at ease in the company of this sandal-clad professor with the gleaming white hair sitting across from me in his office at Yad Vashem. Until this point, he has been extremely enthusiastic about the book, especially the chapters dealing with the youth movements.

He did not know Mother personally, but her diaries were of great service to him in painting the portrait of Mordechai Anielewicz in the first major book he published, *Mered Hanetzurim* (Heb. Uprising of the Besieged). He has been reading through my manuscript out of interest and curiosity, rather than strictly out of professional duty. A thin thread woven out of unspoken words connects us: the Hashomer Hatzair tradition in the ghettos where Gutman grew up, the Warsaw Ghetto Uprising, the subject of his great book *The Jews of Warsaw, 1939–1945*, my memories of the movement. And there's more: Mother's fate echoes that of Israel's son. Nimrod Gutman, who was two years younger than me, was killed during his early military service. He probably committed suicide, but Israel never admitted it.

Yet, while I rely heavily on his books in my research and writing, our views on how the Jewish youth movements transformed into a militant underground resistance diverge. Israel Gutman tends to see this process as an organic transition of strong youth organizations into a new position of leadership in the ghettos.[1] Gutman emphasizes that the youth movements were among the first to become aware of the extermination project and to start establishing militant organizations. On the other hand, based on my mother's diaries and the many sources I have consulted, I tend to see this process of transition as informed by elements of playful risk-taking, youthful romanticism, and military amateurism, all of which led to many painful failures.

Over the years, this conceptual rift has grown wider. Gutman hesitated to accept my request to be my doctoral advisor. While he appreciated my approach in describing the Jewish response to the Holocaust—during the Great *Punkt* in particular—he was reticent regarding the emphasis I put on the Zionist component of the Judenrat and Merin's use of Zionist rhetoric. He disagreed with my "leftist" interpretation of the figure of Anielewicz. When I turned to the writings of Emanuel Ringelblum and interpreted them in the spirit of Walter Benjamin's critical historiography during my later studies in the early 1990s, the differences of opinion between us intensified to the point of an outright clash. I was suspected of being a "new historian" and felt as though I was not welcome at Yad Vashem.

Back in 1986, Gutman, like other members of his generation, wanted me to transmit the story of their heroism to future generations exactly as it was told by those who survived, as recorded in their memory, words, and writings. Whereas I can't help but open the bundle handed to me and rummage through it, invading their memories, their books. I then repack it and hit the road, raising the question: Whose bundle is it that I carry on my back?

The ŻOB in Warsaw

The return of Mordechai Anielewicz to Warsaw at the end of September 1942 was a critical factor in the ŻOB's growth and development. Anielewicz did not experience the failures and frustrations of the young organization's leadership during the Great Deportation. According to Israel Gutman, Anielewicz was "free from the entrenched self-constraint and hesitations that gnawed at the hearts of those who had tried to mobilize and organize resistance at the time of the deportation and were now being held back

1 See Israel Gutman, *B'alata Uvema'avak: Pirkei Iyun Bashoah U'vahitnaggedut Hayehudit* (Hebrew) (Tel Aviv: Moreshet, Sifriat Poalim, and Hebrew University Press, 1985).

by exhaustion from within and, even more so, the overwhelming and paralyzing terror from without."[2] Whereas when Marek Edelman, one of Anielewicz's deputies, was asked about Mordechai's leadership position, he replied: "He very much wanted to be a commander, so we chose him. He was a little childlike in this ambition."[3] Nevertheless, Gutman was right in claiming that Anielewicz filled a leadership void created after the Great Deportation in Warsaw. After all, of the three heads of the Hashomer Hatzair central leadership in Warsaw, he was the only one still alive. In Będzin, Chajka recorded the following:

> During the first deportation there were very heated *asefot* [meetings] in the Warsaw branch. All the young people without exception demanded action against the deportations. They wanted *hagana*. Very embittered about Josef, the people were waiting impatiently for Mordechai [Anielewicz].[4]

Anielewicz's return and commencement of his leadership position in Hashomer Hatzair was therefore a natural development, and with a change of leadership came a change of direction. Anielewicz strove to expand the circle of the ŻOB's partners and participants. At the end of October 1942, contacts were revived with members of the Poalei Zion Left party. The main point of contention between the two was Poalei Zion Left's demand to establish a political umbrella organization to supervise the operations of the militant organization and prevent reckless and irresponsible defensive actions. Anielewicz and Zuckerman objected: the political parties had failed them in the past. All they did during the Great Deportation was argue. They had no right to preach to young people. The establishment of a political umbrella organization would only hinder the establishment of a military headquarters and delay action.[5] Hirsch Berlinski and his friends, however, took up a more careful approach:

> We are fighting to live...We cannot allow for frivolous measures that could lead to the premature liquidation of the Warsaw ghetto...

2 Gutman, *Mered Hanetzurim*, p. 363.

3 Hanna Krall, *The Subtenant/To Outwit God* (Evanston: Northwestern University Press, 1992), p. 134.

4 Klinger, *I Am Writing These Words to You* (1943 diaries), pp. 149–150.

5 Gutman, *The Jews of Warsaw*, pp. 287–288.

> We declare that, as a political party, we are indeed responsible for our actions toward the Jewish masses in the world and to our friends abroad.[6]

They presented their demand for the establishment of a political umbrella organization as non-negotiable. To their surprise, after a break in discussions for consultation purposes, the youth movement accepted their position.

These descriptions, as recorded by Berlinski, point to the divide between the youth movements' position and that of the party. The youth in Warsaw, as in Zagłębie, were motivated by the desire to take revenge and die with dignity. On the other hand, Berlinski and his friends felt the weight of responsibility toward the people in the ghetto. Yet here, unlike in Zagłębie, the adults joined the struggle of the young. Once the partnership with Poalei Zion Left had been established along with the National Jewish Committee supervisory body, the way was paved for other parties to join, including members of the General Zionists. To enlist the Bund, another umbrella organization—the Coordinating Committee—had to be set up. The consolidation of forces in the Warsaw ghetto was also significant in terms of access to weapons. In December 1942, the first ten pistols were transferred to the ghetto from the nationalist underground's Home Army (AK), and in return, on December 2, 1942, its people received the ŻOB's statutes, the names of the participating movements, and its list of objectives. The memorandum was accompanied by a request to receive additional pistols, but this was only answered in late January 1943.[7]

The ŻOB of the winter of 1942–1943 was a different organization than the one that had tried to organize in the summer of 1942. It now included all the underground organizations in the ghetto except for Betar and the Revisionists, who formed their own fighting organization—the Żydowski Związek Wojskowy (Jewish Military Union, ŻZW). In terms of its definition and objectives, it was a Jewish organization that emphasized fighting within the ghetto in contact with the Polish nationalist underground. However, it was obvious that the ŻOB was dominated by two groups: the youth movements and the radical left parties. At the peak of its strength (April 11, 1943), of the ŻOB's twenty-two fighting companies, eleven belonged to the pioneer youth movements (five to

6 Hirsch Berlinski, "Zihronot" (Hebrew), *Yalkut Moreshet*, 1 (November–December, 1963) , pp. 14–15.

7 Gutman, *The Jews of Warsaw*, pp. 299–300.

Dror, four to Hashomer Hatzair, one to Gordonia, and one to Akiva), while eight belonged to the Bund and the communist parties.

On October 29, 1942, Eliyahu (Elik) Różański, a member of Hashomer Hatzair, shot Jakub Lejkin, the commander of the Jewish police, and on November 29, 1942, a squad of Dror men assassinated Izrael Furst, one of the Judenrat's senior employees. The assassinations were successful and made a powerful impression on the Jews of the ghetto. However, neither the Jews nor the Germans saw these as actions perpetrated by a Jewish defense organization. Rather, they assumed that both were cases settling internal accounts.[8] In Będzin, Chajka saw these developments through the prism of her movement:

> When Mordechai returned to Warsaw, they [Hashomer Hatzair members] resumed their previous activity, despite knowing that its scale was minute. As I have already written, the idea of partisan combat had already lost its importance for young Jews. But *hagana* was still an act of historical significance, which was also important for its own sake.
>
> Mordechai became the commander. Their main intention was to fight the inner evil, the Jewish scum. A series of death sentences was passed on the Jewish police commander and Jewish *moiserim*. [Jakub] Lejkin and Szrebniakow were finished off. The plan was to get the *gmina* to revolt. Those acts of terror were of enormous significance for the Jewish society as they awakened its spirit of defiance.[9]

Internal terrorism became the ultimate course of action for young people who, until a few months earlier, were naively trying to fulfill utopian dreams of living the pioneer life inside the ghetto. Anielewicz had undergone this transformation even earlier. Back in Zagłębie, he had already argued to Chajka that their duty was first of all "[to liquidate] the Jewish traitors [collaborating with] the Gestapo."[10] Embracing the idea wholeheartedly, Chajka stated:

> The first, historic—figuratively speaking—shot was also of great significance for our movement. Szmuel [Breslaw] had long been

8 Ibid., pp. 302–304.

9 Klinger, *I Am Writing These Words to You* (1943 diaries), pp. 150–151. The identity of Szrebniakow is unknown.

10 Ibid., p. 100.

> dreaming of killing Lejkin and that was why he was caught on a street with a switchblade. He wanted to do it in a very childish way and had long been contemplating it.
>
> Looking up to Chen, he sought consolation in acts of terror.[11]

Chajka is referring here to Chen, the protagonist of André Malraux's *Man's Fate*, who carries out a political assassination and whose life is driven by the fatal feeling of imminent death until his inevitable demise in a suicide attack. The elimination of the collaborators in the Warsaw ghetto was an opportunity to perpetrate revolutionary terror. In her writings, Chajka described the process of Hashomer Hatzair's transformation from a youth movement to a revolutionary organization with anarchist, if not downright terrorist, leanings. Her way of seeing things was typical of the spirit of the ŻOB during these stages of its organization. Even its more moderate people, such as Yitzhak Zuckerman, seemed to consider acts of internal terrorism and the robbing of the ghetto's rich a necessary condition for the formation and strengthening of the Jewish resistance: "We said to ourselves that if we do not secure the home front, if we don't clear the air in the ghetto, if we don't remove by force everyone who might bring us harm—there can be no uprising in the Warsaw ghetto."[12]

By early January 1943, the ŻOB was well organized but not yet ready for action. When the Germans entered the ghetto once again on January 18, 1943, it caught the young organization by surprise.[13] In Będzin, Chajka recorded the course of events:

> When the deportation campaign began in January they had only a few guns. The people were divided into several groups. The order was not to let oneself be taken alive.
>
> Soldiers walk into a flat and order the resident to dress and follow them. The man leisurely puts on his coat. Suddenly—boom! He takes his hand out, shoots, gets the arms, and flees.
>
> In another apartment the entering gendarme is attacked with a torch, as if with a gun. […]

11 Ibid., p. 151.

12 Zuckerman, *Bageto U'bamered*, p. 142. As far as is known, between thirteen and twenty Jews suspected of collaborating with the Germans were eliminated in Warsaw, a number similar to the number of Germans killed in the Warsaw Ghetto Uprising.

13 Gutman, *The Jews of Warsaw*, p. 307.

> It happens that those who defend themselves, those who are not empty-handed do not die, that *hagana* enthusiasts, who would rather die on the spot than be deported, are those who stay alive.[14]

Chajka's description broadly fits the course of events as we know it. The January deportation campaign in Warsaw targeted approximately 8,000 Jews who lived in the ghetto, and who, according to Heinrich Himmler, exceeded the quota required in the workshops. The campaign caught the leaders of the ŻOB off guard. The companies they had organized were not coordinated, and those that were could not reach the weapons depots, which contained few firearms at any rate. And yet, in Zuckerman's estimation, it was precisely the surprise element that made defensive actions possible. In his view, if there had been time to ask the opinion of the political committee, there would have been no actual resistance.[15]

By comparing the actual number of deportees (4,000) to the planned one (8,000), Gutman found that the resistance impacted the deportation campaign. Most of the Jews hid in their houses and did not respond to the Germans' summonses. Searching houses became a risky activity since resistance fighters would fire at the searchers who, in turn, chose to avoid putting themselves in harm's way in the ghetto's dark stairwells and basements.[16] The Jews of the Warsaw ghetto held their heads high. The Oneg Shabbat group, having expressed doubts about the wisdom of *hagana* on January 18, concluded just four days later that the youth's resistance efforts had forced the Germans to retreat.[17] Zuckerman would state in retrospect that the defensive action of January 1943 gave the fighters the feeling that "it was possible to kill Germans and not die, it was possible to defeat Germans."[18]

The ŻOB in Zagłębie

The developments in Warsaw were closely related to the rise of the underground resistance in Zagłębie. To an extent, the latter operated as a regional branch of the ŻOB. The people of Hashomer Hatzair and Dror saw themselves as subject to orders from Warsaw. Moreover, during

14 Klinger, *I Am Writing These Words to You* (1943 diaries), pp. 151–152.
15 Zuckerman, *Bageto U'bamered*, p. 138.
16 Gutman, *The Jews of Warsaw*, pp. 310–311.
17 Ibid., pp. 312–316.
18 Zuckerman, *Bageto U'bamered*, p. 139.

this period, two central representatives were active in the leadership of the underground organization in Zagłębie: Zvi Brandes from Hashomer Hatzair and Frumka Płotnicka from Dror-Hechalutz, who had returned to Będzin in November or December of 1942. Already active in the ŻOB headquarters in Warsaw, Frumka had ideological and operative authority and soon became the dominant figure in the kibbutz alongside Herszel Szpringer and Baruch Gaftek.[19]

The structure of the joint headquarters of the youth movements in Będzin has never been clear, and in the absence of documents, one can only speculate about its nature. It is not known whether there was a military headquarters whose orders the various movements obeyed. It seems that Hechalutz continued to be the umbrella organization housing the usual pioneer movements—Dror, Hashomer Hatzair, and Gordonia—to which members of Hanoar Hatzioni and Hashomer Hadati were added. Regarding the individual members, opinions are divided: Zvi Brandes is usually mentioned as the representative of Hashomer Hatzair; Józek Kożuch and Israel Diamant as representatives of Hanoar Hatzioni; Herszel Szpringer, Frumka Płotnicka, and Baruch Gaftek as representatives of Dror; and Shlomo Lerner and Shlomo Zimmerman as representatives of Gordonia.[20] Among this leadership group, it seems that no commander in chief had been elected.[21] The headquarters served as a sort of underground coordination committee for the various movements. Unlike in Warsaw, the resistance in Zagłębie did not include any representatives of political parties—the inevitable result of the parties' disappearance from the Jewish public sphere in the region. The organization was run almost entirely by the pioneer youth movements.

It can therefore be stated that the overarching framework of Hechalutz that operated in Będzin and Sosnowiec from the beginning of 1940 became the de facto underground Jewish resistance organization. The communists were not included in this organization, although they did carry out independent resistance actions. Very little is known about the communist group during this period, and the evidence is mostly contradictory. The group was mainly engaged in

19 Naomi Shimshi, "Frumka Płotnicka," in *Guf Shlishi Yahid*, p. 194.

20 Gutman and Gutman-Herzberg, "Bageto Bendin: Protocol," pp. 172–179; Brandes and Reshef, *Zvi Brandes*, p. 129; Myriam Ochs report, Moreshet Archives, Hashomer Hatzair High Command, C.79.03; Judenrat clerk, "Kos Hayegonim shel Yehudey Bendin."

21 Zuckerman, *Bageto U'bamered*, p. 108.

propaganda activity and did not develop into an armed resistance.[22] Members of Betar also renounced joining the resistance. According to Shaya Sfinkelstein, one of the members of the movement in Będzin, Betar was the third largest movement in the region before the war but ceased to function with the beginning of the occupation. Some of its *bogrim* had left, and the rest failed to come up with an action plan. Some of them—following Moshe Glidman's example—became Jewish policemen.[23]

The Couriers: Idzia, Ina, and Astrit

The resistance cells in Zagłębie coordinated with the ŻOB in Warsaw on two main operative objectives: establishing contact with the partisans and acquiring weapons. The January events in Warsaw had an immediate impact on the newly established Zagłębie resistance. Chajka wrote:

> And Warsaw had already had a lot of experience. It had already gone through the January campaign and the first defense.
>
> We were so proud: 40 Germans perished[24] and only a few of ours. It turned out that those who defended themselves were the ones who didn't die.
>
> A decision was made to send somebody to Warsaw: Ina [Gelbard] or Idzia [Pejsachson]?
>
> Idzia was sent as she would accomplish more, clarify our situation, demand aid for us, and learn a practical lesson in Warsaw as to how to operate. And that was another mistake. We shouldn't have sent our best girl, particularly as she wasn't so fit for that. She was shortsighted and shortsighted people are always scared.
>
> Idzia perished on the way, while carrying arms, but she had done a lot for us: she presented our situation in Warsaw and they promised to keep sending arms.[25]

22 Ranz, *In Nazi Claws*, pp. 97–98; Szymon (Shimon) Balicki testimony, YVA, O.3/1246, p. 15; Tosia Herzberg, *Hahol Hatzohek* (Hebrew) (Tel Aviv: Ahi'asaf, 1986), p. 20; D. Liwer, *Ir Hametim*, pp. 107–108; Shalom Herzberg, interview by the author, Ramat Gan, 1988.

23 Moshe Yarkoni, in *Sefer Sosnovitz*, vol. 2, pp. 167–168.

24 In fact, only a few Germans were killed and/or wounded.

25 Klinger, *I Am Writing These Words to You* (1943 diaries), pp. 111–112.

Thus Idzia, the middle daughter of the old Bundist Pejsachson, became the first martyr of the resistance. She and Chajka were alike in their devout faith in the idea of *hagana*, as well as in their rhetorical prowess and unwillingness to compromise. Still, Chajka was also a young woman in love, whereas Idzia's whole being seemed to be consumed by the revolution:

> I can see her [Idzia] standing during a meeting, pale, her eyes burning. She's talking about Jewish dignity, about *hagana*. Her eyes are sparkling. She can analyze events soberly, rationally. Having an intellectual's mind—at the same time she can attract, inspire, and make people follow her. It is utterly silent and everybody is staring at her. I will follow her through fire and water.
>
> She is a revolutionary. Perhaps her father's blood is running in her veins—the blood of old Pejsachson, a 1905 revolutionary.[26]

Chajka—and perhaps David too—had tried to convince her, saying she cannot go, she's too short-sighted and doesn't have the right appearance; she'll fall into their trap. It would be better to send the tall, handsome Ina Gelbard, one of the *bogrim* from Sosnowiec. A natural blond, Ina had the looks of a typical Aryan girl, although deep inside, she was also a romantic who wrote moving poetry.[27] Thanks to Idzia's trip, the Zagłębien Hashomer Hatzair resistance acquired its first weapons. However, Idzia herself did not make it back. A new courier called Astrit[28] returned from Warsaw alone.

Idzia's downfall could have been a severe blow to the organization. In her diary, Chajka hints that Idzia's mission was tinged with more than a touch of naivety. Still, the success of the other liaison Astrit from Warsaw seems to have offset the tragedy: "Astrit [Zosia Miller] arrived with the first pieces. Great sorrow over the loss of Idzia, but also great joy on account of those first weapons."[29]

In her diaries, Chajka paints a bright portrait of Astrit that is full of admiration, hiding perhaps a hint of female jealousy:

> Astrit is a new type of member of our movement—a girl messenger. In normal times she would be a very ordinary type of girl. Yes, boys

26 Ibid., pp. 140–141.

27 For more about Ina Gelbard, see Wajsbort, *Yahad U'badad*, p. 27.

28 Zosia Miller, underground name "Astrit" or "Astrid."

29 Klinger, *I Am Writing These Words to You* (1943 diaries), p. 112.

> would always find her attractive. She's very pretty and shapely, but also flighty and vain. She was talking a lot about clothes, because one had to look neat and pretty on the "Aryan" side. New shoes, shirts, dresses had to be bought every time.
>
> And you couldn't criticize her at all. It had to be so. She was so brave, was such a daredevil, and had so much *chutzpa*. They never stopped her for frisking. Once she brought [arms] in a large teddy bear—she looked so sweet and innocent with it—the second time in a marmalade tin, and the third time simply in her coat pocket. She went back and forth several times—bold, brave, and confident.[30]

Yet, the weapons she brought back from Warsaw were too few. Since the resistance had found almost no other sources from which to obtain weapons, this was the bulk of their armaments. But even the few weapons they did receive were enough to infuse the group with renewed vigor:

> We looked at them as though they were sacred objects. The first lesson. Baruch [Gaftek] is teaching us. I grab one, initially scared that it'll burn me, but then my hands begin to move more confidently and stroke the piece. You feel more confident with it and you gain importance in your own eyes. The boys were making fun of us, "So you can do it too? It's not for you."[31]

Chajka felt an erotic attraction to weapons, guns in particular. They were a tangible and palpable expression of revolutionary romanticism. With a gun in their hands, the young women felt like true revolutionaries in the service of a Jewish and humanitarian cause. Boys being boys, their fascination with weapons was tightly linked with the process of maturing. Referring to an earlier period when they had had no access to firearms, Chajka wrote: "The boys carried large switchblade knives on them, out in the streets. They knew full well how childish it was, that one could be killed on the spot if found with that sort of thing."[32]

The guns were also a kind of game, played by youths who felt like they had been admitted into the revolutionary club. As someone accustomed to strictly observing the Hashomer Hatzair *mitzvot* (commandments) prohibiting smoking and drinking, Chajka regarded this with a critical

30 Ibid., pp. 112–113.

31 Ibid., p. 112.

32 Klinger, 1944 diaries, Haogen II, pp. 4–5.

eye: "The movement became somewhat Bohemian. The girls and boys were smoking and drinking vodka. Each expedition or arms purchase was celebrated. They were partying a lot and eating good food."[33] The guns were the embodiment of the revolutionary dream; those holding them felt that they were part of a great historical act.

The Jews of Zagłębie: Work and Survival

The new enthusiasm of the underground resistance was largely disconnected from the course of affairs in Zagłębie and the activity of the Judenrat. In the fall and winter months of 1942–1943, the Judenrat was engaged in two major undertakings: first, the continued integration of Zagłębien Jews into "productive enterprises"; and second, preparations for the establishment of ghettos in Będzin and Sosnowiec. Arrangements for the transfer of the Jewish population into the ghettos began in September 1942. A rare document from the Będzin municipality attests to a meeting held at city hall with the participation of the Gestapo inspector Dreier, in which the further "implementation of the solution to the Jewish problem" was discussed. According to the meeting minutes, the main idea was to continue deporting Jews "who are not integrated into the work process," while workers were "to be concentrated in a certain part of the city."[34] Similar preparations were also being made in Sosnowiec and the other remaining communities in the area.

However, the process was not quick: The concentration of the Jews of Sosnowiec in the suburb of Środula was completed months later, on April 1, 1943, and the transfer of Będzin's Jews into the suburb of Kamionka was only finished in the middle of May 1943.[35] The delay was due to conflicts within the German regional administration. On the one hand, the Gestapo wanted to continue the process of selective extermination; on the other hand, elements motivated by economic considerations—in particular Organization Schmelt within the SS itself as well as the regional inspector on behalf of Speer's Ministry of Armaments and War Production—sought to preserve the Jewish workforce in the area. It

33 Klinger, *I Am Writing These Words to You* (1943 diaries), p. 152.

34 A photograph of the meeting protocol was found in a collection of Będzin municipality documents from the Nazi occupation period relating to the fate of the Jews (on microfilm). See documents regarding the Jewish community in Bedzin, 1943, YVA, M.54.ZIH/JM/2702/1.

35 Ibid.; Wiederman, *Płowa bestia*, pp. 281–303.

appears that the latter had the upper hand. In the report summarizing the extermination of Polish Jews submitted to Himmler by the statistician Richard Korherr on December 31, 1942, it was stated that Organization Schmelt employed 50,570 Jews, of whom 8,188 were foreign citizens.[36] From this data, it appears that approximately 42,000 of the Jews of Eastern Upper Silesia (i.e., Zagłębie) were working for Organization Schmelt either in labor camps or as part of the workshops established in the region and were therefore protected from deportation to Auschwitz. Overall, the Jews of Zagłębie at that time were organized into twenty-three communities of over 60,000 people in total, in addition to about 10,000 young Jews laboring in the Organization Schmelt camps.[37]

Various documents that will be discussed later imply that the purpose of the ghettos in Zagłębie had changed: they were now supposed to operate as huge labor camps rather than holding pens for Jews for the purposes of selection and extermination. Indeed, from August 1942 until June 1943, no further deportations took place in Zagłębie, with the exception of the deportation of 3,000 Jews from Chrzanów on February 18, 1943.[38] However, every Wednesday, a special Gestapo car would take a number of undocumented Jews or those caught for various crimes to Auschwitz.[39] The threat of Auschwitz therefore continued to loom over the Jews of Zagłębie, but it seemed that those working under the auspices of Organization Schmelt (the Special Commissioner) would be spared the sword.

Following the events of the Great *Punkt*, the conclusion of the majority of Zagłębien Jews—contrary to that of the youth movement activists—was that the process of annihilation was fundamentally selective: the people who failed to prove their vitality to the German system were sent to their deaths. Most of the residents, however, had returned to their homes. The Great *Punkt* was a final stage in the annihilation of the "useless." Hence, if the Jews wished to continue to survive, they had to prove themselves essential to the Germans.

36 Albert Speer, *The Slave State: Heinrich Himmler's Masterplan for SS Supremacy*, tr. by Joachim Neugroschel (London: Weidenfeld and Nicolson, 1981), p. 284.

37 Statistische Angaben des Stands über die Jüdische, Moreshet Archive, Avihu Ronen collection, 235.

38 Bochner, *Sefer Kheshanov [Chrzanów]*, pp. 245–246; Rutka Laskier, *Rutka's Notebook*, p. 43.

39 Yehudit Sinai (Halinka Goldblum) interview; Aharon Brandes testimony at the Barenblatt trial, Moreshet Archive, D.1.5366; D. Liwer, *Ir Hametim*, pp. 78–79.

Thus, from August 12, 1942, onward, the Jews flocked in droves to the gates of the workshops and the other "essential" enterprises. Working for them was henceforth seen as an insurance certificate not only against deportation to the camps but also against death. The work permits handed out by Organization Schmelt became life permits. By the end of April 1943, about 13,000 of the 18,000 Jews of Będzin who had managed to survive until that time were employed as "essential workers."[40] Some of them were elderly people and children as young as ten. A similar proportion was recorded in Sosnowiec.

Among other things, this explains Merin's renewed power and popularity. The idea he championed—"work for rescue"—seemed to have proven itself. By and large, the Jews of Zagłębie appear to have placed their trust in his steady hand to lead them toward survival. Refugees coming in from the Generalgouvernement territories testified to the continuation of the systematic extermination, whereas most Zagłębien Jews were still alive and working. Thus, the move to the ghettos was also seen as a necessary evil on the way to survival. Granted, Środula and Kamionka were dilapidated and poverty-stricken suburbs, but even there it was possible to continue to be productive, and therefore, to live. From Merin's point of view, the only threat to these developments, which seemed to guarantee the survival of the Jews of Zagłębie, was the resistance.

The Judenrat and the Resistance: The First Clash

Did Merin know what the youth of Zagłębie were doing? All evidence leads to the conclusion that he was aware of their underground activity almost as soon as it began. And how could he not have been? Anielewicz was a well-known figure, and Merin's conversation with Nathan Eck indicates that he had heard about the idea of armed defense from the man himself. Besides, the youth movements conducted public propaganda campaigns, and the flyers they pasted in the streets were directed as much against the Judenrat as against the Germans. Moreover, in towns where everyone knew everyone, it was difficult to conduct underground activity without it eventually coming to the attention of community institutions.

During the fall of 1942, it seems that Merin tried to avoid open confrontation with the Jewish public and the youth movements. He did try

40 Documents regarding the Jewish community in Bedzin, 1943, YVA, M.54.ZIH/JM/2702/3, 4, 16, 22, 24.

to quell the growing hostility against the Jewish police and the Judenrat. In view of the behavior of the Jewish police on the day of the Great *Punkt*, Merin decided to reorganize its ranks. Barenblatt was appointed head of the Będzin police, while Romek Goldminc—a close associate of Hanoar Hatzioni—was appointed chief of police on behalf of the Central Judenrat in Sosnowiec.[41] With this well-thought-out move, Merin supposedly renounced the actions of the Jewish police and created a separation between it and the Judenrat. It was a retroactive admission of the violent and corrupt behavior of some Jewish policemen. But this separation between the Jewish police and the Judenrat was for appearances' sake only; in reality, Merin, his brother Chaim, and his deputy Fania Czarna commanded the police directly.

In parallel, Merin made efforts to ingratiate himself with the youth in order to divert them from underground activities. From Chajka's diaries, we learn about at least one meeting that took place between representatives of the movements and those of the Judenrat. In the absence of names and dates, it is difficult to determine who participated in such a meeting and when. Based on the context, we can assume that it included representatives of Hashomer Hatzair as well as other movements and that it was held during the first stages of the organization of the resistance in the fall of 1942. The young activists attended the meeting after already deciding on a pursuit of armed resistance, which meant a fight against the Judenrat. At least among Hashomer Hatzair members, it was obvious that the resistance's first actions would be directed against members of the Jewish police. In her diary, Chajka wrote:

> The struggle against the Jewish *gmina*—against the internal evil and the police. After the disgraceful behavior of the Jewish police during the deportation campaign a decision was made to blind [Romek] Goldminc and Procel with vitriol.
>
> There was also Mordechai's secret order and a resolution of the OKW to liquidate [Moshe] Merin. The Jewish *gmina* was feeling the growing influence on the young and on the sober, defiant part of the society.[42]

41 Wiederman, *Płowa bestia*, pp. 250–255; Hirsch Barenblatt testimony at the Barenblatt trial, Moreshet Archive, D.1.5366.

42 Klinger, *I Am Writing These Words to You* (1943 diaries), pp. 107–108.

Romek Goldminc, as mentioned, was the head of the Jewish police, and Procel must have been one of his men. A plan to blind one of the members of the Jewish police also appears in the testimony of Chana Wiernik referring to that period, and the name of the Jewish policeman mentioned there is Procel.[43] Chajka's words testify to the hatred toward the Jewish police that was felt among the public in general and among members of the youth movements in particular.

The meeting, of which Chajka's is the only testimony in our possession, was very tense. It is not clear whether Merin himself participated in it, and it is possible that the youth activists met, in fact, with Mołczadski, the head of the Judenrat in Będzin. Chajka interpreted the conduct of the Judenrat members at the meeting as betraying fear:

> They began to fear us—hotheads ready for anything. They feared for their own heads, because they were aware that their kingdom resting on clay feet would collapse the moment our first act was discovered. They knew that they would be the first to lose their heads because of us.
>
> They didn't want that to happen, no price was too dear for them to avoid that…[44]

At the meeting, the Judenrat members adopted a two-pronged approach: they spoke in condemnation of the idea of *hagana* and suggested educational avenues for youth movement activity:

> They called us to a meeting.
>
> They criticized those who had brought over "foreign" pessimism and declared that the things happening in the General Government wouldn't happen here.
>
> There's the *Leiter* [Merin] here and the local Jews play a vital economic role—the local Yishuv [Jewish community] will remain.

43 Chana Schlesinger (Wiernik) testimony, Moreshet Archive, A.273. There are several sources of Chana Schlesinger's (Wiernik) testimony that appear throughout this volume: Chana Schlesinger (Wiernik) testimony, Moreshet Archive, A.273; Chana Schlesinger (Wiernik), interview by the author, Ra'anana 1986; Chana Schlesinger-Wiernik, *Hadapim Sheli* (Hebrew) (Ra'anana: self-published, 2004). There are no contradictions between the three. In cases where the same event is described in all of them, the reference is Chana Wiernik testimony. In other specific cases, the reference is to one of the three sources mentioned above.

44 Klinger, *I Am Writing These Words to You* (1943 diaries), p. 108.

> They criticized the young for being *Philistines* [egoistic and narrow-minded persons] and unable to act.
>
> They'd like to go hand in hand with us, as the young have to be taken care of. They'd open clubs, have choirs, singing, and lectures. *Hagana*—very well, they support it too and want to be ready, but we shouldn't do that on our own. We're hotheads, who'll bring ourselves and the *gmina* to ruin.[45]

It is not entirely clear who responded on behalf of the youth movements. Based on the wording and the fact that the speaker's name is not mentioned, we can assume that it was Chajka herself:

> We answered them...
>
> There was a time when we wanted to cooperate with them. Today, after they have undertaken the disgraceful deportation work, we have nothing in common with them. There's too wide a gap between us and too much mutual distrust.
>
> This is no time to educate the young generation when we are in danger of physical extermination.
>
> There was a time when we used to say that we had to survive not only physically, but also morally. We were educating both ourselves and others back then, relentlessly, zealously.
>
> Today, when we see no future ahead of us but only the naked, horrible reality—death in the ovens of Auschwitz—we have to prepare ourselves for something different—for *hagana*. Yes, this is the only plane on which we can reach an agreement. Sometimes we didn't want that agreement either. And we showed them our *partzuf* [face]. They had stopped deluding themselves and began fighting us.[46]

The youth activists thus spoke openly about *hagana*. On the other hand, it is evident that Merin—if he was indeed present—and his people also meant what they said. But by this point it was already too late. As Chajka points out with disdain: "They wanted to give the child a toy. But they were too late."[47]

45 Ibid.

46 Ibid., pp. 108–109.

47 Klinger, 1944 diaries, Haogen II, p. 27.

It was likewise evident that because they had accused Merin and the Judenrat of collaborating with the Germans, not to mention betraying the Jewish People, the youth movement members risked finding their names on the lists of those heading to the labor camps.

The Conflict Is Aggravated

In the winter of 1942–1943, there were several clashes between Judenrat members in Będzin and members of the underground resistance. One of them involved the rescue of a young Gordonia refugee from Warsaw, Shimon Frost, by members of his movement.[48] The Jewish police raided the city in an attempt to locate him. When this failed, Mołczadski arrested all the Gordonia people on the farm, including David Liwer. Mołczadski threatened the members of Gordonia with labor camps if they did not hand Frost over to them, but the young people did not take his words seriously. He would not dare take action against the sons of the community's dignitaries, including his own deputy. And indeed, Mołczadski was forced to forgo punitive action, and the young men were released. Frost himself was transferred to the special refugee work camp the *Arbeitskommando* (AK).[49]

In February–March 1943, Mołczadski was involved in another, far more acute confrontation with Dror. Mołczadski first tried to deal with the members of the kibbutz by forcing them to join the ranks of the Jewish police. An invitation to enlist was sent along with a threat that if they failed to show up, they would be deprived of their workers' IDs (*Sonderkarte*). Nevertheless, the young men refused to obey the summons. Jewish policemen under the command of the deputy police chief Kaufman marched over to the kibbutz and surrounded it. A fight broke out between the policemen and members of Dror. Later, the clash spilled out into the street as well. Kaufman ordered his men to retreat, while Jews who witnessed the scuffle applauded the defeat of the police.

In Sosnowiec, Merin took tougher measures. He knew to pick out the weakest links: the communists and Hashomer Hatzair. The blow inflicted on the communist organization was seemingly intended to be a

48 Shimon Frost belonged to a group of Gordonia people who were smuggled to Zagłębie by Eliezer Geller after the Great Deportation in the summer of 1942.

49 D. Liwer, *Ir Hametim*, pp. 97–100; Shimon Frost, interview by the author, Jerusalem, 1985; Abraham Manela, *Haderech Layare'ah Ha'oleh* (Hebrew) (Kibbutz Lohamei Hageta'ot: Ghetto Fighters' House, 1999), pp. 49–50; Abraham Manela interview.

warning to the resistance but, in fact, the activity of the communist cell was harmless: Loyal to the notion that the only viable solution was struggling alongside the Soviet Union, the members of this organization opposed the idea of *hagana*. Their activity consisted of the distribution of propaganda leaflets and the sale of charity bonds to the communist underground. A Judenrat official who was close to the group turned whistleblower and led to the arrest of young people suspected of communist activity. The arrests were carried out by the Judenrat, which handed the detainees over to the Gestapo. They were interrogated and tortured in the Mysłowice Prison.[50]

Some of the prisoners were from out of town, but the name of two among them carried a special sting. The first was Bobo Graubart, who switched from Hashomer Hatzair to the communists due to ideological differences. He came from a notable family: His grandfather was the city's late rabbi, Issachar Ber Graubart, and his father Benjamin was the former chairman of the Judenrat.[51] The second was the son of Rabbi Bunim Bonhardt, also one of the city's notables. No one could explain why he was included on the list of suspects. Following the arrests and the interrogations, the family members of the detainees were also arrested. According to Liwer, with the exception of the Graubart family, they were all deported to Auschwitz as part of the weekly Wednesday transport.[52] There is no mention of the usual lobbying processes deployed on behalf of the communist group and their families, and it therefore seems that Merin had found a scapegoat without risking losing popularity.

The Dunski and Minc Affair

Hashomer Hatzair was a harder target to hit, but Merin could spot a weakness there. At this time, the Hashomer *ken* in Sosnowiec had no more than ten *bogrim*. Operating as a branch of Hashomer Hatzair in Będzin, it was isolated and weak. This explains why Merin went after them rather than the Będzin group, who were known as the leaders of the resistance.

Opinions differ regarding the immediate cause of the affair. According to Fela Katz, a member of the group, it all started with the

50 Szymon (Shimon) Balicki testimony, YVA, O.3/1246; D. Liwer, *Ir Hametim*, p. 105; Ranz, *In Nazi Claws*, pp. 65–68; Stanisław Wygodski, interview by the author, Ramat Gan, 1986.

51 See Herzberg, *Hahol Hatzohek*, p. 20.

52 D. Liwer, *Ir Hametim*, pp. 108–109.

aforementioned leaflets that Janek Zimmerman, a member of Hanoar Hatzioni, had stuffed into the boots made in the workshops, which were supposed to be sent to the soldiers at the front. The leaflets fell into the hands of the Germans, who put pressure on Merin to find the culprits.[53] According to Chajka, it was the result of the Judenrat's monitoring of the secret radio station and the underground newspaper.[54] And according to Chana Wiernik's testimony, it was the plan concocted by Zvi Dunski and Lipek Minc to blind a Jewish policeman named Procel with acid, which came to the attention of the Jewish police, thanks to Romek Szlezinger, a member of Chana's group in Hashomer Hatzair.[55]

The hunt for Dunski and Minc appears to have begun in late autumn of 1942. Dunski, Minc, and two other instructors from the Sosnowiec *ken* were arrested. The police tried to exert pressure on the boys through their families: Lipek Minc's brother, who served in the Jewish police, was fired from his position, and Zvi Dunski's mother and his ten-year-old sister were imprisoned with him. But at this point, Merin contented himself with threats. After three weeks, the boys and their families were released. Chajka remembered that "Lipek was tasked with telling us that our actions were known to them, that they would not play games with us. We were forced to submit to negotiate."[56]

At any rate, the resistance continued its activity both in Będzin and in Sosnowiec. Although evidence regarding the development of the affair is contradictory and confused, it seems that Merin, having failed again to catch Zvi Dunski, decided to hold Zvi's mother and ten-year-old sister as hostages. At some point, the second sister Genia—a member of Hashomer Hatzair—was also imprisoned with them.[57] When Zvi failed to come forward, the members of his family were transferred to the Będzin orphanage, the usual roundup point for deportations to Auschwitz. There, they were held hostage until Zvi turned himself in to the police. His mother held out defiantly:

> She sent cards. Don't let Zvi come, she wrote. I am not afraid, she said, they will not hurt me. She was called to testify before Merin, asked where her son was, what he was doing, who his associates

53 Chana Schlesinger (Wiernik) testimony, Moreshet Archive, A.273.

54 Klinger, 1944 diaries, Haogen II, p. 31.

55 Chana Schlesinger (Wiernik) interview.

56 Klinger,1944 diaries, Haogen II, p. 31.

57 Chana Schlesinger (Wiernik) interview.

> were. The mother said she knew nothing. She didn't ask Merin for anything, she didn't cry, as mothers usually did. Even her baby was laughing and playing. The mother read a book and so did the little girl. She was a simple woman, she could barely read, but she was made of strong stuff.[58]

Zvi did not come forward. In Sosnowiec, or perhaps among the Będzin leadership, it was decided that he would be safer in Generalgouvernement territory. Ina Gelbard, the movement's courier, was tasked with shepherding him across the border.[59] But Zvi hesitated, and this delay would seal his tragic fate.

On the night of the escape, probably at the beginning of February 1943, Zvi suddenly appeared at the house of Kasia (Miriam, Hela) Szancer. Kasia was his girlfriend, and he asked to spend one last night with her. Kasia was confused. It was past curfew, and walking around on the streets was not allowed. Her parents were religious and opposed her activity in Hashomer Hatzair. Hiding a young man in her home—one wanted for the crime of illicit underground activity to boot—went against all good sense. Without saying a word to her parents, Kasia led Zvi to the attic, brought up a folding bed for him to sleep on, and went back downstairs.[60]

That day, the Judenrat decided to arrest all the members of Hashomer Hatzair in Sosnowiec as hostages subject to Dunski's appearance. Lipek Minc and his girlfriend Chana Wiernik walked home together after a day at the workshop. When they passed by the police station, a light suddenly came on inside. The two concluded that another reprisal was imminent. They took no special measures in response but continued on their way to their respective homes. Chana hurried to get into bed, but a few moments later there was a knock on the door. She refused to open. The door was forced, and three Jewish policemen entered, among them Klajner, the deputy police chief in Sosnowiec. A search was conducted, but the police found nothing. Nevertheless, they arrested Chana.[61]

Concurrently, the other members of Hashomer Hatzair—among them Lipek Minc, Ina Gelbard, and Fela Katz—were also arrested, as were most of their parents and family members. A typewriter was found

58 Klinger, 1944 diaries, Haogen II, p. 32.

59 Chana Schlesinger (Wiernik) interview.

60 Miriam (Kasia) Barenblatt, interview by the author, Tel Aviv, 1985.

61 Chana Schlesinger (Wiernik) testimony, Moreshet Archive, A.273.

in Lipek's home. The police also arrived at Kasia's apartment. Kasia saw them approaching from her window and hurried to lock Zvi in the attic. She locked herself in a nearby room. From above she could see the police combing through the house. Her parents were arrested along with her brother-in-law who was staying with them. Kasia decided to go downstairs. When she entered the living room, her father turned around and slapped her across the face. They were taken together to the police station. However, Zvi was not discovered.[62]

The main focus of the investigation was Chana Wiernik. The police probably chose her because they knew her house served as the main meeting place for the *shomrim*. The investigator was Romek Goldminc, the head of the Jewish police. According to Chana's testimony:

> Since he couldn't get anything out of me, he got angrier and started beating me as the other policemen laughed. I decided not to speak at all. They wouldn't even hear the words: "I don't know" from that point on. This angered Goldminc even more. He hit me on the head, slammed me against the wall, struck me with an iron rod, put me in a special room, and beat me again. Finally, I said: "I haven't seen him, I don't know." He stopped. Suddenly, Romek [Szlezinger] entered the room. Goldminc asked me again: "When did you see Zvi?" Shocked and stunned, I answered: "Two months ago." Now Goldminc turned to Romek, and Romek said: "He was at her house this week." I screamed at Romek with all my might: "Pig!" and didn't add anything more. He exited. I was beaten again. It was a different question now repeating: "Where is Zvi?"[63]

Chana lost consciousness and was taken to a basement holding cell. Fela and Kasia were also interrogated. Fortunately for Fela, she did not know much. Contact with Zvi was maintained mainly by Chana and Ina Gelbard. Fela was not beaten during the interrogation, even though she was also personally questioned by Goldminc.[64] As for Kasia, it seems that the Jewish police did not know about her relationship with Zvi.

The long night continued for the Sosnowiec *shomrim* and their parents. From her cell in the basement, Chana Wiernik suddenly heard a noise followed by shouting. She tried to guess what had happened.

62 Miriam (Kasia) Barenblatt interview.

63 Chana Schlesinger (Wiernik) testimony, Moreshet Archive, A.273.

64 Fela Katz testimony, Moreshet Archive, A.470.

Soon she was taken out once more and found herself facing Chaim Merin. She testified:

> Chaim Merin said: "We caught him." Tears burst from my eyes. "Why are you crying," he asked, "what happened? I want you to go and convince Zvi not to jump." I didn't believe that they had really captured Zvi. I didn't understand what the jumping thing was about. Merin explained: "We found him in a friend's room. He's gone up to the roof and wants to kill himself." For a moment I doubted what I should do and immediately decided to go with them and convince Zvi to jump off the roof. Yes, to jump. Merin couldn't believe I was willing to go, but unfortunately, before I could leave the police station accompanied by the officers, Zvi walked in before us. He was wounded all over and had blood stains on his clothes. They shackled him as they shackle a murderer. I only managed to call out to him: "Haszu!" (that's what we called him). We exchanged glances for a second and I didn't have time to see him again. They took me into the basement. From above came the sound of commotion and noise. It's possible that these were echoes of the policemen celebrating Zvi's capture.[65]

In the basement, she was joined by Kasia, Ina, and their friends. Until the moment she saw Zvi, she had been sure that he was on his way to Generalgouvernement territory. Now, the tears burst forth. "Why did you do that? Why did you delay the departure?" she admonished Ina.[66]

In the morning, the girls and the families were released. The father of one of the girls turned to Kasia and said to her that she could not return home in her state. She came home only a few days later. Rebel though she may have been, she also had a soft heart. She was ready to talk about her relationship with Zvi, lest he jump off the roof, but Chana Wiernik grabbed her hand and said: "You know nothing," and made her sit back down.[67]

The beaten and tortured Zvi and Lipek were transferred to the Będzin orphanage under heavy Jewish police guard. In all likelihood, they were tortured there as well. After a few days, they were handed over to the Gestapo and put in the Sosnowiec prison with the members of the communist cell. According to Chajka, "in prison the boys found out that

65 Chana Schlesinger (Wiernik) testimony, Moreshet Archive, A.273.

66 Ibid.

67 Miriam (Kasia) Barenblatt interview.

Merin and Goldminc had signed a confidential document at the Gestapo, accusing Lipek and Zvi of membership in a secret organization that conducted sabotage against the Germans."[68] Lipek and Zvi's conduct in the German prison elicited their friends' respect and admiration. While the wave of arrests among the members of the communist cell continued, no further members of Hashomer Hatzair were arrested. Hence, the *shomrim* concluded that the two had held up under investigation:

> But he [Lipek] proved resilient to the Germans.
>
> And Cwi, that simple boy devoted to the movement, knew how to be a hero. After every interrogation he would return covered in blood and unconscious. But as soon as he came around, he would take water and wash the others and console them, making them hardier and stronger. And when one of the prisoners who was sleeping in the same cell tried to hang himself, Cwi didn't try to stop him even though he would have been executed for that.[69]

Despite all obstacles, the members of the movement managed to maintain correspondence with Zvi and Lipek. They bribed a warden to smuggle letters out of the prison, hidden inside laundry bundles. It is likely that Merin's continued involvement in the affair came to light thanks to these letters. Apart from the message given to the Gestapo, Merin and his men also gave the Germans a subversive leaflet that the Jewish police had found in Zvi's home. Chajka reported:

> And after all that, Moniek Merin had the nerve to enter Zvi's cell. The Germans sent him there to get some information out of Zvi. Moniek then said, "I, too, am a Zionist, I've come to rescue you." "If you are a Zionist," said Zvi, "then I am not." He then slapped Moniek, and ordered him to get out.[70]

Chajka admired Dunski:

> He was hard-headed, a simple cobbler of a Jewish proletariat origin, with a lot of good sense, a peasant's sense, always pragmatic

68 Klinger, *I Am Writing These Words to You* (1943 diaries), p. 110. David Liwer confirms this. See D. Liwer, *Ir Hametim*, pp. 107–108.

69 Klinger, *I Am Writing These Words to You* (1943 diaries), p. 110.

70 Klinger, 1944 diaries, Haogen II, p. 34.

> and practical. He was very meticulous when it came to work too, very thorough. Punctual to a fault. One could rely on him. He was a *shomer*.
>
> He sent us letters from prison—you wouldn't believe Zvi wrote these letters. They were simple, ordinary words, but there was a kind of inner beauty there, a kind of depth. He wrote about the prison, about being surrounded by bars, about freedom—how he had been more of a prisoner out in the streets, where he could not do what he wanted, while in prison he could laugh at the Germans in the face, he could say what he wanted, out loud, without fear. He had nothing to lose, he knew he wouldn't come out of prison alive. He did not like to deceive himself—he was strong enough to face the truth.
>
> He even got used to the idea of dying. He asked us to send him some cyanide. A man never knows what will happen to him, he might grow weak, he might run out of strength right at the end, although he had faith in himself, since he had survived so far. He might have let them shoot him, to show them how a Jew faces death. But he would not let them hang him, he would take cyanide instead. Our girls sat in the corner, wiping their eyes in secret, so that no one would see. Zvi also wrote that he was proud of [Lipek] for holding up so well, for not falling apart.[71]

Lipek and Zvi were imprisoned in Sosnowiec for two months, after which they were sent to Auschwitz, where they were probably hanged. In another version of events, Zvi was killed in the prison in Sosnowiec, while Lipek was killed in Auschwitz.[72] About a month later, on April 23, 1943, the management of the Central Judenrat published a document signed by Fania Czarna in which the residents of Zagłębie were informed of the hanging of the eight members of the communist cell in Auschwitz in March. It contained no information regarding Zvi or Lipek. Benjamin Graubart, the father of Bobo from the communist cell arrestees, kept this document as a memento of iniquity until after the war.[73]

Ina Gelbard visited Chana Wiernik in a labor camp in Gliwice near Zagłębie, where Chana had been taken on March 13, 1943. Ina told Chana about the death of Lipek and Zvi. By this time, Chana had lost the

71 Ibid., pp. 35–36.

72 Chana Schlesinger (Wiernik) testimony, Moreshet Archive, A.273.

73 D. Liwer, "Hamihteret BeBendin Vehasviva" (Hebrew), in Stein, *Pinkas Bendin*, vol. 2, p. 357; Szymon (Shimon) Balicki testimony, YVA, O.3/1246, p. 16.

will to live. Imprisoned in the camp, cut off from her friends, she asked Ina for cyanide. Ina gave her the dose she had on her, but asked her not to use it: "You will stay alive, I want you to tell people about us. That, too, is an important role. You must stay here in the camp. I don't know when the end will come, but I know I won't be alive to see it."[74]

In Będzin, Chajka summarized the affair in poignant words that were never published:

> The case of Lipek and Cwi is a dark stain on the history of our movement in Zagłębie. Whenever I recall it, I feel ashamed, even today.
>
> There was no need for those victims.
>
> We were still weak back then and not ready to react. So, it was either of the two: react or go to Canossa [humiliating surrender]. Back then we could still go to Merin. We would have avoided the unnecessary victims and even that burning shame caused by their deaths remaining un[avenged]. The response of a fighting revolutionary organization, which we were, should have been either to rescue the boys or kill Goldminc or Merin, and go even more underground and intensify the conspiracy.[75]

It seems that the resistance leadership realized that it would not be possible to react violently to the imprisonment of Lipek and Zvi without then having to go much deeper underground, which was practically impossible in such a small community. If they were to start an open battle on the other hand, the entire organization and perhaps even the community would be eliminated. Frustrated, Chajka wrote: "So we could have taken action and then completely liquidated the organization, but we didn't want to let that happen."[76] One can hear the sensible influence of Zvi Brandes in these words, and perhaps even Frumka Płotnicka's: the organization was too small and weak to react. An immediate reaction could lead to disaster. According to Chajka, the decision they eventually came to was: "We took a step ahead: we 'dissolved' the organization in order to completely 'confuse' the enemy. We already knew that we would never gain prominence without firearms."[77]

74 Chana Schlesinger (Wiernik) testimony, Moreshet Archive, A.273.

75 Klinger, *I Am Writing These Words to You* (1943 diaries), p. 111.

76 Ibid.

77 Ibid.

Whether or not the organization actually disbanded or the move was a ploy to mislead the Judenrat, subsequent developments show that underground operations did not cease. Nevertheless, the resistance's operational plans during this period remained vague. Either way, Merin's tactics seemed to have proven successful. While the Dunski and Minc affair did not lead to a complete paralysis of the resistance, it clearly curbed its actions.

Chapter Fifteen

False Hopes

A Possibility of Rescue

The Dunski and Minc affair came at a time when the youth movements were already debating and reconsidering the wisdom of *hagana*. At the end of 1942, Hanoar Hatzioni held its council in Sosnowiec, and Józek Kożuch said that, in parallel to armed resistance, resources should be directed toward rescue efforts, especially in view of the failure to make contact with the partisans and the lack of weapons. It seems that Gordonia was not wholly on board with the idea of defense either. For the first time in years, a realistic possibility of rescue was in sight. News began to arrive from Switzerland about the possibility of purchasing Latin American passports, which would grant the holder protection until the end of the war. The news arrived in January 1943, and the members of Gordonia embraced this new line of action. The members of Dror and Hashomer Hatzair thus found themselves isolated in their devotion and commitment to *hagana*.

The Citizens Exchange Delegations

Due to its geopolitical situation, Zagłębie at this time became a central hub of communications with *Eretz Israel*. As an area annexed to the German Reich, it was able to maintain postal correspondence with the neutral countries—Switzerland in particular—from where it was possible to maintain continuous contact with the Yishuv. There were also relatively convenient communication channels between the Generalgouvernement territory and Zagłębie, thus it was possible to transfer information quickly from the Polish ghettos—Warsaw chief among them—to this region, which was considered relatively safe. By virtue of this, Zagłębie became a kind of relay station between youth movement activists in Poland and their headquarters in *Eretz Israel*.

Yet contact between the youth movements in Zagłębie and *Eretz Israel* did not stop at postal correspondence. At the end of October 1942, news arrived in Zagłębie that some women and children whose relatives were British citizens or who themselves had British citizenship would be able to leave occupied Poland for Mandatory Palestine as part of a citizens exchange agreement. This hard-earned agreement applied not only to Zagłębie but also to all of occupied Poland. A total of sixty-nine Jews left Poland, including about ten people from Zagłębie.[1] Great excitement stirred around those about to leave. Even though everyone knew that this rescue option was only available to a lucky few, their departure was seen as a breach in the barrier, a gateway to the free world.

Among those who left were Chajka Buchbinder and Sara Rechnitz, members of Kibbutz Degania Bet, who came to visit relatives in Będzin on the eve of the war and got stuck there. The two were associated with both the Judenrat and the youth movements. One of them worked as a clerk in the relief department of the Judenrat in Będzin.[2] Both were close to the pioneer youth circles through the Gordonia movement. Chajka knew both women and mentioned their stay at the farm, but there is no reference to their journey to *Eretz Israel* in her diary. On the eve of their departure from Będzin, a festive party was held in their honor at the orphanage, attended by representatives of both the Judenrat and the youth movements.[3] The two women also met with Eliezer Geller, the leader of Gordonia in Warsaw, who was staying in Będzin at the time, and the information they subsequently brought with them to Mandatory Palestine included many details about the deportations to the extermination camps and about Auschwitz.

The group's arrival in Mandatory Palestine in November 1942 caused a public stir. These survivors were the first eyewitnesses to the

1 Dina Porat, *Hanhaga Bemilkud: HaYishuv Nohach Hashoah, 1942–1945* (Hebrew) (Tel Aviv: Am Oved, 1986), p. 62.

2 Anonymous Judenrat clerk testimony, YVA, O.12/3. This is most likely Sara Rechnitz who worked as a clerk in the relief department of the Judenrat.

3 Ibid.; Shraga Fruchtzweig interview.

systematic extermination of European Jews. As shown by Yoav Gelber and Shabtai B. Beit Zvi, detailed information about the extermination was published in the Yishuv press as early as the beginning of 1942. However, the news was too shocking to be believed, and according to Gelber, the difficult situation in *Eretz Israel* in the spring and summer of 1942—the increasing fears of a possible occupation of Mandatory Palestine by General Erwin Rommel's forces advancing in Egypt—also contributed to the suppression of the ghastly knowledge.[4] Members of the newly arrived group were interrogated immediately by the Jewish Agency and gave living testimonies based on the slaughter they had seen with their own eyes, which made it no longer possible to ignore the horror unfolding in Europe. The Hebrew-speaking Degania companies who had come over to *Eretz Israel* from Będzin played a significant part in this.

The publication of the investigation's findings on November 23, 1942, was effectively an official recognition by the Jewish Agency that a systematic extermination of Jews was underway in Europe. A shockwave now passed over the Yishuv: Days of mourning and fasting were announced, the masses were called to memorial and protest rallies, and petitions were sent around the world. There were cries of contrition for the sin of not knowing and rallies of accusations between members of the Yishuv leadership: "Who gave us permission not to know?" asked Zalman Robashov (Zalman Shazar), "Who allowed us to deceive ourselves?"[5] Harsh allegations were directed against Yitzhak Gruenbaum who, by virtue of his position as head of the Jewish Agency's Committee of Four, was responsible for contact with the Jews of occupied Europe.[6] Among the accusers was Meir Ya'ari who decried: "You ask yourself in a daze: What happened to the Zionist movement? Have all standards and morals been lost?"[7] One might wonder who the target of this reprimand might have been. After all, his own movement had also lost contact with its people in Poland since Mordechai Oren had returned from Geneva

4 Yoav Gelber, "Ha'itonut Ha'ivrit Be'Eretz Yisrael al Hashmadat Yehudey Eropa, 1941–1942" (Hebrew), *Dapim Leheker Hashoah Vehamered*, 2:1 (1970); see the chapter "Deep Silence," in Beit Zvi, *Post-Ugandan Zionism on Trial*. See also Yosef Gorny, *Kriya bein Onim: Ha'itonut Hayehudit BeEretz Yisrael, BeBritaniya, BeArtzot Habrit, U'beBrit Hamo'atzot Linohah Hashoah, 1939–1945* (Hebrew) (Tel Aviv: Hakibbutz Hameuchad and Tel Aviv University Press, 2009).

5 Porat, *Hanhaga Bemilkud*, p. 65.

6 Ibid., pp. 65–66.

7 Meir Ya'ari at a meeting of the Hakibbutz Ha'artzi Executive Committee, December 15, 1942, quoted in Halamish, *Meir Ya'ari*, p. 240.

over two years earlier. Yet, now they sprung to action. Ya'ari and Hazan, his associate in the Hakibbutz Ha'artzi leadership, would over the next few months become the most vocal proponents of a general mobilization of the Yishuv for the sake of rescue operations.

Ya'ari's awakening reflected that of the Yishuv in general. Fundraising for a special rescue mission began in *Eretz Israel*. Young people began urging their leaders to send them to Europe to help the remaining Jews of the exterminated ghettos. In January 1943, the Action Committee for the Rescue of Diaspora Jewry was established on behalf of the Jewish Agency, which—despite everything—was still headed by Yitzhak Gruenbaum. A delegation from the Yishuv gathered in Istanbul, and special attention was paid to the contact center of Hechalutz in Geneva. All these would become important links connecting *Eretz Israel* with occupied Poland, a connection that passed chiefly through Zagłębie.

Halinka's Mission

About three months after the departure of the first group on January 23, 1943, another group of exchange citizens gathered in Zagłębie. The departure of this second group was made possible thanks to a private Jewish initiative as opposed to the institutional intervention of the Jewish Agency.[8] The Jews in this group hailed from Będzin and Sosnowiec only. Among them was the eighteen-year-old Helena (Halinka) Goldblum, a member of Hanoar Hatzioni from Sosnowiec. The youth movements saw her departure as a mission to convey to the Yishuv in the Land of Israel the story of the Jews' annihilation and the good news of the youth movements' preparations for *hagana*. The leadership of the ŻOB in Warsaw hoped that Frumka Płotnicka would be included in one of these exchange deals so that she would get to *Eretz Israel* and renew the severed contacts with her people. However, this could not be arranged, and Frumka went to

8 According to the testimony of Yehudit Sinai (Halinka Goldblum), the delegation was organized by Klajner, whose daughters were rescued in this same mission, allowing their testimony to be quoted more than once in this study. Likewise, according to Ka-Tzetnik's *Sunrise over Hell*, the delegation was arranged by Jews in occupied Poland (Ka-Tzetnik was Halinka's brother-in-law). Ka-Tzetnik, *Sunrise over Hell*, pp. 83–85; Yehudit Sinai (Halinka Goldblum) interview. The preparations for the group's departure caused great excitement in the city. Rutka Laskier wrote in her diary: "There is great excitement in town. A lot of people are about to leave for 'the land of our forefathers,' to [Mandatory] Palestine." Laskier, *Rutka's Notebook*, p. 25.

Sosnowiec to brief Halinka instead. From the testimony of Fredka Mazia (Oksenhendler) it appears that Chajka Klinger was also among those to be briefed.[9] Chajka does not mention Halinka's trip in her diary.

Halinka was instructed to convey several messages to *Eretz Israel*. The first of these was detailed information about the extermination, given to her by Frumka. The young woman also carried intelligence about the activities of the youth movements in Zagłębie, with an emphasis on the establishment of the underground resistance in Zagłębie and Warsaw, their preparations for defensive actions, their difficulties contacting the Polish underground, and their lack of means as well as the vague news that had just arrived about battles breaking out between Jews and German soldiers in Warsaw. At the time of the briefing—the end of January/the beginning of February 1943—Będzin had just received knowledge about the first clashes between the ŻOB and the Germans that had taken place on January 17, 1943. Halinka also brought with her the first request for help and rescue from the Yishuv in Mandatory Palestine, formulated in extremely sharp terms by Frumka. The message made it clear that if the Yishuv did not come to their rescue, the young people in the ghettos may turn to communism.[10]

On the eve of the group's departure, Halinka was given a double farewell. The members of the group were called to appear before Merin, where they received instructions from him and Dr. Bornstein, the representative of the Joint from Warsaw who had fled to Zagłębie and was now living under Merin's protection. Merin added some information about the extermination campaign: the Jews were being killed in Auschwitz by means of lethal gassing. Dr. Bornstein reported "There are no more Jews in Warsaw." And yet, Merin asked the emigrants not to speak publicly about the extermination since the previous declarations following the first group's arrival in *Eretz Israel* had caused great damage and had prevented more people from leaving.[11] Merin remained true to his view that any protest action—even outside Poland—could sabotage the rescue efforts as he saw them.

A second farewell ceremony was held for Halinka by her movement. A member of Halinka's group, Hanka Beatur (later Chana Ben Sira), later described it as follows:

9 Mazia, *Re'im Basa'ar*, p. 114; Yehudit Sinai (Halinka Goldblum) interview.

10 Halinka Goldblum report, Central Zionist Archives, S26/1159.

11 Eliyahu Dobkin from the office of the operating committee of the Histadrut, February 11, 1943, Tnu'at Ha'avoda Archive, Pinchas Lavon Institute for Labour Movement Research.

> Józek Kożuch said a few farewell words. He sent greetings to Kibbutz Tel Yitzhak and Shorashim. He spoke about the struggle of the youth and the preparations for *hagana*, about the weapons they were buying, about the desire and plans to meet with the partisans. Halinka was charged with the duty to speak about the horrors we are going through here—the deportations, the killings. She must tell it all, because all our hearts are with our friends in [*Eretz*] Israel. I hope the building over there goes faster than the destruction over here.[12]

Zvi Brandes was more pessimistic than Kożuch. In a letter dated January 27, 1943, he informed Switzerland of Halinka's departure and the undergoing preparations for *hagana* in bitter code language:

> In recent days, many people have had the opportunity to see Meir [Ya'ari]. You know how much we love him and miss him. But apparently it is not mutual. It seems to me that he has forgotten us. What do you think? In the meantime, I am getting ready to marry Miss Hagniewska [*hagana*].[13]

On February 12, 1943, after a long journey that passed through Vienna, Budapest, Bulgaria, Turkey, Syria, and Beirut, the group arrived in *Eretz Israel.* It consisted of fourteen women and children. Their arrival became another milestone in the Yishuv's awareness of the extermination of European Jews. Just like Merin, the Jews of Mandatory Palestine at the time believed that the systematic extermination had stopped in mid-November 1942 and that the remaining Jews concentrated in fifty-five ghettos around Poland had a shot at survival.[14] However, the evidence delivered by the new arrivals dispelled this conviction, and the Jewish Agency personnel concluded that the Germans intended to continue their extermination campaign. In his speech, the head of the Action Committee Yitzhak Gruenbaum referred to this news and admitted the error of his ways: "Once again we were wrong.... Indeed, no human heart is capable of understanding the schemes of Nazi evil."[15]

12 See the Chana Ben Sira testimony in Mazia, *Re'im Basa'ar*, p. 115.

13 Letter from Zvi Brandes to Artur Rath, January 27, 1943, Moreshet Archive, D.1.1082.

14 Beit Zvi, *Post-Ugandan Zionism on Trial*, p. 91.

15 Minutes of the meeting of the Rescue Commission, Central Zionist Archives, S26/1237; Yitzhak Gruenbaum, *Beyamey Horban Veshoah* (Hebrew) (Tel Aviv: Haverim, 1946), p. 71.

Another shockwave passed over the Jewish Yishuv in the Land of Israel. On February 22, 1943, a day of general mourning was declared. Work ceased, cafés and entertainment parlors closed their doors, while teachers conducted special informational lessons in the classrooms. Frustrated by the lack of action so far, the members of the Histadrut decided to set up a committee, chaired by Golda Meyerson, to deal with special rescue fundraising and to put pressure on the Jewish Agency to increase rescue efforts.[16]

Did Halinka accomplish the other goals of her mission to convey the news about the establishment of the underground resistance and requesting help? As her testimony indicates, Halinka reported that Frumka had received a telegram from Warsaw that read: "We have obtained funds for the purchase of weapons. What happened during the first deportation will not happen again." She also said that "the slogan of the youth is '*hagana*'...Such news about *hagana* preparations is also coming in from other Polish cities."[17]

However, though documented in the Jewish Agency's protocols, this information was not heeded. In February 1943, the Jews of Mandatory Palestine did not see that this young woman from Sosnowiec was the harbinger of the preparations for the ghetto uprising. Eliyahu Dobkin, the Jewish Agency's chief interrogator, concluded from Halinka's testimony that whatever self-defense measures were being taken, they had already been put in place.[18] Even David Ben-Gurion, who had met with Halinka in person, did not take measure of the significance of the news she had brought. The tough and practical man sat across from her for hours, his eyes welling up with tears. Finally, he asked: "If we send a few fellows from the Land Israel, what good will it do?" [19] And even then, Ben-Gurion was talking about help from abroad, from the Land of Israel, not about rebellion in the ghettos themselves.

A chasm of misunderstanding separated the message from "back there" and its listeners "over here." The latter wished to see a Jewish revolt in the Diaspora, which would make them proud as new Jews in their ancestral land. They judged the behavior of their compatriots in Europe based on the stereotype of the submissive and obedient exilic Jew and

16 Porat, *Hanhaga Bemilkud*, pp. 89, 135. This is referring to Golda Meir, who would later become the prime minister of Israel (1969–1974).

17 "Al Tnu'atenu BeZaglembia," Central Zionist Archives, S26/1159.

18 Eliyahu Dobkin report, February 11, 1943, Tnu'at Ha'avoda Archive, Pinchas Lavon Institute.

19 Yehudit Sinai (Halinka Goldblum) interview.

consequently failed to understand that such a rebellion was indeed being organized, that preparations were underway, and that its champions desperately needed their help and support.[20]

Istanbul: Assembling the Delegation

Despite misunderstandings regarding the *hagana*, the news about the extermination had practical consequences. At the end of 1942 and the beginning of 1943, the Yishuv made increased efforts to help the Jews of Europe in some shape or form. This was reflected in the establishment of the delegation in Istanbul (Kushta), which included envoys from the pioneer movements: Wenia Pomeranz (later Ze'ev Hadari), a member of Hakibbutz Hameuchad; and Menahem Bader, a member of Hakibbutz Ha'artzi and Hashomer Hatzair.

Bader was somewhat of an anomaly in his movement. He was an economist by profession and much older than most of his friends in Mandatory Palestine (he was around forty-eight at the time). A practical man, he made it to Istanbul mostly on his own initiative. He had been in Yugoslavia in 1941 on the day of the Nazi invasion and had not ceased demanding to be sent back to Europe ever since. As someone who had seen the Germans and their actions with his own eyes, he harbored ill premonitions regarding the fate of the Jews of Europe and the Hashomer Hatzair trainees there. In the summer of 1942, his petitions were finally answered, but he still had to run around the Jewish Agency's official corridors for about four months in order to obtain the necessary approvals for his trip.[21]

Shortly before his trip, his movement recognized the urgency of the mission. On December 15 or 16, 1942, about a month after the arrival of the women and children from Poland, Hakibbutz Ha'artzi held a dramatic meeting of its Executive Committee in Kibbutz Ein Hahoresh. Meir Ya'ari lamented the plight of the Jewish people and admitted that he was still unable to "face full consciousness of the Holocaust."[22] In a series of decisions, Hakibbutz Ha'artzi determined that they should spearhead

20 For a more detailed analysis of this mission, see Avihu Ronen, "Shlihuta shel Halinka" (Hebrew), *Yalkut Moreshet*, 42 (December 1986), pp. 55–80.

21 Horowitz, "Shlihuto shel Menahem Bader," p. 161. For more on Bader, see Menahem Bader, *Shlihuyot Atzuvot* (Merhavia: Sifriat Poalim, 1954).

22 Meir Ya'ari, "El Mul Pney Ha'ason" (Hebrew)," in Ya'ari, *Bederech Aruka*, pp. 259–261.

the rescue efforts. The movement was tasked with being "a spurring and demanding element that will not allow the Yishuv to return to the normal course of life. As our primary concern in the coming period, we must increase rescue efforts immediately."[23] The measures taken in practice, however, were much more modest: Bader's trip was approved, and it was decided to dispatch a delegation to London and Washington immediately. Of the two, only the first was implemented.

Wenia Pomeranz arrived in Istanbul a little before Bader. To a large extent, this was also a result of his personal efforts. As early as May 1942, Wenia trained in a special course initiated by the Mossad L'Aliyah Bet (the Organization for "Illegal" Immigration, established by the Jewish leadership in Mandatory Palestine) with the aim of training young people to take part in rescue missions in the occupied territories. The news from Poland in November 1942 filled the course organizers with despair and frustration. Shaul Avigur, one of the heads of the Hagana and the Mossad, was pessimistic about their efforts yielding any kind of success but allowed Wenia to give Istanbul a try. And so Wenia went as a representative of Hakibbutz Hameuchad in December 1942.[24]

Pomeranz and Bader's initial action was to renew direct contact with the branches of their movements in Poland. A local Jewess named Sarka Mandelblatt stepped in as their secretary, and her home became the address for any incoming correspondence. On January 20, 1943, Wenia wrote to Frumka and Herszel in Będzin and added a greeting from Bader, but the link failed to be established: Though the letter from Istanbul reached Będzin, Frumka's reply did not make it back.[25] From then on, postal correspondence was maintained mainly through the Hechalutz delegation in Geneva, which delivered copies of the letters from Poland to Istanbul.

Pomeranz and Bader, however, were looking for more than a sparse trickle of letters arriving via a third party. They managed to make contact with a group of double agents, who operated within the framework of the German military intelligence service (the Abwehr) under the command of Wilhelm Canaris and who expressed their willingness to act as couriers and deliver letters and money to occupied Poland.[26]

23 Horowitz, "Shlihuto shel Menahem Bader," p. 159.

24 Wenia Pomeranz, Hagana Historical Archive, 3031. For more on Wenia's activities in Istanbul, see Ze'ev Hadari, *Tzomet Kushta: Shlihut Keneged Kol Hasikuyim, 1942–1945* (Hebrew) (Tel Aviv: Ministry of Defense Press, 1992).

25 Letter from Frumka Płotnicka to Wenia Pomeranz, March 8, 1943, in Ruth Zariz, ed., *Mihtavey Halutzim MiPolin Hakvusha* (Hebrew) (Ramat Efal: Yad Tabenkin, 1994), pp. 157–158.

26 Much has been written about the group of couriers, which in 1944 played a significant

The first courier went out on March 10, 1943, with a letter and money for the underground resistance in Będzin. In the letter, Pomeranz and Bader referred to the deep rift that had been created over the past three years between the people of the Yishuv and the resistance fighters in occupied Poland. The two wrote to their friends in Będzin:

> We knew very well that you must have accumulated quite a bit of resentment in your hearts against our family in [*Eretz*] Israel and the world, for not rushing to your aid until now. The letters of Frumka and Tosia reached us over a month ago, and we felt that they were speaking our common tongue, whereas in *Eretz Israel* only your mute silence reached us. This silence expressed a heavy guilt, and we knew that too. We were powerless to help you, and we are also powerless to justify ourselves.[27]

Was this help effective? The Israeli historiography on this subject—with the exception of Beit Zvi—consistently states that not much could be done. In January 1943, the head of the Action Committee Yitzhak Gruenbaum believed likewise. In a meeting of the Hapoel Hatzioni committee on January 18, 1943, Gruenbaum claimed that "the end of the massacre, rescue" could only be achieved with a victory for the allies, and for that reason, he strongly opposed the allocation of United Israel Appeal (Keren Hayesod) for the rescue of Jews in Europe. Despite the establishment of a rescue fund and increased activity around this issue, the Jewish Yishuv continued to mainly pursue other lines of action, namely enlisting in the British army and developing the country as a place of refuge for survivors. A poster of the revisionist Tel Hai Fund, which appeared on Hanukkah in December 1943, featured a Jewish soldier in a British army uniform, his stern face illuminated, protecting a frightened Jew dressed in black and tearing the Star of David band from his arm.

However, the letters that reached Pomeranz and Bader show that the moral value of maintaining the connection between the youth movements in Poland and their headquarters in the Land of Israel should

role in the attempts to save the Jews of Hungary. See Dalia Ofer, "Pe'ulot Ezra Vehatzala shel Hamishlahat HaEretz Yisraelit BeKushta, 1943" (Hebrew)," *Yalkut Moreshet*, 16 (February 1972), pp. 33–58; Bella Vago, "The Intelligence Aspects of Joel Brand's Mission," *Yad Vashem Studies*, 10 (1975), pp. 111–128; Eliyahu Stern, "Haksharim bein Hamishlahat Bekushta LeYehadut Polin" (Hebrew), *Yalkut Moreshet*, 39 (May 1985), pp. 135–152.

27 Letter from Wenia Pomeranz and Menahem Bader, March 10, 1943, in Zariz, *Mihtavey Halutzim*, p. 229.

not be overestimated. Feelings of disconnect and abandon were indeed common among the leaders of the resistance during this period. They were preparing to defend themselves out of alienation and anger at the world for which they were fighting. Chajka's friend Tosia Altman reported to her movement in *Eretz Israel* as early as July 1942 about the beginning of the extermination with the shocking words: "Israel is dying before my eyes, and I am simply wringing my hands, unable to help it."[28] To this, she added harshly:

> Why [write to *Eretz Israel*] then? You have erased us from your memory, and have we not done likewise? Don't we admit that one should not draw water from a poisoned well.... I hold myself back from giving an outlet to the bitterness that has accumulated over you and your friends, for whom you have forgotten us, such a complete oblivion.... Don't send my regards to anyone [in *Eretz Israel*]. I don't want to know about them. But I would still like to see you again.[29]

These lines were censored when the letter was first published, and some of them were even omitted from *Sefer Hashomer Hatzair*, published in 1956.[30]

The Gordonian leader Eliezer Geller, who became a supporter of armed resistance and joined the new ŻOB, met Chajka Buchbinder and Sara Rechnitz on the eve of their trip from Będzin to Mandatory Palestine in November 1942 but refused to hand them a letter addressed to the leadership of his movement in *Eretz Israel*. Instead, the two delivered the following on his behalf: "His heart is full of bitterness toward you and *Olamowitz* [the world] and he does not wish to write to you anymore. He claims that you deem him unnecessary and, therefore, it would simply be a waste of paper and time."[31]

What could Bader and Pomeranz do except write words of encouragement and comfort? By the time they sent their first letter, a new and ostensibly promising avenue for effective action had presented itself—from the Hechalutz center in Geneva, news came of a rescue plan involving Latin American passports.

28 Shalev, *Tosia Altman*, p. 142.

29 Ibid., pp. 142–143.

30 Beit Zvi, *Post-Ugandan Zionism on Trial*, p. 388; Tosia Altman, "Yisrael Geviya Le'einai," in Dror and Rosenzweig, *Sefer Hashomer Hatzair*, vol. 1, pp. 523–524.

31 Habas, *Mihtavim min Hageta'ot*, p. 38.

Geneva: The Latin American Passport Rescue Plan

As mentioned above, there was really only one channel of communication between the youth movements in Zagłębie and the outside world throughout the entire period of the war, and that was the postal correspondence that connected them with Geneva, in particular with the Swiss office of Hechalutz. Their main liaison was Nathan Schwalb (later Drori), a member of Gordonia and the head of Hechalutz in Switzerland. Schwalb operated alone for a long time: Other emissaries who had been with him prior to mid-1940 returned to Mandatory Palestine, as we may recall. An energetic and active man, Schwalb was left to manage the office's affairs, which he did in an assertive manner while safeguarding the interests of his party (Mapai), and was reluctant to share information with people he considered unqualified to handle it.[32] The copies of the letters he had received from Poland and other countries and had sent off to institutions in Mandatory Palestine and abroad were censored by him for security reasons.

Schwalb was aided by Heini Bornstein, a member of Hashomer Hatzair. In the absence of Mordechai Oren, the authorized representative of the movement, young Heini assumed the duties of liaison with the youth movements. It took some fighting to earn his place in the Hechalutz office beside the suspicious Schwalb, but in early 1943, Heini became the main address for the members of his movement in Będzin.[33]

Also operating from Geneva were both an *Eretz Israel* ministry headed by Chaim Pozner (Pazner) and the RELICO organization headed by Dr. Abraham Silberschein. Alfred Schwarzbaum, an affluent Jew from Będzin whose name has already been mentioned in the chapter about the outbreak of the war, was also active in Geneva at this time. After he had been released from detention and had refused Merin's offer to join the Judenrat, Schwarzbaum managed to do a thing considered impossible in early 1940: He made it to Switzerland with his wife, two daughters, and eight suitcases. It appears that not long after that, he began to make independent efforts to aid Polish Jewry while trying to establish contacts with various parties. Schwarzbaum maintained continuous contact with Zagłębie, providing addresses to the liaison's office, organizing package shipments, and even participating in some of the rescue fundraising drives held in Switzerland. Overall, he played

32 Bornstein, *Ha'i Shvaitz*, pp. 30–36; Geva, *Pe'alo shel Hakibbutz Ha'artzi*, p. 44.

33 Heini had been working at the office since the beginning of the war, but the relationship with the movement grew closer at this time.

a major role in keeping the lines of communication with Zagłębie open throughout the war.

At the end of 1942 however, the Swiss contingent discovered a new way to help the people of occupied Poland—they would help them escape the country using Latin American passports. The idea came from the Agudat Israel circles in Switzerland. The Polish consul in Bern Aleksander Ładoś helped them establish contact with Latin American embassies, obtain forms, and even falsifying them to request citizenship in their countries.[34] The Agudat Israel people filled out these forms with details of their relatives in Poland and attached the appropriate photos. The ambassador then signed them, and the forms were sent to Poland. The recipients of the passports in occupied Poland were henceforth considered foreign citizens (or pending foreign citizens) and were supposed to be arrested by the police and transferred to detention camps for foreign citizens until the end of the war or until the conclusion of a prisoner exchange agreement.[35]

In the final months of the same year, Schwalb and Silberschein also decided to use this plan to try and rescue members of their movements in Poland. Alfred Schwarzbaum, who according to his testimony was the one who told them about the operations of Agudat Israel, took an active part in this endeavor from the beginning. Pozner and Heini Bornstein soon also joined the action. In light of the news of extermination coming from Poland, it seemed futile to proceed with the shipment of packages, whereas the passports seemed a viable way to at least try to save what remained of Polish Jewry. By mid-1943, thousands of passports or "promises"—notifications that the addressee in Poland had received the citizenship of the relevant Latin American country and that the passport would be delivered to them soon—had been sent to Poland. The passport scheme was not confined to Paraguay alone; similar contacts were made

34 The actions of Aleksander Ładoś and his colleagues were rediscovered in the last years by the Polish diplomat Jakub Kumoch. See Jakub Kumoch, Monika Maniewska, Jędrzej Uszyński, and Zygmunt Bartłomiej, *The Ładoś List: An Index of People to Whom the Polish Legation and Jewish Organizations in Switzerland Issued Latin American Passports During the Second World War* (Warsaw: Pilecki Institute, 2020), p. 8.

35 Alf Schwarzbaum, "Pe'ulot Ezra MiShvaitz Bashanim 1940–1945" (Hebrew), *Massuah*, 2 (September 1974), pp. 138–145; Haim Bornstein, "Din Veheshbon al Pe'ulot Ha-misrad Latnu'a Al Yadey Hahanhaga Harashit BeShvaitz Beshnot Hamilhama, 1940–1946," Moreshet Archive, D.1.5466; Nathan Eck, "The Rescue of Jews with the Aid of Passports and Citizenship Papers of Latin American States," *Yad Vashem Studies*, 1 (1957).

with the consulates of other Latin American states, such as Honduras and San Salvador. A number of passports were also obtained from the consulates and missions of Peru, Haiti, and Bolivia.[36]

From a technical point of view, the passport operation did not require special preparations nor did it involve any special risks. It was financed by the funds collected in *Eretz Israel* as well as money coming from local Jewish sources and Dr. Ignatz Schwartzbard, the Zionist representative in the Polish National Council in London. The price of a passport ranged between 900 and 1,800 Swiss francs (about 450–900 US dollars). As far as we know, there was only one case in which one of the passport negotiators (Alfred Schwarzbaum) was arrested by the Swiss police, but he was released after a short investigation.[37]

Zagłębie now became a central hub of correspondence with Switzerland regarding the obtaining of Latin American passports. A huge wave of postcards and letters flooded the post offices of Będzin, Sosnowiec, and Geneva in the first half of 1943.[38]

Będzin: Defense or Rescue

Chajka took an active part in this correspondence and in establishing connections between Będzin and the delegations in Geneva and Istanbul, and through them—*Eretz Israel*. Her diaries record feelings of profound bitterness and disappointment from this relationship. It goes without saying that only a little of what she wrote in 1943 appeared in the printed version of the book:

> That was when we heard from abroad.
>
> Earlier they had been sending us letters in which they wrote about the *moledet* [fatherland] and other things in that vein. Those letters made us laugh. How could we care about that while being engaged in a bloody, daily fight for survival? Was that...

36 Kumoch et al., *The Ładoś List*, pp. 8, 37.

37 Alf Schwarzbaum, interview by the author, Ramat Gan, 1986.

38 The names of 838 Jews from Bedzin, 215 from Sosnowiec, and 71 from Dąbrowa Gornicza were included in the list of people who were in contact with Switzerland. See Kumoch et al., *The Ładoś List*, p. 41. However, it does not mean that they all actually received passports or used them. See the following chapters for more on this subject.

> Those letters caused us pain, but at the same time made us laugh. The most explicit expression of our attitude toward the [*moledet*] overseas was a slightly vulgar saying—*Moledet, Y[ob]. T[voyu]. M[at]*.[39]

By the time Chajka started writing her 1943 diaries, her relationship with "abroad," as she refers to both Geneva and the Yishuv in Mandatory Palestine, had been long and strained. She had reservations about both the letters and the packages that had arrived from Switzerland before:

> But perhaps we were most irritated by Nathan Schwalb (*shvantz* [prick]), who was sending such bullshit in his letters, which were so full of Hebrew sentences that they could give us away ten times in a day.
>
> A parcel delivery campaign was launched. Nathan was unjust, as he was sending disproportionately more to Gordonia than to us. On what grounds? Had they been given a bigger share of *Hechalutz*? [...]
>
> The parcels from abroad didn't bring us much consolation or help. And later we didn't even have that, because the *gmina* began to requisition them.[40]

Communication with Heini Bornstein—a fellow *shomer*—was of some comfort: "Heini had already sent us a letter as early as during that period. His letters made us so happy; they were short but so warm. You could sense a dear, kindred spirit—he was simply our man."[41] Of the passport affair, she reported the following:

> So, what should be our stance on the issue of the *Internierungslager* [internment camps for foreign citizens]?... [A council was called together to decide] and a resolution was adopted against the idea. (Later on, we learned that Warsaw also adopted such a resolution.) We were sending only a *shlichut* [emissaries]. The resolution was adopted by all the youth organizations.
>
> But suddenly after several weeks we learned that some *Gordonia* members had sent [passport photographs]. Papers began to come.

39 This saying is a mix of Hebrew and Russian words. Klinger, *I Am Writing These Words to You* (1943 diaries), p. 113.

40 Ibid., p. 114.

41 Ibid., p. 115.

> There was a commotion in the town. The older generation was outraged at the young for their rejection of a chance to survive. Parents began to appeal to their daughters and sons, achieving partial success.
>
> And the young began to change their minds. *Gordonia* members openly supported the idea of sending the photographs. There was a frantic search for ways of doing that.[42]

Diverse testimonies confirm Chajka's account. Schwalb, who had concentrated his efforts on procuring passports for Hechalutz people, managed to make contact with Warsaw and Zagłębie. It seems that in Warsaw in January 1943, in the midst of preparations for armed defense, the news about the passports option was received with mixed feelings. Schwalb appears to have offered to get part of the leadership of the Hechalutz out of Poland, but they refused. Instead, they asked to send envoys to convey to the free world the information about the ongoing extermination of the Jews.[43]

In Zagłębie too, the passport idea was initially accepted with reservations. At a gathering convened by Liwer at the home of Gedalia Sobkowski from Poalei Zion, where the letter from Schwalb was read, the participants leaned toward rejecting this line of action.[44] However, some of the older members and those with families sent Schwalb their photos, among them Nathan Eck from Warsaw and his family. At the beginning of March, the passports arrived, and on March 6, 1943, they left the city. Nathan Eck was taken to the internment camp for foreign nationals in Tittmoning in Germany.[45] Their departure caused a great uproar in the city.

Prior to that, another meeting was called at the Gordonia headquarters, and the situation was reassessed. Difficult things were said during this poignant discussion, which was held on March 3, 1943, in the midst of the Dunski Affair. Hanka Borenstein hesitated out loud: she had wanted to move forward with *hagana* and even join the partisans. The main thing was to fight for life rather than die passively.[46] But the aid coming from abroad was tipping the scales. It appeared to be effective. Others, such as a certain Zvi from Gordonia, however, were more decisive:

42 Ibid.

43 Letter from Frumka Płotnicka to Nathan Schwalb, January 25, 1943, in Zariz, *Mihtavey Halutzim*, p. 152.

44 D. Liwer, *Ir Hametim*, p. 205.

45 Eck, *Hato'im Bedarkey Hamavet*, pp. 141–149.

46 D. Liwer, *Ir Hametim*, p. 110.

> Defense and rescue are mutually exclusive concepts. Therefore, we have to pick one. Defense is a lost cause. The extermination method leaves us no way to respond appropriately.... Defense for the sake of honor has no value. The world that will be left to judge us is not worth our lives. We must hold on to life at any cost so that we can take revenge on the Germans.[47]

The people of Gordonia wished to live. One can certainly see how this pragmatic stance reflects a less stringent commitment to the idea of *hagana*.

The Role of the Vanguard

The decision made by the Gordonia people and the departure of Nathan Eck caused unrest in Kibbutz Dror.[48] According to Chajka, all the members of the kibbutz wanted to go and felt overlooked because they did not receive passports.[49]

On the other hand, Hashomer Hatzair took a hard stance: they would not apply for passports. Isaac Neuman remembered a meeting attended by thirty members in somebody's attic.[50] The meeting is also mentioned in Chajka's diaries:

> There was almost no controversy in our movement. Perhaps the young did get some stupid ideas, but none of us said anything out loud. On the contrary, when that issue was discussed during a Hashomer Hatzair *asefa* [gathering] everybody was in favor of a *shlichut* [sending out emissaries].
>
> Our *hanhaga* [leadership] went as far as being ready to resign from a *shlichut* [traveling on a mission], which I thought was wrong, just to avoid creating an impression that the leadership of the organization was leaving.[51]

The passport option was thus rejected, with Chajka among its most strident opponents. However, even though a resolution had been reached, it was a tough pill to swallow:

47 Perlis, *Tnu'ot Hano'ar Hehalutziyot*, p. 300.
48 Renia Kukielka, *Escape from the Pit* (New York: Sharon Books, 1947), pp. 73–75.
49 Klinger, *I Am Writing These Words to You* (1943 diaries), p. 115.
50 Isaac Neuman interview.
51 Klinger, *I Am Writing These Words to You* (1943 diaries), p. 116.

> A horrible atmosphere ensued.... We, the Hashomer Hatzair movement, would be isolated. Everybody would get their passports, and there wouldn't be any *hagana* anyway. We were afraid of isolation and that was our mistake. We had strength, so why were we afraid to engage in *hagana* on our own?[52]

Indeed, it appears that Hashomer Hatzair's firm stance on the matter did have an effect. In a letter dated March 8, 1943, Frumka reported to Nathan Schwalb: "As you know, my entire family maintains a very negative relationship with her ways, but according to Zivia's express demand, I must meet with her."[53] Torn between the necessity of her own trip, the pressures from Gordonia and Dror, and the intransigence of Hashomer Hatzair, Frumka finally came up with a compromise proposal that was accepted by all the movements in Hechalutz: The members would send their photos and personal details to Switzerland, but the passports received would not be used for the time being.[54]

We know that at least in Hashomer Hatzair, the passport operation was managed by the leadership. The members submitted their photos and details, but the leadership kept the incoming passports and did not give them out to the members.[55] Chajka and her comrades' resistance to the passport scheme was motivated by one main factor: Acceptance of the passports by the members of the youth movements meant giving up on the idea of self-defense.[56]

Yet, beyond this immediate consideration, there was a deeper reason behind Hashomer Hatzair's reluctance to accept the rescue route, one that was rooted in the tradition on which they had been brought up. They saw themselves as both a national and social vanguard. As mentioned earlier, Hashomer Hatzair adopted the concept of the "vanguard" as an expression of its revolutionary commitment back in the late 1930s. The term was equivalent to "pioneer" and involved not only paving the way but also challenging society's conventions and promoting revolution. Could a pioneer leading the way save herself while her followers were being decimated? The passports did not provide a channel for mass rescue. They were a solution available to only a few—the *bogrim* of the

52 Ibid.

53 Zariz, *Mihtavey Halutzim*, pp. 157–158.

54 According to Renia, Dror finally ruled in favor of *hagana*. Kukielka, *Escape from the Pit*, p. 74.

55 Isaac Neuman interview.

56 Klinger, *I Am Writing These Words to You* (1943 diaries), p. 116.

movement, maybe even only its leaders. It seems that in those days, Chajka and her comrades embraced the notion of the death of the vanguard as a necessity: "If there is no nation, there is no need for its avant-garde. What was it for if not for the nation?!"[57]

Later, when Chajka arrived in *Eretz Israel*, she stated explicitly: "The vanguard has no right to exist while the entire nation is being destroyed."[58] The idea of the vanguard that had been central to their education and the distant echo of Ya'ari's call to revolution now stood the test of continued personal existence. The other option—defending the ghetto—was an act of suicide, as Shmuel Ron admitted years later.[59] Even Chajka, who denied that their struggle stemmed from "extreme pessimism, out of indecision," admitted immediately afterward that "we could never have managed to organize any kind of *hagana* in the ghettos through common sense alone. It was the absolute opposite of logical thinking." Moreover, she asserted that "the path of the *shomrim* especially seemed to lead toward certain doom."[60] It appears that Chajka had been aware from the start that the defense of the ghetto was not a fight for life, but for death.

And yet Hashomer Hatzair accepted the compromise reached at the Hechalutz gathering. Chajka herself sent her and David's photos to Schwalb on February 13, 1943, and on March 24, 1943, Zvi Brandes sent his picture to Heini Bornstein. Other Hashomer Hatzair members—Irka, Idzia, and Lea Pejsachson, Nacia Klugman, and Aharon Brandes—also sent their personal details to Heini.[61] Yet, on May 3, 1943, Zvi Brandes wrote a coded letter to Heini Bornstein:

> This time, I want to make it clear to you why the photo [passport] is not to my liking, and why I do not wish to marry her. As I have already written to you, I have recently gotten to know Agana [*hagana*] very well, and I like her very much. She is a bold and brave young lady, and we have forged a great bond. You and Mendel [Bader, in Istanbul] will not understand my opposition to the photo. But I have talked about it at length with Tosia [the main leadership in Warsaw] and she said that I was right. But to put the matter to

57 Ibid., p. 31.

58 See chapter 25.

59 Shmuel Ron interview.

60 Chajka Klinger, 1944 diaries, notebook C, Moreshet Archive, D.2.211, pp. 2–3.

61 Avihu Ronen, ed., *Mihtavim Bezmanim Afelim: Hitkatvut bein Anshey Hashomer Hatzair Be'Eropa Hakvusha Vemerkaz Hakesher BeShvaitz, Vol. 1: Polin, Slovakia* (Hebrew) (Tel Aviv: Moreshet, 2019), pp. 101–119.

> rest, some more of our family will meet with her [that is, go on a mission]. Please, when you have the chance, tell our grandfather Meir [the leadership of Hashomer Hatzair in *Eretz Israel*], that he too will be pleased with my new bride.[62]

Developments in the Passport Affair

As a whole, the adult Jewish population of Będzin saw the Latin American passports as a viable channel of salvation and were puzzled by the hesitations of the youth. When the first group of passport holders set off on their way to the internment camp, there was uproar in the city in reaction to the youth movements' decision to forego the use of passports. As Chajka described it: "The elders erupted in anger. How can it be, there is a chance to be saved and we don't want to take it? We should take it, and get documents for them too. The parents began to revolt; they were weak, and they gave in."[63]

Isaac Neuman remembered the changing attitude of the relative with whom he was staying when the matter of the passports came to light. This relative, who had been reluctant to take Isaac in because of the danger involved in sheltering a refugee, now requested that he procure him a passport as well.[64] Everyone wanted to live, and the key to preserving one's life was now in the hands of the youth movements who refused to use it. Chajka wrote: "People began to call on us, offering to pay 20,000–50,000 if we could get them a passport. We needed money, and in a few cases, we did get the passports."[65]

Family conflicts erupted. Despite the movement's decision to acquire passports, some key Gordonia activists still refused to use this rescue option. David Liwer's fellow Gordonian Borenstein came to him with tears in his eyes. Hanka, his daughter, did not want to use the passport she had obtained: "We sacrificed our whole lives for our only daughter. She was brought up for Zionist devotion. Are there not many like her in the ranks of the youth? Why would she sacrifice her young life?" Liwer, who was a supporter of the passport scheme, approached Hanka, but her stance was firm: "I feel sorry for my parents, that because of me they will

62 Ibid., p. 121.
63 Klinger, 1944 diaries, notebook C, p. 11.
64 Isaac Neuman interview.
65 Klinger, 1944 diaries, notebook C, p. 11.

miss a chance at salvation. But my private thoughts are of no importance in this matter. Hechalutz has made its decisions, and as a central member I must serve as an example to others."[66] The deputy chairman of the Judenrat, Moshe Manela, used a different tactic. When he despaired of trying to convince his son Abraham—a member of Gordonia—to use a passport, he locked him up in his home with the help of the Jewish police until his transfer to the internment camp.[67] In doing so, the father saved his son's life. Abraham eventually made it to *Eretz Israel*; his father Moshe, who stayed behind, perished.

Merin kept his watchful eye on the affair and saw the passport scheme as a violation of his authority and tried to present it as a potential disaster for the community. He demanded that the people of Hechalutz leave it to the Judenrat to liaise with Geneva.[68] He may have been tipped off by the Gestapo. According to Ada Neufeld's testimony, the Gestapo knew about the connection with Switzerland from a very early stage. In 1941, after visiting Będzin, Tosia Altman asked Ada Neufeld, a member of Hashomer Hatzair, to receive any letters from Switzerland addressed to her. When the letters started to arrive, Ada was called in to the Gestapo headquarters. She was brought there by a Jew, probably a policeman. She was then interrogated about the identities of Schwalb and Tosia as well as about the contents of the packages coming from Switzerland. She managed to evade the questions through pleading. It seemed to Ada that the Germans "ate it up"—they did not beat her, and she was allowed to return home.[69]

Nevertheless, if Merin's opposition to *hagana* could be considered somewhat reasonable, the same cannot be said regarding his reaction to the passports. Had he wanted the scheme to succeed, he would have been better off leaving communication in the hands of private individuals or small movements, whose actions—if discovered—would not endanger the entire Jewish public. Transferring the matter into the hands of the Judenrat, which was closely supervised by the Gestapo, would have been far riskier. Merin's megalomania and paranoia that his position was being undermined were reflected in a speech he gave during this period in which he equated the resistance's defense preparations with the rescue

66 D. Liwer, *Ir Hametim*, pp. 109–110.
67 Ibid.; Abraham Manela, interview.
68 Letter from Merin to Schwarzbaum, June 2, 1943, in A. Liwer, "Asher Lo Yishkach," p. 354.
69 Ada Halperin (Neufeld) interview.

operations: "I know what's going on. Some of you young smart alecks are involved in plots," Merin told listeners gathered in one of the ghetto squares. "Your names are already in my files. You needn't think that I didn't know about the citizenship papers you're doing your best to sneak in behind my back from Switzerland. I'm warning you!... I'll never let a handful of brats interfere with my holy mission. I won't stand for it! I'll say it again and again so no one can say they didn't hear me. I'll fight you to the last one. And may history be my judge."[70]

Indeed, he would be judged by the Jews of Zagłębie but not favorably—the "King of the Jews" had crossed a line. In a conversation with Arie Liwer, who was already in the process of being transferred to the internment camp for foreign nationals, Merin bared his teeth, saying that if the youth movements did not obey his ultimatum to transfer the handling of the passports into his hands, no one would leave Będzin.[71] Arie refused. For once, the power was in the hands of the youth movements. Confined to Zagłębie, Merin had no influence over Schwalb of Hechalutz, Heini of Hashomer Hatzair, or Schwarzbaum, his own personal rival. The young activists knew this and stood firm. The passports kept coming.

On April 7, 1943, a second group of Latin American passport holders was taken into custody by the German police and transferred to a detention camp, from where they would be sent to the foreign nationals' internment camp in Tittmoning. The group consisted of nineteen people, most of them members of Hitachdut or Gordonia, some of them Judenrat officials. To the credit of Gordonia, it should be said that their numbers included several members who were expected to be in immediate danger: Shimon Frost and Aharon Gepner, who were Gordonia refugees from the Generalgouvernement zone, and the parents of Bobo Graubart, who had been hanged for underground activity. The group likewise included Arie Liwer, the Krzesiwo family, and Abraham Manela.[72]

The departure of the group and the good news coming from the detention camp (Arie Liwer even got to visit Będzin toward the end of April) bolstered passport-related activity. Among the youth movements, however, this aroused some indignation: How were the passports arriving? Why were so many of them destined for Gordonia members?

70 Ka-Tzetnik, *Sunrise over Hell*, pp. 134–135. There is no other testimony of this speech at our disposal; however, Merin's attitude here seems in line with his later actions, notably the communication of resistance members' names to the Gestapo.

71 A. Liwer, "Asher Lo Yishkach," p. 354.

72 Abraham Manela interview; Shimon Frost interview; Aharon Gepner testimony, YVA, O.3/2910.

What about the other movements? An upset Chajka wrote: "A number of passports for Gordonia were delivered, while we didn't get any even for our *shlichut* [envoys]. When they already had about 20 passports, we finally got one, and to make matters worse, a Honduran one. I'd like to get a chance to get even with them."[73]

Chajka's judgment was somewhat harsh. She was not overly fond of either Schwalb or Gordonia, and one could certainly point out that the people of Hashomer Hatzair had been in no rush to send in their details and photos. And yet, from the testimonies of Heini Bornstein and Schwarzbaum, we learn that Schwalb's actions were indeed informed by political calculations.[74]

Throughout April, May, and the first half of June, the passport affair continued to sow unrest among the Jews of Zagłębie. Yet, in the meantime, other much stormier events were brewing, and on April 19, 1943, the flag of revolt was raised aloft in the Warsaw ghetto.

73 Klinger, *I Am Writing These Words to You* (1943 diaries), p. 117.

74 Schwarzbaum, "Pe'ulot Ezra MiShvaitz," pp. 138–145; Bornstein, *Ha'i Shvaitz*, p. 244; Postcard from Chajka to Schwalb, March 16, 1943, "Hechalutz," Tnu'at Ha'avoda Archive, Pinchas Lavon Institute, p. 59.

Chapter Sixteen

The Shadow of Warsaw

Mythological Mother: 1970

Other children had a mother waiting for them at 4:00 PM for family time. I had a mythological mother. Her presence on the page made up for her absence from the room. Her figure was embedded in the stories of heroism on which we had been brought up. About two months after her death, we received the Hagana ribbon, awarded to her posthumously.[1] As far as I'm concerned, Mother died in battle. At the end of the 1950s, they held a celebratory assembly in Kibbutz Haogen and read out the names of members who had perished on duty in the Israeli forces, among them Charlie Nomis, the father of Meron from my group.[2] I was excited: they would surely mention Mother's name. But the solemn announcements went on, and it turned out that to my disappointment, Mother was not listed among the fallen. What did her death mean then?

A more distant memory, from when I was around four, takes me back to the green seesaw in the kindergarten yard. At one end there's Yardena, who is two years older than me; at the other end—there's me. Yardena goes up, and I go down. Yardena goes down, and I am tossed skyward. Yardena says: "Everyone dies in the end, not just Haviva Reik the paratrooper," and I am amazed at this piece of information.

1 The Hagana ribbon—a medal of honor—was awarded to Chaya Rosenberg on June 6, 1958, and she also received the Nazi Combatant medal, certificate dated May 7, 1967. See Moreshet Archive, C.36.5.

2 Charlie Nomis was killed in the battle over Iraq Suwaydan on December 28, 1948. May he rest in peace.

Until this moment, I've always thought that death was reserved for heroes alone.

Mother's death was scary and inexplicable. Nitza, a member of the group, told me later that when I left the classroom with Aunt Yaffa on my way to my father's house to receive the news, Ya'ir the teacher explained to the other children: "Avihu's mother died." The children asked the cause of death, and he answered: "Heart attack."[3] This was the official explanation propagated in the kibbutz. An obituary notice on the bulletin board read: "28 of the month of Nisan. Our home mourns the loss of the late Chajka, dead of severe heart disease." An anonymous soul had handwritten the following addition: "The funeral procession will depart from the reading room with the bell at approximately six o'clock."[4] The secret of mother's death was meant to remain well hidden from the children. But secrecy turned into nameless fear. I wasn't the only one to sneak out from the children's house at night. Nitza also ran away more than once to her parents' home. She was afraid that if this could happen to Avihu's mother, it might happen to other mothers as well, maybe even hers. Later, she told me that every year, as the anniversary of my mother's death approached, she and Hagit would watch me with concern and wonder what I was going through that day.[5]

The only solution to the inexplicable presence of death was to make it a heroic death. Mother suddenly joined the list of mythological names taught to us in the kibbutz—Haviva Reik, Mordechai Anielewicz, Uri Ilan. The photograph of Anielewicz's monument at Yad Mordechai hung over our childhood. The story of Haviva Reik's capture and death during the Slovak uprising was recounted to us as children time and time again. The "Mishmar Layeladim" (Children's Guard) section of the *Al Hamishmar* newspaper described Uri Ilan from Kibbutz Gan Shmuel, whose body was returned from Syrian captivity in 1955. Nine notes with words formed from punched out holes had been found on his body. One note read: "*Lo bagadti*" (I did not betray.) What we were not told at the time was that some of Haviva Reik's contacts in Slovakia saw her mission as unnecessary,[6]

3 Nitza Herzog (Pu'a), interview by the author, Kibbutz Haogen, 2009.

4 Anonymous note, Moreshet Archive, C.36.11.

5 Nitza Herzog (Pu'a) interview.

6 Tehila Ofer and Ze'ev Ofer, *Haviva: Sipur Hayeha, Shlihuta, Venefilata shel Hatzanhanit Haviva Reik* (Hebrew) (Bnei Brak: Sifriat Poalim and Moreshet, 2004), p. 275. Based on Haim Hermesh, *Mivtza Amsterdam* (Hebrew) (Tel Aviv: Ma'arahot, 1971).

that Anielewicz had committed suicide in a bunker at 18 Miła Street, and Uri Ilan had taken his own life in a Syrian prison. As a child, I would go back and read about their exploits over and over again, hoping that one day I would grow up to be like them.

The myth continued to resonate even in later years. During the War of Attrition (1967–1970), whenever I would finish preparing the equipment for a cross-border incursion, I would also make sure to write a few lines to some girl. The fact that I didn't have a girlfriend back then did not matter. The main thing was to have a letter out there in case I didn't come back. I could see the letter printed on the first page—or even better the last page—of my memorial booklet. When I finally did find a girlfriend to wait for me back home, it turned out that she wasn't the right audience for my missives. She did not understand why it was so important for me to go into battle and maybe perish in it.

Wars and death became an inseparable part of me—despite the skepticism, despite the criticism, despite the recognition that they were unnecessary. In 1973, during the Yom Kippur War, I was with a group of reserve soldiers. When I swept ahead toward the Egyptians, they grumbled: "Where are you rushing off to?" They had families waiting for them at home. During the First Lebanon War in 1982, Ran Sasson, the only avowed Likudnik in our patrol company, was openly indignant: "These leftists preach against wars, but when they come, they charge into the most dangerous places." Ran was a radio operator, and he did not like to ride with me in the jeep to the distant observation points right in front of the Syrians' eyes.

Maybe that is why I never feel angry at my mother. Several years after her death, I returned from the funeral of a kibbutz member who had also taken his own life. He was buried in the orchard, next to Mother's grave. When we passed by the members' clubhouse, I suddenly heard a kibbutz member say angrily: "What a fool. How could he do that? Leave a wife and two children like that?" The raw fury of the words struck me: I had never thought about it that way. I couldn't get angry. Only in retrospect, when I collected the few childhood memories I had of her, I realized that most of them contained her anger toward me. Mom is mad at me for coming back late from the game on the big lawn; Mom is angry that I forgot to pick up Arnon from kindergarten; Mom is mad that I was rude. But she was allowed to be angry. She was dead. She was a hero.

Documenting the Uprising

In her 1943 diaries, Chajka devoted roughly thirty pages out of a total of 143 pages to the subject she filed under the title "The *Hagana* in Warsaw." One might wonder what made Chajka write at such great length about events that she had not witnessed with her own eyes. It seems that her decision to do so was spurred by two main factors: first, the fact that the Warsaw Ghetto Uprising was a defining event in her life, and second, when she wrote her diaries in the fall of 1943, her assumption was that none of her close friends had survived to testify about what had happened.

When she arrived in *Eretz Israel*, her writings were considered the first detailed report on the uprising and, as such, were accorded great importance. She was the first to do so among the surviving ghetto fighters. Excerpts from her diaries were picked up and widely published in the Israeli press, although they were edited here and there to cover delicate matters. However, in the years that followed, additional reports began to surface based on the fighters' testimonies as well as various documents, and Chajka's testimony was downgraded to a secondary role. After all, she did not participate in the uprising herself. Nonetheless, her reports were reliable—they were based on information from sources on the ground, giving her a sharply critical vision of various events.

One should not be surprised at the large amount of information Chajka had at hand when composing the diaries. Between January and July 1943, there was continuous contact between the ŻOB headquarters in Warsaw and Będzin. The information came in the form of letters couriered by Hashomer Hatzair's liaison officers—mostly Astrit and Ina Gelbard. More detailed information was brought in by Renia Kukielka from Dror, who had been sent to Warsaw in the midst of the uprising and had managed to make contact with one of the ŻOB's liaisons outside the ghetto walls. Though remaining on the outside, Renia witnessed the ghetto burning with her own eyes and caught glimpses of the actual battles happening within.[7] Further valuable information was brought in later by Marek Folman, one of the central Dror activists who had survived the Warsaw Ghetto Uprising, who arrived in Będzin in June 1943.[8] Chajka was therefore up-to-date on the details of most of the main events in the Warsaw ghetto. She described the events of April 19, 1943, in Warsaw as if she had been there:

7 Kukielka, *Escape from the Pit*, pp. 90–94.

8 See chapter 18.

> They've been expecting another campaign in Warsaw for many weeks.
>
> Anxiety. The atmosphere is different. You can already feel that something's up. Patrols keep walking outside our bunkers. The organization has been mobilized and it's waiting, ready for combat.
>
> Final, frantic preparations. Twice a day a roll call of the entire organization. It has a few hundred members. Everybody's armed, everybody's holding some arms.
>
> Orders have been given. Mordechai is the commander-in-chief. None of us can go into the bunkers. The Germans enter the ghetto. There are [resistance] groups in various places.
>
> We're in combat. We're fighting mostly with grenades and bottles of incendiary material. Lithuanians, Ukrainians, and Poles are participating in the campaign. 80 German victims and many wounded. They didn't expect such a resistance and they're retreating toward the ghetto gates.[9]

Later, Israel Gutman would estimate the number of fighters at about 500. Their main equipment consisted of pistols and grenades, but they also had several dozen rifles at their disposal as well as a machine gun that was in the possession of the Jewish Military Union (ŻZW). They were facing approximately 2,100 German, Polish, and Ukrainian military and police personnel.[10] The number of casualties Chajka mentions is based on the estimates given by the ŻOB at the time; however, these turned out to be very much exaggerated. According to the report by General Jürgen Stroop, recounting the German suppression of the Warsaw Ghetto Uprising, twenty-four Germans were wounded on the first day of the fighting, and one was killed. The number of Germans killed during the uprising was no higher than seventeen, with eighty-five wounded.[11]

According to most testimonies—as later reconstructed by Israel Gutman—the actual fighting lasted three days. During this time, two tanks were damaged, one of them by means of a mine, as Chajka specifies:[12]

> The ghetto has been tightly sealed and there's no access to it.
>
> Mordechai writes in his letter that he's happy to have lived until that moment.

9 Klinger, *I Am Writing These Words to You* (1943 diaries), pp. 153–154.

10 Gutman, *The Jews of Warsaw*, pp. 365–366.

11 Ibid., p. 393.

12 Ibid., p. 389.

> The Fighting Organization is spreading terror in the ghetto: the Jews who don't want to fight or threaten *museruf* [informers] are to get a bullet in the head.
>
> After two days they retreat into the bunkers. The Germans are appealing to them to not be afraid to come out. The *gmina* tells the Germans that it has no authority in the ghetto. The Fighting Organization is asked to assume power.
>
> The Germans set out on a rougher course and drop incendiary bombs from aircraft.
>
> Frightened Jews who want to save their lousy lives reveal bunkers by walking into a courtyard and screaming, "*Yiden geht areus es iz schin nach der akzia*" [Jews, go out! The *Aktzia* has ended!].[13]

Already on the second day of the fighting, the ghetto was set ablaze, and the combat tactics of the resistance changed on April 21, 1943—the third day of the uprising—with groups of fighters adopting the technique of surprise ambushes against opportune targets. The retreat to the bunkers took place mainly on the following day.[14] However, new research by Moshe Arens reveals that members of the ŻZW, who were ignored by the sources informing Chajka, continued to wage stubborn battle for several more days after that. It would appear that the success of the initial battles must also be attributed in part to this group, whose people were both better equipped and better trained.[15] Be that as it may, Chajka was soon made aware of Anielewicz's last letter. She was thus able to narrate the fall of the resistance fighters and Mordechai's death:

> And now begins the most tragic period of the Warsaw *hagana*.
>
> Not many people died in combat. Nobody expected that. No way of retreat had been prepared. Our people descended into the sewers. Without food, they were up to their waists in water.
>
> On the "Aryan" side, Yitzhak [Zuckerman] was doing everything he could and sought help from the PPR to get people out of the ghetto. Finally, access to the canals was organized. The entire street was cordoned off by our armed people. Nobody could get through the cordon. 40 people in very bad condition were removed. In the

13 Klinger, *I Am Writing These Words to You* (1943 diaries), p. 154.

14 Gutman, *The Jews of Warsaw*, pp. 381–382.

15 Moshe Arens, *Flags over the Warsaw Ghetto: The Untold Story of the Warsaw Ghetto Uprising* (Jerusalem: Gefen Publishing House, 2011), pp. 212–218.

> meantime, the Germans discovered that there were fighters in the sewers and they sent [poisonous] gas in.
>
> Can you imagine a more horrible death for our people? Death by suffocation.
>
> Some, for instance, Arie Wilner[16] or Bareł [Berl Brojde] were still strong enough to commit suicide by shooting themselves in the temple. Mordechai didn't manage.
>
> The next day, after an inspection of the other bunkers Cywia [Zivia] descends to her comrades and the horrible [scene] unfolds before her eyes.[17]

Chajka's description lines up with the course of events, except that in her account, the rescue of the fighters through the sewers is mixed up with the detonation of smoke grenades in the bunkers. On May 7, 1943, the command bunker at 18 Miła Street was discovered, and therein were the bodies of Mordechai Anielewicz and his friends. Several of them had committed suicide:

> One more group, including Tosia [Altman] and Szyfra [Sokółka], managed to get out. They were in an apartment with a barrel of gunpowder. Somebody accidentally dropped a match, causing an explosion. The people were fleeing from the burning building. Everybody was captured.[18]

In this instance too, Chajka had access to up-to-date information. A fire had broken out in a celluloid factory,[19] and her best friend Tosia Altman was indeed captured by the Germans. The news regarding Tosia's fate was contradictory, and it was unclear whether she had died or survived.

Only a few members of the ŻOB lived to tell their tale. Among them were two of its leaders—Zivia Lubetkin and Antek Zuckerman of Dror-Hechalutz. Of the leadership of Hashomer Hatzair, no one survived.

16 Chajka must have been aware of the important role that Arie Wilner (1917–1943) had played in the ŻOB. Wilner was one of the main activists of Hashomer Hatzair in the ŻOB and perished in the fighters' bunker. See Aya Shahem, "Arie Wilner," in Ronen and Kohavi, *Guf Shlishi Yahid*, pp. 163–257.

17 Klinger, *I Am Writing These Words to You* (1943 diaries), pp. 154–155.

18 Ibid., p. 155.

19 Gutman, *The Jews of Warsaw*, pp. 395–396.

In Love with Death

For Chajka in Będzin, the Warsaw Ghetto Uprising was the fulfillment of her deepest desire. She identified with the combatants fully. In fighting and dying with honor they had also defended her dignity, exacted her revenge:

> [A]fter the incident in Czechoslovakia Republic [the assassination of Heydrich] it was the greatest achievement of the people oppressed by Hitler's regime.
>
> It was a full Jewish compensation on a large scale. For could any of us dream that the Germans would be liquidating the Jewish ghetto for four weeks?
>
> We knew that in the best-case scenario *hagana* would last a couple of hours.
>
> For *hagana* has nothing to do with logic or actual defense.
>
> It simply comes down to dying a human death. But unexpectedly there was a feat that few people living in better conditions could find courage for. For me it was a sigh of relief that we wouldn't be so fiercely condemned.[20]

Yet the feeling of elation and satisfaction here is tempered by a strange comment: "I wonder whether such actions in all the occupied territories would have made the Germans change their tactics in regard to Jews. I don't think so. It could even lead to an aggravation."[21] Chajka's sharp vision made her realize that the ghetto uprising was not likely to change the course of events, and perhaps even hasten the extermination. In retrospect, she turned out to be right: The Warsaw Ghetto Uprising did influence Himmler's decision to eliminate the rest of the "working" Jews in occupied Poland, including the Jews of Zagłębie.[22] Although this recognition did not change her belief in and dedication to revolt, she could not silence the pain:

> But aside from that feeling of pride and compensation, I was also feeling great pain, which was ripping my intestines apart. Everybody

20 Klinger, *I Am Writing These Words to You* (1943 diaries), pp. 118–119.

21 Ibid., p. 119.

22 For Himmler's order of May 21, 1943, regarding the expulsion of the Jews in the territories of the Reich, see chapter 17.

> is dead, having died a tragic death, as it wasn't during combat.
>
> None of our people is alive. There's no *zecher* [trace] of that powerful and beautiful movement that Hashomer Hatzair used to be. There's nobody left to objectively assess our part in that combat.[23]

The people in Warsaw she knew and loved were no longer alive. They had joined Josef Kaplan and Shmuel Breslaw. She had to continue walking in their footsteps. In particular, she felt an obligation toward Mordechai Anielewicz, who remained a spiritual and applied authority for her. In her diary she mentions two letters received from Anielewicz in the period preceding April 1943: "He succinctly described their operation, which we were to emulate. He told us step by step how to develop our organization and how to prepare for action. He demanded action, threatening to stop sending arms."[24] She quotes another letter from memory, which Anielewicz must have written during the period of intense preparations for *hagana*:

> Lots of work. Our arms are dropping off owing to the excess of work—difficult, hard toil.
>
> When you collapse exhausted after a hard day, sad thoughts beset you: that we'll soon see each other there, where none of us is in a hurry to get to. Few of us, veterans, are left. Farewell, dear young friend.[25]

To whom did Anielewicz address this pessimistic letter? Both Brandes and David were older than him. Perhaps he had sensed that his time was near. Chajka retained this letter in her heart. One can assume she saw it as his last testament.

Members of the underground resistance in Będzin passed on the news about the fighters' deaths to *Eretz Israel*. On April 25, 1943, Frumka conveyed to Switzerland news of the death of Tosia Altman and Zivia Lubetkin.[26] This was false information. At this point in time, both women were still alive. Tosia was destined to die only a few days later. It fell to Chajka to inform her movement of the death of Anielewicz and his friends. On May 22, probably after the courier Renia's return, a letter from Chajka arrived in *Eretz Israel* from Będzin:

23 Klinger, *I Am Writing These Words to You* (1943 diaries), p. 119.
24 Ibid., p. 153.
25 Ibid.
26 Zariz, *Mihtavey Halutzim*, p. 170; Habas, *Mihtavim min Hageta'ot*, p. 50.

> I am to ask you to inform Grandfather Meir that his dearest children working for Mrs. *Rashit* [leadership]—Tosia, Mordechai, Mira—have gone to join Josef Kaplan. You did not know Mordechai. He was an exceptionally gifted man. He was the father of *hagana* and he loved her like no man has ever loved his daughter. Grandfather can be proud of his children.[27]

No, "Grandfather" Meir did not know Mordechai. Even after the news was received, it was not clear to which Mordechai the letter referred. In contrast to Josef Kaplan, Anielewicz belonged to the younger generation of *shomrim*. According to Melech Neustadt, a member of the Histadrut's Diaspora Committee, many inquiries were made in order to finally determine that Mordechai Anielewicz was the man in question.[28] The unknown youth would soon become legendary.

Passing along news of her friends' death took a heavy toll on Chajka. Even though she had reported it, she was still having a hard time believing Tosia was really gone. Even in 1944, Chajka appears to have believed that Tosia was still among the living. In fact, the news about her death had been somewhat confused: After she had been taken to the hospital with severe burns, witnesses saw her captured by the Germans, and she had not been seen since. According to a later testimony by Chajka, a man named Adler reported seeing Tosia in Kraków. Adler had recognized her from her picture. "He said he saw her, and she smiled and said: 'I'm already dead.' He mentioned that she had a head injury."[29]

The story sounds too fantastical to be true: Tosia walking around Kraków with a bandage on her head, telling people she had come back from the dead. Yet, Chajka and David wanted it to be true. On June 3, 1943, David wrote to Heini Bornstein that "Tosia sends him her heartfelt congratulations and that she herself is feeling well after her serious illness."[30] Based on this, hope that Tosia might have been rescued was rekindled in Mandatory Palestine.[31] She was seen as the face of the movement, and she

27 The original manuscript of the letter has been lost; however, a copy of the letter remains. Letter from Chajka Klinger to Heini Bornstein, May 22, 1943, quoted in the report given by Heini at the end of his mission, Moreshet Archive, D.1.5466. See also Ronen, *Mihtavim Bezmanim Afelim*, vol. 1, p. 119.

28 Neustadt, *Horban U'mered*, pp. 101–102.

29 Chajka Klinger, minutes of the Executive Committee of Hakibbutz Ha'artzi from March 10, 1944, Moreshet Archive, D.1.1051.

30 Ronen, *Mihtavim Bezmanim Afelim*, p. 134; Bornstein, *Ha'i Shvaitz*, p. 237.

31 Letter from Wenia Pomeranz to Eliyahu Dobkin, June 21, 1943, Moreshet Archive, D.1.713.

was a symbol even in her lifetime. Efforts to locate her continued until the fall of 1943.[32]

Meanwhile, in Będzin, a place where reality had long since become stranger than fiction, Chajka was seeing her comrades transformed into the heroes of her favorite novels:

> The history of the Warsaw *hagana* is the history of another *Musa Dagh*. It's another *Man's Fate* by Malraux. It's Brzozowski's *Płomienie*.
>
> The people of *hagana* are extraordinary individuals, men of the cause, which was closer and dearer to them than life. These are not meaningless words or empty phrases. They gave their lives for them. So young, so young, they loved heroic death unflinchingly. [...]
>
> Will anybody be able to depict our unfathomable tragedy and the heroism of the final days like Malraux rendered China's heroism or like Werfel rendered the tragedy and heroism of the Armenians?[33]

Malraux's heroes achieved the ideal of revolutionary death in different forms. Chen the fatalist turned himself into a living bomb; old Gisors, a rebel commander who believed in man's control over his fate, chose to end his life by ingesting cyanide. The characters of *Płomienie* sacrificed their lives for the revolutionary ideal in which they believed. The protagonist of Malraux's story Gabriel Bagradian and some of his men escaped to the beach, safe only after the demise of Musa Dagh and his men. Chajka identified their deaths with the deaths of her comrades. And after all, were they really any different?

Malraux, Brzozowski, Werfel. These were not stories or symbols of Jewish heroism like that of Masada or Tel-Hai. The heroes of the literature she read sanctified the act of resistance and revolutionary death. The admiration, devotion, jealousy, and perhaps guilt she expresses toward her dead friends, make it possible to understand why she wanted to follow the path of her comrades in Warsaw, even though after the Warsaw Ghetto Uprising, the public consensus said: "Stop. No more." No more uprisings. This was the general opinion in Warsaw, in *Eretz Israel*, and also in Będzin.

32 Bornstein, *Ha'i Shvaitz*, pp. 240–242; Shalev, *Tosia Altman*, pp. 205–207.

33 Klinger, *I Am Writing These Words to You* (1943 diaries), p. 157.

Something Grand

Chajka drew immediate conclusions from the Warsaw Ghetto Uprising. To her mind, the Zagłębien resistance had to follow in the footsteps of the Warsaw *hagana* and perhaps even surpass it: "After the Warsaw feat, a small, minor act would have been meaningless here, and, in our own opinions, insufficient. We had to bring ourselves to do something grand that would if not exceed [the] Warsaw [act], then at least match it."[34]

This was not just her own individual opinion. Her use of the plural indicates the like-mindedness of her comrades. Indeed, activity increased among the two leading movements of the ŻOB in Zagłębie: Hashomer Hatzair and Dror. Renia Kukielka, Dror's courier, had returned from Warsaw and then traveled there several more times. Ina Gelbard, a member of Hashomer Hatzair in Sosnowiec, went with her. In Warsaw, they bought weapons from Terla, a Jew who lived on the Aryan side and with whom contact was established at the time through the chairman of the Pilica Judenrat. The risk was high: Idzia's fate loomed over them. They had to be ready to take a bullet or jump off a moving train. If they did get caught, they had to hold up under interrogation.[35]

The idea of setting the ghetto on fire, inspired by the events in Warsaw, became an actual plan:

> An "Aryan" group was formed. It was sent to places that it was to set ablaze in order for its members to get to know them well. We were frantically buying inflammable materials. The girls who were carrying those cans [with explosives] to the various groups felt so content and important.[36]

This "Aryan group" also appears in the testimonies of people from Sosnowiec. Fela Katz remembered that the group included Kasia (Miriam, Hela) Szancer, Ina Gelbard, and herself.[37] The girls began walking around without yellow patches on their clothing, equipped with false IDs to accustom themselves to the conditions of future operations. Chana Wiernik's testimony also confirms the plan to set the ghetto on fire, although it seems that it had been hatched even before the Warsaw

34 Ibid., p. 119.

35 Kukielka, *Escape from the Pit*, pp. 97–98.

36 Klinger, *I Am Writing These Words to You* (1943 diaries), pp. 119–120.

37 Fela Katz interview.

Ghetto Uprising. She had to stash the cans of gasoline that Zvi Brandes had sent from Będzin in her attic. In the event of another deportation, she and her comrades were to set fire to the entire city.[38]

Diverse testimonies also confirm the existence of workshops for manufacturing firearms. At first the workshop produced cold weapons only—brass knuckles, knives, and so on—but now they had moved on to making grenades, Molotov cocktails, and bombs. Meir Schulman, who arrived in Będzin at the end of February 1943 as a refugee from the decimated community of Chrzanów, played a central role in this activity. Even though Schulman was not a youth movement activist, he had been in contact with the Hechalutz people back in his hometown, where he had used his nimble hands to forge documents for the purposes of smuggling people into the Aryan side. Using instructions that came from Warsaw, Schulman began to produce Molotov cocktails and improvised grenades. He would saw off a metal pipe and fill it with a mixture of sulfur, powdered coal, and sugar. The explosive component was a glass test tube filled with sulfuric acid. A simple iron wire would do for a fuse.[39]

During those months, there was also a marked acceleration in the preparation of bunkers. David Kozłowski of Hashomer Hatzair and Alter Goldblum of Dror had already been overseeing the digging of bunkers—according to instructions received from Warsaw—for a while.[40] But now, the activity spread. Members of Dror and Hashomer Hatzair also began to build bunkers in private houses, initially in their parents' homes, then in other Jewish homes. The young men went from house to house and instructed the residents on bunker mining.[41] Chajka noted:

> I remember those nights when the boys would sneak out of the house dressed in working clothes with spades in hand. It was obvious that they were going to construct the bunker. They used to return tired at dawn and collapse on their beds. Many had to be dragged out by their legs, "Get up, man. Wash yourself before going to bed."[42]

The best bunker was dug in the Kibbutz Dror house, under the laundry room. The diggers taunted Chajka:

38 Chana Schlesinger (Wiernik) interview.

39 Meir Schulman, interview by the author, Tel Aviv, 1986.

40 Kukielka, *Escape from the Pit*, pp. 75–76.

41 Klinger, 1944 diaries, notebook C, p. 13.

42 Klinger, *I Am Writing These Words to You* (1943 diaries), pp. 159–160.

> "The bunker by the laundry will be the best. Even if the Germans bend over backward they won't discover it." "Is there going to be another entrance?" I asked. "No, it can't be made." "So I don't believe in that entire enterprise." They were angry with me that I dared criticize them, as if I knew better. Why, the purpose of the bunker was not to survive the war in it. It was made for us to sit there until we understood the situation, organized everything and then commenced action. We never discussed the subject again. [...]
>
> When it was finally finished, they sighed with relief. They talked secretly with one another about various bunkers, but they still stubbornly claimed that the one by the laundry was the best. "We'll make a bet with you, Chajka, that you won't find the entrance." "We'll see," I smiled ironically.[43]

And indeed, when Chajka went back, she was unable to find the entrance. Only several days later did Baruch finally show her the way in: "You slip out a small board, fixed inside, through the window. The wall is hollow and you slide down the wall. There is electricity, water, and an electric heater inside. It is indeed a first-class bunker."[44]

Yet, as amusing as Chajka's description is, it reveals the problematic nature of the bunkers. They were not built for defense or for long-term survival, but as a place to regroup before returning to action. In conditions of total expulsion, they could become death traps.

A Letter from Warsaw

Yet, in the midst of preparing for armed defense in the months of May and June 1943, the resistance in Będzin received news that hit them like a bucket of cold water. Chajka wrote:

> And then we received a letter from Warsaw, which was a slap in the face that stunned us.
>
> Very resigned and desperate, Yitzhak [Antek Zuckerman] and Cywia [Lubetkin] had changed their minds as to the value of *hagana*.
>
> They had come to the conclusion that it hadn't been worth those victims and their tragic deaths.

43 Ibid., p. 160.
44 Ibid., p. 161.

> This is how we explained it to ourselves: the events had overwhelmed them, they had become afraid of what they had started with their own hands, and the responsibility that had fallen on their shoulders was too great.
>
> They were spiritually exhausted. After so many days of psychological tension, which had reached its zenith, they became depressed.
>
> It's no wonder either that they felt devastated after only 40 of the few hundred members of the ŻOB had left the ghetto or that life had lost its value for them after they became the only survivors from the very many and beautiful hard core [of the organization].[45]

There is no evidence corroborating Chajka's interpretation of the mental state of Zivia Lubetkin and Antek Zuckerman, although her conclusions are not improbable. Later, Zivia Lubetkin would express her feelings after the rescue of the remaining fighters from the ghetto with the following words: "That evening we sat around a bonfire burning in a pit feeling like the last remnants of a nation that had been totally destroyed…We lay there on the ground unable to fall asleep…My heart pounded and pondered relentlessly but there was no answer."[46]

We do know, however, after the fighting had ended in Warsaw, Zivia and Antek were busy taking care of the rest of the fighters as well as maintaining contact with centers abroad. From their hiding place on the Aryan side, hidden threads stretched toward Jews hiding in Warsaw, the group of partisans sent to the forests, to Częstochowa in the Generalgouvernement, to Zagłębie annexed to the Reich. The threads were fragile and loose, but Zivia and Antek became quickly involved in the political organization of the Żydowski Komitet Narodowy (Jewish National Committee, ŻKN). Their main concern was survival and rescue.[47] The words of Zivia Lubetkin testify to the change in her attitude toward the uprising:

> After the uprising in Warsaw, I met with Rivka Glanc and told her: "I think that since this uprising ended as it did, it is better for the partisans to leave, and in this way, you will be able to kill many

45 Ibid., p. 120.

46 Zivia Lubetkin, *In the Days of Destruction and Revolt* (Tel Aviv: Hakibbutz Hameuchad and Am Oved, 1981), pp. 255–256.

47 Zuckerman, *A Surplus of Memory*, pp. 404–409.

> more Germans and save more Jews." She replied: "We want to stay with the Jews until the last moment." And they did stay. They stayed and died.[48]

Underground fighter Rivka Glanc's trip from Częstochowa to Warsaw took place at the end of May or the beginning of June 1943. Immediately afterward, Glanc also visited Będzin.[49] She may have brought Zivia's letter with her. However, the Będzin resistance also refused to accept Zivia and Antek's advice. Chajka wrote:

> But should we have learned a lesson regarding our objective duties from their subjective opinion of the events? No, and that is why their opinion—that after the Warsaw *hagana* there was no need for it here—had absolutely no influence on us.
>
> And one more thing, very important to us.
>
> Were we supposed to live in the shadow of their glory? Were we supposed to live at the price of their deaths and peacefully rest on their laurels?
>
> No, that would have been more than dishonorable. Besides, had any of the main reasons that inclined us to *hagana* changed? No. Not even one. While others were satisfied with the *hechsher* [kosher certification] that Warsaw had given them, we didn't give up our stance.[50]

Chajka and her comrades in Hashomer Hatzair refused to continue living in the shadow of the Varsovians' fame. The interpretation they offered of Zivia and Antek's letter allowed them to bypass the pair's authority, even though the Będzin activists were supposed to be their subordinates—both as part of the Hechalutz organization and within the ŻOB—and their words should have been perceived as instructions or even actual orders. This may have been the context for what Chajka said when she arrived in *Eretz Israel*: "We received orders in Zagłębie not to organize any more *hagana*, since those who were still alive were important for the Yishuv, so they could tell about the history of the movement and everything it went

48 Zivia Lubetkin, *Aharonim al Hahoma* (Hebrew) (Ein Harod: Hakibbutz Hameuchad, 1946), p. 48.

49 Perlis, *Tnu'ot Hano'ar Hehalutziyot*, p. 271.

50 Klinger, *I Am Writing These Words to You* (1943 diaries), pp. 120–121.

through to get to the Yishuv."[51] In this instance too, Chajka emphasized that, at the time, the "objective factors" that justified the organization of armed defense had not changed, and "there was no factor that justified that we should save ourselves of all people. Our decision was firm, to prepare for defense."[52] In military terms this is called refusing an order. If this had actually happened, the refusal would have led to many heroic deaths, following the example of the Warsaw ghetto fighters.

Yet, it is also possible that Chajka was referring to another order—the one that had come from *Eretz Israel.*

A Telegram from the Yishuv

In her 1943 diaries, immediately after her report on the instructions from Warsaw, Chajka wrote the following cryptic passage:

> And then we received Tabenkin's cable, "use all means for immigration," that is, quit *hagana*.
>
> We were outraged: they hadn't contacted us for four years of war, hadn't helped us at all, despite having [had] plenty of opportunities, and now, ignorant of the conditions, they dared tell us what to do.
>
> Could you kindly tell us which possibilities to use? When we received the wire Hashomer Hatzair had three or four papers [passports].
>
> Plenty of means for immigration![53]

A telegram from Tabenkin? To Będzin? In the middle of the war? In the 1950s, this paragraph would provoke intense political controversy. At a time when the ethos of the ghetto fighters became one of the founding legends of the State of Israel, it was akin to Moses breaking the tablets: It implied that Yitzhak Tabenkin, the leader of Hakibbutz Hameuchad in *Eretz Israel*, had suggested to the remnants of the resistance in the Polish ghettos to save themselves in any way possible and to give up fighting.

This telegram stood in clear contrast to the spirit of the news published about the Warsaw Ghetto Uprising. The main headline in

51 Chajka Klinger, minutes of the Executive Committee of the Histadrut from March 15, 1943, Moreshet Archive, C.53.1.24.

52 Ibid.

53 Klinger, *I Am Writing These Words to You* (1943 diaries), p. 121.

the *Davar* newspaper on April 23, 1943, screamed across the entire front page: "The Remnant of the Jewish Diaspora Stands Up for Itself."[54] Special mourning gatherings were held by the Histadrut and the pioneer movements. The people of Hakibbutz Ha'artzi and Hakibbutz Hameuchad appropriated the uprising—members of their movements in Poland, Hashomer Hatzair and Dror-Hechalutz, were at the head of the resistance. On June 2, 1943, this feeling was amplified when a telegram arrived from the surviving fighters via the Polish government-in-exile in London. The telegram was addressed to "Ya'ari-Tabenkin" and was signed by "Hashomer-Hechalutz." It read: "The surviving members of the movement continue to fight for the honor of the remaining nation of Israel in Poland."[55]

The telegram from Poland stirred up great excitement. At the meeting of the Executive Committee of Hakibbutz Ha'artzi in June 1943, Ya'akov Hazan delivered a eulogy for Zivia Lubetkin and Tosia Altman. Both merged in his heart into "one legendary figure." In every word of the telegram, Hazan saw "a symbol, an order, a demand."[56] Meir Ya'ari also paid tribute to Tosia: "The image of Tosia was carved from the bedrock of our movement and we know that she was not alone. Hundreds of Tosias walked in the midst of our camp. Hundreds of Tosias may yet arise to walk the paths of her life." He did not, however, mention Anielewicz.[57] At the time, Zivia Lubetkin was thought to be dead based on false information received from Będzin, among other places. Chajka's letter regarding Mordechai Anielewicz's role in the uprising had not yet been fully understood.

Nevertheless, Ya'ari also had some skeptical reflections regarding how justified the uprising had been:

> The Hashomer and Hechalutz youths in the Warsaw ghetto rose up in flames with weapons in their hands. The precious dead, we used to say, are just in the eyes of judgment. We said: "Such dead command us to live." Yet now, let us not attempt to hide it—a terrible

54 Anonymous, "She'erit Haplita shel Hagola Hayehudit Omedet al Nafsha" (Hebrew), *Davar*, April 23, 1943.

55 "Mivrak el Ya'ari VeTabenkin," in Dror and Rosenzweig, *Sefer Hashomer Hatzair*, vol. 1, p. 582.

56 Ya'akov Hazan, "Ehad Hagoral," in Dror and Rosenzweig, *Sefer Hashomer Hatzair*, vol. 1, p. 590.

57 Me'ir Ya'ari, "Betaba'at shel Ahva Lohemet," in Dror and Rosenzweig, *Sefer Hashomer Hatzair*, vol. 1, pp. 587–588.

> worm of doubt gnaws at us: Do those dead command us to live? Or do they leave behind them eternal death?[58]

Ya'ari, the only one of the Yishuv's leaders to have served as a combat officer in World War I, did not believe in suicide operations.

These doubts were also shared by the Hakibbutz Hameuchad leader Yitzhak Tabenkin. In public he was more resolute than Ya'ari. In June 1943, Tabenkin spoke at the Hanoar Haoved gathering in memory of the fallen and appropriated the fighting in Warsaw to the legacy of scrappy *Eretz Israel*. Referring to the telegram that came from London, he stated firmly: "Are you listening? They called you to stand your ground until the end for the honor of Israel.... The pioneers in the Diaspora died there not for a Polish homeland. They died for their homeland here."[59]

Yet, as much as Tabenkin may have extolled the bravery of the dead combatants in Poland, he secretly sought to save those who had survived. From the letter of Wenia Pomeranz, Hakibbutz Hameuchad's emissary to Istanbul, it appears that in the summer of 1943, a letter had been sent from Istanbul to Antek Zuckerman and Zivia Lubetkin in which it was written: "We want to save you, not for your own sake but for the sake of the people, so that a scion will remain for the family of the ghetto rebels," however it appears that this letter did not reach its destination.[60]

The later testimony of Różka Korczak also confirms this. According to her, upon her arrival in Israel in December 1944, Meir Ya'ari met her and immediately asked her: "'We sent you a telegram—Tabenkin and I—to save yourselves. Did you receive it?' I remember my answer: 'Meir, we didn't receive the telegram, and it's a good thing we didn't, because we wouldn't have listened anyway.'"[61] It is therefore reasonable to assume that there was indeed such a letter and that it had been signed by Ya'ari. Yet the telegram that both Chajka and Różka mention has never been found.

Was it fact or fiction? The telegram could have arrived via the Polish government-in-exile in London, which served as a contact point for the remnants of the ŻOB leadership in Warsaw. The circumstantial evidence, in particular Ya'ari's questioning of Różka and Wenia's letter, implies the

58 Ibid., p. 587.

59 Yitzhak Tabenkin, *Dvarim, Vol. 4: 1943–1949* (Hebrew) (Tel Aviv: Hakibbutz Hameuchad, 1976), pp. 33–36.

60 Anonymous, "Former Emissary in Istanbul Confirms Carmel's Remarks and Decries *Davar* Insinuations," *Davar*, July 1, 1955.

61 Yehuda Tubin, Levi Dror, and Yosef Rav, *Różka Korczak—Lehimata, Haguta, Dmuta* (Hebrew) (Tel Aviv: Moreshet and Sifriat Poalim, 1988), pp. 211–212.

existence of the telegram. All this points to the fact that in early June 1943, the estimated time of the telegram's arrival in Będzin, Ya'ari and Tabenkin—like Zivia and Antek—believed that one uprising had been enough. They wished to see the rest of their friends alive in *Eretz Israel*.[62]

The Path of the *Shomrim*

The sources at our disposal indicate that the special instructions from Warsaw and the telegram from *Eretz Israel* were not the only factors curbing the preparations for the uprising in Będzin. Even Chajka herself did not claim so. In fact, they reinforced a trend that was already prevalent among the youth movements in Zagłębie at the time—the preference for rescue over defense.

New winds were already blowing among the ranks of Hanoar Hatzioni in Będzin and Sosnowiec. Fredka Mazia described the feelings of pride and anxiety that filled her in light of the news broadcast on a secret radio station about the Warsaw Ghetto Uprising. However, at the meeting that gathered afterward, Józek Kożuch made it clear: "There will be no Warsaw ghetto here. Consider our situation. I have, days and nights. I looked for an approach, a solution, a way out—let us not delude ourselves. Our weapons are few, the few pistols we have are not sufficient for the possibility of a fight."[63] Comparing the dense housing structure of the Warsaw ghetto to the wide spaces separating the houses in the Sosnowiec ghetto, Kożuch stated that there was no chance that the *hagana* could actually succeed. "We must increase the rescue efforts...try all possible ways to save the comrades...the uprising in Warsaw has died down and with it died our hopes."[64]

Janek Zimmerman spoke up for the opposition. He did not want to give up the uprising. Would they simply gather again at the assembly points as they did on August 12? Hypek Glitzenstein supported this position. But Kożuch was adamant. With three guns there was no point in *hagana*. It was decided to send Fredka to Kraków in order to contact Zalman Bajuk, the member of Hanoar Hatzioni who could smuggle people into Slovakia, and take advantage of the Latin American

62 Avihu Ronen, "The Cable That Vanished: Tabenkin and Ya'ari to the Last Surviving Ghetto Fighters," *Yad Vashem Studies*, 41:2 (2014), pp. 95–138.

63 Mazia, *Re'im Basa'ar*, pp. 133–135.

64 Ibid.

passport option. If necessary, members could pretend to marry those with foreign passports.[65]

In May 1943, Gordonia members were busy organizing rescue operations using Latin American passports. The next group of departures were to include David Liwer as well as Shlomo Zimmerman, the de facto leader of Gordonia in Będzin. The refusal of Hanka Borenstein and Moshe Manela to be sent to the detention camp for foreign nationals was accepted with understanding but not approval.

Chajka saw these developments as a betrayal of the idea of *hagana*. Elsewhere in her diaries, where she recounted the end of the passport affair, she wrote: "Isn't it funny and outrageous at the same time? The issue of the *Internierungslager* had one consequence: it dampened the enthusiasm and weakened the strength and the concentration of force on our one aim—*hagana*."[66]

It seemed that all these circumstances stacked up against the notion of an attempted uprising. In her 1943 diaries, after describing these three affairs—the directives from Warsaw, the Tabenkin telegram, and the development of the passport affair—Chajka devotes an extensive, soul-searching passage to justifying the idea of hagana:

> What was *hagana* to us actually?[...]
>
> *Hagana* was not only a compensation for the harm and our nation's disgraceful behavior. It was not only a deed for the sake of history, but in my opinion, it was predominantly an individual need in each of us. It was born inside [of] us. We gave birth to that thought in ourselves. It was the best part of our existence. And only thanks to its presence within us could we endure all that humiliation for so long without losing our personal dignity. For each of us knew that the day of reckoning would come.[67]

In the revised 1944 version of the diaries, she returned to this subject; however, editing errors make it unclear whether this passage refers to this period alone or the overall course of the war. Either way, in this text, Chajka formulated her position more sharply and poignantly than ever:

> But the *hagana* could not have been born of dry, rational calculation alone. After all, the *hagana* was in its essence a rejection of reason,

65 Ibid.

66 Klinger, *I Am Writing These Words to You* (1943 diaries), pp. 117–118.

67 Ibid., p. 118.

> of logic. Some kind of inner pathos was at play here, a sense of necessity, springing from an inner conviction, a subjective perception of events. We knew very well that we could never create a force that could truly oppose the Germans. All we could aim for was a dignified death, not in gas chambers, not in baths where they killed you with electricity, but on the battlefield. A chance to avenge our deaths, to make the Germans pay. We knew this was the end, this was death. We were prepared to struggle but it was not an optimistic one, it could not end in victorious life but only in victorious death.[68]

The path of Hanoar Hatzioni and Gordonia was meant to lead to life; Chajka's path, the path of the *shomrim*, would lead to death. Where the people were being exterminated, it was the vanguard's duty to die.

68 Klinger, 1944 diaries, notebook C, pp. 2–3.

Chapter Seventeen

Devastation at the Doorstep

The Ghettos

In her diaries, centered as they are on the actions of the resistance, Chajka hardly refers to the process of ghettoization that took place at that time and the deportations that followed. The only mention of them appears in connection with Merin's operations in Zagłębie:

> They [Merin and his men] received many concessions from the Germans. The Jews had it best in the Dąbrowa Basin. The hunger there was not as bad as in the Generalgouvernement. Jews received the same food rations as the Poles, and those who worked in heavy industry received an additional ration as well. The black market was fully under Jewish control, and they could get by quite well. Moniek Merin had an agreement with the Germans. They sent reports to Berlin regarding the number of Jews settled in the Dąbrowa Basin and those working for the Wehrmacht, which were not quite truthful. So, they left the Basin alone till the very end. In the Generalgouvernement, resettlements from Łódź, Warsaw, Częstochowa, and Kraków had been going on for a long time before the time for Będzin finally came.[1]

German documents make it possible to reconstruct the process of the concentration of Zagłębien Jews in the ghettos in preparation for deportation. By April 1, 1943, the concentration of the Sosnowiec Jews in

1 Klinger, 1944 diaries, notebook C, pp. 58–59.

the ghetto had been completed. Nearly 20,000 Jews were closed off in the suburb of Środula. The turn of Będzin came on April 8, 1943. Between April and May 1943, 18,670 Jews were resettled in the ghettos of Kamionka and Mała Środula (Little Środula).[2] According to estimates, around 6,000 more Jews lived in approximately ten smaller ghettos in the nearby towns of Dąbrowa Górnicza, Zawiercie, Wadowice, and Andrychów. In fact, they were supposed to be large labor camps of sorts, whose inhabitants were considered essential workers of the German war industry.

For Merin, these ghettos were further proof that his chosen path was the Jews' best chance of survival. The neglected and squalid suburbs of Kamionka and Środula were transformed at lightning speed. Relatively early testimony stated:

> The ghetto was established on the basis of productivity. The construction work was done by the Jews themselves, and Moniek Merin worked extensively in this area. The "*Eretz Israel* model" served as the example for construction as well as the organization of life in general. Agricultural enterprise was established for the sake of self-provision.[3]

Liwer's testimony completes the description: "Soon, the area designated as the ghetto shed its old skin and took on a new one.... The ghetto came to life in the hustle and bustle of construction that proceeded at an accelerated pace, and it felt as if we were going to settle in this place for decades."[4]

The Health Department took care of sanitation and hygiene arrangements, the public kitchens were moved to the ghetto, a daycare center was established for small children, and thousands of books accumulated by the Judenrat were transferred to the resettled residents.[5]

During the first months of 1943, most of the population of Będzin in particular and of Zagłębie in general became involved in production and manufacture. Many children and the elderly were integrated into the workshops, and as essential workers they were supposedly protected from deportation. Multiple testimonies of children from Będzin and

2 Documents regarding the Jewish community in Bedzin, 1943, YVA, M.54.ZIH/JM/2702/3, 4, 16, 22, 24.

3 Gutman and Gutman-Herzberg, "Bageto Bendin: Protocol," p. 174.

4 D. Liwer, *Ir Hametim*, p. 104.

5 Mazia, *Re'im Basa'ar*, pp. 124–135; Amos Avni testimony, YVA, O.3/3794; Wiederman, *Płowa bestia*, pp. 351–352.

Sosnowiec indicate as much.[6] Prominent among them is the testimony of ten-year-old Sara Kleiner from Sosnowiec, which was collected in *Eretz Israel* a short time later:[7]

> Because Mother was afraid of deportation, she asked one of the officials of the Council [Judenrat], Diamant, to pull some strings and get me a job at one of the workshops. And so, I entered the forced labor workforce. My job was to make dominoes for hospitalized German soldiers. There were lots of children, maybe as many as 100 or 150, working alongside me. They were all over the age of twelve, I was the only one who'd been accepted at the age of ten, thanks to the strings pulled for me.[8]

Faced with the threat of deportations, there was a shift in attitude toward the labor camps. Despite the hard work and harsh conditions, the camps were now seen as a lesser evil that promised higher chances of survival. Going to a labor camp was also sometimes seen as an act of valor. The young worker was seen as protecting his family from the threat of deportation. Suspicions aside, young Jews were now willing to listen to the arguments of the Judenrat who were once again preaching the merits of voluntary recruitment to the labor camps. For example, David Eisenberg of Dąbrowa Górnicza recalled the following:

> In mid-February 1943, a delegation arrived from Sosnowiec's Central Judenrat (Secretary Czarna, Moniek Merin, and others) and they announced that: "In order to save women and children, you have to report to work in Germany." After that, a group was sent out on March 3. It was the last group, and I was among them. The German Kuczyński checked the men and suddenly asked me: "Do you want to go to Germany or do you prefer to stay home?" I agreed to stay home. Then I regretted it, because all those who remained had only extermination to look forward to.[9]

6 Cypora Plawner-Kochav testimony, YVA, O.3/3230; Abraham Friedman testimony, Moreshet Archive, A.403. The fourteen-year-old Rutka Laskier also got a job in a workshop on March 20, 1943. Laskier, *Rutka's Notebook*, pp. 52–53.

7 The Kleiner family was sent to Mandatory Palestine under the subject exchange agreement in February 1943.

8 Sara Kleiner testimony, YVA, O.12/47.

9 "David Eisenberg testimony," in Gelbart, *Sefer Dombrova Gurnitze* [*Dąbrowa Górnicza*] *Vehurbana*, p. 412.

Nevertheless, as other testimonies show, there were young people who chose to avoid hard labor even at this stage.[10]

A feasible employment solution was even found for the refugees from the Generalgouvernement arriving in Będzin and Sosnowiec in great numbers at that time.[11] Since they had no documents, the Gestapo intended to deport them to Auschwitz in the weekly transports that continued during this period. The responsibility for locating the refugees was assigned to the Jewish police. From September 1942, Jewish policemen had been conducting searches in Będzin and Sosnowiec to find refugees from the Generalgouvernement. Those hunted down would be brought to either the Sosnowiec Dulag transit camp (*Durchgangslager*) or other places of detention, and from there they would be taken to the labor camps or to Auschwitz. Merin proposed to the Germans that the refugees should be concentrated in a special camp under the supervision of the Central Judenrat and employed in various jobs assigned to them by this Jewish Council. The Gestapo approved the arrangement, and thus a new labor camp was established in the beginning of 1943 in the suburb of Środula—the AK Camp (*Arbeitskommando*). The camp was recognized by the members of Organization Schmelt as part of the Jewish labor camp system in the area. In the spring of 1943, the camp held 270 refugees, all of them employed in municipal jobs. Despite the glimmer of hope it offered, many refugees hesitated to report to the camp: to some, the AK Camp looked like a trap from which they would be sent to their deaths in Auschwitz.[12]

Work recruitment under the auspices of the certificates issued by Organization Schmelt was indeed an effective survival mechanism. In May 1943, Będzin received a visit from an inspector on behalf of the Reich Ministry of Armaments and War Production. According to the report he sent to Berlin on May 12, 1943, no less than 13,182 out of the 18,670 Jews in Będzin were employed at that time, meaning that about 70 percent of the Jewish population was contributing to the German war economy.[13] These were very high figures of Jewish survival. Together with the 15,000 young Jews in the Organization Schmelt labor camps,[14] this amounts to

10 See D. Liwer, *Ir Hametim*, pp. 87–88; Meir Pardleski, in *Sefer Sosnovitz*, vol. 2, p. 239.

11 In the spring of 1943, this number was estimated to be at least 600. See documents regarding the Jewish community in Bedzin, 1943, YVA, M.54.ZIH/JM/2702/4.

12 D. Liwer, *Ir Hametim*, pp. 102–103; Documents regarding the Jewish community in Bedzin, 1943, YVA, M.54.ZIH/JM/2702.

13 D. Liwer, *Ir Hametim*, p. 95; Documents regarding the Jewish community in Bedzin, 1943, YVA, M.54.ZIH/JM/2702/3.

14 This figure is based on the statistical proportion of Będzin's population and the

the highest survival rate in all of Poland. While about three-quarters of the Jews of Poland had already perished, nearly two-thirds of the Jews of Zagłębie—approximately 60,000 people—were still alive.

As Chajka speculates, this was not thanks to Merin's efforts alone. In large part, survival was made possible by the influential position of Organization Schmelt, which exploited the work of the Jews both in the ghetto workshops and in the labor camps. As the economic branch of the SS directly subordinate to Himmler, its people had a special status. In many instances, German entrepreneurs—Rossner chief among them—were able to rescue workers from deportation by contacting the organization's representatives in Będzin and Sosnowiec. Rossner, the former socialist and current humanitarian, a less extravagant version of Schindler so to speak, probably enjoyed a special position in Organization Schmelt due to the fact that his factories supplied uniforms to the Luftwaffe, the army offices, the navy, and the police.[15]

This notion was supported by the Ministry of Armaments and War Production under Albert Speer. In his summary report, the inspector wrote:

> All the factories [in Będzin] are of lesser or greater military importance, some of them of decisive importance for the war effort.... A further reduction of the Jewish workforce seems impracticable, since there is no replacement workforce, and crucially, none of equal value. Such an action may jeopardize the continued existence of the factories.... It is in the interest of the nation, the state, and the entire German Defense Authority, as well as the needs of civilians, to maintain production at full capacity, so as not to strain or weaken the welfare of the economy under any circumstance.[16]

But the adamant language of the report fell on deaf ears. At the end of May 1943, an order was given to eliminate the Jews of Eastern Upper Silesia.[17] The decision was connected to the turn in Himmler's global

Korherr Report. See also Statistische Angaben des Stands über die Jüdische, August 24, 1942, Moreshet Archive, Avihu Ronen collection, 235.

15 Documents regarding the Jewish community in Bedzin, 1943, YVA, M.54.ZIH/JM/2702/24.

16 Documents regarding the Jewish community in Bedzin, 1943, YVA, M.54.ZIH/JM/2702/3.

17 Leni Yahil, *The Holocaust: The Fate of European Jewry, 1932–1945* (New York and Oxford: Oxford University Press, 1990), pp. 406–408.

policy regarding the remaining Jews of occupied Poland. At the end of 1942, with the main extermination wave coming to a close, Himmler allowed the continued existence of "productive" Jews, on condition that they be subject exclusively to the SS in concentration camps. The Warsaw Ghetto Uprising, which broke out in the second half of April and lasted until mid-May 1943, brought about a turning point in the Germans' attitude to the exploitation of the Jewish workforce. It provided Himmler with the pretext he needed to overcome factors that had—until now—prevented him from fully realizing the "Final Solution to the Jewish Question."[18]

On May 21, 1943, Himmler gave an order to "deport to the East" (meaning to Auschwitz) all the Jews still remaining in Reich territories by June 30.[19] The testimony of Rudolf Höss, commandant of Auschwitz, confirms this:

> An unequivocal order was received from the SS [Himmler] that the workshops [of Organization Schmelt] must be closed, the Jews and the factories must be transferred to the concentration camp in Auschwitz, and the labor camps closest to factories of decisive importance for the war must be operated under the administration of the Auschwitz concentration camp, or rather, Gross-Rosen. Labor camps outside of these categories must be dissolved, and their residents must be transferred to Auschwitz.[20]

The meaning of the order was clear: Those fit for work would continue to work in the concentration camps; the unfit would be destroyed.

The End of the Passport Affair

At the same time as the fate of Zagłębie's Jewry was being sealed, hopes of salvation by way of procuring foreign passports were also extinguished. The letters that arrived from the first two groups who had left in March

18 Gutman, *The Jews of Warsaw*, pp. 426–429.

19 Eichmann trial verdict, based on document T/1398, https://www.asser.nl/upload/documents/DomCLIC/Docs/NLP/Israel/Eichmann_Judgement_11-12-1961.pdf (accessed August 2024).

20 Nachman Blumental, Józef Kermisz, and Artur Eisenbach, eds., *Dokumenty i Materialy* (Łódź: Centralna Żydowska Komisja Historyczna w Polsce, 1946), doc. no. 173.

and April 1943 for the detention camps for foreign nationals caused a veritable run on passports in Będzin. Hundreds of letters went back and forth from Będzin to Geneva. Members of the youth movements accumulated dozens of certificates, and despite their reservations, a number of passports also arrived for members of Hashomer Hatzair. The passports were held by Zvi Brandes, and it was clear that the fate of those leaving would be decided by the movement as a collective.[21] Passports likewise arrived for Chajka, David, and Zvi, as well as several other members,[22] and while talk in the movement still revolved around missions only, it is likely that doubts were starting to creep in. Yet before they could germinate, the wheel turned a second time, and the passports ceased to be an easy way out.

Complications in the passport affair began due to Merin's involvement. As we may recall, Merin saw the passports as a threat to his control over the lives of the Jews of Zagłębie. He claimed that the passports arriving from Switzerland were endangering the well-being of the entire community.[23] Were he to be placed in charge of the matter, salvation would be guaranteed, and the community would come to no harm. Yet, in this instance, unlike in questions of *hagana*, the youth movements' refusal was unshakable. Following his failure to negotiate with them, Merin went directly to the Hechalutz representatives in Switzerland. Fredka Mazia recounts that a letter arrived from Switzerland, expressing much puzzlement at the fact that veteran Zionists like Merin and Czarna were being left out of the loop and not included in actions and decision-making processes.[24] Still, the youth movements insisted: Merin and Czarna were no longer Zionists, and in light of their current conduct, their past should not be taken into account.[25]

Having failed to advance his position based on his Zionist past, Merin forbade the ghetto inhabitants from contacting anyone abroad, including via letters.[26] Yet, this move also backfired: There were plenty of opportunities to smuggle letters in and out of the relatively open ghetto, and the youth movements took advantage of this to continue their relationships with Switzerland. Merin had no choice but to escalate

21 Isaac Neuman interview.
22 Ronen, *Mihtavim Bezmanim Afelim*, vol. 1, pp. 99–118.
23 A. Liwer, "Asher Lo Yishkach," pp. 354–355.
24 Mazia, *Re'im Basa'ar*, p. 138.
25 Ibid.
26 D. Liwer, *Ir Hametim*, p. 111.

his efforts. On May 24, 1943, the Judenrat issued arrest warrants for about twenty people involved in the passport affair, most of them youth movement activists.[27] Chajka recorded:

> They have arrested some family members of the most active leaders of various organizations, pretending it was because some of them supposedly possessed international passports. The Gestapo had no idea about any of this. Merin threatened these people day after day with exile and resettlement. He wanted the youth movements to settle the whole matter with him, so that he could get something from them too. But no one came to him and Merin, fearful of the consequences, had to let the arrestees go.[28]

The arrests are also mentioned in both Liwer's and Mazia's testimonies. The people of Gordonia, who received a warning from Jewish policemen, managed to escape.[29] In Sosnowiec, Jewish policemen broke into the Kożuch house late at night and arrested Józek Kożuch, his wife Fredka, and his brother Bolek. The police officers refused to inform the detainees of the reason for the arrest.[30]

The arrests achieved the desired result: Even though the youth movement activists assumed that the arrests were the result of a sporadic initiative by Merin related to the passport affair, they feared that the detainees would be sent to Auschwitz on the weekly transport, which was to leave the next day.[31] At a meeting held in Będzin that morning among representatives of all the youth movements, the consensus was that the Germans were not involved in the matter. Therefore, it was decided to wait a few days before sending a delegation to Merin.[32] A similar decision was made in Sosnowiec. At any rate, the members of Hanoar Hatzioni prepared themselves for armed action to free the prisoners if it turned out that they were being taken to the Gestapo.[33]

The tension lasted several days, but the gamble paid off. When the detainees and the other family members were released, it was

27 Mazia, *Re'im Basa'ar*, p. 139.

28 Klinger, 1944 diaries, notebook C, p. 12.

29 D. Liwer, *Ir Hametim*, pp. 111–112.

30 Mazia, *Re'im Basa'ar*, p. 139. Fredka herself was released the same evening.

31 Ibid., p. 140.

32 D. Liwer, *Ir Hametim*, p. 112; Klinger, 1944 diaries, notebook C, p. 12.

33 Mazia, *Re'im Basa'ar*, p. 140.

proof that the Gestapo had not been involved in the arrests.[34] Two letters went out from Zagłębie to Switzerland at the beginning of June 1943. The first was from Liwer, who wrote explicitly that passports should not be sent to the Judenrat because "they are criminals who feed on the blood of Israel."[35] Merin wrote the second letter, on June 2, 1943, in which he asked Schwarzbaum in Switzerland to refrain from being in contact with anyone other than him. He made a similar request to Schwalb.[36]

Even though the Gestapo wasn't directly involved, it is likely that Merin was acting under Gestapo pressure. The Gestapo in the area could not help but notice the strange correspondence that was going on under their noses, and they certainly knew about the departure of the first two groups to the detention camp for foreign nationals. However, with the organization of the third group at the beginning of June, the Gestapo intervened and delayed the departure of additional Jews with Latin American passports.[37] The youth activists were sure that Merin had played a part in the matter. They had long since received an order from Mordechai Anielewicz to eliminate Merin. Now it appeared that the time had come to do it. In her account, Chajka approves of the decision:

> A decision was made to eliminate Moniek Merin. He was ready to do anything and would not let us act.... Everyone agreed to the death sentence issued for Merin in principle, but when it came to carrying out the orders, they began to waver, saying the responsibility was too great, that we were risking everyone's lives, and that this would only speed up the general resettlement.[38]

A plan to assassinate Merin also emerges from the testimony of Tosia Herzberg. Her brother Alex Gutman, then a young member of Hanoar Hatzioni in Będzin, was ordered to dig a grave for Merin.[39]

The various hesitations indicate that the members of the underground resistance in Będzin—unlike those in Warsaw—were not

34 D. Liwer, *Ir Hametim*, p. 112.
35 Ibid., p. 113.
36 A. Liwer, "Asher Lo Yishkach," pp. 354–355.
37 Letter from David Kozłowski to Heini Bornstein, June 3, 1943, Moreshet Archive, D.1.1090.1.
38 Klinger, 1944 diaries, notebook C, p. 14.
39 Tosia and Shalom Herzberg, interview by the author, Ramat Gan, 1990.

prepared to seize internal control of the city. They knew what was at stake: In Będzin, where there had been no *Aktionen* for around a year, the Jews had too much to lose.

And if all else failed, they had the passports. The Hashomer Hatzair command was finally ready to use them for mission purposes. In mid-June, a list arrived from the civilian police headquarters, containing the names of people for whom passports had arrived from abroad. The next day, they were to report to the police building, where they would be arrested as foreign nationals and transferred to the detention camp in Germany. The list was received with mixed feelings at Hashomer Hatzair: "The six of us were on that list. Bleak despair. What now? This could break our discipline. If they don't leave, the campaign against Hashomer Hatzair will resume."[40]

Chajka's notes indicate that a meeting was held to discuss the list of mission candidates. The task of coordinating the mission was to be entrusted to either Chajka or Nacia Klugman. The choice of contenders is easily understandable. Both women were eloquent and were endowed with considerable rhetorical ability. They were regular speakers at movement events on holidays and feast days.[41] Both were well acquainted with the resistance and its mode of operations. It seems that Chajka was initially the favorite, as implied by the following passage she wrote in her diary: "We wanted Nacha [Nacia] to go. It was possible that I wouldn't manage to leave, so she would be a *shlicha* [envoy]."[42]

This is the first time she mentions—rather casually—the fact that she had been selected for a mission, that is, chosen to remain among the living. Later, Shmuel Ron would describe it as being "condemned to life."[43] Her friends assigned her the same role that was assigned to Tosia and Frumka in Warsaw: to survive in order to tell. It is possible that this is what Chajka meant when she described her relationship with David during this period from the third person perspective:

> "If only I could take at least one," he would say. "Chaj," he would tell his girlfriend, "you must survive. You must tell them all about us." [...]
>
> And she didn't dare oppose him, so that he wouldn't accuse her of cowardice.

40 Klinger, *I Am Writing These Words to You* (1943 diaries), p. 121.

41 Ibid., p. 122.

42 Ibid.

43 Shmuel Ron interview.

> And she would have loved to go with him, even to die, for she could not imagine a life without him.[44]

As we learned later, she never agreed to be sentenced to life. However, now it all depended on a formal decision. It is likely that Nacia's name was included on the list submitted by the police, whereas the certificates for Chajka had not yet arrived. It was also decided to approve the departure of Yankale and Dov (Barak) Fruchtzweig as well as that of Hela. Now the names of David and Zvi came up. Both refused. Chajka recorded David's refusal in hindsight: "Dawid was chosen but did not wish to go. He did not wish for cowards to take shelter under his name, happy that they had to go too, that they had been selected. 'Besides, since Dawid is going,' they'd say. Dawid refused."[45]

The last person on the Hashomer Hatzair list was Zvi Brandes: "As for Cwi, his stance was firm and tough: he wasn't going regardless of the consequences."[46] Zvi Brandes was the leading figure in Hashomer Hatzair at this time. He was its representative in Hechalutz and a key member—if not the commander—of the resistance. His departure would have meant giving up on *hagana* altogether. The movement's leadership could not agree to this. Zvi's decision became a litmus test for Hashomer Hatzair's insistence on the principle of *hagana*. Zvi stayed: When the police came to arrest him as a foreign national, he hid and was never found.

The day when the second group of "foreign nationals" left was remembered by many in Będzin and Sosnowiec. It was Saturday, June 19, 1943. Many gathered near the Judenrat building to say goodbye to the lucky few who were going to survive.[47] Among them was Shraga Fruchtzweig, who came to bid farewell to his brother Dov (Barak), one of the four members of Hashomer Hatzair who planned to leave. He remembered that many people handed letters and photographs to the departing group for them to take to *Eretz Israel*.[48] However, happiness for those about to leave was tinged with envy: Sure, they might make it, but what would happen to the rest? Fredka remembered that the departing group was called in to say goodbye to Merin and were forced to listen to a tearful farewell speech. Merin wanted them to

44 Klinger, *I Am Writing These Words to You* (1943 diaries), p. 173.

45 Ibid.

46 Ibid., p. 122.

47 D. Liwer, *Ir Hametim*, p. 114.

48 Shraga Fruchtzweig interview.

tell the world about his efforts and everything he had done for the community: "Let the youth not hold a grudge against him, for even though he was often forced to go against them, Merin's heart was always with them."[49] The truck arrived, and the deportees got on to go to Katowice, from where they would be sent to the detention camp for foreign nationals.

However, they never reached the detention camp. That same day (some say two days later),[50] news arrived that the "foreign detainees" had been taken to Auschwitz. The news was delivered by an electrician, a Christian who was working at the entrance to Auschwitz.[51] However, the photographs the group carried with them would survive and serve as a silent testament to their lives.[52] Chajka in Będzin, was shaken and wrote with great bitterness:

> *Besach hakol* [to sum up]. What good did help from abroad, which was surrounded with all that uproar, do us?
>
> Nacia [Klugman], Jacow [Jacob] [Landau], Berek [Barak] [Fruchtzweig], and Hela were sent to Auschwitz.
>
> God, we are personally responsible for the death of those who were [supposed] to survive.
>
> Making matters worse, we received a wire from [Yitzhak] Tabenkin urging us to use all means for immigration.
>
> Isn't it funny and outrageous at the same time? The issue of the *Internierungslager* had one consequence: it dampened the enthusiasm and weakened the strength and the concentration of force on our one aim—*hagana*.[53]

Her disappointment is easily understood: the rescue hatch that had undermined the movement's efforts to prepare for *hagana* turned out to be a trap. Four of her best friends—among them the gifted Nacia Klugman—were gone, never to return. Her own life and that of Zvi

49 Mazia, *Re'im Basa'ar*, p. 157.

50 D. Liwer, *Ir Hametim*, p. 114.

51 Ibid.

52 These photographs were preserved in the "sauna" at Auschwitz and were displayed for many years after the war. A study conducted at the end of the 1990s revealed that most of them belonged to the residents of Będzin in the 1930s. See Kersten Brandt, Hanno Loewy, and Krystyna Oleksy, eds., *Before They Perished… Photographs Found in Auschwitz* (Oświęcim: Auschwitz-Birkenau State Museum, 2001).

53 Klinger, *I Am Writing These Words to You* (1943 diaries), pp. 117–118.

Brandes had come within a hairsbreadth of being lost as well. Reality had played a bitter joke on them all.

Merin's Demise

That very day, June 19, 1943, a no less momentous occasion took place: Merin himself was deported to Auschwitz. Early in the afternoon, rumors spread throughout Będzin and Sosnowiec that Merin and his entourage had been called to report to the Gestapo headquarters in Katowice. Merin made his way there accompanied by Dr. Bornstein, Dr. Levinstein (the secretary of the Central Judenrat), and Fania Czarna.[54] According to Fredka Mazia's account, members of Hanoar Hatzioni in Sosnowiec placed lookouts on the streets in anticipation of a possible *Aktion*. In the evening, the police chief Romek Goldminc arrived in Fredka and Kożuch's room. "They're all gone!" the cry erupted from his mouth. He said that he had followed the Judenrat officials on his bicycle and waited for them outside the Gestapo headquarters. Suddenly, they began to take the people destined for the *Julags*—the *Judenarbeitslager*, the detention camp for foreign nationals—outside in a most rude fashion, while beating them and shouting; they made them get into a windowless car, the kind in which small groups were transported to Auschwitz. Their packages were taken from them. They looked shocked and depressed. Then, they pushed Merin and his entourage into the same car. Goldminc jumped on his bike and rode away as fast as he could.[55]

Even with the benefit of hindsight, it is difficult to determine whether there was more than a circumstantial connection between the deportation of the "foreign nationals" to Auschwitz and Merin's fate. The Jews of Będzin and Sosnowiec believed that this was no coincidence. Chajka thought it was a case of whistleblowing gone wrong. She wrote: "It was Merin's fault—he had said too much to the Gestapo."[56] This seems to have been the accepted version of events in the resistance circles.

Today we know that the Gestapo had its eye on the passport affair from the beginning. At that exact time (May 1943), the Gestapo itself

54 D. Liwer, *Ir Hametim*, p. 114.

55 Mazia, *Re'im Basa'ar*, pp. 157–158. According to Auschwitz records, forty-five Jews arrived from Sosnowiec on June 20, 1943. These included the thirty-four Jews destined for the foreign nationals' detention camp and eleven Judenrat officials, Merin among them. See Namysło, *Zagłada Żydów Zagłębiowskich*, p. 30.

56 Klinger, *I Am Writing These Words to You* (1943 diaries), p. 122.

was selling passports in Warsaw. Thousands of passports arriving from Switzerland came into the hands of its people, and through the mediation of Jewish agents who worked in its service, these were sold to the highest bidder. The transactions were conducted at the Hotel Polski. In this way, the Gestapo exposed hundreds of Jews who had managed to find a hiding place on the Aryan side of Warsaw after the uprising. In Warsaw as well as in Będzin, certain hopes were pinned on the passports. But their fate was no better than that of the Jews of Będzin, and they also ended up in Auschwitz. In July 1943, the Gestapo surrounded the Hotel Polski and arrested several hundred people. They were taken to the Pawiak Prison. Many of them were shot dead.[57]

In essence, the Gestapo had its own considerations, and those in Warsaw and in Będzin who thought they could influence it were only kidding themselves. In the end, Merin also learned this lesson the hard way and not just in terms of the outcome of the passport affair. He received special treatment from the Germans, who placed him in Block 11 of Auschwitz I, mainly intended for political prisoners. In a rare testimony, Dawid Gertler, the commander of the special department of the Jewish police in Łódź who was arrested on August 12, 1943, stated that Merin had been placed in this block, and he let it be understood that he had most likely been put to death.[58] As far as the Germans were concerned, Merin's part had come to an end, and a few days after his transfer to Auschwitz, the deportations resumed in Będzin.

The Deportation of June 1943

Despite the ominous signs, the deportation that began on June 22, 1943, surprised not only the Jews of Będzin and Sosnowiec but also the resistance. When the deportation began, many believed that—like its predecessors—it would be selective. Chajka wrote:

> Soon after, the resettlement began. It was common knowledge that children and the elderly were the ones being resettled predominantly.

57 Adolf Berman, *Bamakom Asher Ya'ad Li Hagoral: Am Yehudey Varsha, 1939–1942* (Hebrew) (Tel Aviv: Hakibbutz Hameuchad, 1971), pp. 139–140; Eck, "The Rescue of Jews with the Aid of Passports," pp. 93–111; Jonas Turkow, *Sofan shel Ashlayot* (Hebrew) (Tel Aviv: Hamenora, 1973), pp. 54–73.

58 Isaiah Kuperstein interview with Dawid Gertler, Paris, March 6, 1974, YIVO archives New York, CD 3A (transcription by Robert Shapiro).

> Young people, especially those who worked at Rossner's, did not try to hide. This time, however, they were taken too, these young, healthy, energetic men and women. The sisters Lea and [Irka Pejsachson] were among those taken.[59]

Ostensibly, the resistance was well prepared to face this deportation. They had finished constructing a number of bunkers, and according to Chajka, "The order had long been that we weren't going to the [deportation] center."[60] And indeed, members of Hashomer Hatzair and Dror rushed down to the bunkers. According to the testimony of Zippora Szporn, about twenty people went down to the Hashomer Hatzair bunker, including Leibel and Perl Klinger, their daughter Sarah, and her children.[61] Frumka Płotnicka and Herszel Szpringer of Kibbutz Dror ordered their members to go down to the bunkers as well. Yet, at the last minute and with Frumka's consent, Herszel decided that holders of the *sonder* certificates—the workshop employees—did not have to go. He and some other Dror men did not go down to the bunker but joined the Jews who were gathered in a large field.[62] Lea and Irka Pejsachson simply did not reach the bunker in time. Chajka wrote:

> They were at the gathering point together with their father, a remarkable man, an old Bund activist, one of the nicest characters in the town. Really, it was because of him that they were being resettled. He did not want to hunker down in a bunker or hide in general. "I don't want to," he kept saying, "I'll go with all the other Jews." They spent so much time arguing with him that, in the end, the German police came and took them all.[63]

Outside, German guards led the Jews toward a large field. The process was far more brutal this time around, and only a few were released. Kuczyński and Lindner, members of Organization Schmelt, disappeared after taking their share to the labor camps, and Rossner, who had managed to rescue his employees on countless occasions, was denied the opportunity this time around.[64] The task of selection was put in the

59 Klinger, 1944 diaries, notebook C, p. 15.
60 Klinger, *I Am Writing These Words to You* (1943 diaries), p. 122.
61 Zippora Szporn interview.
62 Kukielka, *Escape from the Pit*, p. 99.
63 Klinger, 1944 diaries, notebook C, p. 17.
64 Ibid.

hands of the Gestapo man Dreier. His hands, clad in white gloves and holding a cane, could be seen moving up and down, signaling who lives and who dies.[65]

In the afternoon, when the house searches had ended, those who had gone into hiding began to emerge from the bunkers. Not a single bunker was discovered—they had proven their worth. The Klingers, the Dror people, and the members of Hashomer Hatzair all emerged healthy and unharmed. Yet the scene waiting for them outside chilled their blood:

> Outside: people coming back from police headquarters in tears. One without his mother, others without a father, without a husband, without a son, without a daughter, without a brother or sister. Everybody has lost someone. People passing out in the streets. A mother, driven half mad with grief, runs to join the procession [of deportees]. Three adult sons have been taken from her. Five children return in tears: their father and mother have been taken from them. They have no one to come home to.[66]

According to a German document, seventy-four Jews who had hid or refused to report to the selection point were shot in the streets and in their homes. The youths were shocked to discover the extent of their losses: of the nine Dror members who had remained outside the bunkers during the selection, only two returned. Seven members, including Herszel Szpringer and his brother Joel, were deported. The house of the kibbutz was in a state of utter disarray. Those who had returned there lay down on their beds and indulged in their grief. The "children of the future" shed inconsolable tears. Renia Kukielka recorded those difficult moments:

> Frumka is pulling out her hair and slamming her head against the wall. We fear, God forbid, that she may try to end it all. She shouts loudly: "I am to blame for their death, why did I order them to stay in the rooms? I am their murderer, I am the one who sent them to their deaths." And it is impossible to explain to her no matter how hard we try that it is not her fault.[67]

65 Kukielka, *Escape from the Pit*, pp. 100–101.
66 Ibid.
67 Ibid., p. 102.

According to Max Fischer's testimony, Frumka tried to commit suicide with a knife, and her friends only just managed to get it out of her hands with great difficulty.[68]

The train arrived. The Germans pushed the deportees into the wagons, meting out kicks and blows indiscriminately. The carriages were filled to capacity. When the wagons were found not to have sufficient room, the rest were taken to the old holding places—the Judenrat's orphanage and the old people's home. A heavy guard of Gestapo men and German police encircled the buildings. The detainees looked out of the fourth-floor windows and looked for ways to escape. There were Jewish policemen hanging around the buildings—their families had not been spared this time around, and they were trying to save them with the help of their connections. Rossner returned and managed to free a few people from the orphanage, but many of his workers remained imprisoned to await the train. The Gestapo's objectives had finally prevailed over economic considerations.[69]

Lea and Irka

With the dazed and belated reaction of someone recovering from shell shock, the members of the youth movements again began to mobilize for a response. The deportation took place over the course of two days, and the resistance developed action plans for immediate execution. According to Chajka's testimony, Lea and Irka Pejsachson managed to send letters from the *punkt*: "They wrote letters filled with despair, asking to be sent bottles of explosives: They wanted to do something from the inside, they felt that their days were numbered."[70] Chajka wrote two versions of the operation that followed. In the 1944 diaries, she recorded: "Finally, we decided to liberate the people by force, but in the end the plot was abandoned and instead of a rescue mission, two campaigns to obtain weapons were organized."[71] Whereas, the 1943 diaries read:

68 Max Fischer testimony, GFH, 11578.

69 Kukielka, *Escape from the Pit*, pp. 103–104.

70 Klinger, 1944 diaries, notebook C, p. 15.

71 Ibid.

> A decision was made to carry out a retaliatory campaign in various spots in the town. The workshop was to be set on fire should the campaign continue. It subsided and the plans were changed. Instead of the attack, two expeditions for arms were organized.[72]

The earlier version implies that the decision on general action—including the burning of the ghetto—was to be made only in the event of a total deportation. The cessation of deportations led to the suspension of the plans. The decisive factor: not enough weapons. Instead, the old proposal by Harry Blumenfrucht to steal weapons from German citizens was adopted. Two squads consisting of Dror and Hanoar Hatzioni members were assembled: Jakub (Kuba) Rosenberg, Alex Gutman, Jadzia Szpigelman, and Harry Blumenfrucht from Hanoar Hatzioni, and Baruch Gaftek and Markus Pohorila from Dror. The squads donned Hitler Youth uniforms and set out toward their targets. In one German resident's house, the housekeeper got scared and handed the house owner's gun to the disguised youths. The second operation failed: the landlady identified the boys. They escaped and found refuge nearby, but the ghetto was overrun with German soldiers and Gestapo men because of the *Aktion*. Alex Gutman and Harry Blumenfrucht were discovered by a German guard. Gutman managed to escape, but Harry, a boy of about seventeen, drew his gun and shot a policeman who approached him with a dog. He was caught and transferred to the police headquarters in Katowice, where he was interrogated under torture by the Gestapo.[73]

Brimming with bitter disappointment, Chajka wrote:

> Meanwhile, the resettlement was sped up, everyone was being resettled, including [Irka] and Lea. Under pressure from various city notables, the municipality decided to let one person from the [Pejsachson] family go. They were allowed to choose whom they wanted—let them decide for themselves. The girls decided that the father should go, but he did not want to; after all, another wave of resettlements would happen the next day and they would take all

72 Klinger, *I Am Writing These Words to You* (1943 diaries), p. 123.

73 Ya'akov (Kuba) Rosenberg, "We Looted German Arms," *Yad Vashem Bulletin*, 4/5 (October 1959), p. 12.

> the old people, while the two girls may still have a chance at life. "We will jump out of the carriage and return home," they reassured him. Their father left and they stayed, expecting another escape campaign to be organized from the inside in which they could be involved, or if worse comes to worst, planning to jump out of the carriage. There was no campaign, and they were transported in closed cattle carriages.[74]

Their father was not spared either. Liwer recounts that the old Bund man called out to the Germans as he boarded the train carriage: "Murderers! Your end is approaching! Our blood, the blood of innocents will be avenged upon your heads!" He swallowed a potassium cyanide tablet and fell dead on the spot.[75] Chajka was overcome by conflicting emotions: appreciation for the father and the daughters who went with him, a sense of insurmountable loss, but also a hidden bitterness that when the order was given, Lea and Irka chose to go with their family rather than stay with the movement. In her 1943 diaries, she expressed these feelings in the starkest of terms:

> I don't want to talk now about what Irka and Lea had been for our movement. We were completely disheartened for many days. We couldn't get over their loss, but the most painful thing was that they, who had been on fire and had lived and breathed *hagana*, left quietly together with everybody else, with a transport.[76]

Yet, she was also suffering from the burden of passivity forced upon those left behind. Gnawed by guilt, she noted: "And Irka and Lea left embittered by the fact that we had not brought ourselves to act. They couldn't have taken the beaten track. They might have jumped out the window and been shot, or more likely they took cyanide because they had it on them."[77] As before, regarding the Dunski and Minc affair, Chajka refused to gloss over the harsh truth. She wanted to view her friends as heroes, but spared herself and her peers not an ounce of criticism. The insult of helplessness made her blood boil. As a personal consolation, she imagined Lea and

74 Klinger, 1944 diaries, notebook C, pp. 17–18.

75 D. Liwer, *Ir Hametim*, p. 119.

76 Klinger, *I Am Writing These Words to You* (1943 diaries), p. 122.

77 Ibid., p. 123.

Irka's death as a product of free choice, in the spirit of *Man's Fate*—suicide by cyanide.

Lea and Irka did not go alone. Based on diverse sources, roughly 4,100 Jews were deported from Będzin and Sosnowiec between June 22 and 24, 1943.[78]

78 D. Liwer, *Ir Hametim*, p. 120; Ester Zindman, in *Sefer Sosnovitz*, vol. 2, p. 123; Gutman and Gutman-Herzberg, "Bageto Bendin: Protocol"; Ester Mark, "Din Veheshbon shel Ish Ha'es-es Functzioner (Pakid) Mahane Rikuz Auschwitz" (Hebrew), *Yalkut Moreshet*, 17 (February 1974), p. 185; Szternfinkiel, *Zagłada Żydów Sosnowca*, p. 53. According to Auschwitz records, on May 21, 1943, 1,000 Jews from Sosnowiec were deported to Auschwitz, but there is no record of this deportation among Jewish sources. It is possible that smaller deportations took place over the course of the entire month. On June 24, 1943, 1,600 Sosnowiec Jews arrived in Auschwitz, and on June 25, 1943, 2,500 Będzin Jews followed. Namysło, *Zagłada Żydów Zagłębiowskich*, p. 30.

Chapter Eighteen

David's Death

Chajka and David: Summer 1943

Everything happened so fast: the bitter end of the passport affair, Merin's deportation, the *Aktion* of June 22, 1943. Time and again, Chajka, David, and Zvi were faced with the fact that their fate was not in their hands. Possible rescue opportunities revealed themselves as disastrous dead ends while hopes of *hagana* were dashed yet again. The population of Będzin was reduced by a third, the numbers of their friends steadily dwindling. Ten of their underground friends died before they could carry out their actual mission. In Sosnowiec and Będzin, pictures of those suspected in the weapons heist began to appear on the streets. Jakub Rosenberg of Hanoar Hatzioni—apparently assumed to be the leader—was hurried away to the nearby Beskid Mountains.[1] Gallows were set up in the courtyard of the Katowice Prison, and Harry Blumenfrucht was hanged there.[2] His friends considered him a hero who had refused to betray the resistance,[3] but Chajka found no comfort in this: There had been no real resistance and the members' loot amounted to a couple of pistols, which, as Chajka points out caustically, were confiscated by Hanoar Hatzioni for their own use, and the fact that their pictures had been posted even

1 Rosenberg, "We Looted German Arms," pp. 10–12.

2 Tovka Gutman testimony, Moreshet Archive, C.53.1.5; Mazia, *Re'im Basa'ar*, pp. 177–178.

3 Tovka Gutman testimony, Moreshet Archive, C.53.1.5; "Ha'ari Hatzaluv," in Herzberg, *Hahol Hatzohek*, p. 19.

made her suspect that Blumenfrucht had broken under interrogation.[4] It is no wonder that she summarized the period succinctly: "Those two matters—of the *Internierungslager* and the deportation—depressed us greatly."[5]

In a postcard sent from Będzin to Switzerland on June 27, 1943—five days after the deportation—David Kozłowski reported that four comrades had set off to visit Nathan (Eck) but ended up in Auschwitz instead. With harrowing black humor, he wrote: "They went out to convalesce with Darca [passport] at Mavetia [death]." And added: "We too intend to visit her. There is a lot of work ahead in this regard. We must prepare a lot of food and clothes. And we are especially concerned with *hagana*, a special favorite of ours."[6]

It was their despair that impelled them to continue; the surviving Hashomer Hatzair members clung to each another. At that time, some twenty veteran members were living together in a kind of kibbutz of their own.[7] The need to form a kibbutz—sometimes called a *pluga* (company)—was partly due to the arrival of some Hashomer Hatzair refugees from Żarki, among them Aharon Brandes, Zvi's brother, his sister Pesia, Isaac Neuman, and Zippora Szporn, Abrashka's girlfriend from Chajka's *hachshara*. It is possible that at the time, Chajka and David were living in the kibbutz of the Kamionka ghetto. As in thousands of other places in Poland, social cohesion, sticking desperately close to one another, became a kind of defense against the collapse of reality.

At this time, or perhaps a little earlier, a significant event took place in Chajka and David's lives: they got married. It was only by chance that news of this reached Zippora Szporn, who happened to turn up at the Klingers' home. It seems that Perl Klinger's last wish was to live to see her daughters Chajka and Mania (Malka) married. The two couples went to see a rabbi in secret, and he married them. Chajka and David said nothing about it to their friends in the movement.[8] There is also evidence that Leibel, too, wanted to see his daughters married.[9]

4 Klinger, *I Am Writing These Words to You* (1943 diaries), p. 123.
5 Ibid.
6 Ronen, *Mihtavim Bezmanim Afelim*, vol. 1, p. 141.
7 Isaac Neuman testimony, Moreshet Archive, A.175.
8 Zippora Szporn interview. See also letter from Chajka to Nathan Schwalb, February 12, 1943; Ronen, *Mihtavim Bezmanim Afelim*, vol. 1, p. 101.
9 Ada Blacharz interview with Eliyahu Stern, 1979, Moreshet Archive, Avihu Ronen collection, 235.

In her diaries Chajka avoided any mention of their marriage. However, it is possible that this is what she was alluding to in the special note she later addressed in Hebrew "To My Dear Boy."[10] True to the socialist ideal of renouncing bourgeois terms, she chose the term "my boy" as a euphemism for marital commitment.

According to Zippora Szporn's testimony, Chajka felt closer to her family at this time. She invited Zippora to her sister Sarah's house to play with Sarah's young daughters. However, there is no evidence of any change in Chajka's relationship with her father, although she made sure that every member of her family found refuge in the bunker built by her friends, their hideaway in times of peril.[11] Chajka also tried to look after her sister's family: Despite the passport fiasco, she wrote another letter to Heini Bornstein in Switzerland at the end of July, asking him to hurry up with the arrangements for Ya'akov Mgła's brother and his family. Heini was surprised by this letter as after all, Chajka knew that the passport business had ended badly. Apparently, she wished to protect her family in case of another deportation.[12]

A short time after her wedding, Mania Klinger was sent to a labor camp. Chajka does not mention this fact in her diaries but presumably, she left of her own volition, and Zippora Szporn's two sisters left with her. Their destination was Ludwigsdorf in Germany.[13] Following the deportation in June, Chajka's attitude to labor camps had apparently changed. The youth movements now considered labor camps a possible means of deliverance. Chana Wiernik, Benjamin Szlezinger, and ten other members of Hashomer Hatzair who were prisoners in a labor camp, were given definite orders by Chajka and David not to attempt an escape.[14] Chajka seems to have taken a similar approach in her instructions to Mania—to try and survive in the labor camp. Mania was strong and healthy; it was reasonable to assume that she would survive. There is some later testimony about Mania's actions in the women's camp where she organized a resistance group that planned to escape and to join the partisans.[15]

10 Klinger, *I Am Writing These Words to You* (1943 diaries), p. 166.

11 Zippora Szporn interview.

12 Letter from Ya'akov Mgła to Heini Bornstein, April 27, 1943, Ronen, *Mihtavim Bezmanim Afelim*, vol. 1, p. 118.

13 Zippora Szporn interview.

14 Chana Schlesinger (Wiernik) testimony, Moreshet Archive, A.273.

15 Szymon (Shimon) Balicki testimony, YVA, O.3/1246, p. 55.

The Partisans

Three weeks after the June *Aktion* and the loss of Idzia and Irka, another blow was dealt to the Będzin resistance—the loss of two teams that set off to join the partisans. This setback was even harder for Chajka, for heading one of the teams was her beloved David Kozłowski. In her 1943 diaries, Chajka continues her description of the events in the previous chapter:

> That was when we received news from Częstochowa: A campaign against our people had been carried out there and the bunker had been discovered.
>
> Mojetek, Heniek, and Rywka[16] had perished, some had managed to reach Koniecpol, others had vanished. And there was no *hagana* in Częstochowa. They had been so well prepared—so many grenades, bombs, and handguns. But all of that came to nothing.[17]

The news was brought back by the Dror leader from Warsaw Marek Folman, who was a well-known figure in Będzin. Born in Poland in 1916 to an educated family, he and his siblings were members of the Zionist socialist groups. He had been active in Dror-Freiheit since his early youth, and during the war he had been one of the liaisons for the Hechalutz center in Warsaw. His Aryan good looks had helped him fill the role successfully.[18] The Warsaw Ghetto Uprising brought him back to his city where he took part in the battles. At the end of the uprising, Marek Folman was among the fighters who escaped to the nearby forests and organized a partisan group named after Mordechai Anielewicz. He didn't stay with the partisans for long, instead returning to Warsaw and from there to Częstochowa where the youth movement had organized a resistance group.[19] This ran counter to the orders given by Zivia Lubetkin to Rivka Glanc. Zivia's preference was to join the partisans at this stage, estimating that there was no real chance to mount an armed resistance in the ghettos. Marek, who seemingly disagreed with her, joined the local

16 Mordechai (Motek) Zylberberg and Rivka Glanc were the leading activists of the defense organization in Częstochowa. Heniek is unknown.

17 Klinger, *I Am Writing These Words to You* (1943 diaries), pp. 123–124.

18 Chavka Folman Raban, *They Are Still with Me* (Dalia: Ghetto Fighters' House Museum and Ma'arehet, 2001), pp. 110–114, 116–120; Zuckerman, *A Surplus of Memory*, pp. 405–406.

19 Folman Raban, *They Are Still with Me*, pp. 125–126; Zuckerman, *A Surplus of Memory*, pp. 405–406.

resistance group in Częstochowa, and very soon became its commander. On June 25, 1943, he lined up the fighters for roll call. There were a few dozen of them under his command, as well as pistols, grenades, and even two rifles. The weapons were handed out, and Marek gave the order of the day. He spoke of the bravery of the rebels in Warsaw and called upon them to fight to the last bullet.[20]

However, it turned out that the Germans had tricked them. By three o'clock that afternoon, it seemed that the *Aktion* had been canceled. The alert was called off. Weapons were returned to the cache. An hour later, the Germans attacked the ghetto. Those ghetto fighters who tried to escape to the bunker were trapped. Inside the bunker, Mordechai Zylberberg, one of their commanders, committed suicide. Another member who was there at the time managed to escape. The arms bunker fell into German hands. Only the group under Marek Folman's command managed to take cover in one of the houses. The next day, they decided to leave their position and join the partisans in the neighboring forests. They set off. Six of the fighters stayed where they were under Rivka Glanc's command, defending themselves with two pistols and a single grenade until the end.[21] Marek Folman himself did not stay with the partisans. He crossed the border and arrived in Będzin.

Despite the bitter news about the ŻOB group in Częstochowa, Marek Folman's presence inspired fresh hope. The Będzin underground members considered him one of their own, someone they knew, by now an experienced fighter who had fought in the Warsaw Ghetto Uprising, in the forests, in Częstochowa. He was also seen as an emissary from the central leadership in Warsaw.[22] He believed it was possible to make a difference in Będzin; not through armed resistance but by joining the partisans. Chajka wrote about this with reservations:

> Marek [Folman] came to us and inspired us with the idea of partisan warfare.
>
> We had had a different attitude toward partisan combat. In fact, during that phase of the war partisan combat was of cardinal

20 Aryeh Levi Sarid, *Bemivhan Ha'anut Vehapedut: Hatnuot Hehalutziot Bepolin Bashoah U'le'ahareha, 1939–1949*, vol. 1 (Hebrew) (Tel Aviv: Moreshet, 1997), p. 438.

21 Ibid., p. 439; Mark Gefen, Chajka Grossman, Shalom Cholawski, Yeshayahu Segal, Abba Kovner, and Różka Korczak, eds., *Sefer Hapartizanim Hayehudim*, vol. 2 (Hebrew) (Merhavia: Sifriat Poalim, 1958), pp. 393–394.

22 Zuckerman, *A Surplus of Memory*, p. 405.

> importance to the Soviets and it had only now begun to assume its importance.
>
> But at the same time at that stage of the liquidation of Jewry, when the Jewish Yishuv was no more and the Polish street ceased to regard us as a separate group, partisan warfare had lost its significance to us Jews. [...]
>
> What was important was [that it was] the last act of the dying Jewry. *Hagana* was now more essential than partisan combat, which could be a way for individuals who survive *hagana* to continue to fight. But Marek had an influence on us, especially because, as I have noted, various groups were seeking a way to avoid dying in *hagana*. Consequently, his plan was adopted.[23]

Marek Folman's suggestion had a practical side to it. He said that he had made contact with someone from the local PPR, a Pole by the name of Socha, who introduced himself as a partisan officer. Nothing much was known about the man, but Marek Folman trusted him. Together with Zvi Brandes who took to the idea, he went to Socha's home on Modrzejowska Street. The man, like his house, made a good impression on them: he seemed to be a straightforward and reliable family man. Socha's demands were reasonable: Those who went to the forests were to be armed with guns, be suitably dressed, and carry enough equipment for a long stay in the forests. Folman and Brandes arranged with Socha how they would contact the partisans and what their password would be.[24]

Chajka wrote: "He [Folman] established contact with a PPR representative. The people were happy that long-sought contact had finally been made. But there were secrets in our movement, so even I didn't ask who, what, and how. I only knew that he belonged to the same group as Marek."[25]

When Marek and Zvi returned from meeting Socha, the young people began eager preparations to join the partisans: "Breeches were being sewed frantically. Alter was bringing us a pair of high boots from a shed every day. Plus fours were being stolen. Windcheaters were being made."[26] The youth movements collected donations for the purchase of essential equipment, and for the first time in the history of Zagłębie, the

23 Klinger, *I Am Writing These Words to You* (1943 diaries), p. 124.

24 Brandes and Reshef, *Zvi Brandes*, p. 105.

25 Klinger, *I Am Writing These Words to You* (1943 diaries), pp. 124–125.

26 Ibid., p. 125.

Judenrat also contributed its share. Youth group representatives were sent to Władek (Wolf) Śmietana, who had replaced Merin as head of the Central Judenrat. Śmietana, a veteran of Hanoar Hatzioni with close contacts with others in the youth movements, lent his support to the partisans' plan.[27]

The first group of ten included members of Hashomer Hatzair, Dror, and Gordonia. David Kozłowski was nominated as commander. It was decided that women would not go out with the first group. "And there was so much joy," recalled Chajka, "when we learned that girls would also be able to go with the second group. And then there were arguments as to who would go."[28] The list of names in the first group was fateful for Chajka:

> Dawid was to go as the commander of the first group. I wanted to go with him and share my fate with him, but they didn't let me. Perhaps I'd still get to go as a *shlicha*. (Perhaps) I was [still] too weak physically to go.[29] Dawid was to convince the boys to let us, a couple of girls, stay with them.
>
> I didn't want to be petty and say that either we'd go together or none of us would go. Others, the girls in the kibbutz said so, but I didn't. He left. I knew that I would never see him again.[30]

Shmuel Ron described the eve of their departure for the forest as a "farewell party which, despite the seriousness of the occasion, included humor and a bit of playing soldier." The fighters were given slices of cheesecake in recognition of their mission's importance. When Shmuel Ron shook David's hand in parting, David asked to borrow his khaki trousers so he would look more like a soldier. "I want to die in trousers like these," he said. Shmuel agreed, and they traded pants.[31] Chajka observed them:

> Like peas in a pod—ten tall, strong, young men—the best we had.
>
> They all wore high *Stiefel* [boots], trousers, windcheaters, and jackets, and they had haversacks.

27 Shalom Herzberg interview, 1987.

28 Klinger, *I Am Writing These Words to You* (1943 diaries), p. 125.

29 Chajka is alluding here to the problems she was having with her legs due to an illness in 1942.

30 Klinger, *I Am Writing These Words to You* (1943 diaries), p. 125.

31 Shmuel Ron, in *Sefer Sosnovitz*, vol. 2, p. 180.

> The farewell in the packed room was quiet: a firm handshake, a hard kiss. "Farewell, comrade."
>
> Their eyes were sparkling with joy and happiness. They looked like groomsmen going to a wedding and Dawid seemed younger. My eyes couldn't get enough of the sight of him—a Red *komandir* [commander].[32]

For David this really was a dream come true. At one time, he had written an article addressed to a member of the Red Army: "My brother...I'm with you. I offer you my hand. Take it."[33]

In describing their parting on the night he left, Chajka adopts a distant perspective and speaks of herself in the third person, inadvertently turning into the myth she herself was weaving after the fact:

> They had spent many years together. Never seen apart, they seemed like one person. It's rare for people to complement each other to such an extent, [despite being so] oddly matched.
>
> They were simply comrades, friends, and lovers. "Do you remember, Didia," she used to say, "the time when during our wandering we looked death in the eye when bombs were falling all around us and you lay down on me and I kicked you to get off of me."
>
> "And do you remember, Chaj, the time when you protected me with a knife against that cutthroat?"
>
> He was carrying her in his arms during the fatal illness and he did not wish to live without her.
>
> And when he was about to go to the forest without her, they cried together for a long time at night. But he did not say that he wouldn't go without her and she did not tell him to stay. [...]
>
> Finally they leave and everybody's looking at them with joy and concealed jealousy. "One day I'll go too," everybody's thinking. "But will I manage? Won't there be a deportation first?"[34]

A few days went by, and Socha returned to Będzin. Because he had not been given an address, Markus Pohorila and Marek Folman went to his house. Socha gave them an encouraging report. The comrades had

32 Klinger, *I Am Writing These Words to You* (1943 diaries), p. 174.

33 Ibid., p. 172.

34 Ibid., pp. 173–175.

arrived safely at their destination and were received with open arms by the partisans. "But, he said, in their excitement they had forgotten to write us a note."[35] This was shortly before July 25, 1943, the date that appears on a letter sent to Geneva in which Zvi and Chajka wrote "Didia [David Kozłowski] and his friends have gone to Mr. Ya'arski [*ya'ar*, Heb. forest]."[36]

A second group was organized. There were enough arms for only ten members so the group could not exceed this number. This time two women were included. Once again, there was the joy of setting off, the sadness of parting. "They left feeling quite happy. And we were also very happy. Everybody was getting ready for the next groups."[37]

The second group included Isaac Neuman from Hashomer Hatzair in Żarki. Later, Isaac recounted:

> We passed through the ghetto on our way. It was a hot day, and as soon as we saw the first trees our spirits soared. We took out our weapons. At last our hopes were being fulfilled. We were going off to fight the Nazi foe. We felt like free men. The villagers who knew where we were headed greeted us with open joy. After a five- or six-hour trek we sat down to rest. The Pole said he was going to get water. Then he returned. An hour later he said, "We're coming to the border. I'll go check…" He left and never came back. Suddenly there was gunfire from every direction. In a matter of seconds everyone lay dead. I, too, had fallen, but I wasn't hit. I lay motionless. The Germans walked past us. One of them lifted my legs and shouted "Kaput!" As soon as they were out of sight I got up and started running through the forest, chased by their bullets. I don't know where I got the strength to run so fast. I managed to dodge the bullets.[38]

Isaac fled across the Pilica River, arrived at the train tracks, and followed them until he reached a small village. It was early dawn and the farmers were up early, feeding their animals. Outside the village, a door opened. Isaac introduced himself as a Pole and asked for food. The farmer served him potatoes. In return for his good clothes and wristwatch, Isaac bought some ragged clothes and a train ticket. He traveled back to Będzin. On

35 Kukielka, *Escape from the Pit*, p. 109.

36 Brandes and Reshef, *Zvi Brandes*, p. 130. The word "Ya'arski" was mistakenly understood as "Ya'ari."

37 Klinger, *I Am Writing These Words to You* (1943 diaries), p. 125.

38 Isaac Neuman testimony, Moreshet Archive, A.175; Brandes and Reshef, *Zvi Brandes*, pp. 106–107.

the way, he heard some Poles talking about shots they heard during the night. They guessed that Russian partisans had arrived in the area. With bitterness he recalled Chajka and Zvi's words: "We will die and they will take credit for our blood."[39]

Late at night, Isaac managed to sneak into the ghetto. He headed for the kibbutz. Everyone was asleep. The moment he walked in, they all jumped out of bed. Screams and wailing ensued. People fainted. Isaac himself fainted. When he regained consciousness, he saw some friends lying on the floor and others pouring water over them.[40] Zippora Szporn remembered Isaac looking as though he had come back from the dead. His face was ashen, he could barely walk. She led him to her room and looked after him. Later on, he would say: "You saved my life."[41] But for Chajka, Isaac's return meant only one thing—David was dead. Stunned with grief she remembered: "But the second group almost made me furious. I asked if they had a password. They said they did. But then I found out that it was either not top secret or that there was none."[42]

Had she been responsible for the password? According to Chana Wiernik who was not in the ghetto at the time, Chajka was the one who was supposed to obtain the password.[43] However, there is little evidence to this effect. The main responsibility fell to Zvi and Marek. Zvi wanted to commit suicide. He justified his actions: "Marek had given him that idea and that he had trusted him blindly."[44] Socha, as it turned out, had been a traitor and a Gestapo collaborator, and Zvi could not forgive himself:

> "I've sent them to die. I killed them and Dawid, my dearest friend. I don't want to live anymore."
>
> I had to persuade, beg, and threaten him for a long time. "You are needed here. Without you there won't be anything here. You have to stay."

39 The names of those known to have fallen are: Alter Goldblum, Shmuel Finklestein, Yitzhak Krovka, Lalek Goldstein, Mordehai Bachrzac, Zippora Marder, and Yitzhak (Atid) from Kibbutz Dror; David Kozłowski, Hela Kacengold, and Moshe Auerbach from Hashomer Hatzair; Avraham Tannenberg, Zalman Tannenberg, Yisrael Sheinthal, and Elias Vesala from Gordonia; and another four members from Hanoar Hatzioni and Hashomer Hadati. Max Fischer testimony, GFH, 11578; D. Liwer, *Ir Hametim*, p. 127.

40 Isaac Neuman interview.

41 Zippora Szporn interview.

42 Klinger, *I Am Writing These Words to You* (1943 diaries), p. 126.

43 Chana Schlesinger (Wiernik) interview.

44 Klinger, *I Am Writing These Words to You* (1943 diaries), p. 126.

> In the end I managed to convince him. He said, "If I thought even for one second that I'd survive, I'd finish myself off but I'm sure that I shall die."
>
> There was so much confidence in his words that it scared me. It was like gravitation toward death or some strange fate. Those of us who talked a lot about death died.[45]

They had finally achieved the ideal of a romantic death. In dying, David joined his comrades in the Warsaw ghetto, the heroes of *Płomienie* and *Man's Fate*. Zvi wanted to join them too, but he also wanted to die the right way. The compulsion to commit suicide was characteristic of the Jewish fighters not only in Będzin but also in Warsaw, Białystok, and Częstochowa. It arose in response to the crisis or as the final act in the war against the Nazis.[46] Their futile struggle bore the seal of collective suicide. Surprisingly, it was Chajka—the most romantic of them all—who refused to submit to a meaningless death and persuaded Zvi to go on living.

In her own distinctive way, she elaborated a myth about David's death as well. Perhaps, putting it down on paper, in figurative language, brought her some relief, some semblance of having been with him in his last moments. Perhaps her myth of heroism countered the absurdity of existence and its ending:

> There were ten of them. [...]
>
> Initially, they're walking slowly, scared, their hearts pounding. Then their steps begin to get bolder and more resolute.

45 Ibid., p. 180.

46 In Warsaw, on a September evening in 1942, after the murder of Josef Kaplan and Shmuel Breslaw, a plan was hatched to attack the Germans with stones and knives, and to die fighting (see chapter 13). Some of the fighters in the bunker at Miła 18 presumably committed suicide (see chapter 16). In Białystok, Mordechai Tannenbaum thought of suicide when the news reached him that his comrades in Warsaw had died. Among them was his girlfriend Tama Schneiderman. In Kraków, an agreement was signed by Gusta Davidson and her lover Shimshon Dranger that they would turn themselves in if either were captured by the Germans. Gusta Davidson fulfilled her promise and her footsteps disappeared after she turned herself in. In Częstochowa, one of the commanders of the group, Motek Zylberberg, killed himself when he was trapped in the fighters' bunker (more information in this chapter). In Zagłębie, the idea of suicide using potassium cyanide came up in relation to: the Dunski Affair (see chapter 14); the deportation of Lea and Irka Pejsachson (see chapter 17), and the attempted suicide of Frumka Płotnicka following the deportation of her friends in June 1943 (see chapter 17).

> They enter a forest. Their hearts are swelling with joy and emotion, wanting to jump out of their chests.
>
> "We're finally free. We can hold our heads really high now." They feel like singing but they cannot, because the one walking in front doesn't let them—it's Dawid with the guide. The two men are talking about the Germans, guerrillas, and the life they're about to start. [...]
>
> They walk on, talking calmly with each other. They enter a forest again. The guide leaves them. "Sit," he says. "We'll eat here. I'll fetch water."
>
> They sit down and look at one another, happiness and joy emanating from their eyes. [...]
>
> Suddenly—boom, rattle, noise. They want to get up. Shots. A submachine gun. Grenades. A few dozen armed Germans on horseback are surrounding them.
>
> The men jump to their feet but don't manage to stand. One, two, three of them collapse, dead.
>
> Only Didia [Dawid] managed to take his grenade out and throw it. He didn't know what happened because at that very moment he clutched his chest. He only managed to think, "Farewell, Chaj," and died.[47]

Maybe the real tragedy was that even as she was creating a myth, she couldn't help facing the bitter truth. Time and again she was forced to pay the price of the resistance game, and the price kept getting higher and higher. She could not forgive Marek. A death sentence was passed on Socha, but it was not carried out.[48] Consumed with guilt, Marek Folman left Będzin two days after Isaac Neuman's return. He tried to cross the border, but he was caught, and he too was shot.[49] From the pits of despair, Chajka also did her reckoning with the dead Marek:

> I don't want to suggest that the fact that he was captured during that journey was a punishment. No, because he hadn't wanted the boys

47 Klinger, *I Am Writing These Words to You* (1943 diaries), pp. 174–176.

48 David Liwer wrote that he learned about the trial and execution of Socha in Sosnowiec from a Polish bulletin in May 1945. The bulletin also reported the trial of a Pole named Dodek who had been in contact with the people on the farm and who was executed for turning in twenty-eight members from different movements. See D. Liwer, *Ir Hametim*, pp. 147–148. However, there is no corroboration for this information, and there is evidence to suggest that Socha survived the war.

49 Folman Raban, *They Are Still with Me*, p. 128.

> to die. But how could a responsible organization member have been so naive. Why, I feel ashamed just talking about it.
>
> I bear such a deep grudge against him. I still can't forgive him.[50]

Someone in the throes of anger should not be judged. Folman was a hero in his way. His daring and enterprising spirit was not unlike that of Anielewicz. Under the same conditions, Anielewicz might have made the same mistake. After all, the Warsaw groups that went off to join the partisans were also captured. From now on, Chajka had to deal not only with the blows to the organization as a whole but also with her own personal calamity. Until then, she had seen herself and David as a single entity. She had lost her other half.

Our Hope of Seeing the Homeland Will Not Be Fulfilled

In the days that followed, Chajka plunged into depression. Cruel fate had torn her beloved away, and with him, the dream of *hagana*. It seemed that there was nothing more to do now, all hope was lost:

> We were completely devastated. Our workshop had been closed the moment we had decided to dispatch our major forces into the woods. The reason was that we had been afraid of a search since Hari's [Harry's] [Blumenfrucht] capture. We didn't know how much he had revealed.
>
> We spent many days in the bunker. We had lost our best boys and most of our weapons, which they had taken with [them]. Who could we begin a campaign with now?
>
> Wasn't it too painful?
>
> We've sacrificed so many victims, so many valuable people perished, but we had been afraid to take a risk for *hagana*. Twenty such boys, of whom almost everyone was a commander of a five, might have constituted a hell of a force. That healthy core of our movement had left.[51]

Was this the moment of truth? Hashomer Hatzair was undoubtedly hit worse than other movements that had sent members to join the

50 Klinger, *I Am Writing These Words to You* (1943 diaries), p. 126.
51 Ibid., pp. 126–127.

partisans. Not that they suffered more casualties, but they had lost David, one of their leading triumvirate. The bonds of friendship among the three of them and the parental support they gave to the *ken* affected the entire group. David's death left Zvi just as shattered as Chajka. His name had been added to the list: Idzia, Irka, and Lea Pejsachson; Nacia Klugman; and Hela Kacengold. Other than Rachel Rosenkier, Ada Neufeld, and Chajka, there were no survivors among the founders of the flourishing Będzin *ken*. Moreover, in Sosnowiec, the beloved Kalman Tencer was dead, and Lipek Minc and Zvi Dunski had been executed. In Warsaw, Josef Kaplan, Shmuel Breslaw, Mordechai Anielewicz, Tosia Altman, and Arie Wilner had fallen. Chajka and Zvi had known and loved them all, had dreamed of fighting side by side with them. Now they were bereft.

It is hard to gauge whether Chajka and Zvi had made operative decisions while hiding in the bunker. Judging from their behavior, they had given up on any specific plans for defense during the coming *Aktion*. Instead, they resolved to defend themselves using guns and grenades from the bunkers should they be discovered. In a passage that hints at this, Chajka wrote: "But those who remained knew that they wouldn't let themselves be taken for deportation alive."[52]

The same decision was apparently reached by the other movements as well: the general mood in Dror was not much better after a deportation took away some of its strongest members. Yet, the leaders of Dror had survived: Frumka Płotnicka, Baruch Gaftek, and Herszel Szpringer escaped the June deportation train and returned to Będzin.

Renia remembered the arrival of a note in Herszel's handwriting, asking to be reached at his hiding place in one of the workshops. Escorted by a Jewish policeman, they found him there under a pile of merchandise. "His face was scratched and bruised, his clothes torn, his legs covered with sores. He laughed softly, nestled against us and held us close with real fatherly emotion. Tears ran down his cheeks, tears of happiness that he had come back to us."[53] He told them that when he had tried to break through the floor of the cattle car, the Jews called out: "Are you insane, what are you trying to do? You'll bring disaster on us all and we'll be killed because of you." But Herszel kept at it. When everyone's attention was distracted, he escaped through the window. The Germans fired at him but missed. He saw bodies that had presumably been hit by bullets

52 Ibid., p. 127.

53 Kukielka, *Escape from the Pit*, p. 105.

strewn along the railroad tracks. Slowly he made his way back to Będzin and found a place to hide with the help of the Jewish police.[54]

Just at this time, long-awaited contact with Mandatory Palestine was finally made. On July 17, 1943, a courier from the Istanbul rescue mission arrived in Będzin. There is no mention of this event in Chajka's diary, and it is possible that she was unaware of it. The emissary was apparently Jerzy (Yoszy) Winiger, who had failed in his attempt to reach Będzin two months earlier. He brought many letters with him and a large sum of money: 50,000 Marks.[55]

On his return to Istanbul, Jerzy took a letter written in German by Frumka Płotnicka and signed by the leaders of the underground youth movements: Herszel Szpringer (Dror), Józek Kożuch (Hanoar Hatzioni), Shlomo Lerner (Gordonia), and Zvi Brandes (Hashomer Hatzair). This letter, a crucial document in Holocaust historiography, was filled with despair and longing: "After so long a wait, we were fearsomely happy to receive only today the courier with your letter. To our great sorrow, however, the courier was a little late in arriving. For years we have dreamed of having the chance to tell you about our lives and our war."[56]

Next, the letter contained a detailed account of the annihilation of Polish Jewry with a list of the communities that had been destroyed, the numbers of Jews killed, and the names of the death camps and their extermination methods. "In the Generalgouvernement region, there are no Jewish communities left besides three forced labor camps," they reported dryly. As for the activities of the youth movements, the Będzin members recounted the events of the Warsaw Ghetto Uprising and its outcome, carefully naming the fallen: "No one left from the Ya'ari family: Tosia, Hancheh [Hańcia Płotnicka], Lea Perlstein, Josef Kaplan, Mordechai Anielewicz, and hundreds of others of those closest to us are no longer alive."[57]

About themselves they spoke very little. They reported the failure of the passport rescue operation and about their dwindling numbers: membership in all the youth movements combined had dwindled to a few hundred. They were seeking a way into Hungary, they added, and asked the mission for any and all possible help in this. There was no mention of armed resistance. They closed with the words:

54 Ibid., pp. 106–107.

55 D. Liwer, *Ir Hametim*, pp. 130–131.

56 Brandes and Reshef, *Zvi Brandes*, p. 127.

57 Ibid., p. 128.

> Do everything you can. It is doubtful that you will be able to help us in time because we are facing our last days...Our hopes of seeing the homeland will not be fulfilled, to our greatest sorrow. Send our heartfelt regards to Tabin (Tabenkin), Eliezer (Gravitsky), Bendersky (Bendori), Ya'ari, Kolodny, Goldstein, Pinchas (Lubianker-Lavon), and all our loved ones."[58]

Liwer, who knew about the letter, said a decision was made to use the funds from Istanbul to organize defense. This decision was willingly accepted by the movement representatives.[59] The underground resistance members were determined to die armed, but they no longer believed in the possibility of a real defense of the ghetto.

Chajka mentions nothing about the courier in her diary. Nevertheless, a letter sent from Będzin to Switzerland one week later, on July 25, 1943, signed "Zvi" but written in Chajka's round hand testifies that she knew about it:

> We received regards from Mendel [Menahem Bader] but to our sorrow it arrived too late. All the same we were glad that he hasn't forgotten us or our family. I wrote a few lines to him today and passed on our approval and regards. Please thank him for me and my family.
>
> I am about to be married...to Kilyonsky [*kilyon*, Heb. extermination] We will honor the occasion with our presence. I believe our entire family will very soon move in with Mr. Mavetsky [*mavet*, Heb. death].[60]

Last Rescue Attempts

Despite this sense of doom, the request for help in finding a way into Hungary shows that the youth movements were also looking for a means of escape. Hanoar Hatzioni sought a way out of the condemned ghetto through Slovakia. They began sending contingents of women to Germany disguised as Polish workers.[61] The members of this movement

58 Ibid.

59 D. Liwer, *Ir Hametim*, p. 132.

60 Letter from Zvi (Chajka) to Heini Bornstein, July 25, 1943, Moreshet Archive, D.1.1092.2; Brandes and Reshef, *Zvi Brandes*, p. 130.

61 Mazia, *Re'im Basa'ar*, p. 155; Danka Furstenberg testimony, Moreshet Archive, C.53.1.5.

had organized few if any bunkers. The single bunker that had been built by Hanoar Hatzioni was not big enough to hold all its members.[62]

Regarding Hashomer Hatzair, Dror, and Gordonia, all the active members were organized in bunkers. These movements did not believe in rescue but strove to keep a few members alive as witnesses. Their sense of mission now took new forms. Chajka wrote:

> But there was an intention to rescue a group of people—a *shlichut* [mission]. Some were to go to Warsaw to the "Aryan" side. Ina arrived and said that there was a place for me in a bunker. I don't want to go. I won't go as long as there's somebody here. I won't sit there idly growing fat. Nobody from the hard core went. Nobody was in a hurry to go and nobody went.[63]

As far as we know, the courier from Istanbul asked Frumka Płotnicka to go with him, but she also declined. Like Chajka, she rejected the idea of returning to Warsaw and hiding out on the Aryan side. Later, Chajka would imagine Frumka's last hours:

> "Be quiet!" they tell her. "You could have already been on the Aryan side. Your death here is unnecessary. You should have survived. Who could tell our story better than you? Apparently you wanted our names to sink into oblivion."[64]

When she wrote about Frumka she was writing about herself as well. Time after time, Chajka had been condemned to life by her comrades, but she refused to accept the verdict. Here she defied the decree of the movement.

Nevertheless, Zivia's plan to save a few Będzin members was apparently accepted. In late July 1943, Ina Gelbard and Renia Kukielka set off again on the road to Warsaw. This would be Ina's last trip to Warsaw. At the Generalgouvernement border, she attracted the attention of a female Nazi prison guard and was held for questioning.[65] Renia continued on her own. She arrived in Warsaw, stayed there for a few days, and headed back to Będzin on August 1, carrying twenty-two

62 Tosia Herzberg interview.

63 Klinger, *I Am Writing These Words to You* (1943 diaries), p. 127.

64 Ibid., p. 162.

65 Kukielka, *Escape from the Pit*, pp. 113–115; Fela Katz, "L'lo Het," in Dror and Rosenzweig, *Sefer Hashomer Hatzair*, vol. 1, p. 714.

counterfeit border passes and identification papers. However, as she quickly realized, she was too late.[66]

At the same time, an attempt was made to send a contingent through Hungary. The orders and the financing for the mission likely came from Istanbul. A German railway worker they found agreed to let four of the men cross into Hungary in exchange for 20,000 Marks. Baruch Gaftek from Dror was chosen to captain the team and he was joined by Shmuel Rozencwajg of the "Aryan group" from Hashomer Hatzair, Dov from Gordonia, and a member of Hashomer Hadati. Shmuel recalled that at the farewell party for the group, Zvi Brandes had pulled him aside and made him swear to return with weapons: "Zvi felt hopeless and disappointed. He no longer believed in the conscience of humanity or in any real help from the Jews of the world."[67]

The four of them apparently set off on July 31, 1943, supplied with the false documents of Polish workers. Everything went smoothly all the way to the Auschwitz station, but there, the German railway worker disappeared. The four men, fearing a trap, decided to turn back. They separated into pairs. Gaftek and the Hashomer Hadati man left the station area, while Shmuel and Dov hid in the sewer pipes for the night. In the morning, they headed back to Będzin. As they approached the city, they saw Nazi policemen surrounding the farm. They understood that an *Aktion* was underway and hurried to get away.[68] Baruch Gaftek managed to escape during a guard shift change and returned to his friends. If he was going to die, he wished to die with them.

66 Kukielka, *Escape from the Pit*, p. 117.

67 Shmuel Ron, testimony, Moreshet Archive, A.364; D. Liwer, *Ir Hametim*, p. 148.

68 Shmuel Ron, in *Sefer Sosnovitz*, vol. 2, p. 181.

Chapter Nineteen

The Last Bunker

Where Had the Grandparents Gone? 1957

When Ran would say he was going to stay with his grandparents in Safed over the summer, we would all be jealous. Most of the children in the "Oren" group didn't have grandparents. Gershon had a grandfather, Meron had a grandmother but only an adoptive father as his biological father had been killed in the War of Independence before Meron was born. And I, too, had a grandmother. I was very proud of my grandmother, and every Tuesday, we would take the workers' bus to visit her in the Shikun Vatikim neighborhood in Netanya. She lived in a small house together with another family of immigrants, and she had fruit trees and an old, empty chicken coop in her back garden. A small, gray-haired woman, who always seemed to be smiling at us. She baked *habcsóks*, the Hungarian version of meringue kisses, and made loquat compote. Grandmother also picked up Mother's share of the knitting. In the fall, every mother in the kibbutz would get an allotment of wool, the color and thickness of her choice, and she would then knit sweaters for her children. But Mother didn't knit, and I was slightly ashamed of this fact. I felt like it cost me points in the unspoken competition of whose mother had knitted the nicest sweater. I took comfort in the fact that Grandmother's sweaters were still very handsome. The other children—our group numbered fourteen at this time—had no grandparents.

Where had the grandparents gone? Our parents told us nothing about their absence. They just weren't there. They were never mentioned as part of Shabbat story time. On Saturdays, the fathers were put in charge of the children and took turns to make sure we all got out of bed, had breakfast, and had an afternoon rest. Unlike the rigid schedule we were subjected to the rest of the week, the father on duty was given a free hand in deciding the agenda for Shabbat. Every father brought their own ideas to the table; they even seemed to be competing among themselves. Dubi's father would rouse us with a rooster's call. Esti's father organized wrestling matches on a pile of mattresses. Gershon's father, who was the kibbutz's truck driver, would sometimes take us out to frolic in the fields in Qaqun. But when he distributed the half-tablet of chocolate we were given on Shabbat, it was forbidden for the loser of the weekly "bet" to pay his share to the winner. Uri's dad and Esther's dad would tell stories during our afternoon rest. Nathan's favorite was Mathias Sandor, Jules Verne's Hungarian hero, while Wizo recounted the tales of John Steinbeck. But the grandparents' story was never told.

Who were the grandparents? We didn't ask, and the parents didn't say. A few small cabins were erected next to the "Oren" children's house to accommodate some of the kibbutz members' elderly parents. But only Gershon had a real grandfather there. The old people would stare at passersby from the deck chairs in their little front gardens, sticking out like sore thumbs on the kibbutz landscape. Sometimes we would refer to them as "Grandpa Dogi," or "Sugár Bácsi" and "Sugár Néni," but they were never real grandparents. They were never invited to tell us a story or recount some small excerpt from the tome of their lives. Sometimes we would ask one of the fathers to tell us something about the time when he was young. Once, Aryeh Ya'akov, Avri's dad, told us about a work camp where everyone went hungry, got sick with typhoid, and died en masse. His eyes turned sad and distant all of a sudden. But this story, too, failed to provide the link to the missing grandparents.

The books we read had no mention of them either. Twice a week, at the end of the day's work tending to the livestock or cleaning out the classroom, freshly showered and dressed in sparkling clean whites, we would march down to the children's library. Rivka the librarian would suggest books for each child according to their age and forbid us from reading other books that were deemed not yet appropriate. The most gripping of tales were waiting there on the shelves, translated just for us. We could make our way through the wild forests of America with Leatherstocking, suffer for little Cosette in *Les Miserables* in its abridged Hebrew edition, titled *Gibor Bekabalim* (A Hero in Chains), join the ten-year-old Pyetka and the other Odessa revolutionaries in *A White Sail Gleams*, or compete in long-distance runs across Tel Aviv in Avner

Carmeli's *Olympiadat Hashchunot* (Neighborhood Olympics). The library also had translations from Polish. My favorite among these was Kornel Makuszyński's *Satan from the Seventh Grade*, about a mischievous genius adept at solving logic and detective puzzles, beloved by Wanda with the purple eyes. There was nothing that tied the mystery of the disappearing doors in the country home of a failing mathematician somewhere in rural 1930s Poland with the grandparents who disappeared only a few years later in that very same countryside.

Father never told us about the grandparents either. Sometimes he would take out the big family photograph from grandmother's linen closet and point out Grandfather Moritz who died shortly after I was born. Mother, for her part, said nothing. Once, when I was making a racket during Father's nap, she shushed me angrily: "When my father was resting, no one in the house dared make a peep." Another time, when I was ill, Mother brought me books from the library. Among them was a slim volume that I leafed through hastily and saw that it contained Hasidic tales. The book looked boring to me, but Mother said: "Read it, it's important." That was probably an attempt to bring me closer to her parents' world. Yet she never mentioned their names. On one of our visits to Grandmother's house in Netanya, Mother and I went for a walk and saw a group of children at the edge of a thorn field, digging through piles of rags. I asked her who they were, and she said "the poor." There was something foreign in her voice. Half-scorn, half-fear. "The poor"—up until then I had only seen this word in books. The poverty of the grandparents was only implied, as if there had always been the big lawn and the poinsettia next to the dining hall and the sweaty gang of children playing there until the last glimmer of twilight.

The Eve of the Deportation: Saturday, July 31, 1943

Merin's removal from his position and the deportation of June 1943 led to a sense of the end approaching. In her 1943 diaries, Chajka wrote:

> The anxiety is intensifying. People are saying that it will be on the night between Saturday and Sunday. But I somehow cannot believe it. Why would they ruin their holiday—Sunday? And of course it has not dawned on anybody that there could be a general deportation, *Judenrein* [cleansed of Jews]. Only we, the black ravens, say that if there is a campaign, they will no longer handle

> us with kid gloves—they will finish us off once and for all. For it was as clear as day to us that since they did not take any economic [matters] into account in the entire General Government or in Germany and liquidated *kriegswichtige* [important for the war effort] arms factories, which employed Jews, they surely would not take into consideration our tailoring workshops owned by Rossner, which produce clothes, but only for the *Wehrmacht*. Because Rossner was told during the previous campaign: "*Das ist eine Staadt politische Aktion und es gibt keine Kraft die Stören soll*" [This is a political situation, and there are no forces that can disturb it].[1]

Chajka did not know about the instructions given by Himmler at the end of May 1943, but her intuition was correct. The final elimination was imminent. Additional evidence indicates that on July 31, 1943, the Kamionka and Środula ghettos were buzzing with various rumors about the impending deportation.[2] It seems that the Judenrat also had concerns about an upcoming *Aktion*, although, according to at least one of the testimonies, Mołczadski denied it.[3]

Numerous bunkers were constructed in both ghettos, and guards were placed in their vicinity to sound the alarm in case of an imminent *Aktion*. Wiser and more experienced since the June deportations, the Jews of Będzin and Sosnowiec tried to prepare themselves for a final struggle for survival.[4] As far as we know, the resistance had six bunkers: the central Dror and Hashomer Hatzair bunker under the command of Herszel Szpringer; the bunker at the Kibbutz Dror house, of which Gedalia Sobkowski of Poalei Zion was in charge; the Hashomer Hatzair brigade bunker under the command of Zvi Brandes; the "Laundry" or "Number 5" bunker under the command of Baruch Gaftek and Frumka Płotnicka; the Gordonia greenhouse bunker on the farm; and the Hanoar Hatzioni bunker in Środula. These bunkers were only partially prepared for defensive action, which amounted to opening fire in case the Germans discovered them. At this time, there seems to have been no plan for any major operation, such as burning down the ghetto, or even targeted operations such as attacks on the deportee convoys on their way

1 Klinger, *I Am Writing These Words to You* (1943 diaries), p. 34.

2 Shraga Fruchtzweig interview; Ka-Tzetnik, *Sunrise over Hell*, p. 129.

3 Shraga Fruchtzweig interview.

4 Gutman and Gutman-Herzberg, "Bageto Bendin: Protocol"; Myriam Ochs report, Moreshet Archive, C.79.03; Zippora Szporn interview.

to the train station. The weapons in the hands of all resistance groups combined are estimated to have consisted of about twenty revolvers and several dozen homemade grenades and bombs.

The Deportation Begins: Morning, August 1, 1943

According to a document in which the Sosnowiec police chief summarized the events of the *Aktion*, the Germans were preparing for a large-scale operation with 690 German soldiers and policemen recruited from the entire region in preparation for the task at hand, most of them members of the Schupo, including trainees of the police riding school in Sosnowiec. Overall, 775 policemen and soldiers and twenty-two officers took part in the *Aktion*.[5] Their goal was to swiftly eliminate the Kamionka and Środula ghettos as well as the Jews concentrated in Dąbrowa Górnicza and to deport the 30,000 Jews still living in them to Auschwitz. It would appear that such extensive preparations were prompted by the Warsaw Ghetto Uprising and reports of unrest in the town.[6] For an added element of surprise, the *Aktion* began in the dead of night. Chajka recorded:

> And Saturday came. In the evening, just as it had been for the last couple of days, there were guards in the entire Jewish ghetto, outside every building, including ours. They wake us at 3 AM.
>
> I walk out, anxious. I hear shots. We wake everybody. Cwi [Brandes] opens the hiding place and takes out [several] pieces [guns]. "Why so few?" I ask anxiously. "Has something happened?" He says in a trembling voice that they didn't expect that something would happen, that they had information that nothing would, and that, consequently, everything's at Baruch's [Gaftek], and there's not even one in the main bunker at Herszel's [Szpringer]. Frantic, we clutch our heads. What now? What now? Have we been cultivating the thought of *hagana* in our heads only to be empty-handed now in case nothing happened? I become furiously angry with the OKW and the entire world. But no, we won't let them deport us. We'll do something stupid—maybe only one shot will be fired, but something will happen, something must happen. [...]

5 Deportation operation report, YVA, O.53/10, pp. 367–369. See also Szternfinkiel, *Zagłada Żydów Sosnowca*, pp. 71, 74.

6 Mark, " Din Veheshbon shel Ish Ha'es-es Functzioner," p. 185.

> And we descend through the oven, which is rather uncomfortable. It's Abraham's first time in the bunker, which is very small and awfully uncomfortable, still quite unfinished. We hastily grab two loaves of bread and some water in a pot. We lock the oven. Soon afterward the campaign begins.[7]

Abraham Zilberstein had arrived shortly prior to these events from Częstochowa and was viewed by the people of Będzin as an experienced veteran: He had been a member of Hashomer Hatzair in Warsaw, and had taken part in the attempted uprising in Częstochowa.[8] Fela Katz and Kasia Szancer from Sosnowiec also went down to the same bunker together with Dorka Herzberg, Zvi Brandes's girlfriend from Zawiercie, and his sister Pesia. There was no room in the bunker for every member of Hashomer Hatzair. It was small, with only enough space to accommodate around twenty people. A number of members, including Isaac Neuman and Aharon Brandes, were sent to the central Dror bunker.[9]

Meanwhile, Max Fischer was on duty and woke up the members of Kibbutz Dror.[10] They hurried down to the central bunker. In their haste, they forgot to take important supplies. Chawka Lenczner, a nurse by profession, regretted that they had not taken any medical supplies. Thirty people crowded into the bunker commanded by Herszel Szpringer, including his girlfriend Aliza Zeytenfeld, Chawka, Sara Kukiełka, and about ten children from Kibbutz Atid—children who had been left behind parentless after the previous deportations. The bunker was well organized. It was located under a coal warehouse and had wooden beams built into the walls. There was electricity and even a radio, but there was no direct water supply. Chawka looked around at her friends: no one had had time to get properly dressed. Many had come down in their pajamas. The children looked terror-stricken.[11]

Seven members of Dror hid in the laundry bunker, Frumka Płotnicka and Baruch Gaftek among them. Baruch had returned the day before from a failed attempt to cross the border into Hungary and now assumed command of the bunker. His girlfriend was also here, the second, "beautiful" Frumka (Polna Róża), as they called her. Most of

7 Klinger, *I Am Writing These Words to You* (1943 diaries), pp. 34–36.

8 See Zilberstein, *Bageta'ot Varsha, Tzenstohov*; letter from Abraham Zilberstein to the author, 1986.

9 Brandes and Reshef, *Zvi Brandes*, pp. 135–136.

10 Max Fischer testimony, GFH, 11578.

11 Lenczner, "Parashat Bendin," p. 129.

the guns were also found here—twelve of them.[12] The third bunker, dug under the Kibbutz Dror house, served as the hiding place for members of the Poalei Zion party. There were no Dror members there.

In his home, Liwer woke up to find the guard standing next to him. The latter informed him of a lot of movement happening on the road around Kamionka. Liwer woke his family members and tried to get them to the farm bunker, but the road was already blocked. German guards were stationed at the crossings. The Liwers returned to their home and went down to the small family bunker.[13] A similar bunker had been dug under the building where the Klingers resided. Perl, Leibel, their daughter Sarah Mgłą, and her two daughters, along with a few neighbors and Zippora Szporn presently headed down there to await further developments.[14]

In Sosnowiec too, the *Aktion* caught the members of Hanoar Hatzioni unprepared. Young Fredka was awakened by the sound of her friend's whistle. She and Józek went outside. The ghetto was ablaze. Soldiers stationed on every street corner. Notices were plastered on the walls announcing the final deportation. Everyone was being transferred to Auschwitz-Birkenau. All the Jews were to report to the community field at ten o'clock in the morning. Many had already humbly packed their bundles. Fredka and Józek separated in order to contact their friends and tell them to hide. They had only one bunker at their disposal. Those who could not find a place would have to hide in their neighbors' bunker. Fredka arrived at her parents' house and urged them to go down to the bunker. Then she found a hiding place with Józek in the bunker of an acquaintance.[15]

Yehiel Feiner (Ka-Tzetnik) found himself a space in a bunker with thirty other bewildered Jews. Who could have expected the *Aktion* to commence on a Sunday?[16] Yet, despite the surprise, hundreds, perhaps even thousands of Sosnowiec and Będzin Jews hid underground, which made things rather difficult for the Germans. The police chief in Sosnowiec noted:

> The Jews had long been ready for this *Aktion*. Only the start day was kept secret. A large part of them were found in bunkers outside

12 Klinger, *I Am Writing These Words to You* (1943 diaries), pp. 34–35.

13 D. Liwer, *Ir Hametim*, p. 141.

14 Zippora Szporn interview.

15 Mazia, *Re'im Basa'ar*, pp. 187–188.

16 Ka-Tzetnik, *Sunrise over Hell*, pp. 144–145.

> their apartments. These were well-disguised burrows in the ground, and cellars closed up with construction material, and it took great efforts to catch them.[17]

In the Bunkers: August 1, 1943

Within a few hours, the situation inside the bunkers deteriorated. Most of them were small and built to provide shelter for only a short time. They were not equipped for a prolonged stay. From their hiding places, the Jews listened anxiously to the Germans' voices outside. They huddled in their tiny corners, bit their lips, spoke in whispers, hardly breathing. The mothers gave the babies soporifics and prayed they would not cry. Chajka wrote:

> It was awfully stuffy underground. Some air was coming in only through a tiny hole in the oven and there was such a squeeze that it seemed that we could not endure it. There was no bucket. How horrible it is even for someone who has the most primitive human needs; to satisfy them and other needs in the same place (an empty corner) where he sleeps!... They [the Germans] were hitting the floor with pickaxes. They were trying to open the oven. At one point they were tearing apart the floor just above our heads.... Breathless, we waited to see what would happen. Our only worry was whether we had working guns in our dirty pockets.[18]

Above ground, some of the workshop employees were trying to reach their workplaces, hoping that their presence and their workers' certificates would save them from deportation once more.[19] Without even looking at the certificates, the Germans hurried to evacuate them. They were taken to the roundup points to prepare for transfer.

Judenrat employees and Jewish policemen were also arrested. Ze'ev Londner (later Liron), a boy from Hanoar Hatzioni in Będzin, noticed Barenblatt in the Judenrat building. When the curfew began, Londner—who knew Barenblatt—tried to reach him to ask him for

17 Deportation operation report, YVA, O.53/10, pp. 367–369.

18 Klinger, *I Am Writing These Words to You* (1943 diaries), p. 36.

19 Deportation operation report, YVA, O.53/10, pp. 367–369.

help reaching the farm people. Now he saw that Barenblatt had also been arrested.[20] So had Mołczadski. The Jews who had been rounded up took the opportunity to mock him.[21] Shraga Fruchtzweig would later encounter him in Auschwitz.[22] There, he would be beaten "half to death" by Jews from Będzin who recognized him.[23]

The bunker on the farm was quickly discovered. The Gordonia members there were all arrested, including the leaders of the movement: Shlomo Lerner, Shlomo Zimmerman, and Hanka Borenstein. Together they were led to the deportation point. As they walked, Hanka suggested to Shlomo that they should take action against the Germans even though they were unarmed. Shlomo hesitated; he still hoped that something might happen to change the course of events. Hanka, Idzia, and the other girls whispered to him that they were ready to act as soon as he gave the order. He did not.[24]

In the Klingers' bunker, the youngest of Chajka's sister's daughters breathed her last. They had given the four-year-old girl a sleeping pill, but her crying grew louder precisely when footsteps were heard from above. She was smothered. It is unknown whose hand did the deed. After some time, the bunker was discovered. One man coughed, and the Germans above heard him. The men came out of the bunker, and the Germans made them stand with their hands against the wall. According to the testimony of Zippora Szporn, "the first one who came out received a bullet to the head." Zippora and the Klingers were led to the roundup point. From there, they would be transferred by train to Auschwitz. Somebody asked Chajka's sister Sarah where her youngest was. "She stayed down there," she answered.[25] They would remain alive for the next few hours: Sarah and her nine-year-old daughter Malka, old Leibel with his heavy limp, and Perl the matriarch. Chajka, who was hiding in a different bunker, was ignorant of their fate.

20 Ze'ev Liron testimony at the Barenblatt trial, Moreshet Archive, D.1.5366, pp. 130–136.

21 Ada Balchasz (Chmielnicka), interview by the author, Kiryat Tivon, 1987.

22 Shraga Fruchtzweig interview.

23 Aryeh Ben-Tov, *Uvehalomi Ani Shome'a et Kola shel Imi* (Hebrew) (Tel Aviv: The Aryeh Ben-Tov [Hesenberg] Memorial Foundation, 1999), p. 30.

24 Lenczner, "Parashat Bendin," p. 129.

25 Zippora Szporn interview.

The Deportation: August 1–2, 1943

From the beginning of the operation, the Germans had ordered groups of Jews to collect the remaining Jewish property in the Środula and Kamionka ghettos and evacuate the houses. A group of Jews designated as the so-called Undertaker Commandos, were sent out to collect the corpses from the streets. Abraham Izbicki, a man from Częstochowa who had arrived in Będzin only four months earlier, came out of his hiding place in the AK camp. That morning the camp was also surrounded by armed Germans. When Izbicki heard the shout "All Jews, outside!" he hurried to hide in the small room behind the camp nurse's office. He blocked the opening with a cupboard. A small group of people hid with him. In the evening, he went out and saw bodies littering the street. A group of Jews under German supervision were collecting the bodies on stretchers covered in lime.[26]

It was either on this day or the following day that the first shots were fired by Jews in Sosnowiec. Hypek Glitzenstein of Hanoar Hatzioni fled from the transport armed with a gun. His girlfriend was with him. A German policeman with a big dog approached them. The policeman drew his weapon and asked: "Jude?" Hypek fired. The policeman fell, and other Germans arrived on the scene. Hypek continued to shoot until he fell under a hail of bullets. At another point in Sosnowiec, Janek Zimmerman also tried to escape. He managed to flee the ghetto, but some Polish boys surrounded him and yelled: "Runaway Jew!" At the sound of their shouting, German soldiers approached. Janek opened fire. Soon, he was also killed.[27] Hypek and Janek were proponents of armed resistance within Hanoar Hatzioni and died the way they would have wanted.

The recently married Fredka and Józek Kożuch also emerged from their hiding place. The city was quiet. There was not a soul on the street. According to Fredka's estimate, three trains had already left, transporting 1,000 people each. By morning, a pause was announced. The *Aktion* would resume tomorrow. Józek, the leader of Hanoar Hatzioni, decided to reach out to his people to tell them about the rescue plan that had been formulated over the course of the day. Fredka suggested barricading themselves in one of the houses and fighting to the last bullet. Józek

26 Abraham Izbicki testimony at the Barenblatt trial, Moreshet Archive, D.1.5366, p. 146.

27 Mazia, *Re'im Basa'ar*, pp. 194–195; see also Gutman and Gutman-Herzberg, "Bageto Bendin: Protocol."

rejected her proposal. He went out. After a short time, he came back and then left again. Fredka waited anxiously. The hours passed, and Józek did not return. At 1:40 PM, two shots were heard. Fredka's heart sank. At three o'clock in the morning she went out to look for Józek. She found his body among those piled on top of a cart heading toward the hospital. He was already cold.[28]

The first deportation trains left Będzin. As would later become known, special preparations had been made in Auschwitz to accommodate the victims of the great *Aktion*. The wagons carrying the Będzin deportees arrived at their destination at night. Despite the darkness, Zippora noticed an iron sign that read "Arbeit macht frei"(Work sets you free). Selection commenced. Some people were sent to the right, others to the left. Zippora was ordered to join those on the right. She was granted life. Suddenly she saw Sarah Mgłą lunging toward her: "Pani Szporn, Pani Szporn, take me with you!" Zippora said: "Please." Sarah's nine-year-old daughter was left alone and burst into tears: "Mommy, where are you leaving me?" Among the guards were Polish policemen who understood the girl's screams. They shone their flashlights and located Sarah: "Go to your child," they scolded her. Sarah returned to her daughter. Fifteen minutes had elapsed before the scene repeated itself. Again, Zippora felt Sarah clinging to her. The girl cried again, and the police came and took mother and daughter back to the large group that stood under the gate bearing the "Arbeit macht frei" sign. They waited there until they were taken to the crematorium. Zippora never saw Sarah or her daughter again. Nor did she see Perl and Leibel Klinger, who were with her on the same transport. The selection was carried out in pitch black.[29] Chajka would learn of their fate from Zippora only years later.

The Move to the Central Bunker: August 3–4, 1943

The *Aktion* continued over the following days. The Germans' activity now mostly concentrated on discovering the bunkers. For the first time, voices were heard calling out in Yiddish along with those of the Germans: "Jews, come out of the bunkers! The extermination of the Jews has begun! There will be a *Judenrein*!" In Yehiel Feiner's bunker in Sosnowiec, the situation had reached breaking point. There were dead

28 Mazia, *Re'im Basa'ar*, pp. 190–191.

29 Zippora Szporn interview.

bodies in the corners, among them a baby who had been suffocated by the bunker's occupants. The stench of the corpses mixed with the stench of excrement. Feiner and his girlfriend went outside. He was captured and made to join the Undertaker Commandos. He learned from his coworkers that the evacuation groups were housed in a special camp. The work would continue until there was not a single Jew left in the place.[30]

Things were similarly rough in the Hashomer Hatzair bunker. Due to the overcrowding, it was decided to send messengers to the Aryan side. Kasia Szancer seemed best suited for this task. She had gone on similar missions in the past and was equipped with false papers. Her goal now was to reach Zawiercie. Perhaps things were better there. Those remaining in the bunker sat tight in tense anticipation:

> We spent three days like that. And nobody came to us with any sign of life. We immediately had a bad feeling. *Judenrein*. Cwi says, "I must go to the kibbutz and see what's happened to them." Everybody's worried.... We loved and at the same time respected him so much, as a companion, a brother, and at the same time like a father.
>
> He left. Yet another awful, horrible day ahead of us.
>
> Again the hammering, pounding of the pickaxe, bated breaths, mortal fear, and nervous tension. They were near our bunker for three hours. Perhaps they had heard a murmur. They've torn up half the floor. They're reaching the oven. They call out: "*Juden, geht schon raus*" [Jews, come out at once]. Panic. The people want to get up. There's murmur. With all my willpower I calm everybody down with a quiet hiss: "On the floor." Nobody dares to get up without my order. I have instinctively taken command.
>
> I hoped for one thing—their laziness. And I was not disappointed. They left.
>
> Cwi came back at night with mortal fear in his heart. He had thought that we were already doomed. And he sighed with relief and I did too. I was so happy that he was already back. I felt such a relief. I no longer have to be the only one responsible for what is to happen. It was such a great responsibility on my part.[31]

30 Ka-Tzetnik, *Sunrise over Hell*, pp. 147–153.

31 Klinger, *I Am Writing These Words to You* (1943 diaries), pp. 36–37.

The next day, the water shortage became critical. There was unrest in the bunker. Zvi's sister Pesia began shouting hysterically: "Kill me, I don't want to live anymore! I can't stand it anymore. Finish me off! I am Cwi's sister. I want to die an honorable death."[32] Panic ensued. Her screams were liable to give up their hiding place to the Germans. Zvi took responsibility and decided that everybody should move to the central Dror bunker, while he would stay behind with his sister. He pushed everyone out impatiently. Two by two, the youths began their crawl toward the Dror bunker. Chajka crawled with the eighteen-year-old Israel (Srulik) Warszawski:

> The first stretch is fine. But rockets appear out of the blue, lighting the entire street, and shots begin to be fired from all directions. We hit the dirt. We're doomed. [...]
>
> My heart is thumping and pounding there, so miserable, so very lonely.
>
> And what have I experienced? There have been few good things in my [life]. [I have led] an exhausting life in poverty and indigence. But stop complaining. There have been good moments too. You had good companions and such deep, great love, and such wonderful moments with the man you loved.
>
> And there's a boy lying next to you. An eighteen-year-old boy. What does he know about the world?...
>
> We're lying for a long time, our heads hidden, as if pinned down to the ground. I'm slowly growing calmer (they keep shooting at us and shining lights around us). I must be destined for the same kind of death as Dawid [Kozłowski]. Tough luck. I'm waiting.[33]

At three o'clock, they reached the central Dror bunker. Everyone was already there. Zvi and Pesia had also arrived.

The Fighters' Bunker: August 3, 1943

Yet the relief was short-lived. With Zvi's arrival, it was decided to try to contact Isaac Neuman and Max Fischer from Dror, who had gone to the laundry bunker that day, and most importantly, to get more guns. Isaac and Max also visited the Poalei Zion bunker, which was empty of people

32 Ibid., p. 38.
33 Ibid., pp. 38–39.

but contained some groceries and even a fan. Baruch's bunker—bunker no. 5 or the laundry bunker—was also empty. Depressed, the two made their way back.[34] The news they delivered chilled Chajka's blood:

> Before I can catch my breath, they tell me, "There's nobody at No. 5. It's a ruin. There's nobody there."
>
> I stop dead. Everything inside me stops, freezes for a moment. It feels as if my heart has stopped beating, that I've gone deaf and dumb. I'm sitting like a dead log without a word. So Frumka [Płotnicka], Baruch, Cipora [Zippora] [Bocian], and so many others of our people are already gone. They were so young, in their prime, healthy, full of life and energy, but they're already gone.
>
> Surely I knew that all of us would die, that all of us would perish. But it was to be different.[35]

Max and Isaac did not know at the time what had happened in bunker No. 5, but with the benefit of hindsight, Chajka provided the missing pieces of information:

> A single shot—this is how Baruch killed one, but we lost a dozen. I'm less sorry that they're gone than about the fact that they had done so little, which makes me furious, screams inside me and rips my intestines apart.
>
> I'm sitting without saying a word, but everything inside me is seething.
>
> All of us will come to such an awful end.
>
> There's not even one gun. Cwi came to have a look but he didn't find any. What now? They'll come and take us all empty-handed. No, I swear to myself for the thousandth time that I won't go into a wagon. Let them execute me. I'll run for the nth time, but I won't go. I won't go in alive.[36]

Chajka would continue to reflect on what happened in the laundry bunker for a long time after. In the weeks that followed, Chajka continued to gather details about the battle that took place that day. A detailed and accurate testimony was given to her by Abram Potasz, a Jewish policeman

34 Isaac Neuman interview.

35 Klinger, *I Am Writing These Words to You* (1943 diaries), p. 40.

36 Ibid.

who had cleared the bodies from the laundry bunker. She recorded his account in the last entry of her diary dated December 17, 1943.[37]

According to Potasz, on August 3 he heard gunfire that lasted for over half an hour in the backyard of Kibbutz Dror. Suddenly, two Gestapo officers burst in on him: Walter Baucke and Hans Dreier. They led him to the shooting range. In the kibbutz yard, he was glad to notice two corpses of German SS soldiers from Auschwitz who had been shot by members of Dror. However, his happiness did not last long. Baucke approached him, put a gun to his temple, and ordered him to enter the bunker. The entrance was through the window, but Potasz was ordered to go down through a hole made by a hail of bullets. He fell into the bunker, and a gruesome scene appeared before his eyes: Near the entrance he spotted Tuvia Dworski, his head crushed, his brains splattered on the floor. Next to him was Frumka Płotnicka, a six-shot gun in her hands, the lower half of her body charred. He also recognized Baruch Gaftek and four other girls: Baruch's girlfriend Frumka Polna Róża, Zippora Bocian, Pnina Jakubowicz, and Hedva Brand. Some of them were dead, some in the process of dying. Those who had not yet perished were emitting a shrill, inhuman wail similar to the hum of an air squadron. The bunker looked terrible. The pillows and blankets smelled of charred feathers. Potasz dragged the seven bodies out of the bunker and into the nearby garden. Baucke and Dreier ordered him to lay them down "facing the sky" and to strip the women naked. Though shocked, he had no choice but to follow their order. Then, they commanded him to go back down and get the guns. The Germans estimated that the number of guns should match the number of people in the bunker. Potasz found twelve guns. He brought seven back up with him. He buried the other five in the ground.

When he came up from the bunker, Potasz was ordered to clean the guns and then turn the bodies face down. He was aghast to see that Frumka Płotnicka had raised her head a little and opened her mouth, as if trying to say something. The look in her eyes was terrifying. One of the Gestapo men suggested they wait—she might reveal some secret information; but another Gestapo man approached Frumka and kicked her in the face with his heavy boot with stoic indifference. Her head was dashed against the ground, and she did not move anymore. When the corpses had all been turned face down, the order came: Fire! There came a barrage of bullets from seven machine guns. After the shots subsided, the Nazis trampled the bodies with their feet. This sequence of shocking

37 Ibid., pp. 181–184; see also D. Liwer, *Ir Hametim*, pp. 146–147.

actions confused and stunned Potasz and—perhaps luckily—prevented him from giving way to any normal human reaction.[38]

Based on this and most likely other testimonies, Chajka would later piece together an account of the last moments of the people in the bunker. She described the events as if she had been there herself:

> Dead silence. Baruch has turned his back on the others and is staring at the hole. Somebody embraces him from behind and cuddles up to his side. He's so big and broad-shouldered. He fired the first shot. Maybe he'll defend her. It's Frumka, his girlfriend, who is so beautiful. She resembles her surname—Polna Róża. She looks so much like a rose, red and blooming. And he embraces her so tightly that you can hear her bones crack and says, "You see? I returned to you this night (he was supposed to go to Hungary) to die with you. I was a *hagana* leader, and apparently I have to fire the first shot."
>
> And the other Frumka, Frumka Płotnicka, is standing pale and tall, taller even than she usually seems, smoking one cigarette after another despite the ban in the bunker. And she's holding a revolver ready to shoot. "I told you that I'd perish with you, that I wouldn't survive."[39]

The description of the battle that followed was probably based on information that became available to Chajka later. A car arrived and a group of soldiers and policemen gathered at the scene. A bomb was thrown into the bunker—probably a smoke bomb. Cries were heard from the bunker: "Murderers, barbarians!" A fire broke out in the bunker, and some of the fighters were suffocated by the smoke. According to Chajka, a jet of water was even directed into the bunker from a car brought over from Auschwitz.[40] The rest of the account was based on Potasz's description of events, after which she added her own farewell salute:

> And the Germans are already satiated; they have quenched their savage lust. They have had enough of the sight of blood.
>
> They have left but for one, who is still standing there, looking.
>
> He looks somehow different from the others. His face did not redden with raging blood. He is not laughing. On the contrary, he seems sad, appalled, and repulsed.

38 Klinger, *I Am Writing These Words to You* (1943 diaries), pp. 181–184.

39 Ibid., pp. 161–162.

40 Based on Max Fischer's testimony, GFH, 11578.

> He's looking at one body in particular. It's a woman. She must have still been very young and she had a beautiful body. It seems to me that this body is screaming at him, "Remember, I will take my revenge and you shall not escape me alive."
>
> And those eyes are laughing so. And those teeth, so [white] and large, are bared in anger at him and they're calling, "I will have my revenge. I will come and take you!"
>
> He flees from there as fast as possible, but that image is still chasing him.
>
> He turns back, stops, and suddenly looks around to make sure that nobody is watching him and he takes off his cap. He calms down and slowly walks away, pensive.[41]

Did things transpire as she describes? The chief of police in Sosnowiec added a note to the summary report of the operation that stated: "The Jews partially tried to defend themselves with weapons." He noted three cases in which Jews opened fire, and a battle that took place on the night of August 2–3. The casualties on the German side amounted to two dead and one wounded.[42]

In the Bunker: August 4–6, 1943

The *Aktion* continued and with it the evacuation process. During the first days of the deportation, two liquidation camps were set up for the groups clearing the streets and collecting Jewish property: one in Rossner's workshop and the other in four barracks in Środula. About 200–300 Jews were concentrated in these camps. Roughly 400 bodies were found in the streets of the two ghettos.[43]

Many Jews were still hiding in bunkers: The Liwer family bunker had not yet been discovered nor the bunker where the chief rabbi of Sosnowiec, Rabbi Grossman, was hiding. The youth movements had only one bunker left. About thirty-five people were hiding in the central Dror bunker with two guns in their possession. Chajka wrote:

> Some thought that it would better in the kibbutz bunker than it was in ours. I have the impression that it's worse. It's stuffy as hell.

41 Klinger, *I Am Writing These Words to You* (1943 diaries), pp. 164–165.

42 Deportation operation report, YVA, O.53/10, pp. 367–369.

43 Ibid.

> Everybody's skin is glistening from sweat, of course, and they're walking around half-naked, in pyjamas and shirts. Everybody's lying on the floor, their bodies like corpses. It feels like I won't stand being here for long. It's difficult for me to catch my breath.... The petite Chawka is bustling about by the stove. Everybody's lying on the ground like corpses, and she's cooking lunch plus semolina for Aliza [Zeytenfeld]. I admire her. It's so hot by that stove and she's looking after the people nonstop. She bandages a wound for one, hands talcum powder to another for him to rub on his skin, and orders another to wash himself so that we don't become infested with lice and ill from dirt. And then she washes herself and [we eat] lunch. It's so nice to look at her, so clean and kind.[44]

Toward evening it was decided that, due to the overcrowding in the bunker and the improbability of lasting in these conditions for much longer, a number of people should leave. According to Fela Katz's testimony, it was decided that she would be sent to the Aryan side. She was given money and false papers. Chajka approached her and asked if she knew Christian prayers. The two then memorized prayer passages together. Under the cover of darkness, Fela crept out along with Genia Dunski, the sister of the deceased Zvi. They started crawling but did not get far before a German policeman appeared next to them. They were taken to one of the liquidation camps for questioning. Fela managed to hold out. The police officers who interrogated her were unable to ascertain her Jewishness. They tested her with Christian prayers. She passed the test. She was set free and walked out slowly so as not to arouse suspicion. In a public bathhouse, she bathed and changed her clothes. Then, she left by train in the direction of Zawiercie.[45]

The nearby town of Zawiercie had been spared by the Germans. There, Fela joined some of her friends who had escaped deportation. Shmuel Rozencwajg, who had just returned from a failed mission to Hungary, was there. The Hashomer Hatzair messenger Ina Gelbard, who had returned from Warsaw, also arrived in Zawiercie. She was stopped on the way by the Gestapo, but no evidence was found against her. She managed to swallow the papers in time. Upon her release, she headed to Będzin, but when she saw what was happening there, she

44 Klinger, *I Am Writing These Words to You* (1943 diaries), p. 41.

45 Fela Katz interview.

changed her trajectory and set her sights on Zawiercie.[46] She joined the members of the "Aryan group" from Sosnowiec who harbored hopes of surviving thanks to their appearance. That evening, Chajka ventured into the open air:

> I walk out and look around. There's a bright light out in front. Those are the barracks—the deportation center. The Germans have assembled all the people there and they're watching them. They also put search lights there so that they cannot escape. The victims are being carefully watched. And in the back, behind the hill, there's an observation post and another two on the other side and by the wall near the factory that leads to the "Aryan" district. This must be what a front line looks like. Rockets keep falling and lighting the way. An actual war is being waged against us. I burst out with vacuous laughter. Ha...Ha... War against Jews in bunkers, against my father and mother.[47]

She went back down, back to the stifling air. Inside, she was greeted by shouting. The girls were quarreling. She looked at them in disbelief: Now, with the door open? And over what? A few rags? Had they lost their minds? Too angry to speak, she burst into sobs. Where were Lea, Idzia, Irka, David, all those who had been so dear to her heart? Perhaps it was best that they didn't live to witness this disgrace.

It seems that Dorka Herzberg also left that night. As a daughter of Zawiercie, where there were no deportations, she hoped to find a relatively safe refuge in her city. Dorka wanted Zvi to go with her. Zvi laughed: "How could I leave my group of friends? No matter what it's like."[48] Dorka also asked Chajka to come with her. She also refused. As much as she longed to go out into the open air, she could not do so now; she could not be among the first to leave. Like Zvi, once again, she stayed.[49]

Isaac Neuman also came out of the bunker. It was decided to evacuate some of the Kibbutz Atid children and try to hide them at Rossner's workshop.[50] Isaac brought out around six children, arranged them in a line, ordered them to hold hands, and holding the hand of

46 Katz "L'lo Het," p. 714.

47 Klinger, *I Am Writing These Words to You* (1943 diaries), p. 42.

48 Ibid., p. 45.

49 Ibid.

50 See the testimony of thirteen-year-old Mońek Hoffenberg from Kibbutz Atid, in Bracha Habas, *Yeladim Mutzalim*, pp. 144–146.

the first child led them through the desolate streets. The sky lit up with fireworks; occasionally, shots were heard. Isaac and the children made slow progress and managed to reach their destination.[51]

The Bunker Is Discovered: August 7, 1943

Only about fifteen people remained in the last bunker. The rest had already gone on their way. Herszel and Zvi, and possibly Chajka as well, decided that there was no point in staying in the bunker any longer. Moshe Markus, one of the members of Kibbutz Dror who had arrived from the outside, reported that there was a possibility of reaching one of the liquidation camps where they thought they would have a better chance of survival. It was decided that they would try to reach Wolf (Władysław) Böhm, the former head of the Judenrat in Sosnowiec, who was respected by the youth activists. Böhm would surely agree to help them. However, to help him make up his mind, they decided to tell him that they also had a handsome sum of money.

Max Fischer from Dror set off with two other people. One of them was shot, but the rest arrived safely. Max made contact with Böhm, and the latter promised to help rescue the bunker people. He decided to send two Germans to transfer the people from the bunker to the liquidation camp.[52] When Fischer learned of this, he tried to stop him, as he knew that the people in the bunker had guns, but he was too late.[53] Those in the bunker were ignorant of the plan. Chajka wrote:

> Suddenly we hear a shout—they're reaching us. They're scraping at the coal. The hatch opens. We've been discovered. I don't understand. What's happened? How come? I'm standing transfixed. But there's commotion all around us. The people are hastily getting dressed, grabbing briefcases and bundles. What's happened? What now? We're doomed! What now? There's such commotion, tumult, bustle. A Jew comes down to us. Meir [Schulman] talks to him. Some have to go out and some can stay. Everybody's standing speechless. Nobody moves. For God's sake, somebody has to go out first. Let the girls and children go out. They won't hurt them. I'm still undressed. I hastily

51 Isaac Neuman interview.

52 Lenczner, "Parashat Bendin," p. 130.

53 Max Fischer testimony, GFH, 11578.

> grab my clothes. I have no shoes or anything at all. I put a dress on my naked body. Meir and Necha [Schulman] open the second exit. I want to go out with them through that exit. Suddenly, bang! They close it. There's a sentry post. What now? Nobody wants to go out first.[54]

Chawka Lenczner ended up coming out first. The Germans interrogated her: How many people are in the bunker? Is Herszel Szpringer among them? She hesitated, not knowing what to say. Were they Böhm's messengers? She asked permission to return to the bunker, which was granted. There, according to Chajka's testimony, she reported: "They asked about Herszel. They said that if we came out at once we would go to Talstrasse [to Rossner's workshop].... A ray of hope."[55] There was confusion in the bunker. Herszel believed that the Germans had come to their rescue. He suggested hiding the guns. Zvi thought otherwise:

> So what should we do with our guns?! Cwi says, "No, maybe they're not here for us. Meir! Meir, where are you?" he shouts. "Take your gun and come." But Meir's not there. He's hidden away with Necia [Necha] under the cots.
>
> What now? Suddenly, Chawka descends for the second time and leaves. People, come out, hurrying upward. Herszel must go out. But he's so confused. He doesn't know what's happening with him. Neither does Cwi. I don't recognize them.
>
> Herszel distributes money. He has such a lot of it. I have never seen so much money. We walk out. There are three of them. They frisk us and take away the money. That was the deal that somebody would go out and talk to them about transporting us to Talstrasse in return for the money. Before we manage to get out and say something, they're already frisking us. Weak, Aliza tells them something in a weak voice about transporting us to Talstrasse. I'm standing in the coal cubbyhole, looking at this sad happening and wondering what to do with the money. I'm worried that they're taking away all the money. Where can I hide it? Perhaps in my knickers? Pesa's [Pesia] next to me. "What should I do with my gun? They gave it to me, thinking that they wouldn't frisk the girls." Oh, fools! I got scared, terrified. It should have been used or hidden somewhere deep underground, in the bunker.

54 Klinger, *I Am Writing These Words to You* (1943 diaries), p. 51.

55 Ibid.

> "Put it in the coal," I say. She obeys. [...]
>
> He [a German soldier] descends and takes one step. He picks up a briefcase and reaches inside. He takes out the other gun and bursts out laughing, "*Nicht eure, so?!*" [Not yours, right?!]. He fumbles inside the briefcase. He takes out a *Lichtbild* [photograph] of [Aliza] Zeytenfeld. We can hear their faint voices again. They're laughing. "*So eine Dummheit, [das] Lichtbild übergelassen*" [How dumb to have left the photograph]. Aliza starts talking and pleading. "It's not mine... not mine..." You stupid, stupid girl. Your words are meaningless so at least be brave.
>
> Can they believe your words? They cannot and should not. Would you believe?
>
> And then he points at me. "*Und das ist ihre*" [And this is yours]. It's a done deal. Fate has passed its sentence. "*Was, meine*?" [What, mine?] I say.
>
> He said nothing and only kicked me twice so hard, that I heard a thud. And then he kept hitting me with a wooden pole, one, two, three, four times. And I didn't even squeal, only at the end, when I saw that he was getting furious. Why should he keep hitting me if he's going to shoot me anyway?[56]

At this point, there were eight adults in the bunker—Zvi Brandes, Aharon and Pesia Brandes, Abraham Zilberstein, Herszel Szpringer, Chawka Lenczner, Aliza Zeytenfeld, and Chajka Klinger—and four children from Kibbutz Atid:

> We're lying, waiting for the sentence.
>
> I'm perfectly calm. I'm looking at the sky, looking around greedily, absorbing everything. I'm looking around fully convinced that it's the last time. But why do they make us wait so long? I'd only like to drink some water and then they can finish me off. As long as it's fast and without suffering. I heard that death from a bullet is painless.
>
> They order us to get up. We all gather our bundles. I look at them, confused. What for? I'm forbidden to either put on my shoes or take the briefcase. I must look like a mad woman in the untidy dress, which is dirty from lying on the ground. I can't shake off the dust. I have no shoes. I must look like I'm out of my mind.

56 Ibid., pp. 51–53.

I'm ordered to walk last. "*In Beine werden Sie bekommen*" [I'll hit you on the legs] and he hits me with a [rifle] butt from behind. "*Ich werde sie jetzt erledigen*" [I will finish her off now], I hear him say to another man, but the other man tells him, "Let her be. Don't do anything on our own initiative." He leaves me alone.

Everybody's walking in single file. We arrive at the square opposite the barracks. Lots of soldiers and officers. "*Das sind diese, das sind diese...*" [It's them. It's them...], we hear from all around. They're standing, looking and pointing at us.

Aliza's pleading again, crying. I can't stand listening to it anymore. "You idiot, calm down," I say. "It won't help you. Have some dignity." "I will," she says, shaking like a leaf. "One is not allowed even to speak."

I'm cursing myself and others. Oh, how I'm cursing OKW [the fighting organization in Będzin]. I hate them. Why did they give me a role that disgraces and hurts me? Why can't I now clearly and openly shout in their faces, "Yes, it's mine. It's ours. I wanted to wipe out our disgrace with it and teach you, *Mörder* [murderers], villains, a lesson." Why must I remain silent and lie? Why did they give me such a disgraceful role? I'm so furious that I'm biting my fingers. Why did we put such a burden on weak Aliza's shoulders? "Farewell," I say. "We, Aliza and I, are probably going to be executed." Only Cwi, I only want to drink some water. "Water!" I call in vain.

The deportees are sitting in the barrack. We are forbidden to enter the barrack. They order us to sit down on the ground in front of the barrack. We can get neither water nor food. We are like lepers.[57]

"Beat Her to Death"

Chajka looked around her and saw a wasteland. The streets of the ghetto were frozen. The campaign had been going on for a week. Everyone had been taken away in the wagons. Even the staff of the Judenrat, whose president had been given the honor of a hansom cab ride to Auschwitz. Many had been shot.

And still people were being dragged out of the bunkers. Her heart sank; old Jews and children, how helpless and frightened they all were:

57 Ibid., pp. 53–54.

> And so thirsty. They dash for the water buckets like wild animals. They snatch mugs from one another and fight. They have had no water for three weeks and have been drinking rainwater or urine.
>
> And the Germans are looking at them as if at…exotic animals… And they take pity on them. They have water and bread brought to them. They are merciful and grand in their generosity.
>
> They've brought an old Jewish man with sidelocks. Laughter.
>
> The brethren ask, "Do you have gold? You've hidden it. Give it to us."
>
> Good God, the man looks as if he has never seen a pfennig [penny] in his entire life and they want gold from him.
>
> And one of the soldiers who are frisking him [says], "*Das ist der richtige—'Jude Schwindler'* [That's the real 'Jewish Swindler']. He must have had a lot of gold."
>
> But I know the faces of my Jews. I could swear, that he's another *Boncie Schweig.*[58] He's staring at them and says, "*Ja… was…*" [Yes... What...].
>
> And they just keep laughing.
>
> And it hurts me so much that I can feel something turning and writhing inside me.[59]

As always, Chajka's eyes were wide open, seeing everything. Her hatred of the Germans mingled with the scorn she felt toward the Jews who were ready to do anything to stay alive. She knew that her time was nigh and was filled with both bitterness and disappointment at the sight of their selfish despair:

> Husbands abandon their wives and children; mothers, their children; children, their parents.
>
> I want to save myself. Perhaps a wagon will arrive in the meantime and there will be a deportation? They'll gain one, two days.
>
> Poor, miserable people. Nothing can save them. The death sentence has already been pronounced. "But it might be revoked. A miracle could happen," so the religious think. But I don't believe in miracles. I don't.[60]

58 For Chajka and her comrades in the youth movement, Boncie Schweig (Bontshe shvayg—Bontshe the Silent), the protagonist of a story by I. L. Peretz, represented the tradition Jewish passivity, and they denounced his character.

59 Klinger, *I Am Writing These Words to You* (1943 diaries), pp. 56–57.

60 Ibid., p. 58.

She judged these poor souls by the standard of her own ideals and found them wanting. In her mind, a certainty had already formed that the gun destined to take her life was in close proximity. There was nothing left to do but to aspire to an honorable death:

> They interrupt my reflections. They're calling us, Aliza and me. We are about to be executed. It's a certainty. "Farewell," I say quietly and walk proudly with my head up. I'm strutting boldly. They stop me by the building of the former militia. Aliza walks in and I stay. They order them to watch me, because I could escape. I'm standing, thinking why are they dragging me to a closed building. They don't want witnesses. But far away in a field they won't have any witnesses either. The thought that they would torture me did not cross my mind. Why would they bother? What good would it do? Bidner, whom I know, a former clerk in the *gmina*, walks past me. He has a frightened look on his face. "What are you doing here?" "Nothing really. They want to execute me." "How come? What for? How?" "They have found something in our bunker."
>
> He had a tray of apples. I take one in a most leisurely manner and begin to eat it. He looks at me as if I were out of my mind. Am I? I don't know. Before I can finish eating, they call me. I throw away the rest. "It's the final moment," I'm thinking. "I'll shout out everything. I'll tell them what I think about them." I've already composed the sentence I would tell them. I hope that I'll have the time. "*Mörder—euer Rache tag wird kommen—Für unser Blut wird man Rache nehmen. Euer Ende ist schon nahe*" [Murderers, your day of reckoning will come. Our blood will be avenged. Your end is already near]. To shout, scream it at the top of my lungs for an entire day—is this all that I can do before dying? Interestingly enough, I was not the only one thinking about it. I had an exchange of thoughts with my neighbor, who was thinking about the same thing. And so were the rest at the same moment. It doesn't seem strange to me at all.
>
> As I was walking to the execution site, I wanted to scream, because nobody would hear me in that desolate area. But I managed to control myself. It even seems to me that I asked Cwi and he didn't tell me not to. Besides, I didn't want to for myself, for the sake of the others. Perhaps they will execute only us and leave the rest, who might escape and get away with it. But I felt such an urge to scream. What do I care about the *chevra* [comrades]? I want to die an honorable death. I care about nothing else.

I became silent and calm. Neither Cwi nor the *chevra* had ordered me to.

I went into a room. Aliza is standing in a corner, so miserable, broken, so severely beaten and covered with blood.

So they're going to beat me. I was completely petrified with fear. Endure. Say nothing. Stand tall.

They order me to lie down. "*Totschlagen*" [beat (her) to death], they say. And they began beating me, beating me severely. They were hitting me hard without paying attention where the blows were landing. They injured my whole body. But the worst thing was when they began hitting me on the head. I wanted to show them what a lousy Jewess was capable of. I wanted to refrain from shouting, even at the price of death, but that was not my tactic. I was disclaiming so I had to shout, scream about my innocence. Let that shout pierce their ears. Let them be forced to cover them. "Say whose this is, and we'll leave you alone," they were shouting. "I don't know," I said. "I don't know. I'm innocent. Mama, Mama," I was calling.

Only those three words, again and again during the entire time I was being beaten. They got nothing else out of me. He let me be and moved on to Aliza, which was even worse. I must be a vile animal because I didn't react. I only covered my face. Oh, how humiliated one can become. How could I not walk over and slap him in the face? How could I? But I was preoccupied with myself. Such horrible pain and such fierce joy! I was already sure that I would endure. That I wouldn't give in.

And they started on me again.

He approached me—a tall, skinny greyhound. And those eyes—very familiar eyes of a snoop—green, cold, floating eyes of a fish…I gave him a cold, slightly derisive look. And it still seems to me that that was what he beat me for.

On the cheek, in the face, in my eyes. Blood gushed out. One more centimeter and I would have lost my eye.

He put his sinewy arms around my thin neck and began to strangle me. He was about to strangle me to death. I began to wheeze and he released his hold. I was about to find out at what point one can die. I'd always been curious when the process of dying began. But he stopped beating me. We were escorted out. I heard the word "Auschwitz" as I was passing. I didn't know then that it referred to us.

In the courtyard I heard two Germans whispering and pointing at us: "*Sie halten sich. Ja, sie halten sich*" [They're holding up. Yes, they are holding up].

I was unable to walk. I barely managed to drag myself back to our group. When they saw us they burst into tears and covered their faces.

How did I manage to sit down then? But it was no longer on bare stone, as those who had some towels or shirts had offered them for me to sit on.

But my body was as hard—how should I put it?—as a stone, as hard as rubber. And so black. Not blue, but black. Instead of sitting I curled up like a cat and lay on Pesia. I had no coat, shoes, or stockings.[61]

Death Is No Longer an Old Woman with a Stick

The night of horrors dragged on. During all that time, Zvi was struggling with feelings of guilt and the need to maintain the composure of a leader. Earlier, sitting with the rest of his comrades outside the barrack, he stared into space muttering to his brother: "They went…I sent them… now it's my turn…it's time…" When Chajka and Aliza returned, he felt a shockwave pass through him. Along with everyone, he helped them try to get comfortable. Then everyone sat in silence.[62] Eventually, Zvi stood up, then sat down again. His eyes scanned the area. He turned to his brother: "We need to break through the ghetto and get to Böhm. He's got other Jews with him. He can save us. We have to try… We have to go…"[63] Chajka watched the scene unfold:

> It became dark. The soldiers are preparing wood, old furniture for a bonfire. They're about to light it. Cwi whispers to Uncio [Aharon, his brother], "Now or never." Nobody except for Uncio heard that whisper. He didn't say even as much as a word to the *chevra*.
>
> And he suddenly sprang to his feet and rushed ahead so fast—so fast that your eyes couldn't follow him.
>
> Your heart begins pounding so strongly again, that you think that it will pop out.

61 Ibid., pp. 58–61.

62 Brandes and Reshef, *Zvi Brandes*, pp. 143–144.

63 Ibid., p. 144.

> Commotion among the soldiers. Shots fired one after another. They begin to run. The commander comes, "*Was? Getürmt—Von diese[n]!*" [What? Escaped —Of those!].
>
> He begins to shout at the soldiers. "How could you let that happen? Chase him and bring him back dead or alive."
>
> It's been only a couple of minutes. My heart's pounding, pounding. What will happen? Will he escape?
>
> I'm quietly begging [to] I don't know who, God perhaps, to let him escape and reach his destination alive. The minutes are dragging on forever. They're already coming back. I look at their faces hoping to guess the truth from their expressions. But it's already too dark to see.
>
> But, I can hear one say to another, "*Schon erledigt! Ich habe ihn erwischt*" [Already done! I got him], he brags. My heart stops and then I feel a contraction, a spasm of pain.[64]

Zvi's brother and sister were sitting next to Chajka. They most likely did not speak German. "What did he say?" they asked her. "I don't know," she replied, and she sat there stunned, hard as a stone, wondering why she couldn't feel a thing:

> I'm sitting, unmoved. Why? I know Cwi's dead, so why am I not crying? Why am I not banging my head against a wall? I'm sitting still and my insides feel empty and hollow. If you knocked on me there might be an echo.
>
> Why is it so? Am I already incapable of any human feelings, emotions, pain?!
>
> I don't know. Perhaps it's because I'm so wounded psychically and physically. Perhaps it's the conviction that tomorrow I'll be where he is now. Yes, that could be it. Tomorrow I'll be gone too. A tragedy will happen, but there will not be anybody to care. We will be gone. There won't be anybody.
>
> What is death? It's just a minute. The heart's pounding strongly and then more and more slowly, and then it weakens and falls silent. The end.
>
> It's only a moment. It seems to me that it's not so frightening at all. Even death from torture, from beating—horrible pain, which intensifies until you lose consciousness and then it's over.

64 Klinger, *I Am Writing These Words to You* (1943 diaries), p. 61.

> I used to fear death a lot. I was terrified of it. I didn't want to die not only because I loved life and because every fiber of my being [yearned] for life, but also because the process of dying was something frightening and horrible in my eyes.
>
> Today life has already lost its sense to me and I've already come to hate it. I'm already so exhausted by it. I used to know a poem, which I often repeat now, "*Ich bin des Lebens müde*" [I'm tired of life].[65]
>
> And death is no longer an old woman with a rod in her hand, but a kind, gentle lady.
>
> These might be our final hours, this night outside the barrack.
>
> During my final hours I should be thinking about my life, about unfulfilled dreams, about a song interrupted in the middle. [...]
>
> It's dark. And in darkness thoughts of escape are born. I'll escape. I won't let them deport me. I won't get into a wagon. Perhaps my dead body will. Yes, my dead body but not me.
>
> I do not believe in the afterlife, to use a term popular where I was from. I do not believe that Jews live in Auschwitz, only some individuals at best.
>
> I'm motivated by some mad curiosity to see, discover what is happening there, in Auschwitz. I'm sure that it's another Treblinka. There are the gearwheels nobody escapes from. They're destined for an oven—they see nothing except an oven. They're destined for labor camps—they see nothing except labor camps. The German soldiers who serve in Auschwitz have no idea what's happening there. No living man has left Auschwitz yet.
>
> No, I won't go to Auschwitz. I'll jump out the wagon, even if it kills me. I'll kill myself, shoot myself. I can die like a dog. But I won't go to Auschwitz. This is a promise I've made to myself.
>
> I still don't have the courage. I'm still recalling Cwi before me. And this bonfire is burning so bright. But tomorrow it might be too late. I have to make up my mind. I'm still asking myself.[66]

Auschwitz was pulling her in as if by an invisible string. She wanted to unravel the terrible secret—what happens to people when they die? She was not the only one: On the train that was making its way to Auschwitz during those hours, Yehiel Feiner pondered similar thoughts:

65 This quotation is from an unknown source.

66 Klinger, *I Am Writing These Words to You* (1943 diaries), pp. 61–63.

> Each one yearned to unravel while still alive, the Enigma of "Auschwitz." A word, which for years had pulled at the heart; now in cattle trains; with the lodestar pull of death...Now, with the present knowledge clear to all and sundry that they were departing the world of the living, each craved to see the Secret at the price of his own death, with his own eyes still open to see it.[67]

Unlike Feiner, Chajka decided not to get into the wagon. Perhaps it was, after all, her love of life that continued to churn within her. However, that feeling of having already crossed the boundary between life and death, of having already died, would remain with her throughout her life. She would have wanted to live, but kind and gentle lady death would not let her find peace in life.

Auschwitz

The *Aktion* that was meant to be completed within a week ended up lasting over two weeks. According to Erich Kulka and Ota Krauss, special preparations had been made in Auschwitz in anticipation of the transports from Zagłębie, as mentioned earlier: "Some 30,000 Jews from the Upper Silesia towns of Sosnowiec and Bedzin were liquidated in the Birkenau gas chambers in August 1943, as a reprisal for the discovery of arms in the towns."[68] The camps were closed, armed guards with machine guns were stationed in them, and work had ceased in all camps.

According to a rare testimony recorded on August 12, 1943, by an SS man who worked as a clerk in Auschwitz, these were the peak days of the camp's activity:

> Between August 1 and 3, [1943], fifteen trainloads of Jews, carrying approximately 15,000 people in total, arrived in Auschwitz. Besides that, trucks were going back and forth. A hundred people were crammed into one truck: children, women, and men. The same number of people was squeezed onto the platform attached behind each truck. They arrived in Auschwitz in inhuman conditions. They were then thrown off the trucks into an open field. Children

67 Ka-Tzetnik, *Sunrise over Hell*, pp. 156–157.

68 Erich Kulka and Ota Krauss, *The Death Factory: Document on Auschwitz* (London: Pergamon Press, 1966), pp. 190, 192.

> were trampled underfoot. In the summer heat, the women stood half naked, half dead, beaten bloody, without any help, without a drop of water. Neither words nor the human imagination are capable of describing the hellish tortures undergone by these people, who yearned for death to bring them relief. Innocent children, sick women barely standing on their feet, mercilessly pushed, brutally beaten and kicked. History has never known such an extent of human desolation and in such a manner. No one but the German, who is the bearer of the highest of cultures, could have invented all this.[69]

Records of the numbers tattooed between August 1 and 15, 1943, indicate that during these days 3,537 men and 4,054 women were selected to work in the camp.[70] Yet, even after this selection, the Auschwitz crematoria could not cope with the load. The SS man concluded: "Since the crematoria could not accommodate the large number of people, the bodies were burned in open trenches near Birkenau, and for three days they saw nothing there but huge flames bursting and rising. Deportees also arrived from France and were immediately eliminated in the same way. Birkenau is celebrating: 30,000 people gassed in one day."[71]

Among the tens of thousands of bodies burned in the open pits were Perl and Leibel Klinger, their daughter Sarah, and the Klingers' little granddaughter.

69 Mark, "Din Veheshbon shel Ish Ha'es-es Functzioner," pp. 177–178.

70 Gerald Reitlinger, *The Final Solution: The Attempt to Exterminate the Jews of Europe, 1939–1945* (New York: Beechhurst Press, 1953), p. 304.

71 Mark, "Din Veheshbon shel Ish Ha'es-es Functzioner," pp. 177–178.

Chapter Twenty

I Won't Go to Auschwitz

Stains: 1955

One time I spotted black marks on Mother's thighs. I asked her what they were, and she shook her head dismissively: birthmarks. I must have been about nine years old, because the scene in my memory is situated in my parents' bedroom in the housing complex. Mother was getting dressed, probably for a trip to the beach. It was one of her good periods. The move to a new house in the kibbutz was a source of great excitement. The resin-top table had been placed in the big living room that opened out onto a sunlit veranda leading into the garden, where she could tend to her African daisies.

Mother never spoke to Zvi or me about the war or what she had gone through. It was not a story meant for us. Even when matters less serious than that would come up, the adults would often whisper to each other sullenly: "Nisht vor den Kindern." Not in front of the kids. And not in front of the adults either. Her diary shows that even after the deportation in Będzin she had to hide her wounds as displaying them out in the open could have endangered the other survivors. The documented reports she gave to the Executive Committee of Hakibbutz Ha'artzi and to the Histadrut leadership in Kibbutz Galon in *Eretz Israel* after her arrival in 1944 show that she almost never referenced the severe torture she herself had undergone. A few times she mentioned that two girls had been caught by the Gestapo with guns in their bags, but one would be hard put to gather from her testimony that she had, in fact, been one of them. Even in Kibbutz Haogen, she did not talk much about her personal travails.[1]

She did not show her complete diaries, which include the story of the bunker and her personal experiences, to almost anyone. Later, when Esther Shoshan arrived in Kibbutz Haogen after Chajka's death and read her diary for the first time, she would experience a wave of renewed shock.[2] Yehuda Weiss, a member of Kibbutz Haogen, would write after the publication of *Miyoman Bageto*:

> We have known about this diary since Chajka appeared among us at the beginning of 1944 in Budapest. Rumors about it made the rounds under the cover of anxious silence.... We wanted to hear about it, to have a look at it, but Chajka, in her quiet, kind, and firm way always refused: "It's written in Polish, and in fact, it's not even a diary but lists that were written under harsh underground conditions."[3]

Her "way" reflected that of the movement. In *Sefer Hashomer Hatzair*, published in 1956, the editors chose to tell the story of the movement over those of its members. It was in this book that selected and well-edited parts of Chajka's diary were published for the first time. Not a single word mentioned what she had gone through.[4] The stories of the last bunker and her interrogation had not been included. Chajka's torture was mostly trivial in the eyes of the movement. The same was true in the kibbutz and everywhere else, it seems. The torture was akin to a stain that must remain hidden.

The Morning After

The morning after the interrogation found Chajka and her ten friends confused and wondering what was to come next. All night long they had sat in anticipation of the fateful dawn. They were separated from the other Jews. Wounded and aching, Chajka felt seething scorn toward the

1 Mina's testimony is the only one containing Chajka's personal stories. See Mina Karni, in *Chajka: Hoveret Zikaron*, p. 15.

2 Esther Shoshan interview.

3 Yehuda Weiss, "Yomana shel Chajka" (Hebrew), *Al Hamishmar*, May 15, 1959.

4 Chajka Klinger, "Hashomrim Bebendin al Mishmar Kvod Amam," in Dror and Rosenzweig, *Sefer Hashomer Hatzair*, vol. 1, pp. 691–706.

Jews who were too scared to approach them and offer help. In her 1943 diaries, she wrote:

> We're still sitting on all fours like yesterday. We haven't had anything to eat. We ask the Jews from the barracks to give us some water. Walking right by us, they can give us some water without being noticed. Besides, this German is a good man. I can tell by his expression, his face, and his treatment of the Jews.
>
> But the Jews will not give you anything. Forget it. Why, they're afraid to look at us. They pass us at a distance without looking.
>
> So you ask another. "For God's sake, give us some water at least." Forget it. Nobody wants to. Ha-ha... I'm afraid of a deportation. Ha-ha… These guards—in an hour or two they could be gone.
>
> I loathe them, I hate them so much.
>
> Your nation—this is who you wanted to die for, who you've sacrificed your life for.
>
> It's such a heavy load and I'm so sad.
>
> I understand everything. They are innocent. It was the others who made them what they are.
>
> But my heart's hurting, hurting so much.[5]

This passage, which is not included in the published 1944 diaries, reveals terrible mental distress. She felt as if her act of heroism had been rejected by the very people for whom she had undertaken it. The deep chasm between the dead "avant-garde" and the living "masses" who failed to follow their example hit her like a slap in the face. They did not want her sacrifice. And the ordeal was not over yet:

> Some higher-rank military men approach us, call out four boys and order them to follow. It seems that it's an execution—they'll be executing in groups of four.
>
> The minutes are dragging on forever. But no, they're coming back carrying something. Yes, we had a hunch. It's Cwi's body. How perfidious they are! They took our people to march past us with Cwi's corpse. They want to show us what they're capable of. They're getting closer. His sister is moaning next to me. I want to shout at her to stop, sit quietly, and look proudly into their faces. I won't shed even one tear. Moaning isn't how I want to honor Cwi's death. […]

5 Klinger, *I Am Writing These Words to You* (1943 diaries), pp. 63–64.

> That was Cwi's last *zchut* [privilege], for his comrades to carry him, and they did. Farewell, our dear, righteous friend, as Mordechai [Anielewicz] once wrote to you. We'll soon see each other there, where nobody is in a hurry to go. Yes, your guess was right—you're gone—the two dearest people I've known in our movement.[6]

Zvi got one thing that Mordechai Anielewicz and David did not: a funeral. Abraham Zilberstein, Herszel Szpringer, Aharon Brandes, and a fourth comrade whose name is not mentioned carried his body to the carcass cart. Then they went back to the isolated bunch seated in front of the barracks:

> Afterward we sat there like corpses for a long time. An order came in the evening. I'm to go into the barracks. We're to mix with all the other Jews and share the same fate. "A transport leaves tomorrow," I said at once. "The barracks will be empty tomorrow."
>
> And I became so gripped with fear. What now? I think I'm going to break my vow and go to Auschwitz. I'm so scared, so terrified of Auschwitz. I already have regrets. Why did they put us in the barracks? Outside at night there might be a chance to escape.
>
> Others are content. We blend in with the crowd so there might be a chance to escape.
>
> But there's only fear in me. Herszel is consoling me, "Don't be scared. There won't be a transport just now." [...]
>
> Everybody goes to sleep. It's perfectly quiet. Nobody's shouting or crying. I can only hear a child crying every now and then. A young girl is flirting with a young boy in a corner. She's in such good spirits! I look at her with disdain. But why am I picking on her? Perhaps she just wants to indulge herself before death?
>
> I lie down on the floor next to a married couple and fall asleep. Somebody puts his hand on me and moves it. Ugh! I shake it off.
>
> Somebody's moaning in their sleep. A child is crying. The bloody red glow of the bonfire [can be seen] through the window. German voices. I fall asleep again.[7]

During this second week of the great deportation, small transports continued to leave the liquidation camp for Auschwitz in a car every day

6 Ibid., pp. 64–65.

7 Ibid., pp. 65–66.

or two. For Chajka, if coming back to life meant submissively waiting to be transferred, she wanted no part of it. Time after time she revolted against what she saw as a passive expectation of the end. Strangely enough, it was this inner rebellion that would once again lead to her survival:

> I look at the people again and I wonder again why they're so calm.
>
> They are saying that a car is due to arrive at 10 AM.
>
> Among the deportees is a very young, resourceful boy, who goes out to work every day. He's going today as well. He wants to help us. I believe in him, because he has honest eyes. His name is Berek.
>
> He wants to escort the girls into the kitchen. [...]
>
> I decide to go. I'm waiting for the right moment. A lot of them have just come. They're talking with one another. Berek winks at me. I approach him. "Go to the kitchen *Bau* [building]." "Come with me," I say to him. "No, go alone." I go. A *Wachtmeister* is standing in front of the kitchen. He lets me through.
>
> Aliza, Pesa, Sara [Kukiełka], and Abram join me. We're talking with the militia regarding Herszel. They go there to bring him over.
>
> He [the *Hauptmann*] comes before 10 AM. He'll surely send us back now. He'll surely recognize us, particularly me due to my wounded face.
>
> He'll send us to a transport. Aliza is hiding, but I won't. I can't take it anymore. What now? What now?
>
> The *Hauptmann* [captain, the rank of the commander] comes in. He looks at me for a long time, shakes his head and slowly says, "*Neue Gesichter. Aber nein, sie sollen bleiben.*" [New faces. But no, they should stay].
>
> A strange man.[8]

Once again, she had won life's lottery. It was as if the *kvitl* given to her all those years back by Leibel Klinger, whose body was being reduced to a plume of smoke billowing from the chimneys of Auschwitz during perhaps those very moments, had preserved her. Of all people, the woman who repeatedly told herself that she did not believe in miracles, was granted life time and time again as the result of the accidental caprices of blind fate. The Germans did not shoot her when she left the bunker, nor at the end of her interrogation, and even now, when identified by the *Hauptmann*, she was not sent to Auschwitz. And yet, fortune only smiles

8 Ibid., pp. 68–69.

on those who try their luck. Chajka certainly tried hers. She attempted to influence her destiny even when it seemed that no human power could change a thing about the terrible reality surrounding her.

Herzel Szpringer, on the other hand, preferred to accept the hand dealt to him. He chose not to go out to work with the boys and instead tried to buy his right to life in that manner. Nor did he wish to escape by way of the kitchen with the girls. Chawka Lenczner recounted that when the opportunity to move to the kitchen presented itself, Herszel commanded her: "Go!" and added that he would take care of the rest of the comrades.[9] Yet, he no longer cared to look after himself.

Herszel had already come back from the dead once before. After being put on a deportation wagon in June, he managed to jump off the speeding train to Auschwitz despite the warnings of his fellow passengers. According to Chawka Lenczner, Herszel was deeply shaken by the sight of his girlfriend Aliza's bruised face after her interrogation. Aliza's torture had broken his spirit.[10] Still, he somehow found the strength to care for the other members of the group. Except for himself and three children from Kibbutz Atid, all the bunker survivors moved to the kitchen.[11] He stayed behind. The Jewish policemen sent by Chajka were apparently unable to locate him or assist him. She was told that he had been looking for a way to escape, but there were too many guards watching him, and finally he was pushed into the car going to Auschwitz.[12]

Again, Chajka found herself eulogizing the last of her friends:

> And he walked the Jewish path. It might as well be destiny.
>
> Herszel has so much Jewish folk character in him. *Azoy, ful volkstumlichkeit* [So full of folkishness]. More than any of us. He would find a way to communicate with anybody of common origin: a wagon driver, a caretaker, a tailor, a cobbler, or a butcher. He had lots of true friends of common origin. He could have an honest conversation with anybody, hit the nail on the head, and use the right expression. I often admired him so much because he could find a place and time for even the most trivial matters of people he

9 Lenczner, "Parashat Bendin," p. 131.
10 Chawka Lenczner, interview by the author, Yagur, 1985.
11 Lenczner, "Parashat Bendin," p. 131.
12 Klinger, *I Am Writing These Words to You* (1943 diaries), p. 69.

> didn't know. And he did so much for them, for those simple people whom he didn't know. He was happy to do someone a favor. [...]
>
> Herszel, if you're still alive, do know that you are alive in our memory and hearts, in the memories of many, many people.
>
> Perhaps we'll meet one day. Even if it's a delusion I want to live with it. Even though deep in my heart I know it's just a delusion, I feel good with it.[13]

As was her custom, Chajka sought to keep her friends alive by consoling herself with fantasy. Yet, at the time, no one sent to Auschwitz ever returned.

The Remnant

Herszel's deportation to Auschwitz completed the circle of loss around Chajka. She was now left utterly alone. From the leadership of Hashomer Hatzair, Dror, and Gordonia in Będzin, no one had survived but her. They had all joined the ranks of dead leaders from Warsaw and Sosnowiec. Overall, only a few from among the youth movement leadership circles remained, and most of those who had survived the missions, the passport affair, the forest ambushes, the massacres in the bunkers, were now being sent to Auschwitz. Frumka's summary statement of the outcome of Warsaw was now also true of Będzin: "No one left from the Ya'ari family." Chajka's biological family had perished too. Even if she did not know at the time what had happened to her parents, sister, and nieces, she could venture an educated guess. Somewhere out there, in a labor camp in Germany, her sister Mania was still alive, and in another labor camp, her brother-in-law Ya'akov Mgła was fighting for his life. She, of course, knew nothing about their fate either. In Będzin, she was on her own.

However, she had not yet grasped the full depth of her loneliness. Her mission now was to recover and return to life. She had to fight to survive, like the other youth movement survivors. Their numbers had dwindled to just a few dozen. They were cut off from each other but tried to organize themselves in small groups.

Apart from Chajka, the remaining members of Hashomer Hatzair in the liquidation camp were Abraham Zilberstein, and Aharon and Pesia Brandes. The two other movement members who had been with them

13 Ibid., pp. 69–70.

in the bunker—Isaac Neuman and Israel Warszawski—had been sent to Auschwitz in one of the smaller transports. From Dror, only the girls remained: Chawka Lenczner, Aliza Zeytenfeld, and Sara Kukielka. From Gordonia, only David Liwer along with his wife and son, who had joined the group in the liquidation camp,[14] as well as Abraham Izbicki, who had also managed to escape, remained.[15]

It would appear that in the first days after Będzin became *Judenrein*, the members of the youth movements in the liquidation camp operated separately from each other. They had to protect themselves in order to avoid being put on the daily transfers to Auschwitz. Some escaped: Aharon Brandes hid in the pit of a latrine on the day Herszel was deported. The Germans had no eyes on him, and he managed to get to the Kibbutz Dror laundry. There he hid during the day among piles of clothes, and in the evening, he arrived at the Braun workshop run by Böhm. Chawka Lenczner, who found herself wandering the streets overwhelmed by grief over the deportation of Herszel Szpringer, also arrived there that same day. She joined Max Fischer and Moshe Markus from Dror and several other friends. Only now did they learn the fate of the last bunker, and they felt sick with regret. "'I wanted to go with the Germans,' said one of them. 'I begged them to let us go with the two Germans,' said the other. They cried and lamented, but in vain: Herszel will never come back from Auschwitz."[16]

A small group of Hashomer Hatzair members gathered in nearby Zawiercie. This is where Fela Katz came after leaving the last bunker. Dorka Herzberg, Zvi's girlfriend, also ended up here, and possibly Kasia too. Shmuel Rozencwajg, who returned after the failed mission to Hungary, also managed to reach Zawiercie. His parents still lived here, like the rest of the Jews in the town who had miraculously been spared the sword. Later, Rozencwajg would remember the astonishment that gripped him in the face of the relative peace in which the people of Zawiercie tried to continue their lives. Here, at a distance of only a few dozen kilometers from Będzin and Sosnowiec, the Jews still deluded themselves that they would be saved thanks to the town's factory.[17]

14 D. Liwer, *Ir Hametim*, pp. 143–144.

15 Abraham Izbicki testimony at the Barenblatt trial, Moreshet Archive, D.1.5366.

16 Lenczner, "Parashat Bendin," p. 132; Max Fischer testimony, GFH, 11578.

17 Shmuel Ron, in *Sefer Sosnovitz*, vol. 2, p. 182.

According to Fela Katz's testimony, Ina Gelbard, the movement's liaison, also arrived there around the same time, only to be captured. Ina, who had returned to Będzin on the day of the deportation, was promptly arrested by the Gestapo. She had been assigned to a special car heading to Auschwitz, but on the way, she jumped out of the car and returned to Zawiercie to her Hashomer Hatzair friends. Fela Katz remembered the moment when she had appeared wounded and shocked, and they had been so happy at her return that they forgot to take precautions. A manhunt for Ina was immediately announced in Zawiercie, and twelve local Jews were taken hostage. But before anything could happen, the Jewish police broke into Dorka Herzberg's apartment and captured Ina there. "Get dressed, lady," they told her. Ina put on her coat and went with the police. They said that the Gestapo officer went into a frenzy when he saw her. His Alsatian dog attacked her, ripping chunks of flesh from her body, while she spat in the officer's face. The beautiful Ina was rendered a lump of shredded meat that was tossed into the car. She met her death at Auschwitz.[18]

The fate of the last liaison—Renia from Dror—was slightly less bleak. She also returned from Warsaw on the day the great deportation began, and when she understood what was happening she returned to Warsaw. She stayed in the capital for about two weeks, worried about the fate of her friends in Będzin. Then, a postcard arrived from Będzin, signed by Ilse Heinsdorf from Kibbutz Dror. Ilse asked Renia to come back. In consultation with Yitzhak Zuckerman, it was decided that she should go. Renia was equipped with a large amount of money and two additional transit licenses in addition to her own. Perhaps they could be used to save another two souls. She managed to locate Meir Schulman and Nechama (Necha) his wife in the home of a Pole named Nowak, a mechanic and friend of the Dror people.[19] The two had escaped from the last bunker after hiding under the beds and were now hiding here.

Thus, in the two liquidation camps in Będzin, at the Nowaks' home on the Aryan side, in Zawiercie, and even in Auschwitz, the last youths of Będzin continued to fight for their existence, not knowing what tomorrow would bring, uncertain if they could continue to hold on.

18 Katz, "L'lo Het."

19 Meir and Nechama Schulman, interview by the author, Tel Aviv, 1986.

In the Liquidation Camp

Chajka spent about two weeks in the liquidation camp.[20] According to most evidence, there were about 250 people at the camp, but their numbers changed daily. Sometimes the numbers increased when Jews who had left the bunkers or had been captured by the Germans came to join them, but mostly the number decreased due to the regular transports to Auschwitz. Those in the camp continued to collect Jewish property and clean the houses and streets. As mentioned before, this was not the only camp in the ghettos in the region: There was a second camp nearby, in Rossner's former workshop with roughly 400 Jews, and there was another camp in Sosnowiec. In total, there were about 1,200 Jews across the three camps. The camps that were under German guard and command were actually managed by the surviving members of the Judenrat: In the Będzin camp, Barenblatt was in charge of keeping order, and the Sosnowiec camp was operated by Dr. Hirsch Lieberman, Asher Kleinberg, the former head of the supply department, and Romek Goldminc, the former chief of the Jewish police.[21]

Rossner, who was busy dismantling his factories and preparing them to be transferred to the labor camps, still tried to do as much as he could to protect his surviving workers. He was able to help some, but his influence had waned as his trump card of doing vital work for the war economy no longer held any power. His role had come to an end. A few months later, he would be arrested by the Gestapo. He was executed in January 1944. In 1995, he would be awarded the title of Righteous Among the Nations by Yad Vashem.[22]

For Chajka these were strange days of returning to life and feeling sick of it. The instinct of life pushed her to do everything necessary to ensure her continued existence, yet at the same time, the very presence of life, and especially of other people, aroused her contempt and disgust. She could not forgive them for being willing to pay any price to stay alive:

> Kitchen building [*Bau*]. The transports have left. We are still here. How odd. A two-minute walk from the barrack to the kitchen

20 The bunker was probably discovered on August 7, 1943, and the writing of the diaries in the hideout began on August 26, 1943.

21 D. Liwer, *Ir Hametim*, pp. 149–150, 163.

22 "Alfred Rossner," Yad Vashem, the World Holocaust Remembrance Center, https://www.yadvashem.org/righteous/stories/rossner.html (accessed September 29, 2023).

> has saved me for now from Auschwitz, from death. How strange this whole life of ours is! In the kitchen building, they are cooking for the laborers from the *Stadtverwaltung* [municipality] who are liquidating property—Jewish apartments. [...]
>
> And now I'm going to wash myself. I'm so happy that I'm about to wash my entire body.
>
> I undress and suddenly somebody shouts, "God, look at her!" They begin to [pity] and bemoan me. I cover myself up. I need neither their tears nor their pity. "What good has it done you? What good?" they ask. "You fools! It's you who make us miserable. Be quiet," I shout. "Leave me alone. It's none of your business. You fools, idiots, you walk like cattle to the slaughter," I'm shouting. And then I immediately feel as if I've been banging my head against a wall. I can't even wash myself.[23]

It would appear that, for several days, Chajka was put to work doing liquidation jobs. She could not believe the level of German organization, efficiency, and speed that was now revealed to her:

> One barrack contains carefully arranged blue kitchen utensils. They have been beautifully sorted according to quality. Another barrack contains enamel utensils as well as shining, bright ones, and pots arranged in a row — large, very large, smaller, smallest. And there is glassware, beautifully arranged on the shelves. Another barrack is packed with porcelain arranged in sets on the shelves.
>
> And there is barrack after barrack. Silverware in one, tin and electrical devices in another, and canvas, wool, shoes, silk in other barracks. And this is how the Jewish slaves are working, assembling Jewish goods and objects obtained at the price of hard work and sweat.
>
> And my heart aches and bleeds. They become angry with me. I cannot work anymore. I am dreaming of taking all this glassware and porcelain and smashing it on the floor with a crash.[24]

She especially hated the Jewish girls who received favors from German officers:

23 Klinger, *I Am Writing These Words to You* (1943 diaries), pp. 73–74.

24 Ibid., pp. 74–75.

> And in the kitchen they bake layer cakes and make *Bohne Kaffee* [brewed coffee] for the *Hauptmann* and his cronies.
>
> And the Jewish girls led by the director are smiling affectionately and flirting.
>
> Jewish girls are working in the soldiers' kitchens where they cook and clean. But not just any girl can work there—she has to be pretty, clean, and smartly dressed. And you'd better not approach a chosen one. Don't you dare! They want for nothing, neither beautiful dresses nor good food.
>
> Oh, you Jewish whores! I would strangle you.
>
> Yes, give yourselves away to soldiers, German *Leutnants*. They'll save you, you idiots.... You're as mean as it comes. It's good that your brothers are dead, if there are such women among you.
>
> But why am I angry? Why?
>
> Why, it would suggest that I'm a naive idealist who doesn't know life at all. Why, you know that there are scum and the dregs of society in every nation.
>
> And at times like these, such dregs rise to the surface.
>
> Yes, I know about it but I'm choking in this quagmire. I sometimes think about attacking the *Hauptmann* when he comes over. I won't stand being here much longer.[25]

She had spent the first four years of war on the farm, in the company of her comrades, living and acting according to moral ideals in which she believed with all her heart. This discipline formed the basis for the strong social cohesion that characterized the group of youths growing up on the farm and allowed them to deal rationally with the rapidly changing reality. The behavioral norms they adhered to protected them from that reality and amplified the buffer between them and the Jews on the street. Fortified by her values that marked a clear line between what was appropriate and inappropriate, Chajka's criticism of the conduct of the remaining Jewish survivors was sharp and scathing.

Few of the dozens of Jews who had stayed with Chajka in the liquidation camp and survived to testify saw things as she did. David Liwer, who was appointed the stock keeper of the Jewish property collected from the looted apartments, described in words full of sorrow and grief his feelings at the sight of Będzin emptied of its Jews, the stolen Jewish property piled up on the shelves, the Jews who were captured and taken to the roundup point to

25 Ibid., pp. 75–76.

be sent to Auschwitz.[26] Achingly, he described repeated attempts to ply the German officers with schnapps so that they would not harm the deportees they were escorting to Auschwitz. Where Chajka saw the lowest and most degraded level of human existence, Liwer saw a desperate, dismal attempt to continue living.[27] Whereas Chajka wrote:

> There's no longer a center in the barracks. Whoever comes from a bunker is escorted to us. There is a selection. They segregate. The center is in our building. They make a selection, leaving the young and attractive and sending the old to Braun for deportation.
>
> They sometimes leave the old ones selected a long time ago. At other times they select those to be deported from among them and leave the newcomers.
>
> The old are protesting, shouting, "We'll teach these new ones." [...]
>
> I was to be sent away because of the wound on my face. *Kranke brauchen wir nicht*! [We don't need any sick ones here!]. But they left me without my asking. Others plead, cry, beg and they sometimes do take pity on them. They leave the husbands and wives and send the children for deportation. The parents remain. They rarely go with their children. You can often hear the piercing screams of children. Oh, these poor Jewish children![28]

Everyone wanted to live, and the choice was: your life or mine. Also from Liwer's descriptions, which highlight examples of mutual help in the camp—and indeed there was some—it appears that the fight for existence continued. A group of Jews who were hiding in a bunker, which the camp detainees tried to help, were eventually discovered by the camp's Jewish commander. For a while they still tried to hide in the liquidation camp, but they were eventually deported to Sosnowiec.[29]

The liquidation camp was one more stop on the road to death, a kind of purgatory where everyone awaited their sentence. Now that there were no more illusions left, the Jews tried to cling to the few things they still had—money, clothes, food, sex—all of which could be taken from them in an instant. The vulgarity of human existence overcame them. Appalled, Chajka saw the kitchen manager beating an elderly woman who

26 D. Liwer, *Ir Hametim*, p. 159.

27 Ibid., p. 152.

28 Klinger, *I Am Writing These Words to You* (1943 diaries), pp. 77–78.

29 D. Liwer, *Ir Hametim*, p. 155.

didn't want to scrub floors; fights broke out among women over clothes. She had heard about camp residents feverishly searching for treasure in the abandoned apartments:

> They rush into the apartment like mad and rush to the wardrobes, [and] frames. It's a sacred procession now. They look for money and gold. And they do find them. And then at the market they are asked, "Is it gold? How much?"[30]

In another passage, which was, of course, not included in the published book, she wrote about the desperate debauchery:

> Eroticism
>
> The people are going crazy: the young and the old—everybody. They will not leave you alone. The same vulgar, awful words continuously spoken and heard. They're only looking for an occasion to kiss and perhaps...
>
> Decadents, they want to seize the day because tomorrow they might be dead. The militiamen are just looking for new victims. They can't understand that one might not want to. Why, we might be dead tomorrow.
>
> No, I don't want to be with you. Besides, it's interesting that I somehow don't want to indulge myself before death. It makes me want to vomit. It makes me nauseous.
>
> It's the same with food. The people are binging frantically. They steal, snatch. They just want to eat, eat as much as they can, and drink vodka and wine, whatever they can get their hands on. They gobble and vomit, gobble and vomit. Worse than animals.[31]

In the nearby camp in Środula, Fredka Mazia also went through similar experiences.[32] However, for Chajka it was all too much. She could not continue living in this atmosphere of rampant hedonism. Rumors circulated in the camp that the liquidation work would continue until Passover. The majority of the Jews rejoiced—they had been given another extension.[33] Chajka, however, made up her mind: "I will not stay here. I'll leave. I cannot be part of this effort. I don't want to. And I cannot tolerate

30 Klinger, *I Am Writing These Words to You* (1943 diaries), p. 76.

31 Ibid., p. 77.

32 Mazia, *Re'im Basa'ar*, pp. 246–247.

33 Klinger, *I Am Writing These Words to You* (1943 diaries), p. 78.

being in this quagmire anymore. In a little while this life will have me in its clutches."[34]

Then one day, probably during the third or fourth week of August, Chajka found a breach in the fence and escaped.

Escape

The descriptions of life in the liquidation camp conclude the chronological sequence of Chajka's diaries. She does not describe the circumstances of her escape nor any of the events that followed. It was the end of a chapter, and everything that unfolded after it had no value in her eyes.

According to other testimonies, dozens of Jews managed to escape the liquidation camps in Kamionka and Środula. After the second week of the deportation, the German forces were much reduced, and the camps were not particularly strictly guarded. In fact, the liquidation camps had many breaches, and despite the daily census, it was possible to come and go through their gates without any particular risk, provided that those who remained ensured the German sentries' ignorance by way of census manipulation or bribery. Part of the guard duties were assigned to former Jewish policemen, and they helped the escapees in diverse ways. Later, Barenblatt, one of the leaders of the camp, would claim that he helped Chajka escape.[35] This was not improbable: Barenblatt often visited the farm in Będzin, and for a while he even had a girlfriend there. He socialized in particular with the Gordonia people, and it can be assumed that Chajka knew him. In the atmosphere of the general turmoil in the liquidation camp, old ties dissolved and new ties were formed, including between members of the Jewish police and members of the resistance. No one had anything left to lose except their life. Yet, there was no proof to support Barenblatt's claim. When he was tried in Poland after the war, he asked Chajka to testify in his favor, which she angrily refused to do.[36]

More than the assistance within the camp, the success of the escape was contingent upon finding a safe hiding place on the outside. Meir Schulman and his wife Nechama managed to find such a place in Mrs. Nowak's apartment on the Aryan side of Będzin. There, the survivors of the last bunker had begun to gather.

34 Ibid.

35 Hirsch Barenblatt testimony at the Barenblatt trial, Moreshet Archive, D.1.5366.

36 Ya'akov Rosenberg testimony at the Barenblatt trial, Moreshet Archive, D.1.5366; Final verdict at the Barenblatt trial, Moreshet Archive, D.1.5366.

Chapter Twenty-One

The Diaries

Zagłębie Is *Judenrein*

By the end of August 1943, Zagłębie had become *Judenrein*. The last mass deportation in the region took place on August 26, 1943. About 2,500 Jews from Zawiercie, who had survived until then under the auspices of the factory that produced uniforms for the Luftwaffe, were also deported to Auschwitz. The 500 workers who remained there were deported on October 17, 1943.[1]

Nevertheless, hundreds, possibly even thousands of Jews continued to live in various places in Zagłębie. Some of them were individuals who found a hiding place within Christian families; others hid in small groups bound by relationships that existed before the deportation. The largest groups were concentrated in the liquidation camps, where there were about 2,000 Jews. Although this number gradually decreased due to the continued transports to Auschwitz, those who remained hoped that their continued employment in liquidation work would ensure their survival. This belief was strengthened when at the beginning of October, the small but regular transports to Auschwitz stopped for a period of time.[2]

The Germans, as mentioned, did not guard the liquidation camps very carefully: A sentence had been issued on the Jews of Poland as well as in Zagłębie, which was now virtually empty of Jews, and it would be

1 Spivak, *Sefer Zikaron Lekdoshey Zaviertze Vehasviva*, pp. 296–298; Aharon Brandes, *Ketz Hayehudim Bedrom Ma'arav Polin* (Hebrew) (Merhavia: Sifriat Poalim, 1945), p. 86; Menahem Goldberg testimony, YVA, O.3/3184.

2 D. Liwer, *Ir Hametim*, p. 163.

very difficult for a Jew to find refuge. This belief was strengthened by the numerous instances in which the Polish population was only too eager to cooperate in identifying runaway Jews.[3] The Poles who hid Jews in their homes—and there were quite a few of them in Zagłębie—were usually located far from German eyes. Along with the few who did find a hiding place, were two organized groups of resistance fighters: the Hanoar Hatzioni group and the Hashomer Hatzair-Dror group. These groups engaged in their own survival and rescue efforts while maintaining contact with the liquidation camps.

Rescue in Hanoar Hatzioni

The most organized and powerful group was that of Hanoar Hatzioni. Like the other movements, Hanoar Hatzioni was also dealt a fatal blow during the last deportation. The fall of Józek Kożuch, the revered leader of the movement in Sosnowiec, of Janek Zimmerman and Hypek Glitzenstein, the heads of the militant wing of the movement, severely depleted the group's leadership ranks. However, unlike Dror, Gordonia, or Hashomer Hatzair, their leadership was not eliminated completely. Even after the great deportation, many of its activists remained alive. The most prominent among them were: Leon Blatt and Bolek Kożuch, members of the Hanoar Hatzioni leadership in Sosnowiec; Fredka Oksenhendler, Józek Kożuch's widow; and several other young women—Szewa (Sheva) Ingster, Karola Bojm, Lola (Lolka) Pomeranzblum, and others.

Evidence indicates that, in all likelihood, a meeting of the surviving members of Hanoar Hatzioni after the deportation was held in the first half of August 1943. According to Fredka Mazia, twelve members were present at this meeting, most of them mentioned above. The meeting was held at the home of the Budziej family, a Polish family with whom Leon Blatt had made contact, and where he had apparently hidden during the deportation. The Budziej family had a small villa in the city suburbs, which was an ideal site for the group's headquarters. After they had shared all available information regarding the fate of movement members, the rest of the meeting was devoted to brainstorming rescue options. The ability of Hanoar Hatzioni to recover and quickly move on to outlining plans for organized rescue was rooted in the fact that they had engaged in rescue efforts before the deportation. In fact, by the time the deportation began,

3 See Kukielka, *Escape from the Pit*, p. 132; Brandes, *Ketz Hayehudim*, p. 85.

they had been operating two or three rescue programs simultaneously, the main one involving the smuggling of Jewish girls disguised as Polish workers into Germany. Two such groups had already left for Germany, and good news of a safe arrival had been received from one of them.[4] The second plan consisted of hiding in holiday homes in the mountains. The members of the movement would be sent to the mountains on the Slovakian border under the protection of forged documents, and there they would hide until the danger passed. The idea was to eventually smuggle some of them into Germany. At the same time, a third plan—escape through Slovakia—was being considered.

This latter plan was developed by chance. Jakub (Kuba) Rosenberg arrived in the Beskid Mountains near Slovakia to hide after a failed attempt to steal weapons in which Harry Blumenfrucht had been captured. After a period of several weeks, Kuba Rosenberg made contact with Polish smugglers and gained their trust by presenting himself as a Polish partisan officer. With their help, Rosenberg was able to smuggle Jadzia Szpigelman, a member of the movement with an Aryan appearance, across the Slovak border. The next day he received a note from her saying that she had crossed the border safely but was yet to report that she had reached the Jews.[5]

At the meeting at the Budziej family's house, roles were designated and tasks were assigned: Fredka was to go to Kraków and start obtaining fake documents and lining up contacts for the smuggling operations; Karola, Ruth, and Lolka were tasked with maintaining contact with the people in hiding, while the responsibilities of coordinating the actions and distributing money and clothes fell into the hands of Leon Blatt and Bolek Kożuch, respectively. The group worked quickly and effectively. Fredka went to Kraków, managed to get in touch with the members of the Polish underground whom she had known before, and after spending time with one of them in a German officers' club, obtained everything she needed: documents, transit licenses, and train tickets. That same week, the first group of twelve Hanoar Hatzioni girls left Katowice on their way to Germany.[6]

4 Mazia, *Re'im Basa'ar*, pp. 198–206.

5 Ya'akov (Kuba) Rosenberg, "Bodedim Bama'avak" (Hebrew) Massuah Archive (1974), AR-PS-00089-022, pp. 73–79; Jadzia Szpigelman remembrances in Jane Lipski, *Memories* (Tucson, Arizona, 1990), Massuah Archive, AR-T-00019-024; Mazia, *Re'im Basa'ar*, p. 210.

6 Mazia, *Re'im Basa'ar*, pp. 200–203.

The successful departure of the "group of twelve" filled the remaining members with a sense of purpose and hope for the future. Fredka continued her travels to Kraków, while Bolek and Leon maintained contact with the liquidation camp where they were smuggling goods from Rossner's workshop in order to finance the operations. On August 25, 1943, another group—this time twenty-people strong—left for Vienna equipped with certificates brought by Fredka from Kraków. However, the departure of this group took a heavy toll: Lolka Pomeranzblum, the movement's liaison, went out on her mission and never returned.[7]

In the mountains, having run out of patience awaiting the green light from Jadzia Szpigelman, Rosenberg began to act of his own accord. Despite the opinion of his friends, who believed that the road to Slovakia had not yet been proven to be safe, he smuggled three more people over the border—his mother and two movement members. The long-awaited news from Slovakia arrived most likely at the end of August. According to Fredka, Jadzia wrote: "Karola [Bojm], Azriel [Kożuch], come.[8] Old people, young people, and children. It is paradise here. An open road to Hungary. Jadzia."[9] According to Erwin Steiner, the rescue activist from Slovakia who delivered the message,[10] Jadzia's letter contained a request that the head of the Hanoar Hatzioni group also come to Slovakia.[11]

Immediately after Jadzia's announcement, Chaim Tenenwurcel and Alex Gutman, who had also been hiding in the mountains after the failed operation to obtain weapons, left for Slovakia. In late August or early September 1943, the two arrived in Žilina in Slovakia and met with Steiner. Contact was made.[12] Those coming from Poland now had confirmation that there were still Jews living in Slovakia. Across the mountains in Poland, Rosenberg and Gutman's sister Tosia were already organizing the next groups.

7 Ibid., pp. 206–209.

8 Jadzia, who had left before the great deportation of August 1, 1943, still did not know about the death of Azriel (Józek) Kożuch, the leader of the movement. See Lipski, *Memories*.

9 Ibid.; Mazia, *Re'im Basa'ar*, p. 210.

10 For more about the rescue workers within the Working Group of the Slovakian Jewish leadership, see chapter 22.

11 Erwin Steiner testimony, as quoted in Rinat Gorodemczyk, "Berihat Tnu'ot Hano'ar MiZaglembia 1943–1944" (Hebrew) (master's thesis, Tel Aviv University, 1986), pp. 48–50.

12 Gutman and Gutman-Herzberg, "Bageto Bendin: Protocol," pp. 172–173; Erwin Steiner testimony, in Gorodemczyk, "Berihat Tnu'ot Hano'ar," pp. 48–50.

Survival in Hashomer Hatzair and Dror

A different picture emerges from the testimonies of members of Hashomer Hatzair and Dror. While the members of Hanoar Hatzioni were already on their way to Vienna, Germany, and Slovakia, the remaining members of the other movements were still looking for a solution to the problem of daily existence, mainly finding places to hide from the Germans. The reasons for this radically different pattern of action is clear: the leaderships of these movements were completely decimated along with most of the active adult class, the *Aktiva*. There were only a few women left from the leading ranks: Chajka and Dorka Herzberg from Hashomer, and Aliza Zeytenfeld and Chawka Lenczner from Dror. Chajka, Dorka, and Aliza had all lost their male companions and were mired in the bog of personal grief. It would be a while before they would recover enough strength to take on new responsibilities.

New faces, therefore, had to step into the center of activity, among them Meir Schulman from Chrzanów, who had not been a member prior to the deportation. Schulman, a quick-witted man who knew how to manage in any situation, was the first to find a hiding place on the Aryan side, and it was through him that contact was made with the comrades in the liquidation camps. Schulman also proved to be an excellent organizer, and his initiatives and resourcefulness were of great help to the group members. Nevertheless, it was clear that he could not fill the void left by those who had been lost—Frumka and Herszel, Zvi and David.

The main source of the group's ability to survive now was the courage and efficiency of the members of the "Aryan group" from Sosnowiec who had gathered in Zawiercie—Fela Katz, Kasia Szancer, and Shmuel Rozencwajg. However, even these younger activists, could not serve as a replacement for the lost leadership, and it is, therefore, not surprising that they failed to organize as quickly and efficiently as the Hanoar Hatzioni members. What is astounding is that these broken and tattered remnants of a movement managed to come together and organize at all.

The first shelter was found—as mentioned—by Meir Schulman in the home of the Nowak family in Będzin, where he hid with his wife Nechama. Thanks to this information, it seems that the members began to escape one by one from the liquidation camps and reached Meir Schulman at the Nowaks'. Chajka was among the first to get out, and she hid there for a few days. However, there was not enough space in the Nowaks' home to accommodate everyone who had escaped. Mrs. Nowak did not trust those hiding in her home. She revealed herself to be of a greedy and nervous disposition.[13] According to Fela Katz's testimony, when Chajka arrived there, she feared that the appearance of a Jew would endanger the rest of the household.[14] It was, therefore, necessary to find additional hiding places.

At an earlier date, Kasia and Fela had made connections with the Kobylec family, miners from the village of Michałkowice (today, Siemianowice Śląskie), who for whatever reasons were considered suspicious elements by the Germans—their certificates were stamped with the word "stateless." Expecting to be deported, they felt a closeness to the persecuted Jews. When the son Mietek (Mieczysław) Kobylec brought these two Jewish girls to the family home and presented one of them—Fela Katz—as his fiancée, the father Piotr suggested that Kasia should hide in their home as well: "I can't throw them out," he said.[15] Numerous other testimonies point to old Piotr's sympathy for the Jews and his hostility toward the Germans. According to one such testimony, Kobylec considered the rescue of Jewish people "a Polish patriotic duty that is part and parcel of the war for the Polish people's liberation from the yoke of the Nazi enslavers and an important human act."[16] The Kobylec family's willingness to help went in the face of great risk—people caught hiding Jews in Poland were sentenced to death.

With the Kobylecs' assistance, two new hiding places were arranged—one in the family's home in Michałkowice and the other in the house of Piotr's daughter Klara in the town of Dąbrówka.[17] It was decided that the comrades who had gathered at the Nowak's home should move on, and Chajka and Chawka were transferred to Dąbrówka. Chajka arrived there with Fela Katz.[18]

Others headed to Zawiercie. However, on August 25, 1943, the last deportation in the area was carried out, and the Zawiercie ghetto was liquidated. Aharon Brandes and little Esterka who had been sent there

13 In reference to a later period, see D. Liwer, *Ir Hametim*, pp. 171–172.

14 Fela Katz interview.

15 Anna Poray, "Kobylec, Piotr; Kobylec, Karolina (wife); Kobylec-Banasik, Klara (daughter); Kobylec, Mieczysław (son); Kobylec, Wiktor (son)," Polish Righteous: Those Who Risked Their Life, http://www.savingjews.org/righteous/kv.htm (accessed May 6, 2024). The author relies extensively on Władysław Bartoszewski and Zofia Lewin, eds., *How Poles Helped the Jews, 1939–1945* (London: Earlscourt Publications, 1969).

16 Fela Katz interview; Miriam (Kasia) Barenblatt interview; Shmuel Ron, in *Sefer Sosnovitz*, vol. 2, p. 184.

17 Lenczner, "Parashat Bendin," p. 134.

18 Fela Katz interview.

were forced to return to Będzin.[19] At this point, Shmuel Rozencwajg and probably Dorka Herzberg, who had been in Zawiercie since the beginning of August, also returned to Będzin. The arrival of Rozencwajg, with his Aryan appearance and experience as a former key activist in the Sosnowiec *ken*, served to stabilize the movement's activity. He acted as a liaison between the liquidation camp and the various groups in hiding. The three liaisons from the "Aryan group"—Kasia Szancer, Fela Katz, and Sara Kukielka—worked with him.

The main locus of activity was at the Kobylec house in Michałkowice, which turned out to be the safest. The Kobylecs did not underestimate the value of the money paid to them, but, as mentioned, they also acted with patriotic and humanitarian motives. Schulman and his wife also came to this hideout, as did all those escaping from the liquidation camp from this point on.[20] By the beginning of September 1943, about twenty members of Hashomer Hatzair, Dror, and Gordonia were housed in the various hiding places in Będzin, Katowice, Michałkowice, and Dąbrówka.[21] About twenty other members were still in the liquidation camps, but contact with them was maintained.

Condemned to Life

Shortly after arriving in the village of Dąbrówka, Chajka began writing her diary. The house belonged to Mrs. Klara Banasik (née Kobylec), the aforementioned daughter of Piotr Kobylec, who was considered a *Volksdeutsche* because her husband had served in the German army.[22] Her apartment was quite spacious, and Chajka enjoyed relatively good living conditions, including a radio receiver in her room. Still, even here she had to remain cautious. Fela Katz remembered that when the neighbors came over to visit the owner of the house, Chajka had to hide standing in the closet for hours on end. Only when the neighbor left would the signal be given, and Chajka could leave the closet. She was happy to have

19 Brandes, *Ketz Hayehudim*, p. 87; Lenczner, "Parashat Bendin," p. 134.

20 Shmuel Ron, in *Sefer Sosnowitz*, vol. 2, pp. 183–184; Meir and Nechama Schulman interview.

21 Poray, "Kobylec," Polish Righteous: Those Who Risked Their Life, http://www.savingjews.org/righteous/kv.htm (accessed May 6, 2024).

22 Chajka refers to the owner of the house as "a German woman," hence we can conclude that she considered Banasik to be *Volksdeutsche*. Klinger, *I Am Writing These Words to You* (1943 diaries), p. 47.

visits from Fela. Chajka, who could not go out on the street because of her "Jewish" appearance, told Fela that her visits were like a dose of sunshine, "like a light that suddenly appears."[23]

Much of her time was occupied with writing. Her friends knew that Chajka was recording their stories. This may have been the reason for the relatively good conditions of her hiding place. Some of her comrades were not so lucky. Aharon Brandes and Abraham Zilberstein, for example, were hiding out in a columbarium (located in the Kobylec attic). Shmuel Rozencwajg later noted:

> Chajka Klinger belonged to the few who were "condemned to life" for the sake of witnessing and telling. In every movement there were few who were chosen for this position. As far as I know, those "condemned to life" would usually appeal their "verdict." No *hagana* person wanted to stay alive after the death of their friends and relatives. This was true of Chajka.[24]

The role assigned to Chajka was similar to the one assigned to Hańcia Płotnicka and Mira Fuchrer in Warsaw, who were obliged by the ŻOB's orders to stay alive despite their wish to the contrary.[25] Chajka would later recall a certain Rachel, a member of Hashomer Hatzair from Warsaw who had joined the partisans in the summer of 1942, "a future genius of the shomer movement, who wrote beautifully, and other very valuable individuals."[26] Hańcia, Frumka, and Rachel all perished in battle in the forest and in the ghetto.

If before she refused to survive and testify, she now accepted the verdict. Again, it was not about saving herself while her friends continued to fight. Her friends were among the dead, and she was tasked with telling their stories. And so, while the younger comrades were preoccupied with the struggle of daily existence, the hardships of which made them forget for a moment the wounds of the recent past, her mission was to revisit all that pain and death.

Only now did the magnitude of her loss and the depth of her loneliness enter her consciousness. She who did not cry in front of the

23 Fela Katz interview.

24 Ron, "Im Hofa'at Yoman Hageto shel Chajka Klinger," pp. 21–22.

25 Lubetkin, *Aharonim al Hahoma*, p. 46.

26 Klinger, *I Am Writing These Words to You* (1943 diaries), p. 104. The identity of Rachel is unknown.

German investigators, nor when Zvi died, who had hardened her heart against the wails and sobs of her friends, now cried for the first time while listening to music on the radio receiver. She who had not shed a tear for her family now looked in the face of the proprietress's young son, and realized that the now ten-year-old Malka and little Tamusia, whom she had loved so much, were gone. The composition of her movement's history became for her a long and painful journey of self-awareness. Her descriptions are saturated with bitter and cruel judgment. Description became judgment, and judgment became description. And so, she began to write:

> *Thursday, August 26, 1943*
> So I am alive?! Am I? After all those experiences, I have broken free from that circle, that ambience of death, from the deportation point and I'm sitting here. Alone with Chawka [Lenczner] in a room, detached from the whole [living] world, in silence and peace. I'm resting. I'm resting. I'm living. Apparently, I have already forgotten what "life" means in a normal language.
>
> I am twisting and turning as if in a nightmare because I can still see the barrack full of people, the elderly and the children. That screaming before death, those silent complaints and that quiet waiting for the truck, that is, for death. I can still see the empty, ruined houses; everything turned upside down, the knocked-over furniture such as chairs, stools, eiderdowns, pillows, underwear, clothes, shirts, and silks. Everything lying discarded on the ground. The whole Jewish settlement is deserted, terrifying and dead. There is emptiness and deathly silence wherever you turn your head. Emptiness. Once it was such a blissful place: lots of people, laughter and joy, the cheerful noise of children and now there is this emptiness. Can you imagine it? A vast area covered with houses, so close to one another, so squeezed and not a living soul inside. The houses radiate such absolute, utter horror. And when you go in, you immediately rush out as if hit by a bullet—deathly stuffiness has wafted over you. It is a corpse; old with a yellow face peeking out of the bed. You want to run away, far away, to the end of the world, but you cannot, because they are watching you.
>
> Such images haunt and nag at you. Both by night and by day. And have you already forgotten for a moment the time when we were on our hands and knees outside the barracks [and] when they called out four boys? "At last," you think, relieved. "[They are being

> taken] to be executed." But they come out carrying the corpse of Cwi our dear companion and leader.
>
> And when you looked into the distance, you saw that small house where 12 of your dearest ones died. I'm not thinking anything. I'm twisting and turning as if in a dream. You must not think. Otherwise you will scream, shout, cry, and pull your hair out—either fly into a rage or commit suicide. I think about it a lot. Why? What do I live for? I have lost everything and everybody for whom I wanted to live and for whom life was worth living. The nation is no more. I've lost so much time. Why that path and not another? The path of *Hashomer Hatzair*. I wanted to and I did come to love the Jewish nation. I abandoned the idea of studying, and the idea of a career. The departure for *hachshara* [training] and then to *Eretz* [land (of Israel); also country, homeland]. And now the nation is no more. Seven [*sic*] million Jews deported, murdered, annihilated.
>
> I've lost my family—parents, sister, brother-in-law, and those children, who were so dear to me. I've lost the man whom I loved so much, without whom I neither imagined life, nor wanted to live. He was my companion, friend, and lover. I've lost my beloved companions who were so dear to me.
>
> So what am I living for and why? How can I justify my miserable existence? Initially, I used to say, "I want to live to be able to do something, to take part in *hagana*." And today, when it's already over, why don't you, you miserable creature, have the courage to put an end to your life? I'll try to justify myself, but it won't be true, because deep at heart I want to live. Why and what for? Because of my memory of them, my companions. They had always wanted, and they crammed that into my head day and night, somebody to stay alive and tell their stories. Why shouldn't they come back to life at least on paper? But why should I live forever with the horror of those days and that unfulfilled task?[27]

The necessity of writing seems to have led her to thoughts of suicide for the first time. She had to write because it was the sole remaining reason for her existence, but as the stories were written down, that reason gradually evaporated. The plight of the community was calling for her memories to come to its aid, and these memories overwhelmed her.

27 Ibid., pp. 25–28.

Honest testimony always involves soul-searching, a task that proved unbearably difficult for Chajka:

> Have I fulfilled my duties? I'm so happy that I was accused. It was a kind of debt, which I'm paying off now. It is a debt to *hagana*. I did not beg them. I did not cry in front of them. I walked calmly, silently, without fear.
>
> I ate an apple before I went in. And then they were hitting me, smacking me on the head and face. Even though they injured me so severely, I felt so deeply satisfied. I endured and now I know that I shall endure even worse. I do not need cyanide. That test of mine is a justification of my still being alive today. Perhaps tomorrow I already won't be. They might discover us. And it will all be over. And that debt to my comrades, my comrades who were dearer to me than anything else—is it true? Yes. I loved my poor old father, so why did his passing not hurt me so much? Why am I not always thinking about them [my family]? […]
>
> My dear ones, I can hear music here, in this room and everything inside me tears apart and tugs so and a miracle [has happened]. I've been hard as a rock. I have not cried (except once). But now I've started crying. It's the music. Unheard for four years, it exposed my miserable, inhuman loneliness.
>
> My dear ones, deported, executed comrades; I have a debt with you—to tell of your lives and deaths.
>
> I do not want you to depart forgotten. I want you to come back to life on paper, in people's memories, in the hearts and souls of our companions who are there, far away.
>
> I want your memory to be celebrated, your names to be respected and loved.
>
> But am I capable of it? I have already wanted to put down my pen a few times. I know I am incapable. The words I am writing are chaotic. Chaos still pervades in my heart and soul. One image chases another. I keep having horrible nightmares, too…[28]

Beyond the nightmares that the task of writing and recollecting provoked, she had to find suitable words in which to put these stories down on paper. Would language, which is the main implement of reason, be able

28 Ibid., pp. 28–29.

to grasp a reality that was now devoid of reason all together? Can one use rational means to express a total lack of rationality?

> And isn't the human language too simple to tell all this?
>
> Human language is too inadequate to properly express all that must be told. Indeed every word and expression seems too pale and inappropriate to render our feelings and what we really [went through].
>
> For words able to render our epoch have not been born. [Nor are there words] to render the situation, destiny, and demise of the Jewish nation in this epoch.
>
> I don't want to embellish. I do not want even the slightest exaggeration in my story. I want to depict the naked truth, but I am lost for words, lost for words to describe those horrible days and our terrible experiences. As I have said, the human language was not created for our times. Language and literature grew from a certain reality and conditions. This reality and these conditions are without precedent. Or am I mistaken?[29]

By the end of August 1943, Chajka was certain that there were no more Jews left in Europe, and that with the people, her own movement Hashomer Hatzair had also been lost. Hence, her return to a familiar question: Is there a point in the existence of the avant-garde after the death of its people? Of course, the avant-garde had to die, but it had to die a certain way:

> The whole nation in the European countries [has been annihilated]. There are no Jews in the territories occupied by the Germans. There is no Jewish youth. There is no Hechalutz movement. There is no Hashomer Hatzair movement. The flower of Jewish youth—that which was the most beautiful in our nation, and not only in our nation—[is gone]. Surely in the course of many centuries no such movement or such people have ever been born.
>
> Our movement has died, perished together with the nation (*shtrift fon hertzen*) [Yid. writings from the heart].
>
> But it had to be so. It is good that it happened so.
>
> If there is no nation, there is no need for its avant-garde. What was it for if not for the nation?![30]

29 Ibid., pp. 29–30.
30 Ibid., p. 31.

And so, she told story after story, without sparing herself or her readers a single gruesome detail. Everything had to be said, everything had to be written down, even the most difficult and painful things. She was aware that she was erecting a mausoleum for her friends, but she decided not to be tempted by either glorification or sentimentality. She described Dunski and Lipek as heroes, but explicitly stated that their deaths are "a dark stain on the history of our movement."[31] She described Mordechai Anielewicz with great admiration but did not hold back her criticism of his reckless daredevilry and fickleness. Even Josef Kaplan, whom she loved, is described as she knew him: a good and benevolent man, but not one who could lead the uprising.

The composition of the diaries was a way of reckoning with both her own and her comrades' actions in relation to the central idea that had guided her actions over the past years—the idea of *hagana*. Therefore, it is not surprising that they are full of bitterness and rage. They were not always written in the order in which the events occurred, and yet she insisted on precision not only in capturing the spirit of things but also in the smallest of details. She described living people. She described the horrifying minutia of death. She kept only one piece of the story to herself, as if shielding her most painful intimacy from the curious reader—she did not tell the story of her family. This may be related to the fact that by now, she already knew what had become of them. Later, she told Shmuel Rozencwajg about the death of her four-year-old niece in the bunker.[32] This was the one subject she could not deal with. It was too painful, literally too close to home. It is only unwittingly that sometimes glimpses of it emerged through the lines: "I loved my poor old father, so why did his passing not hurt me so much?"[33]

Her sense of loss appears to have been inextricably entwined with severe feelings of guilt. The dual attitude of the revolutionary toward the people—the attitude of contempt and disgust, on the one hand, and a deep love and willingness to sacrifice, on the other—must have plunged her into a terrible conflict when it came to her relationship with her family. Everything she criticized and hated about her people was embodied in her own family. Her father had been a living emblem of Diaspora Judaism. Her sister had abandoned her daughters in a time of crisis. She loved them, but she had to distance herself from them. Shortly

31 Ibid., p. 111.

32 Shmuel Ron interview.

33 Klinger, *I Am Writing These Words to You* (1943 diaries), p. 29.

before the deportation, however, she had come back to the family home, and relations between them had grown warmer. She even prepared a hiding place for them in a bunker. Still, when the order came, she hid in a bunker with her comrades, ready for armed defense, which was never really put into practice. Irka and Lea preferred to be with their father in his last moments, whereas Chajka made a different choice. And precisely because of that, she was granted life. She never admitted that this life came with the terrible burden of guilt.

Yet there was no choice but to continue writing, sometimes as if possessed by the words themselves, sometimes in the grips of horror and hatred, torturing herself with reproaches of inadequacy:

> God, how very inadequate my words are. Am I able to express what was happening in the souls of the handful of people who were dearest to me? Am I able to express the greatness of their souls? I haven't written for such a long, long time.
>
> Am I not too small a mortal to comprehend and express the breadth of their horizons and their greatness? Surely I am. [...]
>
> So who should I be writing all this for?
>
> Perhaps for my American brothers. Ha-ha-ha! For those fat apes, who tap their bellies with watch chains on them, who think, "If only the Polish Jews went to [Mandatory] Palestine." I hate them. But who do I actually love? How do I not hate? Yes, there was a period when I hated everything and everybody. I was raging with madness and vengeance, that bloody, merciless vengeance. [...]
>
> And then I came to this house. To a German woman, though not native, and her child. She's good to us like a sister. Could I do her any harm? Or harm her child? But when I look at this child, pale and somehow weak, I can see those Jewish children with their rosy cheeks and lively, black eyes. Our sweet, little Tamusia [Mgła]. My heart's aching so much, so much. But I wouldn't be able to hurt this child. I've even grown fond of her. She's not to blame that the world's so cruel, so unjust.[34]

Her hatred was that of a victim toward those who did not share her fate—an intuitive hatred born out of irrational acts of violence, a hatred that creates an unbridgeable chasm between those living in "normal" places and times and those who had been "there." "I'm writing so chaotically, and

34 Ibid., pp. 45–47.

I'm diverting from the topic," Chajka reminds herself, and immediately adds: "Who will understand this epoch? Cwi had a dream, and so did Dawid. I'd like to see somebody from the Kibbutz Artzi [Hakibbutz Ha'artzi] someday. Am I writing for them? Yes, for them. Perhaps they'll understand. If not, then I think I'll have to blow my brains out."[35]

And as she wrote, she had no way of knowing that in the mountains on the Slovakian border, there were organized smuggling stations already up and running. Little by little, with their help, the survivors of Będzin were escaping to the road that led to life.

35 Ibid., pp. 47–48.

Chapter Twenty-Two

The Survivor

The Slovakian Working Group

In the summer of 1943, there were 25,000 Jews living in Slovakia in relative safety. The great wave of deportations that took place in the summer of 1942 had taken with it the majority of the country's Jewry—approximately 65,000 people. Most of those remaining, however, were protected either by official certificates or by passing themselves off as Christians. The surviving Slovakian Jewish leadership credited this, among other things, to the success of its efforts. In Slovakia, under the pro-Nazi state ruled by an autonomous Catholic-Fascist regime, the Ústredňa Židov (the Jewish Center, ÚŽ) was established in September 1940.[1] In terms of its authority and organizational structure, it was the Slovakian equivalent of the Judenrat in Poland. However, while this body fulfilled the orders of the Slovak authorities regarding the confiscation of Jewish property and the organization of deportations to Poland, an alternative leadership sprung up within it. In the spring of 1941, members of the ÚŽ created a "Working Group" that operated illegally. Its key activists included Oskar Neumann, Gisi Fleischmann, and Rabbi Michael Dov Weissmandel. The fact that this organization operated on both levels allowed it a great degree of flexibility and effectiveness in ensuring the rescue and survival of Slovakian Jews. The Working Group became a kind of shadow government and gained the trust of the surviving Slovak Jews.[2]

1 Gila Fatran, *Ha'im Ma'avak al Hisardut: Hanhagat Yehudey Slovakia Bashoah 1938–1940* (Hebrew) (Tel Aviv: Moreshet and Hamahon LeYehadut Zmanenu, Tel Aviv University, 1992), pp. 35–36.

2 Ibid., pp. 163–169.

The Working Group operated in several areas simultaneously: organizing work camps in Slovakia designed to protect everyone who could be saved from the threat of deportation; delivery of material aid to deportees whom they believed to be living somewhere in the camps in Poland; attempting to bribe Dieter Wisliceny, a member of the SS, so that he would stop the transports. They also sought to obtain funds from Jewish organizations abroad, mainly the Joint. In time, Rabbi Weissmandel went so far as to develop an initiative called the "Europa Plan"—a grandiose plan designed to save all remaining European Jews through strategic bribery. However, the initiative was not implemented, and the reasons for its failure remain controversial.[3]

At the end of the summer of 1943, the members of the Working Group took on a new and unusual task: taking in Jewish refugees who were beginning to trickle in from Poland. The Working Group would meet these refugees at the border crossings, transfer them to a safe place in Slovakia, and then smuggle them across the border to Hungary, which was considered safer at that time, the sword of deportation having spared it almost entirely. On September 1, 1943, Gisi Fleischmann informed the Hechalutz center in Geneva that approximately 200 refugees from Poland had arrived in Slovakia, care of the Working Group. Three reports were attached to the letter: one on the events in Będzin and Sosnowiec, the second on the deportations from Slovakia, and the third on the Łódź ghetto. These reports confirmed the existence of extermination camps. Fleischman already knew the names of most of them: Sobibor, Treblinka, Bełżec, and Auschwitz.[4]

The Road to Slovakia

As mentioned, at the end of August 1943, Chaim Tenenwurcel and Alex Gutman, members of Hanoar Hatzioni in Będzin, arrived in Žilina in Slovakia. The first to cross the border after Gutman and Tenenwurcel were Tosia Gutman and her mother Rela. Too impatient to await the news

3 Ibid., pp 185–192; Porat, *Hanhaga Bemilkud*, pp. 328–346; Beit Zvi, *Post-Ugandan Zionism on Trial*, pp. 338–350. The "Europa Plan" sparked great controversy regarding the ability and willingness of the Yishuv to save Jews during the Holocaust.

4 Letter from Gisi Fleischmann to the Hechalutz center in Geneva, September 1, 1943, in Livia Rothkirchen, *Horban Yehudey Slovakia: Ti'ur Histori Beteudot* (Hebrew) (Jerusalem: Yad Vashem, 1961), pp. 231–234. The report on the events in Będzin and Sosnowiec is probably referring to that made by Alex and Tosia Gutman. See Gutman and Gutman-Herzberg, "Bageto Bendin: Protocol," pp. 172–179.

from Slovakia, Tosia and her mother decided to go out with smugglers whom they contacted through Kuba Rosenberg. They walked until they reached a small village at the foot of a mountain on the Slovak side. Tosia decided to go on to Žilina and try to make contact with the Jews there. Once there, she made contact with Alex Hauser, who helped her arrange Rela's transport, and soon the family was reunited.[5]

The two met with Chaim Tenenwurcel as he was setting out on his journey back to Poland, which happened to be his last. Later it would come to light that he was captured and executed; however, from the Slovakian side it looked like his mission had gone well. People from Hanoar Hatzioni in Będzin kept coming from the mountain passes. The bribed gendarmes would bring them to a hiding place in Žilina, and from there the Working Group activists would smuggle them to hideouts in Prešov and other towns. After a short stay in Slovakia they would be smuggled a second time, this time across the Hungarian border. By mid-October, around forty Jews had arrived from Będzin and its surroundings, as Gisi Fleischmann reported to Istanbul. An approximately equal number were on their way, and another 150—according to the report—were hiding in the woods.[6]

Refusal to Leave

The arriving Hanoar Hatzioni activists gave detailed accounts of the events taking place in Zagłębie. The Slovakian Jews now had a complete picture of the Holocaust in Będzin, as well as the first details of the defensive actions and survival of a small group of youth resistance fighters. The letters sent from Slovakia to Istanbul in mid-October 1943, repeatedly mention a group of around fifteen Hashomer and Dror people hiding out in the Będzin area. However, as most of the authors point out with bewilderment, these activists were refusing to come out of their hiding place in order to reach Slovakia.[7]

Contact with this group was maintained mainly through Josef Korniański, a Hechalutz man from Warsaw, who had arrived in Slovakia

5 Gutman and Gutman-Herzberg, "Bageto Bendin: Protocol," p. 177.

6 Letter from Gisi Fleischmann to Istanbul, October 17, 1943, GFH, Hechalutz Archive, 38137.

7 See letter from Josef Korniański to Istanbul, October 15, 1943, and letter from Moshe Dachs to Istanbul, October 18, 1943, GFH, Hechalutz Archive, 29757-IV.

as early as March 17, 1941.[8] Eager to help his fellow Jews, Korniański soon became involved in the activities of the pioneer organizations in Slovakia. His close acquaintance with the comrades in Poland made him an important liaison.

Korniański's correspondence with Poland at this time went mainly through Będzin. There must have been no contacts left in Warsaw. Therefore, he was determined to do as much as possible for the Będzin resistance. According to him, in the first half of 1943, in collaboration with the Hechalutz people in Slovakia, he sent no less than three messengers to Będzin. At least one of these missions appears to have been coordinated together with the delegation in Istanbul. However, all three messengers failed to reach their targets. One was shot, the second was unable to find the activists, and the third was caught and transferred to the Gestapo for interrogation in Vienna, where Korniański's name was passed on to the Slovak police.

During this period, contact between Będzin and Istanbul also ceased. A courier had delivered the last letter from Frumka and her friends, sent on July 17, 1943, announcing the death of the comrades in battle in Poland in early August. "Our hopes of meeting our homeland will not be fulfilled," the letter read.[9] About a week later, Wenia Pomeranz and Menahem Bader sent a letter of reply. In it, they tried to bolster the spirits of the people of Będzin and suggest ways of escape.[10] However, by the time it was sent out—August 10, 1943—most of its recipients were no longer alive. A month later, Nathan Schwalb in Geneva informed Pomeranz that the twenty-two postcards and letters he had recently sent to Będzin were returned to sender. The letters bore the notice: "Addressee absent or departed to unknown destination."[11]

At the beginning of September, a number of postcards from Hungary and Slovakia arrived in Istanbul, announcing the arrival of the first refugees from Będzin but also delivering information about the extermination and the attempted *hagana* in Będzin. Pomeranz and Bader reported to *Eretz Israel*: "Some have managed to escape and we

8 Korniański, *Beshlihut Halutzim*, pp. 87–88.

9 Zariz, *Mihtevey Halutzim*, pp. 200–202.

10 Letters from the Istanbul delegation to Poland, August 10, 1943, Moreshet Archive, Rescue Committee of the Jewish Agency in Istanbul, 149485.

11 Letter from Nathan Schwalb to Wenia Pomeranz, September 17, 1943, Moreshet Archive, Rescue Committee of the Jewish Agency in Istanbul, 149516, p. 19.

are eagerly awaiting news from Bratislava to see if anyone has arrived."[12] Korniański in Budapest also had good news to report: a steady stream of people was arriving from Będzin. But his joy was mixed with grief as these survivors gave, confirmed, and added details about the death of his friends. Korniański's letter to Pomeranz in mid-October hinted (probably based on the survivors' testimonies) that rescue was not at the top of their priorities: "I am sure they tried to do all they could to save themselves," Korniański wrote in Hebrew, "but were unlucky. All their efforts were directed toward *hagana*, which is where they invested a large proportion of the funds they received."[13]

Moshe Dachs, a rescue activist in Slovakia, thought otherwise. Around the same time, he wrote to Istanbul in outright fury:

> But regarding Będzin, I would like to add just a few words. An atmosphere of heroism has developed in our movement, and that is why our members did not pass [across the border], but died defending the honor of Judaism. In Będzin, there are fifteen more members of Ya'ari [Hashomer Hatzair], who are afraid to come, even though Nathan wrote to them to come to us. The incoming friends [Hanoar Hatzioni] also invited them to come with them, and they did not want to come.[14]

Dachs's Hebrew, written in Latin letters, makes it difficult to understand the spirit of what he wished to convey. Did he see the Będzin survivors as heroes who were refusing to cross the border because of their desire to die for the honor of their people? Or did he mean to say that the Będzin people were simply afraid to come out of hiding, contrary to the heroic spirit of Polish Jewry? Oskar Krasnianski, who sent a similar report to Istanbul only five days later, believed that fear was the reason behind the Hashomer Hatzair people's reluctance to flee across the border. It would appear that Krasnianski was quite well informed: he named Chajka as the leader of the group.[15]

12 Letter from Wenia Pomeranz and Menahem Bader to Hakibbutz Hameuchad and Hakibbutz Ha'artzi, September 9, 1943, Moreshet Archive, Rescue Committee of the Jewish Agency in Istanbul, 149394, p. 35.

13 Letter from Josef Korniański to Istanbul, October 15, 1943, GFH, Hechalutz Archive, 29757-IV.

14 Letter from Moshe Dachs to Istanbul, October 18, 1943, GFH, Hechalutz Archive, 29757-IV, p. 27.

15 Letter from Oskar Krasnianski to Istanbul, October 23, 1943, GFH, Hechalutz Archive, 29757-IV.

In Istanbul, Bader and Pomeranz read Dachs's letter to mean that the remaining fighters in Będzin had decided to die a heroic death. Bader asked the leadership in Slovakia to reach out and convince the fighters to flee to Slovakia: "We will need their bravery in our Jewish struggle, which will not end with the end of the war and the coming of victory."[16] Bader did not believe in the valor of suicide.[17] He wanted to see his people alive. None of the members of Hashomer Hatzair or Dror had arrived from Poland. Bader and Pomeranz knew about the battles that had taken place in the ghettos, but they were yet to see any of the members of their movements who survived them.

At the end of November or the beginning of December 1943, news reached the delegation in Istanbul about the presence of a Hashomer group in Będzin and their refusal to cross the border to Slovakia. Dachs even pointed out bitterly that the messenger sent to them, Chaim Tenenwurcel, had been captured and killed, and even though he "gave his life for them," they were refusing to leave.[18] Korniański in Budapest, who relied on other sources, wrote in his letter the correspondence address of Fela Katz and noted that a messenger had been sent to them.[19] In Istanbul, there formed a strong impression that the people of Będzin had decided to die a heroic death rather than be saved. At the end of December, Bader and Pomeranz wrote to *Eretz Israel*: "We told them it wasn't a personal rescue, that we want to save them as an asset to the nation, to the movement, so that they can at least tell us everything they have been through and everything they have been carrying since the beginning of the devastation. Will they listen to us? Who knows."[20]

16 Bader, *Shlihuyot Atzuvot*, p. 91.

17 In a letter that Bader sent to *Eretz Israel* immediately after the Warsaw Ghetto Uprising, he wrote about his reservations of the meaning of the act: "It was not an uprising. It was a resistance and not the first of its kind in Warsaw and other places. And are those who died in the resistance more important than those who died because they were always on the road and risking their lives? Were they more important than those who were led like sheep to the slaughter?" Letter from Menahem Bader to Abramek, April 23, 1943, Moreshet Archive, D.1.700/A.

18 Letter from Moshe Dachs to Istanbul, December 4, 1943, GFH, Hechalutz Archive, 29757-IV, p. 50.

19 Letter from Josef Korniański to Istanbul, November 30, 1943, and December 1, 1943, GFH, Hechalutz Archive.

20 Letter from Menahem Bader and Wenia Pomeranz to dear friends (in *Eretz Israel*), December 31, 1943, GFH, Hechalutz Archive.

Chajka and the Pioneer Resistance in Będzin

To this day, we do not know why the Hashomer Hatzair group chose not to escape through Slovakia in October 1943. It is also unclear on what information Dachs and Korniański based their opinions regarding the matter and its reliability. Tenenwurcel most likely failed to reach the Hashomer people, since none of the many testimonies given by the survivors mention his name. Despite the news that the Hanoar Hatzioni people brought with them to Slovakia regarding their Hashomer Hatzair friends, the two groups operated separately.[21] Later, Leon Blatt, who coordinated rescue operations for Hanoar Hatzioni, would say: "I had to save my people first."[22] His and his friends' efforts bore fruit: Between October and December 1943, the members of Hanoar Hatzioni transferred a total of thirty-five people to Slovakia, including a number of parents and relatives of the group's members.[23]

Chajka did not record this period in her diary. Testimonies indicate that during this time, she only left her hiding place when it was time to find another. After leaving Dąbrówka, she joined the bunker dug under the Kobylec house in Michałkowice. Most of her time was devoted to writing. The private craft of composition had now taken on the character of a collective enterprise. Shmuel Rozencwajg would later recall: "Often, when writing a new chapter, Chajka would present it to a small circle of friends, and then shared memories would surface and find their way, in one form or another, into the 'diary.' The whole group shared a single concern: that Chajka and her diaries stay alive!"[24] Aharon Brandes and Fela Katz also remembered the group readings.[25]

The further Chajka progressed in her writing, the more she freed herself from the darkness to which her first words had drawn her. Having unloaded her emotional burden in the first pages of the diary, the work of documenting became a soothing process. Fela, Kasia, and Shmuel, who were with her during those days, did not remember her being depressed. On the contrary, she regretted her inability to do more for the group. Kasia remembered Chajka helping her take off her

21 According to Fredka Mazia, who was the "liaison" for Hanoar Hatzioni, she had no knowledge of the existence of the underground resistance group. Fredka Mazia interview.

22 Leon Blatt interview.

23 Gutman and Gutman-Herzberg, "Bageto Bendin: Protocol," p. 174.

24 Ron, "Im Hofa'at Yoman Hageto shel Chajka Klinger," pp. 21–22.

25 Fela Katz interview; Aharon Brandes, interview by the author, Negba, 1985.

clothes when she returned from her missions and rushing off to wash them. Her Jewish appearance may have prevented her from moving about on the streets, but she wanted to feel useful, sometimes to Kasia's annoyance: "Why are you taking my clothes off," she would grumble, "I was going to sleep in them."[26]

Was Chajka the leader of the group? Krasnianski's letter from Slovakia implies that she was perceived as such, at least from the outside. The two young female liaisons of Hashomer Hatzair continued to treat her as an authoritative figure: according to Fela Katz, Chajka was "the group's heart and brain." Although the liaisons usually operated independently, Fela mentioned a particular case in which—under Chajka's guidance—she went out to rescue Chana Wiernik from a labor camp in German-occupied Silesia. Fela managed to get to the camp, make contact with Chana, and transfer a letter, food, and money for the escape preparations into her hands. However, she never made it to the camp a second time, and the rescue attempt failed.[27] A later letter indicates that Chajka also tried to rescue Ada Neufeld from the liquidation camp through Fela's mediation and even sent her a sum of money for this purpose.[28] Kasia testified that at a certain point, when tensions arose in the group and she decided to go back to the liquidation camp, it was Chajka who sent her a note asking her to return.[29] The testimony of Abraham Izbicki, who arrived at the same hiding place at a later date, also shows that "Chajka was a central figure in the bunker."[30] It seems that Chajka also took an active part in organizing the economic life of the group in hiding, the narration of her diary often interrupted by lists of groceries and expenses.[31]

Diverse testimonies also emphasize the importance of Meir Schulman.[32] The technical and organizational skills of this young man,

26 Miriam (Kasia) Barenblatt interview.

27 Fela Katz interview. Chana Wiernik would later describe this daring attempt in detail: Fela arrived with Roman Kołodzi, a Pole who helped the group, at the labor camp. She managed to smuggle money, a letter, and food in to her. However, the Jewish police spotted them. One of them even wished to run away with Chana. But Fela was unable to return to the camp after Roman Kołodzi was captured. Schlesinger-Wiernik, *Hadapim Sheli*, pp. 116–121.

28 Letter from Chajka Klinger to Shraga Fruchtzweig, Kfar Saba, February 25, 1947, Moreshet Archive, Avihu Ronen collection, 235.

29 Miriam (Kasia) Barenblatt interview.

30 Abraham Izbicki testimony at the Barenblatt trial, Moreshet Archive, D.1.5366, p. 151.

31 Klinger, *I Am Writing These Words to You* (1943 diaries), pp. 88–89.

32 Shmuel Ron, in *Sefer Sosnovitz*, vol. 2, p. 184.

who never rose through the movement's ranks, were a primary factor in ensuring the survival of its members. Meir dug the bunker at the Kobylec home, assisted in the preparation of false papers, and coordinated financial activity. According to Fela, Chajka and Meir used to consult with one another, but there were also arguments between them that arose from differences in personality and movement affiliation.[33]

Was it Chajka who refused the repeated invitations from Slovakia and Istanbul to cross the border? According to her diaries, she no longer placed her trust in *Eretz Israel*, and accordingly, it is possible that her hesitation was based on ideological concerns. In any case, she did not attach much importance to personal rescue and perhaps believed that she and her friends should either stay in Poland and die there or be freed when the Red Army arrived. A letter sent from Slovakia a little later said of Chajka and her friends that due to the suffering they had undergone, they "hate the Jews, hate their weakness, and their only hope is the Red Army."[34] However, Fela Katz—with the benefit of hindsight—rejected all the above conjectures: "If only there was hope—we would have gone to Slovakia." She heard that Hanoar Hatzioni had a connection with the smugglers, but "we did not," and according to Fela, the voices calling from across the border to come over into Slovakia never reached their group members.[35]

Throughout this period, the group continued to maintain contact with the liquidation camps in Będzin and Środula. Fredka Oksenhendler, Józek Kożuch's widow and the Hanoar Hatzioni liaison who had returned to the Sosnowiec camp after being arrested and released from prison in early December, described the atmosphere in the liquidation camps in a manner similar to the one found in Chajka's diary: "The people got used to the conditions, new groups and families came together from the remains, and they lead a life of 'eat and drink because tomorrow we die.'"[36]

The camps were a temporary solution to the problem of existence. Some members of the pioneer youth movements who could not find another suitable hiding place also lived there. The group's liaisons would periodically venture into the liquidation camps and smuggle objects and

33 Fela Katz interview.

34 Letter from Ya'akov Rosenberg to Menahem Bader, Istanbul, January 3, 1944, Moreshet Archive, D.1.1124.4.

35 Fela Katz interview.

36 Mazia, *Re'im Basa'ar*, p. 246.

money out of them to support the survival of those in hiding. From time to time more people were smuggled out of the camps. Bribery was easily accomplished—from the relevant testimonies it appears that money was abundant in the liquidation camps.[37]

A special relationship had formed between the members of the group and Hirsch Barenblatt, the former head of the Jewish police in Będzin, who now held a position of authority in the camp. Barenblatt, who knew the members of the youth movements from his visits to the farm,[38] protected those who were with him in the liquidation camp by using his connections with the German camp commanders and probably also the money he had accumulated. Kasia, who was cut off from her comrades for a period of time, became Barenblatt's friend.[39] Through the liquidation camp there was also correspondence with Zivia Lubetkin in Warsaw, who used the channel to transfer the funds at her disposal.[40]

In November 1943, the members of the pioneering youth movements began to look for their own way to reach Slovakia. According to Renia Kukielka, this was due to the influence of the letters they received, in particular the message that arrived from Yitzhak Zuckerman and Zivia Lubetkin in Warsaw, saying they should move to Slovakia.[41] Later, a letter from Slovakia would state that the members of the group "decided to come but only after receiving an order from Zivia."[42] In the report she wrote in *Eretz Israel* about these events, Chajka would recount: "We received a message that we must move to Slovakia. December 1943." She did not specify who the author of the message was.[43] As she saw it, she had acted—as always—in accordance with the movement's orders.[44]

37 See D. Liwer, *Ir Hametim*, pp. 171–174.

38 Hirsch Barenblatt testimony at the Barenblatt trial, Moreshet Archive, D.1.5366; Kalman Balchasz testimony at the Barenblatt trial, Moreshet Archive, D.1.5366.

39 Miriam (Kasia) Barenblatt testimony at the Barenblatt trial, Moreshet Archive, D.1.5366.

40 D. Liwer, *Ir Hametim*, pp. 167–168; Kukielka, *Escape from the Pit*, p. 164.

41 Kukielka, *Escape from the Pit*, pp. 164–165.

42 Letter from Moshe Dachs to the delegation in Istanbul, January 5, 1944, GFH, Hechalutz Archive.

43 Chajka Klinger, Statements made at the Histadrut Operational Committee meeting, March 15, 1944, Moreshet Archive, C.53.1.24. See also chapter 24.

44 To this day, most accounts of the youth movement members' escape continue to ignore both their ties with the Jewish policemen and what appears to be the pioneer group's refusal to go to Slovakia. See Sarid, *Bemivhan Ha'anut Vehapedut*, pp. 502–506.

Rescue

The search for the road to Slovakia involved Renia Kukielka, who had just been freed from incarceration during a daring rescue operation. According to her testimony, she had learned that Hanoar Hatzioni had been smuggling people out of Poland for many weeks but were keeping their operations secret "and under no circumstances can we glean from them who these smugglers are."[45] Fela Katz also noted that "Hanoar Hatzioni had a connection with the smugglers. We didn't."[46] In the absence of information and contact, Kasia went into the mountains to locate possible smugglers, but she found no one who could be trusted.[47]

In the end, Mietek Kobylec and his friend Roman Kołodzi, a deserter from the German army, were the ones who made contact with reliable smugglers.[48] On December 10 or 11, a meeting was held in the Kobylecs' bunker. David Liwer, who had just arrived from the liquidation camp, participated in the meeting. An orderly consultation was held, and according to Liwer's testimony, Meir Schulman, Chajka Klinger, Aliza Zeytenfeld, and Chawka Lenczner all took an active part. Meir reported on the financial situation. They had a lot of money—roughly 120,000 Marks, according to Meir. A list of Jews to be extracted from the liquidation camp was drawn up, and there was talk of organizing the departure of the first group to Slovakia. Max Fischer and Abraham Izbicki were set to depart the next morning.[49] On December 12, Fischer and Izbicki reached Slovakia. The news of their arrival probably reached the messengers of the Working Group that same day, and they were welcomed in a village close to the border. There, Fischer and Izbicki sent letters to their friends in Poland and decided to wait for them to arrive. The smugglers returned to Będzin a week later, and their return caused great excitement. Immediate preparations were made for the departure of the second group.

The news of the smugglers' success caused a great stir of interest in the liquidation camp as well. Many asked to join the fugitives. Furthermore, rumors had begun to spread through the camp that its residents' days were numbered. The source of the rumors was Gestapo

45 Kukielka, *Escape from the Pit*, pp. 175–176.

46 Fela Katz interview.

47 Miriam (Kasia) Barenblatt interview.

48 Kukielka, *Escape from the Pit*, p. 176.

49 D. Liwer, *Ir Hametim*, p. 171.

officer Poltin, who was close to Barenblatt. One day in early December, Poltin called Barenblatt and informed him: "If the trousers are ready, we will come and collect them." In the code language they had agreed upon long ago, this meant that the final deportation was approaching.[50] That day, a group of twenty-eight people escaped from the liquidation camp, among them Barenblatt and another Jewish policeman Abram Potasz. They found a hiding place on the Aryan side, where they could await their departure to Slovakia. According to Kasia's testimony, the group escaped from the liquidation camp on December 9—before the first delegation left for Slovakia.[51]

The resistance activists and the Jewish policemen were not particularly fond of each other; however, in this new reality, they were forced to cooperate. The former needed the money and the connections of the latter; the latter wanted to use the escape route found by the former. According to Liwer, one day Kasia came to him and told him: "Mr. Barenblatt wants to live." Liwer proceeded to organize the removal of Barenblatt and his friends from the camp, and he then sent a note to the commander of the bunker to which they had arrived, instructing him to "take Barenblatt, Potasz, and Ehrlich for all they're worth and send them on."[52] The resistance activists managed to extort no less than 70,000 Marks from the Jewish policemen for the general fund.[53] Kasia did not recall this, but she noted the great assistance that Barenblatt had extended to the youth movement members earlier by virtue of his position and connections in the liquidation camp.[54] According to Kasia, it was Chajka who told her to give Barenblatt a gun in exchange for his help, and that was how the relationship between her and Barenblatt had started.[55]

The second group that was about to cross the border did not include any Jewish policemen. Naturally, priority was given to youth movement members, and among them to those with a particularly Jewish

50 In December 1943, 800 Jews were deported from Będzin to Auschwitz. In Sosnowiec, the deportations continued until July 23, 1944, by which date 638 Jews had been deported. It would seem that the liquidation camp in Sosnowiec continued to operate until July 19, 1944. On this date, 317 Jews were deported from Sosnowiec to Auschwitz. See Namysło, *Zagłada Żydów Zagłębiowskich*, p. 31.

51 Miriam (Kasia) Barenblatt testimony at the Barenblatt trial, Moreshet Archive, D.1.5366, p. 141; Miriam (Kasia) Barenblatt interview.

52 David Liwer testimony at the Barenblatt trial, Moreshet Archive, D.1.5366, p. 23.

53 Ibid.

54 Miriam (Kasia) Barenblatt testimony at the Barenblatt trial, Moreshet Archive, D.1.5366, p. 141.

55 Miriam (Kasia) Barenblatt interview.

appearance. The inclusion of Chajka in this group of refugees was of special importance: she was the one who would bring the story of the attempted uprising and the death of Zagłębien Jewry to the free world. Aharon Brandes and his sister Pesa (Pola), Chawka Lenczner from Dror, Renia Kukielka, and young Moshe (Monia) Hochenberg from Kibbutz Atid were also slated to cross the border with her. They were joined by Leon Markowicz who was close to the movement and another Jew whose name remains unknown to make eight in total. December 21, 1943, was set as the departure day.[56]

The journey across the border to Slovakia is not featured in Chajka's diary, but her friends would later describe it in detail. Renia Kukielka remembered the moment when Chawka Lenczner came to her and told her that she should get ready to go.[57] Renia, who was still recovering from her ordeal in prison, did not wish to leave. She hadn't seen her sister Sara, who was on a mission, in two weeks. Chawka and Aliza Zeytenfeld tried to reason with her and convince her that she should go. Both Aliza and Renia's sister Sara were still maintaining contact with the Kibbutz Atid children who were hiding in German peasants' homes. They would come too when they had managed to gather the children. Renia finally agreed to depart.[58]

At six in the morning, Renia and Chawka said goodbye to Mrs. Banasik in Dąbrówka. Mrs. Banasik was excited. She asked the girls to remember her after the war. According to Chajka, the members of the group wanted to take Mrs. Banasik with them to Slovakia.[59] Renia and Chawka walked to Michałkowice. At the train station they met with the other six, including Chajka and Aharon Brandes. Here they also met Mietek Kobylec. Together they boarded the train and traveled to Katowice. From there, they traveled again by train through Bielsko-Biała (Bielsku) to the village of Jeleśnią near the Slovak border. Mietek Kobylec handed them over to the smugglers and turned back, carrying a note to the comrades left behind. In the evening, they headed into the

56 The list of refugees in the second group is based on the testimonies of Renia Kukielka, David Liwer, and Chawka Lenczner.

57 Kukielka, *Escape from the Pit*, p. 177.

58 Ibid., pp. 177–178.

59 Chajka Klinger, statements made at the Histadrut Executive Committee meeting, March 15, 1944, Moreshet Archive, D.1.1051, p. 8. Banasik and her family would later be recognized by Yad Vashem as Righteous Among the Nations. YVA, M.31.2/86, https://collections.yadvashem.org/en/righteous/4044877 (accessed June 9, 2024).

mountains. There were twelve of them: the group of eight refugees, two smugglers, and two guides. For six hours they walked through snow that was 1.5 meters deep in places. It was a difficult climb, and they were not properly equipped. Aharon's shoes were torn, and Renia was without a coat, only a dress covering her body.[60] We can assume that the journey took a toll on Chajka as well. She was never in good health, and her legs were particularly weak. But now she would walk for as long as needed. The boy, Monia Hochenberg, skipped nimbly ahead, as if taunting the clumsy figures stumbling behind him.[61] Late at night, they crossed the watershed at an altitude of 1,500 meters. From there on, the path went downhill. The Slovak forests loomed black in the distance. They quickened their steps, no longer feeling the cold. The sweat made the clothes stick to their bodies. When they reached the valley, they noticed a flickering fire down below—the camp of the Slovak smugglers.

Soon the refugees were warming their frozen bones and wet clothes by the flames. The Slovak smugglers prepared for the rest of the journey while the Polish smugglers left to return to their country. After walking for several more hours, the party reached Mútne, a small Slovak village. It was early morning, and the villagers were still fast asleep. In one of the houses, a door opened to beckon them in. The flame of a lantern illuminated a small stable. On the straw spread out for them and among horses, cows, and pigs, the members of the group finally collapsed. At that moment, they only wanted one thing—to sleep.

At noon, they were woken by the landlady who brought them food. They ate to their hearts' content and went back to sleep. Later, Renia remembered the rays of the December sun shining through the slits in the stable walls, the touch of the bodies of her friends huddled together on the narrow straw mat, her thoughts of those who remained in Poland, before she fell back to sleep.[62]

The next day, Alex Hauser's van took them to the town of Liptovský Mikuláš. On the way, Hauser eagerly pressed them for every detail of their travails. Even though he had probably already transported dozens of Jews, it was still hard for him to believe that the Germans were indeed capable of such heinous acts. For their part, the Będzin refugees marveled at the meticulous planning and coordination of the smuggling operation. In Liptovský Mikuláš they were brought to the Jewish community house,

60 Kukielka, *Escape from the Pit*, pp. 178–182.

61 Ibid.

62 Ibid., pp. 201–202.

and from there to the temporary hostel organized for refugees. Fischer and Izbicki were already waiting for them there. They had finally reached safety. Renia wrote:

> Our joy is great. After all, we are like a bird that has escaped its cage. As free people, we spread our wings. Out of habit, we still talk in whispers, like we did inside the bunker, even though there is no longer any danger of pursuit or death looming over us at any moment. We feel as if we have been forged from different stuff.[63]

Renia recalls that the next day, they were visited by Benito, a member of Hashomer Hatzair in Slovakia.

63 Ibid., p. 203.

On the way to *Eretz Israel*, Istanbul, March 1944.
From left: Ya'akov (Benito) Rosenberg, Chajka Klinger, Yoshko Baumer, Fredka Oksenhandler (Mazia), and Aharon Brandes.

Leaders of four underground youth movements, Mishmar Ha'emek, 1947.
From left: Moshe Alpan, Ya'akov (Benito) Rosenberg, Roszka Korczak, and Chajka Klinger.

Kibbutz Haogen Archive

Chajka and Benito, Kibbutz Haogen, c. 1944.

Chajka and Benito, Kibbutz Haogen, c. 1944.

Kibbutz Haogen Archive

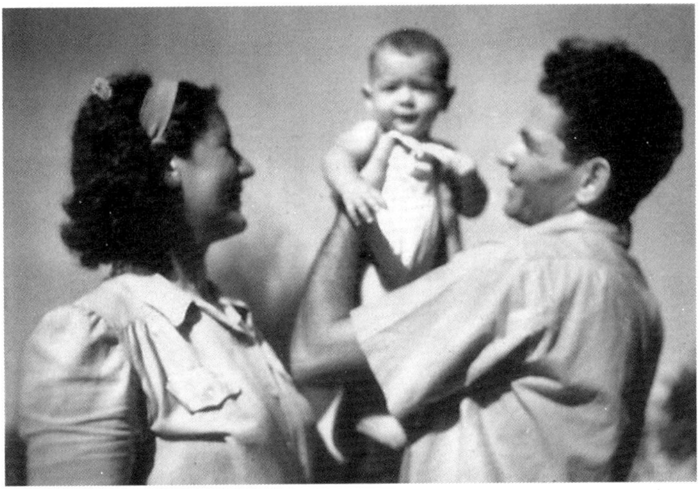

Chajka, Benito, and Zvi, Kibbutz Haogen, 1945.

From left: Chajka, Zippora Sfinkelstein, Zvi, Yosef Sfinkelstein, and Benito, Gan Haim, c. 1946.

Chajka, Benito, and Zvi, Prague, c. 1948.

The four of us, Kibbutz Haogen, c. 1949.

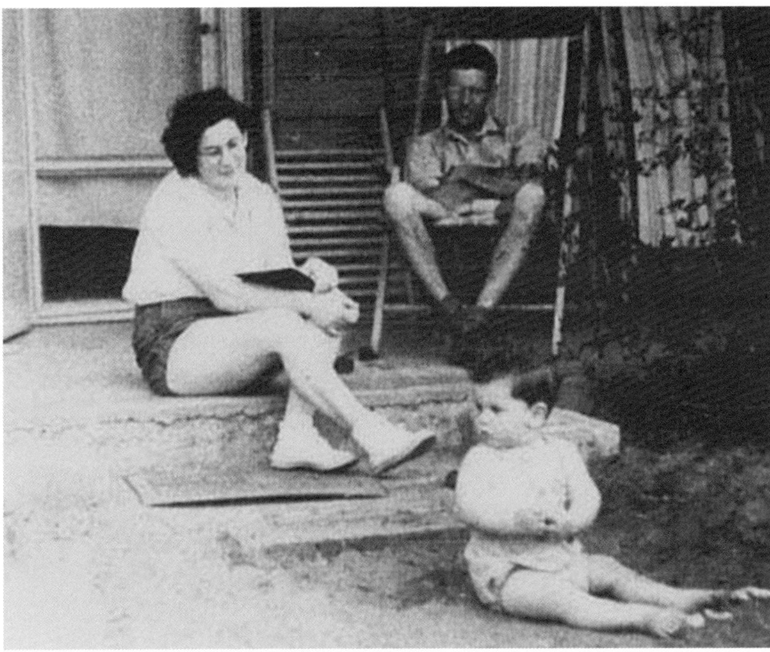

Chajka, Benito, and Avihu, Kibbutz Haogen, c. 1950.

Savta Bella Rosenberg, Benito, Arnon, and Avihu, c. 1959.

From right: Zvi, Avihu, and Arnon, Kibbutz Haogen, c. 1960.

A performance of *Maus* in the Sosnowiec Theater, 2022. Chajka's photo is projected in the background.
Courtesy of the Sosnowiec Theater.

The descendants of the Kobylec family with Chajka's descendants planting an olive tree in memory of Karolina, Piotr, Mieczysław, Alois, and Wiktor Kobylec, and Klara Kobylec-Banasik. Sde Nitzan, 2019.

The last photo. Chajka, Kibbutz Haogen, 1958.

Chapter Twenty-Three

The Harbinger

Father: 1986

Father is cooperating with my project. As usual, he is puzzled by my choices, but when called on to help, he is always willing to clarify obscure details in my mother's diaries and stories or to translate various passages from languages of which I have somewhat limited command. I have always been amazed at the large number of languages he mastered. When we were kids he would translate children's books for us from Russian, in our youth he would quote proverbs in Latin, and his bookshelves housed a wide selection of architecture magazines in German. We, however, inherited only one language from him, the one he was determined to speak and think in exclusively—Hebrew.

Having devoted so many years of his life to building the future, Father now works at preserving the past. Throughout World War II, he kept meticulous records of the movement's resistance efforts, and after managing the Hashomer Hatzair archive (now known as Yad Ya'ari) in Givat Haviva for a while, he established his own archive in Kibbutz Haogen.

Mother's shadow is a barrier between us, but she is also the opportunity to build a bridge. When we were kids, Father rarely talked about Mother, certainly not about the way she died. Her memory has been a charged and silent topic ever since our little family was replenished with the arrival of Malka, Father's second wife. His way of dealing with his misfortune was to transfer the grief from the private sphere to the public sphere. It was thanks to him that the memorial booklet in Mother's honor was published, and without his insistence, the diaries would not have seen the light of day at all. In 1959, when Kibbutz Haogen was required to finance the publication of *Miyoman Bageto* together with Sifriat Poalim, the kibbutz secretariat had reservations. After all, chapters of it had already been printed in various movement publications.[1] Father, as one of the pillars of the kibbutz, was not used to hearing the word "no." He informed the secretariat that if his request was rejected, he would take his Holocaust compensation money and leave the kibbutz with his three children. The request was approved—Father was too important to be allowed to leave.

Father did not add any of his own notes to the texts published in the memorial booklet or to the book. Only now, for the first time, is he passing on to me the eulogy he delivered at Mother's funeral. In it he described in tender, trembling words their first meeting and Mother's struggle to create a new life and forget her years of suffering. "I ask for your forgiveness, Chajka, for not looking after you and your health as well as I should have, for having proven unequal to the task of healing the wounds of your soul."[2]

Father was the kibbutz's custodian of the memory of the Holocaust. After the book was published, he took on the issue of compensation from Germany, which he dealt with for many years. Compensation was received individually, but it was transferred in its entirety to the kibbutz. One member who insisted on receiving his share was forced to leave the kibbutz. The compensation money was tied to the center of Father's activities in the kibbutz—construction. Although some of it was dedicated to the creation of personal pension funds for members, a significant portion was diverted to a special fund that financed the construction of the kibbutz's large public buildings: the members' club, the cultural hall, and the crown jewel of Father's projects—the new dining hall.

In the early 1960s, when Yom Hashoah, the official state Holocaust Remembrance Day, became a properly honored public occasion, my father was made responsible for the annual ceremony in the kibbutz. I was a high school student at the time, and he used to consult me in choosing the literary and musical pieces to be featured. Yet even then, we never spoke about Mother as a person, as a woman.

1 In the minutes of the Kibbutz Haogen secretariat meeting it was recorded: "The diary of Chajka Klinger. It has been reported that the entirety of the article was written by Chajka Grossman and published in *Sefer Hapartizanim Hayehudim*." Kibbutz Haogen Secretariat, December 9, 1958, Kibbutz Haogen Archives, 3/107 (53).

2 Ya'akov Rosenberg, eulogy for Chajka, April 19, 1958, Ya'akov Ronen collection.

Father's own memories of the war were a source of thrill and excitement in our childhood. Stories about his time in prison, border smuggling operations, and his escape from a forced labor brigade were told with good humor and cheer. During his stint in prison, for example, he had noticed that the language of the Hungarian underworld was peppered with Jewish expressions, which were used as code names for the shady dealings of dubious men.[3] Now, when I read the testimony he gave to the historian Yeshayahu Jelínek in the 1960s, it conjures up a different, more sober outlook, yet one never devoid of optimism. Father believed in the possibility of salvation even in the most difficult of times.

Born in 1917 as Ya'akov Rosenberg, he was registered under the Slovak name Tibor, whereas fellow movement members called him "Benito," an ironic nickname inherited from his father, one of the main benefactors of the Prešov community. Later, we would all trade in Rosenberg for the Hebrew surname "Ronen." Following in the footsteps of his siblings, Father joined Hashomer Hatzair at the age of sixteen and soon became a key activist. On the eve of the war, he was already an experienced instructor and a member of the Hashomer Hatzair leadership in Czechoslovakia. Following March 1939, when Czechoslovakia disintegrated with the entry of the Germans into Prague, he became a member of the Hashomer Hatzair leadership in Slovakia.

During the early years of the war, Father was an official worker of the *Umschichtung* department of the ÚŽ. Thanks to this position, he could protect the members of the movement who continued their semi-underground activity in Slovakia, a country that was more than sympathetic toward Germany.[4] When the deportations from Slovakia to Poland began in March 1942, he used both his status and the information he had to warn his friends of what was to come and recommended that they cross the border into Hungary. "If anyone has a real, concrete opportunity to save our people by crossing the border, one should take it," he wrote to his friends in a circular he distributed on March 6, 1942.[5]

In April 1942, after he had successfully transferred around sixty of his comrades to Hungary, the *Umschichtung* department was disbanded, and he also crossed the border into Hungary. There, he joined his friends

3 See Ya'akov Ronen, *Iy Sham BeSlovakia Harehoka* (Hebrew) (Tel Aviv: self-published, 1987). Based on Ya'akov Ronen, *Sipurim LeCarmel* (Hebrew) (Haogen: unpublished, 1985–1986).

4 Ya'akov (Benito) Rosenberg testimony, 1961, Moreshet Archive, A.28.

5 Letter from the Central Hashomer Hatzair leadership in Slovakia to its members, March 6, 1942, Moreshet Archive, C.38.

Joseph (Yoshko) Baumer and Ruth Loránd, both members of Hashomer Hatzair from Slovakia. His underground activities landed him in prison several times, both when he attempted to smuggle people over the border and when he was caught carrying fake papers in Hungary. After his release from prison, he was recruited into a forced labor brigade in Hungary but managed to escape when he received a short leave before the company was sent to the Russian front. The lawyer he consulted explained to him that he had two options: to die by bullet (on the Russian front) or by hanging (as a defector). Father chose a third option and returned to Slovakia. There, he resumed his involvement in underground operations and was assigned a new role welcoming the Jews coming in from Poland. This is how he met Mother.

The Meeting in Liptovský Mikuláš

It was the first time Benito encountered one of those who would later be called the "ghetto fighters." Benito was in close correspondence with Bader and was a link to *Eretz Israel*, the movement, and Ya'ari. Whereas Chajka was the woman "from there," the one who had seen the horrors and experienced them in the flesh, the one who could tell the stories of the lives and deaths of the comrades who had fought or tried to fight. They were both excited. Benito remembered their meeting very well:

> I first met you on a winter's night in a Slovak town close to the Polish border. Your face showed none of the hardships of the road. The ordeal of crossing the border, with all the superhuman efforts it required, had been pushed far behind the months and years of horror, pain, and suffering. Your own personal rescue became a trivial episode in comparison. But the moon, looking down at the cold snow, illuminated the night. And everything was as clear and defined as in daylight. So were Chajka's words that night.
>
> We sat down together by the big stove in the school hall, which had become a hostel for Polish refugees from Zagłębie. And she talked nonstop. It was not the cry of one single person, not the suffering of a lone individual that was emerging from her throat. An entire generation was shouting through her, her words but a tool used to express the entirety of the disaster that had befallen our nation.
>
> She talked without pause, hours upon hours, as if afraid she wouldn't have enough time to tell it all, as if unburdening herself

> of a heavy load, but one that cannot be held with one's hands, for it is all far too much for the logic inherent in the human body to bear. And I, hearing her words, intermittently reached out and held her hand, to feel the person carrying all of this in her heart and soul. Certainly, I knew of the destruction of millions of Jews, among them dozens of friends and relations, but that night, for the first time, I felt their pain, I suffered their fate.[6]

She also had her diaries. It is possible that already that evening she had begun to read and translate them to Benito, as a representative of the movement. Communication was not a problem: both were fluent German speakers. It was the first authentic document smuggled out of Poland containing a detailed description of the events shortly after their occurrence. There was testimony in it that could help their friends in Istanbul and *Eretz Israel* by removing the veil of uncertainty regarding the fate of the movement in Poland. A few days after her arrival, the diary was transferred to the movement's offices, where it was typed up and translated into German. In fact, the diaries arrived in Istanbul two months before Chajka herself, although their translation was not yet complete.[7]

And in the process, Chajka fell in love. The figure of the Slovak activist was like a reincarnation of everything she had lost. He was her age and a movement man. Like her, he was ready to risk his life for comrades, and like her, he believed in the ideas of tomorrow's world. And as luck would have it, the feeling was mutual. Benito felt an urge to protect this black-haired, sad-eyed fugitive. From their corner of the school hall, Max Fischer and Chawka Lenczner watched the pair frequently conferring by the blackboard. Max said to Chawka: "This may grow into a problem," the term they used for a love affair that kindled within the movement.[8] At the same time, Max himself was hoping that something resembling a problem would grow between him and Chawka.

Kasia, too, remembered the beginning of the love affair. She had arrived with the second group and was reunited with Chajka at the school in Liptovský Mikuláš. Chajka was clearly happy to love again, but also a little hesitant: was it appropriate for her to fall in love only four months after David's tragic death? Kasia reassured her. After all, she herself had

6 Ya'akov Rosenberg, eulogy for Chajka, April 19, 1958, Ya'akov Ronen collection.

7 Letter from Ya'akov Rosenberg to dear friends (in Istanbul), January 3, 1944, Moreshet Archive, D.1.1124.4.

8 Chawka Lenczner interview.

been romantically involved with Zvi Dunski, who had been killed in the resistance in Sosnowiec, and now arrived in Slovakia in the company of another man.[9]

Kasia's group also included the Jewish policemen who had joined the remnants of the resistance in their escape. Benito and the other rescue workers eyed Barenblatt and Potasz with suspicion: they had heard about their conduct in the ghettos from Chajka and the others.[10] Later, Benito would write that the surviving resistance fighters even suggested eliminating Barenblatt right there and then.[11] However, Benito and the Slovakian Working Group people were not ones for hasty action.[12] It was decided not to take measures in this regard in Slovakia but to transfer them as quickly as possible to Hungary and let the comrades there know what kind of people they were. And indeed, when Barenblatt and Kasia reached Hungary, they were sequestered, and Barenblatt would later be put on trial by the local Jewish community.[13]

David Liwer and his family also reached Liptovský Mikuláš, as did Abraham Zilberstein of Hashomer Hatzair. They came bearing tragic news: There had been a shooting accident in the Kobylec bunker in which Kobylec's son-in-law Banasik had been injured. The mortally wounded Banasiak did not reveal anything to the police, but the hiding place was no longer viable and the survivors had to move on quickly.[14] At the train station, Shmuel Rozencwajg, Dora Herzberg, and Sara Kukielka said goodbye to the outgoing group. They were supposed to go with the next group. The Liwer party set off and crossed the Slovakian border at night. The next day, they arrived in Liptovský Mikuláš where they were welcomed cordially by Benito and the others.[15]

9 Miriam (Kasia) Barenblatt interview.

10 Ya'akov Rosenberg testimony at the Barenblatt trial, Moreshet Archive, D.1.5366; Ya'akov Ronen interview.

11 Ya'akov Ronen, *Curriculum Vitae*, May 5, 1985, Ya'akov Ronen collection, p. 107.

12 In her letter from September 1, 1943, Gisi Fleischmann wrote "Among the refugees there are many dubious people, who, precisely due to their lack of scruples, were more easily able to make their way to the ranks of the administration. But they are relatively few, and the large part definitely deserves, in all respects, to be saved. In the end, we must see this operation as an act of pure charity, and therefore we must extend the hand of salvation to all who seek our help." Letter from Gisi Fleischmann to the Hechalutz center in Geneva, September 1, 1943, in Rothkirchen, *Horban Yehudey Slovakia*, p. 232.

13 Hirsch Barenblatt testimony at the Barenblatt trial, Moreshet Archive, D.1.5366.

14 D. Liwer, *Ir Hametim*, pp.175–177; Meir and Nechama Schulman interview.

15 D. Liwer, *Ir Hametim*, pp. 172–182.

They were the last members of the group to reach Slovakia. Later, it was revealed to Shmuel Rozencwajg that Roman Brzuchowski, one of the Polish smugglers, had betrayed them. Shmuel was arrested in Bielsko-Biała as was Mietek Kobylec, who was helping smuggle them over the border. A few days later, his father Piotr Kobylec was also arrested, and the two were sent to Auschwitz.[16] Roman Kołodzi, the other Polish liaison of the group, had been shot even earlier while trying to rescue Dr. Lieberman from the liquidation camp in Sosnowiec.[17] The three of them as well as Klara Banasik would later be recognized as Righteous Among the Nations.[18] Rozencwajg was informed that Aliza Zeytenfeld and Sara Kukielka, who had gone to the villages to gather the children of Kibbutz Atid, had also been captured. None of them were ever seen alive again.[19] Meir Schulman and his wife Nechama survived and later made it to Hungary.[20] Fela Katz was destined to continue to fight for her and her family's survival in hiding. Shmuel Rozencwajg became gravely ill and continued to be transferred from camp to camp until the end of the war. While Chajka, who had long since tired of life, was granted it again in a safe haven.

The Conference in Nové Mesto nad Váhom

Chajka and Benito appear to have spent only a few days in Liptovský Mikuláš, after which Benito went out with the Hashomer Hatzair people to his parents' house in Prešov. Aharon Brandes remembered the warm hospitality extended to them by the Rosenbergs, particularly the fact that they bought him shoes and a watch.[21] Moritz Rosenberg, Benito's father, would later also recall that meeting, stating how he could not have imagined that he was hosting his future daughter-in-law.[22] Yet Bella, Benito's mother, felt that something was brewing between her son and

16 Poray, "Kobylec," Polish Righteous: Those Who Risked Their Life, http://www.savingjews.org/righteous/kv.htm (accessed May 6, 2024).

17 D. Liwer, *Ir Hametim*, p. 174.

18 Piotr's wife Karolina and his other son Wiktor were also honored as Righteous Among the Nations. Poray, "Kobylec," Polish Righteous: Those Who Risked Their Life, http://www.savingjews.org/righteous/kv.htm (accessed May 6, 2024).

19 Shmuel Ron, in *Sefer Sosnovitz*, vol. 2, pp. 188–189.

20 Meir and Nechama Schulman interview.

21 Aharon Brandes interview.

22 Moritz Rosenberg testimony, Moreshet Archive, C.38.1.8.

the refugee from Poland. And indeed, as Benito would later testify, the intimate bond between them blossomed with surprising speed.[23]

Chajka was not the only one to have lost a lover and to be in need of warmth and comfort: Benito had been cut off from Ruth Loránd, his bright and charming childhood sweetheart, for over a year.[24] It was a painful episode that would later be erased from his memory. During their stay in Budapest in the second half of 1942, they were both arrested separately, and their false papers were discovered. Ruth did not hold up under interrogation and led the investigators to the house of Peretz Révész, a Maccabi Hatzair man from Slovakia, who had arrived there shortly before her. Peretz evaded the police and reported the incident to members of Hashomer Hatzair.[25] An inquiry was launched, and Ruth was expelled from the movement.[26] Yoshko Baumer, Benito's friend, wrote about the incident to Hakibbutz Ha'artzi in the Land of Israel. Ruth was badly hurt: She would later interpret this letter as an act of revenge by Yoshko, who had tried to take advantage of the imprisoned Benito's absence to win her heart.[27] Ruth was kept in another detention camp for nine months and was later deported to Auschwitz.[28]

Benito, who was in a concentration camp before his forced recruitment into the Hungarian labor division, may have been spared this information. Nevertheless, in Chajka he found a new love. From Prešov, Chajka and Benito traveled to Bratislava, where Chajka met with the heads of the Working Group: Gisi Fleischmann, Oskar Neumann, and Moshe Dachs. Then, toward New Year's Eve, they headed to the town of Nové Mesto nad Váhom in western Slovakia. There, an important conference of the surviving Hashomer Hatzair activists in Slovakia was to be held.

For about a year and a half, Hashomer Hatzair in Slovakia had been operating underground. They had stopped all educational activity. Some of the movement's graduates had found refuge in Hungary, and

23 Ya'akov Rosenberg, *Curriculum Vitae*, p. 112.

24 Ibid., p. 93.

25 Peretz Révész, *Standing Up to Evil: A Zionist's Underground Rescue Activities in Hungary* (Jerusalem: Yad Vashem, 2019), pp. 107–109.

26 Joel Brand, *Beshlihut Nidonim Lamavet* (Hebrew) (Tel Aviv: Eynot, 1956).

27 In an interview conducted in Prague in 1990, Ruth vehemently denied the issue of extradition. Ruth Loránd, interview by the author, Prague, 1990.

28 "She Outsmarted the Nazis and Saved Hundreds," *Aktuálně.cz*, March 3, 2008, https://zpravy.aktualne.cz/she-outsmarted-the-nazis-and-saved-hundreds/r~i:article:523823/ (accessed May 6, 2024).

others were hiding in Slovakia, mainly under the auspices of the Slovak labor camps. In fact, they now numbered no more than a few dozen members. Their ties with the leadership—especially with Benito and Egon Roth—were very loose. The operations of the movement as a whole had almost come to a halt. This may have been one of the reasons behind the tightening of relations with the Communist Party. At that time, there were communist partisan units already operating in Slovakia, and some Hashomer Hatzair members found their way into their ranks. Another important connection to the communists was formed in the Sereď labor camp, where a large and cohesive group of *shomrim* lived. In the debased living conditions of the camp, the connection between these two organized and cohesive cells was only natural. Akiva Nir (Karol Neufeld), one of the group's operators in Sereď, was convinced that the relationship could bring great benefit to both parties.[29]

In recent months, members of Hashomer Hatzair had begun to consider joining the Slovak rebellion. In this matter they acted separately and in contrast to the position of their friends in the other movements. Josef Korniański saw joining the revolt as an act of folly.[30] Korniański, who had also opposed spending funds on armed defense in Będzin, had only one commitment and that was to the Land of Israel. However, the Hashomer Hatzair people in Slovakia—like their comrades in Poland—also had a commitment to socialist values.

This was the context in which the conference in Nové Mesto nad Váhom took place on New Year's Eve of 1943. It was the first time since the beginning of the deportations that all the main activists of the Slovak branch of the movement had gathered under one roof. Some were escapees coming directly from the labor camps, whereas others came from the forests. Benito presided over the meeting, where several key members were due to speak, including Chajka. His friends noticed that there was a spark between him and the black-haired emigrant from Poland.[31]

The first to speak was Rabbi Emanuel (Armin) Frieder, a member of the Working Group who extended his patronage to the young people. As a representative of the moderate religious current of Slovakian Jewry, he was also respected by Hashomer Hatzair. In addition, he happened to operate a shelter for the elderly in Nové Mesto nad Váhom, where the

29 Akiva Nir, *Shvilim Bema'agal Ha'esh* (Hebrew) (Tel Aviv: Sifriat Poalim, 1967), p. 50.

30 Ibid.

31 See a somewhat fictionalized account of the conference in Moshe Alpan, *Be'eyn Hase'ara* (Hebrew) (Tel Aviv: Moreshet, 2001), pp. 168–169.

summit took place. Rabbi Frieder surveyed the situation of Slovakian Jews with optimism. The tactic of bribery that the Working Group had been employing for the past two years had proven effective. At all levels of the Slovak government there were people who were willing to accept bribes and prevent the deportation of the Jews in return. With each passing day, the number of "alibi-ists"—government officials who were undertaking actions on behalf of the Jews to serve as evidence in their favor after the war—was growing. The information services were functioning, and there was hope on the horizon. He recommended that the activists refrain from taking rash measures and trust the leadership of the Slovak Jews.[32]

After Rabbi Frieder's speech, Benito took to the podium. He spoke of the ongoing contact with Bader in Istanbul, about the repeated attempts to reach *Eretz Israel*. A number of immigration certificates had already been received in Budapest, intended among other things for the members of the movement. He himself had been chosen to be among the leaving party. He then talked about the rescue operations and the efforts to smuggle refugees from Poland into Slovakia and Hungary.[33]

Then, it was Chajka's turn to speak. Later, the summit participants remembered the shock that ran through them when they heard her stories. Moshe Alpan (Pil) who was present at the meeting recalled:

> Chajka spoke quietly in fluent German. In the small hall, you could hear a pin drop. Everyone held their breath. Chajka herself was very moved, both due to the events she was recounting and the circumstances. She spoke for over an hour.... It was a lament and perhaps a eulogy for the vast Polish Jewry that had been erased from the map and for its glorious movement, Hashomer Hatzair, which no longer existed.... She dedicated the last few minutes to a number of personal friends who sacrificed their lives in the war against the Nazis.... Her muffled sobs resonated throughout the silent room. She finished by apologizing for her emotional outburst. Only once did Chajka speak about herself, when she expressed shame, almost an apology, for having saved herself and left her family and friends behind, saying that the only meaningful

32 Emanuel Frieder, *To Deliver Their Souls: The Struggle of a Young Rabbi during the Holocaust* (New York: Holocaust Library, 1987), pp. 148–149; David Goldstein, "Tafkidim," in Dror and Rosenzweig, *Sefer Hashomer Hatzair*, vol. 1, pp. 754–755.

33 Akiva Nir, *Yehudey Slovakia Bema'avak* (Hebrew) (Tel Aviv: Moreshet, 1984), p. 20.

> purpose that can grow from it is for her to tell and to warn. It was poor consolation, nothing more.[34]

For her listeners in Nové Mesto nad Váhom, this was the first time they were meeting a representative of the movement in Poland face to face. They knew about what had happened in Poland, however "the personal and vivid descriptions gave Chajka's words a different, almost apocalyptic dimension.… Even the toughest among them wiped the moisture from their eyes."[35]

Chajka had an urgent message to deliver: there must be no illusions about the Germans' intentions. It was best for the Slovak movement to organize for armed defense, since "everything that is to come from now on will be harsher, crueler, and aimed at the total destruction of the Jewish people."[36] Her words made a strong impression. They stood in complete contrast to everything that Rabbi Frieder believed and represented. Later, Benito remembered that Chajka "did not spare the Slovak movement or me personally her criticism regarding our attitude toward resisting the Germans. She reprimanded our complacency and the way we openly went about our daily lives. She interpreted it as sloppiness." He also recalled that back in Liptovský Mikuláš, he had jumped out of the school window when the gendarmes came for a surprise inspection. Chajka had admonished him and interpreted his behavior as cowardice. Benito could not understand her anger. After all, he had to avoid falling into the hands of the gendarmes so that he could continue his underground activity.[37]

A discussion then ensued, inspired by Chajka's words. A number of members asked to conduct an ideological and in-depth discussion, as was customary. Benito objected, claiming that the current situation was not suitable for such matters. A position had to be formulated on a number of practical questions concerning the coming days. In fact, based on the atmosphere in the room, Benito feared that if the movement members were pressed to make an ideological decision, they would reach a resounding answer—no to Zionism.[38] Chajka's report was filled with deep feelings of

34 Alpan, *Be'eyn Hase'ara*, pp. 168–169. Although this is a semi-fictionalized account, this testimony corroborates with previous testimonies given by Alpan and is thus quoted here.

35 Ibid., p. 169.

36 David Goldstein, "Tafkidim," p. 755; Ya'akov Ronen interview.

37 Ya'akov Ronen, *Curriculum Vitae*, pp. 110, 112.

38 Letter from Ya'akov Rosenberg to dear friends (in Istanbul), January 3, 1944, Moreshet Archive, D.1.1124.4.

disappointment at the behavior of the Zionist leadership in Poland. The rapprochement of some of the members with the communists and talk of preparations for a future uprising might have also led to the conclusion that it was necessary to join the Communist Party and the struggle of the peoples of Europe to liberate themselves from the Nazi yoke.[39]

At the end of the day, a kind of compromise was reached: the movement would continue with preparations for combat as well as rescue operations. Three practical decisions were made at the conclusion of the meeting: a) Hashomer Hatzair would join the communist groups organizing for an uprising, facilitate escapes from the labor camps, make preparations to join Slovak partisan units, and build bunkers in the mountains and forests in preparation for the uprising; b) Hashomer Hatzair would continue rescue operation in cooperation with the Working Group; c) Hashomer Hatzair would take care of refugee members and continue efforts to get them to Mandatory Palestine.[40]

Chajka's message was not adopted verbatim, but it certainly left a mark on the position of her friends in Slovakia.

Benito's Letter

Three days after the council in Nové Mesto nad Váhom, on January 3, 1944, Benito sat down and wrote to Bader about the exciting developments of the past month in Slovakia. The letter opened with the good news about the arrival of the comrades from Poland; however, it soon took a pessimistic turn, as if the writer felt the evil wind blowing in from Poland. Inadvertently, Benito poured his own doubts—the shock he experienced at the first meeting with the movement members from Poland and with the person who would later become his wife—into what was supposed to be an official movement missive. He wrote:

> Regarding the state of mind of our friends who have just arrived. Most of their fellows died in the woods. There are twenty more *shomrim* in the forests near Częstochowa, and we will try to save them as well.[41] The violence and the events that they have endured

39 Ibid.

40 Moshe Alpan, interview by the author, Tel Aviv, 1989; Nir, *Yehudey Slovakia Bema'avak*, p. 21; David Goldstein, "Tafkidim," p. 755; Letter from Ya'akov Rosenberg to dear friends (in Istanbul), January 3, 1944, Moreshet Archive, D.1.1124.4.

41 The reference here is to the underground group from Częstochowa that operated

> have shaken them out of their normal equilibrium. They hate the Jews, hate their weakness, and their only hope is the Red Army.[42]

As someone who did not believe in the idea of an uprising and saw rescue, such as the operations in which they had been engaged in Slovakia, as a practical alternative to the idea of defense, he seems to be criticizing the people of Poland. Yet, it is evident that he, too, was troubled by the same thoughts:

> The elimination of Polish Jewry and the acts (deeds) of this war have created in them the same thoughts that I have already expressed to you regarding Zionism and the Jewish question in general. The masses in Central Europe have disappeared, along with most of the pioneer movement, the Jewish masses in the Soviet Union will also be lost to Zionism in the Land of Israel. With whom, then, will our people immigrate to *Eretz Israel*? Who will our instructors educate, for whom will the pioneers pave the way—for our friends? An avant-garde without the masses, pioneers without a people—what is this?[43]

Here, he unwittingly quoted Chajka: "An avant-garde without the masses," was an expression she frequently used to express her doubts about Zionism. He then added:

> Despite this great ideological difference that has entered the brains—and especially the souls of the people and apprentices of the Hashomer movement in Europe—we have stayed together, we are connected with all the pioneering parts of the movement and try to help each other. Of course, our goal is to get to *Eretz Israel*—simply because it is the nearest country to go to for safety reasons. And if it were another country, and not necessarily the goal of Zionism, we would still want to flee for the sake of the people, but only to flee and hide... Zionism has displayed such colossal incompetence in caring for Polish Jewry that even the staunchest followers of Zionism have lost their faith in it. And the remainder...they have been so damaged in their soul and

in the forests of Koniecpol. About half of its members were murdered by Polish nationalist partisans. See Sarid, *Bemivhan Ha'anut Vehapedut*, pp. 441–446.

42 Letter from Ya'akov Rosenberg to dear friends (in Istanbul), January 3, 1944, Moreshet Archive, D.1.1124.4.

43 Ibid.

> body that they will not be able to fulfill any pioneering or even human roles. They will be sick for the rest of their lives. Of the whole nation, there are only disparate individuals left, and they are looking for the citadel, the fortress that will protect them.[44]

There is an almost nihilistic note echoing throughout these lines. The only two options he saw before him were nihilism or communism. The "Polish" despair had managed to infect even a naturally optimistic man such as Benito.

His letter was the fulfillment of the nightmare of Eliyahu Golomb, who at the time was involved in the initiative to send Israeli paratroopers to Europe: "If Zionism does not help," he claimed, "the hatred of those left alive will poison the Zionist enterprise after the war."[45] Unbeknownst to him, Benito's words reiterated the central message of *Eretz Israel* pragmatism, as expressed by the chairman of the Action Committee, Yitzhak Gruenbaum: Zionism could not do much to stop the extermination; its role now was to concentrate on preparing a home to welcome the displaced survivors who will surface once the storm subsides.[46]

At the end of his letter, however, Benito regains his optimistic spirit: "Ask me why—despite everything I have just written—we are still together? Why do we help each other in saving lives? Simply because there is no one to trust."[47]

The Budapest Dilemma

Chajka did not remain in Slovakia for long after the New Year's Eve council. Although she called on her comrades to organize armed defense, she herself could no longer find the strength to continue fighting. She was looking for a place of refuge, but not only that: She also had to continue to tell the world about her friends' actions and their fate, to go through cities and towns and tell the Jews in each one about the destruction of Polish Jewry, to warn

44 Ibid.

45 Eliyahu Golomb to the Mapai Secretariat, December 23, 1943, Mifleget Ha'avoda Archive, Pinchas Lavon Institute for Labour Movement Research, 24/43.

46 Beit-Zvi, *Post-Ugandan Zionism on Trial*, pp. 115–116; Porat, *Hanhaga Bemilkud*, pp. 125, 133. See also Aryeh Morgenstern, "Va'ad Hahatzala Hame'uhad shel Hasohnut Hayehudit 1943–1945," *Yalkut Moreshet*, 13 (June 1971).

47 Letter from Ya'akov Rosenberg to dear friends (in Istanbul), January 3, 1944, Moreshet Archive, D.1.1124.4.

them lest they suffer the same fate. It appears that already at the conference in Slovakia there was talk of her leaving for *Eretz Israel*. Did she only wish to get there in order to find a safe haven, as Benito's letter would imply? It seems unlikely. Although she harbored an intense hatred and bitterness toward those who stayed on the sidelines instead of rushing to help, she also felt a longing for the Land of Israel. And to top it all off, she had no one left now except Esther Shoshan, Shayke Goldrin, and Shmaryahu Milinsky, who were all waiting for her in a small kibbutz on a hill near Nes Ziona.

Her diaries went before her. Bader's heart ached as he read them in German translation; he felt like he knew the diary's author intimately.[48] Meanwhile, Chajka was making her way to Hungary with Renia Kukielka and Moshe Alpan, who was sent to Hungary on behalf of the movement.[49] They crossed the border using one of the typical arrangements organized by the Slovak rescue workers. At first, they traveled by train to a station near the border town of Košice, which had been annexed by Hungary. The girls stayed in the empty train carriage while Moshe Alpan bought tickets for the Hungarian train that was supposed to cross the border from this point on with the carriages locked. They waited all night in the frozen carriage. At dawn, the chief mechanic, who had been bribed, raised a lot of steam from the locomotive's exhaust pipes, and under the cover of this steam, the three made their way onto the Hungarian train. The trip did not go without a hitch: When the Hungarian controller asked to see their tickets, Chajka accidentally handed him the Slovakian train tickets, but thanks to Alpan's intervention—or perhaps the controller's leniency—the incident did not escalate into a problem. Within hours they were in Budapest.[50]

Upon their arrival, Chajka was welcomed by Hashomer Hatzair activists. Here, as in Slovakia, the movement members were well practiced in handling refugees. The latter would receive a small amount of money for initial arrangements and be directed to local Jewish homes. At the same time, efforts were made to regularize their legal status in Hungary, either by contacting the representative office of the Free Polish Government (the Polish government-in-exile led by Władysław Sikorski's people) or by obtaining false papers.[51] Their efforts did not always go

48 Bader, *Shlihuyot Atzuvot*, p. 90; Menahem Bader, "Eulogy," in *Chajka: Hoveret Zikaron*, p. 7.

49 Moshe Alpan interview.

50 Alpan, *Be'eyn Hase'ara*, pp. 178–180.

51 Asher Cohen, *The Halutz Resistance in Hungary 1942–1944* (Boulder: Social Science Monographs and Institute for Holocaust Studies of the City University of New York, 1986), pp. 38–43; Korniański, *Beshlihut Halutzim*, p. 163.

well. As Korniański, who had been helping refugees in Budapest for several months by this time, pointed out: "Hungarian Jews have not excelled in providing shelter to refugees, especially not to those without legal papers."[52] However, the members of the youth movements probably fared better than others due to the patronage of their friends. In Budapest, Chajka was reunited with her friend Tosia Gutman from Hanoar Hatzioni in Będzin. They had attended the Gymnasium together but hadn't seen much of each other during the war years, since both were preoccupied with the affairs of their respective movements. Tosia remembered how happy Chajka was, as if drunk on the feeling of freedom.[53]

Even though Hungary was a German satellite state under a fascist regime, in January 1944, the Jews could walk the streets freely, go shopping, attend theater plays and concerts. Chajka and Tosia were stunned. The two women resided in the same flat, and Tosia remembered giving her a nightgown: "It was so far removed from our way of life, and it was sort of a symbol of the free and beautiful world. Chajka said: 'Oh, it's so beautiful… It's out of this world.'"[54]

Rafi Benshalom, a Hashomer Hatzair activist in Budapest, later wrote his impression of Chajka:

> She was the kind of woman who knew exactly what she wanted, had a very determined outlook on life and a talent for organizing and educating. In Budapest all her latent femininity was reawakened. She enjoyed being a survivor, as well as the quiet, the concerts, the colors of Budapest's streets, the Danube, the castle, the people; in a word—the life—without which she had had to do for so long.[55]

Chajka herself did not record her impressions of Budapest. However, several testimonies of the Będzin survivors who were with her indicate that the intoxicating feeling of freedom only accentuated their awareness of the disaster that had befallen Polish Jewry. Fredka from Hanoar Hatzioni asked herself: "How many kilometers separate Budapest and Auschwitz? A whole world separates them. Free Jews walked the streets. They could not believe our stories, which failed to penetrate their consciousness."[56]

52 Ibid.
53 Tosia Herzberg interview.
54 Ibid.
55 Rafi Benshalom, *We Struggled for Life: The Hungarian Zionist Youth Resistance during the Nazi Era* (Jerusalem: Gefen Publishing House, 2001), p. 17.
56 Mazia, *Re'im Basa'ar*, p. 210.

Despite their bitterness—or perhaps because of it—the picture painted by the Będzin survivors is rather accurate. Hungarian Jews at the beginning of 1944 lived under the impression that they had been spared the sword. Whereas in all the neighboring countries—particularly in Poland and Slovakia—most of the Jewish communities had been destroyed, the Hungarian Jews were still living in relative peace and security. Hungarian Jewry, which at roughly 400,000 people was the third-largest community in Europe before the war, had grown with the annexation of territories from Romania and Slovakia to reach a total of 727,000.[57] Miklós Horthy's fascist regime was not particularly harsh on the Jews. In fact, at this point in 1944, Horthy had withdrawn from his alliance with Hitler. During 1943, he was already seriously exploring options of how to get Hungary out of the war. By the end of 1943, his government even allowed Zionist activity on Hungarian territory and thus, the Zionist movements in Hungary, albeit numbering only a few hundred members each, experienced a boom at the height of the war, the end of which already seemed in sight. Asher Cohen estimates that between 10,000 and 15,000 Jewish refugees arrived in Hungary in 1943 and were received by partisan, Zionist, and pioneer organizations.[58] Some of the refugees became key activists in the smuggling and rescue operations of their movements.[59]

This was the state of affairs that Chajka encountered in her own movement. It would seem that at the beginning of February, she participated in an assembly or several assemblies similar to the one in which she took part in Slovakia. Later, Ephraim Teichman (Agmon), one of the veteran Hashomer Hatzair activists in Hungary, who had been operating underground since October 1943, would recall that it was from Chajka's mouth that he first heard about the extermination. "Before then—nothing!" He added that his uncle had returned from Kamenets-Podolsk (Kam'yanets'-Podil's'kyy) with reports of the slaughter of stateless Jews but that "we saw it as an exceptional incident rather than a harbinger of

57 Randolph L. Braham, "Hungary: Jews during the Holocaust," in Israel Gutman, ed., *Encyclopedia of the Holocaust*, vol. 2 (New York: Macmillan, 1990), p. 698.

58 Cohen, *The Halutz Resistance in Hungary*, p. 35.

59 Examples of such refugees who became key activists are: Dr. Israel Kasztner, Shmuel Springman, and Joel Brand of Ihud, a movement with ties to Mapai in *Eretz Israel*; Zvi Goldfarb from Dror; and Josef Korniański of Hechalutz. The leadership of Hashomer Hatzair, except for the veteran Szilágyi, were, in fact, all refugees: Moshe Alpan, Rafi Benshalom, Dan Zimmerman, Yoshko Baumer, and Benito Rosenberg. All had come over from Slovakia.

our future, the future of Hungarian Jewry."[60] Shmuel Frankel, a member of the movement from Hungary, had a similar reaction:

> Before us sat a comrade who had just arrived from hell, with a tangible description of [what happened to] our people in Poland. Although we knew about the extermination, this living testimony was something we could not bear. An entire people has been wiped out and here no one even knows about it.[61]

Whereas Eugene Kolb, a member of the Borochov circle, an older group that accompanied Hashomer Hatzair in Budapest (and later the director of the Tel Aviv Museum), summed up his impression of Chajka's words in a nutshell: "[That evening] we 'walked past a million corpses.'"[62]

Here, too, Chajka repeated her gloomy prophecies. The Holocaust would reach Hungary eventually. The members of the movement must be willing to stand up for themselves with weapons in hand:

> Haika [Chajka] wanted to clarify one issue: What would our position be in the event of a holocaust? Would it be one of defense, in other words, self-defense in the form of armed combat, or rescue—the use of every possible means in order to save lives?... Haika and Aaron [Rosenfeld] supported a defense tactic. Haika was very enthusiastic about the Warsaw uprising, which she saw as one of the rays of light in our history. She had witnessed first the annihilation of thousands of Jews and, more than anything, had been shocked by their surrender—the way they had gone like "cattle to the slaughter." Her conclusion was that there was no real way out anyway, the Germans were bent on murdering all the Jews slowly and systematically. Since we were still together, we had to start organizing an efficient defense program.[63]

Unlike in Nové Mesto nad Váhom, most of the members in Budapest had reservations regarding her position. Her message did indeed reach their consciousness, helping them cross the thin line separating

60 Ephraim Agmon in the collective testimony of the underground resistance in Hungary, Moreshet Archive, A.655. See also Ephraim Agmon, *Shomer Ahi* (Hebrew) (Kibbutz Dalia: Ma'arahot, 2008), pp. 46–47.

61 Shmuel Frankel testimony, Moreshet Archive, A.155.

62 Benshalom, *We Struggled for Life*, p. 12.

63 Ibid., pp. 14–15.

knowledge from awareness. Yet, to understand does not mean to accept. The comrades in Budapest were of the opinion that under the special circumstances in Hungary, there was no room for armed defense. Rafi Benshalom, who coordinated the movement's activities, believed that it would be possible to save the majority of people by organizing and preparing appropriately. We have already lost many millions, argued Benshalom, and for the existence of the nation, the life of every Jew is so important that any "historical act of courage" can be neither justified nor allowed.[64]

Moshe Alpan voiced a more stringent view:

> I stayed up one night with Chajka Klinger who had come over from Poland, from the Będzin ghetto, and was an older girl…unusually intelligent. And she broke down in tears before me. What was she crying about? She cried about the fact that she had been saved from Będzin, from the ghetto. That the Germans may have killed more Jews after the uprising, while she had been saved. And this was a very drastic thing for me…Then I asked myself...first and foremost to save Jews when there is a desperate situation...If I happen to have a weapon, and the Germans catch me, I will shoot, I will not let myself be killed. Just like that?—No. For nothing?—I'm not going. But from there, under the conditions that existed at the time in Hungary, at the beginning of 1944, to reach a decision that it's necessary to organize an uprising, because all other means have failed? I don't think so. I said: "No, not all means have been exhausted and there is no need to organize an uprising. And I cannot, in this current situation, take responsibility for the fact that thousands of people will be killed, just to go down as a hero in history."[65]

Yoshko Baumer, Benito's friend, who at the time coordinated the movement's rescue and survival operations in Hungary, attributed Chajka's attitude to the terrible pessimism her words betrayed:

> There is no longer a Jewish People. There is no longer anyone to make efforts for because there is no Jewish People. These were the words she told us, and even then, we could not accept it. She had

64 Ibid., p. 15.

65 Moshe Alpan in the collective testimony of the underground resistance in Hungary, Moreshet Archive, A.655.

> buried the Jewish people...She was very skilled at describing the events, but it was hard to hear, and even harder to accept. She was also very pessimistic, even when I spoke to her in person.[66]

Later, Rafi Benshalom would say that the members of the movement in Budapest did not reach a final decision on the questions raised by Chajka. At the time of this summit, the pioneer underground had established a Hagana Committee, and Moshe Alpan began organizing self-defense training. However, overall, Hashomer Hatzair members in Hungary preferred to focus on the rescue channel of action.[67] A letter to Geneva sent a few months later reads as follows:

> Together with our friends from Poland, we have faced the fateful question of life and death: self-defense or rescue. We conducted debates about this when Chajka, Benito, and Yoshko were still here with us. And even then, we came to the final conclusion that our job is to save as many of our members as possible and all of our efforts are concentrated on this.[68]

In February 1944, there were many reasons to believe that the Jews of Hungary would manage to survive. During this period, the movement specialized in smuggling refugees from Poland and Slovakia to Hungary. Their efforts proved productive, and it seemed obvious that running an effective rescue operation was preferable to dying a heroic death. Later, movement member Yitzhak (Mimish) Herbst expressed this sentiment with a witty statement: "I don't want a village in the Land of Israel named after me, I want to live in it."[69]

Looked at from a broader perspective, the dilemma stemmed from the collision of two extreme avant-garde concepts rooted in the Hashomer Hatzair tradition. The heroic-romantic view stated that under conditions of extermination, the function of the avant-garde is to instruct the people in how to die heroically and make a bright mark on the pages

66 Yoshko Baumer testimony, Kibbutz Haogen Archive, Testimonies, p. 128.

67 Benshalom, *We Struggled for Life*, pp. 14–15.

68 Asher Cohen, *Hamahteret Hahalutzit BeHungaria* (Hebrew) (Tel Aviv: Kibbutz Hameuchad and Ghetto Fighters' House, 1984), pp. 178–179. This is the original Hebrew edition of Asher Cohen's *The Halutz Resistance in Hungary 1942–1944*. This quote does not appear in the English edition.

69 Yitzhak (Mimish) Herbst in the collective testimony of the underground resistance in Hungary, Moreshet Archive, A.655.

of history. On the other hand, the pragmatic view stated that the role of the movement was to save its people, the last reserves of Zionism, to ensure the continued existence of the Jewish people.

There is no evidence of Chajka's reaction to the rejection of her proposals, but it is safe to assume she was disappointed. This much can be gleaned from the testimony of her friend Tosia Gutman, with whom, as we recall, she shared a room in Budapest. Here, in this place of refuge, the ideological gap separating them in Poland had been paved over. Both were now refugees and saw themselves as emissaries of the dying Polish Jewry. Tosia felt that the message from Poland failed to reach the people in Hungary, and she was disappointed by the unwillingness of the members of the Hungarian youth movements to prepare for *hagana*.[70]

The Road to *Eretz Israel*

Disappointed and perhaps even bitter, Chajka prepared herself for immigration to *Eretz Israel*. Unlike David Liwer and the members of Hanoar Hatzioni from Będzin, she did not integrate into the activities of her movement in Budapest. Apart from the lectures she gave, she did not engage in educational or organizational activities.[71] Most likely, the main reason for this was that she viewed Budapest as a transit station on her way to Mandatory Palestine. Regardless, in terms of her mental state, she was still far from being fit to return to the activities to which she had devoted her life for the past four years. Her friends in Hungary and Slovakia gave special importance to her departure to Mandatory Palestine as an emissary that would tell the people there what she had told them.

The possibility of emigrating through Budapest arose back in October 1943 after transit permits were received from Bulgaria. Youth movement members could go from Budapest to Istanbul, and from there to Mandatory Palestine. The first to leave in January 1944 were Josef Korniański along with Eliezer Unger from Kraków. They were tasked with telling the people in Mandatory Palestine everything they knew and had witnessed and to demand quick rescue action and increased immigration while it was still possible. Their group included fourteen immigrants,

70 Tosia Herzberg interview.

71 Benshalom, *We Struggled for Life*, p. 17.

eight of whom were children.[72] In Budapest, Chajka, Renia, and Fredka waited impatiently to receive their coveted visas. Bitter conflicts broke out between the leaders of their movements and between them and the people of the Eretz Israel Office. Each movement was anxious to ensure that it would receive its fair share of permits;[73] however, it seems that this was not the cause of the delays. Complications (probably administrative ones) arose before Chajka's departure, and for a moment she stopped believing that the trip would ever take place. She teetered between hope and despair. Yet finally, on one of the first days of March 1944, she found herself standing at the window of the high-speed train to Bucharest. With tears in her eyes, she whispered to friends who had come to say goodbye that she now believed she would make the journey after all.[74]

Several days later, Benito also left on his way to Istanbul with his visa in hand. Benito's four years of wandering through war-torn Eastern Europe were coming to an end. He had been hiding in Hungary for several weeks with false papers. The Hungarian police had registered him as a defector from a labor brigade. The police were looking for him in Slovakia as well. Before leaving Slovakia, he had informed his friends in the underground that if they were ever caught, they should give up his name as the organizer of the operation in question. One of the members, a boy of about sixteen, was caught and most likely followed Benito's instruction. On the Hungarian radio, the comrades heard an announcement that the Hungarian police were looking for him based on the claim of the Slovak authorities. The Slovak teenager Felo Feldman was released from prison but was later caught transferring weapons to the communists and was hanged in public.[75] Benito himself managed to escape once more and for the last time. Now he was also on his way to safe shores. On March 4, 1944, he was reunited with Chajka at a hotel in Istanbul, where she was staying for several days in order to give her first testimony.

Those Who Stayed Behind

Chajka got out at the last moment. Less than three weeks after her departure, on March 19, 1944, the Germans invaded Hungary. A

72 Kornianski, *Beshlihut Halutzim*, p. 194.

73 Kukielka, *Escape from the Pit*, pp. 184–185.

74 Benshalom, *We Struggled for Life*, p. 18.

75 Ya'akov Ronen, interview with Yeshayahu Jelínek, 1961, Moreshet Archive, A.28; Ya'akov Ronen, "Shmi Mofi'a Beplilim," in Ronen, *Sipurim LeCarmel*, p. 85.

German "inspector" was appointed over Horthy. Prime Minister Miklós Kállay was removed and replaced by the pro-Nazi Döme Sztójay. Adolf Eichmann also arrived in Budapest with the German forces, equipped with well-thought-out plans for the extermination of the Hungarian Jews. As early as March 20, the Jews were called to establish a "temporary Jewish council." Eichmann outlined the procedures for assembling the Jews and deporting them to Auschwitz. Within a month, the preparations were complete. In the second half of April, the first transports left for Auschwitz. By July, approximately 435,000 of Hungary's Jews would be deported and effectively sentenced to death.

Rafi Benshalom and Moshe Alpan, who remained in Hungary, now led the Hashomer Hatzair resistance. They acted in line with their previous decision: rescue by all means. Having recovered from the initial shock of the invasion, they began to operate on two levels simultaneously: 1) the production and supply of false papers to their friends and family members; and 2) smuggling as many movement members and Jews as possible across the Slovak and Romanian borders. Using the strategy that became known as "the trip" they managed to smuggle around 1,000 people to Romania. The false papers they initially provided to members of their movement and then to anyone who needed them ended up protecting tens of thousands of Jews. In the children's homes that they had established under the auspices of the Red Cross, they managed to save the lives of around 5,000 Jewish children.[76]

In Slovakia, the long-awaited national uprising broke out on August 28, 1944. Akiva Nir, David Goldstein, and their friends who had heard Chajka speak in Nové Mesto nad Váhom, also remained faithful to their decision. Several dozen members of Hashomer Hatzair played an active role in the fighting as part of various units. Among them was Egon Roth, who had replaced Benito in his leadership position there. They were not the only Jews to go into combat. Later it was estimated that roughly 2,500 Jews had fought in the vicinity of Banská Bystrica. However, the uprising was quickly suppressed, and the deportations had resumed even earlier. By March 1945, around 13,500 of Slovakia's Jews had been deported.

76 Many books have been published over the years about the activities of the pioneer resistance in Hungary after the occupation. See, for example, Benshalom, *We Struggled for Life*; Zvi Goldfarb, *Ad Kav Haketz* (Hebrew) (Tel Aviv: Hakibbutz Hameuchad, 1981); Moshe Alpan, *Be'eyn Hase'ara*; Yoel Palgi, *Into the Inferno: The Memoir of a Jewish Paratrooper behind Nazi Lines* (New Bruswick: Rutger's University Press, 2003); Avihu Ronen, *Hakrav al Hahaim* (Hebrew) (Tel Aviv: Yad Ya'ari, 1994).

There were now no more than 10,000 Jews left in hiding in Slovakia.[77] Among them were Bella and Moritz Rosenberg, Benito's parents, as well as his brother Sani (Sándor) and his family.

By this time, Chajka and Benito would already be very far from the theater of events in Europe. They would be in the small kibbutz near Kfar Saba, moving into a family room. But before they would get there, they would have to go through Istanbul and face their first encounter with the Land of Israel.

77 For more about the actions of the Jewish fighters in Slovakia see Nir, *Shvilim Bema'agal Ha'esh*; Nir, *Yehudey Slovakia Bema'avak*; Fatran, *Ha'im Ma'avak al Hisardut*; Yeshayahu Jelínek, "Yehidat Halohamim Hayehudim Mimahane Novaki Beslovakia," *Yalkut Moreshet* (Hebrew), 1 (1962), pp. 47–67.

Chapter Twenty-Four

The Witness

Chajka in Istanbul

In early March 1944, having traveled by train through Romania and Bulgaria, Chajka arrived in Istanbul.[1] Menahem Bader and Wenia Pomeranz came out to greet the arrivals. It had been a good week. Every day, small groups of immigrants and children had been arriving from Budapest, many of them smuggled there from Poland and Slovakia. Just two or three months earlier, these people had been locked up in bunkers or hiding out in the woods, and now—here they were. Bader recalled the following:

> It was an indescribable joy to see their faces and their eyes beaming through the windows of the train as it slowed down and came to a halt at the station. It was sheer delight to hear them singing and waving their hands and saying *shalom* and calling you by your name. There were among them people from all movements, from all parties of the nation of Israel, men, women, and children. There were also a few familiar faces, some of which belonged to members of the movement. Among them was Chajka. Simple, quiet, as if gathered into herself completely and without reservations.[2]

Having known of Chajka from her letters and the copies of the diaries that had been sent to him from Slovakia, Bader was excited to meet her

1 Kukielka, *Escape from the Pit*, pp. 188–189.

2 Menahem Bader, in *Chajka: Hoveret Zikaron*, p. 5; Bader, *Shlihuyot Atzuvot*, p. 90.

in person.[3] According to his testimony, what little free time he had, he spent with her. However, he restrained himself from asking questions, believing that the refugees should be allowed to enjoy the first days of their liberation without having to summon memories of the horrors left behind. They strolled through the streets of Istanbul. Walking past one of the shops, Bader invited Chajka to go in and choose whatever her heart desired, but her reluctant smile was an answer in and of itself—her thoughts were still with those left behind, and thus, she could not allow herself to return to a life of small pleasures just yet.

Still, there were a few moments of happiness. On March 6, 1944, Benito arrived in Istanbul, and together with Chajka, they went on a tour of the city. A rare photograph shows her leaning on the railing of the boardwalk on the Bosporus waterfront with Benito, Yoshko, and two other friends. She is wearing a long coat and squinting in the intense sunlight. There is a faint smile on her lips, as if placed there for the camera's sake. According to Bader's account, in the hours remaining until the departure of her train, she sat in his room in contemplation, without uttering a word. Only when the time came to say goodbye did she ask if he had read her diaries. He answered that yes, he had. Chajka then asked: "Is there a point, after all that, to keep living?" And Bader replied: "It is our duty. Our duty is to keep living. Our duty is to make every day of life a day of struggle for the glorious future of our nation."[4]

As he accompanied Chajka to the station, he shook her hand and intended to "kiss her head and her sad eyes, which kept asking her earlier question—is there a point after all?" However, the Turkish policemen hastened the passengers into the carriages, and the two were separated before he could do so.[5]

The Train Journey

Bader's account implies that the closer Chajka got to Mandatory Palestine, the more dejected she felt. The gaiety and hedonism of her Budapest days were replaced by intense grief. Her soul oscillated

3 Bader hastened to "photocopy" (take photos with a regular camera) the diaries. Later he would send the copies as a parting gift to Ira Hirschmann, Roosevelt's special envoy representing the War Refugee Board. See the letter from Menahem Bader to Ira Hirschmann, October 1944, Moreshet Archive, C.36.24.

4 Bader, "Eulogy," p. 7.

5 Ibid.

between contrasting extremes: The impulse of life told her to enjoy the freedom she had been given; but all the while, the memory of the comrades who had died before her eyes weighed heavily on her heart, denying her even a moment's peace. She was afraid of the encounter with *Eretz Israel*. Would those living there be able to understand the cry of anguish she was bringing with her from the depths of hell? Would she find the strength inside her for rebirth and renewal? Would she be able to love these people who had not suffered the cataclysm, who seemed to have forgotten all about her and her friends? She was all too aware of the fact that she was coming from a different world. Would she be able to bridge that old world with the new?

A unique passage, the composition of which took place in unclear circumstances and which was inserted at the end of *Miyoman Bageto*, probably gives expression to Chajka's thoughts on the train as it made its way to Aleppo, and from there, via Beirut, to Mandatory Palestine. Reflecting on herself and her friends, Chajka remembered how much they had been changed by the war: how they had been hardened by new needs and new problems; how educational concerns made way for matters of daily survival; how they had taught themselves not to cry when loved ones perished; how they had had to learn to put their feelings aside when faced with a task; how veteran guards lost their rights when they failed the test and broke under pressure; how they had lost their optimism:

> We began to doubt the value of our education. The harsher the times, the thicker our armor had to be to fend off resignation and surrender. First of all, [we had] to learn how to control ourselves and not cry or wring our hands. The deportations were reaping a bitter harvest. It was becoming emptier and emptier around us.
>
> How could one not cry when one's mother, father, and sister were no longer at home? How could one stop oneself from going and joining a transport when one's family was already gone? How could one leave one's old mother at such a moment? We obtained arms and became cynics. Our cynicism beggared belief.[6]

Yet, she feared the influence of cynicism in *Eretz Israel*:

> But cynicism knows no bounds. It wreaks havoc in man's spirit and laughs at what used to be sacred. And this is what happened to

6 Klinger, *I Am Writing These Words to You* (1943 diaries), p. 188.

> our attitude toward *Eretz* [*Israel*]. They left us for the five years of war without any sign of life, without any help. Neither the *mosdot* [institutions], the Hakibbutz Ha'artzi, nor the *chaverim* [members] of the *kibbutzim* [helped us]. We were receiving letters saying that they were thinking of us, loving us, embracing and kissing us, but there was no actual help. Long letters about setting up a new colony or the fact that this or that *kibbutz* became a *hityashvut* [settlement] on the eve of the deportation. We laughed at those letters and did not even wish to read them.[7]

Let us recall that the approaching Red Army had replaced Zionism as rescuer and savior in the eyes of Chajka and some of her younger comrades. She herself seemed to have begun doubting the merits of Zionism. Further on, she states:

> Life ceased to play any role whatsoever. We were rushing to our doom. As for our lifestyle, we became somewhat Bohemian. Did it matter that some [of us] were smoking? We even began to drink enough vodka to relax and become quite free in the sexual sphere. I noticed the same symptoms. That spirit of *carpe diem* [seize the day] had an impact on the nation, on the life of emigrant *shomers* in Slovakia and Budapest. That provisional lifestyle left an indelible imprint on them. [...]
>
> They are like leaves detached from the tree on which they grew, their old mother tree. Swirling in the air, they are unable to find their place. They cannot attach themselves to a new tree, and the old one has been cut down and no longer exists. [...]
>
> Can they find their own places? Will not life seem too confined, petty, and bleak to them? Will they be able to sit in one place? They have always been drawn—[to] somewhere or someplace. Will they be able to satisfy that internal drive?[8]

Though *Eretz Israel* promised safety, it did not offer substitution or even compensation for what had been lost. If Chajka had managed to repress her feelings about her decimated family, she at least admitted to herself—and later publicly—that she felt guilty about her dead friends

7 Ibid., pp. 188–189.
8 Ibid., pp. 190–191.

Later, this feeling of guilt would also manifest itself as an intense hatred and resentment of those who were not like them—those who had been granted life.

Kibbutz Galon

The train pulled into the station in Haifa on March 7, 1944. A few members of Kibbutz Galon were there to greet the new arrivals. Chajka noticed tears in their eyes. Later, she would recall that "it was the first ray of sunlight, the warmth of which began to melt away my hatred."[9] A reporter from the movement newspaper *Al Hamishmar* was also on the platform in Haifa, and he hurried to interview her. The next day he published an article with the headline "Eyewitness Testifies about Będzin Ghetto," which opened with the lines: "Horrifying details from the extermination abyss in Poland…as told by CK, a member of Hashomer Hatzair who had been in the Będzin ghetto." "What is the state of the underground resistance today?" the reporter asked. "There is no movement without a people," his interlocutor answered. "With the elimination of the Jewish *hagana*, the organized youth movement has also been eliminated. Most of the members of the *hagana* have not survived. They have fallen in battle."[10]

Chajka would have many more such meetings in the coming weeks. Here, the excitement stirred by her arrival in Mandatory Palestine was no lesser than that of the comrades in Slovakia and Hungary or that of Bader in Istanbul. More than anything, the people were eager to listen, they wanted to know every detail of the lives and deaths of their loved ones. The second stop on her journey in *Eretz Israel* was Kibbutz Ein Shemer. She was brought there by Zvi Lurie, a member of the movement's global leadership. In Ein Shemer she was reunited with one of the members of her old kibbutz, Shmaryahu Milinsky, who had retrained himself for agricultural work. In the evening she spoke to the kibbutz members. Shmaryahu remembered the following:

> The talk started at a quarter past seven [PM]…. The whole of Kibbutz Ein Shemer sat there and listened until three thirty [AM]... And

9 *Dapim*, internally circulated pamphlet, Kibbutz Hashomer Hatzair Galon, 3rd year, 2 (22), March 10, 1944, p. 1.

10 Anonymous, "Ed Re'iya Mesaper al Hageto BeBendin" (Hebrew), *Al Hamishmar*, March 8, 1944.

> she told us about everything that had happened there. During this period, whenever any news arrived or anyone came, they would sit up all night to listen and to hear. There was quite a bit of insulation. They didn't know what was going on. They had no idea. To this day, we cannot fathom how we could have been so oblivious. The whole world. About what was happening and what was going to happen. When a person came to us, here, from that hell.... You can imagine the excitement, they didn't eat or drink. Not so much as a glass of water. They just sat there silently and listened to Chajka. For hours.... Then we went to Zvi's room and stayed up with her, and she continued telling us her story until the morning light.[11]

Shmaryahu did not exaggerate. Only two months earlier, the 3,000 members of Hakibbutz Hameuchad had sat up and listened all night to the reports of Korniański and Unger who had arrived from Poland and Hungary in Kibbutz Givat Brenner. It was "an evening that will not fade from our hearts," stated the conference summary. "When they saw the familiar faces of the movement members, comrades and friends from the days of the operations in the Diaspora clasped them in their arms, and the audience wept for the great disaster and the small miracle that was taking place at that moment."[12]

As in Givat Brenner, the listeners in Ein Shemer had a cathartic experience. Through the words of Chajka, Korniański, and Unger, they were enabled—if only for a moment—to be with their friends in the Holocaust, to identify with them, to live and die with them. Many of the listeners already knew that they had lost their parents, brothers, friends. It was a kind of affirmation of their mortality. Like the father who insists on seeing with his own eyes the random spot in the desert where his son had fallen, they too wanted to know every detail about the deaths of their loved ones and the stories of the survivors. In the hearts of many, there glimmered an ember of hope that their mother, their brother, or their loved one was still alive, against all odds, and that maybe they would also make it to the Promised Land.

A day or two after the meeting in Ein Shemer, Chajka headed to her own kibbutz, Kibbutz Galon. Aharon Brandes, who had also been assigned to that kibbutz, traveled with her. *Al Hamishmar* published a news item about their arrival that appeared in the center of the back page:

11 Shmaryahu Milinsky interview.

12 "Introduction," 14th meeting of Hakibbutz Hameuchad, 1944, leaflet published by Hakibbutz Hameuchad.

> Remnants of a hero movement: Kibbutz Galon welcomes members who have escaped from hell. Galon (Nes Ziona), Thursday. Hours of excitement and deep emotional shockwaves gripped Kibbutz Galon as it welcomed two members, Chajka Klinger and Aharon Brandes, the first survivors of the Nazi inferno, who left Będzin at the end of 1943 and arrived in *Eretz Israel* on Monday via Turkey. The anticipation reached its peak when the entire kibbutz came out to the *moshava*[13] to welcome the guests of honor. A large crowd of people working in the *moshava* also gathered near the bus station. A chill went through the crowd as the two got out of the car. Cheers and tears erupted from their hearts. Friends from the time of the *ken* and the *hachshara* threw their arms around the arrivals.[14]

The members of the small kibbutz, whose tents were pitched on Givat Michael behind the *moshava*, were already used to welcoming incoming refugees. In 1940, a number of members from the Vilna gathering came to the kibbutz. In October 1942, a group of activists who had traveled for many months from Vilna via Moscow, Tehran, Bombay, and Suez also arrived here.[15] However, in March 1944, the number of those left behind in Poland was still almost equal to those who had arrived in *Eretz Israel*. The occasion of the fifth anniversary of the kibbutz members' immigration to *Eretz Israel*, which had been celebrated recently in the presence of Meir Ya'ari, was marred by pain and loss, and many pages in the anniversary issue of the kibbutz bulletin were dedicated to members who had perished in the war or vanished without a trace.[16]

Shayke Goldrin delivered the opening remarks on the evening of Chajka and Aharon's arrival. As in Kalisz, here, too, he was at the center of things. He said:

> Our joy is not unmitigated this evening. You have arrived but bearing tragic news: our friends who stayed behind have fallen and are no longer among the living. How shall we welcome you? With

13 A *moshava* is a form of agricultural settlement dating from the Ottoman empire wherein the land is privately owned, unlike in a kibbutz or a moshav.

14 "Sridim shel Tnu'at Giborim" (Hebrew), *Al Hamishmar*, March 10, 1944.

15 Moshe (Mosze) Gal, "Al Pney Artzot Veyamim" (Hebrew), *Yalkut Moreshet*, 32 (1981), pp. 71–100.

16 "Hamesh Shanim Lekibbutz Hashomer Hatzair Galon," January 1944, Nes Ziona, Kibbutz Galon Archive, pp. 48–52. The article mentions the names of seventy-three members left behind in Poland and the Soviet Union.

> nothing but blessings and elation, or while doing some deep soul-searching? For five years we have been separated from you, and now it appears that a misunderstanding has arisen between us. It is difficult to convince you that our entire lives here have had one single meaning—our friends in the Diaspora. Tell us what you have been through, it is our great desire to know how Polish Jewry and our members among it lived and died. This enterprise that we have established here is not just ours. It is yours as well.[17]

Then it was Chajka and Aharon's turn to speak. A deathly silence reigned in the dining hall. Here, in Galon, they talked about the death of friends who were very familiar to the listeners. Most of the members of the *hachshara* had been killed: Shoshana Neuman had been killed in Żarki; Shimshon and Mendek had given their lives in service in the Polish army; Dorka Herzberg had disappeared on the road. Their reports about the demise of the two men who were supposed to take leadership positions in the kibbutz—David Kozłowski and Zvi Brandes—were particularly heartrending. Of their trio, Chajka remained the only survivor. Later, Esther Shoshan would remember the terrible silence of the enraptured listeners, broken only by a stifled sob here and there.[18]

For many members, especially those who hailed from Zagłębie, Chajka and Aharon came bearing long-dreaded news. Before the gathering that evening, Abrashka Eisenberg asked them about the fate of his girlfriend Zippora Szporn. Chajka told him that to her knowledge, Zippora had been deported to Auschwitz and added that Auschwitz was a place from which no one returned. Abrashka would later recall this episode, admitting that the rest of the evening was a blur—his personal tragedy had eclipsed all else. And yet, he continued to hope as, after all, there were no witnesses to her death. He kept that hope alive for three more years, until he finally learned that Zippora's name was on the list of survivors from Bergen-Belsen.[19]

The warmth and the sorrow with which Chajka was received in Galon melted some of her hardness and bitterness. For the first time since escaping from the hell of Poland she, too, burst into tears. During a kibbutz meeting, she found out that despite the distance and lack of correspondence over those years, her friends in Galon had kept her alive

17 *Dapim*, 3rd year, 2 (22), March 10, 1944, p. 1.

18 Ibid.; Esther Shoshan interview.

19 Abrashka Eisenberg interview.

in their thoughts. She had not been forgotten after all.[20] Yet, the welcome she felt was immediately mixed with guilt. What was the point if she couldn't write about it to those who hadn't managed to stay alive? Late at night, when she retired to sleep in Chana Lieberman's room, she said to her: "I wish I had stayed there too."[21] Esther Shoshan, who would later recount this, felt "as if a sense of guilt had crept up on her, a feeling of having sinned in being the only one left.... She cried over the great sin of having stayed alive!"[22]

Esther was sensitive enough to notice that Chajka was carrying around a terrible burden; and yet, she had only seen the tip of the iceberg. It consisted not only of guilt but also of a great amount of hatred. In the particularly harrowing passage that closes her diary, Chajka confesses her resentment of the life she saw blossoming all around her: "When I first saw the children, the young, they made me angry about those little, innocent Jewish children who had been murdered, deported, strangled—about the fact that these ones were too well off."[23]

By this time there was a little boy bouncing on Esther's knees. Shayke and his wife were also living in a family room together. The kibbutz members decorated the meager rooms with empty yoghurt jars and made little bookshelves and cupboards out of milk crates. They went out to work every day, carrying the loaf baked for them in the kibbutz kitchen. Some had already become professionals in the fields of construction and agriculture.[24] Whereas Chajka, who was the same age and had come through the same training, had been left behind. She was the woman from back there, still wearing her black beret, as was the fashion of the revolutionaries in Europe, still hurt, still bitter, still grieving.[25]

Hakibbutz Ha'artzi

The next day, Chajka went to attend the meeting of the Executive Committee of Hakibbutz Ha'artzi. Benito, who had arrived in the meantime, was already waiting for her there. At the meeting, Chajka and

20 Letter from Chajka to friends, 1944, Esther Shoshan collection. See also chapter 25.

21 Chana Lieberman interview.

22 Esther Shoshan, in *Chajka: Hoveret Zikaron*, p. 5.

23 Klinger, *I Am Writing These Words to You* (1943 diaries), p. 192.

24 "Hamesh Shanim Lekibbutz Hashomer Hatzair Galon," Kibbutz Galon Archive, pp. 4–5.

25 Esther Shoshan interview.

Aharon Brandes were supposed to present the testimonies from Poland, while Benito and Yoshko Baumer were to report on Hashomer Hatzair's activities in Slovakia and Hungary. The presentation before the Executive Committee of Hakibbutz Ha'artzi was supposed to be the high point of Chajka's lecture tour. This was a powerful institution that oversaw forty-one kibbutzim, an educational movement with thousands of trainees, a publishing house, and an extensive newspaper network. At the meeting, Chajka was supposed to speak in front of the movement's main activists, headed by the man whose name she had spoken with reverence so many times and to whom she had directed her letters—Meir Ya'ari himself. As far as Benito remembered, before the meeting, Meir Ya'ari had a private audience with Chajka.[26] What the first representative of the remaining Hashomer Hatzair activists in Europe said to the father of her movement, we will never know. However, as the meeting that followed revealed, it is very possible that they had stumbled onto a number of disagreements. Chajka opened her speech to the committee as follows:

> For years we have dreamed of seeing the Land of Israel and meeting with Hakibbutz Ha'artzi, and now our dream has come true. We have come to *Eretz Israel* for strange reasons. We have come to tell not only tales of heroism but also all the stories of Hashomer Hatzair and Polish Jewry during the war. I am ashamed to be here. I am not the one who should be standing here before you. Our meeting is symbolic. It should have been the ones who led the organizational work of the movement—they are the ones who should have been in this position, not me.
>
> I'll tell you this for a fact: All the things I have endured throughout this period, none of them have brought me to a state of tears. And yet, yesterday, for the first time, I cried. It was during the kibbutz [Galon] meeting.
>
> The times have left their mark on us. We have become cynical; we mocked *Eretz Israel* and Hakibbutz Ha'artzi, and we dreaded this moment of encounter. You would not believe how much we feared this moment.[27]

26 Ya'akov Ronen interview.

27 Chajka Klinger, speech delivered at a meeting of the Executive Committee of Hakibbutz Ha'artzi, Moreshet Archive, D.1.1051 (Hebrew) (typed document, probably in preparation for publication in *Al Hamishmar*), p. 1.

It was a strange and harsh overture. Instead of expressing joy, she seemed to be apologizing that it was her and not Tosia Altman or Mordechai Anielewicz standing where she was. Instead of breathing a sigh of relief, like a prodigal daughter finally home from exile, she spoke of the anxiety of return. Her role as witness was one she did not take lightly. Would she prove worthy to tell the tale as it should be told? Would her listeners understand?

> A romantic view of our life has emerged in *Eretz Israel*. This view is incorrect and exaggerated. It is a terrible era we are living through. It is a life-and-death struggle and our movement and the Hechalutz movement have served as a singular light shining to reveal the filth of this era. I am plagued by fears that it will become extremely popular and serve as inspiration for cheap literature. It is indeed my duty to tell, but there is a danger of misrepresentation and this we [must] keep in mind.[28]

And so, she began unfolding her tale with little glorification and few superlatives. Her goal was to report the facts as they were. The only liberty she took was to speak in the first-person plural—"we"—even when recounting the uprising in Warsaw. Her listeners knew that she herself had not taken part in it but that she was familiar with all the details of the events and personally knew the people involved. Indeed, most of her presentation was devoted to the Warsaw Ghetto Uprising. The details she gave were consistent with what was known at the time—she described the formation of the Anti-Fascist Bloc and the establishment of contact with Andrzej Szmidt who had been parachuted in from a Russian plane, the attempts to join the partisans during the Great Deportation, the arguments between Kaplan and Anielewicz. She gave an account of Zelcer's betrayal and Kaplan's death, of the formation of the ŻOB, of the revenge actions against Lejkin and others, of the January 1943 uprising, and finally of the ghetto uprising in April and its bitter aftermath. She knew every detail of the fall of the last bunker at Miła 18, as well as the fire that took Tosia Altman's life.

By contrast, she had little to say about Będzin and Zagłębie, as if they had been overshadowed by the Warsaw Ghetto Uprising. When she did speak of her own group and their actions, she seemed regretful, almost apologetic:

28 Ibid.

> We didn't have time to make the necessary preparations. All the weapons were concentrated in one bunker and we did not have the means to distribute them to different locations. It would not be an exaggeration to say that all the Jews in Upper Silesia went into hiding. Entire streets were deserted. The deportation *Aktion* continued for two weeks. Houses were blown up and the whole ghetto looked like a war zone. Resistance was impossible.[29]

She made no mention of Zvi, David, Frumka, or Herszel, and spoke of her own torture only in passing while recounting the weapons incident:

> When leaving the bunker, they found two guns. They asked: Whose are these? Someone pointed out two girls, to whom the guns belonged. The girls, of course, took the blame on themselves. We were taken to the Gestapo. They demanded that we give names and information. We refused. I don't need to tell you the nature of the beatings we received. There was no doubt in our minds that they would kill us. But they did not.[30]

Twice during her speech, she addressed the question of the Soviet Union. First, she talked about the council (which probably took place in Zagłębie) where the movement's sympathetic attitude toward the Soviet Union was made official. However, she stated that she and her friends had opposed those who saw the Soviet Union as the only hope at the expense of their belief in Zionism.[31] Finally, toward the end of her speech, she stated that the process of productivization imposed by the Germans had changed the Jews' attitude to work and had made the younger generation ready to accept a life of labor in the Soviet Union. The approach of the Russian front also increased the fascination with the Red Army. "It was clear that if they should come, we would be swept away by the current. The movement would not be able to withstand the general current and would be dragged along on the waves of red assimilation."[32]

With stark frankness, she confronted her listeners with the question: "What is the future of Zionism in light of the

29 Ibid., p. 7.
30 Ibid., p. 8.
31 Ibid., p. 2.
32 Ibid., p. 9.

extermination of the majority of the subjects of Jewish Zionism?" This was a reformulation of the question of the "avant-garde without a people" with which she had been wrestling for many months. Meir Ya'ari's sharp political senses made him immediately aware of what the question meant. As permitted by the meeting procedures, he fired a question at the speaker: "What is your conclusion?" Like a student stumped by her professor, Chajka replied: "We did not have enough time to establish a position. The disaster came upon us unexpectedly."[33] Yet, she quickly managed to gather her wits and added:

> In 1942, the prevailing opinion was that we should direct our efforts toward participation in the building of the Soviet Union and that all our ideas about Jewish settlement in the Land of Israel should be consigned to history.... We had not had enough time to formulate an ideological position because we had to prepare for defense and death.[34]

Following this, she fired back at the Executive Committee as a whole: "We did not see great concern for the Jewish community in Poland on the part of Hakibbutz Ha'artzi. We needed help, weapons, people. We didn't need you to weep over us. We never said that the path was not worthwhile, even though it was so tragic and so terrible."[35]

Here, according to the printed minutes of the meeting, "Meir Ya'ari gave his answer," yet the answer itself is missing from the document.[36] Only later, when the handwritten minutes of the meeting of the Executive Committee's secretariat came to light, would his answer to all the refugees of Europe, including Benito, Yoshko, and Chajka, be revealed.[37]

33 Ibid., p. 3.
34 Ibid., p. 9.
35 Ibid.
36 Ibid.
37 Meir Ya'ari's remarks, handwritten protocol of the 54th meeting of the Secretariat of the Executive Committee of Hakibbutz Ha'artzi, Hashomer Hatzair Archive, Yad Ya'ari, secretariat log, March 1944, 54(3). It is possible that this manuscript contains the minutes of a meeting of the secretariat that took place on March 27, 1944, with the participation of Chajka, Benito, and Yoshko Baumer.

Ya'ari's Answer

At the time when Chajka presented her report, Meir Ya'ari was at one of the peaks of his glory. The Hakibbutz Ha'artzi organization had continued to develop during the war: the economic situation of the kibbutzim improved, five more kibbutzim were established, and Hashomer Hatzair became a major opposition force on the political scene. Furthermore, as part of the Socialist League, he had won roughly 20 percent of the votes at the Histadrut conference. Yet Ya'ari, who was no stranger to illness, was also tired. The incessant struggles at home and abroad depleted his strength. A few months later, he would ask to resign from his position.[38]

On the other hand, he was once again faced with the question of his movement's position regarding the Soviet Union. During the war, Hashomer Hatzair had strengthened its ties with the Soviet Union and took an active part in the Israeli-Soviet Friendship League established in the summer of 1942 (later renamed the "V League"—the "V" standing for Victory). The visit of two junior Russian diplomats to the Hashomer Hatzair kibbutzim in 1942 was accompanied by a certain sense of intoxication at the prospect of a change in the attitude of the Soviet Union toward the Zionist enterprise.[39] It was Ya'ari's responsibility to dampen the enthusiasm on the left and the skepticism on the right—he had censured the Yakum and Hama'apil people in 1941 for having moved too far to the left.[40] He had also scolded a group of Galon members—who had returned from their travels and told the movement members about what was happening in the Soviet Union—for holding up a "warped mirror" to reality: "It was the travails of the road that made them lose their minds."[41] This may have been the secret of his leadership: Ya'ari always knew how to bring the erring sheep back to the flock. The reprimands were always accompanied by words of reconciliation and comfort.[42] Thus, those who had been admonished,

38 Halamish, *Meir Ya'ari*, pp. 251–254.

39 Ya'ari, *Bederech Aruka*, pp. 251–255.

40 Halamish, *Meir Ya'ari*, pp. 264–265.

41 Ya'ari, *Bederech Aruka*, p. 130. Esther Shoshan spoke about the raging arguments that the head of this group, Moshe Gal, had with Meir Ya'ari. Esther Shoshan interview.

42 Ya'ari concluded his address to Moshe Gal and his friends with the following words: "I do not forget the pioneer loyalty and devotion that served them in everything they set out to do, and there is no doubt that the burdens of their wanderings atone for their mistakes." Ya'ari, *Bederech Aruka*, p. 130.

whether on the left or on the right, would inevitably end up swallowing their insult and remain loyal to the movement.

Later, Benito would recall that at that time, he also met with Ya'ari privately to give him a report on the activities of Hashomer Hatzair in Slovakia. Ya'ari listened in silence without interrupting. His eyes were fixed on the new jacket that Benito's friends had bought for him in Budapest on the eve of his trip. Finally, he said: "Where did you get that beautiful coat?"[43]

Ya'ari's answer to the members who had arrived from devastated Europe was rather confused: "I find it difficult to say anything after listening to you," he opened his remarks at that meeting. He saw Chajka and her friends as the first survivors, the harbingers of more people to come, and emphasized: "The words coming out of your mouths—they are my destiny." Turning to Chajka, he said: "I want to talk to you separately. Together we need to clear up some things regarding the possibilities that might open up there [in Europe]."[44] It would appear that he wished to avoid the ideological debate raised by Chajka's difficult questions as well as Benito's report, as evident from the following statement: "There is no need to preach morality. Those who did not pay too much mind to ideological stringency have done well. It is better to lose the movement member but save the person. The ideological terrain can always be repaired, but only living people can continue fighting." He then addressed Chajka's accusation directly: "I do not accept the claim that we have abandoned our movement abroad." To back up his argument, Ya'ari described Hakibbutz Ha'artzi's efforts to maintain contact with the movement in Europe throughout the war, the members' willingness to join the fight in Europe, the means and labor invested in Bader's mission, the fundraising. "There was no shortage of people ready to join the partisans.... *Eretz Israel* is the only place in the world that managed to raise money."[45]

Yet, while his remarks contained hints of remorse—"We knew that we could not replace Oren in Switzerland, and that was disastrous.... Our failure was that we did not manage to establish a delegation in Switzerland"[46]—he would not admit to more than that. There was no owning up to the abandonment of Hashomer Hatzair envoys during

43 Ya'akov Ronen, interview by the author, Sde Nitzan, 2009.

44 The idea of sending in a parachute brigade was being considered at the time.

45 Meir Ya'ari's remarks, secretariat log, March 1944, Hashomer Hatzair Archive, 54(3).

46 Ibid.

the first years of the occupation, the departure of the central leadership from Poland, the long years of radio silence before Bader's departure to Istanbul, his refusal to acquiesce to Bader's repeated appeals to send a letter to his disciples in the ghettos, the same disciples who frequently used his name as a code name for the entire movement. Chajka herself, in the letter about Anielewicz's death, had written that "Grandfather Meir" could be proud of his children.[47] However, Ya'ari was not about to get reprimanded by his surviving daughter. As it had always been, the role of the scolding parent was reserved for him alone.

Ya'ari also spoke in detail on the matter of the Soviet Union. According to him, had he been in Slovakia, he would have resolved the dispute described by Benito. Ya'ari stressed that despite the Soviet victories, the Land of Israel was the only solution to the Jewish question. "There is a dawn on the horizon of this war. We have created it so that we could absorb the rest of the survivors." His final answer to Chajka and her friends was clear: "We were last in the Diaspora; here we have to be the first. It is not easy to rebuild a nation."[48] Over time, with the arrival of other ghetto fighters bringing with them the good news of victory and struggle, this perception would only be strengthened: "We have much to learn from you about how heroes should die, but when it comes to living a heroic life day in and day out...we ask that you let us teach you a lesson."[49] Ya'ari, as mentioned, did not believe in symbols of self-sacrifice and was not enraptured with the example of the Warsaw Ghetto Uprising.[50] Even though at a gathering in Galon roughly two months prior he had held up the image of Tosia as an exemplary kibbutz member, this was only to encourage her living friends to take their place "on the frontline" of the kibbutz "creation." Never once in his answer to Chajka did he address her own act of resistance or that of her comrades in Europe.

Chajka replied respectfully, almost apologetically, but in a manner that also made it clear that she was not about to retract her claims:

47 See chapter 15.

48 Meir Ya'ari's remarks, secretariat log, March 1944, Hashomer Hatzair Archive, 54(3).

49 Meir Ya'ari, remarks at the meeting of the World Partisan Movement in Evron, November 1945, in Dror and Rosenzweig, *Sefer Hashomer Hatzair*, vol. 2, p. 528.

50 For more on Ya'ari's response to the uprising, see chapter 15, and Neima Barzel, *Ad Kelot U'mineged: Hamifgash bein Manhigey Mered Hageta'ot levein Hahevra HaYisraelit* (Hebrew) (Jerusalem: Hasifriya Hatzionit al Yad Hahistadrut Hatzionit Ha'olamit, 1998), pp. 91–93.

> One has the impression that we have not been properly understood. We couldn't discuss everything at length. The Land of Israel was far away and difficult to reach. Our starting assumption was that the Jews were not participating in the historical struggle taking place right now. That is why we contacted the partisans. People went to the partisans not only for self-preservation. It is difficult to judge someone for associating with communist ideology [based on] their will to live.
>
> We were cut off from *Eretz Israel*, and any knowledge we had was fragmentary. There is no doubt that there was willingness on your part, but in reality, there were no signs of an organized effort to participate in our struggle. What we saw was that over here people stuck to the old ways of building and keeping calm. But the country did not enter the historical struggle. We joined the partisans as an independent stream. With the rise in exterminations, we questioned what would happen to Zionism, and one must not wonder at the fact that we strayed.[51]

Ya'ari then summed up the issue in an ostensibly conciliatory manner: "I approve of self-rescue. I approve of joining the partisans. We never gave explicit instructions to our people to save themselves."[52] Was this last sentence also a kind of belated response to the telegram sent but a few months earlier? Possibly. In the typed version of Chajka's speech, there is no mention of the telegram, but it is possible that she had brought it up in another conversation. In public, of course, Ya'ari had to deny the telegram's existence.

As evident from this exchange, Ya'ari and Chajka's relationship was a far cry from the warm and close bond that had formed between Tabenkin and Zivia Lubetkin in 1946. The two spent three days together in a quiet house in Beit Oren, with Zivia telling her story and Tabenkin listening attentively. Unlike Ya'ari, Tabenkin was ready to admit his own personal responsibility, as well as that of the movement. He had no trouble remembering that he and his fellow leaders had asked Zivia, Antek, and Frumka to stay in Poland when the war broke out. "We tasked them with the mission of remaining at the helm of the movement," he said in his response to Zivia Lubetkin's speech at the Hakibbutz Ha'artzi conference

51 Chajka Klinger's remarks, secretariat log, March 1944, Hashomer Hatzair Archive, 54(3).

52 Meir Ya'ari's remarks, secretariat log, March 1944, Hashomer Hatzair Archive, 54(3).

in June 1946. It is possible that Tabenkin's sympathy also stemmed from his complete identification with the act of revolt: He was convinced that for "the six million who went to the slaughter, resistance was imperative," and that "not resisting did not save anything or anyone."[53]

While Ya'ari was best known as the harsh father of the movement who educated his children with reprimands, the figure of Tabenkin was more in line with the archetype of the gentle, merciful father. And yet, Ya'ari was not entirely devoid of affection or kindness.[54] Over a decade later, when he learned of Chajka's passing, he would take the trouble to write to the secretary of Kibbutz Haogen and to Benito (in that order): "Please accept my deep sympathy in your grief at the passing of Chajka Klinger. To this day, I see her pleasant image before me, and I am still powerfully shaken by her stories about the Holocaust and the struggle in which she took part. Yours, in friendship, Meir Ya'ari."[55]

As usual, Ya'ari's response came a little too late.

Al Hamishmar

A few days later, on March 17, 1944, Chajka's testimony and Brandes's complementary statements were spread across an entire page in the *Al Hamishmar* newspaper. The testimony was presented almost in its entirety, except for a number of modifications (mostly with the intention of softening the depictions) and omissions. Some of these were significant: instead of "we mocked *Eretz Israel* and Hakibbutz Ha'artzi," the text read: "we mocked our holy values." The sentence saying that "resistance [in Będzin] was impossible" was omitted. The problematic paragraph about her doubts regarding the fate of Zionism after the annihilation of the Jewish people was likewise left out.

By devoting an entire page to Chajka and Brandes's reports, the movement in *Eretz Israel* demonstrated the enormous importance it attached to the words of the ghetto fighters but did not refrain from censoring everything that contained a hint of criticism. In particular, the comrades in *Eretz Israel* were not ready to admit that they had sat idly by. Other paragraphs that touched on the elimination of Nazi collaborators,

53 Barzel, *Ad Kelot U'mineged*, p. 152.

54 Halamish emphasizes the warm relationship that formed between Ya'ari and Różka Korczak, but she also notes that it was an exception to the rule. Halamish, *Meir Ya'ari*, pp. 274–275.

55 Chajka Klinger file, Moreshet Archive, C.36.

Zelcer's betrayal, and Tosia's chances of survival were apparently omitted, as publishing such information was risky for underground activists at that time.[56]

Alongside Chajka and Brandes's testimony, the paper included Mordechai Bentov's article titled "Hirhurim Al Gvura" (Reflections on Heroism).[57] Bentov was the paper's editor in chief, and in this article, he tried to expound the lessons that the movement was supposed to derive from Chajka's report. It was a strange article. Bentov starts by admitting that everyone who heard the story of the Będzin group was "upset to the point of agony." Yet he immediately determines that the tidings brought in by the arrivals are really nothing new, and he is therefore puzzled by the "strange and unnatural lust for tragic news" that he has discovered within himself. "From whence does this appetite for scratching wounds that have not yet scabbed over stem?" he ponders. The answer he eventually arrives at is that the "strange and unnatural lust" originates from the listeners' self-hatred for continuing to live their daily lives and shame over their joy-filled existence here as opposed to the terror experienced by the Jews in Europe. He thus gives expression to the feelings of guilt that Chajka's testimony evoked.

Further on in the article, Bentov formulates the movement's attitude toward the ghetto fighters, emphasizing the heroism of the fighters, who fulfilled the movement's ideological promise, and its contrast to the behavior of the Judenrat, the Jewish police, and "the man of the herd laying his head beneath the slaughterer's axe." "They have removed the shame of fear and the stain of disgrace from the Jewish community in exile," he writes, "so that we here and the generations of Jews in [*Eretz*] Israel that follow can walk upright and look into the eyes of others with pride. We will remember—they died for life, for the honor in our lives."[58] Thus Bentov aligns himself with Yonatan Ratosh, the young Tabenkin, and Yitzhak Gruenbaum in expressing the "sense of disgrace and humiliation" inflicted on them by the Diaspora Jews.

When it came to this central point in Chajka's testimony, her messages fell on attentive ears. There was unanimous respect and admiration for the fallen heroes. The living heroes, on the other hand, were more difficult to deal with. The perception of the "death of the avant-garde" that Chajka had brought with her, as well as her claims about the

56 *Al Hamishmar*, March 17, 1944.

57 Mordechai Bentov, "Hirhurim al Gvura" (Hebrew), *Al Hamishmar*, March 17, 1944.

58 Ibid.

Yishuv's failures during the war, made it problematic to have her inducted into the movement's pantheon as the first witness of the ghetto uprising. Nine months later, in December 1944, Różka Korczak, the representative of the Vilna partisans, would arrive in Israel and enter the movement's collective memory as the one who delivered the news of the uprising.

The Histadrut

Five days after her appearance before the Executive Committee of Hakibbutz Ha'artzi, on March 15, 1944, Chajka appeared before the Executive Committee of the Histadrut. Fredka Oksenhendler (Mazia) and Sheva Ingster of Hanoar Hatzioni, who had arrived in *Eretz Israel* with her, also spoke on this occasion. Ben-Gurion was present at the meeting, but he left the assembly hall at some point, and it is not clear whether he heard the testimony.[59]

Chajka began her address by repeating her warning against the temptation to mythologize the uprising, and this time, she phrased it in sharper terms:

> There is much to tell. The heroism of the Hechalutz movement, the youth movements, must be told. But there is a risk that the sacrifices of the pioneering youth might become cheap literature. This must not be allowed to happen. It is not a matter of practicality. We need to establish a large enterprise of remembering what happened there.[60]

She gave vivid depictions of the deportations and the extermination; she described the negative behavior of the Judenrat, the role of the *hagana*, and the difficulties in its organization. She emphasized that many of the Judenräte were headed by Zionists:

> Various communities [Judenräte] were headed by leaders of the Zionist movement, and most of them failed to understand that if they said "A," they had to carry out "B." By the time they started collecting gold and furniture from the Jews, they already had no choice but to help the Germans in preparing the lists of Jews for the

59 Ya'akov Ronen interview.

60 Chaja Klinger, remarks at the meeting of the Executive Committee of the Histadrut, March 1944, Moreshet Archive, C.53.1.24, p. 7.

> labor camps. Once they started establishing the Jewish militia and the deportation operations began, there was no turning back. And precisely because most of the [Judenräte] had Zionists at the helm, it had a negative psychological influence on the masses of Jews with relation to the Zionist idea, and hatred for Zionism grew with every passing day. If, after the war, the same people will once again rise up to lead the Zionist enterprise, it will certainly be difficult to win over the Jewish masses onto the side of Zionism. And one day we will have to pass judgment on these people. We cannot remain silent. It should be said openly and clearly that many Zionists betrayed [the nation], but the Zionist youth remained loyal. Yes, there should be a trial for Chaim Mołczadski, the head of the Keren Kayemet in Będzin, who later became the head of the community [Judenrat], as well as for many others.[61]

The delivery of these allegations in this specific forum was the result of a deliberate choice. Chajka was looking for the right audience to reckon with the Judenrat Zionists. Merin's life had already come to an end in Auschwitz. According to a rare testimony, before his death he had been severely beaten in Auschwitz by Jews from Będzin who had recognized him.[62] Mołczadski would later immigrate to *Eretz Israel* and give his life in combat in the 1948 war. He would be buried in Nahalat Yitzhak under the name Chaim Aharoni.[63] Later, rumors would spread among the members of the Będzin chapter of Hanoar Hatzioni that he may have been killed by one of them. Genia, Mołczadski's widow, who lived in Haifa in the 1980s, refused to testify on this issue.[64] Chaim Merin, Moniek's brother and right-hand man, survived and would be tried in Poland after the war.[65] Barenblatt, too, was supposed to be retried in Poland, having already been prosecuted once by the rescue activists in Budapest. As previously mentioned, when he would later ask Chajka to testify on his behalf, Chajka responded with an outburst of rage.[66] Other Zionists from the Judenrat, such as Michał Laskier who was in the detention camp

61 Ibid., p. 11.

62 Israel Bleichman, interview by the author, Kibbutz Haogen, 1985.

63 "Chaim (Mołczadski) Aharoni," Yizkor, http://www.izkor.gov.il (accessed May 6, 2024).

64 Genia Aharoni, phone interview by the author, Haifa, 1985.

65 Decision of the court for the exoneration and honor trials of liberated Jews in the American Occupied Zone in Munich, May 26, 1949, YVA, M.21.2.20.

66 Ya'akov Rosenberg testimony at the Barenblatt trial, Moreshet Archive, D.1.5366.

for foreign nationals in Germany at the time, may have enjoyed more sympathy on Chajka's part.

It is safe to assume that the link Chajka established between the Judenrat and Zionism was not a comfortable thing for her listeners in *Eretz Israel* to hear, to say the least. Later, this problematic and entangled relationship would become the subject of much controversy among historians. On the other hand, the portrait she presented of the pioneer youth and their actions on the Jewish street stood in stark contrast to the Judenrat Zionists. Here, at the Histadrut, she did not place particular emphasis on Hashomer Hatzair. She mainly related to the question of defense versus rescue, which had come up in the remarks of Fredka, who had spoken before her. The latter described the extensive rescue operations as a reaction to the deportations: "We then said to ourselves: there is no use in continuing like this [as fighters] and we must save those who remain."[67] Whereas Chajka continued to reject the option of rescue even now:

> The pioneering movement is the vanguard of the people. It must not save itself when the entire nation is about to perish. The pioneer of a people without the people has no value. When the question of rescue or non-rescue arose, the youth movements could not take the path of rescue alone. If there is to be rescue, the people must be rescued, and if there is to be annihilation—the pioneer will perish too.[68]

From here, she seamlessly pivoted to the subject of the help that never came, and this time, she named names: "During the war years we received neither support nor help. And there was a time when our bitterness was aimed mainly toward Nathan Schwalb. In the midst of a terrible period of darkness and anguish, in the days of a terrible struggle for our existence, Nathan Schwalb was unable to rise above his ambitions and partisan ways." Unfazed by the interruption of Joseph Baratz, who called out "There is other information!" Chajka continued: "We shall have a discussion together with him one day. The best proof is that in the detention camp [for foreign citizens] you will not find today a single

67 Frida (Fredka) Mazia, remarks at the meeting of the Executive Committee of the Histadrut, March 1944, Moreshet Archive, C.53.1.24, p. 6.

68 Chaja Klinger, remarks at the meeting of the Executive Committee of the Histadrut, March 1944, Moreshet Archive, C.53.1.24, p. 16.

member of Dror or Hashomer Hatzair, but you will find seven members of Gordonia."[69]

She then moved on to describe the events of the uprising in Warsaw while highlighting the purges carried out by the ŻOB among the "informants" and Jewish collaborators. At the end of her remarks, she spoke about the fighting in the bunkers in Będzin but noted ruefully: "However, it was not a big enterprise. In other places, such as Białystok and Warsaw, the *hagana* movement encompassed a wide stratum. If the history of the movement is to be told, it should mainly concern the events of Warsaw and not Zagłębie."

She ended her speech with a summary of the tragic fate of the Jewish youth and pioneer movement in Poland. It would appear that the eyes of her listeners filled with tears at this point; however, she asked her audience not to weep over the movement: "The movement followed the right path, even if that path was awful and tragic. Where the entire people is dying, the avant-garde must die as well." To this, the secretary of the Histadrut David Remez replied: "I weep because it is too late, we really are too late."[70]

69 Ibid., p. 15.
70 Ibid., p. 19.

Chapter Twenty-Five

Chajka R.

Zvi: 1986

I tell my brother Zvi about my research only after its completion. We meet in Tel Aviv and talk at length while strolling along the brightly illuminated city streets. We haven't spoken to each other in years. Zvi is very much interested in my findings and has his own details to add based on childhood memories of Mother. He asks to see the manuscript, which is already a whopping 600 pages long, and promises to photocopy it in its entirety at his workplace. He buys a ream of paper and makes a meticulous copy, on the margins of which he makes notes in his neat handwriting. The hulking volume in which he has bound the photocopied pages would later become the only complete copy of the manuscript.

Zvi is named after Zvi Brandes. He is our parents' firstborn child, having come into the world only a year after they had immigrated to Mandatory Palestine. Now he is a senior engineer at Rafael Advanced Defense Systems. He lives in Karmiel with his wife and two daughters and hardly ever makes it to Tel Aviv. This time he's staying in town a little longer at my request. His memories of Mother are few and far between. He remembers going to Tel Aviv with her to visit our uncles, the conversations they had in Uncle Yosef's bathroom regarding his political views. Mother insisted on explaining the difference between Uncle Yosef's bourgeois lifestyle and the kibbutz lifestyle in which she wholeheartedly believed. He also remembers the children's room in Bratislava during the mission in Slovakia. He had his own toy train there, a remarkable thing for a boy reared on the milk of communal education. Then later, after their return to the kibbutz, Zvi remembers going on Saturday carriage rides in a buggy hitched to Polly, the white horse belonging to the construction division, with the four of us merrily squished in together on the wooden planks that served as our seat. Occasionally, Zvi and I would be allowed to hold the reins.

Zvi also remembers the hard time he had processing his feelings after Mother's suicide. As a young boy, the conclusion he drew from it was that the world was bad and that one must be tough in order to survive its ordeals. From that point on he tried to never let his emotions show. He was considered a terror by the teachers and supervisors at the kibbutz's educational institutions and only went to classes that interested him—mathematics, for example. Alec, a cynical Hungarian-born intellectual who taught all the scientific subjects at the kibbutz, made Zvi his protégé. His efforts soon bore fruit: In the eleventh grade, Zvi, endowed with a confident drawing hand and substantial mathematical abilities, won second place in the Weizmann Institute's mathematical model competition.

Over the years, Mother remained mostly locked away in our own private memories. If there was any anger, it was well suppressed by our efforts to rebuild our lives without her. We continued to drive on Saturdays in Polly's buggy to Kfar Haim for ice cream. From time to time Zvi and I even tried to ride Polly. Later, when the banana plantation near the kibbutz was uprooted and an ancient burial mound was discovered underneath it, we went there to dig in the black soil, unearthing old pottery. Zvi and Father built a mosaic fish pond and populated it with two goldfish—Johnny and Belinda. Father bought Zvi a whittling tool, and he carved an exquisite head of an African woman with a big curly afro out of wood.

And then a new maternal figure—Malka—quietly but determinedly secured her place in our family. Malka was a veteran fighter: She had been one of the pioneers of Kibbutz Ma'anit, and in 1943, despite the movement's reservations, she enlisted in the Auxiliary Territorial Service (ATS) established by the British army. In Italy, where she arrived as a nurse with the British army, she bid farewell to her fellow kibbutz member Haviva Reik. Haviva was on her way to join the Slovak rebels. She never came back from Slovakia. The Germans executed her in Kremnička during the suppression of the Slovak uprising. A new kibbutz was named after her as well as the movement's seminary. There is no kibbutz named after Malka—she returned to live in one. In 1948, Malka participated in the battles that took place in the Ma'anit region. The children and mothers of the kibbutz were evacuated to the nearby Pardes Hanna, but Malka, as a veteran of the British army, remained on guard duty with a rifle in hand. Once, while she was relieving herself near the post, an Iraqi bullet whizzed past her, almost ending her life in a comically grotesque manner. Roughly thirteen years later, Malka arrived in Kibbutz Haogen, married Father, and joined our family. We all needed her, and Malka was ready to step up to the plate. She learned everything there was to know about being a kibbutz mother as she saw it: pedagogy, caretaking, knitting, baking, gardening, party planning.

Zvi and I didn't make things easy for her either. We challenged her whenever we could, but Malka faced our obnoxious hijinks with patience. The same did not apply to five-year-old Arnon, who took to her from the get go, her soul immediately bonding with his. Meanwhile, the image of Mother slowly faded away. The curtains were changed. The house took on a new feel. Malka was there, and we didn't talk about mother. Malka did not ask to be called mother; the word "mother" was shrouded in silence in our patched-up family.

During the Six-Day War, Zvi was seriously injured on the slopes of Qal'a, where his squadron lost their way and got ambushed by Syrian tanks. After rescuing a fellow squadron member from a nearby tank, his own tank was hit by a shell, and Zvi had to walk alone for about 2 kilometers down the steep hillside toward the squadron assembly point. A few days later, an excited Bilha Neshri burst into Father and Malka's room in the kibbutz: "I've found him!" she informed them with a proud smile. "He's at Rambam Hospital." For the next week, Malka stayed at Rambam Hospital, refusing to leave Zvi's bedside. Zvi lay on his back motionless, the large white patch over his eyes staring straight at the ceiling. As usual, he spoke calmly and frankly. There was a good chance he would be able to see again, he explained to me when I came to visit. I was wearing the army-issue trousers I had borrowed so I could continue hitchhiking my way to the girl waiting for me in a kibbutz near the Jordanian border. Last time we saw each other, I couldn't get her bra open, and it slid down to her stomach still fastened. This time I was determined to overcome the tenacious hooks. But she hadn't been waiting for me after all, and when I got home, Malka opened the door and, without asking a single question, allowed me to prostrate myself on the couch in the front room, where I would proceed to wallow for the next three sad days. In the meantime, Zvi got better and moved on.

Farewell to Galon

Chajka spent many more days going from kibbutz to kibbutz and from movement meeting to movement meeting; however, she could put off the decision about where to settle down for only so long. The choice appeared to be self-evident: Galon was her home. This was where all her remaining friends—Esther, Abrashka, Shayke, Shmaryahu, Chaim, Chana—were living. Her dead friends—David, Zvi, and Tosia—were also supposed to live in Kibbutz Galon. Throughout all the terrible years, she had longed to join these distant friends, and they, in turn, had kept her alive in their thoughts and dreams. The joy and sadness of their long-awaited reunion were supposed to stretch over many future years of communal living.

Yet, as always, the choice was not hers alone to make. She had another person's wishes to consider. Since their arrival in Mandatory Palestine, Chajka and Benito's relationship had solidified. Benito had come to Haifa with a certificate bearing the name of a spouse, as a means of enabling two people to travel under one certificate. His supposed wife was Esterka Grinwald, a member of the Slovak branch of Hashomer Hatzair, who had, in fact, been his girlfriend at one time. However, once they had made it across the border to Mandatory Palestine, Benito severed his relationship with Esterka and became Chajka's boyfriend.[1] His affection for the Polish refugee was a known fact.

Benito also had friends eagerly awaiting him, but they were in Kibbutz Haogen. Like the people of Galon, the founders of Haogen had managed to escape at the last moment: In April 1939, a few dozen members from Slovakia had made their *aliya* via an illegal route. They were transferred to a camp near Kfar Saba and immediately began to function as a kibbutz. These were industrious people, some of them technically trained, and they soon discovered a hitherto untapped source of income: car tire puncture repair. British cars were becoming more and more numerous on the roads of Mandatory Palestine, and with the outbreak of the 1948 Arab-Israeli War, the kibbutz's choice of specialization soon proved profitable. Little by little, the small workshop turned into a veritable factory. Haogen's rubber industry thrived on the waves of demand set in motion by the war. The kibbutz also grew rapidly. In 1944, Haogen already had 120 members. Like the members of Galon, those of Haogen were expecting the arrival of dozens of comrades who had been left behind in Europe. Letters arrived from Hungary and Slovakia, letting them know that many of them had

1 Ya'akov Ronen, *Curriculum Vitae*, p. 95.

survived and were now seeking to make their way to *Eretz Israel.*[2] Benito and Yoshko Baumer, who had arrived in March 1944, had been the first swallows of a long-awaited spring.

In the end, Benito and Chajka chose to join Kibbutz Haogen. According to Benito, Chajka's choice was "relatively easy";[3] however, Chajka's letter to her friends in Galon reveals significant internal struggle. She was so ashamed of her decision not to join their kibbutz that she did not have the heart to inform them directly. After making up her mind, she sent Benito to Galon to fetch her suitcase. The letter, which is undated, was probably written in 1944, shortly after she established her residence in Haogen. This is also the first document she wrote in Hebrew, in small, meticulous script written with a fountain pen. At the top of the letter, Chajka added a diagonal line that read "Please excuse the errors":

> [The fact] that I am attached to you—that whenever I think about the past I have to think of you—I don't need to tell you. I am sure you understand that I am ashamed of myself for not joining you now to continue our past together, after all, this is also clear to you. But that is not the only thing that hurts me. How could you not understand that, when I sent Benito to get the suitcase, it was because it hurt me too much for me to go myself. How could you interpret it the other way around? I explained my state of mind to you more than once when I was with you, petty reasons, I know, but they are human ones. I was so tired of life in general, I was in such need of rest, of familial calm, a loved one by my side, that I could not give it up, I had no strength left to fight it. I am sure that with time, you have come to understand my reasons and have forgiven me. In the end, we are all just human.[4]

It was yet another weight added to her already massive burden of guilt: As far as she (and her friends) saw it, her decision to choose "familial calm" and "a loved one by [her] side" over joining Galon amounted to abandoning her comrades. At the end of the letter, she asked her friends to write and come visit her. "I'm worried about Shayke," she added with humor, albeit tinged with real concern. And indeed, Shayke Goldrin

2 Letter from Moshe Ben-David to Abraham Lipsker, Kibbutz Haogen, January 16, 1943, Kibbutz Haogen Archive, container 231.

3 Ya'akov Ronen, *Curriculum Vitae*, p. 118.

4 Letter from Chajka Klinger to friends, 1944, Esther Shoshan collection.

had reprimanded her, as he later testified. He had engaged in a long conversation with Chajka, warning her against going to Haogen: "They have a different mentality. They are Hungarians. They will not understand you." Yet Chajka responded decisively that she was "attached to Benito and did not want them to have to argue."[5]

The letter to Galon also reveals her state of well-being during this early period of her life in *Eretz Israel*. In its opening lines, she wrote: "Well, I'm all settled in. I have a room; it doesn't have many things in it yet, but I'm not worried about that. We will get everything in time, the main thing is that I have a place where I [can] read and study—which is what I've always lacked and always missed having."[6] The room, as Benito would later testify, was nothing more than a shack built out of orange crates, covered with tar paper on the outside and plastered over on the inside.[7] Still, Chajka was happy there. As the daughter of a Hasidic family in Będzin, a trainee of the Kalisz *hachshara*, and an inhabitant of the Kamionka ghetto, she had never had a room of her own. And it seems that she was also privileged in comparison to other members of Haogen, many of whom were still living in tents. Naturally, her relatively luxurious living arrangements made her feel guilty:

> I'm content but I am always plagued by shame. Shame about my past—I am always under the impression that I have not done right by my past.... If I'm happy by day—it comes to me in a dream—and again, the same awful images will not give me peace—when will it end? I think never as long as I live—and I don't want to forget.[8]

Chajka was clearly aware of the emotional baggage she carried and of the deep disparities between her and her friends:

> I did not come to *Eretz Israel* at the same age as you—I came only after having undergone all those things—full of indignation and disappointment regarding the world and mankind. It's a bit strange—when you look at me in my everyday life, you can get the impression that I'm full of life, energetic, and not as serious as I was during our time in Kalisz. But that is not the case. It is just that, with

5 Shayke Goren interview.
6 Letter from Chajka Klinger to friends, 1944, Esther Shoshan collection.
7 Ya'akov Ronen, *Curriculum Vitae*, p. 116.
8 Letter from Chajka Klinger to friends, 1944, Esther Shoshan collection.

> time, I have learned to overcome [my feelings] and be cheerful in everyday life.[9]

She described Kibbutz Haogen soberly, "with no illusions," as she put it. Everything had positive and negative aspects to it, and "Kibbutz Haogen is really a good kibbutz, and the people are fine." She mentioned her struggles to adjust at first but attributed them to her own faults: "I am pretty introverted, but with every day I get closer to the people and the business of the kibbutz."[10] The kibbutz members had welcomed her with open arms. "She had a reputation," Shmuel "Wizo" Klein (Koren), a veteran member of the kibbutz, would later recall. "She was a delicate and very cultured woman. But there was also a shadow of difference, of sadness hovering over her. Once in a while she would get a kind of jolt of cheerfulness, and she'd reveal herself to be a woman of great humor. That caught me by surprise, it didn't fit with the impression I had of her."[11]

Writing and Motherhood

Despite the various hardships, this was a happy period for Chajka. She was living with the man she loved among people who shared her ideas and way of life. She also found family members outside the kibbutz—her mother's cousin, the previously mentioned Yosef Sfinkelstein, and her father's brother, Shmuel Klinger.[12] The two men had immigrated during the third and fourth waves of *aliya*, and their families were warm and welcoming to Chajka. Shortly after her arrival, she had visited the Sfinkelsteins in Tel Aviv and formed a special bond with Yosef's kind and caring wife Zippora as well as their eighteen-year-old daughter Rachel. Zippora and Yosef became substitute parents of sorts for Chajka, and Rachel had traces of her long-lost sister Mania about her. At the time, Chajka still harbored hope that Mania was alive.

May 1944 marked two important beginnings in Chajka's life: She fell pregnant, and at the same time, she began rewriting her diaries. While the former was a secret hidden even from Chajka herself at this point, the latter was public knowledge and probably the reason for the "luxurious"

9 Ibid.
10 Ibid.
11 Shmuel Koren (Klein), interview by the author, Kibbutz Haogen, 2009.
12 There was another cousin on her mother's side, Mendl Kurnik, a Hasidic woman residing in Tel Aviv, but Chajka was not close with her or her family.

living conditions mentioned in her letter. The kibbutz—or perhaps the movement—gave her several months to edit her memoirs and prepare them for publication.

There are no testimonies or documents detailing Chajka's state of mind at the time of writing. Only the diary pages remain, the date of the beginning of their composition recorded as: "Haogen 22.5 [May 22]." Although she was already fluent in Hebrew by this time, this version was also written in Polish. As usual, her handwriting was round and meticulous. She tried to maintain a chronological order and connect segments of her existing diaries and her memories into one logical sequence. This time, she described at length her escape at the beginning of the war and the activities of Hashomer Hatzair in Będzin, chapters that took up approximately half of the new manuscript. Some of the phrasings were softened, but as a rule, Chajka remained faithful to the spirit of her 1943 text. However, there was a noticeable difference between the two versions: While the first was a report on the movement's actions interrupted by fragments of personal testimony, the new version gradually taking shape was a continuous personal account of the actions of the underground resistance in Będzin. And yet, it was destined to remain unfinished. Later, she would write to Chajka Grossman: "Why did I never write anything myself, you ask? At first, there were all kinds of small, cheap, and dubious publications, booklets and reports coming out, while I dreamed of a great big book, and I didn't think I was talented enough for that."[13]

Was she aspiring to write another *Man's Fate* or *The Forty Days of Musa Dagh*? In retrospect, this explanation only hints at part of the answer. The flowing and coherent writing in the revised version also points to a process of distilling memories. These appear alongside various sections that were written separately and remain unconnected, such as the passage about her experience of arriving in Mandatory Palestine. According to an analysis conducted by Różka Korczak, the 1944 version fits the description of events up to the fall of 1942.[14] It seems that this is more or less the stage where Chajka got stuck in her writing. The process of recollection was excruciating. She wanted to both recall the past and run away from it. In 1943, Chajka wrote that her fate had been sealed and that she would have no life after writing.

13 Letter to Chajka Grossman, April 1, 1959, in *Chajka: Hoveret Zikaron*, p. 15.

14 Różka Korczak, handwritten notes to the original diaries of Chajka Klinger, Moreshet Archive, C.36.

Yet, in 1944, the act of writing, which had been her source of life while in hiding, became draining. When it came time to describe the failures of the resistance and her own harrowing experience, she found that she hadn't enough strength to go on. What used to be a process of liberation had become a form of enslavement. She stopped writing. Faced with the dilemma of literature or life, as Jorge Semprún would later put it, Chajka—like Jorge—chose life.[15]

Nevertheless, her efforts had not been for nothing. *Dvar Hapoelet* published the text of her remarks at the Histadrut's Executive Committee meeting in its July 1944 issue. As usual, the text underwent extensive editing. Her harsh criticisms of the Zionists were omitted, while the statement about the "the avant-garde without the people" was spun into the article's encouraging title: "The Pioneer with the People: Words of a Surviving Member."[16] The first excerpts from the diaries were likewise published in the fall of that year, probably near the end of the composition period. It seems that the title under which they were published—"Linkom Velihiyot: Prakim Miyoman Bageto" (To Avenge and to Live: Chapters from a Ghetto Diary)—would later inspire the title of the later book.[17]

Over the next two years, passages from her diaries were published here and there, mostly on Warsaw Ghetto Uprising Remembrance Day. It would appear that she herself composed the texts to be in line with the editors' requests. *Hedim* (Heb. Echoes), the intellectual mouthpiece of the movement, published a short article titled "The Girls in the Underground" in which she described her comrades in the underground.[18] The article in *Hedim* was probably written shortly after Zvi's birth, and although it is based on the diaries, its text differs from both versions. The Hebrew manuscript is written in a large and clumsy hand, a heavy hand that seems reluctant to continue writing about her dead friends.[19] At the end of the article, she attempts for the first time, in defiance to the male world in which she lived, to say something about the unique role of women in the underground and their equal merit to men, both in life and

15 Jorge Semprún, *Literature or Life* (New York: Penguin, 1998).

16 Chaja Klinger, "Hehalutz im Amo: Sipur Havera Shenitzla" (Hebrew), *Dvar Hapoelet*, July 1944.

17 Chaja Klinger, "Linkom Velihiyot: Prakim Miyoman Bageto" (Hebrew), *Mishmar*, September 1, 1944.

18 Chaja Rosenberg, "Haverot Bageto" (Hebrew), *Hedim*, 1945, p. 40. See the section "The Girls in the Underground," in Klinger, *I Am Writing These Words to You*, pp. 136–142.

19 Chajka Klinger file, Moreshet Archive, C. 36.

in death.[20] As usual, her own role in the resistance goes unmentioned. And anyway, she was too busy looking forward to a new life. According to my calculations, when she stopped writing, most likely in the summer or fall of 1944, she was in the advanced stages of pregnancy.

Once she had ceased writing, Chajka's name was incorporated into the kibbutz's work rota, but the pregnancy made it difficult to set her up with a permanent job. According to a later letter, she was forced to switch jobs on several occasions to accommodate the needs of the kibbutz, and this was not to her liking. As the pregnancy progressed, she began suffering from nightmarish hallucinations at night, and Benito found it difficult to calm her down. Later, he would see this as the first signs of "a condition bordering on illness," but at this point, she was making considerable efforts to hide her problems from both him and others.[21] When she finally gave birth on February 24, 1945, she found it to be a very trying experience. In the postcard she sent to Esther in Galon, she wrote:

> Forgive me for writing in pencil, but I am in bed. My turn has finally come, and I have given birth to a son. Yesterday I came back from the hospital: I was convinced that I would have that belly forever. I was as fat as a barrel, and I really thought that I might give birth to two [babies]. Luckily, only one came out. I am still tired, because it was hard going. Benito is going to have to give birth to the next one.[22]

The newborn's name would be a living testament to the memory of Zvi Brandes. She was not quite ready to let go of that part of her past.

Thoughts of Leaving Kibbutz Haogen

On May 8, 1945, World War II officially ended. While the people of Great Britain and the Soviet Union celebrated on the streets, in Mandatory Palestine, Ben-Gurion wrote in his diary "Victory Day—sad, very sad." It is fair to assume that Chajka was in a similar mood. She was unlikely to have been comforted by the knowledge that some of her tormentors were

20 Chaja Klinger, "Haverot Bageto," p. 40.

21 Ya'akov Ronen, *Curriculum Vitae*, p. 118.

22 Postcard from Chajka to Esther Shoshan, February 23, 1945, Esther Shoshan collection.

no longer alive: Albrecht Schmelt, the head of the Forced Labor Division, had committed suicide shortly prior to V-Day, while his subordinates Friedrich Kuczyński and Heinrich Lindner hid, fearing for their lives. Lindner would be caught in 1948 and committed suicide in custody. Kuczyński would be tried and hanged in Sosnowiec in 1949.[23] Yet, Chajka's heart, like the hearts of most survivors, was not set on revenge but rather on the hope of finding family members and friends still alive as well as on the idea of building a new life.

Shortly after Zvi's birth, Chajka received a visit from Shayke Goldrin of Kibbutz Galon. The purpose of the visit was reconciliation. According to Shayke, Chajka was very proud of her son and the name she had given him. When he returned to Galon, he told his friends that he had the impression that Chajka was satisfied and well-adjusted to life in her kibbutz.[24] Motherhood gave her a sense of fulfillment. The kibbutz children and their upbringing became her main focus. A kibbutz member would later say of her:

> She loved the children very much and worried for them. It was nothing unusual—there were other women in the kibbutz who had gone through the experience of concentration camps and the possibility of happiness came as a surprise to them too. During our joint walks with the children through the fields and in the yards, I had several occasions to witness how much she fretted over the children.[25]

That winter, Chajka and Benito lived in a tent. According to him, "these were stormy winter months but we were happy and felt like pioneers in every sense of the word."[26] In the Spartan conditions of kibbutz life in the 1940s, members were allotted their place according to the nature of their work and their profession. There was a clear hierarchy between professionals and regular workers, and between the latter and those who functioned as "plugs,"—workers used to fill holes in the work rota. As usual, things were more difficult for the women. Few of them were assigned to the "productive jobs," and if they could not find a permanent

23 See YVA, O.4 (Documentation about Trials of War Criminals); "Lindner," in Bochner, *Sefer Kheshanov [Chrzanów]*, pp. 245–246.

24 Shayke Goren interview.

25 Shmuel Koren interview.

26 Ya'akov Ronen, *Curriculum Vitae*, p. 116.

place in the kitchen, the clothes warehouse, or the children's house, they were subject to the arbitrariness of the work rota. The members' success in integrating into the kibbutz was thus largely conditioned upon acquiring a profession. Refugees and survivors were not given any preferential treatment—they had to make do like everyone else.

Benito set his sights on becoming a professional builder. Living as he did among his friends from the Slovakian branch of the movement who knew him well and admired his accomplishments during the war, he had no trouble integrating into kibbutz life. During his first year at Haogen, he worked in the repair workshop, which by then had become a small vulcanized rubber factory. In the evenings he devoted his time to cultural activities, held painting exhibitions, and edited the kibbutz bulletin, which had changed its name to *Beitenu* (Heb. Our Home). However, the issue of professional progress was constantly on his mind. In his youth, he had graduated from a scientific Gymnasium and strove to put the knowledge and technical skills he had acquired into practice. He also wished to follow in the footsteps of his brother, the engineer, whom Benito used to help with mapping and measurements as a teen before the war. Later, he would write that he thought about studying at the Technion Institute of Technology.[27] But that thought was too far-reaching as the kibbutz needed working hands, and higher education was out of the question. Benito thus came up with a compromise: to train as a professional builder. A construction course was supposed to open in Kfar Saba, and he asked to enroll. However, the kibbutz members had other plans. They wanted Benito to join the factory management or alternatively, the kibbutz secretariat.[28]

Chajka had her own career plans. Of the various jobs she was engaged in, she loved working with children the most. Giving birth to Zvi and taking care of him as well as the general atmosphere in the small kibbutz, whose members were completely enamored with its twenty children, had erased the resentment she had initially felt toward the children she had encountered upon her arrival in Mandatory Palestine. As her friends would later testify, she sought to make childcare the focal point of her life. However, the competition was tough. In the small kibbutz, there were only two groups of children, and there was no shortage of other candidates for the job. As she would later write to her friend: "I wanted very much to

27 Ibid., p. 136.

28 Letter from Chajka Klinger to Esther Shoshan, January or February 1946, Esther Shoshan collection.

work in the nursery. I worked there for a while, and I did a good job of it too, but then I fell ill and another girl, with more seniority in the kibbutz, took my place and stayed there—and I was doing the rounds again."[29]

For a while, Benito and Chajka considered pursuing their dreams outside of the kibbutz. About six months after Zvi's birth, Chajka consulted Esther Shoshan on this matter:

> During the entire time I was in the kibbutz, I was very distressed because I didn't have a profession. I came over to [*Eretz*] Israel as an adult after all those upheavals and it was difficult for me to start all over again as a "greenhorn" because I was used to having a certain position, whereas here it's "seniority" that counts. Don't get the idea that I don't respect this system, on the contrary. But it was hard for me to stand by the "work rota" [sheet] and wait.[30]

Having led a resistance cell during the war, stood up to the Gestapo, and dared to face off against the movement leadership, Chajka now found herself powerless and at the mercy of the work rota. From now on she was "Chajka" or "Chajka R.," first names being the only identifier a member would be known by in this intimate society, with the exception of nicknames from their youth movement days: Puzo and Wizo, Nushi and Dushi, Poti and Piri, Motyo and Gete, Benito and Chajka. "Chajka R." would be one of the names written on the huge sheet around which the members would gather every evening to find out what job they were assigned to tomorrow.

In her letter, Chajka described how she dealt with the various jobs imposed upon her by the work rota. She was appreciated "as a good worker," and she could "deal with the work as well as any veteran," but she was tired of "doing the rounds," and therefore volunteered to work in a chicken coop, a job she was not particularly fond of. After describing Benito's desire to train as a construction worker, she wrote:

> And so we both decided to leave the kibbutz for a year, against the kibbutz's wishes, and learn a profession. I am at the children's home at Hadassah and he is in Na'ot. I think I will be able to leave the baby at the nursery and "go out" to work as well—he is still very little and he won't feel the lack of his parents' presence as much—and it is

29 Ibid.

30 Ibid.

> time for us to learn a profession—and after that we are thinking of coming to join you.[31]

The decision to move to Galon after finishing their studies was informed by additional considerations. Chajka still felt like a stranger in Haogen. The fact that Hungarian was widely spoken in the kibbutz, especially among the new arrivals, made it difficult for her to fit in. As she wrote to Esther, she did not make many friends in the kibbutz.[32] The memorial booklet confirms that her only friends were Mina Karni, who was also from Poland, and Evka Sharon, the nursery caretaker.[33] The presence of Benito's former girlfriend in the kibbutz also made things uncomfortable for her. According to her letter to Esther, she gave her a lot of "grief."[34] Nevertheless, the letter was not devoid of optimism. News had come in from Bergen-Belsen that her sister Malka (Mania) was ostensibly alive. Zvi was a healthy, well-developed baby, and was already able to sit up on his own. Her and Benito's plans to acquire an education and the decision to dedicate herself to children filled her with hope.

It would appear that the members of Haogen were aware of Chajka and Benito's deliberations. They wanted Benito and Chajka to stay on as active members and tried to find ways to keep them in the kibbutz. Benito was elected secretary of the kibbutz, while Chajka was elected to the "fraction"—a group of the movement's representatives working within the Histadrut. But these appointments only fueled the couple's hesitations—they did not want a life of political wheeling and dealing. All they wanted was a quiet family life and professional fulfillment. Benito appealed the kibbutz's decision, and an alternative plan was formed to send him to school.

Esther replied to Chajka's letter and suggested that she and Benito move to Galon straight away. The suggestion was most likely proffered after a consultation with other kibbutz members, since another letter from Chajka shows that they were awaiting her reply to Esther's offer. Yet, Chajka was in no hurry to give her answer. When she finally wrote on February 10, 1946, the deliberations were over. Benito had enlisted

31 Ibid.

32 Ibid.

33 Mina Karni, in *Chajka: Hoveret Zikaron*, p. 15; Evka Sharon, in *Chajka: Hoveret Zikaron*, pp. 15–16.

34 Letter from Chajka Klinger to Esther Shoshan, January or February 1946, Esther Shoshan collection.

in a construction course, and Chajka had started a training program in the poultry industry in Kibbutz Ramat Hakovesh. Yet, while the kibbutz gave solutions—albeit limited ones—to the professional ambitions of the two, it had its own demands. Benito was made secretary of the kibbutz, and Chajka agreed to train in a profession that was not the one she wanted, but one that was considered productive and useful. It was a compromise that seemed to balance the needs of the society with the needs of the individual. For Benito, it was a path toward realizing his professional ambitions, but for Chajka it was yet another concession. Her dream of becoming a childcare professional seemed destined to remain just that.

Chajka's second letter conveys a sense of reconciling with reality. The plan to move to Galon had been scrapped, but she was now nervous about members of Kibbutz Haogen catching wind of it: "When Abrashka [Eisenberg] was here, I was scared to death that he would start talking to me about it in the dining room." Regarding Benito's election to the kibbutz's secretariat she wrote: "And me? I have come to terms with it, like many other things over time." She reiterated that she wanted a quiet life, and noted with irony that she had become a petty bourgeois ("Kleinburgerlech," she wrote in Yiddish). As for Benito's former girlfriend, she now saw it as an issue "that has more to do with my imagination than with reality." With regard to poultry farming, she wrote: "I'm starting to like the profession and to get a feel for it. I'm also learning a lot of Hebrew and English." She was happy for Benito that he was going to learn the practical aspects of his profession as well as drawing and planning from an engineer acquaintance, and she noted with pride: "There was a tough battle for this profession [training], because there were many serious volunteers, and he is overjoyed to have been chosen." This also had another advantage: "It will also give him a few years off, before the movement renews its demands."[35] It was clear to Chajka as well as to Benito that sooner or later they would be required to resume their movement activity. During her pregnancy with Zvi, Benito had received a proposal to go to Europe as an illegal emissary, but he had flatly refused. It was only a matter of time before a second appeal would arrive.

35 Letter from Chajka Klinger to Esther Shoshan, February 10, 1946, Esther Shoshan collection.

The Mission Abroad

The following year was a busy one for Benito and a relatively calm one for Chajka. The main item on the Kibbutz Haogen agenda was the establishment of a permanent settlement. Heated debates broke out among members who supported the establishment of an agricultural settlement near Mount Tabor, on the one hand, and those on the side of industrial development who wanted to hold on to the land of Wadi Qabbani (Emek Hefer), which was better situated in terms of the rubber plant's transportation requirements, on the other hand. As secretary of the kibbutz, Benito had to navigate this charged topic and begin preparations for the move. In March 1947, he sent a memo to the Jewish Agency in which he proudly detailed the achievements of the kibbutz, which already had 160 full members and 213 residents. The kibbutz possessed agricultural assets, and the main source of his livelihood was industrial enterprise. "There is no other topic or thought on the minds and tongues of all kibbutz members big and small, apart from settlement."[36] At the same time, Benito was making progress in his professional training, completing a course in silicate brick construction that lasted about six months, and he joined the kibbutz's construction group, which hired itself out for contract work in the area. After the course, which effectively made him the only professional builder in the group, he assumed a leadership position.[37]

Chajka, on the other hand, divided her time between her work in the chicken coop and taking care of Zvi in the afternoons. In retrospect, the evidence points to her experiencing job satisfaction and being a devoted mother to Zvi. A letter Chajka sent to Shraga Fruchtzweig during this time points to a general spirit of optimism. Shraga had been through Auschwitz and lived to tell the tale, and though his letter was a direct link to the past, it actually filled her with joy:

> I was very happy to read your letter, I read it several times. I knew you were alive, but I wasn't entirely sure, and here I have decisive proof, a living word from that old world, which cannot be forgotten, which rises from the dream, from the past, from the subconscious. But it is not forgotten, God forbid. It is deeply engraved in my heart,

36 See letter from Ya'akov Rosenberg to the Jewish Agency, March 1947, Kibbutz Haogen Archive.

37 Ya'akov Ronen, *Curriculum Vitae*, p. 135.

> as if branded by white hot iron on the living flesh. One cannot erase it, even if one wanted to, but I don't want to, because it is dear to me, even if it hurts.[38]

She saw him as a fellow soul who had undergone a miraculous twist of fate: "How absurd it all is, but who can fathom the secret workings of life? Remember, Shraga, how very ill I was in 1942—and yet I remained alive. And now the wheel has turned again, new life, new love. And the same goes for you." Later in the letter, she assured Shraga that despite the decrees of the British, he would be able to get a certificate and immigrate to Mandatory Palestine: "There is no future for you there. You are still young, and you will be able to overcome [the difficulties involved], there is no other way."[39] She was once again a Zionist. As for news of herself, the few lines she wrote were brimming with pride over Zvi:

> You know everything there is to know about me, there are no secrets in this world. Yes, I gave birth to a son. After everything that happened to us, we wanted to convince ourselves that it was real, that we had experienced all of it, and so we had a great yearning to have a child. Nowadays, I am an "old" mother already. Zvi turned two this week. I am attaching a picture of him, for you and for Ada [Neufeld].[40]

The past was not dead, but it was new life that mattered most. According to Mina Karni and Evka Sharon, Chajka used to talk about her past during those years. Evka remembered stories about Chajka's home, the *ken*, and her escape from the ghetto. Mina remembered more harrowing tales that showed signs of the scars the horrors of the Holocaust had left upon her. However, even though she told her friends about her past, Chajka felt that her story did not get an adequate reception in Kibbutz Haogen. At this time, several members of the movement arriving from Hungary joined the kibbutz, including Rafi Benshalom and Moshe Alpan. Their optimistic rescue stories became fixed in Haogen as the central memory of the war. Like Benito, they knew how to tell their stories with a good dose of Slovak humor. The story of Chajka's uprising,

38 Letter from Chajka Klinger to Shraga Fruchtzweig, Kfar Saba, February 25, 1947, Shraga Fruchtzweig collection.

39 Ibid.

40 Ibid.

which was naturally full of pessimism, bitterness, and resentment, was pushed to the side. Later she would write that she felt misunderstood by the kibbutz members, that they thought she was bragging and telling tall tales. Therefore, at a certain point, she chose to keep her story to herself.[41] This was yet another concession, but it facilitated her integration. For a certain period of time at least, it seems that Chajka reconciled with her past and came to terms with her present.

The minutes of a kibbutz meeting in the fall of 1946 reveal Chajka's first active participation.[42] She also got involved in political activity. Shmaryahu Milinsky remembered that he met her during the attempt to break the siege on Givat Haim on November 25, 1945. After the Palmach men had blown up a number of British police stations and radars, military forces surrounded the kibbutz, where the Palmach division had made its headquarters at the time. Thousands of volunteers gathered in Kibbutz Ein Hahoresh to break the siege in a nonviolent march. Things escalated, and the British opened fire: eight protestors were killed, and forty-two were injured. Chajka was upset, but told Shmaryahu: "Nothing can compare to the Warsaw Ghetto Uprising."[43]

However, toward the end of 1946, Chajka's life would take yet another turn. Benito was approached by Adam Rand, a representative of the movement, with the request to go on a mission to Czechoslovakia.[44] Benito refused, but the movement did not give up. On March 6, 1947, a tense meeting took place at Haogen. Meir Talmi (Judeks), one of the key people in Hakibbutz Ha'artzi, was present at the conversation. He indicated that over the past five months, the movement had been asking to send an emissary from Kibbutz Haogen to Czechoslovakia, and due to its continued refusal, the kibbutz was to stand before the movement's tribunal. Two candidates were immediately proposed for the emissary position: Avry Goldberger and Benito. Judeks demanded that the matter be settled that very night.[45]

The members were in a bind. The kibbutz needed Avry in the factory and Benito in construction and in the secretariat. And there were also personal factors: Avry was in poor health and Benito was reluctant to leave

41 Letter to Chajka Grossman, April 1, 1959, in *Chajka: Hoveret Zikaron*, p. 15.

42 Minutes of a Kibbutz Haogen meeting, October 16, 1946, Kibbutz Haogen Archive, I/284.

43 Shmaryahu Milinsky interview.

44 Ya'akov Ronen, *Curriculum Vitae*, p. 136.

45 Minutes of a Kibbutz Haogen meeting, March 26, 1947, Kibbutz Haogen Archive, II/284.

the profession he had just acquired. Chajka and her difficulties assimilating in the kibbutz were not mentioned in the conversation. Moshe Ben-David, who had just returned from his mission in Slovakia, sided with the movement's position: "There is no choice but to help the movement in its development. There is a great need for an envoy...a person who knows how to coordinate the movement, and the people who are there now cannot do that. One of the two will have to go." Judeks kept pressing the issue: "It is a question of whether we have a future. Up until two years ago, we weren't sure. We still don't quite have a firm grasp on the movement as it was rebuilt by the people after the war. Without the movement there is no future there, no point, no purpose."[46] The members tended to agree with Judeks.

Benito spoke at length. He was ready to accept the position, but he needed time to prepare. The three years he had spent in the kibbutz were not enough. "He wants to be present when settlement begins," the minute keeper recorded his words, "sometimes a year can be fateful. How can he appear before the Diaspora and talk about things he is not convinced of himself.... [He] is opposed to everything revolving a small number of people, that they should be bothered for the rest of their lives."[47] As one who was seeing the door to a future path close before his eyes, his words had a tone of fatality about them.

Then it was Avry's turn to speak, and he too expressed a preference to decline the position, due to his health problems. A vote was held. Most of the members abstained. Avry was elected by a majority of five to four. The small number of voters was cause for embarrassment, and according to the protocol, a "personal vote" (a secret vote, most likely) was called for. Judeks urged those who were undecided: "This is a difficult situation, but everyone needs to show courage and vote." In the second vote, Benito was elected by a majority of eighteen to eleven.[48] The kibbutz pledged that the mission would not last longer than one year.[49]

It was a mission for two, not one, yet Chajka's reservations were never brought up during the meeting. After all, the man was the emissary, and there was no argument that would tip the scale in the other direction. Even two-year-old Zvi was not a sufficient reason to stay: after all, Avry and Rivka were also parents to four-year-old Ya'ir. And it is possible

46 Ibid.
47 Ibid.
48 Ibid.
49 Minutes of a Kibbutz Haogen meeting, November 6, 1948, Kibbutz Haogen Archive, I/295.

that for Chajka, this was a moment similar to David's departure for the partisans. At such crucial junctures, she could not allow herself to be "petty." Later, Evka would write:

> I remember the kibbutz meeting in which it was decided, at the request of the top leadership, to send Chajka and Benito on a mission abroad. Chajka was so unhappy at the time, she did not want to leave the kibbutz, which had become her home by then. She did not want to leave the country that she had fought so hard to get to. But it was the decree of the movement, and she complied.[50]

However, according to Benito's memoirs: "Chajka was rather hesitant, but once again she showed almost blind loyalty to me and my assignment, and did not set any material conditions despite the hardships that we could expect to encounter in Europe at the time."[51] He himself was upset by the kibbutz's decision, but in the spirit of the times, Benito had to swallow his insult, just as Chajka had to hide her distress. In those days, no one was particularly concerned about the effects such a move might have on a two-year-old child. And so, in the summer of 1947, just as the final decision was made to establish the Kibbutz Haogen settlement in Wadi Qabbani (Emek Hefer), Benito had already started a preparatory course for activists abroad run by the World Zionist Organization.

In early 1947, the Czechoslovakian branch of Hashomer Hatzair was at the height of its activity. The Hashomer graduates who had survived the war were rallying hundreds of children and adolescents to the movement. Approximately 400 graduates had already immigrated to Mandatory Palestine, and more intended to follow in their footsteps. The emissaries sent over from the Yishuv were essential to maintain communication and lend a guiding hand. Benito was an experienced organizer, and his friends in Czechoslovakia accepted his leadership. Although he and Chajka may have harbored heretical thoughts, they were not reflected in their work in practice: the hardships of the individual took a backseat to the demands of society. It is only in retrospect that one can reflect on the sacrifice Chajka was forced to make —giving up her home, the warmth of the kibbutz, and what little peace and quiet she had painstakingly carved out for herself in order to return to the ravaged continent she had escaped only a few years earlier.

50 Evka Sharon, in *Chajka: Hoveret Zikaron*, pp. 15–16.

51 Ya'akov Ronen, *Curriculum Vitae*, p. 119.

Another thing that emerges with the vantage of time is that among the representatives of the movement who demanded that Benito and Chajka be sent to Europe, there were those who had already been involved in her life in one way or another. The movement did not pass judgment on its leadership, except in cases of ideological deviation. Ordinary members such as Chajka, on the other hand, had to accept their rulings. On the eve of the mission, Chajka drove to Mishmar Ha'emek to be briefed by Ya'akov Hazan. An old photograph shows her standing on the kibbutz lawn in the company of Hazan, Benito, and the other emissaries, wearing a floral skirt and white shirt. She levels a worried look at the camera. Hazan is standing with his profile toward the messengers. He is looking out at the future with a smile.

On August 28, 1947, Kibbutz Haogen officially took up its land. Three barracks, a water tower, and a security room were erected in one day on a desolate hill. Hundreds of members from all the surrounding kibbutzim came to help with the building work. In the evening they gathered for a celebration and said the momentous words: "We've planted a stake in Wadi Qabbani."[52] It was right about then that Chajka, Benito, and little Zvi arrived in Czechoslovakia.[53]

Bratislava

The little family settled in Bratislava, and Benito quickly got to work. The apartment was small, and times were still hard in Czechoslovakia with food shortages and long lines in front of the shops. But Chajka could devote all her time to taking care of Zvi and the household. Rachel Zakai, a member of Kibbutz Haogen who was also on the mission, wrote with admiration:

> It is especially fascinating to see how Chajka has gone about getting her son, a member of the kibbutz, accustomed to life outside of the children's house, in a foreign environment, and without knowing the language of the country, and above all how a kibbutz member

52 Shimshon Merer, "Yamim Rishonim BeHaogen," in Dror and Rosenzweig, *Sefer Hashomer Hatzair*, vol. 1, p. 557.

53 Chajka's passport shows August 26, 1947, as her date of entry into Czechoslovakia. Moreshet Archive, C.36.4.

> could set up and manage a private household, something that is so contrary to her entire essence.[54]

Was it really so contrary to her essence? Chajka could do with some petty bourgeois comfort, and it seems that she even drew some pleasure from it. The reunion with Europe and with movement activity even awakened forces that had lain dormant within her. According to Benito, when Zvi started to attend daycare, Chajka began writing articles for the movement newspaper and contributing to other domains.[55] For Zvi, it was a time full of new experiences. He had his own room, and his own little train on the bookcase. He was beginning to chatter in Slovak and was inexhaustibly excited by the public tram where he had a permanent seat on the driver's lap. Nevertheless, he retained some of the habits of the kibbutz children who were brought up to be very independent. Sometimes, he would leave the house by himself, and Chajka and Benito would run out to look for him only to find him sitting at the train station waiting for the train to arrive.[56]

Chajka also found family in Bratislava. Benito's parents Moritz and Bella Rosenberg, who survived the last year of the war hiding in the mountains, lived there.[57] Benito's older brother Sani, his wife Stefi, and their nine-year-old daughter Yulika lived in Košice near Bratislava. Sani, the veteran communist, now held a senior position in the management of a national railway project.[58] Chajka paid frequent visits to the Rosenbergs and forged a close relationship with her mother-in-law Bella. It was Bella who sensed that not everything was right with Chajka. When she noticed the first signs of distress, she shared her concerns with her son, but Benito did not attach much importance to his mother's premonitions.[59] During the mission, Bella and Moritz immigrated to Mandatory Palestine and settled in Hadera, near their daughter Yaffa, a member of Kibbutz Gan Shmuel. It is also possible that during their stay in Czechoslovakia, Chajka met her brother-in-law Ya'akov Mgła, who had survived the labor camps.[60]

54 Rachel Zakai, in *Chajka: Hoveret Zikaron*, p. 16.

55 Ya'akov Ronen, *Curriculum Vitae*, p. 120.

56 Zvi Ronen, interview by the author, Karmiel, October 13, 2008.

57 Moritz Rosenberg testimony, Moreshet Archive, C.38.1.8.

58 Robert Gero, *Jewish Roots—Memoirs* (Ashkelon: self-published, 2008), p. 231.

59 Ya'akov Ronen interview.

60 Ya'akov Mgła got remarried to Rela Rogowsky, and in 1947 they had a daughter named Sonja. The three immigrated to the United States in the early fifties and contact with them, if any, was completely severed.

Despite all this, Chajka spent much of her time alone. Benito was frequently on the road, traveling between the *kens* in Slovakia and the movement's world headquarters in Prague. He traveled on the fast night train, often sleeping in his carriage so as to be ready to leap into action the next morning.[61] His aim was to fulfill the two functions dictated by Meir Ya'ari for the movement during this period: to be "a compass for those who leave, and an anchor for those who stay."[62] Even after the war, Ya'ari did not believe in bringing in the surviving masses before they were properly qualified for *aliya*. Benito had to organize the movement's graduates and prepare the members of the Lehavot Haviva kibbutz for their *aliya*. He also had to take care of the Youth Aliya institutions, where the movement's young trainees were being integrated. As an anchor for those who stayed, Benito had to tour the movement's *kens*, prepare the winter and summer camps, be involved in the discussions of the main leadership in Czechoslovakia, represent the movement in the institutions of the Jewish community—which had been mainly restored within the framework of the Socialist League—and be in continuous contact with the institutions of the Communist Party regarding their policies toward the Jews in Czechoslovakia.[63]

On November 29, 1947, the decision was made in the United Nations to end the British Mandate and establish two states—a Jewish state and an Arab state—on the territory of Mandatory Palestine. Tensions mounted there, and skirmishes flared up in mixed cities and on the roads. On January 15, 1948, Benito wrote to the top leadership in Merhavia: "In my opinion, in light of the current security situation in *Eretz Israel*, the number of emissaries in the Diaspora countries should be reduced to a minimum.... The situation is exacerbating, and a man of my age cannot in good conscience remain removed from participating in the effort demanded by the country today," adding, "Of course, I am writing this letter in Chajka's name as well."[64] Soon after, he received a reply from Levi Grinblatt from the top leadership in Europe, stating that Benito must continue fulfilling his duties in the Diaspora. It was precisely because of the conditions in Mandatory Palestine that the

61 Ya'akov Ronen, *Curriculum Vitae*, pp. 121–122.

62 "Matzpen Leholhim Ogen LeNesharim," in Dror and Rosenzweig, *Sefer Hashomer Hatzair*, vol. 2, pp. 425–426.

63 Letter from Ya'akov Rosenberg and Abraham to the secretariat of Hakibbutz Ha'artzi in Merhavia, October 18, 1947, Hashomer Hatzair Archive, 78.31 (3D).

64 Letter from Ya'akov Rosenberg to the top leadership in Merhavia, January 15, 1948, Hashomer Hatzair Archive, 6.33 (1).

movement had to concentrate on training the youth for *aliya*, because *Eretz Israel* needed young people and pioneers. Even if it were decided to reduce the number of emissaries, their age would not be taken into account, "since there are no emissaries too old to be able to contribute to the country's defense."[65]

In February 1948, there was also political upheaval in Czechoslovakia, with the communists seizing power. Hashomer Hatzair had supported them in the previous elections and couldn't be happier: "We, as socialist Zionists, see the recent events in Czechoslovakia as a consistent and necessary development that will lead to the strengthening and stability of popular democracy and socialism," proclaimed the movement's publications on March 18, 1948.[66] As a sign of support for the new regime, the graduates of Hashomer Hatzair asked to take part in the major economic-educational project of the time in Czechoslovakia—the Youth Railway, which aimed to erect a railway line through the center of Slovakia. Their request was approved, and the Haviva Reik Brigade would become legendary among railroad builders, its output, measured in cars unloaded and tracks laid, sometimes reached 450 percent of the standard norm. In the evenings, the youths attended classes with Benito as one of the lecturers.[67]

The trust between the young administration and Hashomer Hatzair was expressed, among other things, in a report on the activities of Hashomer Hatzair, which Benito submitted every week to Bedřich Geminder, head of the International Department of the Communist Party Secretariat. The report was delivered in German: Geminder, whose Jewish parents had emigrated from Poland, spoke no Czech at all. A few years later, Geminder's nonexistent command of Czech would be proof of his disloyalty to Czechoslovakia. He was executed after the Prague show trials (1951–1952) with Rudolf Slánský and eleven other defendants, most of them Jewish.[68]

65 Letter from Levi Grinblatt to Ya'akov Rosenberg, January 23, 1948, Hashomer Hatzair Archive, 6.33 (1).

66 Yehoshua Bichler, "Yemey Hahra'a," in Yosef Rav, ed., *Shomrim Tamid: Hashomer Hatazir BeCzechoslovakia, 1920–1950* (Hebrew) (Givat Haviva: Yad Ya'ari and Hitagdut Yotzey Hashomer Hatzair BeCzechoslovakia, 1994), p. 253.

67 Zvi (Rubi) Berenstein, "Mesilat Hano'ar," in Rav, *Shomrim Tamid*, pp. 290–299.

68 Helaine Blumenthal, "Communism on Trial: The Slansky Affair and Anti-Semitism in Post-WWII Europe," UC Berkeley: Berkeley Program in Soviet and Post-Soviet Studies, pp. 12–13, http://escholarship.org/uc/item/4wr2g4kf (last accessed May 6, 2024).

Shortly after, on May 14, 1948, the State of Israel was established. Czechoslovakia became a pillar of support and assistance for the young country. Arms shipments came from Prague and Bratislava. For the first time it was possible for graduates of the movement to legally immigrate to Israel. However, the activists' joy was clouded by constant debates around Ya'ari's conflicting orders: Were they to accelerate the immigration of graduates to Israel or to continue to strengthen the movement in Czechoslovakia? The regime's sympathetic attitude toward the young State of Israel as well as Hashomer Hatzair's rising influence in the small Jewish community, which numbered around 45,000 people, seemed to dictate that their efforts in Czechoslovakia must continue. Benito worked relentlessly—in training courses, winter camps, movement councils, the endless meetings of various institutions. Meanwhile, Chajka took care of Zvi and spent long hours standing in line for milk in a city that had not yet recovered from the horrors of war. What little spare time she had she devoted to movement work.[69] A rare photograph shows her sitting next to the poet Avraham Shlonsky during his visit to Europe while the emissary Haim Zakai is delivering a passionate oration next to them. Shlonsky, his hands resting on the table, looks pensive. Chajka's gaze appears unfocused, as if turned inward, perhaps sifting through memories of her time in the *ken* in Będzin.[70]

In June 1948, Benito was asked to travel to Israel to promote the appointment of his fellow kibbutz member Rafi Benshalom to the position of consul at the Israeli Embassy in Prague.[71] It was decided that during his absence, Chajka should travel to Budapest, where Yoshko Baumer and Munshel (Haim) and Rachel Zakai of Kibbutz Haogen were acting as the movement's emissaries. The trip was a kind of reminder of home:

> Chajka spent about two weeks with us, the children were happy. She was a bit of home company.... Most of the hospitality duties fell on Rachel. It was the fate of the emissaries' wives to be the keepers of the kibbutz home, and they bore much of the responsibility for the children's upbringing while adhering devoutly to the rules of

69 According to Benito's letter on November 17, 1947, Chajka was supposed to start helping out with office work and Hebrew classes.

70 This photograph can be found in the Givat Oz Archive. In the photo, Munshel (Haim Zakai) is identified as the speaker.

71 Ya'akov Ronen, *Curriculum Vitae*, p. 123.

> elementary kibbutz education.... The kids were still little at this time, but there was also talk of a "follow up" and above all of the need to return as soon as possible home, to the kibbutz, "for their sake" if nothing else.[72]

"For their sake" was a fundamental factor in these conversations about shortening the time spent abroad. For Chajka, the idea went deeper than personal, familial concerns:

> "There are frighteningly few of us left," she used to say, especially when she was told about the displaced survivors in Germany, among them a few of her own movement friends from back in the desperate days in Zagłębie. And we knew the role that Chajka played during that period of extermination. We remembered what she told us when she came to [*Eretz*] Israel among the first of the survivors.[73]

Rachel's testimony touches on two events. First, the aforementioned "follow up" was already on its way. At the time of her stay in Budapest, Chajka was in the third month of her second pregnancy. She was due to give birth in December. And second, among the "few of us left," there was no sign of her sister Mania. Upon her return to Israel in 1949, she would be reunited with Zippora Szporn who had witnessed the demise of Chajka's family in Będzin and had been placed in a women's labor camp in Germany with Mania Klinger. While the conditions in the camp were relatively reasonable, and most of the girls survived, Mania died in an accident when she fell from the couplings of a tractor pulling a cart.[74]

It was a final and terrible blow. None of Chajka's immediate family survived. The children were supposed to be an answer to the loss. They were supposed to serve as the anchor and compass of Chajka's life. But the dead were also a kind of anchor, pulling her down, distorting the readings of the compass, and threatening to drown her. Ya'ari's metaphor could be read both ways.

72 Rachel and Munshel Zakai, in *Chajka: Hoveret Zikaron*, pp. 16–17.

73 Ibid.

74 Zippora Szporn interview. See also Szymon (Shimon) Balicki testimony, YVA, O.3/1246, p. 55.

Second Birth and Breakdown

As her pregnancy progressed, Chajka decided to return to Israel and give birth to her second child there. Benito was supposed to join her a little later, in time for the birth. From September 1948, he and Chajka desperately pressed the movement's institutions in Israel to find a replacement for Benito. As was common practice in the movement, another member from Kibbutz Haogen, Ya'akov Ernest (Arden) would take his place. But Ernest's departure was delayed due to difficulties obtaining permits to leave the country. The movement's top leadership in Merhavia informed Benito that even after Ernest arrived, he would have to remain in Bratislava for a few weeks longer so as to train the new emissary before departing.[75] Chajka would have to go back and face the possibility that the father of her child would not be there to see it born. However, there were other practical matters to consider: her ability to communicate with the Czech hospital nurses, Zvi's integration in the kibbutz children's house after the birth, the support of Zippora Sfinkelstein, who was waiting for her in Tel Aviv. At the end of the day, the kibbutz was her home and Israel was her country.

In the fall of 1948, Chajka and Zvi boarded a Dakota airplane heading to Israel. It was raining, and in the middle of the flight, Zvi got up and ran to the cockpit. Chajka had to fetch him and bring him back to his seat.[76] They landed in Israel on October 26 with the war still raging.[77] Two days later saw the launch of Operation Hiram to occupy the Galilee. On December 22, Operation Horev to conquer the Negev began. Kibbutz Haogen had not yet completed its transfer from Kfar Saba to Wadi Qabbani. Those members who were not serving in the army were scattered between the two locales. It was not a particularly suitable time to give birth.

When Chajka arrived at the kibbutz, she hastened to check whether Ya'akov Ernest, the emmisary appointed to replace Benito, had left for Czechoslovakia. The subject was even brought up at a kibbutz meeting about two weeks after her arrival. However, it turned out that Ernest's departure was delayed due to arrangements that had to be made for his

75 Letter from S. Shebretz to the central leadership in Bratislava, March 9, 1949, Hashomer Hatzair Archive, 78.31 (D3).

76 Zvi Ronen interview.

77 Chajka's passport, Moreshet Archive, C.36.4.

girlfriend who wished to join him.[78] Chajka anxiously reported this news to Benito, who informed the top leadership in his region that his work in Czechoslovakia would be over by the end of December even if the new emissary failed to arrive.[79] Both were sensing the hardships that lay ahead.

On December 8, Benito was told by the leadership in Merhavia that Ya'akov Ernest had left, but they asked him to extend his stay in Czechoslovakia beyond the end of December.[80] A letter sent on the same day to the leadership in Bratislava explained the reasons for this request: In the fall of 1948, the Jews of Czechoslovakia, frightened by the new communist regime, began to pack their belongings in preparation for mass immigration to Israel. Benito reported to Israel that the increased immigration of families was beginning to impact regular operations of the movement's *kens*. Other Zionist youth movements had already begun shutting down activity. In light of this, Benito suggested that Hashomer Hatzair cease its educational activities and focus instead on organizing immigration groups.[81] After consulting with Meir Ya'ari himself, the leadership wrote back: "The complete liquidation of our movement is inconceivable.... The central leadership and the key instructors must remain on their guard as long as there are Jewish youths in the country."[82] Faithful to his orders, Benito remained even after Ya'akov Ernest had arrived in Bratislava. And so, Ya'ari's invisible hand had once again unwittingly circumscribed Chajka's fate—his decision meant that her husband could not be by her side during the birth of her second child.

On December 19, 1948, in a hospital in Kfar Saba, Chajka gave birth to a second son—me. My name—Avihu—was picked by Munshel Zakai who had returned from Hungary shortly after Chajka's arrival in Israel. The events of the birth and what followed can only be reconstructed in fragments. It was another difficult birth. I weighed a hefty 4.150 kilograms. It seems that following my birth, Chajka went into postpartum depression that intensified over time. It is impossible

78 Minutes of a Kibbutz Haogen meeting, November 6, 1948, Kibbutz Haogen Archive, I/295.

79 Letter from Ya'akov Rosenberg to the top leadership in Merhavia, November 20, 1948, Hashomer Hatzair Archive, 78.31 (D3).

80 Letter from S. Shebertz to Ya'akov Rosenberg, December 8, 1948, Hashomer Hatzair Archive, 78.31 (D3).

81 Letter from Ya'akov Rosenberg and Zvi Borenstein to the top leadership in Merhavia, November 17, 1948, Hashomer Hatzair Archive, 78.31 (D3).

82 Letter from S. Shebretz to the central leadership in Bratislava, December 8, 1948, Hashomer Hatzair Archive, 78.31 (D3).

to say how known or diagnosed the phenomenon was at that time; however, weeks after the birth, she had difficulty functioning. Zippora Sfinkelstein's daughter Rachel later remembered Chajka being very ill in their apartment on HaAliya Street in Tel Aviv. She recalled Chajka saying that she was losing fluids and was going to die. She refused to have a urine test for fear of losing even more fluids; she refused to take medicine for fear that she would be poisoned. She had lost her trust in people, including Benito.

According to Rachel, it was the Sfinkelsteins who had decided to hospitalize against her will. Rachel said that later, Chajka could not forgive Father for this.[83] It is unclear whom she had meant by "Father": her father, Yosef, or my father, Benito, who was abroad at the time. However, it is possible that it was the members of the kibbutz who had decided to hospitalize Chajka and to take responsibility for the care of her son. Later, Evka summarized the events as follows:

> On her return from the mission, she had her second son, but her prolonged illness prevented her from taking care of him for a while. When I visited her in the convalescent home, she asked a lot about the boys, about the house, about every single detail. She longed to go back.[84]

No additional testimony regarding Chajka during this period has been found.

Benito returned to Israel about two and a half months later, in early March 1949. At the beginning of the new year, he received a telegram from the kibbutz that he must return as soon as possible, because Chajka had fallen ill. The nature of the illness was not specified.[85] Benito tried to finish his mission in an orderly manner, which meant training his replacement.[86] During these months, the position of Hashomer Hatzair in Czechoslovakia worsened. In the spirit of Ya'ari's instructions, on January 4, 1949, the movement's council made a public decision against the cessation of the movement's educational activities in the Diaspora. Nevertheless, in practice, the numbers of graduates who were

83 Rachel Sfinkelstein, interview by the author, Savyon, 1985.

84 Evka Sharon, in *Chajka: Hoveret Zikaron*, p. 16.

85 The telegram from the kibbutz to Benito was lost. Ya'akov Ronen interview.

86 Ya'akov Ronen, *Curriculum Vitae*, pp. 124–125.

immigrating continued to rise.[87] In an "exclusively internal" letter, written a little later, the liaison office of Hashomer Hatzair in Prague reported that there were clear signs that the communist regime intended to "dissolve" (meaning ban) Zionist activity in Czechoslovakia after the *aliya* of most of the Jews who wished to immigrate.[88] The accelerated immigration of graduates demanded Benito's presence. The movement's orders once again superseded personal hardships.

Benito set out on February 12, 1949, on a small ship named *Madex* accompanied by a large group of Hashomer Hatzair youths, among them 110 graduates of the movement. About three weeks later he arrived in Haifa.[89] Upon his arrival, he was greeted by Mori Farkash, a member of Gan Shmuel who had been with him early on in the mission, and who informed him that his father Moritz had passed away two weeks earlier.[90] Benito had to face a new reality: his wife was in hospital, his father was dead, and he had a new son whom he was yet to meet. His parents, who had asked to be admitted to Kibbutz Gan Shmuel where their daughter Yaffa resided, were rejected by the kibbutz, perhaps due to Bella's insistence on cooking kosher food at home. In Hadera, the Rosenbergs had lived in squalor, and Benito felt guilty that his father died without him by his side.[91]

In his memoirs, Benito did not elaborate on his feelings during his reunion with his wife and sons. He only pointed out that "Zvi, who was fluent in Slovak, abandoned it in an instant, probably in order not to stand out from the other children."[92] For his part, Zvi remembered that Benito had brought gifts for all the children in the group: blue dolls for the boys, pink dolls for the girls. He was upset because he had wanted a pink doll.[93] Elsewhere, Benito noted the difficulties he experienced in reintegrating into the construction group: "I found myself preoccupied with Chajka's health problems and taking care of two children whose

87 Bichler, "Yamey Hahra'a," pp. 260–263.

88 Letter from Ya'akov Mayus to the central office in Tel Aviv, January 23, 1949, Hashomer Hatzair Archive, 68.31(1).

89 This date is estimated based on a telegram Benito received in Kfar Saba on March 6, 1949, regarding *aliya* arrangements for the youths. Yad Ya'ari Archive, 33.4 (5).

90 According to Benito, it was one week earlier. Ya'akov Ronen interview. Moritz Rosenberg died on February 17, 1949.

91 Ya'akov Ronen, *Curriculum Vitae*, p. 127.

92 Ibid., p. 125.

93 Zvi Ronen interview.

mother was not at home."[94] Later, he would record that his life had been turned upside down: "Chajka's behavior became more and more difficult to deal with from day to day. We had to isolate her from the children and watch over her at the same time. The doctors established the diagnosis of her mental illness unequivocally."[95] He does not, however, specify what that diagnosis was.

Later, according to Benito, she was admitted to the Geha Psychiatric Hospital and was treated by Prof. Winnik and Dr. Ruth Yaffe.[96] These were two of the finest professionals in the field of psychiatry at the time, but the treatment of survivors was then only in its infancy. Concepts such as "collective trauma," "post-traumatic stress," and even "postpartum depression" did not yet exist as we know them today. The term "mental illness" was an umbrella that covered a variety of mental phenomena and irrational behaviors, and commitment was the only solution available. Later, Winnik would write: "It was assumed that, in any case, the whole problem would become a thing of the past within a few years, and it was not worth bothering with the research effort." Only in retrospect was it discovered that "we were facing an enormous devastation in the mental field."[97] Only in the late 1950s and early 1960s were comprehensive studies on the subject beginning to be published, and even then the researchers had to admit that they had not yet been able to properly define the new psychopathological conditions they were studying.[98]

We do not know exactly how long Chajka remained in hospital, but it appears that it was not a prolonged stay. However, in the eyes of the kibbutz, she was marked with what was considered a stain in those days. If she had already been trying to hide her struggles before, she now had to try even harder to pretend to be calm and happy, not only for the sake of the kibbutz but also for the sake of her children.

94 Ya'akov Ronen, *Curriculum Vitae*, p. 140.

95 Ibid.

96 Ya'akov Ronen interview.

97 Heinz Zvi Winnik, "Holi Hanefesh Hame'uhar (Ketotza'a shel Pgi'at Hashoah)," in Tommy Spencer, ed., *Harefu'a Vehashoah: Ma'amarim Mitoch "Harefua"* (Hebrew) (Ramat Gan: Hahistadrut Harefu'it BeYisrael, 2006), p. 77.

98 In his article, Winnick refers to two groundbreaking studies on the subject: W. Ritter Von Baeyer, H. Haefner, and K. P. Kisker, *Psychiatrie der Vervolgen* (Berlin: Springer Verlag, 1964); Leo Eitinger, *Concentration Camp Survivors in Norway and Israel* (Oslo and London: Universitetsforlaget and Allen and Unwin, 1965).

CHAPTER TWENTY-SIX

Mother

Hybrid Birth: 2009

The social worker says: "What we can do is issue you a hybrid birth certificate. This document will confirm that you are the son of your biological mother, and her name can also appear on your ID card, in parentheses, next to the name of the adoptive mother. The process must, of course, be approved by the Family Court." She speaks softly and has warm eyes, as befits a social worker. On the phone, we agreed to skip the preparatory step of opening the adoption file. The adopted child is arguably a grown up, and there is not much risk of him experiencing an identity crisis at this juncture. Nevertheless, I am a little excited to be sitting here, in the spacious office located in a high-ceilinged Arabic-style building in the Lower Town area of Haifa. The validation of my adoption process by the Child Services Department at the Ministry of Welfare is necessary for me to reach the next and final stage in my research: the retrieval of my mother's files from Geha Psychiatric Hospital. I have not been able to view them because my ID card does not list Chajka Klinger as my mother.

The adoption file, dated November 24, 1966, is as thin as I remember it. I recall informing Zacharia Goren, our eleventh-grade teacher, that tomorrow I would be absent from school because I had to go to Tel Aviv. "I'm being adopted," I explained to him, barely managing to contain my giddiness at the thought of the fun day that awaited me in Tel Aviv. Maybe I would have enough time to catch a matinee at the Paris Cinema and bring back a chocolate-covered marshmallow treat from the big city for Hagit. I was no stranger to Tel Aviv: Once a month I reported to the treasurer of the educational department at the kibbutz to receive travel expenses and a check made out to Uzi Wiesel for my Tuesday cello lessons. Uzi listened to me play with concentration, but it was evident that he was far from satisfied. He had agreed to take me on as a student a few months earlier, after hearing me at the annual students' recital at the Ramot Hefer school in Ma'abarot. I played the prelude from Bach's first suite by heart. It all went pretty smoothly, but at the end, as usual, I rushed through the long chords. The maestro's face twitched slightly: "Is it so hard to count four crochets?" Nevertheless, he decided to give me a trial run.

I remember the puzzled look that Zacharia gave me, but he didn't ask any questions. It was clear to me that he was fuzzy on the details of this adoption business, but he still approved. The meeting at the office in Jaffa took no time at all. It was 1966, and I didn't quite understand why I had to meet with a social worker. Still, I answered her questions willingly. "No, I have no objection to the adoption." "Yes, I remember my mother well, and I don't mean to forget her." "Yes, they've spoken to me and explained that this was important to them." "No, why would I consider it a violation of Mother's memory?" "Yes, if it's what my parents want, then I'm ready." "No, I haven't talked to my brother about it." "No. We don't talk about things like that." The social worker saw it fit to suggest at the end: "Maybe you should talk to Zvi after all." "What for?" She wrote down the answers, and I headed for the bus going to Hayarkon Street with plenty of time to make it to the screening at the Paris Cinema.

"That's right," I affirm to the social worker in present-day Haifa. "I really didn't care back then. I did it for them, because they asked me to. I was seventeen and used to making my own decisions." Yet in 1966, they forgot to tell me one small detail: When an adoption decree is issued by a court, the adoptee gets a new birth certificate, bearing only the name of the adoptive mother.[1] The name of the biological mother is erased from the certificates and kept only in the state's adoption register.[2] Only now, during this conversation in Haifa, do I realize that the state has been issuing its own—legal—fake certificates. The social worker casually explains that until about twenty years ago it was not possible to fix this either, but then a special law was enacted allowing the biological mother's name to be featured in parentheses on the adoptee's ID card. This is conditioned

1 Population Registry Law, 1965, paragraph 20, http://main.knesset.gov.il/EN/About/History/Documents/kns5_population_eng.pdf (accessed May 6, 2024).

2 Adoption of Children Law, 5741-1981, paragraph 29, https://www.nevo.co.il/law_html/Law01/055_075.htm#Seif69 (Hebrew) (accessed May 6, 2024).

on the opening of the adoption file and the issuance of a "hybrid" birth certificate. "But what did people do before this law?" She doesn't know. "What about the Yemenite children?"[3] I can't help but asking. "At least I knew my biological mother. If their adoptive parents didn't bother telling them they were adopted, they never even had the chance of finding out who they really were before the state faked their identity." She looks at me quizzically—what have I got to do with the Yemenite children? She would rather talk about my feelings and my current relationship with Zvi.

The historian's habit kicks in like a conditioned reflex. ID card. January 1966. About a year before I was supposed to get my first ID card. Zvi was already in the army, and it was too late to adopt him. Arnon's adoption was obvious; as a ten-year-old he adopted Malka as much as she adopted him. The date of my adoption, however, testifies to what was never explicitly said: Just as I was about to be permanently recognized by the state as my mother's son, I was legally adopted according to my express consent, and my mother's name was deleted from my birth certificate.

About a month or more after the meeting in Haifa, the hybrid birth certificate finally arrives, and a new problem arises. The Family Court secretary, who validated the document on January 24, 1966, recorded Mother's last name as "Ronen (Rosenberg)," even though our surname was changed by family decision only two or three years after her death. However, as far as the state is concerned, I am the son of "Chaja Ronen," a fictitious character whose name suggests just how fully she must have acclimatized to Israel. I go back and insist that the "Ronen (Rosenberg)" be changed to "Rosenberg (Klinger)." After a phone call with the director of the head office, the error is partially amended: the new hybrid birth certificate I receive lists "Chaja Rosenberg" as my biological mother. The retrieval of the lost "Klinger" requires a court order.

But that is where my journey down the winding bureaucratic path ends. Viewing the file at Geha Psychiatric Hospital requires the approval of all first-degree blood relatives, and Zvi, with whom I discuss the matter, does not approve. He adamantly insists that Mom would not want us to see the file and that a person's wishes must be honored even after they're dead. He is probably right.

3 This is referring to the Yemenite Children Affair, which saw the disappearance of between 1,000 and 5,000 Yemenite Jewish babies and toddlers of immigrants to the newly founded State of Israel between 1948 and 1954.

At the Kibbutz

More bewildering than the fact that Chajka took her own life fifteen years after having escaped from the pits of hell is the fact that she managed to keep living as long as she did. Her story was not one of survival but of struggle. In Chajka's belief system—and that of the kibbutz society in which she lived—in order to have value, life had to have meaning. It did not have inherent value independent of that. "Real" life consisted of creation and struggle. Members of the kibbutzim, after having read from their specially adapted secular Haggada on Passover, raised a glass to the socialist struggle and meant it. In Kibbutz Haogen, as in other kibbutzim, every action was seen as part of a huge creative enterprise, whether it was building housing, making rubber balls, planting an orchard, harvesting potatoes, or raising children. Every action had a unique Zionist, socialist, and above all "constructive" significance. They believed the great and powerful Soviet Union to be the "world of tomorrow": Mapam (Mifleget Hapo'alim Hameuhedet, The United Workers' Party), which had just been established in 1948, was the second largest party in Israel; the Haogen factory was an impressive economic success; and the birth rate in the kibbutz was particularly high. In 1953, there were already 126 children in the kibbutz, a third of the local population.[4] "For us and our children and our children's children forever and ever" the kibbutz painter Shraga Weil had written on a scroll buried in the foundations of the new dining hall.

The few remaining pieces of evidence indicate that Chajka preserved her beliefs in collective education and Marxism. However, she had another struggle to wage: the struggle for her own soul. Whether she wanted to or not, she had to continue dealing with her past. Holocaust survivors did not receive special treatment in Israeli society.[5] At Kibbutz Haogen, which took in about forty members who had been through the concentration, death, and labor camps, no one was called a "survivor." They were sometimes called "Slovaks," "Hungarians," "Viennese," and so on, but mostly they were divided into "veterans," "newbies," "auxiliary workers," and "parentless youths." Holocaust survivors identified themselves as "partisans" or "resistance fighters." The term "hero" was reserved for Haviva Reik alone. The survivors did not talk much about

4 Demographic evolution of Kibbutz Haogen, Kibbutz Haogen Archive, 112/5.

5 See Hanna Yablonka, *Ahim Zarim: Nitzoley Hashoah Bimedinat Yisrael, 1948–1952* (Hebrew) (Jerusalem and Be'er Sheva: Yad Ben Zvi and Ben-Gurion University, 1994), pp. 175–189.

their past. The fact that some of them had a blue number tattooed on their arm, took part in the partisan operations in Slovakia, or worked in the Polish ghettos, was not given special importance in the kibbutz. What mattered was their integration into the kibbutz's work life, their social and political activity, and their adherence to the rules of collective behavior. The present and the future were the central concern, the past was marginal.

Once a year, on the 27th of Nisan—Ghetto Fighters' Remembrance Day—the members of the kibbutzim would travel en masse to the Yad Mordechai memorial rally. As Chajka Grossman's testimony shows, Chajka Klinger rode in the jeep with her to one of the rallies. Chajka Grossman was younger; she had arrived in Israel in 1948 after participating in the uprising in Białystok, fighting alongside the partisans, and leading the remnants of her movement for a time after the war. Because of her pro-Soviet leanings, she also had had her clashes with the Hashomer leadership.[6] Nevertheless, by this time, she had already published her book, *Anshei Hamahteret* (The People of the Resistance), which became a canonical text within the movement.[7] The two Chajkas were talking, and it is possible that the elder of the two mentioned the existence of her as yet unpublished diaries.[8]

They had a lot in common, but they did not keep in touch over the years. Once they had made it to *Eretz Israel*, the surviving ghetto fighters of Hakibbutz Ha'artzi lived in different kibbutzim, and apart from a failed attempt to gather a group of partisans in Ein Hahoresh, no movement effort was made to build a common home for them.[9] That is not to say it couldn't be done. Over in Tabenkin's sister movement Hakibbutz Hameuchad, Kibbutz Lohamei HaGeta'ot (Ghetto Fighters' Kibbutz) was founded in 1949 in Western Galilee. Most of the kibbutz members were not fighters, but their shared past and the joint leadership of Antek Zuckerman and Zivia Lubetkin gave them the strength to live and remember.

The younger Chajka (Grossman) was proud of her past, and the uprising in Białystok and the efforts of the partisans were considered a success. On the other hand, the older Chajka (Klinger) saw the resistance

6 Ziva Shalev, *Chajka* (Hebrew) (Tel Aviv: Moreshet, 2005), part II, pp. 29–35; Barzel, *Ad Kelot U'Mineged*, p. 231.

7 Chajka Grossman, *Anshey Hamahteret* (Hebrew) (Merhavia: Hakibbutz Ha'artzi, Hashomer Hatzair, 1950).

8 Chajka Grossman interview; Chajka Grossman, in *Chajka: Hoveret Zikaron*, p. 39.

9 Barzel, *Ad Kelot U'mineged*, pp. 76–84.

operations in Będzin as a failure. Through her book, Chajka Grossman reached out to the past and drew empowerment from it, whereas Chajka Klinger-Rosenberg's connection to her past was complicated. Memories of the past continued to disturb her nights, and she did not live to see the publication of her diaries. She did not make much effort to keep in touch with any of her resistance friends who slowly made their way to Israel. She did encounter Ada Neufeld randomly once and told her that "they need to talk more."[10] Chana (Wiernik) and Benjamin Schlesinger tried to keep in touch with her, but when they expressed a desire to visit her at Haogen, they were told that she was not in good health and that the visit may be detrimental to her.[11] Abraham Izbicki too, her fellow escapee from Slovakia, visited her during her illness, but she could not talk to him.[12] On another occasion, Shmuel Ron met with her and asked her to give him her diaries to read.[13] No letters from this period remain, only a distant childhood memory from an apartment in Netanya of my mother talking to another woman in a foreign language.

Chajka did not ask for special consideration at Kibbutz Haogen, neither in light of her distant past nor due to recent events. As kibbutz member Shmuel "Wizo" Klein later testified, Chajka's hospitalization was never discussed at the kibbutz: "Such things were considered 'taboo' back then. They said neither good nor bad things about them, they simply did not talk about them. People knew that it was beyond their understanding and that they were better off keeping their distance from the subject."[14] Wizo had held key positions in the kibbutz at the time, and according to him, if there had been talk, it is likely that he would have heard about it.[15] As it turns out, the "taboo" also included the horrors of the Holocaust. Chajka and other survivors at Kibbutz Haogen barely spoke about what they had gone through in the camps. Their kibbutz friends, who did not experience the Holocaust, could not comprehend the depth of the survivors' personal trauma. "Only later did we begin to understand," Wizo said, "that people who went through so much, none of them came out unscathed."[16]

10 Ada Halperin (Neufeld) interview.

11 Chana (Wiernik) and Benjamin Schlesinger interview.

12 Abraham Izbicki at the Barenblatt trial, Moreshet Archive, D.1.5366.

13 Letter from Benito to Menahem Bader, January 9, 1959, Chajka Klinger file, Moreshet Archive, C.36.

14 Shmuel Koren interview.

15 Ibid.

16 Ibid.

That said, Chajka made a quick recovery. After her hospitalization, she spent some time in a convalescent home, and then returned to the kibbutz. In one of the few remaining photographs of her from that time, she is seen hoisting up a several-month-old baby, the expression on her face happy and proud. Another photograph is one of the four of us sitting in a field of flowers on a winter's day. The youngest of the bunch (me) is about a year old. Mom's face is calm. Dad is smiling at the camera. During this period, my parents were living in a shack just by the kibbutz fence; beyond it were the open fields. They had been allotted one room but with the toilets nearby—a stone building with public facilities for the whole neighborhood. The shared shower was also quite close. In the evening hours, friends passing by on the path behind the shack used to call Dad to go with them to the showers. Sometimes, Mom would send me there to fetch him back, and I would look in amazement at the steam-filled space and the nude men bent over in a vain search for spare wooden clogs or standing in front of the mirror, their faces half-covered in white shaving foam.

Work

After this, Chajka resumed her work duties in the kibbutz. For a while, she worked as a kitchen cook before she was moved to the children's clothing warehouse. She was also assigned various committee coordination duties. As Mina Karni later wrote in the memorial booklet:

> When we moved to the settlement, like most of the members, you were required to work in service jobs. By working in the kitchen, in the children's [clothing] warehouse, you could serve as a role model in caring for the children despite the insufficient help and the difficult conditions. The kibbutz could rest assured that every job assigned to you would be in faithful hands. Whether it was labor or coordinating committees—you could do it all![17]

Though posthumous praise is likely to be hyperbolic, Mina emphasized that Chajka was well enough that the kibbutz society could entrust her with any task. In the summer of 1950, she attended the Mapam party seminar in Givat Haviva. In March 1951, it was proposed that she

17 Mina Karni, in *Chajka: Hoveret Zikaron*, p. 15.

become the second instructor of the kibbutz's parentless youth group,[18] at the end of 1952 she was chosen to be the coordinator of the members' committee,[19] and about a year later, she became the coordinator of the children's clothing warehouse. The minutes of the kibbutz meetings in the years 1951–1952 indicate that Chajka was an active participant in the conversations, above what was customary for female kibbutz members. (Whether they were intended to be so or not, kibbutz meetings were run mainly by the men.) Wizo's testimony confirms this: "You could tell that before the hospitalization she had been an active and opinionated woman. She participated a lot in the meetings and her Hebrew was good, which was not the case for all of us."[20]

Most of Chajka's remarks during these meetings concerned work and appointments. That was the general spirit of the kibbutz meetings at Haogen, whose members were practical and not prone to bickering. The women would take the floor mainly when the discussion concerned their work in the "service branches"—the accepted name for jobs that were not considered strictly productive. This was the glass ceiling of kibbutz society; neither Mina nor Chajka could shatter it, nor did they try to do so. The romantic literature they read could provide them with role models for revolutionary women in conditions of war or with women fighting to be integrated into the labor force in the 1920s, but there were no books featuring female characters who were equal to men in everyday kibbutz life. Though Hakibbutz Ha'artzi demanded that much attention be paid to the state of the community in any given kibbutz, in practice, the women found themselves going back and forth between the kitchen and the clothes warehouse. The lucky ones got to work in education. In Kibbutz Haogen, with the exception of two treasurers, all the key positions were filled by men, although they were often inferior in their skills to the educated female kibbutz members.[21]

Chajka's comments during the kibbutz meetings show how committed she was to work. In the kibbutz meeting of November 22, 1952, she said: "Every female member has to have a turn at working in the kitchen. I stand by my right to finish my turn. That is why I don't want to work in the clothes

18 Chajka Klinger, "Beseminarion Hamiflaga BeGivat Haviva" (Hebrew), *Beitenu*, 26 (June 24, 1950). See also minutes of a Kibbutz Haogen meeting, March 3, 1951, Kibbutz Haogen Archive, I/286.

19 Minutes of a Kibbutz Haogen meeting, November 22, 1952, Kibbutz Haogen Archive, III/286.

20 Shmuel Koren interview.

21 Ibid.

warehouse."[22] In a previous meeting on July 14, 1952, when the burden of additional tasks on the kitchen workers was discussed, she passionately defended her work: "It is not true that the kitchen workers do not work a full eight hours. They start in the morning at a quarter past five and finish at two. And in the afternoon—from twelve to nine in the evening."[23] When she finally took over coordinating the clothes warehouse, she wrote a long article in which she described her work in detail.[24]

She no longer spoke about her aspirations of further education. Only a fraction of the kibbutz members were high school graduates, and their skills were rarely in demand. Some were sent to be trained as teachers; however, in the 1950s, all the teachers were men, except for Tzipi Sadeh, who taught first graders. The women were assigned the job of custodian. Educated women could demonstrate their skills by writing for the kibbutz newspaper, organizing holiday festivities, or sometimes by being active in the Mapam party or the Hakibbutz Ha'artzi movement. A few women, such as Miriam Goldberger, did manage to make cultural activity the center of their work alongside their regular duties. The kibbutz Passover and harvest ceremonies she organized were spectacular productions involving all the members of the kibbutz and their children.

Chajka, on the other hand, whose skills were basically in the realms of literature and ideology, did not find a place where she could apply them, or else, she simply did not aspire to demonstrate them externally. She returned from the party seminar satisfied and particularly impressed by Hazan who was skilled at answering questions before they could even be raised. Wizo remembered a rare instance of a literary gathering held in the kibbutz in which Chajka asked for permission to speak. According to him, Chajka's knowledge of fine literature surprised him and everyone present at the gathering.[25]

A rare letter preserved by Ruth Klinger, a cousin of Chajka's who was residing abroad at the time, presents an accurate picture of Chajka's state of mind in 1953:

22 Minutes of a Kibbutz Haogen meeting, November 22, 1952, Kibbutz Haogen Archive, III/286.

23 Minutes of a Kibbutz Haogen meeting, July 14, 1952, Kibbutz Haogen Archive, III/286.

24 Chajka Klinger, "Miba'ayot Mahsan Habegadim" (Hebrew), *Beitenu*, 82 (August 11, 1953), pp. 5–6.

25 Klinger, "Beseminarion Hamiflaga BeGivat Haviva"; Shmuel Koren interview.

> Greetings to all, Ruth and Rafi!
>
> Unfortunately, I am the one to bring shame on my family, since they've all finished writing their letters, and only Mom… But that's the way of the world, the mothers are always busy and preoccupied to no end, especially mothers in Israel, even if they are kibbutz mothers.
>
> I am currently working at the children's clothes warehouse. Imagine having to provide clothes for 150 children for the winter, for hot weather, for when it rains. Whether you have the budget or not, and even if the treasurer has quit or been replaced. So where does one find the time for letter writing? And yet, here I am. […]
>
> As for me? What else is new? Slowly but surely the boys are starting to take first place in our lives. They're getting bigger, growing up nicely, they're quick boys, diligent and gentle. Every mother must say these things about her children, and I am no exception. (And you Ruth? Aren't you getting ready to be a mother in Israel? Do not discount this most important role! It is best to be a young mom and finish having children early so as to be a free person again afterward.) But it's good to enjoy yourself now too, since you're already abroad, why shouldn't you?[26]

Photographs from this period confirm the calm disposition conveyed by this letter. Most of them are family photographs or shots of Purim costumes. At the time there were two or three members in Kibbutz Haogen who were allowed to have cameras. Not as private property, of course, but as a means of capturing moments of the joy and creativity of the collective and the individuals within the kibbutz. Rafi Benshalom, Benito's friend who had returned from his mission as first secretary at the embassy in Prague, seems to have been the family's photographer. In one photograph, Mom and Dad are sitting on the shack's veranda. Dad is relaxing in a deck chair, his hands folded restfully. Mom is wearing shorts and sitting on the steps with a book in her hand. Her eyes, through the lenses of her glasses, are following their two-year old toddler. A soft smile graces both their faces. I am looking to the side in consternation. In another photograph, it is a winter's day on a stony path leading up to a house whose façade is obscured by climbing vines. Grandmother is sitting in the middle of the frame—a small woman dressed in black.

26 Letter from Chajka to Ruth and Rafi Klinger, September 15, 1953, Ronen family archive.

Mom and Dad are standing to either side of her, each of them holding a child by the hand. Mom, wearing a sweater, has her gaze directed straight at the camera. It is a cheerful gaze, seemingly at peace. Her days seem to have been bright and stable during those years. As for her nights, they are shrouded from view.

Family

During those years, family members often came to visit us in the kibbutz, and Chajka and Benito traveled to see them frequently as well. Thanks to Benito's influence as a returning emissary, his mother, Grandmother Bella Rosenberg—Moritz's widow—got an apartment in a small duplex in a senior housing complex in Netanya. The small one-bedroom apartment quickly became the center of the Rosenberg family gatherings and our family's holiday destination. Bella was a great cook, and her special lunches, where she served Benito beer and fish before the soup, were full of flavors from another place and time, both strange and magical. Benito's two sisters—my aunts Yaffa and Zippora—would also come with their families to the gatherings on Bella's birthday or on Passover, and the square next to Grandmother's house would be filled with screaming children.

Yosef and Zippora Sfinkelstein liked to come from Tel Aviv to Haogen on Shabbat, and their new apartment on Hashoftim Street, which was very spacious by the standards of the time, became an alternative place to go to during the holidays. Chajka went to visit Yosef and Zippora regularly. According to Benito, Zvi stayed with Yosef and Zippora one year for a whole week alone.[27]

As for motherhood, it appears from Chajka's letter that it occupied a central place in her life. The transfer of the children to the nursery and the children's house did not bother her; she wholeheartedly believed in raising children collectively. The few hours in the afternoon she devoted to spending time with the children were intense. Among the few childhood memories I have left, there is a snippet of us in the shack in winter in front of the oil stove. Zvi and Dad are down on the carpet playing Meccano, an assembly game with screws and perforated metal plates that they had brought back from the mission. Mom is teaching me to read and write and is tickled every time I pick up a new letter or word. By the time I

27 Letter from Benito to Ruth and Rafi Klinger, September 15, 1953, Ronen family archive.

started first grade, I could already read and write. Another snippet: Mom is walking with me along the main path and asks me what kind of things I wish for. As a member of the kibbutz, I reply in the name of the collective that I wish there were no more poor people and no more wars. Mom asks skeptically: Don't you think poverty leads to wars? She was devoted to Marxism to the end. Standing at her grave, Dad said:

> It is not easy to find another example of the same loving care that she invested in raising her sons in their early days. Not by indulging them but by presenting life as it is, a gentle mother leading her sons by the hand and teaching them to jump across the slippery rocks in the stream of life and when they slipped, she showed them how to get up and keep going.[28]

Another childhood flashback: Mom and I are at the beach. I don't know how to swim yet. Mom is holding me afloat and then suddenly lets go. I panic and thrash around in the water, looking for solid ground. But a few seconds later, she is holding me again, smiling: This is how you learn to swim. As far as we can remember, Zvi was a father's boy, and I was a mother's boy. Zvi sometimes found it difficult to remain seated in the classroom, and he would run to the construction sites to look for Father.[29] School at Haogen was quite strict, and sometimes the teachers would use force out of helpless rage toward the children with whom they had to spend a large part of their day. The Education Committee would convene for urgent meetings, but the beatings and shouting continued.

Mom's upbringing was strict, but it involved neither shouting nor violence. She got angry sometimes, of course, but only once did she slap me, probably in response to a particularly audacious act of rebellion. She never spoke about it again. "Indulgence" was the word she and Dad employed to describe any inappropriate display of childishness. It was the spirit of the times: chasing sweets and complaining about toothaches were also considered indulgent. To me, my mother seemed no different than any other mother. There was only one thing that set her apart: she did not knit. Was it a sign of otherness or an attempt to avoid becoming yet another small, petty bourgeois woman? Who can tell. As children we

28 Ya'akov Rosenberg, eulogy for Chajka, April 19, 1958, Ya'akov Ronen collection.
29 Zvi Ronen, remarks at Father's 90th birthday, Sde Nitzan, 2007.

did not notice the signs of Mom's psychological troubles. In the three afternoon hours we spent at our parents' house, hours that were dedicated to us, she managed to push them aside.

In general, the adult world was separated from us by the impenetrable partition of *Nisht vor den Kindern*. At Haogen, children were not allowed to enter the dining room during dinner, the adults' Purim party was off-limits to us, and the few movies shown at the kibbutz were sometimes stopped midway through if they happened to feature a kiss. The Holocaust, too, was *Nisht vor den Kindern*. They wanted to protect us from the shadows of their past. They were looking out for us.

In 1949, the polio epidemic hit the children of the kibbutz, and nine small graves were dug on the western outskirts of the settlement. More children suffered permanent disfigurement of their arms, legs, or faces. Any minor illness would send the sick child into quarantine. Yet, the quarantine had a silver lining—it allowed these children to spend several more hours with their parents. When Ya'akov Shenfeld's daughter Edna fell ill, he went with her to Vienna for treatment. The coordination of the "group"—the kibbutz leadership—was then assigned to Benito.

A New Home

In the fifties, Benito made a career for himself in the construction business. The big project at that time was rebuilding the factory in the new settlement, and Benito was mainly involved in the ironwork. With the completion of the factory, residential units were added to the building, which would later be designated as "veterans' housing." The new units were erected by the Solel Boneh company, and the members of the construction group were assigned to other roles. Benito's position was now defined as building coordinator. As a man of initiative, he quickly expanded his role to become a kind of overseer of all construction projects in the kibbutz, coordinating between the planners, the main contractor, and the subcontractors.[30] He was in charge of making sure that the construction corresponded to the kibbutz's blueprints, took an active part in designing the settlement, and oversaw the implementation process. His time was divided between various foundations and scaffoldings, and his office on the second floor of the water tower that was erected next to

30 Ya'akov Ronen, *Curriculum Vitae*, pp. 140–142.

the shack. Within six years he managed to build a factory, several barns, a dairy, a nursery and a daycare, two classroom buildings, living quarters, and a large dining room. Still, the rate of construction barely kept up with the rate of growth of the kibbutz, which in 1953 already counted 393 members.[31]

In 1955, he was finally able to build a house for his own family as well. At the foot of the first veterans' housing, a second housing complex was built with an apartment for him and Chajka. The apartment was considered large at the time—around 40–50 square meters—and included two rooms, a balcony, a toilet, and a shower. New furniture was brought into the apartment—a wooden table and matching chairs. Dad spent quite a few days polishing the new furniture, and when the job was done, we were strictly forbidden from putting our feet on the table top. In a small garden plot allotted to them, Mom began growing African daisies and water arums. Dad planted a pecan tree, as did his old friend Yoshko Baumer, who moved into the adjacent apartment with his wife Marta.

Dad had his own original ways of expressing his artistic and archaeological ambitions. Later Zvi would say:

> When our parents were able to move into the veterans' housing, we had a family meeting and decided that we would add a special decoration to the square in front of the house. Father got a copy of Picasso's painting of the dove of peace, and we used it as a guide to make a painted mosaic on the ground, with wooden molds, and finally we poured red mortar over them to fasten the stones to the picture.[32]

Mom, too, was in the mood to celebrate. She held a small tea party on the new balcony. Despite the usual custom, I was allowed to take part, dressed in white boxers and a tank top, the children's recess uniform. Smiling, Mom pointed to a crack in the balcony ceiling and said: "As usual, the shoemaker's children go barefoot." But, of course, she was overjoyed: this was the first time she got to live in her own brick and mortar apartment. At that time, she was on her third pregnancy. According to Dad's testimony, one of the kibbutz women had tried to convince him that Chajka should

31 Letter from Benito to Ruth and Rafi Klinger, September 15, 1953; see also Ya'akov Ronen, "Habniya BeKibbutz Haogen," Ronen family archive.

32 Zvi Ronen, interview, 2007.

have an abortion. He refused: "I decided that, no matter what happened, I wouldn't make Chajka feel that the fruit of her womb, our child, hers and mine, was unwanted."[33]

The Edek Affair

The joys of creation and newness kept the kibbutz members insulated from the hardships all around them. The hired laborers in the factory and the construction group at Haogen came from poor immigrant backgrounds and lived in difficult conditions in Kfar Yona or Netanya. A new parentless youth group made up of emigrants from Islamic countries was formed and immediately gained a reputation as a "problem group"; we, the kibbutz members, were warned not to play with them. The nearby Arab villages were out of bounds and under harsh military rule.

Even the stories of Holocaust survivors both inside and outside the kibbutz were still "out of bounds." In the short-term Israeli memory, the Holocaust played a dual role. It was the justification for the State of Israel as the home and safe haven of the Jewish people, but it was also the negation of that people, the failure and demise of the Diaspora. The "From Holocaust to Revival" slogan that was prevalent at the time was too flimsy to bridge this contradiction. The new Israeli Jew was a hero—there was no question about that. But who was the survivor? A lamentable memorial to Jewish misery, to the need to survive at any cost, even if that cost is the death of others?

The defamation suit filed in 1953 by Israel Kasztner, one of the leaders of the Rescue Committee in Hungary, against Malchiel Gruenwald, who accused him of collaborating with the Nazis, raised these questions into the public conscience. Thanks to Shmuel Tamir, a sophisticated lawyer with clear political motivations, the Gruenwald trial became the Kasztner trial. Kasztner, who initially managed to present himself as responsible for saving thousands of Hungarian Jews, was accused by Tamir of having made a deal with the Nazis in which he was promised that his and his associates' lives would be spared in exchange for his silence on the subject of extermination. The accusations were unfounded, but Judge Binyamin Halevi accepted Tamir's claims, and in the ruling issued on June 22, 1955, he acquitted Gruenwald of most

33 Ya'akov Ronen, *Curriculum Vitae*, p. 135.

of the charges, stating that "Kasztner sold his soul to Satan." Halevi's statement resonated throughout the country. Fierce debates broke out between supporters of the ruling and its critics. However, overall public opinion, influenced by Tamir's public appearances and the articles in *Ha'olam Ha'ze*, sided with Judge Halevi. Soon, the expression "Kasztnerism" became a byword for collaborationism.

The ruling was pronounced only a few weeks before the next Knesset elections. Accusations were exchanged between the different parties. Everyone wanted to prove that the collaborators were identified with the other party, while the fighters and rebels were members of their own movement in the Diaspora. At this time, Maki (the Israeli Communist Party) was competing with Mapam—the party of Kibbutz Haogen and its members—over the same voter base. Maki completely agreed with Halevi's ruling, and its organ *Kol Ha'am* was quick to point out that Kasztner was aided by Mapam activists who had worked with him in Hungary, thus associating them with the "Quisling."[34]

In particular, their arrows were aimed at Rafi Benshalom, a member of Haogen and a well-known public figure, who was accused of having worked with Kasztner and was tainted with the stain of collaborationism. Mapam reacted quickly. At an election rally held the next day, Shimon Avidan, the legendary commander of the Givati Brigade, stated that Rafi Benshalom had freed many Jews from the Nazi prison. However, *Kol Ha'am* had another bomb at the ready. In an item published on July 1, 1955, the byline proclaimed: "The Leadership of Hashomer Hatzair in Israel Opposed the Armed Struggle in the Polish Ghettos."[35] The inner pages of the paper contained three columns of an article signed by "Edek" who was presented as a Hashomer Hatzair activist in Poland during World War II. Edek wrote:

> At the end of 1942, while Mordechai Anielewicz's people made one single plea—"Save Agana" [the underground nickname for *hagana*]—and called for help with their armed revolt, they received one single answer from the Land of Israel: "Agana—no!" The greetings sent in the name of "Meir" also stated that demands for "Agana" were not being taken seriously.[36]

34 Ronen, "The Cable That Vanished," pp. 101–102.

35 *Kol Ha'am*, July 1, 1955.

36 Edek, "Me'ahorei Masach Hashoah" (Hebrew), *Kol Ha'am*, July 1, 1955.

Edek then presented Anielewicz as someone who worked for the *hagana* out of anti-fascist idealism in alliance with the communists.[37]

Al Hamishmar, the mouthpiece of the Hashomer Hatzair movement and Mapam, first tried to mitigate the impact of this allegation by casting doubt over the existence of Edek.[38] However, Edek promptly stated in another article that he was very much alive and real, and that he had written his initial article because he was shocked by the verdict in the Kasztner trial and not for political motivations. He called on his friends in Hashomer Hatzair to speak up. "He has reason to believe," Edek wrote, "that those people whose lives he, Edek, saved, and who saved his life in return, will never remain silent."[39] With these words, Edek hit on a Mapam sore spot—the fear that some of the members of the kibbutzim, who were fans of the Soviet Union, would switch over to the Communist Party. In response, the party went on the offensive. A "special correspondent" refuted Edek's claims one by one in a four-column article in *Al Hamishmar*, titled "Provocateurs Bad-Mouth Anielewicz."[40]

In the following days, a Mapam spokesman came out with a new slogan: "The popular masses shall put their faith in the party of Mordechai Anielewicz and his comrades!"[41] However, on July 10, *Kol Ha'am* published a third article by Edek, titled "May the Voice of Conscience Be Heard!" In it he suggested that Mapam voters should seek out members of Kibbutz Negba and Kibbutz Haogen who will confirm his words, because during the preparations for the Warsaw Ghetto Uprising, missives from the Land of Israel instructed the fighters: "Agana—no!"[42] *Al Hamishmar* chose not to respond.

The affair was over, but the clues Edek had given in order to prove his existence and the reliability of his sources had exposed him. There were only two ghetto fighters in Haogen and Negba: Chajka Klinger and Aharon Brandes, respectively, and the members of Hakibbutz Ha'artzi's Security Department quickly put two and two together. The Security Department was a body whose official function was to maintain contact with soldiers from the kibbutzim; however, in the early fifties, its people

37 Ibid.

38 "Ad Heihan Shifluta shel Maki Magia?" (Hebrew), *Al Hamishmar*, July 3, 1955.

39 "Hahisteria Ha'anti-komunistit BeMapam Goveret Miyom Leyom: Edek Mezim et Haziyufim Vehashikutzim be'al Hamishmar" (Hebrew), *Kol Ha'am*, July 4, 1955.

40 "Provokatorim Mitnaklim Lesh'mo shel Anilevitz" (Hebrew), *Al Hamishmar*, July 5, 1955.

41 "Yitnu Hamonei Ha'am Emunam Bemiflagtam shel Mordechai Anilevitz Vehaverav" (Hebrew), *Al Hamishmar*, July 10, 1955.

42 Edek, "Yishama Kol Hamatzpun" (Hebrew), *Kol Ha'am*, July 10, 1955.

were also involved in political espionage.[43] It is reasonable to assume that it was the members of this department who uncovered the recording devices planted in Meir Ya'ari's office by head of Mossad Isser Harel.[44] Malka Ronen (Lipner), who had worked in the Security Department in the years 1951–1953, remembered that the department was also involved in spying on communist kibbutzim members—or "Sneh-ists" as they were called then, after Moshe Sneh of the Socialist Left. This covert activity was not documented. "It was forbidden to write anything down," said Malka later.[45]

The members of the Security Department did not take long to discover Edek's identity. The mysterious whistleblower turned out to be none other than Shmuel Rozencwajg (Ron), from the Sosnowiec resistance, who at the time had Chajka's notebooks in his possession, possibly to use as inspiration for his own memoirs.[46] In the early 1950s, Rozencwajg had adhered to the Socialist Left Party, a faction that withdrew from Mapam along with their leader Moshe Sneh and joined Maki in 1954. Among Sneh's people there was a small but prominent group of ghetto fighters and partisans led by Adolf Berman, a member of the Knesset and former head of the Jewish National Committee in the Warsaw ghetto. Among them were Shmuel Rozencwajg and Abraham Zilberstein, members of the Będzin-Sosnowiec underground. In the tangled politics of memory, in the 1950s, members of this group fought for their place in history.

Rozencwajg's accusations were based on a phrase that repeated itself several times in Chajka's diary, regarding the wording of the Tabenkin telegram: "Use all means for immigration."[47] Rozencwajg had sharpened it to "Agana—no!" and attributed it indirectly to the leadership of Hashomer Hatzair in Mandatory Palestine, meaning Ya'ari. The editorial titles in *Kol Ha'am* implied that it was Ya'ari who had sent the telegram and that the path of the pro-communist Anielewicz was not the same path as Hashomer Hatzair in *Eretz Israel.*

43 Isser Harel, *Rigul Sovieti: Komunism BeEretz Yisrael* (Hebrew) (Tel Aviv: Idanim and Yedi'ot Aharonot, 1987), pp. 101–104. For more on the department's underground activity before 1952, see Ze'ev Tzahor, *Ya'akov Hazan—Tnu'at Hayim: Hashomer Hatzair, Hakibbutz Ha'artzi, Mapam* (Hebrew) (Jerusalem: Yad Ben Zvi, 1997), pp. 197–203.

44 Harel, *Rigul Sovieti*, p. 201.

45 Malka Ronen, interview by the author, Sde Nitzan, 2009.

46 Shmuel Ron interview.

47 Klinger, *I Am Writing These Words to You* (1943 diaries), pp. 48, 117, 121.

One day in July 1955, Chajka and Benito, accompanied by a member of the Security Department, traveled to Jerusalem, where Shmuel Rozencwajg was residing at the time.[48] Chajka was eight months pregnant but still keen to obey the movement's orders. They located Rozencwajg's apartment and there, at the entrance of the building, a brief and difficult conversation took place. Chajka demanded that Shmuel return her notebooks and retract his accusations. According to Rozencwajg, she even threatened to use physical force. Benito's testimony implies that she did not need to. Rozencwajg stood before her like a scolded pupil. It seems that the presence of the Security Department man also contributed to the matter's speedy end. The notebooks were returned that same night, and Edek never published another article. Chajka believed that some pages had gone missing from the notebooks, and later, when Benito took on the task of publishing the diaries, he wrote to Menahem Bader to ask for the photocopy that he had made in Istanbul in order to check if anything was missing.[49]

Despite this incident, Shmuel continued to admire Chajka. He would later say that in the ghetto, she had been nicknamed "La Pasionaria," after Dolores Ibárruri, the communist leader who had fanned the flames of the Spanish Civil War.[50] In a letter he wrote to Benito after her death, he thanked him for sending him the memorial booklet, noting bitterly "I owe you a thank you for seeing it fit to include me—if only in this way—in the circle of those who cherish the memory of Chajka."[51] With the publication of *Miyoman Bageto*, Shmuel Ron published a scathing review in *Yediot Yad Vashem* as someone who had witnessed the writing of the diaries and was now outraged and insulted by their revision.[52] One day, when I went to visit Mom's grave with Father, we found a bouquet of flowers there. Father believed that "one of Mom's trainees in Jerusalem" had placed them there.

How did the Edek affair affect Chajka's life? It can be safely assumed that it did her very little good. The diaries, which she had put aside for a long time, came back to haunt her. Once again, she had to face the tension between her criticism of and her commitments to the

48 Ya'akov Ronen interview.

49 Shmuel Ron interview; Ya'akov Ronen interview; letter from Benito to Menahem Bader, January 9, 1959, Chajka Klinger file, Moreshet Archive, C.36.

50 Shmuel Ron interview.

51 Letter from Shmuel Ron to Benito, June 2, 1958, Moreshet Archive, C.36.11.

52 Ron (Rozencwajg), "Im Hofa'at Yoman Hageto shel Chajka Klinger," pp. 21–22.

movement, the unresolved conflict between the fragments of her past, the supposedly united present, and the future that held a new promise in the form of another child. Before the birth of her third son, the fickle hand of fate summoned her yet again to a reunion with the past that refused to die.

The Third Birth

Arnon was born on August 19, 1955. It was the summer holidays, and we were at a summer camp in Mihmoret. When we returned to the kibbutz, Dad came to meet us coming off the truck and told me that I had a little baby brother. There is an image in my memory of a pram in the nursery, containing a chubby, dusky-skinned baby. I was proud. At my suggestion, he was named Arnon, after Zvi's group's summer camp instructor. Mom's presence, however, does not feature in my memories of that time. Zvi accompanied Mom on her way from the maternity hospital and insisted on carrying Arnon to the car in the blue baby carrier. There were two baby carriers in the kibbutz: a blue one for boys and a pink one for girls. The ten-year-old Zvi was elated that Arnon got the blue one.[53]

According to the separate testimonies of both Benito and Rachel Sfinkelstein, Chajka collapsed and was hospitalized for a second time after Arnon's birth. Rachel remembered that her mother Zippora would travel to stay with Chajka in the kibbutz during certain periods, but it is not clear whether her testimony is referring to the first or second breakdown.[54] According to Benito, upon Chajka's return to the kibbutz she made great efforts to maintain her mental balance due to her awareness of her illness and due to the torments she had suffered at the mental hospital both times.[55] After her first hospitalization, Chajka told Esther Shoshan about the harsh approach of the hospital staff, who had berated her, claiming that "she has no nerve," and she told Esther that "those who have been through the Holocaust have nerves of steel."[56] She was determined not to be hospitalized again. An independent witness testified that during the treatments she underwent, she was forced to relive her torture at the hands of the Gestapo.[57] It is not clear whether

53 Zvi Ronen interview.

54 Rachel Sfinkelstein interview.

55 Ya'akov Ronen, *Curriculum Vitae*, p. 131.

56 Esther Shoshan interview.

57 Dalia Amotz, interview by the author, Jerusalem, 1986.

she was also given medication. At any rate, there were no antidepressants available at the time.

As children, we were not aware of any of this. I remember my first years of school as a happy and carefree time. I focused on the life of the children's group, on the books I devoured. There were children in the "Oren" group who did not take well to collective upbringing. One of the members of the group later wrote that he suffered terribly when our parents took us back to the children's house every evening.[58] Another group member wrote about being abused by the school teacher.[59] Vulnerable children were taken away by a secret organization called Neged. Sometimes I would tussle with Dubi or Avri, but we still went to look for birds' nests together, milked Tikva, the stubborn goat at the children's farm, together, and mourned the death of Kushi, the "Oren" group's dog that had been run over, together. Togetherness was all that mattered.

Mom shows up in these memories from time to time, mostly as a strict but caring figure. Once, by the hospital bed in the quarantine ward. Another time in the children's warehouse in the evening. Mom teaching me how to sew a button: "Boys need to know how to sew too," she says with a smile. Another time in the Sukkah where I was anxiously waiting for her, anxious lest she be late to the party (she wasn't). Another time near the "big lawn," when I went to play with my friends instead of going to my parents' house. She insisted that I promise not to do it again. I refused. I wasn't sure I could keep that promise, and I didn't want to lie. I couldn't understand why she had been so hurt by my actions. I remember bursting into my parents' room at the head of a group of jubilant children celebrating Rachel's, Avri's, and my birthdays. Mom looks surprised: "Why didn't you say anything, I would've baked a cake," and she immediately whips out the small box containing the few sweets left over from the weekly rations. The photographs from this period continue to commemorate a smiling family: the five of us sitting between each other's legs in a sort of pyramid. Mom is at the top, and below her, in descending order, are Dad and the three of us boys. Zvi and I are smiling wide: He has a mouth full of teeth, whereas I have two black gaps in mine. Arnon is squinting in the sun.

Then the tide turned. Mom sitting in the deck chair, a towel on her head. "Your mom's not feeling well," Dad explains. "You mustn't disturb

58 Nahshon Lustig, *Shir Ha'eres Ha'ilem* (Hebrew) (Tel Aviv: Yaron Golan, 1995), p. 52.

59 Uri Yungris, "Rishayon La'alot Lamosad" (Hebrew), digital materials from the Kibbutz Haogen Archive.

her." We go out to the poppy fields to gather the flowers bursting with seeds from the cracks in the black earth. The whole kibbutz is there, except Mom. She couldn't come due to her illness. Another dim memory of Mom's voice in the other room. She is crying. Mom and Dad talking about a fire that had broken out in a children's house at a different kibbutz and a girl was killed.[60] The word "guilt" filters through the walls and into my ears. And another memory of a cheerful walk at dusk along the path leading to the central warehouse, with an unfamiliar thought echoing in my head: Will I be sad if Mom dies? On my way from the children's house to my parents' house I was supposed to pick two-year-old Arnon up from daycare. One time, I forgot. Mom was so angry. "How could you?" she admonished me, while I thought: What is she angry about? After all, it's her job.

Another time I wanted to surprise her by weeding her flower garden while she was visiting the neighbors. When Mom came back and saw the job I'd done she smiled, but the smile immediately turned into a frown: I had inadvertently also uprooted some of the African daisies she had just planted. She was hard to please.

During Passover vacation in third grade, I fell out of a tree. We had built a tree house in the big eucalyptus tree next to the chicken coop. I went up on the well-secured platform, about 4 meters above ground, and crouched down to pull an asbestos board up with a rope. The next thing I remember is light flickering between the eucalyptus leaves above me, the feeling of my face covered in water, and Itzu, who had been working in the nearby coop, bending over me with a worried expression, then leaving the kibbutz clinic in an ambulance with Mom. I stayed in Beilinson Hospital for four days; Mom was by my side most of that time. The letter I addressed to the children of the "Oren" group was written in her handwriting. According to the timeline I've been reconstructing, this is my penultimate memory of Mom. It was the spring of 1958.

I have no memory of Dad from the hospital. In my mind, he was always associated with construction. Whenever I came to visit him in his office, he would take out some colored pencils and copy paper so that I could draw until he finished his work. "Just a few more seconds. I'm coming," he used to say. I can see Dad next to a rattling concrete mixer that's churning the gray paste fed into it bucket after bucket by three sweaty workers in overalls; Dad taking us to "water the concrete" at noon on a Saturday, because after casting, the concrete must be

60 The fire in the children's house at a different kibbutz took place in 1957.

wetted to prevent it from cracking. Zvi and I were allowed to take turns holding the rubber hose and saturating the thirsty concrete with water. I used to have a recurring thought that maybe, if we watered the concrete enough, it would grow branches and its roots would burrow deep into the earth.

Dad's career was on the rise and he had gained a reputation within the movement. The contracting company established by the Hakibbutz Ha'artzi—Mahleket Bniya—asked for his help at the company offices in Tel Aviv. In 1957, he started work in the technical department, where he dealt with construction proposals and contractors' accounts.[61] He took driving lessons, and the company provided him with a van, a rare thing in those days. Sometimes he would spend the night in Tel Aviv. I remember my mother and I coming with him to visit a small apartment on Mazeh or Nahmani Street and talking to the landlady. An ironic smirk appears in Mom's eyes as she asks questions about the sleeping arrangements.

She seems to have been still working in the clothing warehouse at the time, sometimes doing extra work painting rubber balls at the factory. It is possible that during these years she began thinking about completing or even publishing her book. In 1956, *Sefer Hashomer Hatzair* appeared—a huge volume, 879 pages long, that recounted the history of the movement from the day it was founded until the end of World War II. The book included a fifteen-page article signed in Chajka's name and titled "The *Shomrim* in Będzin Guarding Their People's Honor."[62] As was the custom back in the day, Mother's article was edited in order to transform it into a heroic story worthy of the movement's canon. The story of the last deportation was mentioned in three short lines. There was, certainly, no place in it for the account of Chajka's interrogation. Sensitive issues were omitted: the Tabenkin telegram, Zelcer's betrayal, the passport affair, her criticism of Schwalb. Her description of the activists' admiration of the Soviet Union were also toned down so as not to betray communist leanings.

It can be presumed that Mom felt a certain pride about the fact that excerpts from her diaries had appeared in print. Both Aharon Brandes's and Abraham Zilberstein's books had long since been published as pocket paperbacks accessible to every worker. Renia had published her memoirs under the title *Benidudim Uvamahteret* (In Wandering

61 Ya'akov Ronen, *Curriculum Vitae*, p. 143.

62 Klinger, "Hashomrim BeBendin al Mishmar Kvod Amam," pp. 691–706.

and in the Underground).[63] Mother was mentioned in them, but it was not her book. Now, she had won her place of honor. However, she was perturbed by the editorial interventions. Later, she would write to Chajka Grossman that "in the book [*Sefer Hashomer Hatzair*] there were some interferences and inaccuracies that were not to my liking."[64]

According to Shayke Goren (Goldrin), who went to visit her toward the end of 1957, Chajka talked about her desire to publish her diaries.[65] It may have been influenced by the fact that the remaining fighters and partisans were organizing to produce another book to commemorate the resistance fighters who perished during the Holocaust. Not only that but Chajka Grossman, Abba Kovner, Shalom Cholawski, and other members of Hashomer Hatzair were also planning to write and publish a comprehensive anthology of Jewish combat during the Holocaust. The book would be called *Sefer Hapartizanim Hayehudim* (The Book of Jewish Partisans).[66] Chajka's diaries, which had been returned to the movement archive, had a prominent place in this plan. They were and still remain the most comprehensive and faithful documentation of the resistance in Zagłębie. Chajka Grossman wrote to her: "I will admit without shame that I have read chapter after chapter from it with unusual excitement. And I will also admit that I have found quite a bit of myself in it, even though our life experiences have not been exactly the same."[67]

On January 19, 1958, Mom responded to Chajka Grossman's request:

> I will admit that I am not looking forward to publishing excerpts from my diary. Why? I was among the first to come to [*Eretz*] Israel after the Holocaust. I saw it as a duty, a bequest to tell, to give an account of what happened there. I had a need to erect a monument and honor, in particular, the society in which I had lived. They were great and wonderful people (it wasn't time or circumstances that made them that way either, and I have never since met anyone like them in our kibbutz [Hakibbutz Ha'artzi]). And I traveled from kibbutz to kibbutz and delivered [the message] and told stories. But

63 The Brandes, Zilberstein, and Renia books appeared as early as 1945; Różka Korczak's book *Lehavot Ba'afar* was published by Sifriat Poalim in 1945.

64 Letter from Chajka Klinger to Chajka Grossman, January 19, 1958, in *Chajka: Hoveret Zikaron*, p. 40.

65 Shayke Goren interview.

66 Gefen et al., *Sefer Hapartizanim Hayehudim*, vol. 1.

67 Letter from Chajka Grossman to Chajka Klinger, January 12, 1958, Moreshet Archive, C.36.18.

> I was misunderstood—the members of my kibbutz thought I was bragging and making up tall tales, even though I never spoke about my own part in the events. And so I retreated into silence. This is the reason why I am not eager to publish. Yet, for their sake, for the sake of those who are dearest to me still, to this day, toward whom I feel a sense of guilt because their names are not mentioned or memorialized anywhere, I agree to your request.[68]

Even though she did not wish to publish herself, she trusted Chajka Grossman to make appropriate use of her diary. "It was a day of joy when they were published, Różka's book and yours [Chajka Grossman], and blessed be the hands that do this holy work."[69] She would not get to see her own "day of joy." The book was one child she could not birth.

The End

In October 1957, Kibbutz Haogen celebrated its tenth anniversary. There was great excitement in the air. Shraga Weil, the kibbutz artist, designed a large exhibition. His graphs and placards as well as the enlarged photographs taken by the members of the kibbutz were decorated with small wooden dolls that had been whittled by the carpenter Moshe Glanzman. The exhibition and the accompanying speeches detailed the achievements of Haogen—200 members, 193 children, and a total of 539 people residing in the kibbutz.[70] The rubber factory, which had expanded its product line into plastics, was the pride of collective industry.[71] The kibbutz's gardening team had developed a special variety of melon—the Haogen melon. The melons were grown—for the first time in Israel—under plastic greenhouses, the sheeting for which was manufactured at the Haogen factory and exported to London.[72] It was said that the queen of England would not sit down to breakfast if it didn't include a melon from Kibbutz Haogen. The new swimming pool had been inaugurated only a year earlier, and the members were very proud of it. They had

68 Letter from Chajka Klinger to Chajka Grossman, January 19, 1958, in *Chajka: Hoveret Zikaron*, p. 40.

69 Ibid.

70 Demographic evolution of Kibbutz Haogen, Kibbutz Haogen Archive, 112.5.

71 Haya Ben David, "Yitzu Haplastika Beshnot Hahamishim Vehashishim" (Hebrew), *Haogen Shelanu*.

72 Nathan Miller, "Anaf Hamelonim BeKibbutz Haogen" (Hebrew), *Haogen Shelanu*.

participated in the construction work—under Dad's guidance—and thus had saved on costs.[73]

The celebrations also included a play called *Sysyphus Vehamavet* (Sysyphus and Death), put on by the members and directed by Eli Friedman. We—the children—also performed. For many weeks we had been rehearsing a "pioneer show" under the guidance of the energetic Miriam Goldberger. Divided into groups that represented the different work tools of the pioneer, we sang in unison: "The hammer rose and fell / Concrete roads stretched through the sand! / Awaken, oh wilderness, the hour is nigh / We come to redeem your precious land!" I was in the "sledgehammers" group, which meant wielding cardboard cylinders and swinging them in a circular motion to the rhythm of the song.

I don't remember Mom being present at the celebrations. As the kibbutz's tenth anniversary approached, celebratory articles appeared in *Al Hamishmar*, and in one of them, several key kibbutz members were interviewed. I read the article and proudly told her about it. She grumbled: "Your father has done equally important things." But she said nothing about herself: the memory of the Holocaust was not part of the kibbutz celebrations. *Bli Mizvadot* (Without Suitcases), a play written for the occasion by Nathan Shaham—one of the young writers in the movement—was rejected by the members and shelved.[74]

The play dealt with Hashomer Hatzair activists in Slovakia and their rescue operations. In the play, a Chajka-like character, "Avram," a refugee from Warsaw, appears to warn the Slovak resistance about imminent annihilation, claiming that a fighting movement must struggle with the people to the end, so that the nation should know that they did not go quietly. "Diuro," a Slovak underground activist modeled on Moshe Alpan and Rafi Benshalom, disagrees. He wants not to die the death of heroes but to ensure the continued existence of the people through rescue and immigration to the Land of Israel. The debate is resumed with the appearance of "Judka" (Haviva Reik), the paratrooper from *Eretz Israel*, who declares that one must be able to sacrifice everything in order to fight. "Diuro" rejects her claims as well: "We don't fight to make a good impression on the world…We fight when we have a chance to win and stay alive." The play was not particularly flattering to those resistance

73 Minutes of a kibbutz meeting of September 28, 1952, Kibbutz Haogen Archive, III/286; see also Ya'akov Ronen, "Habniya Bekibbutz Haogen," Ronen family archive.

74 Ben Ami Feingold, "Lehatzil o lo Lehatzil" (Hebrew), *Yediot Aharonot*, May 2, 1986. Nathan Shaham's play was written in 1954–1955.

factions who chose rescue over fighting. And even though the play still served the purpose of perpetuating accepted myths,[75] it was not to the liking of the kibbutz members, who believed that the festivities should touch on topics to which all members could relate.

In the period that followed, Mom's depression returned. As mentioned above, according to Shayke Goren, he learned that Chajka was ill and came to visit her about six months before she died. He spent time with her and the children, and accompanied her to the children's house where, as far as he remembered, she worked at the time.[76] Upon his return to Galon, he gathered some of his friends and told them that he thought Chajka was isolated at Haogen, and they renewed their invitation for her to join their kibbutz. Chajka told him that her love for the children was the "thing that keeps me going," and added that "when we parted, I saw that she was ill."[77] Rachel Sfinkelstein also had the same impression, although the details of her testimony do not entirely match those of Shayke. According to her, during this period, Zippora used to stay with Chajka while Benito was at work. Chajka was not working at the time. In the mornings, they would get up together, Benito would go to work, and Chajka would stay home. About a week before her death, she scrubbed the house, washed and ironed all the clothes. She seemed to be turning a corner.[78]

For decades Dad struggled to tell me the full story of Mom's death, and some of the details I initially learned from Malka. The aggravating depression was accompanied by suicide attempts. Dad tried to convince her to return to the hospital one more time or to receive medical treatment without hospitalization, but she was determined not to go back there. "Her trauma from the previous internments was probably so deep that she decided to put an end to her unbearable torment."[79] According to Rachel, "she didn't want the children to think they had an insane mother."[80] Was it "for the sake of the children" then? For our sake?

Finally, she ostensibly agreed to be committed and prepared herself for the trip to the hospital. Late in the evening, after the echoes of Ya'ir the teacher's rhythmic steps had died down in the hallway, Mom and Dad

75 Ibid.

76 I remember my mother at dinner time with my group in the third grade. According to a member of the group, Nitza Herzog (Pua), she replaced Sarah as our custodian for a while.

77 Shayke Goren interview.

78 Rachel Sfinkelstein interview.

79 Ya'akov Ronen, *Curriculum Vitae*, p. 131.

80 Rachel Sfinkelstein interview.

suddenly appeared in the children's house. Mom was dressed in a long coat, as if she were ready for a trip. They said that Mom wanted to say goodbye before she left. Later, Dad would recount that afterward they both went to bed peacefully. Dad fell asleep. When he woke up, Mom was not at his side. He went outside and found her hanging from the big tree across from the neighbors' garden. It was the eve of Yom Hashoah, Holocaust Remembrance Day. She had finally joined her friends.

Chapter Twenty-Seven

Reconciliation

In April 2008, we convene at the grave. Fifty years later, we are all here for the first time together. Over the many years that have passed, each of us has carried Mom's memory in our own way. Around Passover, at least one of us would walk the path through the orchard to the cemetery, clean the grave, and linger there a little while. Some years, I would come to Haogen from my new kibbutz in the Negev, and my father and I would go there together with a bouquet of flowers that Malka had prepared in advance. About ten years ago, when Zvi, Arnon, and I returned from our war veterans' tour of the north, we came here for the first time with the children. In the years that followed, we would sometimes meet up with Zvi and Nili at the orchard gate. But we have never gathered here together. All of us.

The gate leading to the cemetery is locked, and we have to make a telephone call to obtain the key. There is no way around it, as father must be driven along the old orchard path, which has now become a paved road. He is ninety years old now. We celebrated his ninetieth birthday in December in Sde Nitzan where he has been living for about fifteen years with Malka, next to Arnon and Judy's house. We can see the cemetery down the road, only a few hundred meters from the kibbutz fence. The orchard was uprooted several years ago. Back in the day, it was called the "young orchard" to distinguish it from the "old orchard"—an abandoned Arab orchard near the village of Qaqun. The young orchard was planted by the kibbutz pioneers in the 1950s as one of the new sources of employment for the "boys." Those same boys—the first kibbutz children—would end up uprooting the orchard a few decades later.

The liquidation of the orchard was one of the symptoms of the major crisis that the kibbutz had been undergoing. The industrial glory and social prestige of Kibbutz Haogen faded sometime in the 1980s, during the economic crisis that swept across all the Israeli kibbutzim. The factory had been operating at a loss for five years, and by 1989, the kibbutz was 40 million shekels in debt. Serious tensions arose between the younger generation and the veterans as the youths wanted to use the "Natzhut" compensation fund to repay the debt, whereas the veterans refused out of a desire to protect their pensions. The conflict eroded the solidarity that had kept the kibbutz society together. Members of Haogen, who had always prided themselves on their social cohesion and their economic security (guaranteed by the factory), felt that the era of the cooperative had passed. In the 2000s, the kibbutz began to go through a gradual process of privatization. The children's farm was closed, followed by the dining room. An open-air function hall was opened on the lawn in front of the meeting hall. Cars appeared outside the residential buildings.

None of us live in the kibbutz anymore. Zvi and I have come in from up north; Arnon and Dad drove up from the Negev. Our children are scattered around Tel Aviv, Haifa, and Jerusalem. Only the grave is still here, with "Chajka" embossed upon the tombstone in black marble letters. The rest of the writing is etched in the stone and has to be repainted from time to time. The name remains, but the big tamarisk tree that used to shield it from the sun was uprooted several years ago, and there is no longer any need to clear its needle-like leaves off the grave. All there remains to do is water the flowers and dust the marble. At the time of its digging, it was only the second grave to appear on the other side of the low breeze-block wall delineating the boundaries of the large and empty cemetery. Now it is almost full, and new graves are popping up rather frequently. Every year, after I visit Mom, I take a tour to see the "new arrivals." Her kibbutz friends are now resting here beside her. She is no longer alone.

We encircle the grave, and I say a few words. Arnon's son Yotam films the proceedings. He and Keren, who is standing by his side, have founded a group of political photographers. They call themselves Activestills and are mostly devoted to documenting acts of oppression in the West Bank. The group operates according to the strict principles of a political artistic collective. The first name of the photographers does not appear in exhibitions and publications; the credit belongs to the group alone. The act of documenting is what matters, not the photographer behind it. A significant part of the group's work involves street exhibitions. They plaster enlarged photographs around the streets of Tel Aviv to provoke passersby, to startle them out of their complacency with images of the reality they are trying suppress: the Israeli-West Bank barrier, Palestinians humiliated at checkpoints, and so on. Yotam's brother Ben couldn't make it. He is currently doing the rounds among anarchist communes in Brazil. Before heading to South America, he took an active part in the huge demonstrations in Germany against the G8. In the electrifying new collectives that he has encountered in the slums of Rio and in the landless peasant camps that have taken over the *latifundium* (landed estates) who robbed them of their land, he has found a new and exciting kind of struggle. But Nimrod is here, and so is Daniel. Arnon has made sure to instill Mom's fighting spirit in them as well. For years, every Friday, Arnon stood at the Gush Katif junction, wielding signs calling on Israeli settlers to leave the place and stop obstructing the possibility of peace.

I tell Chajka's story. That is my role in the family, I'm the so-called yahrzeit candle (memorial candle). Some of the children already know it by heart. Twelve years ago, in 1996, we organized a family roots trip to Hungary, Slovakia, and Poland. During the trip, my daughter Ayelet read *Miyoman Bageto*, while Ofer was content with just hearing the stories at the time. Ayelet's eyes remind me of my mother's soft eyes in the photograph from the ghetto days. She is twenty-six now, Mom's age in the photo. When she was born, we considered naming her after Mom, but we ended up getting cold feet. The name sounded too old-fashioned, too foreign, inappropriate for someone born in this country. Ayelet is now studying at Tel Aviv University for a master's degree in the philosophy of education, having already obtained a bachelor's degree in literature. Ofer, who read his grandmother's book eventually, has returned from his travels and has begun studying musicology and philosophy at the Hebrew University. Mother's dreams of education have been fulfilled through them, and the subjects they have chosen are also in the spirit of what she would have wished for them—not to bring them material benefit but to enrich their spiritual worlds. And perhaps, unwittingly, the forgotten spirit of Grandfather Leibel Klinger has also crept in there somehow. After all, is there really that much difference between a Bible scholar, a philosopher, a historian, a researcher of children's literature, and a musicologist?

Zvi is listening attentively. He's always been a good listener—that is Dad's legacy right there. He fulfilled our father's dream of studying at the Technion and becoming an engineer. He is sixty-three years old, just retired from Rafael Advanced Defense Systems, and he has already found a new job in another factory for advanced technology. We do not know much about his work: It is highly confidential, and his lips are sealed. All we know is that he held a senior position at Rafael and managed sensitive projects. When he travels abroad, he always raises alarms as he passes the metal detector. There is about a pound of shrapnel rattling around his body, a souvenir from the terrible battle of Qal'a in the Six-Day War, and it never fails to beep. Nili, his partner, is standing beside him. Next to them, I see Zvi's daughter Carmel, and her husband Ronen who is holding their one-year-old daughter Ma'ayan. They are both young psychologists, just starting their journey on this arduous professional path. Their eldest son, five-year-old Nadav, was left at home, an echo of the old kibbutz maxim—*Nisht for den Kindern*—no doubt. Zvi's second daughter Neri stayed home due to illness. She is about to get married soon.

My account of Mom's life is peppered with childhood memories. The transition from "Chajka" to "Mom" and from the role of all-knowing, omniscient narrator to that of witness-participant is difficult for me. When Zvi spoke at Dad's ninetieth birthday party, he used the same terms consistently: "Dad," "Mom," "I," and "we." His memory is more limber than mine, and he has no trouble connecting to it. Some of what he said was probably difficult for Malka to hear, but as usual, she said nothing; she wanted to rejoice in Benito's happiness. She is not here today, but she is with us in spirit. Malka is ninety-two years old, and her life is still packed full of activity. She is still cooking, knitting woolen hats for every new baby born in the moshav, tending her plants, and following the news of the world from the small house Dad built for them in the empty shed in Arnon's backyard. When we return from a visit to Sde Nitzan, the bag of fresh *habcsóks* she entrusts to us is always accompanied by a warning: "And don't eat everything on the way. Leave something for the children." Without her, it is doubtful whether the family would have recovered after Mom's death. Only in retrospect did we learn how hard she struggled to take her place in the family and in the kibbutz.

I finish speaking. Dad's voice suddenly emerges from the silence, deep and decisive. He addresses Mother directly, as if talking to her. He tells her story, her pain, and her loss. I listen to his words and come to the conclusion that if he was ever angry with her over the years for leaving him alone with three children, he has made his peace with her. Dad tells Mom about the family that has expanded and put down roots all over the place. He speaks warmly of Malka, who took her place by his side. Unusually for him, he does not read from a script, but the words come out of his mouth fluent and clear. For the first time in fifty years he is talking to her and about her before all of us. It is not an easy thing for him to do; his voice cuts off at times, but he remains standing, leaning a little on his cane for support, and carries his speech through to the end. From a distance, the kibbutz houses that he built overlook him and the large family crowded around him.

Arnon is listening to our father speak of our mother. Chajka did not make much of an impression on the memories of the two-and-a-half-year-old toddler. Malka, who arrived three years after her death, was his mother. Of the three of us, he takes care of Dad and Malka the most. He has also come closest of all of us to working the land and living the collective lifestyle his parents wished for him. His mango, dragon fruit, and flower orchards stretch across the plains of the Western Negev. He was the first in Israel to grow cactus fruit such as dragon fruit and the Peruvian apple cactus. This year he will pick pomegranates for the first time. As part of his toast at Dad's birthday celebrations, he said that he had been "born with a spoon full of concrete in his mouth" and was "destined to a life of creativity." Because a kid who "grows up from age zero in the shadows of scaffolding," he continued, "and sees a huge structure rising out of the big lawn at Haogen, which up until that day slumbered peacefully except when harvest parades and local football games disturbed its calm, slowly shedding the wooden planks of its foundry molds, that kid has almost no other options in life than vision, planning, and action." His wife Judy could not be here. She is on duty at Soroka Hospital, and as a midwife her hands are always full. Her willingness to take in Dad and Malka and to live nearby with Arnon breathed new life into them. She turned their home into the central gathering point for both their families; ours in Israel and hers in England.

My son Ofer takes out the guitar and gives it a quick tuning. He unfolds the piece of paper with the chords and lyrics of the song he found on the Internet just two days ago. He didn't know "Tahat Ziv Kohvey Shamayim" (Under the Light of the Heavenly Stars), and I was afraid that he wouldn't have time to learn it. The lyrics of the song were written by Abraham Sutzkever, whom the *New York Times* once proclaimed "the greatest poet of the Holocaust."[1] We chose this song over the "Partisans' Hymn." After all, we live here, and we no longer need "our marching steps to ring out: 'We are here!'"

1 Arthur Cohen, "God the Implausible Kinsman," *The New York Times*, June 17, 1984.

Mom's contrarian spirit has trickled down to her grandchildren: Ben, Nimrod, and Ofer all refused to serve in the IDF, and we supported them. Yotam, too, has refused to serve in the occupied territories. Between them and Chajka there are Zvi, Arnon, and myself, with two or three wars under each of our belts. We were given the weapons and military training that she so sorely lacked in the ghetto. All three of us were commanding officers. But Mom's legacy was never militaristic. She was a rebel. Consciously or unconsciously, we followed her. Arnon was the first refusenik in the family and was imprisoned in 1989 for thirty days for refusing to serve in the occupied territories. When I was called up to serve in the territories at the same time, I sent a letter of conscientious refusal to the commander of the Leadership Development School where I was serving in the reserves, but he preferred to ignore it. Instead, he made me write a book about leadership. Then came the boys of the next generation, each one with his own doubts, considerations, and decisions. When Nimrod appeared before the IDF's Conscientious Objection Committee, he mentioned his grandmother, the ghetto fighter. The members of the committee were quick to pounce on this piece of information and asked if he shouldn't follow her path. Nimrod replied that he also had a grandfather who in the same situation chose to save lives.

"Every word of mine is a tear, please take it to your breast," Ofer sings in a low voice. Raya joins him. She is Ofer's mother, my wife. Raya is a theater teacher and serves as the family's "cultural committee." When we gather in Sde Nitzan on Passover, she is the one who directs the reading of the Haggada. (Yes, we still read from the secular kibbutz Haggada.) She conducts the family in the singing of "Had Gadya," in which everyone must play the various roles: Daniel is the goat, Ayelet is the cat, and Nimrod is the butcher. For years she has accompanied me on my journey to find my mother. I've always been afraid to open the box of the past and rummage around, but she encourages me to dare. When the music is over, she is the first to place a small stone on the grave. We join her.

For some time after that, we sit in front of the grave in silence, each with their own thoughts. And then, as usual, we turn toward each other to catch up, share experiences, chat. Passover is approaching. Who will play the role of the fire, and who will play the role of the water this year?

Acknowledgments

Many people have accompanied me on the long journey of writing this book. In the decades that have elapsed since its beginning, some of them have passed on, and I can but hope that the work to which they have contributed will in some way stand as a worthy testament to their lives.

First and foremost, I would like to thank the witnesses who were kind and open enough to speak about their past before me. It was not an easy thing to do back in 1985, the year I started my research. While writing, I was also documenting the pain involved in giving testimony and the unique experience of listening to it. The names of the witnesses—to all of whom I am eternally grateful—appear in the bibliography. Among them, I would like to give special thanks to the members of Kibbutz Galon: Esther Shoshan, Shayke Goren, Abrashka Eisenberg, and Shmaryahu Milinsky; the youth movement activists from Będzin and Sosnowiec: Tosia and Shalom Herzberg, and Fredka Mazia; the resistance fighters: Fela Katz, Abraham Fiszel, Ada Halperin, Chawka Lenczner, and Shmuel Ron. Thanks to their living memory, I was able to not only discover details that were missing from the documents at my disposal but also—and most importantly—to get a sense, albeit a very limited one, of the era and its spirit.

I was also greatly aided by the archive workers (also mentioned in the bibliography), among them, initially Shmuel Frankl and Yehoshua Bichler and later Daniela Ozacky-Stern of the Moreshet Archive as well as

Talma Nasi and Yosefa Pecher of Yad Ya'ari. At the Yad Vashem Archives, I received the kind help of Hadassa Modlinger; at Ghetto Fighters' House that of Zvika Oren, the dedicated head of the photo archive; and at the Massuah Archive that of Naftali Tzachar. To them and all the other archive workers who do such diligent and painstaking work, I express my heartfelt gratitude.

At the beginning of my research, I received priceless encouragement from Professor Israel Gutman. Professor Gutman read many parts of the manuscript in its early stages and then became my thesis supervisor together with Professor Saul Friedländer. I was also helped at the beginning of my journey by Professor Dina Porat in whose seminar I had the opportunity to speak about my research for the first time. Although we did not always see eye to eye on everything, I owe them a debt of deepfelt gratitude. During those early years, I was also lucky enough to have the unforgettable figure of Professor Yehuda Elkana by my side. Yehuda's continued support has served as an example to me throughout my career, even when I pivoted from the philosophy and history of science to a different, more personal research direction.

When I returned to the research in 2008 with the intention of turning it into a book, I received much needed encouragement from a number of colleagues who read my drafts, made important comments and suggestions, and pushed me to publish. Among them were Professor Ruth Linn of Haifa University, Professor Hanna Yablonka of Ben-Gurion University of the Negev, Professor Moshe Zuckermann of Tel Aviv University, and Professor Dalia Ofer of the Hebrew University of Jerusalem. It is hard to put into words how much inspiration and strength I drew from them and in particular from Muky Tsur, whose faith in the book sometimes seemed to me to exceed my own. To all of them I give my sincere thanks.

I have likewise been fortunate enough to work with exceptional colleagues when it came to the tasks of both preparing and editing the book for publication in Hebrew. Dganit Regev did a thorough and meticulous job of digitizing the original manuscript, which had originally been produced on a typewriter. The benevolent spirit and wisdom of Gabriela Avigur-Rotem hovers over every page of this book. Her editorial guidance allowed me to present Chajka's narrative in a more concise and consistent fashion while retaining the original spirit of my writing. For me, working with Gabriela was an extraordinary experience of true collaboration based on mutual understanding. When it came to making some tough decisions, her insights and counsel were absolutely indispensable.

The publication of the English edition of this book I owe first and foremost to the team at Yad Vashem Publications led by Dr. Ella Florsheim and Idit Zaken, who took it upon themselves to see this extensive and expensive project through to completion. The translation was no easy task since, alongside the translation of the Hebrew text, it required the translation of excerpts from Chajka Klinger's diaries in Polish and integrating sections that had been translated earlier as part of the English edition of the diaries. Avital Tsype of Academic Language Experts, who was entrusted with all of these tasks, did a superb job of transferring the spirit of the Hebrew book into English as well as successfully editing and combining the sections that were translated from Polish and creating a uniform English version that tells a complete and consistent story. My deepest gratitude goes to her. I would also like to thank Avi Staiman of Academic Language Experts, who oversaw the administrative aspects of the translation, and the other translators whose work appears in the book: Maria Gajewska of Academic Language Experts, Anna Brzostowska, and Jerzy Giebułtowski for their work on the Polish translation, and Betsy Rosenberg for her work on the Hebrew translation. I would be remiss not to mention the immense contribution of Paula Sznejder, who transcribed the original diaries in Polish and whose work served as the basis for the abovementioned translations. Last but not least, I want to express my gratitude to Adina Mendelsohn for her careful editing of the English edition of the book and for keeping it true to the original.

I do not think I will ever be able to properly express just how grateful I am to my family. A book such as this, written about the family and in the context of the family, is a shared journey into the past. It confronts one with many moments of loneliness and despair, which only the kind words or warm feedback of a loved one can dispel. Dad in particular had a tough time of it, but his willingness to face the past in order to contribute to my present endeavor was endlessly appreciated. Zvi and Arnon, my brothers, gave me precious encouragement and support. Zvi read and commented on the original manuscript, and Arnon, after reading the updated manuscript, was the first to respond and confirm to me that my writing was indeed in line with my intentions.

My spouse Raya has been a pillar of patience both in the initial writing period and during the time that marked my return to the research. Without her initiative and her wise answers to all my various questions and qualms, it is doubtful whether I would have even taken up this project, let alone completed it. The feedback and comments I received from my children Ayelet and Ofer have likewise been invaluable. I am so lucky to not only have a loving son and daughter but also two lively partners in conversation, brimming with bright ideas and witty remarks. Certain chapters and passages in this book were directly inspired by them. Yotam, Ben, Nimrod, and Daniel—Arnon and Judy's children—also gave me plenty of encouragement. They all read the manuscript, and I found the way they engaged with and responded to the text immensely moving. After all, like Ayelet and Ofer, they are the generation of readers that I would most like to reach.

And speaking of the younger generation, I would like to thank my students of whom there are multitudes. I tend to mention that I have a personal connection to the subject matter I discuss in class only on the rarest of occasions, but their interest and curiosity about the various topics raised in this book have been a kind of backwind pushing me forward when the going got tough. I hope that they will take the time to read this book, which in many ways is written for them, and that it will speak to them beyond the letters printed on the page.

And finally, there's Mother, Mom, Chajka. Chajka Klinger. I do not know whether to thank her for her life, her work, her writing, and the life she has given me or to ask for her forgiveness, in the manner of Orthodox Jews asking the dead to forgive them before their time is up, in case I have written a thing or two out of line. Probably both. May your words, Mom, like you, rest in peace. I hope to have realized even a small part of what you intended for them.

Bibliography

Writings by Chajka Klinger

Diaries

I Am Writing These Words to You: The Original 1943 Diaries, Będzin 1943, ed. by Avihu Ronen (Jerusalem and Givat Haviva: Yad Vashem and Moreshet, 2017).

1944 diaries (handwritten notebooks in Polish, written at Kibbutz Haogen from May 22, 1944: Haogen I notebook; Haogen II notebook; notebook C), Moreshet Archive, D.2.211.

Other publications (in chronological order)

CH.K.A.B. "Ele Divrey Ha'edut" (Hebrew), *Mishmar*, March 17, 1944.

Klinger, Chaja, "Hehalutz im Amo: Sipur Havera Shenitzla" (Hebrew), *Dvar Hapoelet*, July 1944.

Klinger, Chaja, "Linkom Velihiyot: Prakim Miyoman Bageto" (Hebrew), *Mishmar*, September 1, 1944.

Klinger, Chaja, "Hara'ayon Shehasir et Ruhenu" (Hebrew), *Mishmar*, April 20, 1945.

Rosenberg, Chaja, "Haverot Bageto" (Hebrew), *Hedim*, 1945, p. 40.

Klinger, Chajka, "Shney Bikurim: Kitey Yoman" (Hebrew), *Al Hamishmar*, April 18, 1947.

Klinger, Chajka, "Beseminarion Hamiflaga BeGivat Haviva" (Hebrew), *Beitenu*, 26 (June 24, 1950).

Klinger, Chajka, "Miba'ayot Mahsan Habegadim" (Hebrew), *Beitenu*, 82 (August 11, 1953).

Klinger, Chajka, "Hashomrim Bebendin al Mishmar Kvod Amam," in *Sefer Hashomer Hatzair*, vol. 1 (Hebrew) (Merhavia: Sifriat Poalim, 1956), pp. 691–706.

Chajka: Hoveret Zikaron (Hebrew) (Kibbutz Haogen: Haogen, 1958).
Klinger, Chajka, *Miyoman Bageto* (Hebrew) (Merhavia: Sifriat Poalim and Kibbutz Haogen, 1959).
Klinger, Chajka, "Pamiętniki Chajki Klinger," in *Zagłada Żydów: Studia i Materiały, Pismo Centrum Badań nad Zagładą Żydów*, 9 (2013), pp. 335–379.

Archives

Central Zionist Archives, Jerusalem
Ghetto Fighters' House Museum (GFH), Kibbutz Lohamei Hageta'ot
Gordonia Archive, Kibbutz Hulda
Hagana Historical Archive, Tel Aviv
Hashomer Hatzair Archive, Yad Ya'ari, Givat Haviva
Hechalutz Archive, GFH, Kibbutz Lohamei Hageta'ot
Jewish Historical Institute (AŻIH), Warsaw
Kibbutz Galon Archive
Kibbutz Haogen Archive
Massuah Archive, Kibbutz Tel Yitzhak
Moreshet Archive, Givat Haviva
Pinchas Lavon Institute for Labour Movement Research, Tel Aviv
Wiener Library for the Study of the Nazi Era and the Holocaust, Tel Aviv University
Yad Vashem Archives (YVA), Jerusalem

Private Archival Collections

Avihu Ronen collection
Esther Shoshan collection
Shraga Fruchtzweig collection
Ya'akov Ronen collection
*Private collections can be found in the Avihu Ronen collection, Moreshet Archive, 235.

Interviews (Oral Testimony Collected by the Author)

Alpan, Moshe (Tel Aviv, 1989)
Amotz, Dalia (Jerusalem, 1986)
Balchasz (Chmielnicka), Ada (Kiryat Tivon, 1987)
Barenblatt, Miriam (Kasia, Hela) (Tel Aviv, 1985)
Blatt, Leon (Tel Aviv, 1986)
Bleichman, Israel (Kibbutz Haogen, 1985)
Bojm, Karola (Tel Aviv, 1985)
Bornstein, Heini (Lehavot Habashan, 1985)
Brandes, Aharon (Negba, 1985)
Danzygier, Zvi (Tel Aviv, 1985)
Drexler, Michael (Ramat Gan, 1989)
Dreksler, Tonia (Tel Aviv, 1986)
Efron (Kamiński), Joshua (Tel Aviv, 1985)
Eisenberg, Abrashka (Kibbutz Galon, 1985)
Feder, Naftali (Tel Aviv, 1986)
Fiszel, Abraham (Lod, 1988)
Frost, Shimon (Jerusalem, 1985)
Fruchtzweig, Shraga (Tel Aviv, 1985)
Goren (Goldrin), Shayke (Kibbutz Galon, 1985)
Granek, Wladek (Ramat Gan, 1987)
Grinn, Abraham (Tel Aviv, 1987)
Grossman, Chajka (Tel Aviv, 1986)
Halperin (Neufeld), Ada (Tel Aviv, 1985)
Herzberg, Shalom (Ramat Gan, 1986–1990)
Herzberg (Gutman), Tosia (Tel Aviv, 1985–1990
Herzog (Pu'a), Nitza (Kibbutz Haogen, 2009)
Ingster, Sheva (Szewa) (Tel Aviv, 1985)
Katz (Weintraub), Fela (Tel Aviv, 1985)
Klinger (Lev), Rina (Tel Aviv, 2008)
Klinger (Zelinger), Ruth (Tel Aviv, 2009)
Klinger, Yitzhak (Rehovot, 2008)
Koren (Klein), Shmuel ("Wizo") (Kibbutz Haogen, 2009)
Lenczner, Chawka (Yagur, 1985)
Lieberman, Chana (Kibbutz Galon, 1985)
Loránd, Ruth (Prague, 1990)

Manela, Abraham (Netanya, 1986 and 1987)
Mazia, Fredka (Kibbutz Haogen, 1986 and 1987)
Milinsky, Shmaryahu (Kibbutz Galon, 1985)
Neuman, Isaac (Ramat Hasharon, 1985)
Orbach, Moshe (Ramat Gan, 1989)
Plotnik (Chmielnicka), Bracha (Mishmar Hasharon, 1985)
Ron (Rozencwajg), Shmuel (Jerusalem, 1985 and 1986)
Ronen (Lipner), Malka (Sde Nitzan, 2009)
Ronen, Ya'akov (Kibbutz Haogen, 1986; Sde Nitzan, 2009)
Ronen, Zvi (Karmiel, 2008)
Rosenberg, Eliezer (Kiryat Tivon, 1987)
Rosenberg, Jakub ("Kuba") (Tel Aviv, 1985)
Rosenkier (Schwarz), Rachel (Haifa, 1987)
Schlesinger, Benjamin (Ra'anana, 1985)
Schlesinger (Wiernik), Chana (Ra'anana, 1985)
Schulman, Meir (Tel Aviv, 1986)
Schulman, Nechama (Necha) (Tel Aviv, 1986)
Schwarzbaum, Alfred (Ramat Gan, 1986)
Sfinkelstein, Rachel (Savyon, 1985)
Sfinkelstein, Shaya (Kiron, 1985)
Sfinkelstein, Yosef (Tel Aviv, 1985)
Shoshan (Zborowska), Esther (Kibbutz Galon, 1985)
Sinai (Goldblum), Yehudit (Halinka) (Tzahala, 1986)
Stern, Eliyahu (Kibbutz Lohamei Hageta'ot, 1985)
Swinkelstein, Shlomo (Tel Aviv, 1985)
Szporn (Eisenberg), Zippora (Kibbutz Galon, 1985)
Tzachar, Naftali (Tel Yitzhak, 1986)
Tzur, Idzia (Yehudit) (Kiryat Tivon, 1998)
Tzur, Zvi (Kiryat Tivon, 1987)
Wygodski, Stanisław (Ramat Gan, 1986)

Documents and Document Collections in Print

"Barenblatt vs. The Legal Adviser, criminal appeal 77/64," *Piskey Beit Din shel Beit Hamishpat Ha'elyon* (Hebrew) (Jerusalem: Nevo, 1989).

Berenstein, Tatiana, and Artur Eisenbach, eds., *Faschismus — Ghetto — Massenmord: Dokumentation über die Ausrottung und Wiederstand der Juden in Polen während des zweiten Weltkrieges* (Frankfurt am Main: Roderberg, 1961).

Blumental, Nachman, Józef Kermisz, and Artur Eisenbach, eds., *Dokumenty i materiały do dziejów okupacji niemieckiej w Polsce* (Łódź: Centralna Żydowska Komisja Historyczna w Polsce, 1946).

Boda-Krężal, Zofia, and Osojca Jadwiga, eds., "Dokumenty o eksterminacji Żydów Zagłębie Dąbrowskiego podczas okupacji hitlerowskiej," *Biuletyn Żydowskiego Instytutu Historycznego w Polsce*, 3–4 (43–44) (1962).

Borsztein, Szyja, *Ludność Żydowska w Polsce w Okresie Miedzywojennym* (Wrocław: Zakład Narodowy im. Ossolińskich, 1963).

Brandt, Kersten, Hanno Loewy, and Krystyna Oleksy, eds., *Before They Perished...: Photographs Found in Auschwitz* (Oświęcim: Auschwitz-Birkenau State Museum, 2001).

"Dokumenty o Likwidacji Gett na Śląsku," *Biuletyn Żydowskiego Instytutu Historycznego*, 38 (1961).

Fatal-Knaani, Tikva, ed., *The Jewish Underground Press in Warsaw*, 3 vols. (Jerusalem: Yad Vashem, 2018–2021).

Gotthelf, Yehuda, and Avraham Cohen, eds., *Sefer Hashomrim: Antologia Leyovel Hashomer Hatzair, 1913–1933* (Warsaw: Hahanhaga He'elyona Lehistadrut Hashomer Hatzair, 1934).

Habas, Bracha, ed., *Mihtavim min Hageta'ot* (Hebrew) (Tel Aviv: Am Oved, 1943).

Kermish, Joseph, ed., *Itonut Hamahteret Hayehudit Bageto Varsha: Vol. 6, March 1942–July 1944* (Hebrew) (Jerusalem: Yad Vashem, 1997).

Kulka, Erich, and Ota Krauss, *The Death Factory: Document on Auschwitz* (London: Pergamon Press, 1966).

Neustadt, Melech, *Horban U'mered shel Yehudey Varsha* (Hebrew) (Tel Aviv: Hava'ad Hapo'el shel HaHistadrut Hakelalit shel Ha'ovdim Ha'Ivrim BeEretz Yisrael, Va'adat Hagola, 1946).

Zariz, Ruth, ed., *Mihtavey Halutzim MiPolin Hakvusha* (Hebrew) (Ramat Efal: Yad Tabenkin, 1994).

Zayit, David, and Yosef [Josef] Shamir, eds., *Me'ir Ya'ari: Diyukano shel Manhig Ke'adam Tza'ir—Pirkey Hayim, 1897–1929* (Hebrew) (Givat Haviva: Yad Ya'ari, 1992).

Online Documents

"Będzin Census of 1939," Jewish Historical Institute Archives (AŻIH), 212/11, https://www.jewishgen.org/databases/Holocaust/0128_Bedzin_census.html.

"Izkor," The Commemoration Site of Fallen Defense and Security Forces of Israel," Ministry of Defense, The Families, Commemoration and Heritage Department, https://www.izkor.gov.il/en/.

"Jakub Sandzer (Sander) testimony," http://polishjews.org/shoahtts/007one.htm.

"Kobylec, Piotr; Kobylec, Karolina (wife); Kobylec-Banasik, Klara (daughter); Kobylec, Mieczysław (son); Kobylec, Wiktor (son)," Polish Righteous: Those Who Risked Their Life, http://www.savingjews.org/righteous/kv.htm.

Newspaper Articles (chronological order)

"She'erit Haplita shel Hagola Hayehudit Omedet al Nafsha" (Hebrew), *Davar*, April 23, 1943.

"Ed Re'iya Mesaper al Hageto Giborim" (Hebrew), *Al Hamishmar*, March 8, 1944.

"Sridim shel Tnu'at Giborim" (Hebrew), *Al Hamishmar*, March 10, 1944.

Bentov, Mordechai, "Hirhurim al Giborim" (Hebrew), *Al Hamishmar*, March 17, 1944.

Edek, "Me'ahorei Masach Hashoah" (Hebrew), *Kol Ha'am*, July 1, 1955.

"Ad Heihan Shifluta shel Maki Magia?" (Hebrew), *Al Hamishmar*, July 3, 1955.

"Hahisteria Ha'anti-komunistit BeMapam Goveret Miyom Leyom: Edek Mezim et Haziyufim Vehashikutzim be'al Hamishmar" (Hebrew), *Kol Ha'am*, July 4, 1955.

"Provokatorim Mitnaklim Lesh'mo shel Anilevitz" (Hebrew), *Al Hamishmar*, July 5, 1955.

Edek, "Yishama Kol Hamatzpun" (Hebrew), *Kol Ha'am*, July 10, 1955.

"Yitnu Hamonei Ha'am Emunam Bemiflagtam shel Mordechai Anilevitz Vehaverav" (Hebrew), *Al Hamishmar*, July 10, 1955.

Diaries, Written Testimonies, and Memoirs

Agmon, Ephraim, *Shomer Ahi* (Hebrew) (Kibbutz Dalia: Ma'arahot, 2008).

Alpan, Moshe, *Be'eyn Hase'ara* (Hebrew) (Tel Aviv: Moreshet, 2001).

Bader, Menahem, *Shlihuyot Atzuvot* (Hebrew) (Merhavia: Sifriat Poalim, 1954).

Ben-Aryeh, Katri'el, *September 1939* (Hebrew) (Tel Aviv: Lavi, 1987).

Benshalom, Rafi, *We Struggled for Life: The Hungarian Zionist Youth Resistance during the Nazi Era* (Jerusalem: Gefen Publishing House, 2001).

Berlinski, Hirsch, "Zihronot" (Hebrew), *Yalkut Moreshet*, 1 (November–December, 1963).

Berman, Adolf, *Bamakom Asher Ya'ad Li Hagoral: Am Yehudey Varsha, 1939–1942* (Hebrew) (Tel Aviv: Hakibbutz Hameuchad, 1971).

Bornstein, Heini, *Ha'i Shvaitz: Pe'ulot Ezra Vehatzala Bashanim 1939–1946* (Hebrew) (Tel Aviv: Moreshet, 1996).

Brand, Joel, *Beshlihut Nidonim Lamavet* (Hebrew) (Tel Aviv: Eynot, 1956).

Brandes, Aharon, *Ketz Hayehudim Bedrom Ma'arav Polin* (Hebrew) (Merhavia: Sifriat Poalim, 1945).

Brandes, Aharon, and Haim Reshef, *Zvi Brandes: Mirashey Hamahteret Hehalutzit BeZaglembia* (Hebrew) (Tel Aviv: Moreshet and Sifriat Poalim, 1978).

Eck, Nathan, *Hato'im Bedarkey Hamavet: Hav'vai Vehagut Beyemey Hakilayon* (Hebrew) (Jerusalem: Yad Vashem, 1966).

Folman Raban, Chavka, *They Are Still with Me* (Dalia: Ghetto Fighters' House Museum and Ma'arehet, 2001).

Frieder, Emanuel, *To Deliver Their Souls: The Struggle of a Young Rabbi during the Holocaust* (New York: Holocaust Library, 1987).

Geva, Hava, *Pe'alo shel Hakibbutz Ha'artzi Le'ezrat Hatnu'a Beshtahey Hakivush ad 1942* (Hebrew) (unpublished).

Grossman, Chajka, *Anshey Hamahteret* (Hebrew) (Merhavia: Hakibbutz Ha'artzi, Hashomer Hatzair, 1950).

Gruenbaum, Yitzhak, *Beyamey Horban Veshoah* (Hebrew) (Tel Aviv: Chaverim, 1946).

Gutman, Alexander, and Esther Gutman-Herzberg, "Bageto Bendin: Protocol" (Hebrew), Massuah Archive, AR-PS-00089-012 (1973), pp. 172–179.

Habas, Bracha, *Yeladim Mutzalim* (Hebrew) (Tel Aviv: Am Oved, 1945).
Hazan, Ya'akov, *Reshit Hadasha* (Hebrew) (Tel Aviv: Sifriat Poalim, 1988).
Herzberg, Tosia, *Hahol Hatzohek* (Hebrew) (Tel Aviv: Ahi'asaf, 1986).
Ka-Tzetnik 135633 (Yehiel De-Nur), *Sunrise over Hell* (London: W.H Allen, 1977).
Klausa, Udo, *Erlebt—Überlebt, Erster Teil, 1916–1945* (unpublished).
Korczak, Różka, *Lehavot Ba'afar* (Hebrew) (Merhavia: Sifriat Poalim, 1945).
Korniański, Josef, *Beshlihut Halutzim* (Hebrew) (Tel Aviv: Hakibbutz Hameuchad and Ghetto Fighters' House, 1979).
Krall, Hanna, *The Subtenant/To Outwit God* (Evanston: Northwestern University Press, 1992).
Kukielka, Renia, *Escape from the Pit* (New York: Sharon Books, 1947).
Laskier, Rutka, *Rutka's Notebook: January–April 1943* (Jerusalem: Yad Vashem, 2007).
Lenczner, Chawka, "Parashat Bendin" (Hebrew), *Mibifnim*, June 1944, pp. 123–134.
Lipski, Janet, *Memories* (Tucson, Arizona, 1990), Massuah Archive, AR-T-00019-024.
Liwer, David, *Ir Hametim* (Tel Aviv: Twersky, 1946).
Lubetkin, Zivia, *Aharonim al Hahoma* (Hebrew) (Ein Harod: Hakibbutz Hameuchad, 1946).
______, *In the Days of Destruction and Revolt* (Tel Aviv: Hakibbutz Hameuchad and Am Oved, 1981).
Manela, Abraham, *Haderech Layare'ah Ha'oleh* (Hebrew) (Kibbutz Lohamei Hageta'ot: Ghetto Fighters' House, 1999).
Mazia, Fredka, *Re'im Basa'ar: No'ar Tzioni Bema'avak im HaNatzim* (Hebrew) (Jerusalem: Yad Vashem, 1964).
Neumann, Boaz, *Land and Desire in Early Zionism* (Chicago: University of Chicago Press, 2011).
Nir, Akiva, *Shvilim Bema'agal Ha'esh* (Hebrew) (Tel Aviv: Sifriat Poalim, 1967).
______, *Yehudey Slovakia Bema'avak* (Hebrew) (Tel Aviv: Moreshet, 1984), p. 20.
Palgi, Yoel, *Into the Inferno: The Memoir of a Jewish Paratrooper behind Nazi Lines* (New Brunswick: Rutgers University Press, 2003).
Ranz, Jochanan, *In Nazi Claws: Bendzin 1939–1944* (New York: J. Ranz, 1956).

Révész, Peretz, *Standing Up to Evil: A Zionist's Underground Rescue Activities in Hungary* (Jerusalem: Yad Vashem, 2019).

Ringelblum, Emanuel, *Notes from the Warsaw Ghetto: The Journal of Emanuel Ringelblum* (New York: Ibooks, 2006).

Ron, David, *Hem Yorim: Eliezer Geler Mefaked Ezor Bemered Geto Varsha* (Hebrew) (Tel Aviv: Tarbut Vehinuch, 1960).

Ron, Shmuel, "Im Hofa'at Yoman Hageto shel Chajka Klinger" (Hebrew), *Yediot Yad Vashem*, 21–22 (1959).

Ronen, Ya'akov, *Sipurim LeCarmel* (Hebrew) (unpublished, 1985).

______, *Iy Sham BeSlovakia Harehoka* (Hebrew) (Tel Aviv: self-published, 1987).

Rosenberg, Ya'akov (Kuba), "Bodedim Bama'avak" (Hebrew), Massuah Archive, AR-PS-00089-022 (1974), pp. 73–79.

______, "We Looted German Arms," *Yad Vashem Bulletin*, 4/5 (October 1959).

Schlesinger-Wiernik, Chana, *Hadapim Sheli* (Hebrew) (Ra'anana: self-published, 2004).

Speer, Albert, *The Slave State: Heinrich Himmler's Masterplan for SS Supremacy*, tr. by Joachim Neugroschel (London: Weidenfeld and Nicolson, 1981).

Tenenbaum-Tamaroff, Mordechai, *Dapim Min Hadlika* (Hebrew) (Jerusalem: Yad Vashem, 1985).

Turkow, Jonas, *Sofan shel Ashlayot* (Hebrew) (Tel Aviv: Hamenora, 1973).

Wajsbort, Inka, *Yahad U'badad Mul Ha'eyma* (Hebrew) (Tel Aviv: Moreshet, 1992).

Wiederman, Pawel, *Płowa Bestia* (Munich: Eucom, 1948).

Wiernik (Schlesinger), Chana, "Edut Ahat," *Yalkut Moreshet*, 1 (Hebrew) (November–December 1963), pp. 73–78.

Zilberstein, Abraham (Adam), *Bageta'ot Varsha, Tzenstohov [Warsaw, Częstochowa]* (Hebrew) (Merhavia: Sifriat Poalim, 1945).

Zuckerman, Yitzhak (Antek), *Prakim min Ha'izavon* (Hebrew) (Tel Aviv: Ghetto Fighters' House, 1984).

______, *A Surplus of Memory: Chronicle of the Warsaw Ghetto Uprising* (Berkeley: University of California Press, 1993).

______, *Bageto U'bamered* (Hebrew) (Tel Aviv: Ghetto Fighters' House and Hakibbutz Hameuchad, 1985).

Jewish Community Memorial Books

Bochner, Mordechai, ed., *Sefer Kheshanov [Chrzanów]: Lezihram shel Kedoshei Ha'ir Shenisfu Bashoah* (Hebrew) (Tel Aviv: Hotza'ot Avivim and Irgun Yotzei Kheshanov BeYisrael, 1992).

Even-Shoshan, Shlomo, Haim Dan, and Yishayahu Stavi, eds., *Gushey Hachshara Mesaprim: Kibbutz Al Shem B. Borochov, Gushey Kiltz VeBendin* (Hebrew) (Tel Aviv: Ghetto Fighters' House and Hakibbutz Hameuchad, 1983).

Gelbart, Mordehai, et al., eds., *Sefer Dombrova Gurnitze* [*Dąbrowa Górnicza*] *Vehurbana* (Hebrew) (Tel Aviv: Irgun Yotzey Dombrova Gurnitze BeYisrael, 1974).

Geshuri, Meir Shimon, ed., *Sefer Sosnowitz Vehasviva BeZaglembia*, 2 vols. (Hebrew) (Tel Aviv: Igud Yotzey Zaglembia Vehasviva BeYisrael, 1973).

Goldwasser, Pinhas, and Elimelech Gross, eds., *Kehilat Tshebin [Trzebinia]* (Hebrew) (Haifa: Irgun Yotzey Tshebin BeYisrael, 1969).

Jakubowicz, David, ed., *Sefer Zikaron Lekehilot Vadovitze, Andrihov, Kalvarya, Mishlenitze, Suka* [*Wadowice, Andrychów, Kalvarija, Myslenice, Sucha*] (Hebrew) (Givata'im and Ramat Gan: Massada Press, 1967).

Jasny, Abraham Wolf, ed., *Yizker Buch fun der Farpeynikter Klobutsker Kehile* (Yiddish) (Tel Aviv: Irgun Yotzey Klobuck, 1960).

Miron, Eliyahu, ed., *Bielitz-Biala (Bielsko-Biala): Bruchschnitte aus vergangenen Zeiten* (German and Hebrew) (Jerusalem: E. Miron, 1973).

Rapaport, Izaac, ed., *Pinkas Zaglembia* (Yiddish and Hebrew) (Tel Aviv: Hamenora, 1972).

Shenar, Mordehai, ed., *In Pintshev Togt Shoyn Nisht / Sefer Zikaron Lekehilat Pintshev* (Yiddish and Hebrew) (Tel Aviv: Irgun Yotzey Pintshev BeYisrael U'vatefutzot, 1970).

Spivak, Shlomo, ed., *Sefer Zikaron Lekdoshey Zavirtshe [Zawiercie] Vehasviva* (Hebrew and Yiddish) (Tel Aviv: Irgun Yotzey Zavirtshe Vehasviva, 1958).

Stein, Avraham S., ed., *Pinkas Bendin*, 2 vols. (Hebrew and Yiddish) (Tel Aviv: Irgun Yotzey Bendin BeYisrael, 1959).

Volnerman, Haim, Aviezer Burstein, and Meir Shimon Geshuri, eds., *Sefer Oshpitsin: Oshviyentshim–Oshvits* (Hebrew and Yiddish) (Jerusalem: Irgun Yotzey Oshpitsin BeYisrael, 1977).

Yashiv, Zvi, ed., *Olkush [Elkish]: Sefer Zikaron Lekehila Shehuheda Bashoah* (Hebrew) (Tel Aviv: Irgun Yotzey Olkush BeYisrael, 1972).

Anthologies

Al Masu'ot Polin (Merhavia: Hakibbutz Ha'artzi and Hashomer Hatzair, 1940).

Beyamey Shoah: Mipi Shlihim Lehehalutz (Hebrew) (Ein Harod: Hahistadrut Haklalit shel Ha'ovdim Be'Eretz Yisrael, Hakibbutz Hameuchad, 1940).

Dror, Levi, and Israel Rosenzweig, eds., *Sefer Hashomer Hatzair*, 2 vols. (Hebrew) (Merhavia: Sifriat Poalim, 1956).

Gefen, Mark, Chajka Grossman, Shalom Cholawski, Yeshayahu Segal, Abba Kovner, and Różka Korczak, eds., *Sefer Hapartizanim Hayehudim*, 2 vols. (Hebrew) (Merhavia: Sifriat Poalim, 1959).

Hertz, J. S., ed., *Doires bundistn* (Yiddish) (New York: Farlag Unser Tsait, 1956).

Kehilateinu (Hebrew) (Jerusalem: Yad Ben Zvi, 1922).

Rav, Yosef, ed., *Shomrim Tamid: Hashomer Hatazir BeCzechoslovakia, 1920–1950* (Hebrew) (Givat Haviva: Yad Ya'ari and Hitagdut Yotzey Hashomer Hatzair BeCzechoslovakia, 1994).

Ronen, Avihu, and Joachim Kohavi, eds., *Guf Shlishi Yahid: Biographiyot shel Havrey Tnu'ot No'ar Betkufat Hashoah*, 2 vols. (Hebrew) (Haifa: Ghetto Fighters' House, and Yad Ya'ari, 1994).

Zuckerman, Yitzhak, and Moshe Basok, eds., *Sefer Milhemet Hageta'ot: Bein Hahomot, Bageta'ot, Baye'arot* (Hebrew) (Tel Aviv: Ghetto Fighters' House, 1954).

Research Literature: Books and Articles

Arens, Moshe, *Flags over the Warsaw Ghetto: The Untold Story of the Warsaw Ghetto Uprising* (Jerusalem: Gefen Publishing House, 2011).

Bartoszewski, Władysław, *War Crimes in Poland: Erich Von dem Bach* (Sudbury: Chilton Books, 1961).

Bartoszewski, Władysław, and Zofia Lewin, eds., *How Poles Helped the Jews, 1939–1945* (London: Earlscourt Publications Ltd., 1969).

Barzel, Neima, *Ad Kelot U'mineged: Hamifgash bein Manhigey Mered Hageta'ot levein Hahevra HaYisraelit* (Hebrew) (Jerusalem: Hasifriya Hatzionit al Yad Hahistadrut Hatzionit Ha'olamit, 1998).

Bauer, Yehuda, *Hashoah—Hebetim Historim* (Hebrew) (Tel Aviv: Moreshet, 1982).

______, *Tguvot Be'et Hashoah* (Hebrew) (Tel Aviv: Misrad Habitahon, 1983).

Beit Zvi, Shabtai B., *Post-Ugandan Zionism on Trial: A Study of the Factors that Caused the Mistakes Made by the Zionist Movement during the Holocaust* (Tel Aviv: Shabtai B. Beit Zvi, 1991).

Blumenthal, Helaine, "Communism on Trial: The Slansky Affair and Anti-Semitism in Post-WWII Europe," UC Berkeley: Berkeley Program in Soviet and Post-Soviet Studies, retrieved from: http://escholarship.org/uc/item/4wr2g4kf.

Cohen, Asher, *The Halutz Resistance in Hungary 1942–1944* (Boulder: Social Science Monographs and Institute for Holocaust Studies of the City University of New York, 1986).

______, *Hamahteret Hahalutzit BeHungaria* (Hebrew) (Tel Aviv: Kibbutz Hameuchad and Ghetto Fighters' House, 1984).

"Correspondenzia Pnimit" (Hebrew), *Dapim Leheker Hashoah Vehamered*, 1 (April 1951).

Dawidowicz, Lucy, *The War Against the Jews: 1933–1945* (Toronto: Bantam Books, 1986).

Eck, Nathan, "The Rescue of Jews with the Aid of Passports and Citizenship Papers of Latin American States," *Yad Vashem Studies*, 1 (1957), pp. 93–111.

Elkana, Margalit, *Hashomer Hatzair: Medat Ne'urim Lemarksism Mahap'hani, 1913–1936* (Hebrew) (Tel Aviv: Hakibbutz Hameuchad, 1971).

Eshkoli, Hava, *Ilem: Mapai Lenohah Hashoah, 1939–1942* (Hebrew) (Jerusalem: Yad Yitzhak Ben Zvi, 1994).

Fatran, Gila, *Ha'im Ma'avak al Hisardut: Hanhagat Yehudey Slovakia Bashoah 1938–1940* (Hebrew) (Tel Aviv: Moreshet and Hamahon LeYehadut Zmanenu, Tel Aviv University, 1992).

Friedman, Philip, "Two 'Saviors' Who Failed: Moses Merin of Sosnowiec and Jacob Gens of Vilna," *Commentary*, 26 (1958), pp. 479–491.

Gorny, Yosef, *Kriya bein Onim: Ha'itonut Hayehudit BeEretz Yisrael, BeBritaniya, BeArtzot Habrit, U'beBrit Hamo'atzot Linohah Hashoah* (Hebrew) (Tel Aviv: Hakibbutz Hameuchad and Tel Aviv University Press, 2009).

Goshen, Ze'ev, "Mivtza Nisko" (Hebrew), *Dapim Leheker Tkufat Hashoah*, 2 (1982), pp. 179–183.

Gumkowski, Janusz, and Kazimierz Leszczynski, *Poland under Nazi Occupation* (Warsaw: Polonia Publishing House, 1961).

Gutman, Israel, *Mered Hanetzurim: Mordechai Anilevitz Vemilhemet Geto Varsha* (Hebrew) (Jerusalem and Givat Haviva: Yad Vashem and Moreshet, 2013).

______, *The Jews of Warsaw 1939–1943: Ghetto, Underground, Revolt* (Bloomington: Indiana University Press, 1982).

______, *B'alata Uvema'avak: Pirkei Iyun Bashoah U'vahitnaggedut Hayehudit* (Hebrew) (Tel Aviv: Moreshet, Sifriat Poalim, and Hebrew University Press, 1985).

Hadari, Ze'ev, *Tzomet Kushta: Shlihut Keneged Kol Hasikuyim, 1942–1945* (Hebrew) (Tel Aviv: Ministry of Defense Press, 1992).

Halamish, Aviva, *Meir Ya'ari: Biografia Kibbutzit Hamishim Hashanim Harishonot, 1897–1947* (Hebrew) (Tel Aviv: Am Oved, 2009).

Hilberg, Raul, *The Destruction of the European Jews* (New York: Holmes & Meier, 1961).

Horowitz, Ariel, "Shlihuto shel Menahem Bader BeKushta U'maga'ey Hashomer Hatzair im Yehudey Eropa Hakvusha" (Hebrew), *Yalkut Moreshet*, 35 (1983), pp. 153–202.

Jaros, Jerzy, "Grabież mienia Żydów przez wladze hitlerowskie w swietle akt Urzędu Powierniczego w Katowicach," *Biuletyn Żydowskiego Instytutu Historycznego*, 38 (1961), pp. 105–117.

Kirschner, Ann, *Sala's Gift: My Mother's Holocaust Story* (New York: Free Press, 2006).

Konieczny, Alfred, "Die Zwangsarbeit der Juden in Schlesien im Rahmen der 'Organisation Schmelt,'" in Götz Aly et al., *Sozialpolitik und Judenvernichtung: Gibt es eine Ökonomie der Endlösung?* (Berlin: Rotbuch, 1987), pp. 91–110.

Krausnick, Helmut, and Hans-Heinrich Wilhelm, *Die Truppe des Weltanschauungskrieges: Die Einsatzgruppen der Sicherheitspolizei und des SD, 1938–1942* (Stuttgart: Deutsche Verlags-Anstalt, 1981).

Kumoch, Jakub, Monika Maniewska, Jędrzej Uszyński, and Zygmunt Bartłomiej, *The Ładoś List: An Index of People to Whom the Polish Legation and Jewish Organizations in Switzerland Issued Latin American Passports during the Second World War* (Warsaw: Pilecki Institute, 2020).

Madajczyk, Czestaw, *Polityka III Rzeszy w okupowanej Polsce* (Warsaw: Państwowe Wydawnictwo Naukowe, 1970).

Morgenstern, Aryeh, "Va'ad Hahatzala Hame'uhad shel Hasohnut Hayehudit 1943–1945" (Hebrew), *Yalkut Moreshet*, 13 (June 1971), pp. 60–103.

Namysło, Aleksandra, ed., *Zagłada Żydów Zagłębiowskich* (Będzin: Instytut Pamięci Narodowej—Komisja Ścigania Zbrodni przeciwko Narodowi Polskiemu, Oddział w Katowicach, 2004).

Norwid-Neugebauer, Mieczysław, *The Defence of Poland* (London: M.I. Kolin, 1942).

Ofer, Dalia, "Pe'ulot Ezra Vehatzala shel Hamishlahat HaEretz Yisraelit BeKushta, 1943" (Hebrew), *Yalkut Moreshet*, 16 (February, 1972), pp. 33–58.

Ofer, Tehila, and Ze'ev Ofer, *Haviva: Sipur Hayeha, Shlihuta, Venefilata shel Hatzanhanit Haviva Reik* (Hebrew) (Bnei Brak: Sifriat Poalim and Moreshet, 2004).

Oppenheim, Israel, *Tnu'at Hehalutz BePolin, 1929–1939* (Hebrew) (Be'er Sheva: Hamerkaz Lemoreshet Ben Gurion, Ben-Gurion University, 1993).

Paldiel, Mordecai, "Alfred Rossner: The German Hemophiliac Who Died Attempting to Save Jewish Laborers," in Mordechai Paldiel, *Saving the Jews: Amazing Stories of Men and Women Who Defied the "Final Solution"* (Rockville: Schreiber Publishing, 2000), pp. 126–132.

Perlis, Rivka, *Tnu'ot Hano'ar Hehalutziyot Bepolin Hakvusha* (Hebrew) (Tel Aviv: Ghetto Fighters' House and Hakibbutz Hameuchad, 1987).

Piper, Franciszek, *Ilu ludzi zginęło w KL Auschwitz* (Oświęcim: Państwowego Muzeum w Oświęcimiu, 1992).

Porat, Dina, *Hanhaga Bemilkud* (Hebrew) (Tel Aviv: Am Oved, 1986).

Reitlinger, Gerald, *The Final Solution: The Attempt to Exterminate the Jews of Europe, 1939–1945* (London: Vallentine, Mitchell, 1953).

Ronen, Avihu, "Institutionen, Politik und Identität der Jüdischen Selbstverwaltung im Getto von Zaglembie," in D. Kiesel et al., eds., *Wer zum Leben, Wer zum Tod...* (Frankfurt and New York: Campus Verlag, 1992), pp. 97–114.

______, *Hakrav al Hahaim* (Hebrew) (Tel Aviv: Yad Ya'ari, 1994).

______, "Moshe Merin," in Gershon Hundert, ed., *The YIVO Encyclopedia of Jews in Eastern Europe* (New York and London: Yale University Press 2008), pp. 1157–1158.

______, ed., *Mihtavim Bezmanim Afelim: Hitkatvut bein Anshey Hashomer Hatzair Be'Eropa Hakvusha Vemerkaz Hakesher BeShvaitz, Vol. 1: Polin, Slovakia* (Hebrew) (Tel Aviv: Moreshet, 2019).

______,"The Cable That Vanished: Tabenkin and Ya'ari to the Last Surviving Ghetto Fighters," *Yad Vashem Studies*, 41:2 (2014), pp. 95–138.

______, "Women as Leaders in the Jewish Undergrounds in Poland during the Holocaust," in Paula E. Hyman, Dalia Ofer, and Alice Shalvi, eds., *Jewish Women: A Comprehensive Historical Encyclopedia* (Jerusalem: Shalvi Publishing, 2006).

Rosenkranz, Herbert, *Verfolgung und Selbstbehauptung: Die Juden in Österreich 1938–1945* (Vienna: Herold, 1978).

Rothkirchen, Livia, *Horban Yehudey Slovakia: Ti'ur Histori Beteudot* (Hebrew) (Jerusalem: Yad Vashem, 1961).

Sarid, Levi Aryeh, *Hehalutz Vetnu'ot Hano'ar BePolin, 1917–1939* (Hebrew) (Tel Aviv: Am Oved, 1979).

______, *Bemivhan Ha'anut Vehapedut: Hatnuot Hehalutziot Bepolin Bashoah Ule'ahareha, 1939–1949,* vol. 1 (Hebrew) (Tel Aviv: Moreshet, 1997).

Schwarzbaum, Alf, "Pe'ulot Ezra MiShvaitz Bashanim 1940–1945" (Hebrew), *Massuah*, 2 (September 1974), pp. 138–145.

Shalev, Ziva, *Tosia Altman—Mihahanhaga Harashit shel Hashomer Hatzair Lemefakedet Ha'irgun Hayehudi Halohem* (Hebrew) (Tel Aviv: Moreshet and Tel Aviv University Press, 1992).

______, *Chajka* (Hebrew) (Tel Aviv: Moreshet, 2005).

Stern, Eliyahu, "Hamivrak shel Tabenkin el Hamahteret Hehalutzit BeBendin" (Hebrew), *Mibifnim*, 41 (1979), pp. 323–325.

______, "Haksharim bein Hamishlahat Bekushta LeYehadut Polin" (Hebrew), *Yalkut Moreshet*, 39 (May 1985), pp. 135–152.

Szaniawski, Maciej, "Likwidacja Ludności Żydowskiej w Zagłębiu Dąbrowskim w Świetle Dokumentów Archiwum Akt Nowych w Warszawie," *Zeszyty Zagłębiowskie*, 5 (2000), pp. 101–110.

Szternfinkiel, Natan Eliasz, *Zagłada Żydów Sosnowca* (Katowice: Centralnej Żydowskiej Komisji Historycznej w Polsce, 1946).

Trunk, Isaiah, *Judenrat: The Jewish Councils in Eastern Europe under Nazi Occupation* (New York: Stein and Day, 1977).

Tzahor, Ze'ev, *Ya'akov Hazan—Tnu'at Hayim: Hashomer Hatzair, Hakibutz Ha'artzi, Mapam* (Hebrew) (Jerusalem: Yad Ben Zvi, 1997).

Tzur, Eli, *Lifney Bo Ha'afela: Hashomer Hatzair Bepolin U'veGalitzia, 1930–1940* (Hebrew) (Sde Boker: Ben Gurion Institute, Yad Ya'ari, and Ben Gurion University, 2006).

Unger, Michal, *The Last Ghetto: Life in the Lodz Ghetto, 1940–1944* (Jerusalem: Yad Vashem, 1999).

Vago, Bella, "The Intelligence Aspects of Joel Brand's Mission," *Yad Vashem Studies*, 10 (1975), pp. 111–128.

Weiss, Aharon, "Dfusey Hatguva Hayehudit BeZaglembia Betkufat Hashoah" (Hebrew), *Dapim Leheker Tkufat Hashoah*, 1 (1979), pp. 55–76.

Weiss, Aharon, and Abraham Wein, eds., *Pinkas Hakehilot Polin: Entziklopediya shel Hayishuvim Hayehudiyim Lemin Hivasdam Ve'ad Le'ahar Sho'at Milhemet Ha'olam Hashniya, Vol. 3, Galitziya Hama'aravit VeSileziya* (Hebrew) (Jerusalem: Yad Vashem, 1984).

Weiss, Ann, *The Last Album: Eyes from the Ashes of Auschwitz-Birkenau* (New York: W. W. Norton & Co., 2001).

Weitz, Yechiam, *The Man Who Was Murdered Twice: The Life, Trial and Death of Israel Kasztner* (Jerusalem: Yad Vashem, 2011).

Yablonka, Hanna, *Ahim Zarim: Nitzoley Hashoah Bimedinat Yisrael, 1948–1952* (Hebrew) (Jerusalem and Be'er Sheva: Yad Ben Zvi and Ben-Gurion University, 1994).

Yahil, Leni, *The Holocaust: The Fate of European Jewry, 1932–1945* (New York and Oxford: Oxford University Press, 1990).

Philosophy and Ideology

Benjamin, Walter, *Selected Writings*, vol. 2 (Cambridge MA, and London: Belknap Press of Harvard University Press, 1996).

Bernfeld, Siegfried, *Ha'am Vehano'ar* (Hebrew) (Merhavia: Sifriat Poalim, 1948).

Blüher, Hans, *Die Deutsche Wandervogelbewegung als Erotisches Phänomen: Ein Beitrag zur Erkenntnis der Sexuellen Inversion* (Berlin-Tempelhof: Weise, 1912).

Borochov, Ber, *Selected Works of Ber Borochov* (N.p.: CreateSpace Independent Publishing Platform, 2011).

Engels, Friedrich, and Karl Marx, *The Communist Manifesto: A Modern Edition* (London: Verso, 2012).

Marx, Karl, *Das Kapital: A Critique of Political Economy* (Washington DC: Regnery Publishing, 2012).

Ya'ari, Meir, *Bepetah Tkufa: Prakim Lediyun Likrat Hamo'atza Hashishit shel Hakibbutz Ha'artzi Hashomer Hatzair* (Hebrew) (Merhavia: Hakibbutz Ha'artzi, 1942).

______, *Bederech Aruka* (Hebrew) (Merhavia: Sifriat Poalim, 1947).

Index

Names and Organizations

Places

* *Będzin, Sosnowiec, and Zagłębie are not included in the index.*